American Government and Politics Today

2004 - 2005 BRIEF EDITION

Steffen W. Schmidt
Iowa State University

Mack C. Shelley
Iowa State University

Barbara A. Bardes
University of Cincinnati

THOMSON

WADSWORTH

American Government and Politics Today: 2004–2005 Brief Edition
by Steffen W. Schmidt, Mack C. Shelley, and Barbara A. Bardes

PUBLISHER: Clark Baxter
ACQUISITIONS EDITOR: David Tatom
DEVELOPMENT EDITOR: Catherine A. Wein
ASSISTANT EDITOR: Rebecca F. Green
EDITORIAL ASSISTANT: Reena Thomas
MARKETING MANAGER: Janise A. Fry
ADVERTISING MANAGER: Stacey Purviance
PRINT/MEDIA BUYER: Judy Inouye
PERMISSIONS EDITOR: Elizabeth Zuber

INTERIOR DESIGN/PRODUCTION: Ann Borman & Ann Hoffman
COVER DESIGN: Ann Borman
COPY EDITOR: Beverly Peaver
PROOFREADERS: Suzie DeFazio, Mary C. Berry
INDEXER: Bob Marsh
COVER IMAGES: Photonica, Corbis-Sygma
COMPOSITOR: Parkwood
PRINTER: Webcom, Ltd., Ontario, Canada

Printed in Canada

1 2 3 4 5 6 7 05 04

For more information about our products, contact us at:
Thomson Learning Academic Resource Center
1-800-423-0563

For permission to use material from this text, contact us :
Phone: **1-800-730-2214**
Fax: **1-800-730-2215**
Web: **http://www.thomsonrights.com**

Thomson/Wadsworth
10 Davis Drive
Belmont, CA 94002-3098
USA

ASIA
Thomson Learning
60 Albert Street, #15-01
Albert Complex
Singapore 189969

AUSTRALIA
Nelson Thomson Learning
102 Dodds Street
South Melbourne, Victoria 3205
Australia

CANADA
Nelson Thomson Learning
1120 Birchmount Road
Toronto, Ontario M1K 5G4
Canada

EUROPE/MIDDLE EAST/AFRICA
Thomson Learning
Berkshire House
168-173 High Holborn
London WC1 V7AA
United Kingdom

LATIN AMERICA
Thomson Learning
Seneca, 53
Colonia Polanco
11560 Mexico D.F.
Mexico

SPAIN
Paraninfo Thomson Learning
Calle/Magallanes, 25
28015 Madrid, Spain

Library of Congress Control Number: 2003115695

ISBN: 0-534-63180-0

Contents in Brief

iii

Contents

Part Two

The Politics of American Democracy

Part Three
The Institutions of American Government

Part Four

Policymaking

Preface

The terrorist acts of September 11, 2001, marked a pivotal moment for the American people, their government, and their political system. Throughout this Brief Edition of *American Government and Politics Today*, you will read about how our government's responses to the events of that day have affected the course of American government and politics. The war on terrorism has meant tightened domestic security, and many citizens have expressed concerns over the effect of these measures on our civil rights and liberties. Wars against terrorist-friendly governments in Afghanistan and Iraq have raised major questions about what the United States should do to help rebuild those countries. These and other aspects of the war on terrorism are addressed not only in the text of this edition but also in a special new feature entitled *America's Security* that appears in many chapters.

This edition is basically a condensed and updated version of the larger editions of *American Government and Politics Today*. It has been created specifically for those of you who want, for reasons of course length or design, a text that presents the fundamental components of the American political system while retaining the quality and readability of the larger editions. You will find that this edition is up to date in every respect. The text, figures, tables, and all pedagogical features are current so that your students have the latest available data. We have also included coverage of all recently issued laws, regulations, and court decisions that have—or will have—a significant impact on American society and our political system.

As with the larger editions, this volume places a major emphasis on political participation and involvement. Our *At Issue* features present controversial issues that can elicit classroom debate, and each one ends with a *For Critical Analysis* question that encourages students to think critically about a specific aspect of the issue under discussion. Finally, we have added for this edition a special new feature entitled *Making a Difference* that gives students practical information on political participation and involvement.

The Most Complete Web Connection

While this edition may be physically brief, its scope is enlarged by numerous resources that are available on the World Wide Web. Your students can access these resources to gain a fuller understanding of the political issues dominating today's politics. Students can begin their journey by accessing a Web site specific to the Brief Edition:

http://politicalscience.wadsworth.com/schmidtbrief2004

At this address, students will find:

- **Internet Activities**—three exercises for each chapter. Each activity takes the student to a specific online site for research. The activities also provide essay questions that can be automatically e-mailed to the instructor.
- **The Citizen's Survival Guide**—answers questions such as "How do I vote?" and "Who can vote?"
- **Issues in the News**—highlights key issues, updated monthly.
- **Current Events Quiz**
- **Thinking Globally, Acting Locally**
- **English/Spanish Glossary**
- **Links to political science Web sites**
- **InfoTrac American Government Reader**—a list of key words by topic that makes searching in InfoTrac a breeze.
- **Career Resources**
- **American Government Internet Activities**—provides activities that take students through the best sites available on the Web.
- **InfoTrac College Edition**—an online search engine that will take the student exactly where he or she needs to go to find relevant information, including full-text articles in important political science journals and other sources. A special icon in the text margin indicates that InfoTrac will provide information and links relating to the particular topic being discussed in the text.
- **InfoTrac College Edition Student Guide for Political Science**—shows students how to use InfoTrac College Edition, searching tips, and useful key-word search terms and suggestions by subject area.

High-Interest Features

In this edition, we have included two special features designed to pique the student's interest. These features are interspersed throughout the text.

At Issue Features

Each *At Issue* feature focuses on a controversial topic and concludes with a *For Critical Analysis* question to invite critical thinking. Some examples of the *At Issue* topics are the following:

- Should National Security Outweigh Civil Liberties? (Chapter 1).
- Same-Sex Marriages (Chapter 3).

- Does the Endangered Species Act Cause More Harm Than It Prevents? (Chapter 11).
- The Debate over Marijuana (Chapter 13).
- Should the United States Abandon the UN and Go It Alone? (Chapter 14).

America's Security Features

Each *America's Security* feature looks at an issue raised by the events of 9/11 and our government's responses to the terrorist attacks. Each feature ends with a *Critical Analysis* question. Some of the topics addressed in these features are listed here.

- Military Tribunals for Suspected Terrorists (Chapter 2).
- Should We Shut the Immigration Door? (Chapter 5).
- Was the Airline Bailout Necessary? (Chapter 9).
- The President's Role in Wartime (Chapter 10).
- Nuclear Proliferation and Terrorists (Chapter 14).

Making a Difference Features

Finally, at the end of every chapter, a new feature titled *Making a Difference* enhances our emphasis on participation. These features provide the student with information useful for active citizenship. We give the students tips on how to find information on issues, how to learn about their elected representatives, how to join and participate in advocacy organizations, how to protect their civil rights and liberties, and more.

Other Special Pedagogical Aids

The 2004–2005 Brief Edition of *American Government and Politics Today* retains many of the pedagogical aids and features of the larger editions, including the following:

- **Key Terms**—Important terms that are boldfaced and defined in the text when they are first used. These terms are defined in the text margins, listed at the end of the chapter with the page numbers on which they appear, and included in the Glossary at the back of the book.
- **Chapter Summary**—A point-by-point summary of the chapter text.
- **Selected Print and Electronic Resources**—Suggested readings and media resources on topics covered in the chapter text.
- **Logging On**—A section at the end of each chapter that lists and briefly describes important Web sites relating to topics covered in the chapter.
- **Using the Internet for Political Analysis**—A feature concluding each chapter that takes the student to the Internet Activities mentioned earlier and to other resources for a better understanding of American government.

Appendices

The Brief Edition of *American Government and Politics Today* includes, as appendices, both the Declaration of Independence (Appendix A) and the U.S. Constitution (Appendix B). The text of the Constitution has been annotated to help students understand the meaning and significance of the various provisions in this important document. New to this edition is an appendix presenting *The Federalist Papers* No. 10 and No. 51. These selections are also annotated to help students grasp their importance in understanding the American philosophy of government.

A Complete Supplements Package for Instructors

We are proud to be the authors of a text that has the most complete, accessible, and fully integrated supplements package on the market. The text, along with the supplements listed below, constitute a total learning/teaching package for you and your students. For further information on any of these supplements, contact your West/Wadsworth/Thomson Learning sales representative.

Instructor's Resource CD-ROM

This invaluable resource contains the *Instructor's Manual*, the Test Bank, ExamView, and text-specific Microsoft PowerPoint slides.

- **Instructor's Manual**—includes learning objectives, outlines, teaching suggestions, examples, presentation suggestions, and a wealth of ideas for supplementing your lectures. It also contains references to the InfoTrac articles and other supplemental materials, and correlations to the CCN video clips and to the acetate package (see below).
- **Test Bank**—gives you a strong mix of multiple-choice, short-answer, and essay questions.
- **ExamView**—Create, deliver, and customize text-specific tests and study guides (both print and online) in minutes with this easy-to-use assessment and tutorial system. You can build tests of up to 250 questions using up to 12 question types, enter an unlimited number of new questions, or edit existing questions.

Other Supplements for Instructors

- **American Government Transparency Acetate Package**—Illustrate and enhance your lectures with more than seventy full-color acetates featuring diagrams, charts, tables, and figures from the text and additional sources.
- **Multimedia Manager for Political Science 2004**—If you would rather display text images electronically, you can! This powerful set includes images from the transparency package above on multiplatform CD-ROM. This is a Microsoft PowerPoint Link Tool, and is available for Windows and Macintosh.
- **Political Science Video Library**—An exciting collection of videos to enrich your lectures and extend discussions of text materials.
- **Video Case Studies in American Government**—Twelve new video case studies, free to instructors, serve as lecture launchers for classroom use. Each case study covers a contemporary policy issue and concludes with questions for classroom discussion. A free instructor's manual provides suggestions on how to best use this resource.

- **CNN Today: American Government Today**—Get students involved, excited, and engaged with these four to six-minute video clips featuring point-counterpoint debates on current and controversial issues. Four tapes are available, ranging from forty-five to sixty minutes in length. Topics include the Internet and free speech, negative campaign ads, gun control, executive privilege, the death penalty in the United States, the fight against terrorism, and the elections of 2000 and 2002.
- **America's New War: CNN Looks at Terrorism**—This great discussion starter includes sixteen two- to five-minute segments featuring news footage, commentary, and speeches dealing with the terrorist attacks on U.S. targets throughout the world. Topics include anthrax and biological warfare, new security measures, Osama bin Laden, al Qaeda, asset freezing, homeland defense, and more.

Supplements for Students

- **Study Guide**—The Study Guide has been updated and is now offered free on the text Web site. The Study Guide includes chapter summaries, key terms, and practice exams.
- **Readings in American Government, Fourth Edition**—Written by Steffen W. Schmidt, Mack C. Shelley, and Jane E. Clayton. This volume contains numerous readings that deal with controversial issues, legal conflicts, and ethical judgment calls directly related to academia and students. The reader is free when bundled with this text.
- **American Government: Using MicroCase ExplorIt, Eighth Edition**—This award-winning workbook contains fifteen computer-based assignments, MicroCase's Student ExplorIt software, and the highest-quality data sets available to professional researchers. Each assignment is packed with dozens of issues that are guaranteed to grab students' interest.
- **An Introduction to Critical Thinking and Writing in American Politics**—Helps students question and think critically about the political process and write a successful research paper. This handy booklet is filled with useful rules, guidelines, and techniques.
- **Grade Improvement: Taking Charge of Your Learning Video**—An upbeat video that gives first-year and reentry college students tips on how to better enjoy success in school.
- **The College Survival Guide: Hints and References to Aid College Students**—By Bruce M. Rowe.
- **America at Odds CD-ROM**—The America at Odds CD-ROM will engage students in the study of American government through twenty interactive modules covering enduring and multidimensional issues in American politics. These issues are presented in a rich mix of media including digital video and audio, photos, graphics, text, and Internet technology.
- **InfoTrac College Edition Student Guide for Political Science**—Shows students how to use InfoTrac College Edition, searching tips, and useful key-word search terms and suggestions by subject area.

- **American Government Internet Activities, Third Edition**—Contains activities for all major topics in the text. Students are asked to surf the Web to obtain answers to thought-provoking questions.
- **HITS on the Web: Political Science**—An exciting, class-tested product specially designed to help students use the Internet for studying, conducting research, and completing assignments. This guide provides quick links to hundreds of valuable online resources: free interactive study aids, course quizzing, exercises to reinforce student knowledge, Web activities, up-to-date topical content, and related materials.
- **Election 2002: An American Government Supplement**—Election 2002 is a unique supplemental booklet with analysis that includes maps, charts, and graphs. Some factors discussed by the authors are the unpredictable national political climate after September 11 and subsequent economic slowdown, how congressional redistricting may affect the partisan control of the House and Senate, and the impact of the thirty-two gubernatorial elections across the country. The use of real examples in this election booklet makes the concepts covered come alive.
- **9/11: The Giant Awakens**—A short text that puts the tragic events of 9/11 into political context. The focus is on how the American political system is responding to the challenges posed by the 9/11 terrorist attacks. The author looks at how the major institutions, such as the presidency, the Congress, and our system of civil liberties and rights, is changing in response to this challenge. The book also provides historical context by considering how other major crises have been handled.
- **Handbook of Selected Court Cases**—Includes over thirty Supreme Court cases.
- **Handbook of Selected Legislation and Other Documents**—Includes excerpts from twelve laws passed by the U.S. Congress that have had a significant impact on American politics.
- **American Government: Readings and Responses**—Monica Bauer, Metropolitan State College of Denver, has assembled an impressive selection of up-to-date, universally themed readings to illustrate the main debates of key issues in American government. The readings cover both pro and con positions on various issues, and major writers from right, left, and center are represented. In a unique feature, the author includes an edited dialogue among students of varying political orientations. This anthology also includes Web site selections, press releases, congressional testimony, and student-led interviews with major political figures.
- **Thinking Globally, Acting Locally**—By John Soares. Designed to help students get involved and become active citizens. Topics include writing letters to the editor, volunteering, changing laws, and registering to vote.

For Users of the Previous Edition

We thought that those of you who have been using the Brief Edition of *American Government and Politics Today* would like to know what major changes have been made for the 2004–2005 Brief Edition. Generally, we have rewritten much of the text; added numerous new features, as described on previous pages; and updated the text to reflect the latest developments in the war on terrorism. Each chapter contains updated information and tabular data, and, whenever feasible, the most current information available on the problems facing the nation. The effects of emerging technology, including the Internet, are emphasized throughout. To draw student attention, we make more use of political cartoons. In addition, we have made other significant changes in many chapters, as described next.

- Chapter 1 (The Foundations of American Government)—This chapter has been almost completely rewritten to better capture the student's interest. It begins by examining the concepts of order and liberty in the context of post-war Iraq. There is new material on theories of American politics. The concluding section on ideology now separates social liberalism and conservatism from economic liberalism and conservatism for a more detailed analysis.
- Chapter 3 (Federalism)—We now include a section on state governments.
- Chapter 4 (Civil Liberties)—We have added a new, more compelling introduction.
- Chapter 6 (Public Opinion, Political Socialization, and the Media)—The chapter has new analyses of the impact of religion and economic class on political socialization. These updates reflect the expanded treatment of ideology in Chapter 1.
- Chapter 7 (Interest Groups and Political Parties)—We have included additional material on campaign finance. The history of political parties in the United States has been completely rewritten to more fully describe the impact of cultural and economic factors on the evolving two-party system. In particular, we note the importance of cultural factors in the post–Civil War period and the current era. The discussion of the two-party system now contrasts the American and European experiences more strongly.
- Chapter 8 (Campaigns, Elections, and Voting Behavior)—We have made major updates to the discussion of voting behavior based on the most recent research.
- Chapter 9 (The Congress)—The chapter contains new material on congressional committees.
- Chapter 10 (The Presidency)—The text has been updated to describe more fully the administration of President George W. Bush.
- Chapter 11 (The Bureaucracy)—The chapter has a new, more lively introduction. The treatment of the history of the civil service has been improved.
- Chapter 13 (Domestic and Economic Policy)—We have added new material on the war against terrorism and a new discussion of federal drug policy. The discussions of welfare and Social Security have been revised to improve student understanding of these issues.
- Chapter 14 (Foreign Policy)—The chapter has been revised to reflect the dramatic developments in foreign policy in the years following the terrorist attacks of September 11, 2001. In addition, the discussion of Chinese-American relations has been updated, and the sections on the Middle East, the Balkans, and Africa have been rewritten to bring out more completely the underlying causes of conflict in these regions.

Acknowledgments

Since we started this project a number of years ago, a sizable cadre of individuals has helped us in various phases of the undertaking. The following academic reviewers offered numerous constructive criticisms, comments, and suggestions during the preparation of all previous editions:

Randall Adkins
University of Nebraska at Omaha

Danny M. Adkison
Oklahoma State University

Sharon Z. Alter
William Rainey Harper College, IL

William Arp III
Louisiana State University

Kevin Bailey
North Harris
Community College, TX

Evelyn Ballard
Houston Community College

Orlando N. Bama
McLennan Community College, TX

Dr. Charles T. Barber
University of Southern Indiana,
Evansville

Clyde W. Barrow
Texas A&M University

David S. Bell
Eastern Washington University

David C. Benford, Jr.
Tarrant County Junior College

John A. Braithwaite
Coastline College

Lynn R. Brink
North Lake College, Irving, TX

Barbara L. Brown
Southern Illinois University at
Carbondale

Richard G. Buckner
Santa Fe Community College

Kenyon D. Bunch
Fort Lewis College, Durango, CO

Ralph Bunch
Portland State University, OR

Mark Byrnes
Middle Tennessee State University

Carol Cassell
University of Alabama

Janet E. Clark
State University of West Georgia

Frank T. Colon
Lehigh University, PA

Frank J. Coppa
Union County College,
Cranford, NJ

Robert E. Craig
University of New Hampshire

Doris Daniels
Nassau Community College, NY

Carolyn Grafton Davis
North Harris County College, TX

Paul B. Davis
Truckee Meadows Community
College, NV

Richard D. Davis
Brigham Young University

Ron Deaton
Prince George's Community
College, Maryland

Marshall L. DeRosa
Louisiana State University,
Baton Rouge

Michael Dinneen
Tulsa Junior College, OK

Gavan Duffy
University of Texas at Austin

George C. Edwards III
Texas AM University

Gregory Edwards
Amarillo College, TX

Mark C. Ellickson
Southwestern Missouri State
University, Springfield

Larry Elowitz
Georgia College

John W. Epperson
Simpson College, Indianola, IN

Daniel W. Fleitas
University of North Carolina
at Charlotte

Elizabeth N. Flores
Del Mar College, TX

Joel L. Franke
Blinn College, Brenham, TX

Barry D. Friedman
North Georgia College

Robert S. Getz
SUNY–Brockport, NY

Kristina Gilbert
Riverside Community College, CA

William A. Giles
Mississippi State University

Paul Goren
Arizona State University

Daniel Gregory
El Camino College, CA

Donald Gregory
Stephen F. Austin State University

Forest Grieves
University of Montana

Dale Grimnitz
Normandale Community College,
Bloomington, MN

Stefan D. Haag
Austin Community College, TX

Willie Hamilton
Mount San Jacinto College, CA

Jean Wahl Harris
University of Scranton, PA

David N. Hartman
Rancho Santiago College,
Santa Ana, CA

Robert M. Herman
Moorpark College, CA

Richard J. Herzog
Stephen F. Austin State University,
Nacogdoches, TX

Paul Holder
McClennan Community College,
Waco, TX

Michael Hoover
Seminole Community College,
Sanford, FL

Jessie C. Horton
San Antonio College, TX

Robert Jackson
Washington State University

Willoughby Jarrell
Kennesaw College, GA

Loch K. Johnson
University of Georgia

Donald L. Jordan
United States
Air Force Academy, CO

John D. Kay
Santa Barbara City College, CA

Charles W. Kegley
University of South Carolina

Bruce L. Kessler
Shippensburg University, PA

Jason F. Kirksey
Oklahoma State University

Nancy B. Kral
Tomball College, TX

Dale Krane
Mississippi State University

Samuel Krislov
University of Minnesota

William W. Lamkin
Glendale Community College

Harry D. Lawrence
Southwest Texas Junior College,
Uvaide, TX

Ray Leal
Southwest Texas State University,
San Marcos

Sue Lee
Center for Telecommunications,
Dallas County Community College
District

Carl Lieberman
University of Akron, OH

Orma Linford
Kansas State University

James J. Lopach
University of Montana

Eileen Lynch
Brookhaven College, TX

William W. Maddox
University of Florida

S. J. Makielski, Jr.
Loyola University, New Orleans

Jarol B. Manheim
George Washington University

J. David Martin
Midwestern State University, TX

Bruce B. Mason
Arizona State University

Thomas Louis Masterson
Butte College, CA

Steve J. Mazurana
University of Northern Colorado

James D. McElyea
Tulsa Junior College, OK

Thomas J. McGaghie
Kellogg Community College, MI

William P. McLauchlan
Purdue University, IN

Stanley Melnick
Valencia Community College, FL

Robert Mittrick
Luzurne County Community
College, PA

Helen Molanphy
Richland College, TX

James Morrow
Tulsa Community College

William Murin
University of Wisconsin at Parkside

Keith Nicholls
University of Alabama

Stephen Osofsky
Nassau Community College, NY

John P. Pelissero
Loyola University of Chicago

Neil A. Pinney
Western Michigan University

George E. Pippin
Jones County Community
College, MI

Walter V. Powell
Slippery Rock University, PA

Michael A. Preda
Midwestern State University, TX

Mark E. Priewe
University of Texas at San Antonio

Charles Prysby
University of North Carolina

Donald R. Ranish
Antelope Valley College, CA

John D. Rausch
Fairmont State University, WV

Renford Reese
California State Polytechnic
University—Pomona

Curt Reichel
University of Wisconsin

Russell D. Renka
Southeast Missouri State University

Paul Rozycki
Charles Stewart Mott Community
College, Flint, MI

Gilbert K. St. Clair
University of New Mexico

Bhim Sandhu
West Chester University, PA

Pauline Schloesser
Texas Southern University

Eleanor A. Schwab
South Dakota State University

Len Shipman
Mount San Antonio College, CA

Scott Shrewsbury
Mankato State University, MN

Steven Shull
University of New Orleans

James D. Slack
University of Alabama at
Birmingham

Alton J. Slane
Grand Valley State University, MI

Joseph L. Smith
Grand Valley State University, MI

Michael W. Sonnlietner
Portland Community College, OR

Mark Springer
University of Nebraska—Lincoln

Jay Stevens
California State University at Long Beach

Carol Stix
Pace University, Pleasantville, NY

Gerald S. Strom
University of Illinois at Chicago

John R. Todd
North Texas State University

Ron Velton
Grayson County College, TX

Albert C. Waite
Central Texas College

Benjamin Walter
Vanderbilt University, TN

B. Oliver Walter
University of Wyoming

Mark J. Wattier
Murray State University, KY

Thomas L. Wells
Old Dominion University, VA

Jean B. White
Weber State College, UT

Lance Widman
El Camino College, CA

Allan Wiese
Mankato State University, MN

J. David Woodard
Clemson University, SC

Robert D. Wrinkle
Pan American University, TX

In preparing this edition of *American Politics and Government Today*, Brief Edition, we were the beneficiaries of the expert guidance of a skilled and dedicated team of publishers and editors. We would like, first of all, to thank Susan Badger, the president of Wadsworth Publishing Company, for the support she has shown for this project. We have benefited greatly from the supervision and encouragement given by Clark Baxter, editorial director, and David Tatom, acquiring editor. Catherine Wein, our developmental editor, also deserves our thanks for her efforts in coordinating reviews and in many other aspects of project development. The contributions of Rebecca F. Green, assistant editor, were enormously helpful. We are also indebted to Reena Thomas, editorial assistant, for her contribution to this project.

We are grateful to Bill Stryker, our production manager, for making it possible to get the text out on time and to Ann Borman, his assistant, for a remarkable design. We also thank Ann Hoffman, who worked on graphical issues. In addition, our gratitude goes to all of those who worked on the various supplements offered with this text and to Melinda Newfarmer, who coordinates the Web site and other multimedia offerings. We would also like to thank Janise Fry, executive marketing manager, for her tremendous efforts in marketing the text.

Many other people helped during the research and editorial stages of this edition as well. Gregory Scott skillfully coordinated the authors' efforts and provided editorial and research assistance from the outset of the project through its final stages. Beverly Peavler's copyediting and proofreading abilities contributed greatly to the book. We also thank Roxie Lee for her proofreading and other assistance, which helped us to meet our ambitious publishing schedule, and Sue Jasin of K&M Consulting for her contributions to the smooth running of the project. Finally, we are grateful for the proofreading services provided by Mary C. Berry and Suzie DeFazio.

Any errors, of course, remain our own. We welcome comments from instructors and students alike. Suggestions that we have received on previous editions have helped us to improve this text and to adapt it to the changing needs of instructors and students.

CHAPTER 1

The Foundations of American Government

POLITICS, FOR MANY PEOPLE, is "the great game"—better than football, better than golf. Scores may only be tallied every two years, at elections, but the play continues at all times. The game, furthermore, is played for high stakes. Politics can affect what you have in your purse or wallet. It can determine what you can legally do in your spare time. In worst-case circumstances, it can even threaten your life. Few topics are so entertaining—and so important.

Politics and Government

What is politics? **Politics** can be defined as the struggle or process that people engage in to decide which members of society get certain benefits or privileges and which members of society are excluded from benefits or privileges. More specifically, politics is the struggle over power or influence within organizations or informal groups that can grant benefits or privileges.

We can identify many such groups and organizations. In families, all members may meet together to decide values, priorities, and actions. Wherever there is a community that makes decisions through formal or informal rules, politics exists. For example, when a church decides to build a new building or hire a new minister, the decision may be made politically. Politics can be found in schools, social groups, and any other organized collection of people. Of all of the organizations that are controlled by political activity, however, the most important is the government.

What is the government? Certainly, it is an **institution**—that is, an ongoing organization with a life separate from the lives of the individuals who are part of it at any given moment in time. The **government** can be defined as the institution within which decisions are made that resolve conflicts or allocate benefits and privileges. The government is also the *preeminent* institution within society. It is unique because it has the ultimate authority within society for making decisions and allocating values.

Politics The struggle over power or influence within organizations or informal groups that can grant or withhold benefits or privileges.

Institution An ongoing organization that performs certain functions for society.

Government The institution in which decisions are made that resolve conflicts or allocate benefits and privileges. It is unique because it has the ultimate authority within society.

Why Is Government Necessary?

Perhaps the best way to assess the need for government is to examine circumstances in which government, as we normally understand it, does not exist. What happens when multiple groups compete with each other for power within a society? There are places around the world where such circumstances exist. A current example is the African nation of Somalia. Since 1991, Somalia has not had a central government. Such authority as exists in Somalia is in the hands of local clan-based warlords or, in the best of circumstances, local governments. Mogadishu, the capital, is divided among several warlords, each of whom controls a bloc of neighborhoods. When Somali warlords compete over the control of a particular locality, the result is war, generalized devastation, and famine. In general, multiple armed forces compete by fighting, and the absence of a unified government is equivalent to civil war.

The Need for Security

Order A state of peace and security. Maintaining order by protecting members of society from violence and criminal activity is the oldest purpose of government.

As the example of Somalia shows, one of the original purposes of government is the maintenance of security, or **order.** By keeping the peace, the government protects the people from violence at the hands of private or foreign armies. It dispenses justice and protects the people against the violence of criminals. If order is not present, it is not possible to provide any of the other benefits that people expect from government.

Consider the situation in Iraq. In March and April 2003, U.S. and British coalition forces entered that nation, which was governed by the dictator Saddam Hussein. The relatively small number of coalition troops had little trouble in defeating their military opponents, but they experienced serious difficulties in establishing order within Iraq when the war was over. Once it became clear that Saddam Hussein was no longer in control of the country, widespread looting broke out. Ordinary citizens entered government buildings and made off with the furniture. Looters stole crucial supplies from hospitals, making it difficult to treat Iraqis injured during the war. Thieves stripped the copper from electrical power lines, which made it impossible to quickly restore electrical power. In various localities, demonstrators confronted coalition troops, often with fatal results. Groups who had benefited from Saddam Hussein's regime organized ambushes of American soldiers. Only when security and order were restored was it possible to begin the reconstruction of Iraqi society. Order is a political value that we will return to later in this chapter.

Limiting Government Power

Order cannot be the only important political value. Under Saddam Hussein, Iraq certainly experienced a kind of order. For many unfortunate Iraqi citizens, that order took the form of the "peace of the grave"—large numbers of people were killed by Saddam Hussein's security forces, sometimes for trivial reasons. Protection from the violence of domestic criminals or foreign armies is not enough. Citizens also need protection from abuses of power by the government.

U.S. President George W. Bush and British Prime Minister Tony Blair believed that Saddam Hussein possessed weapons of mass destruction, and eliminating these weapons was a principal goal of the war. A second major goal, however, was to promote stability in the broader Middle East by freeing the Iraqi people from a despotic regime. Even before the war, the U.S. government recognized that eliminating Saddam Hussein would not be enough to guarantee the freedom of the Iraqi people. Iraqis are divided among themselves by religion and language. How could each of the various groups that make up Iraq be prevented from oppressing the others? To protect the liberties of the Iraqi people, it would be necessary to limit the powers of the new Iraqi government.

Liberty—the greatest freedom of the individual consistent with the freedom of other individuals—is a second major political value, along with order. Liberty is a value that may be promoted by government but can also be invoked *against* government. We will discuss this value further later in this chapter.

Democracy and Other Forms of Government

There are a variety of different types of government, which can be classified according to which person or group of people controls society through the government.

Types of Government

At one extreme is a society governed by a **totalitarian regime.** In such a political system, a small group of leaders or a single individual—a dictator—makes all political decisions for the society. Every aspect of political, social, and economic life is controlled by the government. The power of the ruler is total (thus, the term *totalitarianism*).

A second type of system is authoritarian government. **Authoritarianism** differs from totalitarianism in that only the government itself is fully controlled by the ruler. Social and economic institutions exist that are not under the government's control.

Many of our terms for describing the distribution of political power are derived from the ancient Greeks, who were the first Western people to study politics systematically. A society in which political decisions were controlled by a small group was called an **oligarchy,** meaning rule by a few members of the **elite,** who generally benefited themselves. Another form of rule by the few was known as **aristocracy,** literally meaning rule by the best. In practice, this meant rule by wealthy members of ancient families. Later in European history, aristocracy meant rule by the titled nobility.

The Greek term for rule by the people was **democracy.** Although most Greek philosophers did not believe that democracy was the best form of government, they understood and debated the possibility of such a political system. Within the limits of their culture, some of the Greek city-states operated as democracies.

Direct Democracy as a Model

From the ancient Greek city-states comes a model for governance that has framed the modern debate over whether the people can make decisions about their own government and laws. The Athenian system of government is usually considered the

Liberty The greatest freedom of individuals that is consistent with the freedom of other individuals in the society.

Totalitarian Regime A form of government that controls all aspects of the political and social life of a nation.

INFOTRAC
To find out more about this topic, use the term "totalitarianism" in the Subject guide.

Authoritarianism A type of regime in which only the government itself is fully controlled by the ruler. Social and economic institutions exist that are not under the government's control.

Oligarchy Rule by an elite group.

Elite An upper socioeconomic class that controls political and economic affairs.

Aristocracy Rule by the "best"; in reality, rule by an upper class.

Democracy A system in which ultimate political authority is vested in the people.

Direct Democracy
A system in which political decisions are made by the people directly, rather than by their elected representatives.

Legislature A governmental body primarily responsible for the making of laws.

Initiative A procedure by which voters can propose a law or a constitutional amendment.

Referendum An act of referring legislative or constitutional measures to the voters for approval or disapproval.

Recall A procedure allowing the people to vote to dismiss an elected official before his or her term has expired.

Consent of the People The idea that governments and laws derive their legitimacy from the consent of the governed.

Republic A form of government in which sovereignty rests with the people, who elect agents to represent them in lawmaking and other decisions.

model for **direct democracy** because the citizens of that community debated and voted directly on all laws, even those put forward by the ruling council of the city. The most important feature of Athenian democracy was that the **legislature** was composed of all of the citizens. Women, foreigners, and slaves, however, were excluded because they were not citizens. This early form of government required a high level of participation from every citizen; that participation was seen as benefiting the individual and the city-state.

Direct democracy has also been practiced in some Swiss cantons and, in the United States, in New England town meetings and in some midwestern township meetings. At New England town meetings, which can include all of the voters who live in the town, important decisions are made for the community—such as levying taxes, hiring city officials, and deciding local ordinances—by majority vote. Some states provide a modern adaptation of direct democracy for their citizens; in most states, representative democracy is supplemented by the **initiative** or the **referendum**—a process by which the people may vote directly on laws or constitutional amendments. The **recall** process, which is available in over one-third of the states, allows the people to vote to remove an official from state office.

The Dangers of Direct Democracy

Although they were aware of the Athenian model, the framers of the U.S. Constitution—for the most part—were opposed to such a system. For many centuries preceding this country's establishment, any form of democracy was considered to be dangerous and to lead to instability. But in the eighteenth and nineteenth centuries, the idea of government based on the **consent of the people** gained increasing popularity. Such a government was the main aspiration of the American Revolution, the French Revolution in 1789, and many subsequent ones. The masses, however, were considered to be too uneducated to govern themselves, too prone to the influence of demagogues (political leaders who manipulate popular prejudices), and too likely to abrogate minority rights to enjoy a pure democracy.

James Madison defended the new scheme of government set forth in the U.S. Constitution, while warning of the problems inherent in a "pure democracy":

> A common passion or interest will, in almost every case, be felt by a majority of the whole . . . and there is nothing to check the inducements to sacrifice the weaker party or an obnoxious individual. Hence it is that such democracies have ever been spectacles of turbulence and contention, and have ever been found incompatible with personal security or the rights of property; and have in general been as short in their lives as they have been violent in their deaths.[1]

Representative Democracy

The framers of the U.S. Constitution chose to craft a **republic,** meaning a government in which the people elect representatives to govern them and to make the laws and policies. To eighteenth-century Americans, the idea of a republic also meant a government based on common beliefs and virtues that would be fostered within

Although a direct democracy may be impractical in the United States, many Americans think that the people should have a more direct say in government. Certainly, the protesters shown here thought that Al Gore, who won more popular votes than George W. Bush did, should have become president.

© AP/Wide World Photos

small communities. The rulers were to be amateurs—good citizens—who would take turns representing their fellow citizens.

The U.S. Constitution created a form of republican government that we now call a **representative democracy.** The people hold the ultimate power over the government through the election process, but all policy decisions are made by elected officials. Even this distance between the people and the government was not sufficient. Other provisions in the Constitution made sure that the Senate and the president would be selected by political elites rather than by the people, although later changes to the Constitution allowed the voters to elect members of the Senate directly. Representative democracy has come to be widely accepted throughout the Western world as a compromise between the desire for democratic control and the needs of the modern state.

Principles of Democratic Government.   All representative democracies rest on the rule of the people as expressed through the election of government officials. In the 1790s in America, only free white males were able to vote, and in some states they had to be property owners as well. Women did not receive the right to vote in national elections in the United States until 1920, and the right to vote was not secured in all states by African Americans until the 1960s. Today, **universal suffrage** is the rule.

To ensure that **majority rule** does not become oppressive, modern democracies also provide guarantees of minority rights. If minorities were not protected, the majority might violate the fundamental rights of members of certain groups, especially groups that are unpopular or dissimilar to the majority population. In the past,

Representative Democracy A system in which representatives elected by the people make laws and policies.

Universal Suffrage The right of all adults to vote for their representatives.

Majority Rule A basic democratic principle: the greatest number of citizens should select officials and determine policies.

Volunteers register voters in the Spanish Harlem section of New York City. By setting up a table in the neighborhood, the election officials make registration more convenient and less threatening for voters. Both political parties often conduct voter-registration drives in the months before general elections.

© Lisa Quionones, Black Star

the majority has imposed such limitations on African Americans, Native Americans, and Japanese Americans, to name only a few.

One way to guarantee the continued existence of a representative democracy is to hold free, competitive elections. Thus, the opposition always has the opportunity to win elective office. For such elections to be totally open, freedom of the press and speech must be preserved so that opposition candidates may present their criticisms of the government.

Constitutional Democracy.   Another key feature of Western representative democracy is that it is based on the principle of **limited government.** Not only is the government dependent on **popular sovereignty,** but the powers of the government are also clearly limited, either through a written document or through widely shared beliefs. The U.S. Constitution sets down the fundamental structure of the government and the limits to its activities. Such limits are intended to prevent political decisions based on the whims or ambitions of individuals in government rather than on constitutional principles.

Limited Government
The principle that the powers of government should be limited, usually by institutional checks.

Popular Sovereignty
The concept that ultimate political authority is based on the will of the people.

What Kind of Democracy Do We Have?

Political scientists have developed a number of theories about American democracy, including majoritarian theory, elite theory, and theories of pluralism. Advocates of these theories use them to describe American democracy either as it actually is or as their advocates believe it should be.

Democracy for Everyone

Many people believe that in a democracy, the government ought to do what the majority of the people want. This simple proposition is the heart of majoritarian theory. As a theory of what democracy should be like, **majoritarianism** is popular among both political scientists and ordinary citizens. Many scholars, however, consider majoritarianism to be a surprisingly poor description of how American democracy actually works. They point to the low level of turnout for elections. Polling data have shown that many Americans are neither particularly interested in politics nor well informed. Few are able to name the persons running for Congress in their districts, and even fewer can discuss the candidates' positions. For the average citizen, the national government may seem too remote, too powerful, and too bureaucratic to be influenced by one vote.

Majoritarianism A political theory holding that in a democracy, the government ought to do what the majority of the people want.

Democracy for the Few

If ordinary citizens are not really making policy decisions with their votes, who is? One answer suggests that elites really govern the United States. American democracy, in other words, is a sham democracy. **Elite theory** is usually used simply to describe the American system. Few people today believe it is a good idea for the country to be run by a privileged minority. In the past, however, many people believed that it was appropriate for the country to be run by an elite. Consider the words of Alexander Hamilton, one of the framers of the Constitution:

Elite Theory A perspective holding that society is ruled by a small number of people who exercise power in their self-interest.

> All communities divide themselves into the few and the many. The first are the rich and the wellborn, the other the mass of the people. . . . The people are turbulent and changing; they seldom judge or determine right. Give therefore to the first class a distinct, permanent share in the government. They will check the unsteadiness of the second, and as they cannot receive any advantage by a change, they therefore will ever maintain good government.[2]

Some versions of elite theory posit a small, cohesive, elite class that makes almost all the important decisions for the nation,[3] whereas others suggest that voters choose among competing elites. New members of the elite are recruited through the educational system so that the brightest children of the masses allegedly have the opportunity to join the elite stratum.

Economic and social developments in the last several years have strengthened the perception that America is governed by an elite, privileged group. Political campaigns are expensive, and campaign costs have increased steadily each year. Today, candidates for political office, unless they can raise campaign funds from wealthy supporters or interest groups, have to drop out of the race—or not enter it in the first place.

Democracy for Groups

A different school of thought holds that our form of democracy is based on group interests. Even if the average citizen cannot keep up with political issues or cast a deciding vote in any election, the individual's interests will be protected by groups that represent her or him.

Certain groups within the United States insist on maintaining their own cultural beliefs and practices. The Amish, pictured here, are descended from German religious sects. The more conservative Amish groups do not use modern conveniences, such as automobiles or electricity, and have resisted immunizations and mandatory schooling for their children.

© Brooks Kraft, Corbis Sygma

Pluralism A theory that views politics as a conflict among interest groups. Political decision making is characterized by bargaining and compromise.

Theorists who subscribe to **pluralism** see politics as a struggle among groups to gain benefits for their members. Given the structures of the American political system, group conflicts tend to be settled by compromise and accommodation so that each interest is satisfied to some extent. Because there are a multitude of interests, no one group can dominate the political process. Furthermore, because most individuals have more than one interest, conflict among groups need not divide the nation into hostile camps.

Many political scientists believe that pluralism works very well as a descriptive theory. As a theory of how democracy should function, however, pluralism has problems. Poor citizens are rarely represented by interest groups. At the same time, rich citizens are often overrepresented. There are also serious doubts as to whether group decision making always reflects the best interests of the nation.

Indeed, critics see a danger that groups may become so powerful that all policies become compromises crafted to satisfy the interests of the largest groups. The interests of the public as a whole, then, are not considered. Critics of pluralism have suggested that a democratic system can be virtually paralyzed by the struggle among interest groups.

Some scholars argue that none of these three theories—majoritarianism, elite theory, or pluralism—fully describes the workings of American democracy. These experts say that each theory captures a part of the true reality but that we need all three theories to gain a full understanding of American politics.

Fundamental Values

There is considerable consensus among American citizens about certain concepts basic to the U.S. political system. Given that the vast majority of Americans are descendants of immigrants having diverse cultural and political backgrounds, how can we account for this consensus? Primarily, it is the result of **political socialization**—the process by which beliefs and values are transmitted to new immigrants and to our children. The nation depends on several different agents to transmit the precepts of our national culture.

The most obvious source of political socialization is the family. Parents teach their children about the value of participating in the political system through their example and through their approval. One of the primary functions of the public education system in the United States is to teach the values of the political culture to students through history courses, discussions of political issues, and the rituals of pledging allegiance to the flag and celebrating national holidays. Traditionally, political parties also have played a role in political socialization as a way to bring new voters to their ranks.

The most fundamental concepts of the American political culture can be considered those of the **dominant culture.** The dominant culture in the United States has its roots in Western European civilization. From that civilization, American politics has inherited a bias toward individualism, private property, and Judeo-Christian ethics. Other cultural heritages honor community or family over individualism and sometimes place far less emphasis on materialism. Additionally, changes in our own society have brought about the breakdown of some values, such as the sanctity of the

Political Socialization The process through which individuals learn political attitudes and form opinions about social issues.

Dominant Culture The values, customs, and language established by the group or groups that traditionally have controlled politics and government in a society.

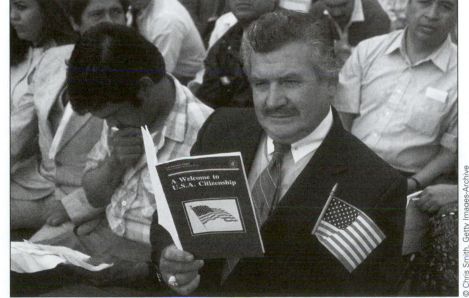

Each year thousands of immigrants are sworn in as new U.S. citizens. The U.S. Constitution, in Article I, Section 8, declares that Congress shall have the power to "establish a uniform Rule of Naturalization." Naturalization is the process by which individuals become U.S. citizens.

© Chris Smith, Getty Images-Archive

AT ISSUE: Should National Security Outweigh Civil Liberties?

In the wake of the terrorist attacks in New York City and Washington, D.C., on September 11, 2001, federal, state, and local governments took steps to strengthen domestic security. For example, the USA Patriot Act, signed into law in October 2001, allows the federal government to detain noncitizens indefinitely, without trial or hearing, on the attorney general's finding of "reasonable grounds to believe" the individuals are involved in terrorism. In the weeks following September 11, the federal government detained approximately 1,200 people. In November 2001, President George W. Bush issued an executive order authorizing nonciti-zens charged in connection with the terrorist attacks to be tried by military tribunals, in which "it is not practicable to apply . . . the principles of law and the rules of evidence generally recognized in the trial of criminal cases in the United States dis-trict courts." In addition, wiretapping laws were modified to give agents of the Federal Bureau of Investigation more freedom to track and monitor the activities of suspected terrorists.

Some of these steps infringe on individual civil liberties highly valued in the United States. Yet these and other government actions following the attacks are a relief to many Americans who fear more terrorism. To others, who fear the erosion of civil liberties protected by the Constitution, they are a cause of great concern.

CIVIL LIBERTIES AND AMERICAN DEMOCRACY

In the Declaration of Independence, Thomas Jefferson declared that "men are . . . endowed by their Creator with certain unalienable rights." The pro-tection of these rights against abuses by government was the basis of the American Revolution. The framers of the Constitution and the Bill of Rights hoped to protect the individual from the tyranny of the central government. In their experience, the great-est threat to the common person, both in Great

family structure, and the acceptance of others, such as women's pursuit of careers in the workplace.

Liberty versus Order

In the United States, our civil liberties include religious freedom—both the right to practice whatever religion one chooses and freedom from any state-imposed religion. Our civil liberties also include freedom of speech—the right to express our opinions freely on all matters, including government actions. Freedom of speech is perhaps one of our most prized liberties, because a democracy could not endure without it. These and other basic guarantees of liberty are found not in the body of the U.S. Constitution but in the Bill of Rights, the first ten amendments to the Constitution.

Liberty, however, is not the only value widely held by Americans. A substantial portion of the American electorate believes that certain kinds of liberty threaten the traditional social order. The right to privacy is a particularly controversial liberty. The United States Supreme Court has held that the right to privacy can be derived from other rights that are explicitly stated in the Bill of Rights. The Supreme Court has also held that under the right to privacy, the government cannot ban either abor-tion[4] or private homosexual behavior by consenting adults.[5] Cultural conservatives

Britain and in the colonies, was the unbridled power wielded by the government. Only by securing the written promises contained in the Bill of Rights, the framers believed, could the people be guaranteed the right to the "pursuit of happiness" for which the Revolution had been fought.

CIVIL LIBERTIES ARE NOT ABSOLUTE

The civil liberties guaranteed by the Bill of Rights are a cornerstone of American democracy. But they are not absolute. For example, a person cannot, without reason, shout "fire" in a crowded room, causing a panic that endangers people's safety. The United States Supreme Court has described some of the circumstances under which the government may encroach on civil liberties: "When clear and present danger of riot, disorder, . . . or other immediate threat to public safety, peace, or other, appears, the power of the State to prevent or punish is obvious."* The issue is, at what point does the exercise of one person's civil liberties create a danger to others?

In the case of *Terminiello v. City of Chicago*,† a man was arrested and convicted for inciting an angry crowd to a breach of the peace. His conviction was overturned by the United States Supreme Court on the ground that the city ordinance under which he was convicted violated his First Amendment right to free speech. In his famous dissent, Justice Robert Jackson argued that government could limit certain liberties if doing so would prevent outbreaks of violence. "There is danger that, if the Court does not temper its doctrinaire logic with a little practical wisdom, it will convert the constitutional Bill of Rights into a suicide pact."

Justice Jackson is frequently quoted by those who argue that the rigid protection of civil liberties in the war against terrorism will expose U.S. citizens to further attack. Upholding the Bill of Rights could be suicide, they argue. Others, however, assert that by infringing on constitutionally protected civil liberties, the government itself could become an instrument of terror.

FOR CRITICAL ANALYSIS

What liberties and privacy rights would you be willing to sacrifice in order to achieve protection against terrorist acts?

* *Cantwell v. State of Connecticut,* 310 U.S. 296 (1940).
† 337 U.S. 1 (1949).

---

believe that such rights threaten the sanctity of the family and the general cultural commitment to moral behavior. Of course, other Americans disagree with this point of view.

Security is another issue. When Americans feel particularly fearful or vulnerable, the government has emphasized national security over civil liberties. Such was the case after the Japanese attack on Pearl Harbor in 1941, which led to the U.S. entry into World War II. Thousands of Japanese Americans were held in internment camps, based on the assumption that their loyalty to this country was in question. More recently, the terrorist attacks on the Pentagon and the World Trade Center on September 11, 2001, renewed calls for greater security at the expense of certain civil liberties. (See this chapter's feature entitled *At Issue: Should National Security Outweigh Civil Liberties?*)

INFOTRAC
For updates on this issue, use the term "terrorism civil liberties" in Keywords.

Equality versus Liberty

The Declaration of Independence states, "All men are created equal." The proper meaning of equality, however, has been disputed by Americans since the Revolution.[6] Much of American history—and indeed, world history—is the story of how the value of **equality** has been extended and elaborated.

Equality As a political value, the idea that all people are of equal worth.

First, the right to vote was granted to all adult white males regardless of whether they owned property. The Civil War resulted in the end of slavery and established that in principle, at least, all citizens were equal before the law. The civil rights movement of the 1950s and 1960s sought to make that promise of equality a reality for African Americans. Other movements have sought equality for other racial and ethnic groups, for women, for persons with disabilities, and for gay men and lesbians.

To promote equality, it is often necessary to place limits on the right to treat people unequally. In this sense, equality and liberty are conflicting values. Today, the right to refuse equal treatment to the members of a particular race has very few defenders. Yet as recently as fifty years ago, this right was a cultural norm.

Economic Equality.

Equal treatment regardless of race, religion, gender, and other characteristics is a popular value today. Equal opportunity for individuals to develop their talents and skills is also a value with substantial support. Equality of economic status, however, is a controversial value.

For much of history, the idea that the government could do anything about the division of society between rich and poor was not something about which people even thought. Most people assumed that such an effort was either impossible or undesirable. This assumption began to lose its force in the 1800s. As a result of the growing wealth of the Western world, and a visible increase in the ability of government to take on large projects, some people began to advocate the value of universal equality, or *egalitarianism*. The value of egalitarianism was especially strong in the European socialist movements. The socialists dreamed of a revolutionary transformation of society that would establish an egalitarian system, that is, a system in which wealth and power were redistributed on a more equal basis.

Many others rejected this vision but still came to endorse the values of eliminating poverty and at least reducing the degree of economic inequality in society. Antipoverty advocates believed then and believe now that such a program could prevent much suffering and reduce the desperation that leads to crime and alcoholism. In addition, reducing economic inequality would promote fairness and enhance the moral tone of society generally as people came to consider the needs of others and not only their own selfish interests.

The Right to Property.

Property Anything that is or may be subject to ownership.

The value of reducing economic inequality is in conflict with the right to **property.** This is because reducing economic inequality typically involves the transfer of property (usually in the form of money) from some people to others. For many people, liberty and property are closely entwined. Certainly, such a connection is widely accepted in the modern-day United States. Our capitalist system is based on private property rights. Indeed, Americans place great value on owning land, acquiring material possessions, and seeking profits through new business ventures.

Property can be seen as giving its owner political power and the liberty to do whatever he or she wants. At the same time, the ownership of property immediately creates inequality in society. The desire to own property, however, is so widespread among all classes of Americans that socialist movements have had a difficult time securing a wide following here.

Political Ideologies

An **ideology** is a closely linked set of beliefs about the goal of politics and the most desirable political order. Political ideologies offer their adherents well-organized theories that propose goals for the society and the political means by which those goals can be achieved. At the core of every political ideology is a set of values that guides its theory of governmental power. The two ideologies most commonly referred to in discussions of American politics are *liberalism* and *conservatism*.

Ideology A comprehensive set of beliefs about the nature of people and about the role of government.

Liberalism versus Conservatism

The set of beliefs called **liberalism** includes advocacy of government action to improve the welfare of individuals, support for civil rights, and tolerance for social change. American liberals believe that government should take positive action to solve the nation's economic and social problems. Liberals usually support programs to reduce poverty, endorse progressive taxation to redistribute income from wealthier classes to poorer ones, and favor government regulation of the economy. Liberals are an influential force within the Democratic Party.

The set of beliefs called **conservatism** includes a limited role for the government in helping individuals. Conservatism also includes support for traditional values and lifestyles. These values usually include a strong sense of patriotism. Conservatives believe that the private sector probably can outperform the government in almost any activity. Believing that the individual is primarily responsible for his or her own well-being, conservatives typically oppose government programs to redistribute income or change the status of individuals. Conservatives play a dominant role in the Republican Party.

Liberalism A set of beliefs that includes the advocacy of positive government action to improve the welfare of individuals and support for civil rights.

Conservatism A set of beliefs that includes a limited role for the national government in helping individuals and support for traditional values.

The Traditional Political Spectrum

A traditional method of comparing political ideologies is to array them on a continuum from left to right, based primarily on how much power the government should exercise to promote economic equality. Table 1–1 on page 14 shows how ideologies can be arrayed in a traditional political spectrum. In addition to liberalism and conservatism, this example includes the ideologies of socialism and libertarianism.

Socialism falls on the left side of the spectrum. Socialists play a minor role in the American political arena, although socialist parties and movements have been important in other countries around the world. In the past, socialists typically advocated government ownership of major businesses. In more recent times, socialists in Western Europe have advocated more limited programs that redistribute income.

On the right side of the spectrum is **libertarianism,** a philosophy of skepticism toward most government activities. Libertarians strongly support property rights and typically oppose regulation of the economy and redistribution of income. Libertarians also tend to oppose government attempts to regulate personal behavior and promote moral values.

Socialism A political ideology based on strong support for economic and social equality. Socialists traditionally envisioned a society in which businesses were taken over by the government or by employee cooperatives.

Libertarianism A political ideology based on skepticism or opposition toward almost all government activities.

TABLE 1–1	The Traditional Political Spectrum			
	SOCIALISM	LIBERALISM	CONSERVATISM	LIBERTARIANISM
How much power should the government have over the economy?	Active government control of major economic sectors.	Positive government action in the economy.	Positive government action to support capitalism.	Almost no regulation of the economy.
What should the government promote?	Economic equality, community.	Economic security, equal opportunity, social liberty.	Economic liberty, morality, social order.	Total economic and social liberty.

Problems with the Traditional Political Spectrum. Many political scientists believe that the traditional left-to-right spectrum is not sufficiently complete. Take the example of libertarians. In Table 1–1, libertarians are placed to the right of conservatives. If the only question is how much power the government should have over the economy, this is where they belong. Libertarians, however, advocate the most complete possible freedom in social matters. They oppose government action to promote traditional moral values, although such action is often favored by other groups on the political right. Their strong support for civil liberties seems to align them more closely with liberals than with conservatives.

Liberalism is often described as an ideology that supports "big government." If the objective is to promote equality, the description has some validity. In the moral sphere, however, conservatives tend to support more government regulation of social values and moral decisions than do liberals. Thus, conservatives tend to oppose gay rights legislation and propose stronger curbs on pornography. Liberals usually show greater tolerance for different life choices and oppose government attempts to regulate personal behavior and morals.

FIGURE 1–1 A Four-Cornered Ideological Grid

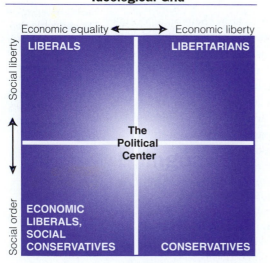

Economic equality ⟷ Economic liberty

Social liberty

LIBERALS　　　　　LIBERTARIANS

The Political Center

Social order

ECONOMIC LIBERALS, SOCIAL CONSERVATIVES　　　CONSERVATIVES

A Four-Cornered Ideological Grid. For a more sophisticated breakdown of American popular ideologies, many scholars use a four-cornered grid, as shown in Figure 1–1. The grid provides four possible ideologies. Each quadrant contains a substantial portion of the American electorate. Individual voters may fall anywhere on the grid, depending on the strength of their beliefs about economic and social issues.

Note that there is no generally accepted term for persons in the lower-left position, which we have labeled "economic liberals, social conservatives." Some scholars have used terms such as *populist* or *communitarian* to describe this point of view, but these words can be misleading.

Individuals who are economic liberals and social conservatives tend to support government action both to promote the values of economic equality and fairness and to defend traditional values. These individu-

MAKING A DIFFERENCE : Seeing Democracy in Action

One way to begin to understand the American political system is to observe a legislative body in action. There are thousands of elected legislatures in the United States at all levels of government. You might choose to visit a city council, a school board, a township board of trustees, a state legislature, or the U.S. Congress.

BACKGROUND PREPARATION

To find out when and where local legislative bodies meet, look up the number of the city hall or county building in the telephone directory, and call the clerk of the council. In many communities, city council meetings and county board meetings can be seen on public access TV channels. Many cities and almost all state governments have Internet Web sites.

Before attending a business session of the legislature, try to find out how the members are

elected. Are the members chosen by the "at-large" method of election so that each member represents the whole community, or are they chosen by specific geographic districts or wards? Is there a chairperson or official leader who controls the meetings and who may have more power than the other leaders? What are the responsibilities of this legislature?

WHEN YOU VISIT

When you visit the legislature, keep in mind the theory of representative democracy. The legislators or council members are elected to represent their constituents (those who voted them into office). Observe how often the members refer to their constituents or to the special needs of their community or electoral district. Listen carefully for the sources of conflict within a community. If there is a debate, for

example, over a zoning proposal that involves the issue of land use, try to figure out why some members oppose the proposal. It is important to remember that the council or board is also supposed to be working toward the good of the whole; listen for discussions of the community's priorities.

If you want to follow up on your visit, try to get a brief interview with one of the members of the council or board. In general, legislators are very willing to talk to students, particularly students who also are voters. Ask the member how he or she sees the job of representative. How can the wishes of the constituents be identified? How does the representative balance the needs of the ward or district with the good of the whole community? You can write to many legislators via e-mail. You might ask how much e-mail they receive and who actually answers it.

als may describe themselves as conservative or moderate. They are more likely to be Democrats than Republicans but often do not identify strongly with any party.

Libertarian, as a position on our two-way grid, does not refer to the small Libertarian Party, which has only a minor role in the American political arena. Rather, libertarians more typically support the Republican Party. They are more likely than conservatives to vote for a compatible Democrat, however.

KEY TERMS

aristocracy 3

authoritarianism 3

consent of the people 4

conservatism 13

democracy 3

direct democracy 4

dominant culture 9

elite 3

elite theory 7

equality 11

government 1

ideology 13

initiative 4

institution 1

legislature 4

liberalism 13

libertarianism 13

liberty 3

limited government 6

majoritarianism 7

majority rule 5

oligarchy 3

order 2

pluralism 8

political socialization 9

politics 1

popular sovereignty 6

property 12

recall 4

referendum 4

representative democracy 5

republic 4

socialism 13

totalitarian regime 3

universal suffrage 5

CHAPTER SUMMARY

1 Politics is the process by which people decide which members of society get certain benefits or privileges and which members do not. It is the struggle over power or influence within institutions and organizations that can grant benefits or privileges. Government is the institution within which decisions are made that resolve conflicts or allocate benefits and privileges. It is unique because it has the ultimate authority within society.

2 Two fundamental political values are order, which includes security against violence, and liberty, the greatest freedom of the individual consistent with the freedom of other individuals. Liberty can be both promoted by government and invoked against government.

3 In a direct democracy, such as ancient Athens, the people themselves make the important political decisions. The United States is a representative democracy, where the people elect representatives to make the decisions.

4 Theories of American democracy include majoritarianism, in which the government does what the majority wants; elite theory, in which the real power lies with one or more elites; and pluralist theories, in which organized interest groups contest for power.

5 Fundamental American values include liberty, order, equality, and property. Not all of these values are fully compatible. The value of order competes with civil liberties, and economic equality competes with property rights.

6 Popular political ideologies can be arrayed from left (liberal) to right (conservative). We can also analyze economic liberalism and conservatism separately from social liberalism and conservatism.

SELECTED PRINT AND MEDIA RESOURCES

Suggested Readings

Gamble, Andrew. *Politics and Fate (Themes for the 21st Century)*. Malden, Mass.: Blackwell Publishers, 2000. The author contends that many people have become disenchanted with the traditional view that politics is a means used by societies to exercise control over their fate. In this book, Gamble comes to the defense of politics, explaining why we cannot do without politics and political processes.

Lasswell, Harold. *Politics: Who Gets What, When and How*. New York: McGraw-Hill, 1936. This classic work defines the nature of politics.

Stanley, Harold W., and Richard G. Niemi. *Vital Statistics on American Politics 2001–2002*, 8th ed. Washington, D.C.: Congressional Quarterly Press, 2001. This valuable reference work contains over two hundred tables and figures on a wide range of topics covering almost all aspects of American politics.

Tocqueville, Alexis de. *Democracy in America*. Edited by Phillips Bradley. New York: Vintage Books, 1945. Life in the United States was described by a French writer who traveled through the nation in the 1820s.

Wolfe, Alan. *One Nation, After All: How the Middle Class Really Think about God, Country, and Family*. New York: Viking Press, 1998. Based on the results of a survey he conducted, sociologist Alan Wolfe concludes that middle-class Americans are far less polarized politically, far less judgmental, and much more tolerant and willing to compromise than is often thought.

Zakaria, Fareed. *The Future of Freedom: Illiberal Democracy at Home and Abroad*. New York: W. W. Norton & Co., 2003. The author argues that democratic elections are likely to lead to negative results unless liberal values have been established first. Liberal values, in this sense, include provisions for limited government, civil liberties, and minority rights.

Media Resources

The Conservatives—A program that shows the rise of the conservative movement in America from the 1940s through the presidential candidacy of Barry Goldwater to the presidency of Ronald Reagan. In addition to Goldwater and Reagan, leaders interviewed include William F. Buckley, Jr., Norman Podhoretz, and Milton Friedman.

Liberalism vs. Conservatism—A 2001 film from Teacher's Video that focuses on two contrasting views of the role of government in society.

The Values Issue and American Politics: Values Matter Most—Ben Wattenberg travels around the country in this 1995 program speaking to a broad range of ordinary Americans. He examines what he calls the "values issue"—the issues of crime, welfare, race, discipline, drugs, and prayer in the schools. Wattenberg believes that candidates who can best address these issues will win elections.

LOGGING ON

The World Wide Web is becoming a virtual library, a telephone directory, a contact source, and a vehicle to improve your learning and understanding of issues. It is therefore important that you become familiar with Web resources. To help you do this, we have included *Logging On* sections at the end of each chapter in this book. Each of these sections contains a list of Internet addresses, or uniform resource locators (URLs), followed by a series of Internet exercises. The URLs will help you find information on topics covered within the chapters,

as well as on related topics. We hope this feature will lead you to some of the most interesting and productive Web locations.

The Internet should be approached with care. You should be very cautious in giving out information about yourself. You also need to use good judgment, because the reliability or intent of any given Web site is often unknown. Some sites are more concerned with accuracy than others, and some sites are updated to include current information, while others are not. Also, realize that sites come and go continually, so some of the Web sites that we include in these *Logging On* features may not exist by the time you read this book.

We also have a powerful and interesting Web site for the textbook, which you can access through the Wadsworth Political Science Resource Center. You can also find additional information and learning opportunities at this site. Go to http://politicalscience. wadsworth.com.

You may want to visit the home page of Dr. Politics—offered by Steffen Schmidt, one of the authors of this book—for some interesting ideas and activities to help you understand American government and politics. Go to http://www.public.iastate. edu/~sws/homepage.html.

For discussion of current political issues, try the resources at the Institute for Philosophy and Public Policy at http://www.puaf.umd.edu/IPPP.

Information about the rules and requirements for immigration and citizenship can be found at the Web site of the U.S. Bureau of Citizenship and Immigration Services: http://www.immigration.gov/graphics/index.htm.

For a basic "front door" to almost all U.S. government Web sites, visit the very useful site maintained by the University of Michigan: http://www.lib.umich.edu/govdocs/govweb.html.

USING THE INTERNET FOR POLITICAL ANALYSIS

Go to this text's Web site at http://politicalscience. wadsworth.com/schmidtbrief2004. Select "Chapter 1" in the box at the top of the window. Then, in the column on the left-hand side of the window, under "Chapter Resources," click on "Internet Exercises." The Web site will then display the following Internet exercises that you can perform to learn more about topics covered in this chapter.

Activity 1–1: Initiative and Referendum
Activity 1–2: A Quiz for New Citizens
Activity 1–3: Populism and Communitarianism

ONLINE STUDY GUIDE AND ADDITIONAL RESOURCES

At http://politicalscience.wadsworth.com/schmidtbrief2004 you will find a free Study Guide to this book that includes tutorial quizzes, essay questions, practice exams, chapter outlines, learning objectives, the glossary, flashcards, crossword puzzles, and Microsoft PowerPoint presentations. Also included in the American Government Resource Center for Chapter 1:

- **InfoTrac® Reader**—Democracy in Iraq; immigration policy in the United States; liberals and conservatives; the American left.
- **You Are There Simulation**—Democracy.
- **Participation Activities**—Support a local public issue of great interest to you; explore the balance of constitutional rights and liberties and the need for increased national security.

- **MicroCase Exercise**—Democracy and political theory.
- **Related Links**—Democracy and political theory.
- **Video Case Study**—Desires of the founders.
- **Source Readings**—By Alexis de Tocqueville, Henry David Thoreau, Herbert Croly, and President John Kennedy.

The site also contains the Citizen's Survival Guide, information on how to get involved in politics locally and globally, as well as regularly updated features including a Current Events Quiz, In the News, Election Links, updates on the war on terrorism, and more.

CHAPTER 2

Forging a New Government: The Constitution

We the People of the United States, in Order to form a more perfect Union, establish Justice, insure domestic Tranquility, provide for the common defence, promote the general Welfare, and secure the Blessings of Liberty to ourselves and our Posterity, do ordain and establish this Constitution for the United States of America.

E VERY SCHOOLCHILD IN AMERICA has at one time or another been exposed to these famous words from the Preamble to the U.S. Constitution. The document itself is remarkable. The U.S. Constitution, compared with others in the states and in the world, is relatively short. Because amending it is difficult, it also has relatively few amendments. Perhaps even more remarkable is the fact that it has remained largely intact for over two hundred years. To a great extent, this is because the principles set forth in the Constitution are sufficiently broad that they can be adapted to meet the needs of a changing society.

How and why the U.S. Constitution was created is a story that has been told and retold. It is worth repeating, because the historical and political context in which this country's governmental machinery was formed is essential to understanding American government and politics today. In the years between the first settlements in the New World and the writing of the Constitution, Americans had developed a political philosophy about how people should be governed and had tried out numerous forms of government. These experiences gave the founders the tools with which they constructed the Constitution.

The Colonial Background

In 1607, the English government sent a group of farmers to establish a trading post, Jamestown, in what is now Virginia. The Virginia Company of London was the first to establish a permanent English colony in the Americas. The king of England gave the backers of this colony a charter granting them "full power and authority" to make laws "for the good and welfare" of the settlement. The colonists at Jamestown instituted a **representative assembly,** setting a precedent in government that was to be observed in later colonial adventures.

Separatists, the *Mayflower,* and the Compact

The first New England colony was established in 1620. A group of mostly extreme Separatists, who wished to break with the Church of England, came over on the ship *Mayflower* to the New World, landing at Plymouth (Massachusetts). Before going onshore, the adult males—women were not considered to have any political status—drew up the Mayflower Compact, which was signed by forty-one of the forty-four men aboard the ship on November 21, 1620. The reason for the compact was obvious. This group was outside the jurisdiction of the Virginia Company of London, which had chartered its settlement in Virginia, not Massachusetts. The Separatist leaders feared that some of the *Mayflower* passengers might conclude that they were no longer under any obligations of civil obedience. Therefore, some form of public authority was imperative. As William Bradford (one of the Separatist leaders) recalled in his accounts, there were "discontented and mutinous speeches that some of the strangers amongst them had let fall from them in the ship; That when they came a shore they would use their owne libertie; for none had power to command them."[1]

The compact was not a constitution. It was a political statement in which the signers agreed to create and submit to the authority of a government, pending the receipt of a royal charter. The Mayflower Compact's historical and political significance is twofold: it depended on the consent of the affected individuals, and it served as a prototype for similar compacts in American history. According to Samuel

In 1620, the Mayflower Compact was signed by almost all of the men aboard the ship Mayflower. It stated, "We . . . covenant and combine ourselves togeather into a civil body politick . . . ; and by vertue hearof to enacte, constitute, and frame such just and equal laws . . . as shall be thought [necessary] for the generall good of the Colonie."

The Granger Collection

Eliot Morison, the compact proved the determination of the English immigrants to live under the rule of law, based on the *consent of the people*.[2]

More Colonies, More Government

Another outpost in New England was set up by the Massachusetts Bay Colony in 1630. Then followed Rhode Island, Connecticut, New Hampshire, and others. By 1732, the last of the thirteen colonies, Georgia, was established. During the colonial period, Americans developed a concept of limited government, which followed from the establishment of the first colonies under Crown charters. Theoretically, London governed the colonies. In practice, owing partly to the colonies' distance from London, the colonists exercised a large measure of self-government. The colonists were able to make their own laws, as in the Fundamental Orders of Connecticut in 1639. The Massachusetts Body of Liberties in 1641 supported the protection of individual rights and was made a part of colonial law. In 1682, the Pennsylvania Frame of Government was passed. Along with the Pennsylvania Charter of Privileges of 1701, it established the rationale for our modern Constitution and Bill of Rights. All of this legislation enabled the colonists to acquire crucial political experience. After independence was declared in 1776, the states quickly set up their own constitutions.

The Road to Independence

The conflict between Britain and the American colonies, which ultimately led to the Revolutionary War, began in the 1760s when the British government decided to raise revenues by imposing taxes on the American colonies. Policy advisers to Britain's young King George III, who ascended the throne in 1760, decided that it was only logical to require the American colonists to help pay the costs of Britain's defending them during the French and Indian War (1756–1763). The colonists, who had grown accustomed to a large degree of self-government and independence from the British Crown, viewed the matter differently.

In 1764, the British Parliament passed the Sugar Act. Many colonists were unwilling to pay the tax imposed by the act. Further regulatory legislation was to come. In 1765, Parliament passed the Stamp Act, providing for internal taxation—or, as the colonists' Stamp Act Congress, assembled in 1765, called it, "taxation without representation." The colonists boycotted the purchase of English commodities in return. The success of the boycott (the Stamp Act was repealed a year later) generated a feeling of unity within the colonies. The British, however, continued to try to raise revenues in the colonies. When duties on glass, lead, paint, and other items were passed in 1767, the colonists again boycotted English goods. The colonists' fury over taxation climaxed in the Boston Tea Party: colonists dressed as Mohawk Indians dumped almost 350 chests of British tea into Boston Harbor as a gesture of tax protest. In retaliation, the British Parliament passed the Coercive Acts (the "Intolerable Acts") in 1774, which closed Boston Harbor and placed the government of Massachusetts under direct British control. The colonists were outraged—and they responded.

The Colonial Response:
The Continental Congresses

New York, Pennsylvania, and Rhode Island proposed the convening of a colonial congress. The Massachusetts House of Representatives requested that all colonies hold conventions to select delegates to be sent to Philadelphia for such a congress.

The First Continental Congress

The First Continental Congress was held at Carpenter's Hall on September 5, 1774. It was a gathering of delegates from twelve of the thirteen colonies (delegates from Georgia did not attend until 1775). At that meeting, there was little talk of independence. The Congress passed a resolution requesting that the colonies send a petition to King George III expressing their grievances. Resolutions were also passed requiring that the colonies raise their own troops and boycott British trade. The British government condemned the Congress's actions, treating them as open acts of rebellion.

National Portrait Gallery

King George III (1738–1820) was king of Great Britain and Ireland from 1760 until his death on January 29, 1820. Under George III, the first attempt to tax the American colonies was made. Ultimately, the American colonies, exasperated at renewed attempts at taxation, proclaimed their independence on July 4, 1776.

The Second Continental Congress

By the time the Second Continental Congress met in May 1775 (this time all of the colonies were represented), fighting already had broken out between the British and the colonists. One of the main actions of the Second Congress was to establish an army. It did this by declaring the militia that had gathered around Boston an army and naming George Washington as commander in chief. The participants in that Congress still attempted to reach a peaceful settlement with the British Parliament. One declaration of the Congress stated explicitly that "we have not raised armies with ambitious designs of separating from Great Britain, and establishing independent states." But by the beginning of 1776, military encounters had become increasingly frequent.

Public debate was acrimonious. Then Thomas Paine's *Common Sense* appeared in Philadelphia bookstores. The pamphlet was a colonial best seller. (To do relatively as well today, a book would have to sell between eight and ten million copies in its first year of publication.) Many agreed that Paine did make common sense when he argued that

a government of our own is our natural right: and when a man seriously reflects on the precariousness [instability, unpredictability] of human affairs, he will become convinced, that it is infinitely wiser and safer, to form a constitution of our own in a cool and deliberate manner, while we have it in our power, than to trust such an interesting event to time and chance.[3]

Students of Paine's pamphlet point out that his arguments were not new—they were common in tavern debates throughout the land. Rather, it was the near poetry of his words—which were at the same time as plain as the alphabet—that struck his readers.

Declaring Independence

On July 2, 1776, the Resolution of Independence was adopted by the Second Continental Congress:

> RESOLVED, That these United Colonies are, and of right ought to be free and independent States, that they are absolved from allegiance to the British Crown, and that all political connection between them and the state of Great Britain is, and ought to be, totally dissolved.

The actual Resolution of Independence was not legally significant. On the one hand, it was not judicially enforceable, for it established no legal rights or duties. On the other hand, the colonies were already, in their own judgment, self-governing and independent of Britain. Rather, the Resolution of Independence and the subsequent Declaration of Independence were necessary to establish the legitimacy of the new nation in the eyes of foreign governments, as well as in the eyes of the colonists themselves. What the new nation needed most were supplies for its armies and a commitment of foreign military aid. Unless it appeared in the eyes of the world as a political entity separate and independent from Britain, no foreign government would enter into a contract with its leaders.

July 4, 1776—The Declaration of Independence

On adoption of the Resolution of Independence, Thomas Jefferson argued that a declaration clearly putting forth the causes that compelled the colonies to separate from Britain was necessary. The Second Congress assigned the task to him. He had already been at work writing such a declaration and had soon completed a draft. Jefferson's declaration, which enumerated the colonists' major grievances against Britain, was passed on July 4, 1776. On July 19, a modified draft became "the unanimous declaration of the thirteen United States of America." On August 2, it was signed by the members of the Second Continental Congress.

The Declaration of Independence has become one of the world's most famous and significant documents. The words opening the second paragraph of the Declaration indicate why this is so:

> We hold these Truths to be self-evident, that all Men are created equal, that they are endowed by their Creator with certain unalienable Rights, that among these are Life, Liberty, and the Pursuit of Happiness—That to secure these Rights, Governments are instituted among Men, deriving their just Powers from the Consent of the Governed, that whenever any Form of Government becomes destructive of these Ends, it is the Right of the People to alter or abolish it, and to institute new Government.

Members of the Second Continental Congress adopted the Declaration of Independence on July 4, 1776. On July 19, the modified draft became the "unanimous declaration of the thirteen United States of America."

Photo Researchers, Van Bucher

Natural Rights and a Social Contract

Natural Rights
Rights held to be inherent in natural law, not dependent on governments.

The assumption that people have **natural rights** ("unalienable Rights"), including the rights to "Life, Liberty, and the Pursuit of Happiness," was a revolutionary concept at that time. Its use by Jefferson reveals the influence of the English philosopher John Locke (1632–1704), whose writings were familiar to educated American colonists, including Jefferson.[4] Locke had argued that all people possess certain natural rights, including the rights to life, liberty, and property, and that the primary purpose of government was to protect these rights. Furthermore, government was established by the people through a **social contract**—an agreement among the people to form a government and abide by its rules. As you read earlier, such contracts, or compacts, were not new to Americans. The Mayflower Compact was the first of several documents that established governments or governing rules based on the consent of the governed.

Social Contract A voluntary agreement among individuals to secure their rights and welfare by creating a government and abiding by its rules.

In citing the "pursuit of happiness" as a right, in place of "property," Jefferson clearly meant to go beyond Locke's thinking. After setting forth basic principles of government, the Declaration of Independence goes on to justify the colonists' revolt against Britain. Much of the remainder of the document is a list of what "He" (King George III) had done to deprive the colonists of their rights. (See Appendix A at the end of this book for the complete text of the Declaration of Independence.)

The Rise of Republicanism

Although the colonists had formally declared independence from Britain, the fight to gain actual independence continued for five more years—until the British General Cornwallis surrendered at Yorktown in 1781. In 1783, after Britain formally recognized the independent status of the United States in the Treaty of Paris, Washington disbanded the army. During these years of military struggles, the states faced the additional challenge of creating a system of self-government for an independent United States.

Some colonists in the middle and lower southern colonies had demanded that independence be preceded by the formation of a strong central government. But the anti-Royalists in New England and Virginia, who called themselves Republicans, were against a strong central government. They opposed monarchy, executive authority, and virtually any form of restraint on the power of local groups. These Republicans were a major political force from 1776 to 1780. Indeed, they almost prevented victory over the British by their unwillingness to cooperate with any central authority.

During this time, all of the states adopted written constitutions. Eleven of the constitutions were completely new. Two of them—those of Connecticut and Rhode Island—were old royal charters with minor modifications. Republican sentiment led to increased power for the legislatures. In Pennsylvania and Georgia, **unicameral** (one-body) **legislatures** were unchecked by executive or judicial authority. Basically, the Republicans attempted to maintain the politics of 1776. In almost all states, the legislature was predominant.

The Articles of Confederation: Our First Form of Government

The fear of a powerful central government led to the passage of the Articles of Confederation, which created a weak central government. The term **confederation** is important; it means a voluntary association of *independent* **states,** in which the member states agree to only limited restraints on their freedom of action. As a result, confederations seldom have an effective executive authority.

In June 1776, the Second Continental Congress began the process of drafting what would become the Articles of Confederation. The final form of the Articles was achieved by November 15, 1777. Under the Articles, the thirteen original colonies, now states, established on March 1, 1781, a government of the states—the Congress of the Confederation. The Congress was a unicameral assembly of so-called ambassadors from each state, with each state possessing a single vote. Each year, the Congress would choose one of its members as its president, but the Articles did not provide for a president of the United States.

The Congress was authorized in Article X to appoint an executive committee of the states "to execute in the recess of Congress, such of the powers of Congress as the United States, in Congress assembled, by the consent of nine [of the thirteen] states, shall from time to time think expedient to vest with them." The Congress was also allowed to appoint other committees and civil officers necessary for managing the general affairs of the United States. In addition, the Congress could regulate foreign affairs and establish coinage and weights and measures. But it lacked an independent source of revenue and the necessary executive machinery to enforce its decisions throughout the land. Article II of the Articles of Confederation guaranteed

Unicameral Legislature A legislature with only one legislative body, as opposed to a bicameral (two-house) legislature, such as the U.S. Congress. Nebraska is the only state with a unicameral legislature.

Confederation A voluntary association of independent states, in which the member states agree to limited restraints on their freedom of action by a central authority.

State A group of people occupying a specific area and organized under one government; may be either a nation or a subunit of a nation.

that each state would retain its sovereignty. Table 2–1 below summarizes the powers—and the lack of powers—of Congress under the Articles of Confederation.

Accomplishments under the Articles

The new government had some accomplishments during its eight years under the Articles of Confederation. Certain states' claims to western lands were settled. Maryland had objected to the claims of Massachusetts, New York, Connecticut, Virginia, the Carolinas, and Georgia. It was only after these states consented to give up their land claims to the United States as a whole that Maryland signed the Articles of Confederation. Another accomplishment under the Articles was the passage of the Northwest Ordinance of 1787, which established a basic pattern of government for new territories north of the Ohio River.

Weaknesses of the Articles

In spite of these accomplishments, the Articles of Confederation had many defects. Although Congress had the legal right to declare war and to conduct foreign policy, it did not have the right to demand revenues from the states. It could only *ask* for them. Additionally, the actions of Congress required the consent of nine states. Any amendments to the Articles required the unanimous consent of the Congress and confirmation by every state legislature. Furthermore, the Articles did not create a national system of courts.

Basically, the functioning of the government under the Articles depended on the goodwill of the states. Article III of the Articles simply established a "league of friendship" among the states—no national government was intended.

TABLE 2–1	Powers of the Congress of the Confederation
CONGRESS HAD POWER TO	CONGRESS LACKED POWER TO
• Declare war and make peace. • Enter into treaties and alliances. • Establish and control armed forces. • Requisition men and money from states. • Regulate coinage. • Borrow money and issue bills of credit. • Fix uniform standards of weight and measurement. • Create admiralty courts. • Create a postal system. • Regulate Indian affairs. • Guarantee citizens of each state the rights and privileges of citizens in the several states when in another state. • Adjudicate disputes between states on state petition.	• Provide for effective treaty-making power and control foreign relations; it could not compel states to respect treaties. • Compel states to meet military quotas; it could not draft soldiers. • Regulate interstate and foreign commerce; it left each state free to set up its own tariff system. • Collect taxes directly from the people; it had to rely on states to collect and forward taxes. • Compel states to pay their share of government costs. • Provide and maintain a sound monetary system or issue paper money; this was left up to the states, and monies in circulation differed tremendously in value.

Probably the most fundamental weakness of the Articles, and the most basic cause of their eventual replacement by the Constitution, concerned the lack of power to raise money for the militia. The Articles lacked any language giving Congress coercive power to raise money (by levying taxes) to provide adequate support for the military forces controlled by Congress. Due to a lack of resources, the Continental Congress was forced to disband the army, even in the face of serious Spanish and British military threats.

Shays' Rebellion and the Need for Revision of the Articles

Because of the weaknesses of the Articles of Confederation, the central government could do little to maintain peace and order in the new nation. The states bickered among themselves and increasingly taxed each other's goods. At times, they prevented trade altogether. By 1784, the country faced a serious economic depression. Banks were calling in old loans and refusing to give new ones. People who could not pay their debts were often thrown into prison.

In August 1786, mobs of musket-bearing farmers led by former revolutionary captain Daniel Shays seized county courthouses and disrupted the trials of debtors in Springfield, Massachusetts. Shays and his men then launched an attack on the federal arsenal at Springfield, but they were repulsed. Shays' Rebellion demonstrated that the central government could not protect the citizenry from armed rebellion or provide adequately for the public welfare. The rebellion spurred the nation's political leaders to action.

Drafting the Constitution

The Virginia legislature called for a meeting of all the states to be held at Annapolis, Maryland, on September 11, 1786. Among the important problems to be solved were the relationship between the states and the central government, the powers of the national legislature, the need for executive leadership, and the establishment of policies for economic stability. At the meeting, a call was issued to all of the states for a general convention to meet in Philadelphia in May 1787 "to consider the exigencies of the union."

The Philadelphia convention, later known as the Constitutional Convention, was formally opened in the East Room of the Pennsylvania State House on May 25, 1787.[5] Fifty-five of the seventy-four delegates chosen for the convention actually attended. Rhode Island was the only state that refused to send delegates.

Factions among the Delegates

We know much about the proceedings at the convention because James Madison kept a daily, detailed personal journal. A majority of the delegates were strong nationalists—they wanted a central government with real power, unlike the central government under the Articles of Confederation. George Washington and Benjamin Franklin preferred limited national authority based on a separation of powers.

Among the nationalists, some—including Alexander Hamilton—went so far as to support monarchy. Another important group of nationalists were of a more democratic stripe. Led by James Madison of Virginia and James Wilson of Pennsylvania, these nationalists wanted a central government founded on popular support.

Among the other factions was a group of delegates who were totally against a national authority. Two of the three delegates from New York quit the convention when they saw the nationalist direction of its proceedings.

Politicking and Compromises

INFOTRAC

To find out more about James Madison, use the term "Madison, James" in the Subject guide.

The debates at the convention started on the first day. James Madison had spent months reviewing European political theory. When his Virginia delegation arrived ahead of most of the others, it got to work immediately. By the time George Washington opened the convention, Governor Edmund Randolph of Virginia was prepared to present fifteen resolutions. In retrospect, this was a masterful stroke on the part of the Virginia delegation. It set the agenda for the remainder of the convention—even though, in principle, the delegates had been sent to Philadelphia for the sole purpose of amending the Articles of Confederation. They had not been sent to write a new constitution.

The Virginia Plan. Randolph's fifteen resolutions proposed an entirely new national government under a constitution. It was, however, a plan that favored the large states, including Virginia. Basically, it called for the following:

Bicameral Legislature A legislature made up of two parts called chambers. The U.S. Congress, composed of the House of Representatives and the Senate, is a bicameral legislature.

1. A **bicameral** (two-house) **legislature,** with the lower chamber chosen by the people and the smaller upper chamber chosen by the lower chamber from nominees selected by state legislatures. The number of representatives would be proportional to a state's population, thus favoring the large states. The legislature could void any state laws.

2. The creation of an unspecified national executive, elected by the legislature.

3. The creation of a national judiciary appointed by the legislature.

It did not take long for the smaller states to realize they would fare poorly under the Virginia plan, which would enable Virginia, Massachusetts, and Pennsylvania to form a majority in the national legislature. The debate on the plan dragged on for a number of weeks. It was time for the small states to come up with their own plan.

The New Jersey Plan. On June 15, lawyer William Paterson of New Jersey offered an alternative plan. After all, argued Paterson, under the Articles of Confederation all states had equality; therefore, the convention had no power to change this arrangement. He proposed the following:

1. The fundamental principle of the Articles of Confederation—one state, one vote—would be retained.

2. Congress would be able to regulate trade and impose taxes.

3. All acts of Congress would be the supreme law of the land.

4. Several people would be elected by Congress to form an executive office.

George Washington presided over the Constitutional Convention of 1787. It formally opened in Philadelphia in the East Room of the Pennsylvania State House (later named Independence Hall) on May 25, 1787. Only Rhode Island did not send any delegates.

The Granger Collection

5. The executive office would appoint a Supreme Court.

Basically, the New Jersey plan was simply an amendment of the Articles of Confederation. Its only notable feature was its reference to the **supremacy doctrine,** which was later included in the Constitution.

The "Great Compromise."
The delegates were at an impasse. Most wanted a strong national government and were unwilling even to consider the New Jersey plan. But when the Virginia plan was brought up again, the small states threatened to leave. It was not until July 16 that the **Great Compromise** was achieved. Roger Sherman of Connecticut proposed the following:

1. A bicameral legislature in which the House of Representatives would be apportioned according to the number of free inhabitants in each state, plus three-fifths of the slaves.

2. An upper house, the Senate, which would have two members from each state elected by the state legislatures.

This plan, also called the Connecticut Compromise because of the role of the Connecticut delegates in the proposal, broke the deadlock. It did exact a political price, however, because it permitted each state to have equal representation in the Senate. Having two senators represent each state in effect diluted the voting power of citizens living in more heavily populated states and gave the smaller states disproportionate political powers. But the Connecticut Compromise resolved the large-state/small-state controversy. In addition, the Senate acted as part of a checks-and-balances system

Supremacy Doctrine
A doctrine that asserts the priority of national law over state laws. This principle is rooted in the Constitution, which states that the Constitution, the laws passed by the national government, and treaties constitute the supreme law of the land.

Great Compromise
The compromise between the New Jersey and Virginia plans that created one chamber of the Congress based on population and one chamber representing each state equally; also called the Connecticut Compromise.

against the House, which many feared would be dominated by, and responsive to, the masses.

The Three-Fifths Compromise.

The Great Compromise also settled another major issue—how to deal with slaves in the representational scheme. Slavery was still legal in many northern states, but it was concentrated in the South. The South wanted slaves to be counted equally in determining representation in Congress. Delegates from the northern states objected. Sherman's three-fifths compromise solved the issue, satisfying those northerners who felt that slaves should not be counted at all and those southerners who wanted them to be counted in the same way as free whites. Actually, Sherman's Connecticut plan spoke of three-fifths of "all other persons" (and that is the language in the Constitution itself). It is not hard to figure out, though, who those other persons were.

The slavery issue was not completely eliminated by the three-fifths compromise. Many delegates were opposed to slavery and wanted it banned entirely in the United States. Charles Pinckney of South Carolina led strong southern opposition to the idea of a ban on slavery. Finally, the delegates agreed that Congress could limit the importation of slaves after 1808. The compromise meant that the issue of slavery itself was never addressed. The South won twenty years of unrestricted slave trade and a requirement that escaped slaves in free states be returned to their owners in slave states.

Export Taxes.

The agrarian South was also worried that the northern majority in Congress would pass legislation unfavorable to its economic interests. Because the South depended on exports of its agricultural products, it feared the imposition of export taxes. In return for acceding to the northern demand that Congress be given the power to regulate commerce among the states and with other nations, the South obtained a promise that export taxes would not be imposed. Even today, such taxes are prohibited. The United States is among the few countries that do not tax their exports.

Working toward Final Agreement

The Connecticut Compromise was reached by mid-July. The make-up of the executive branch and the judiciary, however, was left unsettled. The remaining work of the convention was turned over to a five-man Committee of Detail, which presented a rough draft of the Constitution on August 6. It made the executive and judicial branches subordinate to the legislative branch.

The Madisonian Model—Separation of Powers.

The major issue of **separation of powers** had not yet been resolved. The delegates were concerned with structuring the government to prevent the imposition of tyranny—either by the majority or by a minority. It was Madison who proposed a governmental scheme—sometimes called the **Madisonian model**—to achieve this: the executive, legislative, and judicial powers of government were to be separated so that no one branch had enough power to dominate the others. The separation of powers was by function, as well as by personnel, with Congress passing laws, the president enforcing and administering laws, and the courts interpreting laws in individual circumstances.

Separation of Powers The principle of dividing governmental powers among the executive, legislative, and judicial branches of government.

Madisonian Model A structure of government proposed by James Madison in which the powers of the government are separated into three branches: executive, legislative, and judicial.

Each of the three branches of government would be independent of the others, but they would have to cooperate to govern. According to Madison, in *Federalist Paper* No. 51 (see Appendix C), "the great security against a gradual concentration of the several powers in the same department consists in giving to those who administer each department the necessary constitutional means and personal motives to resist encroachments of the others."

The Madisonian Model—Checks and Balances.

The "constitutional means" Madison referred to is a system of **checks and balances** through which each branch of the government can check the actions of the others. For example, Congress can enact laws, but the president has veto power over congressional acts. The Supreme Court has the power to declare acts of Congress and of the executive unconstitutional, but the president appoints the justices of the Supreme Court, with the advice and consent of the Senate. (The Supreme Court's power to declare acts unconstitutional was not mentioned in the Constitution, although arguably the framers assumed that the Court would have this power—see the discussion of judicial review later in this chapter.) Figure 2–1 on the next page outlines these checks and balances.

In the years since the Constitution was ratified, the checks and balances built into it have evolved into a sometimes complex give-and-take among the branches of government. Generally, for nearly every check that one branch can exercise over another, the branch that has been checked has found a way of getting around it. For example, suppose that the president checks Congress by vetoing a bill. Congress can override the presidential veto by a two-thirds vote. Additionally, Congress holds the "power of the purse." If it disagrees with a program endorsed by the executive branch, it can simply refuse to appropriate the funds necessary to operate that program. Similarly, the president can impose a countercheck on Congress if the Senate refuses to confirm a presidential appointment, such as a judicial appointment. The president can simply wait until Congress is in recess and then make what is called a "recess appointment," which does not require the Senate's approval.

The Executive.

Some delegates favored a plural executive made up of representatives from the various regions. This was abandoned in favor of a single chief executive. Some argued that Congress should choose the executive. To make the presidency completely independent of the proposed Congress, however, an **electoral college** was adopted. To be sure, the electoral college created a cumbersome presidential election process. The process even made it possible that a candidate who came in second in the popular vote would become president by being the top vote getter in the electoral college. The electoral college insulated the president, however, from direct popular control. The seven-year single term that some of the delegates had proposed was replaced by a four-year term and the possibility of reelection.

The Final Document

On September 17, 1787, the Constitution was approved by thirty-nine delegates. Of the fifty-five who had attended originally, only forty-two remained. Three delegates

Checks and Balances A major principle of the American government system whereby each branch of the government exercises a check on the actions of the others.

Electoral College A group of persons called electors selected by the voters in each state and (since 1961) Washington, D.C.; this group officially elects the president and vice president of the United States.

FIGURE 2–1   **Checks and Balances**

The major checks and balances among the three branches are illustrated here. The Constitution does not mention some of these checks, such as judicial review—the power of the courts to declare federal or state acts unconstitutional—and the president's ability to refuse to enforce judicial decisions or congressional legislation. Checks and balances can be thought of as a confrontation of powers or responsibilities. Each branch checks the action of another; two branches in conflict have powers that can result in balances or stalemates, requiring one branch to give in or both to reach a compromise.

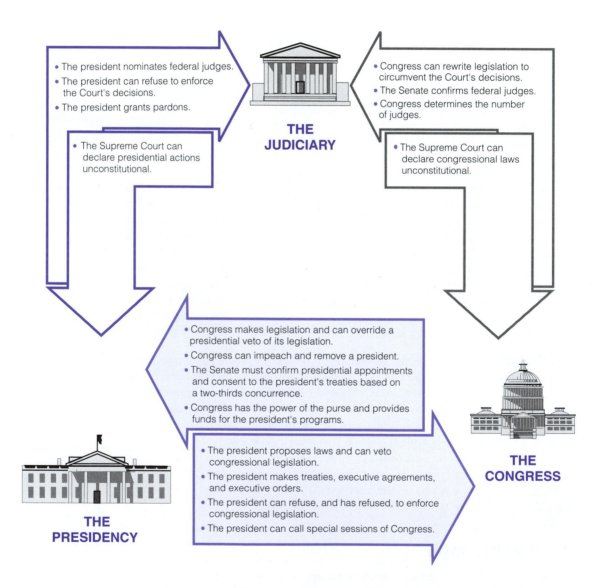

THE JUDICIARY

- The president nominates federal judges.
- The president can refuse to enforce the Court's decisions.
- The president grants pardons.

- The Supreme Court can declare presidential actions unconstitutional.

- Congress can rewrite legislation to circumvent the Court's decisions.
- The Senate confirms federal judges.
- Congress determines the number of judges.

- The Supreme Court can declare congressional laws unconstitutional.

- Congress makes legislation and can override a presidential veto of its legislation.
- Congress can impeach and remove a president.
- The Senate must confirm presidential appointments and consent to the president's treaties based on a two-thirds concurrence.
- Congress has the power of the purse and provides funds for the president's programs.

- The president proposes laws and can veto congressional legislation.
- The president makes treaties, executive agreements, and executive orders.
- The president can refuse, and has refused, to enforce congressional legislation.
- The president can call special sessions of Congress.

THE PRESIDENCY

THE CONGRESS

refused to sign the Constitution. Others disapproved of at least parts of it but signed anyway to begin the ratification debate.

The Constitution that was to be ratified established the following fundamental principles:

1. Popular sovereignty, or control by the people.
2. A republican government in which the people choose representatives to make decisions for them.
3. Limited government with written laws, in contrast to the powerful British government against which the colonists had rebelled.
4. Separation of powers, with checks and balances among branches to prevent any one branch from gaining too much power.
5. A federal system that allows for states' rights, because the states feared too much centralized control.

INFOTRAC
To find out more about the Constitution, use the term "United States Constitution" in the Subject guide, and then go to subdivision "history."

The Difficult Road to Ratification

The founders knew that **ratification** of the Constitution was far from certain. Indeed, because it was almost guaranteed that many state legislatures would not ratify it, the delegates agreed that each state should hold a special convention. Elected delegates to these conventions would discuss and vote on the Constitution. Further departing from the Articles of Confederation, the delegates agreed that as soon as nine states (rather than all thirteen) approved the Constitution, it would take effect, and Congress could begin to organize the new government.

Ratification Formal approval.

The Federalists Push for Ratification

The two opposing forces in the battle over ratification were the Federalists and the Anti-Federalists. The **Federalists** favored a strong central government and the new Constitution. The **Anti-Federalists** wanted to prevent the Constitution as drafted from being ratified.[6]

Federalist An individual who favored the adoption of the U.S. Constitution.

Anti-Federalist An individual who opposed the ratification of the new Constitution in 1787.

The Federalist Papers. In New York, opponents of the Constitution were quick to attack it. Alexander Hamilton answered their attacks anonymously in newspaper columns and secured two collaborators—John Jay and James Madison. In a very short time, those three political figures wrote a series of eighty-five essays in defense of the Constitution and of a republican form of government.

These widely read essays, called *The Federalist Papers*, appeared in New York newspapers from October 1787 to August 1788 and were reprinted in the newspapers of other states. Although we do not know for certain who wrote every one, it is apparent that Hamilton was responsible for about two-thirds of the essays. These included the most important ones interpreting the Constitution, explaining the various powers of the three branches, and presenting a theory of judicial review. Madison's *Federalist Paper* No. 10 (see Appendix C), however, is considered a classic in political theory; it deals with the nature of groups—or factions, as he called them. In spite of the rapidity with which *The Federalist Papers* were written, they are considered by many to be perhaps the best example of political theorizing ever produced in the United States.[7]

The Anti-Federalist Response. Many of the Anti-Federalists' attacks against the Constitution were also brilliant. The Anti-Federalists claimed that the Constitution was written by aristocrats and would lead to aristocratic tyranny. More important, the Anti-Federalists believed that the Constitution would create an overbearing and overburdening central government hostile to personal liberty. (The Constitution said nothing about freedom of the press, freedom of religion, or any other individual liberty.) They wanted to include a list of guaranteed liberties, or a bill of rights. Finally, the Anti-Federalists decried the weakened power of the states.

The Anti-Federalists cannot be dismissed as unpatriotic extremists. They included such patriots as Patrick Henry and Samuel Adams. They were arguing what had been the most prevalent view of the time. This view derived from the French political philosopher Montesquieu (1689–1755), who believed that liberty was safe only in relatively small societies governed by direct democracy or by a large legislature with small districts. The Madisonian view favoring a large republic, particularly expressed in *Federalist Papers* No. 10 and No. 51 (see Appendix C), was actually the more *un*popular view at the time. Indeed, some researchers believe it was mainly the bitter experiences with the Articles of Confederation, rather than Madison's arguments, that persuaded the state conventions to ratify the Constitution.[8]

INFOTRAC

To find out more about this subject, use the term "Anti-Federalists" in Keywords.

The March to the Finish

The struggle for ratification continued. Strong majorities were procured in Delaware, Pennsylvania, New Jersey, Georgia, and Connecticut. After a bitter struggle in Massachusetts, that state ratified the Constitution by a narrow margin on February 6, 1788. By the spring, Maryland and South Carolina had ratified by sizable majorities. Then, on June 21 of that year, New Hampshire became the ninth state to ratify. Although the Constitution was formally in effect, this meant little without Virginia and New York—the latter did not ratify for another month. (Was the Constitution actually favored by a majority of citizens at the time? See this chapter's feature *At Issue: Did the Majority of Americans Support the Constitution?*)

The Bill of Rights

The U.S. Constitution would not have been ratified in several important states if the Federalists had not assured the states that amendments to the Constitution would be passed to protect individual liberties against incursions by the national government. Many of the recommendations of the state ratifying conventions included specific rights that were considered later by James Madison as he labored to draft what became the Bill of Rights.

Madison had to cull through more than two hundred state recommendations. It was no small task, and in retrospect he chose remarkably well. One of the rights that he left out was equal protection under the laws—but that was not commonly regarded as a basic right at that time. Not until 1868 did the states ratify an amend-

AT ISSUE: Did the Majority of Americans Support the Constitution?

In 1913, historian Charles Beard published *An Economic Interpretation of the Constitution of the United States.** This book launched a debate that has continued ever since—the debate over whether the Constitution was supported by a majority of Americans.

BEARD'S THESIS

Beard's central thesis was that the Constitution had been produced primarily by wealthy property owners who desired a stronger government able to protect their property rights. Beard also claimed that the Constitution had been imposed by undemocratic methods to prevent democratic majorities from exercising real power. He pointed out that there was never any popular vote on whether to hold a constitutional convention in the first place.

Furthermore, even if such a vote had been taken, state laws generally restricted voting rights to property-owning white males, meaning that most people in the country (white males without property, women, Native Americans, and slaves) were not eligible to vote.

STATE RATIFYING CONVENTIONS

As for the various state ratifying conventions, the delegates had been selected by only 150,000 of the approximately four million inhabitants of the country. That does not seem very democratic—at least not by today's standards. Some historians

have suggested that if a Gallup poll could have been taken at that time, the Anti-Federalists would probably have outnumbered the Federalists.[†]

Certainly, some of the delegates to state ratifying conventions from poor, agrarian areas feared that an elite group of Federalists would run the country just as oppressively as the British had governed the colonies.

WIDESPREAD SUPPORT

Much has also been made of the various machinations used by the Federalists to ensure the Constitution's ratification (and they did resort to a variety of devious tactics, including purchasing at least one printing press to prevent the publication of Anti-Federalist sentiments). Yet the perception that a strong central government was necessary to keep order and protect the public welfare appears to have been fairly pervasive among all classes—rich and poor alike.

FOR CRITICAL ANALYSIS

Massachusetts delegate Jonathan Smith posited an example to make his point that the Constitution should be ratified: "Suppose two or three of you had been at the pains to break up a piece of rough land, and sow it with wheat; would you let it lie waste because you could not agree on what sort of a fence to make?" What light, if any, does this sentiment shed on the American political process generally?

*Charles A. Beard, *An Economic Interpretation of the Constitution of the United States* (New York: Macmillan, 1913; New York: Free Press, 1986).

[†]Jim Powell, "James Madison—Checks and Balances to Limit Government Power," *The Freeman,* March 1996, p. 178.

ment guaranteeing that no state shall deny equal protection to any person. (An ongoing issue is whether noncitizens should have equal protection under federal law—see the *America's Security* feature on page 38.)

The final number of amendments that Madison and a specially appointed committee came up with was seventeen. Congress tightened the language somewhat and eliminated five of the amendments. Of the remaining twelve, two—dealing with the apportionment of representatives and the compensation of the members of Congress—were not ratified immediately by the states. Eventually, Supreme Court decisions led to reforms of the apportionment process. The amendment on the compensation of members of Congress was ratified 203 years later—in 1992!

On December 15, 1791, the national Bill of Rights was adopted when Virginia agreed to ratify the ten amendments. On ratification, the Bill of Rights became part of the U.S. Constitution. The basic structure of American government had already been established. Now the fundamental rights and liberties of individuals were protected, at least in theory, at the national level. The proposed amendment that Madison characterized as "the most valuable amendment in the whole lot"—which would have prohibited the states from infringing on the freedoms of conscience, press, and jury trial—had been eliminated by the Senate. Thus, the Bill of Rights as adopted did not limit state power, and individual citizens had to rely on the guarantees contained in a particular state constitution or state bill of rights. The country had to wait until the violence of the Civil War before significant limitations on state power in the form of the Fourteenth Amendment became part of the national Constitution.

Altering the Constitution

The U.S. Constitution consists of 7,000 words. It is shorter than any state constitution except that of Vermont, which has 6,880 words. One of the reasons the federal Constitution is short is that the founders intended it to be only a framework for the new government, to be interpreted by succeeding generations. One of the reasons it has remained short is that the formal amending procedure does not allow for changes to be made easily. Article V of the Constitution outlines the ways in which amendments may be proposed and ratified (see Figure 2–2).

FIGURE 2–2   **The Formal Constitutional Amending Procedure**

There are two ways of proposing amendments to the U.S. Constitution and two ways of ratifying proposed amendments. Among the four possibilities, the usual route has been proposal by Congress and ratification by state legislatures.

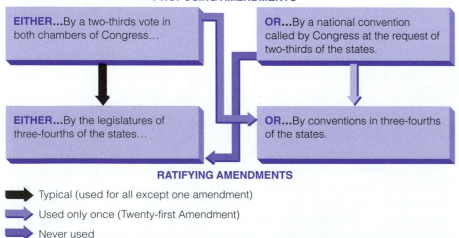

PROPOSING AMENDMENTS

EITHER... By a two-thirds vote in both chambers of Congress...

OR... By a national convention called by Congress at the request of two-thirds of the states.

EITHER... By the legislatures of three-fourths of the states...

OR... By conventions in three-fourths of the states.

RATIFYING AMENDMENTS

➡ Typical (used for all except one amendment)

➡ Used only once (Twenty-first Amendment)

➡ Never used

Two formal methods of proposing an amendment to the Constitution are available: (1) a two-thirds vote in each chamber of Congress or (2) a national convention that is called by Congress at the request of two-thirds of the state legislatures (the second method has never been used).

Ratification can occur by one of two methods: (1) by a positive vote in three-fourths of the legislatures of the various states or (2) by special conventions called in the states for the specific purpose of ratifying the proposed amendment and a positive vote in three-fourths of them. The second method has been used only once, to repeal Prohibition (the Twenty-first Amendment).

Congress has considered more than eleven thousand amendments to the Constitution. Only thirty-three have been submitted to the states after having been approved by the required two-thirds vote in each chamber of Congress, and only twenty-seven have been ratified—see Table 2–2. (The full, annotated text of the U.S. Constitution, including its amendments, is presented in Appendix B at the end of this book.) It should be clear that the amendment process is much more difficult than a graphic depiction such as Figure 2–2 can indicate. Because of competing social and economic interests, the requirement that two-thirds of both the House and the Senate approve the amendments is difficult to achieve.

TABLE 2–2	Amendments to the Constitution		
AMENDMENT	SUBJECT	YEAR ADOPTED	TIME REQUIRED FOR RATIFICATION
1st–10th	The Bill of Rights	1791	2 years, 2 months, 20 days
11th	Immunity of states from certain suits	1795	11 months, 3 days
12th	Changes in electoral college procedure	1804	6 months, 3 days
13th	Prohibition of slavery	1865	10 months, 3 days
14th	Citizenship, due process, and equal protection	1868	2 years, 26 days
15th	No denial of vote because of race, color, or previous condition of servitude	1870	11 months, 8 days
16th	Power of Congress to tax income	1913	3 years, 6 months, 22 days
17th	Direct election of U.S. senators	1913	10 months, 26 days
18th	National (liquor) prohibition	1919	1 year, 29 days
19th	Women's right to vote	1920	1 year, 2 months, 14 days
20th	Change of dates for congressional and presidential terms	1933	10 months, 21 days
21st	Repeal of the Eighteenth Amendment	1933	9 months, 15 days
22d	Limit on presidential tenure	1951	3 years, 11 months, 3 days
23d	District of Columbia electoral vote	1961	9 months, 13 days
24th	Prohibition of tax payment as a qualification to vote in federal elections	1964	1 year, 4 months, 9 days
25th	Procedures for determining presidential disability and presidential succession and for filling a vice presidential vacancy	1967	1 year, 7 months, 4 days
26th	Prohibition of setting minimum voting age above eighteen in any election	1971	3 months, 7 days
27th	Prohibition of Congress's voting itself a raise that takes effect before the next election	1992	203 years

AMERICA'S SECURITY

Military Tribunals for Suspected Terrorists

About two months after 9/11, Attorney General John Ashcroft and Vice President Dick Cheney announced that suspected terrorists would be prosecuted in American military tribunals. There was an immediate outcry against this violation of constitutional safeguards. Nonetheless, President George W. Bush called military trials "absolutely the right thing to do."

In times of crisis, particularly war, the United States has routinely used military tribunals. During the Civil War, for example, the Union Army conducted over four thousand trials by military tribunals. In the last days of the war, several nonmilitary personnel were hanged after being convicted by military tribunals of spying for the South. In 1942, during World War II, German agents who had traveled by submarine to Florida, Long Island, and New York were convicted and sentenced to death by military tribunals.

REDUCED RIGHTS OF THE ACCUSED

In November 2001, President Bush promulgated an executive order setting up military tribunals for noncitizens. The defendant was to have far fewer rights than any military defendant facing a court-martial.

In March 2002, in response to significant public criticism of the proposed tribunals, the Pentagon made public a revised set of rules that allow suspected terrorists to have the presumption of innocence and the right to remain silent. The prosecution must prove that the defendant is guilty beyond a reasonable doubt. The military judges can convict a defendant by a two-thirds majority vote. For the death penalty to be imposed, the judges' decision must be unanimous.

Defendants in such trials, however, do not have the right to a jury trial. Hearsay can be accepted as evidence. Finally, there can be no civilian review of the judges' decisions.

THE REASONING BEHIND MILITARY TRIBUNALS

The Bush administration argued that, in view of these "extraordinary times," secret military tribunals were necessary to safeguard evidence that could be used to prevent future terrorist attacks on Americans and their country. Moreover, the government does not want to give terrorist leaders and supporters a forum for expressing their anti-American views.

Consider also that in a normal criminal trial, evidence can be thrown out based on the exclusionary rule—which is used to keep evidence that is gathered illegally from being admitted in court. The administration does not think that people bent on destroying this country should have such constitutional rights.

FOR CRITICAL ANALYSIS

Under what circumstances should terrorist suspects have the same constitutional rights that criminal suspects have in our normal criminal justice system?

After approval by Congress, the process becomes even more arduous. Three-fourths of the state legislatures must approve the amendment. Only those amendments that have wide popular support across parties and in all regions of the country are likely to be approved.

Why was the amendment process made so difficult? The framers feared that a simple amendment process could lead to a tyranny of the majority, which could pass amendments to oppress disfavored individuals and groups. The cumbersome amendment process does not seem to stem the number of amendments that are proposed each year in Congress, however, particularly in recent years.

Informal Methods of Constitutional Change

INFOTRAC
To find out more about the amendment process, use the term "United States Constitution" in the Subject guide, and then go to subdivision "amendments."

Looking at the sparse number of formal constitutional amendments gives us an incomplete view of constitutional change. The brevity and ambiguity of the original document have permitted great changes in the Constitution by way of varying interpretations over time. As the United States grew, both in population and territory, new social and political realities emerged. Congress, presidents, and the courts found it necessary to interpret the Constitution's provisions in light of these new realities. The Constitution has proved to be a remarkably flexible document, adapting itself time and again to new events and concerns.

Actions by Congress and the President

The Constitution gives Congress broad powers to carry out its duties as the nation's legislative body. For example, Article I, Section 8, of the Constitution gives Congress the power to regulate foreign and interstate commerce. Although there is no clear definition of foreign commerce or interstate commerce in the Constitution, Congress has cited the *commerce clause* as the basis for passing thousands of laws.

Similarly, although the Constitution does not expressly authorize the president to propose bills or even budgets to Congress, presidents since the time of Woodrow Wilson (who served as president from 1913 to 1921) have proposed hundreds of bills to Congress each year. Presidents have also relied on their Article II authority as commander in chief of the nation's armed forces to send American troops abroad into combat, although the Constitution provides that Congress has the power to declare war. Presidents have also conducted foreign affairs by the use of **executive agreements,** which are legally binding documents made between the president and a foreign head of state. The Constitution does not mention such agreements.

Executive Agreement A binding international agreement between chiefs of state that does not require legislative approval.

Judicial Review

Another way of changing the Constitution—or of making it more flexible—is through the power of judicial review. **Judicial review** refers to the power of U.S. courts to invalidate actions undertaken by the legislative and executive branches of government. A state court, for example, may rule that a statute enacted by the state legislature is unconstitutional. Federal courts (and ultimately, the United States Supreme Court) may rule unconstitutional not only acts of Congress and decisions of the national executive branch but also state statutes, state executive actions, and even provisions of state constitutions.

Judicial Review The power of the Supreme Court or any court to declare unconstitutional federal or state laws and other acts of government.

INFOTRAC

To find out more about this topic, use the term "judicial review" in the Subject guide.

The Constitution does not specifically mention the power of judicial review. In 1803, the Supreme Court claimed this power for itself in *Marbury v. Madison*,[9] in which the Court ruled that a particular provision of an act of Congress was unconstitutional.

Through the process of judicial review, the Supreme Court adapts the Constitution to modern situations. Electronic technology, for example, did not exist when the Constitution was ratified. Nonetheless, the Supreme Court has used the Fourth Amendment guarantees against unreasonable searches and seizures to place limits on the use of wiretapping and other electronic eavesdropping methods by government officials. At some point, the Court may need to decide whether certain new antiterrorism laws passed by Congress or state legislatures violate the Fourth Amendment or other constitutional provisions. Additionally, the Supreme Court has changed its interpretation of the Constitution in accordance with changing values. It ruled in 1896 that "separate-but-equal" public facilities for African Americans were constitutional; but by 1954 the times had changed, and the Supreme Court reversed that decision.[10] Woodrow Wilson summarized the Supreme Court's work when he described it as "a constitutional convention in continuous session." Basically, the law is what the Supreme Court says it is at any point in time.

Interpretation, Custom, and Usage

The Constitution has also been changed through its interpretation by both Congress and the president. Originally, the president had a staff consisting of personal secretaries and a few others. Today, because Congress delegates specific tasks to the president and the chief executive assumes political leadership, the executive office staff alone has increased to several thousand persons. The executive branch provides legislative leadership far beyond the intentions of the Constitution.

Changes in the ways of doing political business have also altered the Constitution. The Constitution does not mention political parties, yet these informal, "extraconstitutional" organizations make the nominations for offices, run the campaigns, organize the members of Congress, and in fact change the election system from time to time. The emergence and evolution of the party system, for example, have changed the way the president is elected. The Constitution calls for the electoral college to choose the president. Today, the people vote for electors who are pledged to the candidate of their party, effectively choosing the president themselves. Perhaps most striking, the Constitution has been adapted from serving the needs of a small, rural republic to providing a framework of government for an industrial giant with vast geographic, natural, and human resources.

MAKING A DIFFERENCE:
How Can You Affect the U.S. Constitution?

The Constitution is an enduring document that has survived more than two hundred years of turbulent history. It is also a changing document, however. Twenty-seven amendments have been added to the original Constitution. How can you, as an individual, actively help to rewrite the Constitution?

Consider how one person decided to affect the Constitution. Shirley Breeze, head of the Missouri Women's Network, decided to bring the Equal Rights Amendment (ERA) back to life after its "death" in 1982. She spearheaded a movement that gained significant support. Today, bills to ratify the ERA have been introduced not only in Missouri but also in other states that did not ratify it earlier, including Illinois, Virginia, and Oklahoma.

TAKING ACTION ON AN AMENDMENT

At the time of this writing, national coalitions of interest groups are supporting or opposing a number of proposed amendments. One hotly debated proposed amendment concerns abortion. If you are interested in this issue and would like to make a difference, you can contact one of several groups.

An organization whose primary goal is to secure the passage of the Human Life Amendment is:

American Life League
P.O. Box 1350
Stafford, VA 22555
540-659-4171
http://www.all.org

The Human Life Amendment would recognize in law the "personhood" of the unborn, secure human rights protections for an unborn child from the time of fertilization, and prohibit abortion under any circumstances.

A political action and information organization working on behalf of "pro-choice" issues—that is, the right of women to have control over reproduction—is:

NARAL Pro-Choice America (formerly the National Abortion and Reproductive Rights Action League)
1156 15th St., Suite 700
Washington, DC 20005
202-973-3000
http://www.naral.org

PROTECTING RIGHTS AND LIBERTIES

There is also another way that you can affect the Constitution—by protecting your existing rights and liberties under the Constitution. In the wake of the 9/11 attacks, a number of new laws have been enacted that many believe go too far in curbing our constitutional rights. If you agree and want to join with others who are concerned about this issue, a good starting point is the Web site of the American Civil Liberties Union (ACLU) at http://www.aclu.org.

KEY TERMS

Anti-Federalist 33

bicameral legislature 28

checks and balances 31

confederation 25

electoral college 31

executive agreement 39

Federalist 33

Great Compromise 29

judicial review 39

Madisonian model 30

natural rights 24

ratification 33

representative assembly 20

separation of powers 30

social contract 24

state 25

supremacy doctrine 29

unicameral legislature 25

CHAPTER SUMMARY

1 The first permanent English colonies were established at Jamestown in 1607 and Plymouth in 1620. The Mayflower Compact created the first formal government for the British colonists. By the mid-1700s, other British colonies had been established along the Atlantic seaboard from Georgia to Maine.

2 In 1763, the British tried to reassert control over their increasingly independent-minded colonies through a series of taxes and legislative acts. The colonists responded with boycotts of British products and protests. Representatives of the colonies formed the First Continental Congress in 1774. The delegates sent a petition to the British king expressing their grievances. The Second Continental Congress established an army in 1775 to defend colonists against attacks by British soldiers.

3 On July 4, 1776, the Second Continental Congress approved the Declaration of Independence. Perhaps the most revolutionary aspects of the Declaration were its assumptions that people have natural rights to life, liberty, and the pursuit of happiness; that governments derive their power from the consent of the governed; and that people have a right to overthrow oppressive governments. During the Revolutionary War, all of the colonies adopted written constitutions that severely curtailed the power of executives, thus giving their legislatures predominant powers. By the end of the Revolutionary War, the

states had signed the Articles of Confederation, creating a weak central government with few powers. The Articles proved to be unworkable because the national government had no way to assure compliance by the states with such measures as securing tax revenues.

4 General dissatisfaction with the Articles of Confederation prompted delegates to call a convention at Philadelphia in 1787. Although the delegates originally convened with the idea of amending the Articles, the discussions soon focused on creating a constitution for a new form of government. The Virginia plan and the New Jersey plan were offered but did not garner widespread support. A compromise offered by the state of Connecticut helped to break the large-state/small-state disputes dividing the delegates. The final version of the Constitution provided for the separation of powers, checks and balances, and a federal form of government.

5 Fears of a strong central government prompted the addition of the Bill of Rights to the Constitution. The Bill of Rights secured for Americans a wide variety of freedoms, including the freedoms of religion, speech, and assembly. It was initially applied only to the federal government, but amendments to the Constitution following the Civil War made it clear that the Bill of Rights would apply to the states as well.

6 An amendment to the Constitution may be proposed either by a two-thirds vote in each house of Congress or by a national convention called by Congress at the request of two-thirds of the state legislatures. Ratification can occur either by a positive vote in three-fourths of the legislatures of the various states or by special conventions called in the states for the specific purpose of ratifying the proposed amendment and a positive vote in three-fourths of these state conventions. Informal methods of constitutional change include congressional legislation, presidential actions, judicial review, and changing interpretations of the Constitution.

SELECTED PRINT AND MEDIA RESOURCES

Suggested Readings

Bailyn, Bernard. *To Begin the World Anew: The Genius and Ambiguities of the American Founders*. New York: Knopf, 2003. In a series of essays, a two-time Pulitzer Prize winning historian discusses the themes of order and liberty in *The Federalist Papers* and the advantages of the founders' provincialism. Bailyn also examines contradictions between theory and practice in the lives of Benjamin Franklin and Thomas Jefferson.

Dahl, Robert A. *How Democratic Is the American Constitution?* New Haven, Conn.: Yale University Press, 2002. This book compares the U.S. Constitution with the constitutions of other democratic countries in the world.

Hamilton, Alexander, *et al. The Federalist: The Famous Papers on the Principles of American Government*. Benjamin F. Wright, ed. New York: Friedman/Fairfax Publishing, 2002. This is an updated version of the famous papers written by Alexander Hamilton, James Madison, and John Jay, and published in the *New York Packet*, in support of the ratification of the Constitution.

Orwell, George. *1984*. New York: Knopf, 1992. This is a classic novel about a society in which the totalitarian government ("Big Brother") watches over all. Originally published in 1949, this book is especially relevant today in view of the increased surveillance of the public in the interests of security against terrorism.

Sheldon, Charles H., and Stephen L. Wasby. *Essentials of the American Constitution*. Boulder, Colo.: Westview Press, 2001. The authors present a readable and readily understandable analysis of the concepts set forth in our founding document.

Media Resources

In the Beginning—A 1987 Bill Moyers program that features discussions with three prominent historians about the roots of the Constitution and its impact on our society.

John Locke—A 1994 video exploring the character and principal views of John Locke.

Thomas Jefferson—A 1996 documentary by acclaimed director Ken Burns. The film covers Jefferson's entire life, including his writing of the Declaration of Independence, his presidency, and his later years in Virginia. Historians and writers interviewed include Daniel Boorstin, Garry Wills, Gore Vidal, and John Hope Franklin.

LOGGING ON

For U.S. founding documents, including the Declaration of Independence, scanned originals of the U.S. Constitution, and *The Federalist Papers*, go to Emory University School of Law's Web site at **http://www.law.emory.edu/FEDERAL**.

The University of Oklahoma Law Center has a number of U.S. historical documents online, including many of those discussed in this chapter. Go to **http://www.law.ou.edu/hist**.

The National Constitution Center provides information on the Constitution—including its history, current debates over constitutional provisions, and news articles—at the following site: **http://www.constitutioncenter.org**.

To look at state constitutions, go to **http://www.findlaw.com/casecode/state.html**.

USING THE INTERNET FOR POLITICAL ANALYSIS

Go to this text's Web site at **http://politicalscience. wadsworth.com/schmidtbrief2004**. Select "Chapter 2" in the box at the top of the window. Then, in the column on the left-hand side of the window, under "Chapter Resources," click on "Internet Exercises." The Web site will then display the following Internet exercises that you can perform to learn more about topics covered in this chapter.

Activity 2–1: Constitutions of Other Nations
Activity 2–2: James Madison: His Legacy
Activity 2–3: Proposals for the Bill of Rights

ONLINE STUDY GUIDE AND ADDITIONAL RESOURCES

At **http://politicalscience.wadsworth.com/ schmidtbrief2004** you will find a free Study Guide to this book that includes tutorial quizzes, essay questions, practice exams, chapter outlines, learning objectives, the glossary, flashcards, crossword puzzles, and Microsoft PowerPoint presentations. Also included in the American Government Resource Center for Chapter 2:

- **InfoTrac® Reader**—Original intent; James Madison.
- **You Are There Simulation**—The Constitution.
- **Participation Activities**—Explore the prayer in public schools amendment debate; investigate current congressional proposals for constitutional amendments.
- **MicroCase Exercise**—The Constitution.

- **Related Links**—The Constitution.
- **Video Case Study**—The Constitution and impeachment.
- **Source Readings**—By James Madison, Robert Yates, Abraham Lincoln, and Thomas Paine, plus the Mayflower Compact and *Marbury v. Madison*.

The site also contains the Citizen's Survival Guide, information on how to get involved in politics locally and globally, as well as regularly updated features including a Current Events Quiz, In the News, Election Links, updates on the war on terrorism, and more.

CHAPTER 3

Federalism

I N THE UNITED STATES, RIGHTS AND POWERS are reserved to the states by the Tenth Amendment. It may appear that since September 11, 2001, the federal government, sometimes called the national or central government, predominates. Nevertheless, that might be a temporary exaggeration, for there are 87,900 separate governmental units in this nation.

Visitors from France or Spain are often awestruck by the complexity of our system of government. Consider that a criminal action can be defined by state law, by national law, or by both. Thus, a criminal suspect can be prosecuted in the state court system or in the federal court system (or both). Often, economic regulation over exactly the same matter exists at the local level, the state level, and the national level—generating multiple forms to be completed, multiple procedures to be followed, and multiple laws to be obeyed. Numerous programs are funded by the national government but administered by state and local governments.

Relations between central governments and local units are ordered in various ways. *Federalism* is one of these ways. Understanding federalism and how it differs from other forms of government is important in understanding the American political system. Indeed, many political issues today would not arise if we did not have a federal form of government in which governmental authority is divided between the central government and various subunits.

Three Systems of Government

There are almost two hundred independent nations in the world today. Each of these nations has its own system of government. Generally, though, we can describe the way nations order relations between central governments and local units in terms of three models: (1) the unitary system, (2) the confederal system, and (3) the federal system. The most popular, both historically and today, is the unitary system.

A Unitary System

A **unitary system** of government is the easiest to define. Unitary systems allow ultimate governmental authority to rest in the hands of the national, or central, government. Consider a typical unitary system—France. There are departments and municipalities in France. Within the departments and the municipalities are separate government entities with elected and appointed officials. So far, the French system appears to be very similar to the U.S. system, but the similarity is only superficial. Under the unitary French system, the decisions of the governments of the departments and municipalities can be overruled by the national government. The national government also can cut off the funding of many departmental and municipal government activities. Moreover, in a unitary system such as that in France, all questions of education, police, the use of land, and welfare are handled by the national government. Great Britain, Sweden, Japan, Israel, Egypt, Ghana, and the Philippines also have unitary systems of government, as do most countries today.[1]

A Confederal System

A **confederal system** of government is the opposite of a unitary governing system. It is a league of independent states in which a central government or administration handles only those matters of common concern expressly delegated to it by the member states. The central governmental unit has no ability to make laws directly applicable to individuals unless the member states explicitly support such laws. The United States under the Articles of Confederation was a confederal system.

Few, if any, confederations of this kind exist in the world today. One possible exception is the European Union, a league of countries that is developing unifying institutions such as a common currency. Countries also have formed organizations with one another for limited purposes, such as military or peacekeeping cooperation. Examples are the North Atlantic Treaty Organization and the United Nations. These organizations, however, are not true confederations.

A Federal System

The federal system lies between the unitary and confederal forms of government. In a **federal system,** authority is divided, usually by a written constitution, between a central government and regional, or subdivisional, governments (often called constituent governments). The central government and the constituent governments both act directly on the people through laws and through the actions of elected and appointed governmental officials. Within each government's sphere of authority, each is supreme, in theory. Thus, a federal system differs sharply from a unitary one in which the central government is supreme and the constituent governments derive their authority from it. Australia, Canada, Mexico, India, Brazil, and Germany are examples of nations with federal systems. See Figure 3–1 for a comparison of the three systems.

FIGURE 3–1 The Flow of Power in Three Systems of Government

In a unitary system, power flows from the central government to the local and state governments. In a confederal system, power flows in the opposite direction—from the state and local governments to the central government. In a federal system, the flow of power, in principle, goes both ways.

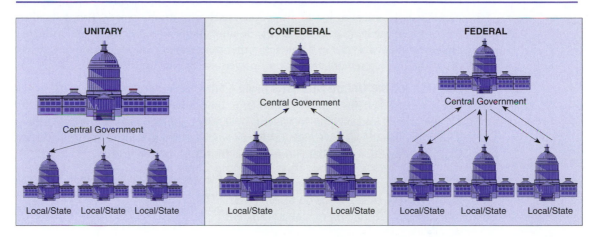

Why Federalism?

Why did the United States develop in a federal direction? We look here at that question as well as at some of the arguments for and against a federal form of government.

A Practical Solution

The historical basis of our federal system was laid down in Philadelphia at the Constitutional Convention, where advocates of a strong national government opposed states' rights advocates. This dichotomy continued through the ratifying conventions in the several states. The resulting federal system was a compromise. The supporters of the new Constitution were political pragmatists—they realized that without a federal arrangement, there would be no ratification of the new Constitution. The appeal of federalism was that it retained state traditions and local power while establishing a strong national government capable of handling common problems.

Even if the colonial leaders had agreed on the desirability of a unitary system, the problems of size and regional isolation would have made such a system difficult operationally. At the time of the Constitutional Convention, the thirteen colonies taken together were much larger geographically than England or France. Slow travel and communication, combined with geographic spread, contributed to the isolation of many regions within the colonies. It could take up to several weeks for all of the colonies to be informed about a particular political decision.

Other Arguments for Federalism

The arguments for federalism in the United States and elsewhere involve a complex set of factors, some of which we already have noted. Even with modern transportation and communications systems, the large area or population of some nations makes it impractical to locate all political authority in one place. Also, federalism brings government closer to the people. It allows more direct access to, and influence on, government agencies and policies, rather than leaving the population restive and dissatisfied with a remote, faceless, all-powerful central authority.

Benefits for the United States.   In the United States, federalism historically has yielded many benefits. State governments long have been a training ground for future national leaders. Many presidents made their political mark as state governors. The states themselves have been testing grounds for new government initiatives. As United States Supreme Court justice Louis Brandeis once observed:

Ron Watts, Black Star

Air pollution in Los Angeles, California. In our federal system of government, states have often been the testing grounds for programs later adopted by the federal government for nationwide implementation. Air-pollution control, for example, was initiated in California to cope with the threatening conditions produced by a large population in a relatively enclosed valley.

It is one of the happy incidents of the federal system that a single courageous state may, if its citizens choose, serve as a laboratory and try novel social and economic experiments without risk to the rest of the country.[2]

Examples of programs pioneered at the state level include unemployment compensation, which began in Wisconsin, and air-pollution control, which was initiated in California. Currently, states are experimenting with policies ranging from educational reforms to the medical use of marijuana. Since the passage of the 1996 welfare reform legislation, which gave more control over welfare programs to state governments, states have also been experimenting with different methods of delivering welfare assistance.

Federalism Allows for Many Political Subcultures.   The American way of life always has been characterized by a number of political subcultures, which divide along the lines of race and ethnic origin, region, wealth, education, and, more recently, degree of religious fundamentalism and sexual preference. The existence of diverse political subcultures would appear to be incompatible with a political authority concentrated solely in a central government. Had the United States developed into a unitary system, various political sub-cultures certainly would have been less able to influence government behavior than they have been, and continue to be, in our federal system.

Arguments against Federalism

Not everyone thinks federalism is such a good idea. Some see it as a way for power-ful state and local interests to block progress and impede national plans. Smaller political units are more likely to be dominated by a single political group, and the dominant groups in some cities and states have resisted implementing equal rights for minority groups. (This was essentially the argument that James Madison put forth in *Federalist Paper* No. 10, which you can read in Appendix C of this text.) Some argue, however, that the dominant factions in other states have been more progressive than the national government in many areas, such as the environment.

Others see dangers in the expansion of national powers at the expense of the states. President Ronald Reagan (1981–1989) said, "The Founding Fathers saw the federalist system as constructed something like a masonry wall. The States are the bricks, the national government is the mortar. . . . Unfortunately, over the years, many people have increasingly come to believe that Washington is the whole wall."[3]

The Constitutional Basis for American Federalism

No mention of the designation "federal system" can be found in the U.S. Constitution. Nor is it possible to find a systematic division of governmental author-ity between the national and state governments in that document. Rather, the Constitution sets out different types of powers. These powers can be classified as (1) the powers of the national government, (2) the powers of the states, and (3) pro-hibited powers. The Constitution also makes it clear that if a state or local law con-flicts with a national law, the national law will prevail.

Powers of the National Government

The powers delegated to the national government include both expressed and implied powers, as well as the special category of inherent powers. Most of the pow-ers expressly delegated to the national government are found in Article I, Section 8, of the Constitution. These **enumerated powers** include coining money, setting stan-dards for weights and measures, making uniform naturalization laws, admitting new states, establishing post offices, and declaring war. Another important enumerated power is the power to regulate commerce among the states—a topic we deal with later in this chapter.

Enumerated Powers
Powers specifically granted to the national government by the Constitution.

The Necessary and Proper Clause.   The implied powers of the national govern-ment are also based on Article I, Section 8, which states that the Congress shall have the power

[t]o make all Laws which shall be necessary and proper for carrying into Execution the foregoing Powers, and all other Powers vested by this Constitution in the Government of the United States, or in any Department or Officer thereof.

Elastic Clause, or Necessary and Proper Clause The clause in the Constitution that grants Congress the power to do whatever is necessary to execute its specifically delegated powers.

This clause is sometimes called the **elastic clause,** or the **necessary and proper clause,** because it provides flexibility to our constitutional system. It gives Congress all of those powers that can be reasonably inferred but that are not expressly stated in the brief wording of the Constitution. The clause was first used in the Supreme Court decision of *McCulloch v. Maryland*[4] (discussed later in this chapter) to develop the concept of implied powers. Through this concept, the national government has succeeded in strengthening the scope of its authority to meet the numerous problems that the framers of the Constitution did not, and could not, anticipate.

Inherent Powers.   A special category of national powers that are not implied by the necessary and proper clause consists of what have been labeled the inherent powers of the national government. These powers derive from the fact that the United States is a sovereign power among nations, and so its national government must be the only government that deals with other nations. Under international law, it is assumed that all nation-states, regardless of their size or power, have an *inherent* right to ensure their own survival. To do this, each nation must have the ability to act in its own interest among and with the community of nations—by, for instance, making treaties, waging war, seeking trade, and acquiring territory. Note that no specific clause in the Constitution says anything about the acquisition of additional land. Nonetheless, through the federal government's inherent powers, we made the Louisiana Purchase in 1803 and then went on to acquire Florida, Texas, Oregon, Alaska, Hawaii, and other lands. The United States grew from a mere thirteen states to fifty states, plus several "territories."

Powers of the State Governments

The Tenth Amendment states that the powers not delegated to the United States by the Constitution, nor prohibited by it to the states, are reserved to the states or to the people. These are the reserved powers that the national government cannot deny to the states. Because these powers are not expressly listed—and because they are not limited to powers that are expressly listed—there is sometimes a question as to whether a certain power is delegated to the national government or reserved to the states. State powers have been held to include each state's right to regulate commerce within its borders and to provide for a state militia. States also have the reserved power to make laws on all matters not prohibited to the states by the national or state constitutions and not expressly, or by implication, delegated to the national government. Furthermore, the states have **police power**—the authority to legislate for the protection of the health, morals, safety, and welfare of the people. Their police power enables states to pass laws governing such activities as crimes, marriage, contracts, education, traffic, and land use.

Police Power The authority to legislate for the protection of the health, morals, safety, and welfare of the people. In the United States, most police power is a reserved power of the states.

The ambiguity of the Tenth Amendment has allowed the reserved powers of the states to be defined differently at different times in our history. When there is wide-

AP Photo/Ed Bailey

A New York police officer questions a truck driver on the Queensboro Bridge shortly after the attacks on the World Trade Center on September 11, 2001. Because homeland security is a massive job, cooperation among all levels of government is needed.

spread support for increased regulation by the national government, the Tenth Amendment tends to recede into the background. When the tide turns the other way (in favor of states' rights), the Tenth Amendment is resurrected to justify arguments supporting increased states' rights.

Concurrent Powers

In certain areas, the states share **concurrent powers** with the national government. Most concurrent powers are not specifically stated in the Constitution; they are only implied. An example of a concurrent power is the power to tax. The types of taxation are divided between the levels of government. States may not levy a tariff (a set of taxes on imported goods); the federal government does not tax real estate; and neither may tax the facilities of the other. If the state governments did not have the power to tax, they would not be able to function other than on a ceremonial basis.

Other concurrent powers include the power to borrow money, to establish courts, and to charter banks and corporations. To a limited extent, the federal government exercises police power, and to the extent that it does, police power is also a concurrent power. Concurrent powers exercised by the states are normally limited to the geographic area of each state and to those functions not delegated by the Constitution exclusively to the national government.

Concurrent Powers
Powers held jointly by the national and state governments.

Prohibited Powers

The Constitution prohibits or denies a number of powers to the national government. For example, the national government has expressly been denied the power to impose taxes on goods sold to other countries (exports). Moreover, any power not delegated expressly or implicitly to the federal government by the Constitution is prohibited to it. For example, the national government cannot create a national public school system. The states are also denied certain powers. For example, no state is allowed to enter into a treaty on its own with another country.

The Supremacy Clause

Supremacy Clause
The constitutional provision that makes the Constitution and federal laws superior to all conflicting state and local laws.

The supremacy of the national constitution over subnational laws and actions can be found in the **supremacy clause** of the Constitution. The supremacy clause (Article VI, Clause 2) states the following:

> This Constitution, and the Laws of the United States which shall be made in Pursuance thereof; and all Treaties made . . . under the Authority of the United States, shall be the supreme Law of the Land; and the Judges in every State shall be bound thereby, any Thing in the Constitution or Laws of any State to the Contrary notwithstanding.

In other words, states cannot use their reserved or concurrent powers to thwart national policies. All national and state officers, as well as judges, must be bound by oath to support the Constitution. Hence, any legitimate exercise of national governmental power supersedes any conflicting state action.[5] Of course, deciding whether a conflict actually exists is a judicial matter, as you will soon read when we discuss the case of *McCulloch v. Maryland.*

National government legislation in a concurrent area is said to *preempt* (take precedence over) conflicting state or local laws or regulations in that area. One of the ways in which the national government has extended its powers, particularly during the twentieth century, is through the preemption of state and local laws by national legislation. In the first decade of the twentieth century, fewer than 20 national laws preempted laws and regulations issued by state and local governments. By the beginning of the twenty-first century, the number had risen to nearly 120.

Some political scientists believe that national supremacy is critical for the longevity and smooth functioning of a federal system. Nonetheless, the application of this principle has been a continuous source of conflict. Indeed, as you will see, the most extreme example of this conflict was the Civil War.

Interstate Relations

So far we have examined the relationship between central and state governmental units. The states, however, have constant commercial, social, and other dealings among themselves. The national Constitution imposes certain "rules of the road" on interstate relations, which have had the effect of preventing any one state from setting itself apart from the other states. The three most important clauses governing interstate relations in the Constitution, all taken from the Articles of Confederation, require each state to do the following:

1. Give full faith and credit to every other state's public acts, records, and judicial proceedings (Article IV, Section 1).

2. Extend to every other state's citizens the privileges and immunities of its own citizens (Article IV, Section 2).

3. Agree to return persons who are fleeing from justice in another state back to their home state when requested to do so (Article IV, Section 2).

Following these constitutional mandates is not always easy for the states. For example, one question that has arisen in recent years is whether states will be constitutionally obligated to recognize same-sex marriages performed in other states. For a discussion of this topic, see this chapter's feature entitled *At Issue: Same-Sex Marriages* on page 55.

Defining Constitutional Powers— The Early Years

Constitutional language, to be effective and to endure, must have some degree of ambiguity, thus leaving the door open for different interpretations. Certainly, disputes over the boundaries of national versus state powers have characterized this nation from the beginning. In the early 1800s, the most significant disputes arose over differing interpretations of the implied powers of the national government under the necessary and proper clause and over the respective powers of the national government and the states to regulate commerce.

Although political bodies at all levels of government play important roles in the process of settling such disputes, ultimately it is the Supreme Court that casts the final vote. As might be expected, the character of the referee will have an impact on the ultimate outcome of any dispute. From 1801 to 1835, the Supreme Court was headed by Chief Justice John Marshall, a Federalist who advocated a strong central

Robert Brenner, PhotoEdit

Interstate compacts have long been used as a way to address issues that affect more than one state. An interstate compact between New York and New Jersey in 1921 created the Port Authority of New York and New Jersey to develop and maintain harbor facilities in that area, including the Port Authority Bus Terminal shown here. Today, there are over two hundred interstate compacts.

INFOTRAC

To find out more about John Marshall, use the term "Marshall, John" in the Subject guide.

government. We look here at two cases decided by the Marshall Court: *McCulloch v. Maryland*[6] and *Gibbons v. Ogden*.[7] Both cases are considered milestones in the movement toward national government supremacy.

McCulloch v. Maryland (1819)

The U.S. Constitution says nothing about establishing a national bank. Nonetheless, at different times Congress chartered two banks—the First and Second Banks of the United States—and provided part of their initial capital; thus they were national banks. The government of Maryland imposed a tax on the Second Bank's Baltimore branch in an attempt to put that branch out of business. The branch's cashier, James William McCulloch, refused to pay the Maryland tax. When Maryland took McCulloch to its state court, the state of Maryland won. The national government appealed the case to the Supreme Court.

One of the issues before the Court was whether the national government had the implied power, under the necessary and proper clause, to charter a bank and contribute capital to it. The other important question before the Court was the following: If the bank was constitutional, could a state tax it? In other words, was a state action that conflicted with a national government action invalid under the supremacy clause?

Chief Justice John Marshall held that if establishing such a national bank aided the national government in the exercise of its designated powers, then the authority to set up such a bank could be implied. Having established this doctrine of implied powers, Marshall then answered the other important question before the Court and established the doctrine of national supremacy. Marshall ruled that no state could use its taxing power to tax an arm of the national government. If it could, "the declaration that the Constitution . . . shall be the supreme law of the land, is [an] empty and unmeaning [statement]."

Marshall's decision enabled the national government to grow and to meet problems that the Constitution's framers were unable to foresee. Today, practically every expressed power of the national government has been expanded in one way or another by use of the necessary and proper clause.

Gibbons v. Ogden (1824)

Commerce Clause
The section of the Constitution in which Congress is given the power to regulate trade among the states and with foreign countries.

One of the most important parts of the Constitution included in Article I, Section 8, is the so-called **commerce clause,** in which Congress is given the power "[t]o regulate Commerce with foreign Nations, and among the several States, and with the Indian Tribes." The meaning of this clause was at issue in *Gibbons v. Ogden*.

The background of the case was as follows. Robert Fulton and Robert Livingston secured a monopoly on steam navigation on the waters in New York State from the New York legislature in 1803. They licensed Aaron Ogden to operate steam-powered ferryboats between New York and New Jersey. Thomas Gibbons, who had obtained a license from the US. government to operate boats in interstate waters, decided to compete with Ogden, but he did so without New York's permission. Ogden sued Gibbons. The New York state courts prohibited

AT ISSUE:
Same-Sex Marriages

The Constitution requires that each state give full faith and credit to every other state's public acts. If you are legally married under the laws of Nevada, the other forty-nine states have to recognize that marriage. What if you live in a state that recognizes same-sex marriages? Does that mean that all other states must recognize such marriages and give each partner to the marriage the same privileges and benefits accorded to partners in opposite-sex marriages?

HAWAII TAKES THE LEAD

In 1993, the Hawaii Supreme Court ruled that banning same-sex marriages might violate the equal protection clause of the Hawaii constitution. The court stated that unless Hawaii could offer a "compelling" reason to maintain this discriminatory practice, it must be abandoned. The Hawaii Supreme Court then sent the case back to the trial court to determine if the state did indeed have such a compelling reason. In 1996, the trial court ruled that the state had failed to meet this burden and therefore the ban on same-sex marriages violated the state constitution.

Congress quickly passed the Defense of Marriage Act of 1996, which allowed state governments to ignore same-sex marriages performed in other states. Somewhat ironically, the Hawaii court decisions came to naught. In 1998, the residents of that state voted for a state constitutional amendment that allows the Hawaii legislature to ban same-sex marriages.

VERMONT AND MASSACHUSETTS

In 1999, the Vermont Supreme Court ruled that same-sex couples should be entitled to benefits of marriage identical to those of opposite-sex couples. The court said that it was up to the Vermont legislature to implement the decision. According to the court, the legislature could either allow gay and lesbian couples to marry or allow them to register as "domestic partners," as long as they would have the same rights and benefits as married couples.

Subsequently, in April 2000, the Vermont legislature passed a law permitting gay and lesbian couples to form "civil unions." Partners forming civil unions would be entitled to receive state benefits available to married couples. Vermont civil unions, however, would not be recognized by the federal government and thus would not entitle partners in those unions to any federal benefits.

In November 2003, the Massachusetts Supreme Judicial Court ruled that same-sex couples have a right to civil marriage under the Massachusetts state constitution. This made Massachusetts the first state to allow same-sex marriages, not just civil unions. The Massachusetts ruling immediately became an issue in the 2004 presidential election campaign.

If a state law allows for same-sex marriages, are other states obligated to recognize those marriages under the "full faith and credit" clause of the Constitution? According to the Defense of Marriage Act, they will not be. Nevertheless, we can be sure that someone will challenge the constitutionality of the Defense of Marriage Act. Until the Supreme Court rules on the question, we do not know how the Constitution will apply to this issue.

FOR CRITICAL ANALYSIS

Opinion polls routinely show that the majority of Americans are against same-sex marriages. Should such polls influence legislators on this issue?

Gibbons from operating in New York waters. Gibbons appealed to the Supreme Court.

There were actually several issues before the Court in this case. The first issue was how the term *commerce* should be defined. New York's highest court had defined the

John Marshall (1755–1835) was the fourth chief justice of the Supreme Court. Some scholars have declared that Marshall is the true architect of the American constitutional system.

term narrowly to mean only the shipment of goods, or the interchange of commodities, not navigation or the transport of people. The second issue was whether the national government's power to regulate interstate commerce extended to commerce within a state (*intra*state commerce) or was limited strictly to commerce among the states (*inter*state commerce). The third issue was whether the power to regulate interstate commerce was a concurrent power (as the New York court had concluded) or an exclusive national power.

Marshall defined *commerce* as *all* commercial intercourse—all business dealings—including navigation and the transport of people. Marshall also held that the commerce power of the national government could be exercised in state jurisdictions, even though it cannot reach *solely* intrastate commerce. Finally, Marshall emphasized that the power to regulate interstate commerce was an exclusive national power. Marshall held that because Gibbons was duly authorized by the national government to navigate in interstate waters, he could not be prohibited from doing so by a state court.

Marshall's expansive interpretation of the commerce clause in *Gibbons v. Ogden* allowed the national government to exercise increasing authority over all areas of economic affairs throughout the land. Congress did not immediately exploit this broad grant of power. In the 1930s and subsequent decades, however, the commerce clause became the primary constitutional basis for national government regulation, as you will read later in this chapter.

INFOTRAC

To find out more about the war, use the term "United States Civil War" in the Subject guide.

States' Rights and the Resort to Civil War

The controversy over slavery that led to the Civil War took the form of a dispute over national government supremacy versus the rights of the separate states. Essentially, the Civil War brought to an ultimate and violent climax the ideological debate that had been outlined by the Federalist and Anti-Federalist parties even before the Constitution was ratified.

The Shift Back to States' Rights

As we have seen, while John Marshall was chief justice of the Supreme Court, he did much to increase the power of the national government and to reduce that of the states. During the Jacksonian era (1829–1837), however, a shift back to states' rights began. The question of the regulation of commerce became one of the major issues in federal-state relations. When Congress passed a tariff in 1828, the state of South

Carolina unsuccessfully attempted to nullify the tariff (render it void), claiming that in cases of conflict between a state and the national government, the state should have the ultimate authority over its citizens.

Over the next three decades, the North and South became even more sharply divided—over tariffs that mostly benefited northern industries and over the slavery issue. On December 20, 1860, South Carolina formally repealed its ratification of the Constitution and withdrew from the Union. On February 4, 1861, representatives from six southern states met at Montgomery, Alabama, to form a new government called the Confederate States of America.

War and the Growth of the National Government

The ultimate defeat of the South in 1865 permanently ended any idea that a state could successfully claim the right to secede, or withdraw, from the Union. Ironically, the Civil War—brought about in large part because of the South's desire for increased states' rights—resulted in the opposite: an increase in the political power of the national government.

Thousands of new employees were hired to run the Union war effort and to deal with the social and economic problems that had to be handled in the aftermath of war. A billion-dollar ($1.3 billion, which is over $11.5 billion in today's dollars) national government budget was passed for the first time in 1865 to cover the increased government expenditures. The first (temporary) income tax was imposed on citizens to help pay for the war. Both the increased national government spending and the nationally imposed income tax were precursors to the expanded future role of the national government in the American federal system.[8] Civil liberties were curtailed in the Union and in the Confederacy in the name of wartime emergency. The distribution of pensions and widow's benefits also boosted the national government's social role. The North's victory set the nation on the path to a modern industrial economy and society.

The Library of Congress

INFOTRAC

To find out more about this issue, use the term "state rights" in the Subject guide.

The Civil War was a fight over the supremacy of the national government as well as over slavery. Had the South won, presumably any state or states would have the effective right to secede from the Union.

The Continuing Dispute over the Division of Power

Although the outcome of the Civil War firmly established the supremacy of the national government and put to rest the idea that a state could secede from the Union, the war by no means ended the debate over the division of powers between the national government and the states. In fact, many current political issues raise questions about states' rights and federalism. The debate over the division of powers in our federal system can be viewed as progressing through at least two general stages since the Civil War: dual federalism and cooperative federalism.

Dual Federalism

Dual Federalism A system in which the states and the national government remain supreme within their own spheres. The doctrine looks on nation and state as co-equal sovereign powers.

During the decades following the Civil War, the prevailing model was that of **dual federalism**—a doctrine that emphasizes a distinction between federal and state spheres of government authority. Various images have been used to describe different configurations of federalism over time. Dual federalism is commonly depicted as a layer cake, because the state governments and the national government are viewed as separate entities, like separate layers in a cake.

Generally, in the decades following the Civil War the states exercised their police power to regulate affairs within their borders, such as intrastate commerce, and the national government stayed out of purely local affairs. The courts tended to support the states' rights to exercise their police power to regulate intrastate activities. For example, in 1918, the Supreme Court ruled that a 1916 federal law banning child labor was unconstitutional because it attempted to regulate a local problem.[9] In the 1930s, however, the doctrine of dual federalism receded into the background as the nation attempted to deal with the Great Depression.

INFOTRAC

To find out more about the New Deal, use the term "New Deal, 1933–1939" in the Subject guide.

Cooperative Federalism A system in which the states and the national government cooperate in solving problems.

Cooperative Federalism

Franklin D. Roosevelt was inaugurated on March 4, 1933, as the thirty-second president of the United States. In the previous year, nearly 1,500 banks had failed (and 4,000 more would fail in 1933). Thirty-two thousand businesses had closed down, and one-fourth of the labor force was unemployed. The public expected the national government to do something about the disastrous state of the economy. But for the first three years of the Great Depression, the national government did very little. That changed with the new Democratic administration's energetic intervention in the economy. FDR's "New Deal" included a large number of government spending and welfare programs, in addition to voluminous regulations on economic activity.

Some political scientists have described the era since 1937 as characterized by **cooperative federalism,** in which the states and the national government cooperate in solving complex common problems. The New Deal programs of Franklin Roosevelt, for example, often involved joint action between the national government and the states. The pattern of national-state relationships during these years gave rise to a new metaphor for federalism—that of a marble cake.

The 1960s and 1970s saw an even greater expansion of the national government's role in domestic policy. Today, few activities are beyond the reach of the regulatory arm of the national government.

Federal Grants-in-Aid

Even before the Constitution was adopted, the national government gave grants to the states in the form of land to finance education. The national government also provided land grants for canals, railroads, and roads. In the twentieth century, the federal grants-in-aid program increased significantly, especially during Roosevelt's administration during the Great Depression and again during the 1960s, when the dollar amount of grants-in-aid quadrupled. The grants were used for improvements in education, pollution control, recreation, and highways. With this increase in grants, however, came a bewildering number of restrictions and regulations.

By 1985, **categorical grants-in-aid** amounted to more than $100 billion a year. They were spread out across four hundred separate programs, but the largest five accounted for over 50 percent of the revenues spent. These five programs involved Medicaid, highway construction, unemployment benefits, housing assistance, and welfare programs to assist mothers with dependent children and people with disabilities. For fiscal year 2003, the national government gave an estimated $238 billion to the states through grants-in-aid.

Why have federal grants to the states increased so much? The main reason is that to state officials they appear to be "free." After all, state officials do not have to tax their constituents more if the federal government pays for a new bridge, a museum improvement, or a new highway.

Categorical Grants-in-Aid Federal grants-in-aid to states or local governments that are for specific programs or projects.

In the 1800s, very young children worked in coal mines. Today, federal child-labor laws prohibit employers from hiring such young workers. Why do you think the parents of these children allowed them to work at such dangerous jobs?

The Library of Congress

This housing development in Minnesota was one of the projects sponsored by the New Deal's Works Progress Administration (WPA) in the 1930s. The federal government's efforts to alleviate unemployment (in this case, among construction workers) during the Great Depression signaled a shift from dual to cooperative federalism.

Minnesota Historical Society

Feeling the Pressure—The Strings Attached to Federal Grants.

No dollars sent to the states are completely free of "strings," however; all funds come with requirements that must be met by the states. Often, through the use of grants, the national government has been able to exercise substantial control over matters that traditionally fell under the purview of state governments. When the federal government gives federal funds for highway improvements, for example, it may condition the funds on the state's cooperation with a federal policy. This is exactly what the federal government did in the 1980s and 1990s to force the states to raise their minimum drinking age to twenty-one.

Block Grants
Federal programs that provide funds to state and local governments for general functional areas, such as criminal justice or mental-health programs.

Block Grants.

Block grants lessen the restrictions on grants-in-aid given to state and local governments by grouping a number of categorical grants under one broad purpose. Governors and mayors generally prefer block grants because they give the states more flexibility in how the money is spent.

One major set of block grants provides aid to state welfare programs. The Personal Responsibility and Work Opportunity Reconciliation Act of 1996 ended the previously existing program and substituted for it a welfare block grant to each state. Each grant has an annual cap. According to some, this is one of the more successful block grant programs.

Although state governments desire block grants, Congress generally prefers categorical grants because the expenditures can be targeted according to congressional priorities. These priorities include programs, such as those for disadvantaged groups and individuals, that significantly benefit many voters.

Federal Mandates.

For years, the federal government has passed legislation requiring that states improve environmental conditions and the civil rights of certain groups. Since the 1970s, the national government has enacted literally hundreds of **federal mandates** requiring the states to take some action in areas ranging from the way voters are registered, to ocean-dumping restrictions, to the education of persons with disabilities. The Unfunded Mandates Reform Act of 1995 requires the Congressional Budget Office to identify mandates that cost state and local governments more than $50 million to implement. Nonetheless, the federal government routinely continues to pass mandates for state and local governments to implement that cost more than that. Consider a recent federal mandate involving the expansion of eligibility for Medicaid, the federally subsidized but state-operated health-care program for low-income Americans. Some researchers believe that this mandate alone will cost the states $70 billion a year during the first half of the 2000s.

Federal Mandate A requirement in federal legislation that forces states and municipalities to comply with certain rules.

Federalism and the Supreme Court

The United States Supreme Court, which normally has the final say on constitutional issues, necessarily plays a significant role in determining the line between federal and state powers. Consider the decisions rendered by Chief Justice John Marshall in the cases discussed earlier in this chapter. Since the 1930s, Marshall's broad interpretation of the commerce clause has made it possible for the national government to justify its regulation of virtually any activity, even when an activity would appear to be purely local in character.

Since the 1990s, however, the Supreme Court has been reining in the national government's powers under the commerce clause somewhat. The Court has also given increased emphasis to state powers under the Tenth and Eleventh Amendments to the Constitution.

INFOTRAC
To find out more about this topic, use the term "federal mandates" in Keywords.

Reining in the Commerce Power

In a widely publicized 1995 case, *United States v. Lopez*,[10] the Supreme Court held that Congress had exceeded its constitutional authority under the commerce clause when it passed the Gun-Free School Zones Act in 1990. The Court stated that the act, which banned the possession of guns within one thousand feet of any school, was unconstitutional because it attempted to regulate an area that had "nothing to do with commerce, or any sort of economic enterprise." This marked the first time in sixty years that the Supreme Court had placed a limit on the national government's authority under the commerce clause.

In 2000, in *United States v. Morrison*,[11] the Court held that Congress had overreached its authority under the commerce clause when it passed the Violence against Women Act in 1994. The Court invalidated a key section of the act that provided a federal remedy for gender-motivated violence, such as rape. The Court noted that in enacting this law Congress had extensively documented that violence against women had an adverse "aggregate" effect on interstate commerce. Nonetheless, the Court held that evidence of an aggregate effect on commerce was not enough to justify national regulation of noneconomic, violent criminal conduct.

State Sovereignty and the Eleventh Amendment

In its 1999–2000 term, the Supreme Court issued a series of decisions that bolstered the authority of state governments under the Eleventh Amendment to the Constitution. As interpreted by the Court, that amendment precludes lawsuits against state governments for violations of rights established by federal laws unless the states consent to be sued. For example, in a 1999 case, *Alden v. Maine*,[12] the Court held that Maine state employees could not sue the state of Maine for violating the overtime pay requirements of a federal act. According to the Court, state immunity from such lawsuits "is a fundamental aspect of the sovereignty which [the states] enjoyed before the ratification of the Constitution, and which they retain today."

In 2000, in *Kimel v. Florida Board of Regents*,[13] the Court held that the Eleventh Amendment precluded employees of a state university from suing the state to enforce a federal statute prohibiting age-based discrimination. In 2003, however, in *Nevada v. Hibbs*, the Court ruled that state employers must abide by the federal Family and Medical Leave Act (FMLA). The reasoning was that the FMLA seeks to outlaw gender bias, and government actions that may discriminate on the basis of gender must receive a "heightened review status" compared with actions that may discriminate on the basis of age or disability.[14]

The Tenth Amendment

The Tenth Amendment states: "The powers not delegated to the United States by the Constitution, nor prohibited by it to the States, are reserved to the States respectively, or to the people." The Court has issued rulings based on this amendment. In

1997, in *Printz v. United States*,[15] the Court struck down the provisions of the federal Brady Handgun Violence Prevention Act of 1993 that required state employees to check the backgrounds of prospective handgun purchasers. Said the Court:

> [T]he federal government may neither issue directives requiring the States to address particular problems, nor command the States' officers, or those of their political subdivisions, to administer or enforce a federal regulatory program.

The Court held that the provisions violated "the very principle of separate state sovereignty," which was "one of the Constitution's structural protections of liberty."

State Governments Today

As we observed at the beginning of this chapter, the United States has more than 87,000 separate government units. State and local governments provide a wide variety of highly visible functions, such as education, police, and fire protection.

State constitutions are often very long and are subject to frequent alteration. Louisiana, for example, has had eleven different constitutions in its history; the constitution of Alabama has been amended 743 times. The framers of state constitutions often included much material because they lacked confidence in the state legislatures. Another reason for highly detailed state constitutions is that state courts have been reluctant to interpret state constitutions as freely as the United States Supreme Court interprets the U.S. Constitution.

The Three Branches of Government

All state governments have executive, legislative, and judicial branches. Here, however, the similarity with the federal government ends. State governments do not always have strong executive branches.

The State Executive Branch.   In colonial times, colonial governors had extensive powers, and the colonies' revolt against British rule centered on these all-powerful governors. When the first states were formed after the adoption of the Declaration of Independence, new constitutions ensured a weak executive branch and an extremely powerful legislative branch. In addition, in the 1800s there was an effort to democratize state governments by popularly electing as many officials as possible. The direct election of so many executive officials makes it likely that none of them will have much power over the government as a whole.

Nonetheless, governors have exercised the authority of their office with increasing frequency in recent years. Governors have become a significant force in legislative policymaking. Most governors also have the power to veto legislation passed by the state legislature, just as the president of the United States can veto legislation passed by the U.S. Congress. In forty-three states, the governor has some form of **item veto** power on appropriations bills—that is, bills that authorize spending. If the governor does not like one item, or line, in an appropriations bill, he or she can veto that item. This is a power that the president of the United States does not have.

Item Veto The power to veto particular sections or items of an appropriations bill while signing the remainder of the bill into law. The governors of most states have this power.

MAKING A DIFFERENCE : Writing Letters to the Editor

Just about every day an issue concerning federalism is discussed in the media. Advocates of decentralization—a shift of power from federal to state or local governments—argue that we must recognize the rights of states to design their own destinies and master their own fates. Advocates of centralization—more power to the national government—see a shift toward decentralization as undermining the national purpose, common interests, and responsibilities that bind us together in pursuit of national goals.

POSSIBLE ISSUES

A big question is how much the national government should do for the people. Is it within the power of the national government to decide what the law should be on abortion? Who should be responsible for the homeless? Should the national government subsidize state and local efforts to help them?

You may have valid, important points to make on these or other issues. One of the best ways to make your point is by writing an effective letter to the editor of your local newspaper (or even to a national newspaper such as the *New York Times*).

EXPRESS YOUR VIEWS

First, familiarize yourself with the kinds of letters that are accepted by the newspapers to which you want to write. Then follow these rules for writing an effective letter:

1. Use a computer, and double-space the lines. If possible, use a spelling checker and grammar checker.
2. Your lead topic sentence should be short, to the point, and powerful.
3. Keep your thoughts on target—choose only one topic to discuss in your letter. Make sure it is newsworthy and timely.

4. Make sure your letter is concise; never let your letter exceed a page and a half in length (double-spaced).
5. If you know that facts were misstated or left out in current news stories about your topic, supply the facts. The public wants to know.
6. Don't be afraid to express moral judgments. You can go a long way by appealing to readers' sense of justice.
7. Personalize the letter by bringing in your own experiences, if possible.
8. Sign your letter, and give your address (including your e-mail address, if you have one) and your telephone number.
9. Send your letter to the editorial office of the newspaper or magazine of your choice. Virtually all publications now have e-mail addresses and home pages on the Web. The Web sites usually give information on where you can send mail.

The State Legislature. State legislatures deal with such matters as taxes, schools, highways, and welfare. They also must redraw state and federal legislative districts each decade to ensure that every person's vote is roughly equal to that of every other person and that minorities are adequately represented in both the state legislature and Congress.

State legislatures have been criticized for being unprofessional and less than effective. In fact, though, state legislators are often given few resources with which to work. In many states, legislators are limited to meeting for only part of the year. Legislative pay is often quite low. A number of states have also imposed term limits that restrict the number of terms a legislator can serve.

The State Judiciary.   Each of the fifty states, as well as the District of Columbia, has its own court system. These systems include trial courts, the state supreme court, and, in about three-quarters of the states, intermediate appellate courts. In some states, state judges are appointed in much the same way that federal judges are appointed. In others, some or all of the judges must run for election, either on a partisan or nonpartisan ballot.

State Finances

State and local government spending is concentrated in the areas of education, public welfare, highways, health, and police protection. State services are funded primarily by sales taxes and state income taxes. Local services are typically financed by property taxes.

During the economic boom years of the 1990s, state tax revenues grew sharply, and many states experienced substantial budget surpluses. As a result, spending rose in most states, and a number of states cut taxes. Beginning with the economic downturn in 2001, however, these state budget surpluses were replaced by large budget deficits. State governments have been faced with the choice of whether to increase taxes or reduce spending.

Neither choice is appealing, and many state legislatures have been reluctant to do either. Because every state except Vermont is required to balance its budget, the result has been a widespread crisis in state finances. In fact, the financial crisis of the states is one of the most important issues facing the country today.

KEY TERMS

block grants **60**

categorical grants-in-aid **59**

commerce clause **54**

concurrent powers **51**

confederal system **46**

cooperative federalism **58**

dual federalism **58**

elastic clause **50**

enumerated powers **49**

federal mandate **61**

federal system **46**

item veto **63**

necessary and proper clause **50**

police power **50**

supremacy clause **52**

unitary system **46**

CHAPTER SUMMARY

1 There are three basic models for ordering relations between central governments and local units: (a) a unitary system (in which ultimate power is held by the national government), (b) a confederal system (in which ultimate power is retained by the states), and (c) a federal system (in which governmental powers are divided between the national government and the states). A major reason for the creation of a federal system in the United States is that it reflected a compromise between the views of the Federalists (who wanted a strong national government) and those of the Anti-Federalists (who wanted the states to retain their sovereignty).

2 The Constitution expressly delegated certain powers to the national government in Article I, Section 8. In addition to these expressed powers, the national government has implied and inherent powers. Implied powers are those reasonably necessary to carry out the powers expressly delegated to the national government. Inherent powers are those held by the national government as a sovereign state with the right to preserve itself.

3 The Tenth Amendment states that powers not delegated to the United States by the Constitution, nor prohibited by it to the states, are reserved to the states, or to the people. The Constitution provides for concurrent powers, such as the power to tax, which are held jointly by the national and state governments. The Constitution also denies certain powers to both the national government and the states.

4 The supremacy clause of the Constitution states that the Constitution, congressional laws, and national treaties are the supreme law of the land. States cannot use their reserved or concurrent powers to override national policies.

5 The three most important clauses in the Constitution on interstate relations require that (a) each state give full faith and credit to every other state's public acts, records, and judicial proceedings; (b) each state extend to every other state's citizens the privileges and immunities of its own citizens; and (c) each state agree to return persons who are fleeing from justice back to their home state when requested to do so.

6 Two landmark Supreme Court cases expanded the constitutional powers of the national government. Chief Justice John Marshall's expansive interpretation of the necessary and proper clause in *McCulloch v. Maryland* (1819) enhanced the implied power of the national government. Marshall's broad interpretation of the commerce clause in *Gibbons v. Ogden* (1824) further extended the regulatory powers of the national government.

7 The controversy over slavery that led to the Civil War took the form of a fight over national government supremacy versus the rights of the separate states. Ultimately, the effect of the South's desire for increased states' rights and the subsequent Civil War was an increase in the political power of the national government.

8 Since the Civil War, federalism has evolved through at least two general phases: dual federalism and cooperative federalism. In dual federalism, each of the states and the federal government remain supreme within their own spheres. The era since the Great Depression has sometimes been labeled one of cooperative federalism, in which states and the national government cooperate in solving complex common problems.

9 Categorical grants-in-aid from the federal government to the states help finance many projects, such as Medicaid, highway construction, unemployment benefits, and welfare programs. By attaching conditions to the grants, the national government can effect policy in areas typically governed by the states. Block grants, which group a number of categorical grants together, usually have fewer strings attached, giving state and local governments more flexibility in using funds. Federal mandates—laws requiring states to implement certain policies—have generated controversy because of their cost.

10 The United States Supreme Court plays a significant role in determining the line between state and federal powers. Since the 1990s, the Court has been reining in somewhat the national government's powers under the commerce clause and has given increased emphasis to state powers.

⑪ Like the federal government, state governments are divided into executive, legislative, and judicial branches. Because all states except Vermont must balance their budgets, recent sharp reductions in state tax revenues have caused widespread financial crises.

SELECTED PRINT AND MEDIA RESOURCES

Suggested Readings

Farber, Daniel A. *Lincoln's Constitution*. Chicago: University of Chicago Press, 2003. The author discusses the Constitution as Lincoln found it on taking office. He then looks at the unprecedented constitutional issues that Lincoln faced during the Civil War.

Hamilton, Alexander, *et al. The Federalist: The Famous Papers on the Principles of American Government.* Benjamin F. Wright, ed. New York: Friedman/Fairfax Publishing, 2002. These essays remain an authoritative exposition of the founders' views on federalism.

Nagel, Robert F. *The Implosion of American Federalism.* New York: Oxford University Press, 2002. The author contends that despite the states' rights trend of recent years, the nation faces the danger of increasingly centralized power.

Warren, Robert Penn. *All the King's Men*, rev. ed. Chicago: Harcourt Brace, 2001. A fictionalized account of Governor Huey Long of Louisiana, one of our "most astounding politicians."

Media Resources

Can the States Do It Better?—A 1996 film in which various experts debate how much power the national government should have. The film uses documentary footage and other resources to illustrate this debate.

City of Hope—A 1991 movie by John Sayles. The film is a story of life, work, race, and politics in a modern New Jersey city. An African American alderman is one of the several major roles.

The Civil War—The PBS documentary series that made director Ken Burns famous. *The Civil War*, first shown in 1990, marked a revolution in documentary technique. Photographs, letters, eyewitness memoirs, and music from the period are used to bring the war to life. The DVD version was released in 2002.

McCulloch v. Maryland and *Gibbons v. Ogden*—These programs are part of the series *Equal Justice under Law: Landmark Cases in Supreme Court History*. They provide more details on cases that defined our federal system.

LOGGING ON

You can learn how some communities have benefited from implementing online government through EzGov, Inc., by reading some of the comments at EzGov's Web site. Go to http://www.ezgov.com/news_main.jsp.

To learn the founders' views on federalism, you can access *The Federalist Papers* online at http://www.law.emory.edu/FEDERAL.

The following site has links to U.S. state constitutions, *The Federalist Papers*, and international federations, such as the European Union: http://www.constitution.org/cs_feder.htm.

The following Web site of the Council of State Governments is a good source for information on state responses to federalism issues: http://www.csg.org.

Another good source of information on issues facing state governments and federal-state relations is the National Governors Association's Web site at http://www.nga.org.

You can find a directory of numerous federalism links at http://www.gmu.edu.

The Brookings Institution's policy analyses and recommendations on a variety of issues, including federalism, can be accessed at http://www.brook.edu.

For a libertarian approach to issues relating to federalism, go to the Cato Institute's Web page at http://www.cato.org.

USING THE INTERNET FOR POLITICAL ANALYSIS

Go to this text's Web site at http://politicalscience.wadsworth.com/schmidtbrief2004. Select "Chapter 3" in the box at the top of the window. Then, in the column on the left-hand side of the window, under "Chapter Resources," click on "Internet Exercises." The Web site will then display the following Internet

exercises that you can perform to learn more about topics covered in this chapter.

Activity 3–1: *McCulloch v. Maryland*
Activity 3–2: American Federalism Today
Activity 3–3: State-Federal Relations

ONLINE STUDY GUIDE AND ADDITIONAL RESOURCES

At http://politicalscience.wadsworth.com/schmidtbrief2004 you will find a free Study Guide to this book that includes tutorial quizzes, essay questions, practice exams, chapter outlines, learning objectives, the glossary, flashcards, crossword puzzles, and Microsoft PowerPoint presentations. Also included in the American Government Resource Center for Chapter 3:

- **InfoTrac® Reader**—Welfare reform; states' rights; term limits; federal mandates.

- **You Are There Simulations**—Federalism; state and local government.

- **Participation Activities**—Research an issue of importance to you that involves federalism; find a newsgroup discussion on a federalism issue; explore local commissions; investigate your state's spending on higher education.

- **MicroCase Exercises**—Federalism; state and local government.

- **Related Links**—Federalism; state and local government.

- **Video Case Studies**—Defining constitutional powers; states' rights; three systems of government; drinking.

- **Source Readings**—By John Marshall, Daniel Webster, Robert Toombs, and presidents Thomas Jefferson, Theodore Roosevelt, and Ronald Reagan.

The site also contains the Citizen's Survival Guide, information on how to get involved in politics locally and globally, as well as regularly updated features including a Current Events Quiz, In the News, Election Links, updates on the war on terrorism, and more.

CHAPTER 4

Civil Liberties

"THE LAND OF THE FREE." When asked what makes the United States distinctive, Americans will commonly say that it is a free country. Americans have long believed that limits on the power of government are an essential part of what makes this country free. The first ten amendments to the U.S. Constitution—the Bill of Rights—place such limits on the national government. Of these amendments, none is more famous than the First Amendment, which guarantees freedom of religion, speech, the press, and other rights.

Most other democratic nations have laws to protect these and other **civil liberties,** but none of the laws is quite like the First Amendment. Take the issue of "hate speech." What if someone makes statements that stir up hatred toward a particular race or other group of people? In Germany, where memories of Nazi anti-Semitism remain fresh, such speech is unquestionably illegal. In the United States, the issue is not so clear. The courts have often extended constitutional protection to this kind of speech.

In this chapter, we describe the civil liberties provided by the Bill of Rights and some of the controversies that surround them. In addition to First Amendment liberties, we look at the right to privacy and the rights of defendants in criminal cases.

Civil Liberties
Personal freedoms that are protected for all individuals— restraints on the government's actions against individuals.

The Bill of Rights

Like the rest of the Constitution, the Bill of Rights is relatively brief. The framers set forth broad guidelines, leaving it up to the courts to interpret these constitutional mandates and apply them to specific situations. Thus, judicial interpretations shape the true nature of the civil liberties and rights that we possess. Because judicial interpretations change over time, so do our liberties and rights. As you will read in the following pages, there have been many conflicts over the meaning of such simple phrases as *freedom of religion* and *freedom of the press*. To understand what freedoms we actually have, we need to examine how the courts—and particularly the United States Supreme Court—have resolved some of those conflicts. One important conflict was over the issue of whether the Bill of Rights in the federal Constitution limited state governments as well as the national government.

Extending the Bill of Rights to State Governments

Many citizens do not realize that, as originally intended, the Bill of Rights limited only the powers of the national government. At the time the Bill of Rights was ratified, there was little concern over the potential of state governments to curb civil liberties. For one thing, state governments were closer to home and easier to control. For another, most state constitutions already had bills of rights. Rather, the fear was of the potential tyranny of the national government. The Bill of Rights begins with the words, "Congress shall make no law . . . ." It says nothing about *states* making laws that might abridge citizens' civil liberties. In 1833, in *Barron v. Baltimore*,[1] the United States Supreme Court held that the Bill of Rights did not apply to state laws.

We mentioned that most states had bills of rights. These bills of rights were similar to the national one, but there were some differences. Furthermore, each state's judicial system interpreted the rights differently. Citizens in different states, therefore, effectively had different sets of civil rights. It was not until after the Fourteenth Amendment was ratified in 1868 that civil liberties guaranteed by the national Constitution began to be applied to the states. Section 1 of that amendment provides, in part, as follows:

> No State shall . . . deprive any person of life, liberty, or property, without due process of law.

Incorporation of the Fourteenth Amendment

There was no question that the Fourteenth Amendment applied to state governments. For decades, however, the courts were reluctant to define the liberties spelled out in the national Bill of Rights as constituting "due process of law," which was protected under the Fourteenth Amendment. Not until 1925, in *Gitlow v. New York*,[2] did the United States Supreme Court hold that the Fourteenth Amendment protected the freedom of speech guaranteed by the First Amendment to the Constitution.

Incorporation Theory
The view that most of the protections of the Bill of Rights apply to state governments through the Fourteenth Amendment's due process clause.

Only gradually, and never completely, did the Supreme Court accept the **incorporation theory**—the view that most of the protections of the Bill of Rights are incorporated into the Fourteenth Amendment's protection against state government actions. Table 4–1 shows the rights that the Court has incorporated into the Fourteenth Amendment and the case in which it first applied each protection. As you can see in that table, in the fifteen years following the *Gitlow* decision, the Supreme Court incorporated into the Fourteenth Amendment the other basic freedoms (of the press, assembly, the right to petition, and religion) guaranteed by the First Amendment. These and the later Supreme Court decisions listed in Table 4–1 have bound the fifty states to accept for their respective citizens most of the rights and freedoms that are set forth in the U.S. Bill of Rights. We now look at some of those rights and freedoms, beginning with the freedom of religion.

TABLE 4–1	Incorporating the Bill of Rights into the Fourteenth Amendment		
Year	Issue	Amendment Involved	Court Case
1925	Freedom of speech	I	*Gitlow v. New York*, 268 U.S. 652.
1931	Freedom of the press	I	*Near v. Minnesota*, 283 U.S. 697.
1932	Right to a lawyer in capital punishment cases	VI	*Powell v. Alabama*, 287 U.S. 45.
1937	Freedom of assembly and right to petition	I	*De Jonge v. Oregon*, 299 U.S. 353.
1940	Freedom of religion	I	*Cantwell v. Connecticut*, 310 U.S. 296.
1947	Separation of church and state	I	*Everson v. Board of Education*, 330 U.S. 1.
1948	Right to a public trial	VI	*In re Oliver*, 333 U.S. 257.
1949	No unreasonable searches and seizures	IV	*Wolf v. Colorado*, 338 U.S. 25.
1961	Exclusionary rule	IV	*Mapp v. Ohio*, 367 U.S. 643.
1962	No cruel and unusual punishment	VIII	*Robinson v. California*, 370 U.S. 660.
1963	Right to a lawyer in all criminal felony cases	VI	*Gideon v. Wainwright*, 372 U.S. 335.
1964	No compulsory self-incrimination	V	*Malloy v. Hogan*, 378 U.S. 1.
1965	Right to privacy	I, III, IV, V, IX	*Griswold v. Connecticut*, 381 U.S. 479.
1966	Right to an impartial jury	VI	*Parker v. Gladden*, 385 U.S. 363.
1967	Right to a speedy trial	VI	*Klopfer v. North Carolina*, 386 U.S. 213.
1969	No double jeopardy	V	*Benton v. Maryland*, 395 U.S. 784.

Freedom of Religion

In the United States, freedom of religion consists of two principal precepts as they are presented in the First Amendment. The first guarantees the separation of church and state, and the second guarantees the free exercise of religion.

The Separation of Church and State—The Establishment Clause

The First Amendment to the Constitution states, in part, that "Congress shall make no law respecting an establishment of religion." In the words of Thomas Jefferson, the **establishment clause** was designed to create a "wall of separation of Church and State." Perhaps Jefferson was thinking about the religious intolerance that characterized the first colonies. Although many of the American colonies were founded by groups who were in pursuit of religious freedom, nonetheless the early colonists were quite intolerant of religious beliefs that did not conform to those held by the majority of citizens within their own communities. Jefferson undoubtedly was also aware that state churches were the rule; among the original thirteen American colonies, nine of them had official churches.

As interpreted by the Supreme Court, the establishment clause in the First Amendment means at least the following:

> Neither a state nor the federal government can set up a church. Neither can pass laws which aid one religion, aid all religions, or prefer one religion over another. Neither can

INFOTRAC

To find out more about this issue, use the term "freedom of religion" in the Subject guide.

Establishment Clause The part of the First Amendment prohibiting the establishment of a church officially supported by the national government.

force nor influence a person to go to or to remain away from church against his will or force him to profess a belief or disbelief in any religion. No person can be punished for entertaining or professing religious beliefs or disbeliefs, for church attendance or nonattendance. No tax in any amount, large or small, can be levied to support any religious activities or institutions, whatever they may be called, or whatever form they may adopt to teach or practice religion. Neither a state nor the federal government can, openly or secretly, participate in the affairs of any religious organizations or groups and vice versa.[3]

The establishment clause covers all conflicts about such matters as the legality of state and local government aid to religious organizations and schools, allowing or requiring school prayers, the teaching of evolution versus fundamentalist theories of creation, the posting of the Ten Commandments in schools or public places, and discrimination against religious groups in publicly operated institutions.

Aid to Church-Related Schools.   In the United States, fully 12 percent of school-age children attend private schools, of which 85 percent have religious affiliations. Many cases have reached the Supreme Court in which the Court has tried to draw a fine line between permissible public aid to students in church-related schools and impermissible public aid to religion. These issues have arisen most often at the elementary and secondary levels.

In 1971, in *Lemon v. Kurtzman,*[4] the Court ruled that direct state aid could not be used to subsidize religious instruction. The Court in the *Lemon* case gave its most general statement on the constitutionality of government aid to religious schools, stating that the aid had to be secular in aim, that it could not have the primary effect of advancing or inhibiting religion, and that the government must avoid "an excessive government entanglement with religion." All laws under the establishment clause are now subject to the three-part *Lemon* test. How the test is applied, however, has varied over the years.

In a number of cases, the Supreme Court has held that state programs helping church-related schools are unconstitutional. The Court has also denied state reimbursements to religious schools for field trips and for developing achievement tests. In a series of other cases, however, the Supreme Court has allowed states to use tax funds for lunches, textbooks, diagnostic services for speech and hearing problems, standardized tests, and transportation for students attending church-operated elementary and secondary schools.

A Change in the Court's Position.   Generally, today's Supreme Court has shown a greater willingness to allow the use of public funds for programs in religious schools than was true at times in the past. Consider that in 1985, in *Aguilar v. Felton,*[5] the Supreme Court ruled that state programs providing special educational services for disadvantaged students attending religious schools violated the establishment clause. In 1997, however, when the Supreme Court revisited this decision, the Court reversed its position; in *Agostini v. Felton,*[6] the Court held that *Aguilar* was "no longer good law."

School Vouchers.   Questions about the use of public funds for church-related schools are likely to continue as state legislators search for new ways to improve the educational system in this country. An issue that has come to the forefront in recent years is school vouchers. In a voucher system, educational vouchers (state-issued credits) can be used to "purchase" education at any school, public or private.

School districts in Florida, Ohio, and Wisconsin have all been experimenting with voucher systems. In 2000, the courts reviewed a case involving Ohio's voucher program. Under that program, some $10 million in public funds is spent annually to send 4,300 Cleveland students to fifty-one private schools, all but five of which are Catholic schools. The case presented a straightforward constitutional question: Is it a violation of the principle of separation of church and state for public tax money to be used to pay for religious education?

In 2002, the Supreme Court held that the Cleveland voucher program was constitutional, even though more than 95 percent of the students use the vouchers to attend Catholic or other religious schools. The Court's majority reasoned that the program did not unconstitutionally entangle church and state because families theoretically could use the vouchers for their children to attend schools of any type.

Children pray in school. Officially organized prayer in public schools is in violation of Supreme Court rulings based on the First Amendment. A Supreme Court ruling does not necessarily carry with it a mechanism for enforcement everywhere in the United States, however.

Bruce Flynn, Picture Group

The Issue of School Prayer—*Engel v. Vitale.* Do the states have the right to promote religion in general, without making any attempt to establish a particular religion? That is the question in the issue of school prayer and was the precise question presented in 1962 in *Engel v. Vitale*,[7] the so-called Regents' Prayer case in New York. The State Board of Regents of New York had suggested that a prayer be spoken aloud in the public schools at the beginning of each day. The recommended prayer was as follows:

Almighty God, we acknowledge our dependence upon Thee,
And we beg Thy blessings upon us, our parents, our teachers, and our Country.

Such a prayer was implemented in many New York public schools.

The parents of a number of students challenged the action of the regents, maintaining that it violated the establishment clause of the First Amendment. At trial, the parents lost. The Supreme Court, however, ruled that the regents' action was unconstitutional because "the constitutional prohibition against laws respecting an establishment of a religion must mean at least that in this country it is no part of the business of government to compose official prayers for any group of the American people to recite as part of a religious program carried on by any government."

The Debate over School Prayer Continues. Although the Supreme Court has ruled repeatedly against officially sponsored prayer and Bible-reading sessions in public schools, other means for bringing some form of religious expression into public education have been attempted. In 1983, the Tennessee legislature passed a bill requiring public school classes to begin each day with a minute of silence. Alabama had a similar law.

In *Wallace v. Jaffree* [8] (1985), the Supreme Court struck down as unconstitutional the Alabama law authorizing one minute of silence for prayer or meditation in all public schools. Applying the three-part *Lemon* test, the Court concluded that the law violated the establishment clause because it was "an endorsement of religion lacking any

INFOTRAC
To find out more about this debate, use the term "prayer public schools" in the Subject guide.

clearly secular purpose." Since then, the lower courts have interpreted the Supreme Court's decision to mean that states can require a moment of silence in the schools as long as they make it clear that the purpose of the law is secular, not religious.

Prayer outside the Classroom.   The courts have also dealt with cases involving prayer in public schools outside the classroom, particularly prayer during graduation ceremonies. In 1992, in *Lee v. Weisman*,[9] the Supreme Court held that it was unconstitutional for a school to invite a rabbi to deliver a nonsectarian prayer at graduation. The Court said nothing about *students* organizing and leading prayers at graduation ceremonies and other school events, however, and these issues continue to come before the courts. A particularly contentious question in the last few years involves student-initiated prayers before sporting events, such as football games. In 1999, a federal appellate court held that while school prayer at graduation did not violate the establishment clause, students could not use a school's public address system to lead prayers at sporting events.[10] In 2000, the Supreme Court affirmed this decision.[11]

Forbidding the Teaching of Evolution.   For many decades, certain religious groups, particularly in the southern states, have opposed the teaching of evolution in the schools. To these groups, evolutionary theory directly counters their religious belief that human beings did not evolve but were created fully formed, as described in the biblical story of the creation. State and local attempts to forbid the teaching of evolution, however, have not passed constitutional muster in the eyes of the United States Supreme Court. For example, in 1968 the Supreme Court held, in *Epperson v. Arkansas*,[12] that an Arkansas law prohibiting the teaching of evolution violated the establishment clause, because it imposed religious beliefs on students. The Louisiana legislature passed a law requiring the teaching of the biblical story of the creation alongside the teaching of evolution. In 1987, in *Edwards v. Aguillard*,[13] the Supreme Court declared that this law was unconstitutional, in part because it had as its primary purpose the promotion of a particular religious belief.

Subsequently, a Louisiana school board required teachers in its district to recite disclaimers that evolution lessons are "not intended to influence or dissuade the Biblical version of Creation or any other concept." In 2000, a federal appellate court held that the disclaimer violated the establishment clause because it was aimed at the "protection and maintenance of a particular religious viewpoint."[14]   Nonetheless, state and local groups around the country, particularly in the so-called Bible Belt, continue their efforts against the teaching of evolution.

Religious Speech.   Another controversy in the area of church-state relations has to do with religious speech in public schools or universities. For example, in *Rosenberger v. University of Virginia*,[15] the issue concerned whether the University of Virginia violated the establishment clause when it refused to fund a Christian group's newsletter but granted funds to more than one hundred other student organizations. The Supreme Court ruled that the university's policy unconstitutionally discriminated against religious speech. The Court pointed out that the money came from student fees, not general taxes, and was used for the "neutral" payment of bills for student groups.

This five-foot stone slab bearing the Ten Commandments sits near the steps of the capitol building in Austin, Texas. In 2002, a federal district court held that this particular display did not violate the Constitution's establishment clause, primarily because the monument served secular (historical), not religious, purposes.

AP Photo/Harry Cabluck

The Free Exercise Clause

The First Amendment constrains Congress from prohibiting the free exercise of religion. Does this **free exercise clause** mean that no type of religious practice can be prohibited or restricted by government? Certainly, a person can hold any religious belief that he or she wants, or a person can have no religious belief. When, however, religious *practices* work against public policy and the public welfare, the government can act. For example, regardless of a child's or parent's religious beliefs, the government can require certain types of vaccinations. Additionally, public school students can be required to study from textbooks chosen by school authorities.

The extent to which government can regulate religious practices has always been subject to controversy. For example, in 1990, in *Oregon v. Smith*,[16] the Supreme Court ruled that the state of Oregon could deny unemployment benefits to two drug counselors who had been fired for using peyote, an illegal drug, in their religious services. The counselors had argued that using peyote was part of the practice of a Native American religion. Many criticized the decision as going too far in the direction of regulating religious practices.

In 1993, Congress responded to the public's criticism by passing the Religious Freedom Restoration Act (RFRA). One of the specific purposes of the act was to overturn the Supreme Court's decision in *Oregon v. Smith*. The act required national, state, and local governments to "accommodate religious conduct" unless the government

Free Exercise Clause The provision of the First Amendment guaranteeing the free exercise of religion.

could show that there was a *compelling* reason not to do so. Moreover, if the government did regulate a religious practice, it had to use the least restrictive means possible.

Some people believed that the RFRA went too far in the other direction—it accommodated practices that were contrary to the public policies of state governments. Proponents of states' rights complained that the act intruded into an area traditionally governed by state laws, not the national government. In 1997, in *City of Boerne v. Flores*,[17] the Supreme Court agreed and held that Congress had exceeded its constitutional authority when it passed the RFRA. According to the Court, the act's "sweeping coverage ensures its intrusion at every level of government, displacing laws and prohibiting official actions of almost every description and regardless of subject matter."

Freedom of Expression

Perhaps the most frequently invoked freedom that Americans have is the right to free speech and a free press without government interference. Each of us has the right to have our say, and all of us have the right to hear what others say. For the most part, Americans can criticize public officials and their actions without fear of reprisal by any branch of our government.

No Prior Restraint

Prior Restraint
Restraining an action before the action has occurred. When expression is involved, this means censorship.

Restraining an activity before that activity has actually occurred is called **prior restraint.** When expression is involved, prior restraint means censorship, as opposed to subsequent punishment. Prior restraint of expression would require, for example, that a permit be obtained before a speech could be made, a newspaper published, or a movie or TV show exhibited. Most, if not all, Supreme Court justices have been very critical of any governmental action that imposes prior restraint on expression.

One of the most famous cases concerning prior restraint was *New York Times v. United States*[18] (1971), the so-called Pentagon Papers case. The *Times* and the *Washington Post* were about to publish the Pentagon Papers, an elaborate secret history of the U.S. government's involvement in the Vietnam War (1964–1975). The secret documents had been obtained illegally by a disillusioned former Pentagon official. The government wanted a court order to bar publication of the documents, arguing that national security was threatened. The Supreme Court ruled six to three in favor of the newspapers' right to publish the information. This case affirmed the no-prior-restraint doctrine.

In 1999 the California Supreme Court issued a ruling that, according to some commentators, amounts to prior restraint in the workplace. The case involved several Hispanic employees who claimed that their supervisor's insults and racist comments had created a hostile work environment. The lower court agreed and awarded damages to the employees. In upholding the ruling, the California Supreme Court took the bold step of issuing a list of offensive words that can no longer be used in any workplace in the state, even among Hispanic Americans themselves. Three justices harshly dissented from the majority opinion, referring to it as "the exception that swallowed the First Amendment."[19]

The Protection of Symbolic Speech

Not all expression is in words or in writing. Gestures, movements, articles of clothing, and other forms of expressive conduct are considered **symbolic speech.** Such speech is given substantial protection today by our courts. For example, in a landmark decision issued in 1969, *Tinker v. Des Moines School District*,[20] the Supreme Court held that the wearing of black armbands by students in protest against the Vietnam War was a form of speech protected by the First Amendment.

In 1989, in *Texas v. Johnson*,[21] the Supreme Court ruled that state laws that prohibited the burning of the American flag as part of a peaceful protest also violated the freedom of expression protected by the First Amendment. Congress responded by passing the Flag Protection Act of 1989, which was ruled unconstitutional by the Supreme Court in June 1990.[22] Congress and President George H. W. Bush immediately pledged to work for a constitutional amendment to "protect our flag"—an effort that has yet to be successful.

In 2003, however, the Supreme Court held that a Virginia statute prohibiting the burning of a cross with "an intent to intimidate" did not violate the First Amendment. The Court concluded that a burning cross is an instrument of racial terror so threatening that it overshadows free speech concerns.[23]

The Protection of Commercial Speech

Commercial speech is usually defined as advertising statements. Can advertisers use their First Amendment rights to prevent restrictions on the content of commercial advertising? Until the 1970s, the Supreme Court held that such speech was not protected at all by the First Amendment. By the mid-1970s, however, more and more commercial speech had been brought under First Amendment protection. According to Justice Harry A. Blackmun, "Advertising, however tasteless and excessive it sometimes may seem, is nonetheless dissemination of information as to who is producing and selling what product for what reason and at what price."[24] Generally, the Supreme Court will consider a restriction on commercial speech valid as long as it (1) seeks to implement a substantial government interest, (2) directly advances that interest, and (3) goes no further than necessary to accomplish its objective. In particular, a business engaging in commercial speech can be subject to liability for factual inaccuracies in ways that do not apply to noncommercial speech.

Les Stone, Corbis Sygma

These protesters are burning an American flag as a symbolic expression of their opposition to government policy. Would a constitutional amendment to prohibit such actions place unacceptable limitations on symbolic speech?

Symbolic Speech
Nonverbal expression of beliefs, which is given substantial protection by the courts.

Commercial Speech
Advertising statements.

An interesting question is whether speech by a corporation is commercial when it does not take the form of an obvious advertisement. In 2003, in a surprise decision, the United States Supreme Court reversed itself and refused to hear *Nike v. Kasky*,[25] a case in which the California Supreme Court had held that almost any statement by a corporation constituted commercial speech. The case was settled out of court later in 2003.

Permitted Restrictions on Expression

At various times, restrictions on expression have been permitted. A description of several such restrictions follows.

Clear and Present Danger.   When a person's remarks present a clear and present danger to the peace or public order, they can be curtailed constitutionally. Justice Oliver Wendell Holmes used this reasoning in 1919 when examining the case of a socialist who had been convicted for violating the Espionage Act. Holmes stated:

> The question in every case is whether the words are used in such circumstances and are of such a nature as to create a *clear and present danger* that they will bring about the substantive evils that Congress has a right to prevent. It is a question of proximity and degree. [Emphasis added.][26]

Clear and Present Danger Test A test for determining when government may restrict free speech. Restrictions are permissible only when speech presents a "clear and present danger" to the public order.

Bad-Tendency Rule A rule stating that speech or other First Amendment freedoms may be curtailed if there is a possibility that such expression might lead to some "evil."

According to the **clear and present danger test,** then, expression may be restricted if evidence exists that such expression would cause a condition, actual or imminent, that Congress has the power to prevent.

Modifications to the Clear and Present Danger Rule.   Since it was first enunciated, the United States Supreme Court has modified the clear and present danger rule. In *Gitlow v. New York*,[27] the Court introduced the **bad-tendency rule.** According to this rule, speech or other First Amendment freedoms may be curtailed if there is a possibility that such expression might lead to some "evil." In the *Gitlow* case, a member of a left-wing group was convicted of violating New York State's criminal anarchy statute when he published and distributed a pamphlet urging the violent overthrow of the U.S. government. In its majority opinion, the Supreme Court held that although the First Amendment afforded protection against state incursions on freedom of expression, Gitlow could be punished legally in this particular instance because his expression would tend to bring about evils that the state had a right to prevent.

The Supreme Court took a somewhat different direction in 1969. In that year, in *Brandenburg v. Ohio*,[28] the Court overturned the conviction of a Ku Klux Klan leader for violating a state statute. The statute prohibited anyone from advocating "the duty, necessity, or propriety of sabotage, violence, or unlawful methods of terrorism as a means of accomplishing industrial or political reform." The Court held that the guarantee of free speech does not permit a state "to forbid or proscribe advocacy of the use of force or of law violation except where such advocacy is directed to inciting or producing imminent lawless actions and is likely to incite or produce such action." The "incitement test" enunciated by the Court in this case is a difficult one for prosecutors to meet. As a result, the Court's decision significantly broadened the protection given to advocacy speech.

Unprotected Speech: Obscenity

A large number of state and federal statutes make it a crime to disseminate obscene materials. Generally, the courts have not been willing to extend constitutional protections of free speech to what they consider obscene materials. But what is obscenity? Justice Potter Stewart once stated, in *Jacobellis v. Ohio,*[29] a 1964 case, that even though he could not define obscenity, "I know it when I see it."

Definitional Problems.   The Supreme Court has grappled from time to time with the problem of specifying an operationally effective definition of obscenity. In 1973, in *Miller v. California,*[30] Chief Justice Warren Burger created a formal list of requirements that currently must be met for material to be legally obscene. Material is obscene if (1) the average person finds that it violates contemporary community standards; (2) the work taken as a whole appeals to a prurient interest in sex; (3) the work shows patently offensive sexual conduct; and (4) the work lacks serious redeeming literary, artistic, political, or scientific merit. The problem, of course, is that one person's prurient interest is another person's medical interest or artistic pleasure. The Court went on to state that the definition of *prurient interest* would be determined by the community's standards. The Court avoided presenting a definition of obscenity, leaving this determination to local and state authorities. Consequently, the *Miller* case has had widely inconsistent applications.

Protecting Children.   The Supreme Court has upheld state laws making it illegal to sell materials showing sexual performance by minors. In 1990, in *Osborne v. Ohio,*[31] the Court ruled that states can outlaw the possession of child pornography in the home. The Court reasoned that the ban on private possession is justified because owning the material perpetuates commercial demand for it and for the exploitation of the children involved. At the federal level, the Child Protection Act of 1984 made it a crime to receive knowingly through the mails sexually explicit depictions of children.

A significant problem facing Americans and their lawmakers today is how to control obscenity and child pornography that are disseminated via the Internet. For a further discussion of this topic, see this chapter's feature entitled *At Issue: Should the Internet Be Censored?* on the following page.

INFOTRAC

For updates on this topic, use the term "Internet censorship" in Keywords.

Unprotected Speech: Slander

Can you say anything you want about someone else? Not really. Individuals are protected from **defamation of character,** which is defined as wrongfully hurting a person's good reputation. The law imposes a general duty on all persons to refrain from making false, defamatory statements about others. Breaching this duty orally is the wrongdoing called **slander.** Breaching it in writing is the wrongdoing called *libel,* which we discuss later. The government itself does not bring charges of slander or libel. Rather, the defamed person may bring a civil suit for damages.

Legally, slander is the public uttering of a false statement that harms the good reputation of another. Public uttering means that the defamatory statements are made

Defamation of Character Wrongfully hurting a person's good reputation.

Slander The public uttering of a false statement that harms the good reputation of another.

AT ISSUE: Should the Internet Be Censored?

Americans have conflicting views as to what, if anything, should be done to curb uses of the Internet that are perceived to be harmful to society. Some contend that the government should prohibit certain types of speech on the Internet. After all, they claim, restraints on speech are not new. Defamatory speech is not protected by the First Amendment, for example; neither are obscene speech and certain other forms of speech. Other groups argue that freedom of speech is one of our most important rights and that the government should let the Internet alone.

FEDERAL RESTRICTIONS ON INTERNET SPEECH

In fact, the federal government has already made several attempts to censor the Internet. The Communications Decency Act (CDA) of 1996, which made it a criminal offense to make "patently offensive" and "indecent" speech available online to minors, was ruled unconstitutional by the Supreme Court because it infringed too much on speech protected under the First Amendment.*

Later attempts by Congress to curb pornography on the Internet also encountered constitutional stumbling blocks. For example, the Child Online Protection Act (COPA) of 1998 banned the distribution of material "harmful to minors" without an age-verification system to separate adult and minor users. In 2002, the Supreme Court upheld a lower court injunction suspending COPA but narrowed the grounds on which it could be found unconstitutional.† In 2000, Congress enacted the Children's Internet Protection Act (CIPA), which requires public schools and libraries to install filtering software on their computers to prevent children from viewing Web sites with "adult" content. In 2002, a U.S. district court found CIPA unconstitutional when applied to public libraries. In 2003, however, the

*Reno v. American Civil Liberties Union, 521 U.S. 844 (1997).
†Ashcroft v. American Civil Liberties Union, 535 U.S. 564 (2002).

to, or within the hearing of, persons other than the defamed party. If one person calls another dishonest, manipulative, and incompetent to his or her face when no one else is around, that does not constitute slander. The message is not communicated to a third party. If, however, a third party accidentally overhears defamatory statements, the courts have generally held that this constitutes a public uttering and therefore slander, which is prohibited.

Campus Speech Codes

Some state universities have issued codes that challenge the boundaries of the protection of free speech provided by the First Amendment. These codes are designed to prohibit so-called hate speech—abusive speech attacking persons on the basis of their ethnicity, race, or other criteria. For example, a University of Michigan code banned "any behavior, verbal or physical, that stigmatizes or victimizes an individual on the basis of race, ethnicity, religion, sex, sexual orientation, creed, national origin, ancestry, age, marital status, handicap" or Vietnam-veteran status. A federal court found that the code violated students' First Amendment rights.[32]

Supreme Court reversed the district court and upheld the act.[†]

SHOULD "VIRTUAL" PORNOGRAPHY BE DEEMED A CRIME?

Recently, the Supreme Court agreed to review a case challenging the constitutionality of another federal act attempting to protect minors in the online environment—the Child Pornography Prevention Act (CPPA) of 1996. This act made it illegal to distribute or possess computer-generated images that appear to depict minors engaging in lewd and lascivious behavior. At issue was whether digital child pornography should be considered a crime when no actual children are involved, only digitally rendered images.

The Supreme Court, noting that virtual child pornography is not the same as child pornography, held that the CPPA's ban on virtual child pornography restrained a substantial amount of lawful speech.[§] The Court stated, "The statute proscribes the visual depiction of an idea—that of teenagers engaging in sexual activity—that is a fact of modern society and has been a theme in art and literature throughout the ages." The Court

concluded that the act was overbroad and thus unconstitutional.

ENFORCEMENT PROBLEMS

Extreme hate speech appears on the Internet, including racist materials and Holocaust denials. Can the federal government restrict this type of speech? Should it? Content restrictions can be difficult to enforce. Even if Congress succeeded in passing a law prohibiting certain speech on the Internet, an army of federal "Internet watchers" would be needed to enforce it. Also, what if other countries attempt to impose their laws that restrict speech on U.S. Web sites? This is not a purely theoretical issue. In 2000, a French court found Yahoo in violation of French laws banning the display of Nazi memorabilia. In 2001, however, a U.S. district court held that this ruling could not be enforced against Yahoo in the United States.[¶]

FOR CRITICAL ANALYSIS

What is the difference between the regulation of explicitly sexual material in magazines, which can be purchased in most jurisdictions by adults, and the regulation of explicitly sexual materials on the Web?

[†]*U.S. v. American Library Ass'n, Inc.,* 123 S.Ct. 2297 (2003).
[§]*Ashcroft v. Free Speech Coalition,* 122 S.Ct. 1389 (2002).

[¶]*Yahoo! Inc. v. La Ligue Contre le Racisme et l'Antisemitisme,* 169 F.Supp.2d 1181 (N.D.Cal. 2001).

Although the courts generally have held, as in the University of Michigan case, that campus speech codes are unconstitutional restrictions on the right to free speech, such codes continue to exist. Whether hostile speech should be banned on high school campuses has also become an issue. In view of school shootings and other violent behavior in the schools, school officials have become concerned about speech that consists of veiled threats or that could lead to violence. Some schools have prohibited students from wearing clothing, such as T-shirts, bearing verbal messages (such as sexist or racist comments) or symbolic messages (such as the Confederate flag) that might generate "ill will or hatred."[33]

Freedom of the Press

Freedom of the press can be regarded as a special instance of freedom of speech. Of course, at the time of the framing of the Constitution, the press meant only newspapers, magazines, and books. As technology has modified the ways in which we disseminate information, the laws touching on freedom of the press have been modified.

What can and cannot be printed still occupies an important place in constitutional law, however.

Defamation in Writing

Libel A written defamation of a person's character, reputation, business, or property rights.

Libel is defamation in writing (or in pictures, signs, or films, or any other communication that has the potentially harmful qualities of written or printed words). As with slander, libel occurs only if the defamatory statements are observed by a third party. If one person writes another a private letter wrongfully accusing him or her of embezzling funds, that does not constitute libel. It is interesting that the courts have generally held that dictating a letter to a secretary constitutes communication of the letter's contents to a third party, and therefore, if defamation has occurred, the wrongdoer can be sued.

Public Figures Public officials, movie stars, and other persons known to the public because of their positions or activities.

New York Times Co. v. Sullivan[34] (1964) explored an important question regarding libelous statements made about **public figures**—public officials and employees who exercise substantial governmental power, as well as any persons who are generally in the public limelight. The Supreme Court held that only when a statement was made with **actual malice**—that is, with either knowledge of its falsity or a reckless disregard of the truth—against a public official could damages be obtained.

Actual Malice Either knowledge of a defamatory statement's falsity or a reckless disregard for the truth.

A Free Press versus a Fair Trial: Gag Orders

INFOTRAC

To find out more about libel, use the term "libel" in the Subject guide.

Another major freedom of the press issue concerns media coverage of criminal trials. The Sixth Amendment to the Constitution guarantees the right of criminal suspects to a fair trial. In other words, the accused have rights. The First Amendment guarantees freedom of the press. What if the two rights appear to be in conflict? Which one prevails?

Jurors certainly may be influenced by reading news stories about the trial in which they are participating. In the 1970s, judges increasingly issued **gag orders,** which restricted the publication of news about a trial in progress or even a pretrial hearing. In a landmark 1976 case, *Nebraska Press Association v. Stuart*,[35] the Supreme Court unanimously ruled that a Nebraska judge's gag order had violated the First Amendment's guarantee of freedom of the press. Some justices even went so far as to indicate that gag orders are never justified.

Gag Order An order issued by a judge restricting the publication of news about a trial or a pretrial hearing to protect the accused's right to a fair trial.

In spite of the *Nebraska Press Association* ruling, the Court has upheld certain types of gag orders. In *Gannett Co. v. De Pasquale*[36] (1979), for example, the highest court held that if a judge found a reasonable probability that news publicity would harm a defendant's right to a fair trial, the court could impose a gag rule: "Members of the public have no constitutional right under the Sixth and Fourteenth Amendments to *attend* criminal trials."

Films, Radio, and TV

As we have noted, only in a few cases has the Supreme Court upheld prior restraint of published materials. The Court's reluctance to accept prior restraint is less evident with respect to motion pictures. In the first half of the twentieth century, films were

Radio "shock jock" Howard Stern apparently offended the sensitivities of the Federal Communications Commission (FCC). That regulatory body fined Stern's radio station hundreds of thousands of dollars for Stern's purportedly obscene outbursts on radio.

Bill Swersey, Getty Images

routinely submitted to local censorship boards. In 1968, the Supreme Court ruled that a film can be banned only under a law that provides for a prompt hearing at which the film is shown to be obscene. Today, few local censorship boards exist. Instead, the film industry regulates itself primarily through the industry's rating system.

Radio and television broadcasting has the most limited First Amendment protection. In 1934, the national government established the Federal Communications Commission (FCC) to regulate electromagnetic wave frequencies. No one has a right to use the airwaves without a license granted by the FCC. The FCC grants licenses for limited periods and imposes a variety of regulations on broadcasting. For example, the FCC can impose sanctions on radio or TV stations that broadcast "filthy words," even if the words are not legally obscene.

The Right to Assemble and to Petition the Government

The First Amendment prohibits Congress from making any law that abridges "the right of the people peaceably to assemble, and to petition the Government for a redress of grievances." Inherent in such a right is the ability of private citizens to communicate their ideas on public issues to government officials, as well as to other individuals. The Supreme Court has often put this freedom on a par with the freedom of speech and the freedom of the press. Nonetheless, it has allowed municipalities to require permits for parades, sound trucks, and demonstrations, so that public officials may control traffic or prevent demonstrations from turning into riots.

This became a major issue in 1977 when the American Nazi Party wanted to march through the largely Jewish suburb of Skokie, Illinois. The American Civil Liberties Union defended the Nazis' right to march (in spite of its opposition to the

INFOTRAC

To learn about protests about the war against Iraq, use the term "anti-war demonstrations" in the Subject guide.

With their right to assemble and demonstrate protected by the Constitution, members of the modern Ku Klux Klan march in Wilmington, North Carolina. The police escort is charged with making sure that neither the marchers nor the observers provoke any violence.

Paul Miller, Stock Photo

Nazi philosophy). The Supreme Court let stand a lower court's ruling that the city of Skokie had violated the Nazis' First Amendment guarantees by denying them a permit to march.[37]

An issue that has surfaced in recent years is whether communities can prevent gang members from gathering together on the streets without violating their right of assembly or associated rights. Although some actions taken by cities to prevent gang members from gathering together or "loitering" in public places have passed constitutional muster, others have not.

Matters of Privacy

No explicit reference is made anywhere in the Constitution to a person's right to privacy. In the 1960s, however, the highest court began to infer such a right from the various constitutional freedoms provided in the Bill of Rights. In 1965, in *Griswold v. Connecticut*,[38] the Supreme Court overthrew a Connecticut law that effectively prohibited the use of contraceptives, holding that the law violated the right to privacy. Justice William O. Douglas formulated a unique way of reading this right into the Bill of Rights. He claimed that the First, Third, Fourth, Fifth, and Ninth Amendments created "penumbras, formed by emanations from those guarantees that help give them life and substance," and he went on to talk about zones of privacy that are guaranteed by these rights. When we read the Ninth Amendment, we can see the foundation for his reasoning: "The enumeration in the Constitution, of certain rights, shall not be construed to deny or disparage others retained by the people." In other words, just because the Constitution, including its amendments, does not specifically talk about the right to privacy does not mean that this right is denied to the people.

Some of today's most controversial issues relate to privacy rights. One issue is the erosion of privacy rights in an information age, as computers make it easier to compile and distribute personal information. Other issues are abortion and the "right to die." Since the terrorist attacks of September 11, 2001, Americans have faced another crucial question regarding privacy rights: To what extent should Americans sacrifice privacy rights in the interests of national security?

Privacy Rights in an Information Age

An important privacy issue, created in part by new technology, is the amassing of information on individuals by government agencies and private businesses, such as marketing firms. The average American citizen is the subject of personal information filed away by dozens of agencies—such as the Social Security Administration and the Internal Revenue Service. Because of the threat of indiscriminate use of private information by nonauthorized individuals, Congress passed the Privacy Act in 1974. This was the first law regulating the use of federal government information about private individuals. Under the Privacy Act, every citizen has the right to obtain copies of personal records collected by federal agencies and to correct inaccuracies in such records.

The ease with which personal information can be obtained by those using the Internet for marketing and other purposes has led to unique challenges to privacy rights. Some fear that privacy rights in personal information may soon be a thing of the past. Whether privacy rights can survive in an information age is a question that Americans and their leaders continue to confront.

Privacy Rights and Abortion

Historically, abortion was not a criminal offense before the first movement of the fetus in the uterus, usually between the sixteenth and eighteenth weeks of pregnancy. By 1973, however, performance of an abortion at any time during pregnancy was a criminal offense in a majority of the states.

Roe v. Wade.   In *Roe v. Wade*[39] (1973), the United States Supreme Court ruled that the laws against abortion violated "Jane Roe's" right to privacy under the Constitution. The Court held that during the first trimester (three months) of pregnancy, abortion was an issue solely between a woman and her doctor. The state could not limit abortions except to require that they be performed by licensed physicians. During the second trimester, to protect the health of the mother, the state was allowed to specify the conditions under which an abortion could be performed. During the final trimester, the state could regulate or even outlaw abortions except when necessary to preserve the life or health of the mother.

During the 1980s, the Court twice struck down laws that required a woman who wished to have an abortion to undergo counseling designed to discourage abortions. In the late 1980s and early 1990s, however, the Court took a more conservative approach. For example, in *Webster v. Reproductive Health Services*[40] (1989), the Court upheld a Missouri statute that, among other things, banned the use of public hospitals or other taxpayer-supported facilities for performing abortions. And, in *Planned Parenthood v. Casey*[41] (1992), the Court upheld a Pennsylvania law that required pre-abortion counseling, a waiting period of twenty-four hours, and, for girls under the age of eighteen, parental or judicial permission. As a result, abortions are now more difficult to obtain in some states than others.

The Controversy Continues.   Abortion continues to be a divisive issue. Because of several episodes of violence at abortion clinics, in 1994 Congress passed the Freedom of Access to Clinic Entrances Act. The act prohibits protesters from blocking entrances to such clinics. In 1997, the Supreme Court upheld the constitutionality of prohibiting protesters from entering a fifteen-foot "buffer zone" around abortion clinics and from giving unwanted counseling to those entering the clinics.[42]

In 2000, the Supreme Court again visited the abortion issue when it reviewed a Nebraska law banning "partial birth" abortions. Similar laws have been passed by at least twenty-seven states. A partial-birth abortion, which doctors call intact dilation and extraction, is a procedure that can be used during the second trimester of pregnancy. Abortion rights advocates claim that in limited circumstances the procedure is the safest way to perform an abortion, and that the government should never outlaw specific medical procedures. Opponents argue that the procedure has no medical merit and that it ends the life of a fetus that might be able to live outside the womb. The Supreme Court invalidated the Nebraska law on the ground that, as written, the law could be used to ban other abortion procedures and because it contained no provisions for protecting the health of the pregnant woman.[43] In 2003, a law similar to the Nebraska statute was passed by the U.S. Congress and signed into law by president George W. Bush. It was immediately challenged in court.

Privacy Rights and the "Right to Die"

The 1976 case involving Karen Ann Quinlan was one of the first publicized right-to-die cases.[44] The New Jersey Supreme Court ruled that the right to privacy includes the right of a patient to refuse treatment and that patients unable to speak can exercise that right through a family member or guardian. Since the 1976 *Quinlan* decision, most states have enacted laws permitting people to designate their wishes concerning life-sustaining procedures in "living wills" or durable health-care powers of attorney. These laws largely have resolved this aspect of the right-to-die controversy.

In the 1990s, however, another issue surfaced: Do privacy rights include the right of terminally ill people to end their lives through physician-assisted suicide? In 1997, in *Washington v. Glucksberg*,[45] the Court stated that the liberty interest protected by the Constitution does not include a right to commit suicide, with or without assistance. In effect, the Supreme Court left the decision in the hands of the states. Since then, assisted suicide has been allowed in only one state—Oregon.

Privacy Rights versus Security Issues

As former Supreme Court Justice Thurgood Marshall once said, "Grave threats to liberty often come in times of urgency, when constitutional rights seem too extravagant to endure." Not surprisingly, anti-terrorist legislation since the attacks on September 11, 2001, has eroded certain basic rights, in particular the Fourth Amendment protections against unreasonable searches and seizures. Current legislation allows the government to conduct "roving" wiretaps. Previously, only specific telephone numbers, cell phone numbers, or computer terminals could be tapped.

Now a specific person under suspicion can be monitored electronically no matter what form of electronic communication he or she uses. Such roving wiretaps go against the Supreme Court's interpretation of the Fourth Amendment, which requires a judicial warrant to describe the *place* to be searched, not just the person. One of the goals of the framers was to avoid *general* searches. Further, once a judge approves an application for a roving wiretap, when, how, and where the monitoring occurs will be left to the FBI's discretion. As an unavoidable result, a third party will have access to the conversations and e-mails of hundreds of people who falsely believe them to be private.

The Great Balancing Act: The Rights of the Accused versus the Rights of Society

The United States has one of the highest violent crime rates in the industrialized world. It is not surprising, therefore, that many citizens have extremely strong opinions

More and more state and local governments have adopted laws that inform citizens when criminal sexual offenders move into their neighborhood. Do such laws violate the rights of individuals who have "paid their debt to society," or do they rightfully forewarn a community of potential danger?

A. Ramey, PhotoEdit

about the rights of those accused of criminal offenses. When an accused person, especially one who has confessed to some criminal act, is set free because of an apparent legal "technicality," many people believe that the rights of the accused are being given more weight than the rights of society and of potential or actual victims. Why, then, give criminal suspects rights? The answer is partly to avoid convicting innocent people but mostly because all criminal suspects have the right to due process of law and fair treatment.

The courts and the police must constantly engage in a balancing act of competing rights. At the basis of all discussions about the appropriate balance is, of course, the U.S. Bill of Rights. The Fourth, Fifth, Sixth, and Eighth Amendments deal specifically with the rights of criminal defendants. (You will learn about some of your rights under the Fourth Amendment in the *Making a Difference* feature at the end of this chapter.)

Rights of the Accused

The basic rights of criminal defendants are outlined below. When appropriate, the specific constitutional provision or amendment on which a right is based also is given.

Limits on the Conduct of Police Officers and Prosecutors
- No unreasonable or unwarranted searches and seizures (Amend. IV).
- No arrest except on probable cause (Amend. IV).
- No coerced confessions or illegal interrogation (Amend. V).
- No entrapment.
- On questioning, a suspect must be informed of her or his rights.

Defendant's Pretrial Rights

Writ of *Habeas Corpus* *Habeas corpus* means "you have the body." A writ of *habeas corpus* requires jailers to bring a prisoner before a court or judge and explain why the person is being held.

- **Writ of *habeas corpus*** (Article I, Section 9).
- Prompt arraignment (Amend. VI).
- Legal counsel (Amend. VI).
- Reasonable bail (Amend. VIII).
- To be informed of charges (Amend. VI).
- To remain silent (Amend. V).

Trial Rights
- Speedy and public trial before a jury (Amend. VI).
- Impartial jury selected from a cross-section of the community (Amend. VI).
- Trial atmosphere free of prejudice, fear, and outside interference.
- No compulsory self-incrimination (Amend. V).
- Adequate counsel (Amend. VI).
- No cruel and unusual punishment (Amend. VIII).
- Appeal of convictions.
- No double jeopardy (Amend. V).

Extending the Rights of the Accused

During the 1960s, the Supreme Court, under Chief Justice Earl Warren, significantly expanded the rights of accused persons. In a case decided in 1963, *Gideon v. Wainwright*,[46] the Court held that if a person is accused of a felony and cannot afford an attorney, an attorney must be made available to the accused person at the government's expense. Although the Sixth Amendment to the Constitution provides for the right to counsel, the Supreme Court had established a precedent twenty-one years earlier in *Betts v. Brady*,[47] when it held that only criminal defendants in capital cases automatically had a right to legal counsel.

Miranda v. Arizona. In 1966, the Court issued its decision in *Miranda v. Arizona*.[48] The case involved Ernesto Miranda, who was arrested and charged with the kidnapping and rape of a young woman. After two hours of questioning, Miranda confessed and was later convicted. Miranda's lawyer appealed his conviction, arguing that the police had never informed Miranda that he had a right to remain silent and a right to be represented by counsel. The Court, in ruling in Miranda's favor, enunciated the *Miranda* rights that are now familiar to virtually all Americans:

> Prior to any questioning, the person must be warned that he has a right to remain silent, that any statement he does make may be used against him, and that he has a right to the presence of an attorney, either retained or appointed.

Two years after the Supreme Court's Miranda decision, Congress passed the Omnibus Crime Control and Safe Streets Act of 1968. Section 3501 of the act reinstated a rule that had been in effect for 180 years before *Miranda*—that statements by defendants can be used against them if the statements were voluntarily made. The Justice Department immediately disavowed Section 3501 as unconstitutional and has continued to hold this position. As a result, Section 3501, although it was never repealed, has never been enforced. In 2000, after a federal appellate court stunned the criminal justice community by holding that the all-but-forgotten provision was enforceable, the Supreme Court held that the *Miranda* warnings were constitutionally based and could not be overruled by a legislative act.[49]

Exceptions to the *Miranda* Rule. Still, the Supreme Court has made a number of exceptions to the *Miranda* rule. In 1991, the Court stated that a suspect's conviction will not be automatically overturned if the suspect was coerced into making a confession. If the other evidence admitted at trial is strong enough to justify the conviction without the confession, then the fact that the confession was obtained illegally can be, in effect, ignored.[50] In yet another case, in 1994, the Supreme Court ruled that suspects must unequivocally and assertively state their right to counsel in order to stop police questioning. Saying, "Maybe I should talk to a lawyer" during an interrogation after being taken into custody is not enough. The Court held that police officers are not required to decipher the suspect's intentions in such situations.[51]

The Exclusionary Rule

At least since 1914, judicial policy has prohibited the admission of illegally seized evidence at trials in federal courts. This is the so-called **exclusionary rule.** Improperly obtained evidence, no matter how telling, cannot be used by prosecutors. This includes evidence obtained by police in violation of a suspect's *Miranda* rights or of the Fourth Amendment. The Fourth Amendment protects against unreasonable searches and seizures and provides that a judge may issue a search warrant to a police

Exclusionary Rule A policy forbidding the admission at trial of illegally seized evidence.

MAKING A DIFFERENCE : Your Civil Liberties: Searches and Seizures

What happens if you are stopped by police officers? Your civil liberties protect you from having to provide information other than your name and address. Normally, even if you have not been placed under arrest, the officers have the right to frisk you for weapons, and you must let them proceed. The officers cannot, however, check your person or your clothing further if, in their judgment, no weaponlike object is produced.

SEARCHES OF YOUR PERSON

The officers may search you only if they have a search warrant or probable cause to believe that a search will likely produce incriminating evidence. What if the officers do not have probable cause or a warrant? Physically resisting their attempt to search you can lead to disastrous results. It is best simply to refuse orally to give permission for the search, preferably in the presence of a witness. Being polite is better than acting out of anger and making the officers irritable. It is usually advisable to limit what you say to the officers. If you are arrested, it is best to keep quiet until you can speak with a lawyer.

SEARCHES OF YOUR CAR

If you are in your car and are stopped by the police, the same fundamental rules apply. Always be ready to show your driver's license and car registration. You may be asked to get out of the car. The officers may use a flashlight to peer inside if it is too dark to see otherwise. None of this constitutes a search. A true search requires either a warrant or probable cause. No officer has the legal right to search your car simply to find out if you may have committed a crime. Police officers can conduct searches that are incident to lawful arrests, however.

SEARCHES OF YOUR HOME

If you are in your home and a police officer with a search warrant appears, you can ask to examine the warrant before granting entry. A warrant that is correctly made out will state the place or persons to be searched, the object sought, the date of the warrant (which should be no more than ten days old), and it will bear the signature of a judge or magistrate. If the warrant is in order, you need not make any statement. If you believe the warrant to be invalid, or if no warrant is produced, you should make it clear orally that you have not consented to the search, preferably in the presence of a witness. If the search later is proved to be unlawful, normally any evidence obtained cannot be used in court.

Officers who attempt to enter your home without a search warrant can do so only if they are pursuing a suspected felon into the house. Rarely is it advisable to give permission for a warrantless search. You, as the resident, must be the one to give permission if any evidence obtained is to be considered legal. The landlord, manager, or head of a college dormitory cannot give legal permission. A roommate, however, can give permission for a search of his or her room, which may allow the police to search areas where you have belongings.

If you are a guest in a place that is being legally searched, you may be legally searched also. But unless you have been placed under arrest, you cannot be compelled to go to the police station or into a squad car.

If you would like to find out more about your rights and obligations under the laws of searches and seizures, you might wish to contact the following organization:

The American Civil Liberties
    Union
125 Broad St., 18th Floor
New York, NY 10004
212-549-2500
http://www.aclu.org

officer only on probable cause (a demonstration of facts that permit a reasonable belief that a crime has been committed). The exclusionary rule was first extended to state court proceedings in a 1961 Supreme Court decision, *Mapp v. Ohio*.[52]

The reasoning behind the exclusionary rule is that it forces police officers to gather evidence properly, in which case their due diligence will be rewarded by a conviction. The exclusionary rule has always had critics, however, who argue that it permits guilty persons to be freed because of innocent errors.

Over the last several decades, the Supreme Court has diminished the scope of the exclusionary rule by creating some exceptions to its applicability. For example, in 1984 the Court held that illegally obtained evidence could be admitted at trial if law enforcement personnel could prove that they would have obtained the evidence legally anyway.[53] In another case decided in the same year, the Court held that a police officer who used a technically incorrect search warrant form to obtain evidence had acted in good faith and therefore the evidence was admissible at trial. The Court thus created the "good faith" exception to the exclusionary rule.[54]

KEY TERMS

actual malice **82**

bad-tendency rule **78**

civil liberties **69**

clear and present danger test **78**

commercial speech **77**

defamation of character **79**

establishment clause **71**

exclusionary rule **89**

free exercise clause **75**

gag order **82**

incorporation theory **70**

libel **82**

prior restraint **76**

public figures **82**

slander **79**

symbolic speech **77**

writ of *habeas corpus* **88**

CHAPTER SUMMARY

1 Originally, the Bill of Rights limited only the power of the national government, not that of the states. Gradually and selectively, however, the Supreme Court accepted the incorporation theory, under which no state can violate most provisions of the Bill of Rights.

2 The First Amendment protects against government interference with freedom of religion by requiring a separation of church and state (under the establishment clause) and by guaranteeing the free exercise of religion. Controversial issues that arise under the establishment clause include aid to church-related schools, school prayer, the teaching of evolution versus creationism, school vouchers, and discrimination against religious speech. The

government can interfere with the free exercise of religion only when religious practices work against public policy or the public welfare.

3 The First Amendment protects against government interference with freedom of speech, which includes symbolic speech (expressive conduct). The Supreme Court has been especially critical of government actions that impose prior restraint on expression. Commercial speech (advertising) by businesses has received limited First Amendment protection. Restrictions on expression are permitted when the expression presents a clear and present danger to the peace or public order. Speech that has not received First Amendment protection includes expression judged to be obscene or slanderous.

4 The First Amendment protects against government interference with the freedom of the press, which can be regarded as a special instance of freedom of speech. Speech by the press that does not receive protection includes libelous statements. Publication of news about a criminal trial may be restricted by a gag order in some circumstances.

5 The First Amendment protects the right to assemble peaceably and to petition the government. Permits may be required for parades, sound trucks, and demonstrations to maintain the public order, and a permit may be denied to protect the public safety.

6 Under the Ninth Amendment, rights not specifically mentioned in the Constitution are not necessarily denied to the people. Among the unspecified rights protected by the courts is a right to privacy, which has been inferred from the First, Third, Fourth, Fifth, and Ninth Amendments. A major privacy issue today is how best to protect privacy rights in cyberspace. Whether an individual's privacy rights include a right to an abortion or a "right to die" continue to provoke controversy. Another major challenge concerns the extent to which Americans may forfeit privacy rights to control terrorism.

7 The Constitution includes protections for the rights of persons accused of crimes. Under the Fourth Amendment, no one may be subject to an unreasonable search or seizure or be arrested except on probable cause. Under the Fifth Amendment, an accused person has the right to remain silent. Under the Sixth Amendment, an accused person must be informed of the reason for his or her arrest. The accused also has the right to adequate counsel, even if he or she cannot afford an attorney, and the right to a prompt arraignment and a speedy and public trial before an impartial jury selected from a cross-section of the community.

8 In *Miranda v. Arizona* (1966), the Supreme Court held that criminal suspects, before interrogation by law enforcement personnel, must be informed of certain constitutional rights, including the right to remain silent and the right to counsel.

9 The exclusionary rule forbids the admission in court of illegally seized evidence. There is a "good faith exception" to the exclusionary rule: illegally seized evidence need not be thrown out owing to, for example, a technical defect in a search warrant.

SELECTED PRINT AND MEDIA RESOURCES

Suggested Readings

Epps, Garrett. *To an Unknown God: Religious Freedom on Trial*. New York: St. Martin's Press, 2001. The author chronicles the journey through the courts of *Oregon v. Smith*, a case concerning religious practices decided by the Supreme Court in 1990. The author regards this case as one of the Supreme Court's most momentous decisions on religious freedom in the last fifty years.

Gottlieb, Roger S. *Joining Hands: Politics and Religion Together for Social Change*. Boulder, Colo.: Westview Press, 2002. In this exploration of the political role of religion and the spiritual component of politics, the author argues that religious belief and spiritual practice are integral to the politics of social change in the United States.

Leone, Richard C., and Anrig Greg, Jr., eds. *The War on Our Freedoms: Civil Liberties in an Age of Terrorism*. New York: PublicAffairs, 2003. In this book, experts from various fields argue that measures taken since the attacks of September 11, 2001, threaten our liberties.

Media Resources

The Abortion War: Thirty Years after Roe v. Wade—An ABC News program released in 2003 that examines the current state of the abortion issue.

Gideon's Trumpet—An excellent 1980 movie about the *Gideon v. Wainwright* case. Henry Fonda plays the role of the convicted petty thief Clarence Earl Gideon.

May It Please the Court: The First Amendment—A set of audiocassette recordings and written transcripts of the oral arguments made before the Supreme Court in sixteen key First Amendment cases.

Skokie: Rights or Wrong?—A documentary by Sheila Chamovitz. The film documents the legal and moral crisis created when American Nazis attempted to demonstrate in Skokie, Illinois, a predominantly Jewish suburb that was home to many concentration camp survivors.

LOGGING ON

The Liberty Counsel describes itself as "a nonprofit religious civil liberties education and legal defense organization established to preserve religious freedom." The URL for its Web site is http://www.lc.org.

Summaries and the full text of Supreme Court constitutional law decisions, plus a virtual tour of the Supreme Court, are available at http://www.oyez.org/oyez/frontpage.

If you want to read historic Supreme Court decisions, you can find them, listed by name, at http://supct.law.cornell.edu/supct.

The Center for Democracy and Technology (CDT) focuses on how developments in communications technology are affecting the constitutional liberties of Americans. You can access the CDT's site at http://www.cdt.org.

The American Library Association's Web site provides information on free speech issues, especially issues of free speech on the Internet. Go to http://www.ala.org.

You can find current information on Internet privacy issues at the Electronic Privacy Information Center's Web site. Go to http://www.epic.org/privacy.

For the history of flag protection and the First Amendment, as well as the status of the proposed flag amendment in Congress, go to http://www.freedomforum.org/packages/first/Flag/timeline.htm.

USING THE INTERNET FOR POLITICAL ANALYSIS

Go to this text's Web site at http://politicalscience.wadsworth.com/schmidtbrief2004. Select "Chapter 4" in the box at the top of the window. Then, in the column on the left-hand side of the window, under "Chapter Resources," click on "Internet Exercises." The Web site will then display the following Internet exercises that you can perform to learn more about topics covered in this chapter.

Activity 4–1: Human Rights in the United States
Activity 4–2: Civil Liberties and the Supreme Court
Activity 4–3: Students and Symbolic Speech

ONLINE STUDY GUIDE AND ADDITIONAL RESOURCES

At http://politicalscience.wadsworth.com/schmidtbrief2004 you will find a free Study Guide to this book that includes tutorial quizzes, essay questions, practice exams, chapter outlines, learning objectives, the glossary, flashcards, crossword puzzles, and Microsoft PowerPoint presentations. Also included in the American Government Resource Center for Chapter 4:

- **InfoTrac® Reader**—Euthanasia; religion in the public schools.
- **You Are There Simulations**—Church and state; freedom of speech.
- **Participation Activities**—Enact your right to freedom of expression by creating your own Web page; find a newsgroup discussion on civil liberties.

- **MicroCase Exercise**—Civil liberties.
- **Related Links**—Civil liberties.
- **Video Case Study**—Abortion.
- **Source Readings**—By John Locke, Thomas Jefferson, and Elizabeth Cady Stanton, plus a collection of important court cases and statutes.

The site also contains the Citizen's Survival Guide, information on how to get involved in politics locally and globally, as well as regularly updated features including a Current Events Quiz, In the News, Election Links, updates on the war on terrorism, and more.

CHAPTER 5

Civil Rights

EQUALITY IS AT THE HEART of the concept of civil rights. Generally, the term **civil rights** refers to the rights of all Americans to equal treatment under the law, as provided for by the Fourteenth Amendment to the Constitution. Although the terms *civil rights* and *civil liberties* are sometimes used interchangeably, scholars make a distinction between the two. Civil liberties are basically *limitations* on government; they specify what the government *cannot* do. Civil rights, in contrast, specify what the government *must* do—to ensure equal protection and freedom from discrimination.

Essentially, the history of civil rights in America is the story of the struggle of various groups to be free from discriminatory treatment. In this chapter, we first look at two movements that had significant consequences for the history of civil rights in America: the civil rights movement of the 1950s and 1960s and the women's movement, which began in the mid-1800s and continues today. Each of these movements resulted in legislation that secured important basic rights for all Americans—the right to vote and the right to equal protection under the laws. We then explore a question with serious implications for today's voters and policymakers: What should the government's responsibility be when equal protection under the law is not enough to ensure truly equal opportunities for Americans?

Civil Rights
Generally, all rights rooted in the Fourteenth Amendment's guarantee of equal protection under the law.

African Americans and the Consequences of Slavery in the United States

Before 1863, the Constitution protected slavery and made equality impossible in the sense in which we use the word today. The constitutionality of slavery was confirmed just a few years before the outbreak of the Civil War in the famous *Dred Scott v. Sanford*[1] case of 1857. The Supreme Court held, among other things, that slaves were not citizens of the United States, nor were they entitled to the rights and privileges of citizenship. The *Dred Scott* decision had grave consequences. Most observers contend that the ruling contributed to making the Civil War inevitable.

Ending Constitutional Servitude

With the emancipation of the slaves by President Lincoln's Emancipation Proclamation in 1863 and the passage of the Thirteenth, Fourteenth, and Fifteenth Amendments during the Reconstruction period following the Civil War, constitutional inequality was ended.

The Thirteenth Amendment (1865) states that neither slavery nor involuntary servitude shall exist within the United States. The Fourteenth Amendment (1868) tells us that *all* persons born or naturalized in the United States are citizens of the United States. It states, furthermore, that "[n]o State shall make or enforce any law which shall abridge the privileges or immunities of citizens of the United States; nor shall any State deprive any person of life, liberty, or property, without due process of law; nor deny to any person within its jurisdiction the equal protection of the laws." Note the use of the terms *citizen* and *person* in this amendment. *Citizens* have political rights, such as the right to vote and run for political office. All *persons*, however, including non-citizen immigrants, have a right to due process of law and equal protection under the law. The Fifteenth Amendment (1870) states: "The right of citizens of the United States to vote shall not be denied or abridged by the United States or by any State on account of race, color, or previous condition of servitude."

The Civil Rights Acts of 1865 to 1875

From 1865 to 1875, Congress passed a series of civil rights acts that were aimed at enforcing these amendments. The Civil Rights Act of 1866 extended citizenship to anyone born in the United States and gave African Americans full equality before the law. The act further authorized the president to enforce the law using the national armed forces. The Enforcement Act of 1870 set out specific criminal sanctions for interfering with the right to vote as protected by the Fifteenth Amendment and by the Civil Rights Act of 1866. Equally important was the Civil Rights Act of 1872, known as the Anti–Ku Klux Klan Act. This act made it a federal crime for anyone to use law or custom to deprive an individual of rights, privileges, and immunities secured by the Constitution or by any federal law. The Second Civil Rights Act, passed in 1875, declared that everyone is entitled to full and equal enjoyment of public accommodations, theaters, and other places of public amusement, and it imposed penalties for violators.

The Ineffectiveness of the Civil Rights Laws

These Reconstruction statutes, or civil rights acts, ultimately did little to secure equality for African Americans in their civil rights, however. Both the *Civil Rights Cases* and the case of *Plessy v. Ferguson* effectively nullified these acts. Additionally, various barriers were erected that prevented African Americans from exercising their right to vote.

The *Civil Rights Cases*.   The Supreme Court invalidated the 1875 Civil Rights Act when it held, in the *Civil Rights Cases*[2] of 1883, that the enforcement clause of the Fourteenth Amendment (which states that "[n]o State shall make or enforce any law which shall abridge the privileges or immunities of citizens") was limited to correcting actions by states in their *official* acts; thus, the discriminatory acts of *private* citizens were not illegal. ("Individual invasion of individual rights is not the subject matter of the Amendment.")

The 1883 Supreme Court decision met with widespread approval throughout most of the United States. Twenty years after the Civil War, the white majority was all too willing to forget about the Civil War amendments and the civil rights legislation of the 1860s and 1870s. The other civil rights laws that the Court did not specifically invalidate became dead letters in the statute books, although they were never repealed by Congress. At the same time, many former proslavery secessionists had regained political power in the southern states.

Plessy v. Ferguson: Separate but Equal.   A key decision during this period concerned Homer Plessy, a Louisiana resident who was one-eighth African American. In 1892, he boarded a train in New Orleans. The conductor made him leave the car, which was restricted to whites, and directed him to a car for nonwhites. At that time, Louisiana had a statute providing for separate railway cars for whites and African Americans.

Plessy went to court, claiming that such a statute was contrary to the Fourteenth Amendment's equal protection clause. In 1896, the United States Supreme Court rejected Plessy's contention. The Court concluded that the Fourteenth Amendment "could not have been intended to abolish distinctions based upon color, or to enforce social . . . equality." The Court indicated that segregation alone did not violate the Constitution: "Laws permitting, and even requiring, their separation in places where they are liable to be brought into contact do not necessarily imply the inferiority of either race to the other."[3] So was born the **separate-but-equal doctrine.**

Separate-but-Equal Doctrine The doctrine holding that separate-but-equal facilities do not violate the equal protection clause.

Plessy v. Ferguson became the judicial cornerstone of racial discrimination throughout the United States. Even though *Plessy* upheld segregated facilities in railway cars only, it was assumed that the Supreme Court was upholding segregation everywhere as long as the separate facilities were equal. The result was a system of racial segregation, particularly in the South—supported by laws collectively known as Jim Crow laws—that required separate drinking fountains; separate seats in theaters, restaurants, and hotels; separate public toilets; and separate waiting rooms for the two races. "Separate" was indeed the rule, but "equal" was never enforced, nor was it a reality.

White Primary A state primary election that restricts voting to whites only; outlawed by the Supreme Court in 1944.

Voting Barriers.   The brief enfranchisement of African Americans ended after 1877, when the federal troops that occupied the South during the Reconstruction era were withdrawn. Southern politicians regained control of state governments and, using everything except race as a formal criterion, passed laws that effectively deprived African Americans of the right to vote. By using the ruse that political parties were private bodies, the Democratic Party was allowed to keep black voters from its primaries. The **white primary** was upheld by the Supreme Court until 1944 when, in *Smith v. Allwright,*[4] the Court ruled it a violation of the Fifteenth Amendment.

Another barrier to African American voting was the **grandfather clause,** which restricted voting to those who could prove that their grandfathers had voted before 1867. **Poll taxes** required the payment of a fee to vote; thus, poor African Americans—as well as poor whites—who could not afford to pay the tax were excluded from voting. Not until the Twenty-fourth Amendment to the Constitution was ratified in 1964 was the poll tax eliminated as a precondition to voting. **Literacy tests** were also used to deny the vote to African Americans. Such tests asked potential voters to read, recite, or interpret complicated texts, such as a section of the state constitution, to the satisfaction of local registrars (who were, of course, never satisfied).

The End of the Separate-but-Equal Doctrine

A successful attack on the separate-but-equal doctrine began with a series of lawsuits in the 1930s that sought to admit African Americans to state professional schools. By 1950, the Supreme Court had also ruled that African Americans who were admitted to a state university could not be assigned to separate sections of classrooms, libraries, and cafeterias.

In 1951, Oliver Brown decided that his eight-year-old daughter, Linda Carol Brown, should not have to go to an all-nonwhite elementary school twenty-one blocks from her home, when there was a white school only seven blocks away. The National Association for the Advancement of Colored People (NAACP), formed in 1909, decided to help Oliver Brown. The outcome would have a monumental impact on American society.

Jim Crow laws required the segregation of the races, particularly in public facilities such as this theater. The name "Jim Crow" came from a vaudeville character who was called Jim (a common name) Crow (for a black-colored bird). Thus, the name "Jim Crow" was applied to laws and practices affecting African Americans.

Brown v. Board of Education of Topeka. The 1954 unanimous decision of the United States Supreme Court in *Brown v. Board of Education of Topeka*[5] established that segregation of races in the public schools violates the equal protection clause of the Fourteenth Amendment. Chief Justice Earl Warren said that separation implied inferiority, whereas the majority opinion in *Plessy v. Ferguson* had said the opposite.

"With All Deliberate Speed." The following year, in *Brown v. Board of Education*[6] (sometimes called the second *Brown* decision), the Court declared that the lower courts needed to ensure that African Americans would be admitted to schools on a nondiscriminatory basis "with all deliberate speed." The district courts were to consider devices in their desegregation orders that might include "the school transportation system, personnel, [and] revision of school districts and attendance areas into compact units to achieve a system of determining admission to the public schools on a nonracial basis."

Grandfather Clause A device used to keep African Americans from voting by restricting the vote to those whose grandfathers had voted before 1867.

Poll Tax A tax that must be paid as a qualification for voting.

Literacy Test A test used as a precondition for voting.

In Little Rock, Arkansas, Governor Orval Faubus sent in the state's National Guard to prevent African American students from entering Central High School on September 2, 1957. On September 24, President Dwight Eisenhower sent in five hundred soldiers to enforce integration.

Burt Glinn, Magnum

INFOTRAC

To find out more about segregation, use the term "segregation" in the Subject guide.

De Facto **Segregation** Racial segregation that occurs because of past social and economic conditions and residential patterns.

De Jure **Segregation** Racial segregation that occurs because of laws or administrative decisions by public agencies.

Reactions to School Integration

The white South did not let the Supreme Court ruling go unchallenged. Governor Orval Faubus of Arkansas used the state's National Guard to block the integration of Central High School in Little Rock in September 1957. The federal court demanded that the troops be withdrawn. Finally, President Dwight Eisenhower had to federalize the Arkansas National Guard and send in the 101st Airborne to quell the violence. Central High became integrated.

The universities in the South, however, remained segregated. When James Meredith, an African American student, attempted to enroll at the University of Mississippi in Oxford in 1962, violence flared there, as it had in Little Rock. President John Kennedy sent federal marshals and ordered federal troops to maintain peace and protect Meredith.

An Integrationist Attempt at a Cure: Busing

In most parts of the United States, residential concentrations by race have made it difficult to achieve racial balance in schools. Although it is true that a number of school boards in northern districts created segregated schools by drawing school district lines arbitrarily, the residential concentration of African Americans and other minorities in well-defined geographic locations has contributed to the difficulty of achieving racial balance. This concentration results in *de facto* **segregation,** as distinct from *de jure* **segregation,** which results from laws or administrative decisions.

Court-Ordered Busing.   The obvious solution to both *de facto* and *de jure* segregation seemed to be transporting some African American schoolchildren to white schools and some white schoolchildren to African American schools. Increasingly, the courts ordered school districts to engage in such **busing** across neighborhoods. Busing led to violence in some northern cities, such as in south Boston. In that instance, black students were bused into blue-collar Irish Catholic neighborhoods. Indeed, busing was unpopular with many groups. In the mid-1970s, almost 50 percent of African Americans interviewed were opposed to busing, and approximately three-fourths of the whites interviewed held the same opinion. Nonetheless, through the next decade, the Supreme Court fairly consistently upheld busing plans in the cases it decided.

The End of Integration?   By the late 1990s and early 2000s, however, the federal courts had become increasingly unwilling to uphold race-conscious policies designed to further school integration and diversity—outcomes that are not mandated by the Constitution. For example, in 2001, a federal appellate court held that the Charlotte-Mecklenburg school district in North Carolina had achieved the goal of integration,[7] meaning that race-based admission quotas could no longer be constitutionally imposed.

The Resurgence of Minority Schools.   Today, schools around the country are again becoming segregated, in large part because of *de facto* segregation. In the largest U.S. cities, fifteen out of sixteen African American and Hispanic students go to schools with almost no non-Hispanic whites. Generally, Americans are now taking another look at what desegregation means. The attempt to integrate the schools, particularly through busing, has largely failed to improve educational resources and achievement for African American children. The goal of racially balanced schools envisioned in the 1954 *Brown v. Board of Education of Topeka* decision is giving way to the goal of educating children better, even if that means educating them in schools in which students are of the same race or in which race is not considered.

The Civil Rights Movement

The *Brown* decision applied only to public schools. Not much else in the structure of existing segregation was affected. In December 1955, a forty-three-year-old African American woman, Rosa Parks, boarded a public bus in Montgomery, Alabama. When the bus became crowded and several white people stepped aboard, Parks was asked to move to the rear of the bus, the "colored" section. She refused, was arrested, and was fined $10; but that was not the end of the matter. For an entire year, African Americans boycotted the Montgomery bus line. The protest was headed by a twenty-seven-year-old Baptist minister, Dr. Martin Luther King, Jr. During the protest period, he went to jail, and his house was bombed. In the face of overwhelming odds, King won. In 1956, a federal district court issued an injunction prohibiting the segregation of buses in Montgomery. The era of civil rights protests had begun.

King's Philosophy of Nonviolence

The following year, in 1957, King formed the Southern Christian Leadership Conference (SCLC). King advocated nonviolent civil disobedience as a means to achieve racial justice. He used tactics such as demonstrations and marches, as well as

Busing The transportation of public school students from areas where they live to schools in other areas to eliminate school segregation based on residential patterns.

INFOTRAC
To find out more about busing, use the term "school busing" in the Subject guide.

purposeful, public disobedience of unjust laws, while remaining nonviolent. King's followers successfully used these methods to gain wider public acceptance of their cause.

For the next decade, African Americans and sympathetic whites engaged in sit-ins, freedom rides, and freedom marches. In the beginning, such demonstrations were often met with violence, and the contrasting image of nonviolent African Americans and violent, hostile whites created strong public support for the civil rights movement.

The Birmingham Protest

One of the most famous of the violence-plagued protests occurred in Birmingham, Alabama, in the spring of 1963, when Police Commissioner Eugene "Bull" Connor unleashed police dogs and used electric cattle prods against the protesters. People throughout the country viewed the event on national television with indignation and horror. King himself was thrown in jail. The media coverage of the Birmingham protest and the violent response it elicited played a key role in the process of ending Jim Crow conditions in the United States. The ultimate result was the most important civil rights act in the nation's history, the Civil Rights Act of 1964 (to be discussed shortly).

AP Photo

Dr. Martin Luther King, Jr., acknowledges the crowd at the August 1963 March on Washington for Jobs and Freedom. Nearly a quarter-million African Americans and whites participated in the march. The march is best remembered for King's eloquent "I have a dream" speech and the assembled multitude singing "We Shall Overcome," the anthem of the civil rights movement.

King's March on Washington

In August 1963, King organized the massive March on Washington for Jobs and Freedom. Before nearly a quarter-million white and African American spectators and millions watching on television, King told the world his dream: "I have a dream that my four little children will one day live in a nation where they will not be judged by the color of their skin but by the content of their character."

Modern Civil Rights Legislation

Police-dog attacks, cattle prods, high-pressure water hoses, beatings, bombings, and the March on Washington—all of these events and developments led to an environment in which Congress felt compelled to act on behalf of African Americans. The second era of civil rights acts, sometimes referred to as the second Reconstruction period, was under way.

The Civil Rights Act of 1964

As the civil rights movement mounted in intensity, equality before the law came to be "an idea whose time has come," in the words of conservative Senate Minority Leader Everett Dirksen. The Civil Rights Act of 1964, the most far-reaching bill on civil rights in modern times, forbade discrimination on the basis of race, color, religion, gender, and national origin. The major provisions of the act were as follows:

1. It outlawed arbitrary discrimination in voter registration.

2. It barred discrimination in public accommodations, such as hotels and restaurants, whose operations affect interstate commerce.

3. It authorized the federal government to sue to desegregate public schools and facilities.

4. It expanded the power of the Civil Rights Commission and extended its life.

5. It provided for the withholding of federal funds from programs administered in a discriminatory manner.

6. It established the right to equality of opportunity in employment.

Title VII of the Civil Rights Act of 1964 is the cornerstone of employment discrimination law. It prohibits discrimination in employment based on race, color, religion, gender, or national origin. Under Title VII, executive orders were issued that banned employment discrimination by firms that received any federal funding. The 1964 Civil Rights Act created a five-member commission, the Equal Employment Opportunity Commission (EEOC), to administer Title VII.

The Voting Rights Act of 1965

As late as 1960, only 29.1 percent of African Americans of voting age were registered in the southern states, in stark contrast to 61.1 percent of whites. The Voting Rights Act of 1965 addressed this issue. The act had two major provisions. The first one outlawed discriminatory voter-registration tests. The second authorized federal registration of persons and federally administered voting procedures in any political subdivision or state that discriminated electorally against a particular group. In part, the act provided that certain political subdivisions could not change their voting procedures and election laws without federal approval. The act targeted counties, mostly in the South, in which less than 50 percent of the eligible population was registered to vote. Federal voter registrars were sent to these areas to register African Americans who had been kept from voting by local registrars. Within one week after the act was passed, forty-five federal examiners were sent to the South. A massive voter-registration drive covered the country.

The Civil Rights Act of 1968 and Other Housing Reform Legislation

The Civil Rights Act of 1968 forbade discrimination in most housing and provided penalties for those attempting to interfere with individual civil rights (giving protection to civil rights workers, among others). Subsequent legislation added enforcement provisions to the federal government's rules against discriminatory mortgage-lending practices. Today, all lenders must report to the federal government the race, gender, and income of all mortgage-loan seekers, along with the final decision on their loan applications.

Increased Political Participation by African Americans

As a result of the Voting Rights Act of 1965, its amendments, and the large-scale voter-registration drives in the South, the number of African Americans registered to vote climbed dramatically. By 1980, 55.8 percent of African Americans of voting age in the South were registered. In recent elections, the percentage of voting-age African Americans who have registered to vote has been about equal to the percentage of voting-age whites who have registered to vote.

Today, there are more than 8,500 African American elected officials in the United States. The movement of African American citizens into high elected office has thus been sure, if exceedingly slow. Notably, recent polling data show that most Americans do not consider race a significant factor in choosing a president. In 1958, when the Gallup poll first asked whether respondents would be willing to vote for an African American as president, only 38 percent of the public said yes. By 2003, this percentage had reached 95 percent.

Political Participation by Other Minorities

The civil rights movement focused primarily on the rights of African Americans. Yet the legislation resulting from the movement has ultimately benefited virtually all minority groups. The Civil Rights Act of 1964, for example, prohibits discrimination against any person because of race, color, or national origin. Subsequent amendments to the Voting Rights Act of 1965 extended its protections to other minorities, including Hispanic Americans, Asian Americans, Native Americans, and Native Alaskans. To further protect the voting rights of minorities, the act now provides that states must make bilingual ballots available in counties where 5 percent or more of the population speak a language other than English.

Immigration and the Civil Rights Agenda

Among those who have benefited from civil rights legislation are various immigrant groups. One of the questions facing Americans and their political leaders today is the effect of immigration on American politics and government. Another issue is the impact of immigration and interracial marriages on the traditional civil rights agenda. (Still another issue is whether immigrants from countries where some citizens are known to support terrorism should be allowed to enter this country at all. See this chapter's *America's Security* feature for a discussion of this question.)

AMERICA'S SECURITY

Should We Shut the Immigration Door?

S oon after the attacks on the World Trade Center and the Pentagon, many political leaders began looking at our immigration policies with security issues in mind. After all, the terrorists were from other countries (mainly Saudi Arabia). The most vocal critics of our immigration policy literally want to shut America's door to immigrants. That the terrorist attacks occurred while the American economy was suffering from a recession did not, of course, help matters. Anti-immigrant forces often have used high unemployment as a reason to restrict immigration.

STUDENT VISAS— THEN AND NOW

Several of the 9/11 hijackers were in this country legally on student visas. Indeed, newly approved student visas for two of the hijackers arrived at their flight school in Florida two months *after* the attacks, emphasizing how inefficient, understaffed, and underfunded the U.S. agency handling immigration services has been for years.

According to those who support reducing immigration to further America's security, all visa applicants from suspect areas of the world should be subject to stricter scrutiny. This includes travelers from any nations in which anti-American groups such as al Qaeda have found supporters—for example, Somalia, Pakistan, Bosnia, the Philippines, Indonesia, and Saudi Arabia.

PROPOSED SECURITY GUIDELINES

U.S. authorities give out over 500,000 student visas each year. Many of these visas go to individuals from countries where some residents are known to support terrorism. Under proposed security guidelines, U.S. authorities will have to conduct additional checks on these students. Universities will have to report to the government whether students who requested visas actually enroll at their campuses. After all, many of the 9/11 hijackers never showed up for classes despite having received valid student visas.

FOR CRITICAL ANALYSIS

Would it ever be possible to close off the borders of the United States entirely? What practical constraints are there on such an action?

The Continued Influx of Immigrants

Today, immigration rates are among the highest they have been since their peak in the early twentieth century. Currently, about one million people a year immigrate to this country, and those who were born on foreign soil now constitute over 10 percent of the U.S. population—twice the percentage of thirty years ago. Since 1977, four out of five immigrants have come from Latin America or Asia. Hispanics are now overtaking African Americans as the nation's largest minority.

Some regard our high rate of immigration as a plus for America because it offsets our low birthrate and aging population. Immigrants expand our work force and help

INFOTRAC

For updates and more information about this topic, use the term "immigration" in the Subject guide.

In Los Angeles, Mexican Americans celebrate Cinco de Mayo. Is the United States a nation of many ethnic cultures existing separately, or is it a melting pot of diverse cultures?

David Young-Wolff, PhotoEdit

to support, through their taxes, government programs that benefit older Americans, such as Medicare and Social Security.

The Problem of Racial Classifications

A challenge facing the government today is that the lines separating racial groups are becoming increasingly blurred. About 25 percent of Hispanics marry persons outside their group, as do nearly one-third of the Asians living in America; and many African Americans have both a black and a white heritage. The blurring of racial distinctions is significant for the civil rights agenda because the U.S. Census Bureau and other federal and state agencies traditionally have used racial classifications to determine who is eligible for certain benefits. Since 1977, for example, the federal government has identified Americans using the following racial categories: black, white, American Indian, Alaskan native, and Asian/Pacific islander. ("Hispanic" is a separate category—Hispanics can be of any race.) Yet how can these classifications be applied to the millions of Americans with mixed ethnic and racial backgrounds? In the 2000 census, the government tried to address this problem by allowing respondents to check more than one racial box.

Women's Struggle for Equal Rights

Like African Americans and other minorities, women have had to struggle for equality. During the first phase of this struggle, the primary goal of women was to obtain the right to vote. Some women had hoped that the founders would provide such a right in the Constitution. The Constitution did not include a provision guaranteeing women the right to vote, but neither did it deny to women—or to any others—this right. Rather, the founders left it up to the states to decide such issues, and, as mentioned earlier, by and large, the states initially limited the franchise to adult white males who owned property.

Early Women's Political Movements

In 1848, Lucretia Mott and Elizabeth Cady Stanton organized the first women's rights convention in Seneca Falls, New York. The three hundred people who attended approved a Declaration of Sentiments: "We hold these truths to be self-evident: that all men *and women* are created equal." In the following twelve years, groups of women's rights supporters held seven conventions in different cities in the Midwest and East. With the outbreak of the Civil War, however, advocates of women's rights were urged to put their support behind the war effort, and most agreed.

In 1869, Susan B. Anthony and Elizabeth Cady Stanton formed the National Woman Suffrage Association. In their view, women's **suffrage** was a means to achieve major improvements in the economic and social situation of women in the United States. In other words, the vote was to be used to seek broader goals. Lucy Stone, however, a founder of the rival American Woman Suffrage Association, believed that the vote was the only major issue. In 1890, the two organizations joined forces. The National American Woman Suffrage Association had only one goal—the enfranchisement of women—but it made little progress.

Suffrage The right to vote; the franchise.

By the early 1900s, small radical splinter groups had been formed. These groups took to the streets; parades, hunger strikes, arrests, and jailings ensued. Finally, in 1920, seventy-two years after the Seneca Falls convention, the Nineteenth Amendment was passed: "The right of citizens of the United States to vote shall not be denied or abridged by the United States or by any State on account of sex." (Today we typically use the word *gender* in place of sex.) Although it may seem that the United States was slow to give women the vote, it was really not behind the rest of the world (see Table 5–1 on the following page).

The Modern Women's Movement

After gaining the right to vote in 1920, women engaged in little organized political activity until the 1960s. The civil rights movement of that decade resulted in a growing awareness of rights for all groups, including women. Additionally, the publication of Betty Friedan's *The Feminine Mystique* in 1963 focused national attention on the unequal status of women in American life.

In 1966, Friedan and others formed the National Organization for Women (NOW). NOW immediately adopted a blanket resolution designed "to bring women into full participation in the mainstream of American society *now*, exercising all the privileges and responsibilities thereof in truly equal partnership with men."

NOW has been in the forefront of what is often called the *feminist movement*. The goal of **feminism** is political, social, and economic equality for women. The initial focus of the modern women's movement was not on expanding the political rights of women. Rather, leaders of NOW and other liberal women's rights advocates sought to eradicate gender inequality through a constitutional amendment.

Feminism The movement that supports political, economic, and social equality for women.

The Equal Rights Amendment.

The proposed Equal Rights Amendment (ERA) states as follows: "Equality of rights under the law shall not be denied or abridged by the United States or by any state on account of sex." It was approved by both chambers of Congress and sent to the state legislatures for ratification in 1972. The necessary thirty-eight states failed to ratify the ERA within the seven-year period specified by Congress, however. To date, efforts to reintroduce the amendment have not succeeded.

Challenging Gender Discrimination in the Courts.

When ratification of the ERA failed, women's rights organizations began to challenge discriminatory statutes and policies in the federal courts, contending that **gender discrimination** violated the Fourteenth Amendment's equal protection clause. Since the 1970s, the Supreme Court has tended to scrutinize gender classifications closely and has invalidated many such statutes and policies. For example, in 1977 the Court held that police and firefighting units cannot establish arbitrary rules, such as height and weight requirements, that tend to preclude women from joining those occupations.[8] In 1983, the Court ruled that insurance companies cannot charge different rates for women and men.[9] The Court held in 1996 that the state-financed Virginia Military Institute's policy of accepting only males violated the equal protection clause.[10]

Gender Discrimination Any practice, policy, or procedure that denies equality of treatment to an individual or to a group because of gender.

Women in Politics Today.

The efforts of women's rights advocates have helped to increase the number of women holding political offices at all levels of government. Although a men's club atmosphere still prevails in Congress, the number of women holding congressional seats has increased significantly in recent years. Elections during the 1990s brought more women to Congress than either the Senate or the House had seen before. In 2001, for the first time, a woman was elected to a leadership post in Congress. Nancy Pelosi, of California, was elected as the Democrats' minority whip in the House of Representatives. In 2002, she became minority leader.

TABLE 5–1	Years, by Country, in Which Women Gained the Right to Vote		
1893: New Zealand	1919: Germany	1945: Italy	1953: Mexico
1902: Australia	1920: United States	1945: Japan	1956: Egypt
1913: Norway	1930: South Africa	1947: Argentina	1963: Kenya
1918: Britain	1932: Brazil	1950: India	1971: Switzerland
1918: Canada	1944: France	1952: Greece	1984: Yemen

SOURCE: Center for the American Woman and Politics.

Although no woman has yet been nominated for president by a major political party, in 1984 a woman, Geraldine Ferraro, became the Democratic nominee for vice president. Another woman, Elizabeth Dole, made a serious run at the Republican presidential nomination in the 2000 campaigns. Notably, a recent Gallup poll found that 92 percent of Americans said that they would vote for a qualified woman for president if she were nominated by their party.

Increasing numbers of women are also being appointed to cabinet posts. More women are sitting on federal judicial benches as well. President Ronald Reagan was credited with a historic first when he appointed Sandra Day O'Connor to the Supreme Court in 1981. President Bill Clinton appointed a second woman, Ruth Bader Ginsburg, to the Court. For all their achievements in the political arena, however, the number of women holding political offices remains disproportionately low compared with their participation as voters.

Gender-Based Discrimination in the Workplace

Traditional cultural beliefs concerning the proper role of women in society continue to be evident not only in the political arena but also in the workplace. Since the 1960s, however, women have gained substantial protection against discrimination through laws mandating equal employment opportunities and equal pay.

Title VII of the Civil Rights Act of 1964.
Title VII of the Civil Rights Act of 1964 prohibits gender discrimination in employment and has been used to strike down employment policies that discriminate against employees on the basis of gender. In 1978, Congress amended Title VII to expand the definition of gender discrimination to include discrimination based on pregnancy.

Sexual Harassment.
The Supreme Court has also held that Title VII's prohibition of gender-based discrimination extends to **sexual harassment** in the workplace. Sexual harassment occurs when job opportunities, promotions, salary increases, and so on are given in return for sexual favors. A special form of sexual harassment, called hostile-environment harassment, occurs when an employee is subjected to sexual conduct or comments that interfere with the employee's job performance or are so pervasive or severe as to create an intimidating, hostile, or offensive environment.

Wage Discrimination.
By 2010, women will constitute a majority of U.S. workers. Although Title VII and other legislation since the 1960s have mandated equal employment opportunities for men and women, women continue to earn less, on average, than men do.

The issue of wage discrimination was first addressed during World War II (1939–1945), when the War Labor Board issued an "equal pay for women" policy. In implementing the policy, the board often evaluated jobs for their comparability and required equal pay for comparable jobs. The board's authority ended with the war. Supported by the next three presidential administrations, the Equal Pay Act was finally enacted in 1963 as an amendment to the Fair Labor Standards Act of 1938.

Basically, the Equal Pay Act requires employers to provide equal pay for substantially equal work. In other words, males cannot legally be paid more than females

Sexual Harassment
Unwanted physical or verbal conduct of a sexual nature that interferes with a recipient's job performance or creates a hostile work environment.

INFOTRAC

For updates and more information about this issue, use the term "sexual harassment" in the Subject guide.

who perform essentially the same job. The Equal Pay Act did not address the fact that certain types of jobs traditionally held by women pay lower wages than the jobs usually held by men. For example, more women than men are salesclerks and nurses, whereas more men than women are construction workers and truck drivers. Even if all clerks performing substantially similar jobs for a company earned the same salaries, they typically would still be earning less than the company's truck drivers.

Civil Rights: Beyond Equal Protection

As noted earlier in this chapter, the Civil Rights Act of 1964 prohibited discrimination against any person on the basis of race, color, national origin, religion, or gender. The act also established the right to equal opportunity in employment. A basic problem remained, however: minority groups and women, because of past discrimination, often lacked the education and skills to compete effectively in the marketplace. In 1965, the federal government attempted to remedy this problem by implementing the concept of affirmative action. **Affirmative action** policies attempt to "level the playing field" by giving special preferences in educational admissions and employment decisions to groups that have been discriminated against in the past. These policies go beyond a strict interpretation of the equal protection clause of the Fourteenth Amendment.

Affirmative Action A policy in admissions or hiring that gives special consideration to traditionally disadvantaged groups to overcome present effects of past discrimination.

Affirmative Action

In 1965, President Lyndon Johnson ordered that affirmative action policies be undertaken to remedy the effects of past discrimination. All government agencies, including those of state and local governments, were required to implement such policies. Additionally, affirmative action requirements were imposed on companies that sell goods or services to the federal government and on institutions that receive federal funds. Affirmative action policies were also required whenever an employer had been ordered to develop such a plan by a court or by the Equal Employment Opportunity Commission because of evidence of past discrimination. Finally, labor unions that had been found to discriminate against women or minorities in the past were required to establish and follow affirmative action plans.

Affirmative action programs have been controversial because they sometimes result in discrimination against majority groups, such as white males (or discrimination against other minority groups that may not be given preferential treatment under a particular affirmative action program). At issue in the current debate over affirmative action programs is whether such programs, because of their inherently discriminatory nature, violate the equal protection clause of the Fourteenth Amendment to the Constitution.

The *Bakke* Case

The first Supreme Court case addressing the constitutionality of affirmative action programs examined a program implemented by the University of California at Davis. Allan Bakke, a white student who had been turned down for medical school at the Davis campus, discovered that his academic record was better than those of some of the minority applicants who had been admitted to the program. He sued the

University of California regents, alleging **reverse discrimination.** The UC–Davis Medical School had held sixteen places out of one hundred for educationally "disadvantaged students" each year, and the administrators at that campus admitted to using race as a criterion for admission for these particular minority slots.

In 1978, the Supreme Court handed down its decision in *Regents of the University of California v. Bakke.*[11] The Court did not actually rule against affirmative action programs. Rather, it held that Bakke must be admitted to the UC–Davis Medical School because its admissions policy had used race as the sole criterion for the sixteen "minority" positions. The Court indicated that while race can be considered "as a factor" among others in admissions (and presumably hiring) decisions, race cannot be the sole factor. So affirmative action programs, but not specific quota systems, were upheld as constitutional.

Reverse Discrimination The charge that an affirmative action program discriminates against those who do not have minority status.

Further Limits on Affirmative Action

A number of cases decided during the 1980s and 1990s placed further limits on affirmative action programs. In a landmark decision in 1995, *Adarand Constructors, Inc. v. Peña,*[12] the Supreme Court held that any federal, state, or local affirmative action program that uses racial or ethnic classifications as the basis for making decisions is subject to "strict scrutiny" by the courts. Under a strict-scrutiny analysis, to be constitutional, a discriminatory law or action must be narrowly tailored to meet a *compelling* government interest.

In 1996, a federal appellate court went even further. In *Hopwood v. State of Texas,*[13] two white law school applicants sued the University of Texas School of Law in Austin, alleging that they had been denied admission because of the school's affirmative action program. The program allowed admissions officials to take race and other factors into consideration. The federal appellate court held that the program violated the equal protection clause because it discriminated in favor of minority applicants. Significantly, the court directly challenged the *Bakke* decision by stating that the use of race even as a means of achieving diversity on college campuses "undercuts the Fourteenth Amendment."

In 2003, however, in two cases involving the University of Michigan, the Supreme Court indicated that limited affirmative action programs continued to be acceptable and that diversity was a legitimate goal. The Court struck down the affirmative action plan used for undergraduate admissions at the university, which automatically awarded a substantial number of points to

On the University of Michigan campus, students react to a federal appeals court decision in 2002 to uphold the use of race in admissions to the university's law school. Supporters of affirmative action formed a group called the Fight for Equality by Any Means Necessary (BAMN).

applicants based on minority status.[14] At the same time, it approved the admissions plan used by the law school, which took race into consideration as part of a complete examination of each applicant's background.[15]

State Ballot Initiatives

INFOTRAC

For updates and more information about this topic, use the term "affirmative action" in the Subject guide.

A ballot initiative passed by California voters in 1996 amended that state's constitution to end all state-sponsored affirmative action programs. The law was immediately challenged in court by civil rights groups and others. These groups claimed that the law violated the Fourteenth Amendment by denying racial minorities and women the equal protection of the laws. In 1997, however, a federal appellate court upheld the constitutionality of the amendment. Thus, affirmative action is now illegal in California in all state-sponsored facilities, including state agencies and educational institutions. In 1998, Washington voters also approved a law banning affirmative action in that state.

Bilingual Education

INFOTRAC

For updates and more information about this issue, use the term "bilingual education" in the Subject guide.

The continuous influx of immigrants into this country presents an ongoing challenge—how to overcome language barriers. Language issues have been particularly difficult for the schools. Some schools have attempted to address these issues through bilingual education programs, which teach children in their native language while also teaching them English. To some extent, today's bilingual education programs are the result of the government policies favoring multiculturalism that grew out of the civil rights movement. Multiculturalism includes the belief that the government should accommodate the needs of diverse cultural groups and should protect and encourage ethnic and cultural differences.

Congress authorized bilingual education programs in 1968 when it passed the Bilingual Education Act, which was intended primarily to help Hispanic children learn English. In a 1974 case, *Lau v. Nichols*,[16] the Supreme Court bolstered the claim that children have a right to bilingual education. In that case, the Court ordered a California school district to provide special programs for Chinese students with language difficulties if a substantial number of these children attended school in the district. Today, most bilingual education programs are for Hispanic American children, particularly in areas of the country, such as California and Texas, where there are large numbers of Hispanic residents.

The bilingual programs established in the 1960s and subsequently have increasingly come under attack. In 1998, California residents passed a ballot initiative that called for the end of bilingual education programs in that state. The law allowed schools to implement "English-immersion" programs instead. The law was immediately challenged in court on the ground that it unconstitutionally discriminated against non-English-speaking groups. A federal district court, however, concluded that the new law did not violate the equal protection clause and allowed the law to stand. Subsequently, Arizona and Massachusetts also decided to ban bilingual education.

Special Protection for Older Americans

Americans are getting older. In colonial times, about half the population was under the age of sixteen. In 1990, fewer than one in four Americans was under the age of sixteen, and half the population was aged thirty-three or older. By 2050, at least half could be aged thirty-nine or older.

Today, about 35 million Americans (nearly 13 percent of the population) are aged sixty-five or older. As can be seen in Figure 5–1 on the following page, by 2020, this figure is projected to reach about 54 million. By 2040, the portion of the population over age sixty-five will have more than doubled.

Older citizens face a variety of problems unique to their group. One problem that seems to endure, despite government legislation designed to prevent it, is age discrimination in employment.

Age Discrimination in Employment

Age discrimination is potentially the most widespread form of discrimination, because anyone—regardless of race, color, national origin, or gender—could be a victim at some point in life. The unstated policies of some companies not to hire or to demote or dismiss people they feel are "too old" have made it difficult for some older workers to succeed in their jobs or continue with their careers. Additionally, older

INFOTRAC

To find out more about this topic, use the term "age discrimination" in the Subject guide.

FIGURE 5–1 Population Projections: Persons Aged 65 or Older (in Millions)

As shown here, the number of Americans sixty-five years of age or older will grow dramatically during the next decade. The number will more than double between 2005 and 2040. The political power of these older Americans will grow as their numbers increase.

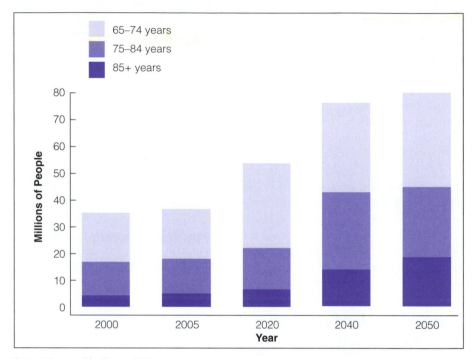

SOURCE: Bureau of the Census, 2003.

workers have fallen victim at times to cost-cutting efforts by employers. To reduce operational costs, companies may replace older, higher-salaried workers with younger, lower-salaried workers.

The Age Discrimination in Employment Act of 1967

In an attempt to protect older employees from such discriminatory practices, Congress passed the Age Discrimination in Employment Act (ADEA) in 1967. The act, which applies to employers, employment agencies, and labor organizations and covers individuals over the age of forty, prohibits discrimination against individuals on the basis of age unless age is shown to be a bona fide occupational qualification reasonably necessary to the normal operation of the particular business.

To succeed in a suit for age discrimination, an employee must prove that the employer's action, such as a decision to fire the employee, was motivated, at least in part, by age bias. Even if an older worker is replaced by a younger worker falling under the protection of the ADEA—that is, by a younger worker who is also over the age of forty—the older worker is entitled to bring a suit under the ADEA.[17]

The ADEA, as initially passed, did not address one of the major problems facing older workers—**mandatory retirement** rules, which require employees to retire when they reach a certain age. Mandatory retirement rules often meant that competent, well-trained employees who wanted to continue working were unable to do so. In 1978, in an amendment to the ADEA, Congress prohibited mandatory retirement rules for most employees under the age of seventy. In 1986, Congress outlawed mandatory retirement rules entirely for all but a few selected occupations, such as firefighting.

Mandatory Retirement Forced retirement when a person reaches a certain age.

Securing Rights for Persons with Disabilities

Like older Americans, persons with disabilities did not fall under the protective umbrella of the Civil Rights Act of 1964. In 1973, Congress passed the Rehabilitation Act, which prohibited discrimination against persons with disabilities in programs receiving federal aid. A 1978 amendment to the act established the Architectural and Transportation Barriers Compliance Board. Regulations for ramps, elevators, and the like in all federal buildings were implemented. Congress passed the Education for All Handicapped Children Act in 1975. It guarantees that all children with disabilities will receive an "appropriate" education. The most significant federal legislation to protect the rights of persons with disabilities, however, is the Americans with Disabilities Act (ADA), which Congress passed in 1990.

The ADA requires that all public buildings and public services be accessible to persons with disabilities. The act also mandates that employers must reasonably accommodate the needs of workers or potential workers with disabilities. Physical access means ramps; handrails; wheelchair-accessible rest rooms, counters, drinking fountains, telephones, and doorways; and more accessible mass transit. In addition, other steps must be taken to comply with the act. Car rental companies must provide cars with hand controls for disabled drivers. Telephone companies are required to have operators to pass on messages from speech-impaired persons who use telephones with keyboards.

The ADA requires employers to "reasonably accommodate" the needs of persons with disabilities unless to do so would cause the employer to suffer an "undue hardship." The ADA defines persons with disabilities as persons who have physical or mental impairments that "substantially limit" their everyday activities. Health conditions that have been considered disabilities under federal law include blindness, alcoholism, heart disease, cancer, muscular dystrophy, cerebral palsy, paraplegia, diabetes, acquired immune deficiency syndrome (AIDS), and infection with the human immunodeficiency virus (HIV) that causes AIDS.

The ADA does not require that *unqualified* applicants with disabilities be hired or retained. If a job applicant or an employee with a disability, with reasonable accommodation, can perform essential job functions, however, then the employer must make the accommodation. Required accommodations may include installing ramps for a wheelchair, establishing more flexible working hours, creating or modifying job assignments, and creating or improving training materials and procedures.

INFOTRAC

For updates and more information about this issue, use the term "Americans with Disabilities Act" in the Subject guide.

Beginning in 1999, the Supreme Court has issued a series of decisions that effectively limit the scope of the ADA. In 1999, for example, the Court held in *Sutton v. United Airlines, Inc.*[18] that a condition (in this case, severe nearsightedness) that can be corrected with medication or a corrective device (in this case, eyeglasses) is not considered a disability under the ADA.

In a 2002 decision, the Court held that carpal tunnel syndrome did not constitute a disability under the ADA. The Court stated that although an employee with carpal tunnel syndrome could not perform the manual tasks associated with her job, the injury did not constitute a disability under the ADA because it did not "substantially limit" the major life activity of performing manual tasks.[19]

The Rights and Status of Gay Males and Lesbians

On June 27, 1969, patrons of the Stonewall Inn, a New York City bar popular with gay men and lesbians, responded to a police raid by throwing beer cans and bottles because they were angry at what they believed was unrelenting police harassment. In the ensuing riot, which lasted two nights, hundreds of gay men and lesbians fought with police. Before Stonewall, the stigma attached to homosexuality and the resulting fear of exposure had tended to keep most gay men and lesbians quiescent. In the months immediately after Stonewall, however, "gay power" graffiti began to appear in New York City. The Gay Liberation Front and the Gay Activist Alliance were formed, and similar groups sprang up in other parts of the country. Thus, Stonewall has been called "the shot heard round the homosexual world."

Growth in the Gay Male and Lesbian Rights Movement

The Stonewall incident marked the beginning of the movement for gay and lesbian rights. Since then, gay men and lesbians have formed thousands of organizations to exert pressure on legislatures, the media, schools, churches, and other organizations to recognize their right to equal treatment.

To a great extent, lesbian and gay groups have succeeded in changing public opinion—and state and local laws—relating to their status and rights. Nevertheless, they continue to struggle against age-old biases against homosexuality, often rooted in deeply held religious beliefs, and the rights of gay men and lesbians remain an extremely divisive issue in American society. These biases were clearly illustrated in a widely publicized case involving the Boy Scouts of America. The case arose after a Boy Scout troop in New Jersey refused to allow gay activist James Dale to be a Scout leader. In 2000, the case came before the Supreme Court, which held that, as a private organization, the Boy Scouts had the right to determine the requirements for becoming a Scout leader.[20]

State and Local Laws against Gay Men and Lesbians

Before the Stonewall incident, forty-nine states had sodomy laws that made various kinds of sexual acts, such as homosexual acts, illegal. (Illinois, which had repealed its sodomy law in 1962, was the only exception.) During the 1970s and 1980s, more than half of these laws were either repealed or struck down by the courts.

INFOTRAC

For updates and more information about gay rights, use the term "gay liberation movement" in the Subject guide.

MAKING A DIFFERENCE : Dealing with Discrimination

When you apply for a job, you may be subjected to a variety of possibly discriminatory practices based on your race, color, gender, religion, age, national origin, sexual preference, or disability. You may also be subjected to a battery of tests, some of which you may believe are discriminatory.

TAKING THE FIRST STEPS

If you believe that you have been discriminated against by a potential employer, consider the following steps:

1. Evaluate your own capabilities, and determine if you are truly qualified for the position.

2. Analyze the reasons why you were turned down. Would others agree with you that you have been the object of discrimination, or would they uphold the employer's claim?

3. If you still believe that you have been unfairly treated, you should first speak to the personnel director of the company and politely explain that you believe you have not been adequately evaluated. If asked, explain your concerns clearly and in detail, and indicate that you believe you may have been discriminated against.

CONTACTING AGENCIES

If a second evaluation is not forthcoming, contact the local branch of your state employment agency. If you still do not obtain adequate help, contact one or more of the following state agencies, usually found by looking in your telephone directory under "State Government" listings.

1. If a government entity is involved, a state ombudsperson or citizen aide may be available.

2. You can contact the state civil rights commission, which will at least give you advice even if it does not take up your case.

3. The state attorney general's office will normally have a division dealing with discrimination and civil rights.

4. There may be a special commission or department specifically set up to help you, such as a women's status commission or a commission on Hispanics or Asian Americans.

Finally, at the national level, you can contact the Equal Employment Opportunity Commission, 1801 L St. N.W., Washington, DC 20507, 202-663-4900, or go to

http://www.eeoc.gov

The trend toward repealing state antigay laws was suspended in 1986 with the Supreme Court's decision in *Bowers v. Hardwick*.[21] In that case, the Court upheld, by a five-to-four vote, a Georgia law that made homosexual conduct between two adults a crime. In 2003, however, the Court reversed itself in *Lawrence v. Texas*.[22] In this case, the Court held that laws against sodomy violate the due process clause of the Fourteenth Amendment. The Court stated: "The liberty protected by the Constitution allows homosexual persons the right to choose to enter upon relationships in the confines of their homes and their own private lives and still retain their dignity as free persons." The result of *Lawrence v. Texas* was to invalidate all remaining sodomy laws throughout the country.

Today, twelve states[23] and more than 230 cities and counties have special laws protecting lesbians and gay men against discrimination in employment, housing, public accommodations, and credit. At one point, Colorado adopted a constitutional amendment to invalidate all state and local laws protecting homosexuals from discrimination. Ultimately, however, the Supreme Court, in *Romer v. Evans,*[24] invalidated the amendment, ruling that it violated the equal protection clause of the U.S. Constitution because it denied to homosexuals in Colorado—but to no other Colorado residents—"the right to seek specific protection of the law."

KEY TERMS

affirmative action **108**

busing **99**

civil rights **94**

de facto segregation **98**

de jure segregation **98**

feminism **106**

gender discrimination **106**

grandfather clause **97**

literacy test **97**

mandatory retirement **113**

poll tax **97**

reverse discrimination **109**

separate-but-equal doctrine **96**

sexual harassment **107**

suffrage **105**

white primary **96**

CHAPTER SUMMARY

1 The civil rights movement started with the struggle by African Americans for equality. Before the Civil War, most African Americans were slaves, and slavery was protected by the Constitution. Constitutional amendments after the Civil War ended slavery, and African Americans gained citizenship, the right to vote, and other rights. This legal protection became largely a dead letter by the 1880s, however.

2 Legal segregation was declared unconstitutional by the Supreme Court in *Brown v. Board of Education of Topeka* (1954), in which the Court stated that separation implied inferiority. In *Brown v. Board of Education* (1955), the Supreme Court ordered federal courts to ensure that public schools were desegregated "with all deliberate speed." Segregationists resisted with legal tactics and violence. Integrationists responded with court orders, federal marshals, and busing. Also in 1955, the modern civil rights movement began with a boycott of segregated buses in Montgomery, Alabama. The Civil Rights Act of 1964 banned discrimination on the basis of race, color, religion, gender, or national origin in employment and public accommodations.

3 The Voting Rights Act of 1965 outlawed discriminatory voter-registration tests and authorized federal registration of voters in any state or political subdivision evidencing electoral discrimination or low registration rates. The Voting Rights Act and other protective legislation apply not only to African Americans but to other ethnic groups as well. Minorities have been increasingly represented in national and state politics, although they have yet to gain representation proportionate to their numbers.

4 Today, more than a million immigrants from other nations enter the United States each year, and over 10 percent of the U.S. population consists of foreign-born persons. Civil rights legislation has helped immigrants to overcome some of the effects of discrimination against them.

5 In the early United States, women were considered citizens, but they had no political rights. After the first women's rights convention in 1848, the women's movement gained momentum. Not until 1920, when the Nineteenth Amendment was ratified, did women finally obtain the right to vote. The modern women's movement began in the 1960s in the wake of the civil rights movement. When efforts to secure the ratification of the Equal Rights Amendment failed, the women's movement began to focus on litigation and increased political representation of women to further the goal of gender equality.

6 Women continue to struggle against gender discrimination in employment. Federal government efforts to eliminate gender discrimination in the workplace include Title VII of the Civil Rights Act of 1964, which prohibits, among other things, gender-based discrimination, including sexual harassment on the job. Wage discrimination also continues to be a problem for women.

7 Affirmative action programs have been controversial because they can lead to reverse discrimination against majority groups or even other minority groups. Supreme Court decisions have limited affirmative action programs but have not ruled out such programs altogether. Voters in California and Washington passed initiatives banning state-sponsored affirmative action in those states.

8 Bilingual education programs teach children in their native languages while also teaching them English. Like affirmative action, these programs have come under attack in recent years.

9 The Age Discrimination in Employment Act of 1967 prohibits job-related discrimination against individuals who are over forty years old on the basis of age, unless age is shown to be a bona fide occupational qualification. Amendments to the act prohibit mandatory retirement except in a few selected professions.

10 The Rehabilitation Act of 1973 prohibited discrimination against persons with disabilities in programs receiving federal aid. Regulations implementing the act provide for ramps, elevators, and the like in federal buildings. The Education for All Handicapped Children Act (1975) provides that children with disabilities should receive an "appropriate" education. The Americans with Disabilities Act of 1990 prohibits job discrimination against persons with physical and mental disabilities. The act also requires expanded access to public facilities, including transportation, and to services offered by private concerns.

11 Gay and lesbian rights groups first began to form in 1969. These groups work to promote laws protecting gay men and lesbians from discrimination and to repeal antigay laws. After 1969, sodomy laws were repealed or struck down by the courts in all but eighteen states, and in 2003 the Supreme Court invalidated all remaining sodomy laws nationwide. Twelve states and more than 230 cities and counties now have laws prohibiting discrimination based on sexual orientation.

SELECTED PRINT AND MEDIA RESOURCES

Suggested Readings

Friedan, Betty. *The Feminine Mystique*. New York: W. W. Norton & Co., 2001. Friedan's work is the feminist classic that helped launch the modern women's movement in the United States. This edition contains an up-to-date introduction by columnist Anna Quindlen.

Hansen, Drew W. *The Dream: Martin Luther King, Jr. and the Speech That Inspired a Nation*. New York: Ecco, 2003. The author examines the background of King's famous speech and analyzes it in detail.

Walker, Alice. *The Color Purple*. Chicago: Harcourt Brace, 1992. This Pulitzer Prize–winning novel, which was originally published in 1982, is about a black woman's struggle for justice, dignity, and empowerment.

Media Resources

Beyond the Glass Ceiling—A CNN–produced program showing the difficulties women face in trying to rise to the top in corporate America.

Dr. Martin Luther King: A Historical Perspective—One of the best documentaries on the civil rights movement, focusing on the life and times of Martin Luther King, Jr.

Separate but Equal—A video focusing on Thurgood Marshall, the lawyer (and later Supreme Court justice) who took the struggle for equal rights to the Supreme Court, and on the rise and demise of segregation in America.

LOGGING ON

For information on, and arguments in support of, affirmative action and the rights of the groups discussed in this chapter, a good source is the American Civil Liberties Union's Web site. Go to **http://www.aclu.org**.

The National Organization for Women (NOW) offers online information and updates on the status of women's rights, including affirmative action cases involving women. Go to **http://www.now.org**.

You can find information on the Americans with Disabilities Act (ADA) of 1990, including the act's text, at **http://www.jan.wvu.edu/links/adalinks.htm**.

You can access the Web site of the Human Rights Campaign Fund, the nation's largest gay and lesbian political organization, at **http://www.hrc.org**.

USING THE INTERNET FOR POLITICAL ANALYSIS

Go to this text's Web site at **http://politicalscience. wadsworth.com/schmidtbrief2004**. Select "Chapter 5" in the box at the top of the window. Then, in the column on the left-hand side of the window, under "Chapter Resources," click on "Internet Exercises." The Web site will then display the following Internet

exercises that you can perform to learn more about topics covered in this chapter.

Activity 5–1: **Slavery Reparations**
Activity 5–2: **Affirmative Action in California**
Activity 5–3: **Gay Rights in the Public Schools**

ONLINE STUDY GUIDE AND ADDITIONAL RESOURCES

At **http://politicalscience.wadsworth.com/ schmidtbrief2004** you will find a free Study Guide to this book and a wealth of other material. For Chapter 5, you will also find in the American Government Resource Center:

- **InfoTrac® Reader**—Race relations and affirmative action; women and the struggle for equality.
- **You Are There Simulations**—Civil rights legislation; affirmative action.

- **Participation Activities**—Find a newsgroup discussion on civil rights; explore political advocacy groups.
- **MicroCase Exercise**—Civil rights.
- **Related Links**—Civil rights.
- **Video Case Studies**—State ballot initiatives—affirmative action; the *Bakke* case; civil rights legislation.
- **Source Readings**—By Standing Bear, plus important court cases and statutes.

CHAPTER 6

Public Opinion, Political Socialization, and the Media

I N A DEMOCRACY, THE ABILITY of the people to freely express their opinions is fundamental. Americans can express their opinions in many ways. They can write letters to newspapers. They can organize politically. They can vote. They can respond to public opinion polls.

President George W. Bush found out how important public opinion was when he announced that the administration was going to try terrorist defendants in military tribunals where the defendants would have few rights. Public opinion was so negative that Bush felt forced to announce new rules for the tribunals that gave defendants more rights. In contrast, Bush's war on terrorism received widespread support from Americans. This support bolstered the Bush administration's authority during a time of crisis.

In this chapter, we discuss how public opinion polls can capture the popular attitudes that shape elections. We discuss how these popular attitudes are formed—that is, the process of political socialization. Finally, we discuss the role of the media, which is an important force in shaping public opinion and in reflecting that opinion back to the political leadership.

Defining Public Opinion

There is no single public opinion, because there are many different "publics." In a nation of about 295 million people, there may be innumerable gradations of opinion on an issue. What we do is describe the distribution of opinions among members of the public about a particular question. Thus, we define **public opinion** as the aggregate of individual attitudes or beliefs shared by some portion of the adult population.

Typically, public opinion is distributed among several different positions, and the distribution of opinion can tell us how divided the public is on an issue and whether compromise is possible. When a large proportion of the American public appears to express the same view on an issue, we say that a **consensus** exists, at least at the moment the poll was taken. Figure 6–1 on the next page shows a pattern of opinion

Public Opinion The aggregate of individual attitudes or beliefs shared by some portion of the adult population.

Consensus General agreement among the citizenry on an issue.

119

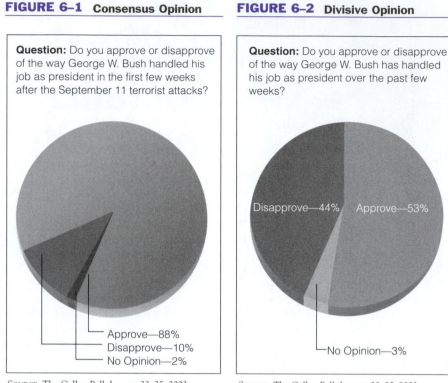

FIGURE 6–1 Consensus Opinion

Question: Do you approve or disapprove of the way George W. Bush handled his job as president in the first few weeks after the September 11 terrorist attacks?

Approve—88%
Disapprove—10%
No Opinion—2%

SOURCE: The Gallup Poll, January 23–25, 2003.

FIGURE 6–2 Divisive Opinion

Question: Do you approve or disapprove of the way George W. Bush has handled his job as president over the past few weeks?

Disapprove—44% Approve—53%

No Opinion—3%

SOURCE: The Gallup Poll, January 23–25, 2003.

Divisive Opinion
Public opinion that is polarized between two quite different positions.

Opinion Poll A method of systematically questioning a small, selected sample of respondents who are deemed representative of the total population.

that might be called consensual. Issues on which the public holds widely differing attitudes result in **divisive opinion** (see Figure 6–2). Sometimes, a poll shows a distribution of opinion indicating that most Americans either have no information about the issue or are not interested enough in the issue to formulate a position.

An interesting question arises as to when *private* opinion becomes *public* opinion. Everyone probably has a private opinion about the competence of the president, as well as private opinions about more personal concerns, such as the state of a neighbor's lawn. We say that private opinion becomes public opinion when the opinion is publicly expressed and concerns public issues. When someone's private opinion becomes so strong that the individual is willing to go to the polls to vote for or against a candidate or an issue—or is willing to participate in a demonstration, discuss the issue at work, speak out on television or radio, or participate in the political process in any one of a dozen other ways—then the opinion becomes public opinion.

Measuring Public Opinion

In a democracy, people express their opinions in a variety of ways. One of the most common means of gathering and measuring public opinion on specific issues is, of course, through the use of **opinion polls.**

The History of Opinion Polls

Opinion polls as we know them are a relatively recent development. In the early twentieth century, the magazine *Literary Digest* mailed large numbers of questionnaires to individuals, many of whom were its own subscribers, to determine their political opinions. From 1916 to 1936, more than 70 percent of the magazine's election predictions were accurate. In 1936, however, the magazine predicted that Republican candidate Alfred Landon would win over Democratic candidate Franklin D. Roosevelt. Landon won in only two states. A major problem was that in 1936, at the bottom of the Great Depression, the *Digest's* subscribers were considerably more affluent than the average American. In other words, they did not accurately represent all of the voters in the U.S. population.

Several newcomers to the public opinion poll industry accurately predicted Roosevelt's landslide victory. These newcomers are still active in the poll-taking industry today: the Gallup poll of George Gallup and the Roper poll, founded by Elmo Roper. Using personal interviews with small samples of selected voters (less than a few thousand), they showed that they could predict with accuracy the behavior of the total voting population.

Sampling Techniques

How can interviewing fewer than two thousand voters tell us what tens of millions of voters will do? Clearly, it is necessary that the sample of individuals be representative of all voters in the population.

The most important principle in sampling, or poll taking, is randomness. Every person should have a known chance, and especially an *equal chance,* of being sampled. If this happens, then a small sample should be representative of the whole group, both in demographic characteristics (age, religion, race, region, and the like) and in opinions. The ideal way to sample the voting population of the United States would be to put all voter names into a jar—or a computer—and randomly sample, say, two thousand of them. Because this is too costly and inefficient, pollsters have developed other ways to obtain good samples. One technique is simply to choose a random selection of telephone numbers and interview the respective households. This technique produces a relatively accurate sample at a low cost.

To ensure that the random samples include respondents from relevant segments of the population—rural, urban, northeastern, southern, and so on—most survey organizations randomly choose, say, urban areas that they will consider as representative of all urban areas. Then they randomly select their respondents within those areas. A generally less accurate technique is known as *quota sampling.* Here, survey researchers decide how many persons of certain types they need in the survey—such as minorities, women, or farmers—and then send out interviewers to find the necessary number of these types. Not only is this method often less accurate, but it also may be biased if, say, the interviewer refuses to go into certain neighborhoods or will not interview after dark.

Generally, the national survey organizations take great care to select their samples randomly, because their reputations rest on the accuracy of their results. The Gallup

INFOTRAC
To find out more about polls, use the term "public opinion polls" in the Subject guide.

and Roper polls usually interview about 1,500 individuals, and their results have a very high probability of being correct—within a margin of 3 percentage points.

Problems with Polls

Public opinion polls are snapshots of the opinions and preferences of the people at a specific moment in time and as expressed in response to a specific question. Given that definition, it is fairly easy to understand situations in which the polls are wrong. For example, opinion polls leading up to the 1980 presidential election showed President Jimmy Carter defeating challenger Ronald Reagan. Only a few analysts noted the large number of "undecided" respondents a week before the election. Those voters shifted massively to Reagan at the last minute, and Reagan won the election.

The famous photo of Harry Truman showing the front page that declared his defeat in the 1948 presidential elections is another tribute to the weakness of polling. Again, the poll that predicted his defeat was taken more than a week before election day.

Sampling Error The difference between sample results and the true result if the entire population had been interviewed.

Sampling Errors.   Polls may also report erroneous results because the pool of respondents was not chosen in a scientific manner. That is, the form of sampling and the number of people sampled may be too small to overcome **sampling error,** which is the difference between the sample results and the true result if the entire population had been interviewed. The sample would be biased, for example, if the poll inter-

President Harry Truman holds up the front page of the Chicago Daily Tribune *issue that predicted his defeat on the basis of a Gallup poll. The poll was completed more than a week before the election, so it missed a shift by undecided voters to Truman. Truman won the election with 49.9 percent of the vote.*

Corbis, UPI/Bettmann

viewed people by telephone and did not correct for the fact that more women than men answer the telephone and that some populations (college students and very poor individuals, for example) cannot be found so easily by telephone. Furthermore, as election day nears, some pollsters use a series of questions and other weighting methods to try to identify "likely voters" as opposed to eligible voters. Poll results can change dramatically when they report only the responses of likely voters.

Poll Questions. The results of a poll will depend on the questions that are asked. One of the problems with many polls is the yes/no answer format. For example, suppose that a poll question asks, "Are you in favor of abortion?" A respondent who is in favor of abortion in some circumstances but not in others has no way of indicating this view because "yes" and "no" are the only possible answers. Furthermore, respondents' answers are also influenced by the order in which questions are asked, by the possible answers from which they are allowed to choose, and, in some cases, by their interaction with the interviewer. To some extent, people try to please the interviewer. They answer questions about which they have no information and avoid some answers to try to measure up to the interviewer's expectations.

"One final question: Do you now own or have you ever owned a fur coat?"

Drawing by Mick Stevens, *The New Yorker*.

Push Polls. Most recently, some campaigns have been using "push polls," in which the respondents are given misleading information in the questions asked to get them to vote against a candidate. Obviously, the answers given are likely to be influenced by such techniques.

Telephone Polling Problems. During the 1970s, telephone polling began to predominate over in-person polling. Somewhat ironically, the success of telephone polling has created major problems for the technique. The telemarketing industry in general has become so pervasive that people increasingly refuse to respond to telephone polls. The nonresponse rate has increased to as high as 80 percent for most telephone polls. In most cases, polling only 20 percent of those on the list cannot lead to a random sample.

Political Socialization

Most Americans are willing to express opinions on political issues when asked. How do people acquire these opinions and attitudes? Most views that are expressed as political opinions are acquired through the process of *political socialization*. By this we mean that people acquire their political attitudes, often including their party identification, through relationships with their families, friends, and co-workers.

Although family and teachers were once seen as the primary agents of political socialization, many scholars today believe the media are displacing these traditional avenues. Busy families and large class sizes have decreased the amount of individual, face-to-face contact young people have with parents and teachers, while time spent with television and the Internet has increased. But the media are agents of

INFOTRAC

To find out more about this topic, use the term "political socialization" in the Subject guide.

socialization by default, not by design.[1] The implications of the increased role of the media in political socialization are under scrutiny by political and social scientists.

The Importance of the Family

Family plays a vital role in political socialization. Not only do our parents' political attitudes and actions affect our adult opinions, but the family also links us to other socialization forces, such as ethnic identity, social class, educational opportunities, and religious beliefs. How do parents transmit their political attitudes? Studies suggest that the influence of parents is due to two factors: communication and receptivity. Parents communicate their feelings and preferences to children constantly. Because children have a strong need for parental approval, they are very receptive to their parents' views.[2] Parents are less receptive to children's views and expect greater deference from their children. Nevertheless, studies show that if children are exposed to political ideas at school and in the media, they will share these ideas with their parents, giving the parents what some scholars call a "second chance" at political socialization.

Educational Influence on Political Opinion

From the early days of the republic, schools were perceived to be important transmitters of political information and attitudes. Children in the primary grades learn about their country mostly in patriotic ways. They learn about the Pilgrims, the flag, and some of the nation's presidents. They also learn to celebrate national holidays. Later, in the middle grades, children learn more historical facts and come to understand the structure of government and the functions of the president, judges, and Congress. By high school, students have a more complex understanding of the political system, may identify with a political party, and may take positions on issues.

Generally, education is closely linked to political participation. The more education a person receives, the more likely it is that the person will be interested in politics, be confident in his or her ability to understand political issues, and be an active participant in the political process.

Peers and Peer Group Influence

Once a child enters school, the child's friends become an important influence on behavior and attitudes. For children and for adults, friendships and associations in **peer groups** affect political attitudes. We must, however, separate the effects of peer group pressure on opinions and attitudes in general from peer group pressure on political opinions. For the most part, associations among peers are nonpolitical. Political attitudes are more likely to be shaped by peer groups when the peer groups are involved directly in political activities.

Individuals who join interest groups based on ethnic identity may find, for example, a common political bond through working for the group's civil liberties and rights. African American activist groups may consist of individuals who join together to support government programs that will aid the African American population. Members of a labor union may be strongly influenced to support certain pro-labor candidates.

Peer Group A group consisting of members sharing common social characteristics.

Religious Influence

Traditionally, scholars have examined the impact of religion on political attitudes by dividing the population into such categories as Protestant, Catholic, and Jewish. In recent decades, however, such a breakdown has become much less valuable as a means of predicting someone's political values. To be sure, Jewish respondents continue to be notably more liberal than members of other groups, both on economic issues and on social issues. Persons reporting no religion are very liberal on social issues but have mixed economic views. Protestants and Catholics, however, do not differ greatly from each other after we correct for various differences such as the fact that more Protestants than Catholics live in the South.

Nevertheless, two factors do turn out to be major predictors of political attitudes among members of the various Christian denominations. One is the degree of religious commitment, as measured by such actions as regular churchgoing. The other is the degree to which the respondent adheres to religious beliefs that (depending on the denomination) can be called conservative, evangelical, or fundamentalist. High scores on either factor are associated with social conservatism on political issues—that is, with beliefs that place a high value on social order. These factors have much less influence on economic views.

The Influence of Economic Status

Family income is a strong predictor of economic liberalism or conservatism. Those with low incomes tend to favor government action to benefit the poor or to promote economic equality. Those with high incomes tend to oppose government intervention in the economy or to support it only when it benefits business. One useful way to evaluate a respondent's commitment to economic equality is to ask whether the government should guarantee everyone a job.

Interestingly, upper-class respondents are more likely to endorse social liberalism, and lower-class people are more likely to favor social conservatism. Support for the right to have an abortion, for example, rises with income. It follows that libertarians—those who oppose government action on both economic and social issues—are concentrated among wealthier voters. Those who favor government action both to promote traditional moral values and to promote economic equality—economic liberals, social conservatives—are concentrated among less well off groups.

The Influence of Political Events

People's political attitudes may be shaped by political events and the nation's reactions to them. In the 1960s and 1970s, the war in Vietnam—including revelations about the secret bombing in Cambodia—and the **Watergate break-in** and subsequent presidential cover-up fostered widespread cynicism toward government.

When events produce a long-lasting political impact, **generational effects** result. Voters who grew up in the 1930s during the Great Depression were likely to form lifelong attachments to the Democratic Party, the party of Franklin D. Roosevelt. There was some evidence that the years of economic prosperity under Ronald

Watergate Break-In
The 1972 illegal entry into the Democratic National Committee offices by participants in President Richard Nixon's reelection campaign.

Generational Effect
A long-lasting effect of events of a particular time on the political opinions of those who came of political age at that time.

Reagan during the 1980s may have influenced young adults to identify with the Republican Party. President George W. Bush's immediate and decisive response to the events of 9/11 may have a similar effect. The extent to which the Bush administration's actions since 9/11 will affect the party identification of young voters, however, remains to be seen.

Opinion Leaders' Influence

Opinion Leader One who is able to influence the opinions of others because of position, expertise, or personality.

We are all influenced by those with whom we are closely associated or whom we hold in high regard—friends at school, family members and other relatives, teachers, and so on. In a sense, these people are **opinion leaders,** but on an informal level; that is, their influence over us is not necessarily intentional or deliberate. We are also influenced by formal opinion leaders, such as presidents, lobbyists, congresspersons, news commentators, and religious leaders, who have as part of their jobs the task of swaying people's views. Their interest lies in defining the political agenda in such a way that discussions about policy options will take place on their terms.

Media Influence

Media The channels of mass communication.

Clearly, the **media**—newspapers, television, radio, and Internet sources—strongly influence public opinion. This is because the media inform the public about the issues and events of our times and thus have an agenda-setting effect. In other words, to borrow from Bernard Cohen's classic statement on the media and public opinion, the media may not be successful in telling people what to think, but they are "stunningly successful in telling their audience what to think about."[3]

Today, many contend that the media's influence on public opinion has grown to equal that of the family. For example, in her analysis of the role played by the media in American politics,[4] media scholar Doris A. Graber points out that high school students, when asked where they obtain the information on which they base their attitudes, mention the mass media far more than they mention their families, friends, and teachers. This trend, combined with the increasing popularity of such information sources as talk shows and the Internet, may significantly alter the nature of the media's influence on public debate in the future. The media's influence is discussed in more detail later in this chapter.

The Influence of Demographic Traits

Finally, where you live, what racial group you identify with, and which gender you are can influence your political attitudes. Although regional differences are less important today than just a few decades ago, there is a tendency, at least in national elections, for the South, the Great Plains, and the Rocky Mountain states to favor the Republicans and for the West Coast and the Northeast to favor the Democrats. Perhaps more important than region is residence—urban, suburban, or rural. People in big cities tend to be liberal and Democratic. Those who live in smaller communities tend to be conservative and Republican.

An event such as the terrorist attacks of September 11, 2001, can influence opinions and attitudes of Americans for many years. The political leadership shown during such a time of crisis is also influential on public opinion. President George W. Bush, shown here at the site of the World Trade Center collapse in New York City, received high public approval ratings for his leadership during the crisis.

AP Photo/Doug Mills

African Americans tend to be more liberal than whites on social-welfare issues, civil liberties, and even foreign policy. Since the 1930s, party preference and voting among African Americans have supported the Democrats very heavily.

It is somewhat surprising that a person's chronological age has comparatively little impact on political preferences. Still, young adults are somewhat more liberal than older people on such issues as pornography, civil disobedience, and racial and gender equality.

The Gender Gap

Until the 1980s, there was little evidence that men's and women's political attitudes were very different. Beginning with the election of Ronald Reagan in 1980, however, political scientists began to see what came to be called the **gender gap.** A May 1983

Gender Gap The difference between the percentage of women who vote for a particular candidate and the percentage of men who vote for the candidate.

Gallup poll revealed that more men than women approved of Reagan's job performance. The gender gap reappeared in subsequent presidential elections, with women more likely than men to support the Democratic candidate. In the 2000 elections, 54 percent of women voted for Democrat Al Gore, compared with 42 percent of men. A similar gender gap was evident in the 2002 midterm elections: 55 percent of women favored Democratic candidates, compared with 43 percent of men.

Women appear to hold different attitudes from their male counterparts on a range of issues other than presidential preferences. They are much more likely than men to oppose capital punishment and the use of force abroad. Studies have also shown that women are more concerned about risks to the environment, more supportive of social welfare, and more supportive of extending civil rights to gay men and lesbians than are men. Women also are more concerned than men about the security issues raised by the events of 9/11, however. If this fact causes women to vote more frequently for the Republicans, then the gender gap may be less important, at least in the immediate future.

Public Opinion and the Political Process

Public opinion affects the political process in many ways. Politicians, whether in office or in the midst of a campaign, see public opinion as important to their careers. The president, members of Congress, governors, and other elected officials realize that strong support by the public as expressed in opinion polls is a source of power in dealing with other politicians. It is far more difficult for a senator to say no to the president if the president is immensely popular and if polls show approval of the president's policies. Public opinion also helps political candidates identify the most important concerns among the people and may help them shape their campaigns successfully.

Nevertheless, surveys of public opinion are not equivalent to elections in the United States. Although opinion polls may influence political candidates or government officials, elections are the major vehicle through which Americans can bring about changes in their government.

Political Culture and Public Opinion

Americans are divided into a multitude of ethnic, religious, regional, and political subgroups. Given the diversity of American society and the wide range of opinions contained within it, how is it that the political process continues to function without being stalemated by conflict and dissension? One explanation is rooted in the concept of the American **political culture,** which can be described as a set of attitudes and ideas about the nation and the government. Our political culture is widely shared by Americans of many different backgrounds. To some extent, it consists of symbols, such as the American flag, the Liberty Bell, and the Statue of Liberty. The elements of our political culture also include certain shared beliefs about the most important values in the American political system, including (1) liberty, equality,

Political Culture The collection of beliefs and attitudes toward government and the political process held by a community or nation.

and property; (2) support for religion; and (3) community service and personal achievement. The structure of the government—particularly federalism, the political parties, the powers of Congress, and popular rule—is also an important value.

The political culture provides a general environment of support for the political system. If the people share certain beliefs about the system and a reservoir of good feeling exists toward the institutions of government, the nation will be better able to weather periods of crisis.

The political culture also helps Americans evaluate their government's performance. At times in our history, **political trust** in government has reached relatively high levels. As you can see in Table 6–1, a poll taken two weeks after the 9/11 attacks found that trust in government was higher than it had been for more than three decades. At other times, political trust in government has fallen to low levels. For example, during the 1960s and 1970s, during the Vietnam War and the Watergate scandals, surveys showed that the overall level of political trust in government had declined steeply. This index of political trust reached an all-time low in the early 1990s but then climbed steadily until 2001 (see Table 6–1).

Public Opinion about Government

A vital component of public opinion in the United States is the considerable ambivalence with which the public regards many major national institutions. Table 6–2 on the following page shows trends from 1977 to 2003 in opinion polls asking respondents, at regularly spaced intervals, how much confidence they had in the institutions listed. Over the years, military and religious organizations have ranked highest. Note, however, the decline in confidence in churches in 2002 following a substantial number of sex abuse allegations against Catholic priests. Note also the heightened regard for the military after the first Gulf War in 1991. Table 6–2 on the following page shows that in 1991, the public had more confidence in the military than it did in churches or organized religion, in newspapers, or in any institution of government. In 2002 and 2003, confidence in the military again soared, most likely because Americans recognized the central role to be played by the military in the war on terrorism.

Political Trust The degree to which individuals express trust in the government and political institutions.

INFOTRAC

To find out more about this topic, use the term "political culture" in the Subject guide.

TABLE 6–1	Trends in Political Trust

QUESTION: *How much of the time do you think you can trust the government in Washington to do what is right—just about always, most of the time, or only some of the time?*

	1968	1972	1974	1976	1978	1980	1982	1984	1986	1988	1990	1992	1994	1996	1998	2000	2001	2002
Percentage saying:																		
Always/Most of the time	61	53	36	33	29	25	32	46	42	44	27	23	20	25	34	40	64	46
Some of the time	36	45	61	63	67	73	64	51	55	54	73	75	79	71	66	59	35	52

SOURCES: *New York Times*/CBS News Surveys; the University of Michigan Survey Research Center, National Election Studies; the Pew Research Center for the People and the Press; Council for Excellence in Government; a *Washington Post* poll, September 25–27, 2001; and a Gallup poll, September 2–4, 2002.

TABLE 6–2	Confidence in Institutions Trend

QUESTION: *I am going to read a list of institutions in American society. Would you please tell me how much confidence you, yourself, have in each one—a great deal, quite a lot, some, or very little?*

	\multicolumn{15}{c}{Percentage Saying "Great Deal" or "Quite a Lot"}
	1977	1979	1981	1983	1985	1987	1989	1991	1993	1995	1997	1999	2001	2002	2003
Military	57	54	50	53	61	61	63	69	67	64	60	68	66	79	82
Church or organized religion	65	65	64	62	66	61	52	56	53	57	56	58	60	45	50
Banks and banking	NA	60	46	51	51	51	42	30	38	43	41	43	44	47	50
U.S. Supreme Court	46	45	46	42	56	52	46	39	43	44	50	49	50	50	47
Public schools	54	53	42	39	48	50	43	35	39	40	40	36	38	38	40
Television	NA	38	25	25	29	28	NA	24	21	33	34	34	34	35	35
Newspapers	NA	51	35	38	35	31	NA	32	31	30	35	33	36	35	33
Congress	40	34	29	28	39	NA	32	18	19	21	22	26	26	29	29
Organized labor	39	36	28	26	28	26	NA	22	26	26	23	28	26	26	28
Big business	33	32	20	28	31	NA	NA	22	23	21	28	30	28	20	22

NA = Not asked.

SOURCE: Gallup poll, June 9–10, 2003.

The United States Supreme Court has scored well over time. Less confidence is expressed in newspapers, television, big business, and organized labor. In 1991, following a scandal involving congressional banking practices, confidence in Congress fell to a record low of 18 percent. Confidence in Congress has yet to return to the levels reported in the 1970s and 1980s.

At times, popular confidence in all institutions may rise or fall, reflecting optimism or pessimism about the general state of the nation. For example, between 1979 and 1981 there was a collapse of confidence affecting most institutions. This reflected public dissatisfaction with the handling of the hostage crisis in Iran and with some of the highest levels of inflation in U.S. history.

Although people may not have much confidence in government institutions, they nonetheless turn to government to solve what they perceive to be the major problems facing the country. Table 6–3, which is based on Gallup polls conducted from the years 1975 to 2003, shows that the leading problems have changed over time. The public tends to emphasize problems that are immediate. It is not at all unusual to see fairly sudden, and even apparently contradictory, shifts in public perceptions of what government should do. In recent years, education, the economy, and terrorism have reached the top of the problems list.

Public Opinion and Policymaking

Public opinion plays an important role in policymaking. Policymakers cannot always be guided by opinion polls, however. In the end, politicians must make choices. When they do so, their choices necessarily involve trade-offs. If politicians vote for

TABLE 6–3	Most Important Problem Trend, 1975 to Present		
1975	High cost of living, unemployment	1990	War in Middle East
1976	High cost of living, unemployment	1991	Economy
1977	High cost of living, unemployment	1992	Unemployment, budget deficit
1978	High cost of living, energy problems	1993	Health care, budget deficit
1979	High cost of living, energy problems	1994	Crime, violence, health care
1980	High cost of living, unemployment	1995	Crime, violence
1981	High cost of living, unemployment	1996	Budget deficit
1982	Unemployment, high cost of living	1997	Crime, violence
1983	Unemployment, high cost of living	1998	Crime, violence
1984	Unemployment, fear of war	1999	Crime, violence
1985	Fear of war, unemployment	2000	Morals, family decline
1986	Unemployment, budget deficit	2001	Economy, education
1987	Unemployment, economy	2002	Terrorism, economy
1988	Economy, budget deficit	2003	Terrorism, economy
1989	War on drugs		

SOURCES: *New York Times*/CBS News poll, January 1996; Gallup polls, 2000, 2002, and 2003.

increased spending to improve education, for example, by necessity there must be fewer resources for other worthy projects. Individuals who are polled do not have to make such trade-offs when they respond to questions. Indeed, survey respondents usually are not even given a choice of trade-offs in their policy opinions. Moreover, to make an informed policy choice requires an understanding not only of the policy area but also of the consequences of any given choice. Virtually no public opinion polls make sure that those polled have such information.

Finally, government decisions cannot be made simply by adding up individual desires. Politicians engage in a type of "horse trading." All politicians know that they cannot satisfy every desire of every constituent. Therefore, each politician attempts to maximize the *net* benefits to his or her constituents, while keeping within whatever the politician believes the government can afford.

The Media and Politics

The study of people and politics—of how people gain the information that they need to be able to choose between political candidates, to organize for their own interests, and to formulate opinions on the policies and decisions of the government—must take into account the role played by the media. Historically, the printed media played the most important role in informing public debate. The printed media developed, for the most part, our understanding of how news is to be reported. Today, however, more than 90 percent of Americans use television news as their primary source of information. In addition, the Internet has become a source for political communication and fund-raising.

The mass media perform a number of different functions in any country. In the United States, we can list at least six. Almost all of them can have political implications, and some are essential to the democratic process. These functions are as follows: (1) entertainment, (2) reporting the news, (3) identifying public problems, (4) socializing new generations, (5) providing a political forum, and (6) making profits.

Entertainment

By far the greatest number of radio and television hours are dedicated to entertaining the public. The battle for prime-time ratings indicates how important successful entertainment is to the survival of networks and individual stations.

Although there is no direct linkage between entertainment and politics, network dramas often introduce material that may be politically controversial and that may stimulate public discussion. An example is *The West Wing*, a TV series that many people believe promotes liberal political values. Made-for-TV movies have focused on a number of controversial topics, including AIDS, incest, and wife battering.

Reporting the News

A primary function of the mass media in all their forms—newspapers and magazines, radio, television, cable, and online news services—is the reporting of news. The media provide words and pictures about events, facts, personalities, and ideas. The protections of the First Amendment are intended to keep the flow of news as free as possible, because it is an essential part of the democratic process. If citizens cannot get unbiased information about the state of their communities and their leaders' actions, how can they make voting decisions? One of the most incisive comments about the importance of the media was made by James Madison, who said, "A people who mean to be their own governors must arm themselves with the power knowledge gives. A popular government without popular information or the means of acquiring it, is but a prologue to a farce or a tragedy or perhaps both."[5]

Identifying Public Problems

Public Agenda
Issues that are perceived by the political community as meriting public attention and governmental action.

The power of the media is important not only in revealing what the government is doing but also in determining what the government ought to do—in other words, in setting the **public agenda.** The mass media identify public issues; for example, the placement of convicted sex offenders in residential neighborhoods on release from prison. The media then influence the passage of legislation, such as "Megan's Law," which requires police to notify neighbors about the release and/or resettlement of certain offenders. American journalists also work in a long tradition of uncovering public wrongdoing, corruption, and bribery and of bringing such wrongdoing to the public's attention. Closely related to this investigative function is that of presenting policy alternatives. Public policy is often complex and difficult to make entertaining, but programs devoted to public policy increasingly are being scheduled for prime-time television. Most networks produce shows with a "news magazine" format that sometimes include segments on foreign policy and other issues.

Socializing New Generations

As mentioned earlier, the media, and particularly television, strongly influence the beliefs and opinions of Americans. Because of this influence, the media play a significant role in the political socialization of the younger generation, as well as immigrants to this country. Through the transmission of historical information (sometimes fictionalized), the presentation of American culture, and the portrayal of the diverse regions and groups in the United States, the media teach young people and immigrants about what it means to be an American. TV talk shows, such as *Oprah*, sometimes focus on controversial issues (such as abortion or assisted suicide) that relate to basic American values (such as liberty). Many children's shows are designed not only to entertain young viewers but also to instruct them in the traditional moral values of American society. In recent years, the public has become increasingly concerned about the level of violence depicted on children's programs and on other shows during prime time.

Providing a Political Forum

As part of their news function, the media also provide a political forum for leaders and the public. Candidates for office use news reporting to sustain interest in their campaigns, whereas officeholders use the media to gain support for their policies or

Providing a forum for political leaders is one of the functions of the media. Here, President George W. Bush uses the media to announce to the public his decision to use military force against Iraq in March 2003. What factors might limit the president's success in appealing directly to the public?

AP Photo / via APTN

to present an image of leadership. Presidential trips abroad are an outstanding way for the chief executive to get colorful, positive, and exciting news coverage that makes the president look "presidential." The media also offer ways for citizens to participate in public debate, through letters to the editor, televised editorials, or electronic mail.

Making Profits

Most of the news media in the United States are private, for-profit corporate enterprises. One of their goals is to make profits—for employee salaries, for expansion, and for dividends to the stockholders who own the companies. Profits are made, in general, by charging for advertising. Advertising revenues usually are related directly to circulation or to listener/viewer ratings. We address the question of how advertising and other commercial considerations may affect reporting in this chapter's *At Issue* feature.

Several well-known outlets, in contrast, are publicly owned—public television stations in many communities and National Public Radio. These operate without extensive commercials, are locally supported, and are often subsidized by the government and corporations. A complex relationship exists among the for-profit and nonprofit media, the government, and the public. Throughout the rest of this chapter, we examine some of the many facets of this relationship.

The Primacy of Television

Television is the most influential medium. It is also big business. National news TV personalities such as Peter Jennings may earn millions of dollars per year from their TV news contracts alone. They are paid so much because they command large audiences, and large audiences command high prices for advertising on national news shows.

The Increase in News-Type Programming

In 1963, the major networks—ABC, CBS, and NBC—devoted only eleven minutes daily to national news. A twenty-four-hour-a-day news cable channel—CNN—started operating in 1980. By 2004, the amount of time networks devoted to news-type programming had increased to about three hours. With the addition of CNN Headline News, CNBC, MSNBC, Fox News, and other news-format cable channels since the 1980s, the amount of news-type programming continues to increase. In recent years, all of the major networks have also added Internet sites to try to capture that market, but they face hundreds of competitors on the Internet.

INFOTRAC

To find out more on this subject, use the term "television and politics" in the Subject guide.

Television's Influence on the Political Process

Television's influence on the political process today is recognized by all who engage in the process. Television news is often criticized for being superficial, particularly compared with the detailed coverage available in the *New York Times,* for example. In fact,

AT ISSUE: Profits and News Coverage

For the most part, the media depend on advertisers to obtain revenues to make profits. Media outlets that do not succeed in generating sufficient revenues from advertising either go bankrupt or are sold. Consequently, news reporters often feel pressure from media owners and from advertisers.

SYNERGY AND THE MEDIA BUSINESS

Many media owners also own other companies. Within the past decade, all of the prime-time television networks have been purchased by major American corporations and have become part of corporate conglomerates. The Turner Broadcasting/CNN network was purchased by a major corporation, Time Warner. Later, Time Warner was acquired by America Online (AOL), a merger that combined the world's then-largest media company with the world's then-largest online company. Fox Television is a part of Rupert Murdoch's publishing and media empire. In addition to these mergers and acquisitions, many of these corporations have formed partnerships with computer software makers, such as Microsoft, for joint electronic publishing ventures.

Not surprisingly, media owners view their media outlets as places to promote their other businesses. They see nothing unethical about such a practice. In addition, media owners often take their cues from what advertisers want. If an important advertiser does not like the political bent of a particular reporter, the reporter may be asked to alter his or her "style" of writing. The Project for Excellence in Journalism in 2001 discovered that 53 percent of local news directors said that advertisers try to tell them what to air and what not to air.[*]

BEHOLDEN TO ADVERTISERS

Advertisers have been known to pull ads from newspapers and TV stations when they read or view negative publicity about their own company or product. For example, when CBS ran a *60 Minutes* show about store security guards at Dillard's and other department stores using excessive force and racial profiling, Dillard's pulled its ads from CBS. This example can be multiplied many times over.

FOR CRITICAL ANALYSIS

How can a news organization remain independent of the pressure to generate ever-increasing profits through more ad revenues?

[*]*Columbia Journalism Review,* November/December 2001.

television news is constrained by its technical characteristics, the most important being the limitations of time; stories must be reported in only a few minutes.

The most interesting aspect of television is, of course, the fact that it relies on pictures rather than words to attract the viewer's attention. Therefore, the videotapes or slides that are chosen for a particular political story have exaggerated importance. Viewers do not know what other photos may have been taken or what other events may have been recorded—they see only those appearing on their screens.

In addition, some critics suggest that there is pressure to produce television news that has a "story line," like a novel or movie. The story should be short, with exciting pictures and a clear plot. In the extreme case, the news media are satisfied with a **sound bite,** a several-second comment selected or crafted for its immediate impact on the viewer.

Sound Bite A brief, memorable comment that can be easily fit into news broadcasts.

It has been suggested that these formatting characteristics—or necessities—of television increase its influence on political events. (Newspapers and news magazines are also limited by their formats, but to a lesser extent.) As you are aware, real life is usually not dramatic, nor do all events have a neat or an easily understood plot. Political campaigns are continuing events, lasting perhaps as long as two years. The significance of their daily turns and twists is only apparent later. The "drama" of Congress, with its 535 players and dozens of important committees and meetings, is also difficult for the media to present. What television requires is dozens of daily three-minute stories.

The Revolution in the Electronic Media

Technology is increasing the number of alternative news sources today. The advent of pay TV, cable TV, subscription TV, satellite TV, and the Internet has completely changed the electronic media landscape. With hundreds, if not thousands, of potential outlets for specialized programs, the electronic media are becoming more and more like the printed media in catering to specialized tastes. This is sometimes referred to as **narrowcasting.** Both cable television and the Internet offer the public unparalleled access to specialized information on everything from gardening and home repair to sports and religion.

Narrowcasting Broadcasting that is targeted to one small sector of the population.

In recent years, narrowcasting has become increasingly prevalent. The broadcast networks' audiences are declining. Between 1982 and 2004, their share of the audience fell from 72 percent to 55 percent. At the same time, the percentage of households having access to the Internet grew from zero to more than 65 percent.

Talk-Show Politics and Internet Broadcasting

Multiple news outlets have given rise to literally thousands of talk shows, whether on television, radio, or the Internet. By 2004, there were more than two dozen national television talk shows; their hosts ranged from Jerry Springer, who is regarded as a sensationalist, to Larry King, whose show has become a political necessity for candidates. Arnold Schwarzenegger actually announced his candidacy for governor of California in 2003 on Jay Leno's *Tonight Show.*

The real blossoming of "talk" has occurred on the radio. The number of radio stations that program only talk shows has increased from about 300 in 1989 to more than 1,200 today. The topics of talk shows range from business and investment, to psychology, to politics. There has been considerable criticism of the political talk shows, especially those hosted by conservatives, such as Rush Limbaugh. Critics contend that such shows increase the level of intolerance and irrationality in American politics. The listeners to those shows are self-selected and tend to share the viewpoint of the host. Similarly, the Internet makes it possible for a Web site to be highly ideological or partisan and to encourage online chat with others of the same persuasion. One of the potential hazards

INFOTRAC

To find out more on this subject, use the term "talk shows" in the Subject guide.

of narrowcasting of this kind is that people will be less open to dialogue with those whose opinions differ from their own, resulting in increased political extremism.

The Media and Political Campaigns

All forms of the media—television, newspapers, radio, magazines, and online services—have an enormous political impact on American society. Media influence is most obvious during political campaigns.

Because television is the primary news source for the majority of Americans, candidates and their consultants spend much of their time devising strategies that use television to their benefit. Three types of TV coverage are generally used in campaigns for the presidency and other offices: advertising, management of news coverage, and campaign debates.

Advertising

Perhaps one of the most effective political ads of all time was a thirty-second spot created by President Lyndon Johnson's media adviser. In this ad, a little girl stood in a field of daisies. As she held a daisy, she pulled the petals off and quietly counted to herself. Suddenly, when she reached number ten, a deep bass voice cut in and began

TOLES © 2004 *The Washington Post*. Reprinted with permission of Universal Press Syndicate.

a countdown: "10, 9, 8, 7, 6 . . . ." When the voice intoned "zero," the unmistakable mushroom cloud of an atomic bomb began to fill the screen. Then President Johnson's voice was heard: "These are the stakes. To make a world in which all of God's children can live, or to go into the dark. We must either love each other or we must die." At the end of the commercial, the message read, "Vote for President Johnson on November 3."

To understand how effective this "daisy girl" commercial was, you must know that Johnson's opponent was Barry Goldwater, a Republican conservative candidate known for his expansive views on the role of the U.S. military. The ad's implication was that Goldwater would lead the United States into nuclear war. Although the ad was withdrawn within a few days, it has a place in political campaign history as the classic negative campaign announcement. The ad's producer, Tony Schwartz, describes the effect in this way: "It was comparable to a person going to a psychiatrist and seeing dirty pictures in a Rorschach pattern. The daisy commercial evoked Goldwater's pro-bomb statements. They were like dirty pictures in the audience's mind."[6]

Since the daisy girl advertisement, negative advertising has come into its own. Candidates vie with one another to produce "attack" ads and then to counterattack

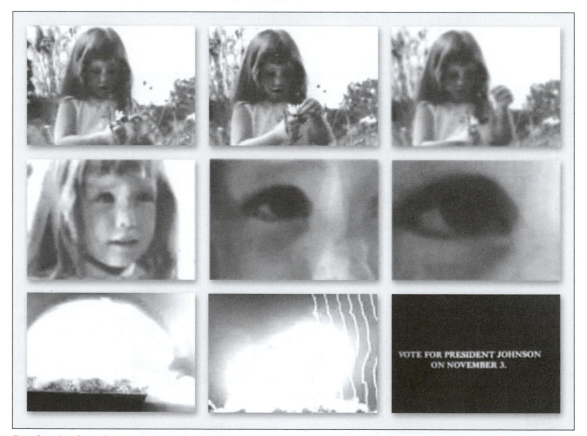

President Lyndon Johnson's "daisy girl" ad contrasted the innocence of childhood with the horror of an atomic attack.

when the opponent responds. In recent elections, candidates have gone to great lengths to paint their opponents in unfashionable colors. The public claims not to like negative advertising, but as one consultant put it, "Negative advertising works." The most important effect of negative advertisements may not be to transfer votes from the candidate who is under attack to the candidate running the ads. Rather, the negative ads can demoralize the supporters of the candidate who is under attack. Some supporters, as a result, may not bother to vote. The widespread use of negative ads, therefore, can lead to reduced political participation and a general cynicism about politics.

Management of News Coverage

Using political advertising to get a message across to the public is a very expensive tactic. Coverage by the news media, however, is free; it simply demands that the campaign ensure that coverage takes place. In recent years, campaign managers have shown increasing sophistication in creating newsworthy events for journalists to cover. As Doris Graber points out, "To keep a favorable image of their candidates in front of the public, campaign managers arrange newsworthy events to familiarize potential voters with their candidates' best aspects."[7]

The campaign staff uses several methods to try to influence the quantity and type of coverage the campaign receives. First, the campaign staff understands the technical aspects of media coverage—camera angles, necessary equipment, timing, and deadlines—and plans political events to accommodate the press. Second, the campaign organization is aware that political reporters and their sponsors—networks or newspapers—are in competition for the best stories and can be manipulated through the granting of favors, such as personal interviews with the candidate. Third, the scheduler in the campaign has the important task of planning events that will be photogenic and interesting enough for the evening news. A related goal, although one that is more difficult to attain, is to convince reporters that a particular interpretation of an event is correct.

Today, the art of putting the appropriate **spin** on a story or event is highly developed. Each presidential candidate's press advisers, often referred to as **spin doctors,** try to convince the journalists that their interpretations of political events are correct. For example, in the 2000 primaries George W. Bush's camp played down his loss to John McCain in the Michigan primary by using the spin that Michigan independents who normally vote Democratic voted in the Republican primary to defeat Bush. Journalists have begun to report on the different spins and on how the candidates are trying to manipulate campaign news coverage.

Spin An interpretation of campaign events or election results that is favorable to the candidate's campaign strategy.

Spin Doctor A political campaign adviser who tries to convince journalists of the truth of a particular interpretation of events.

Going for the Knockout Punch—Presidential Debates

In presidential elections, perhaps of equal importance to political advertisements is the performance of the candidate in televised presidential debates. After the first such debate in 1960, in which John Kennedy, the young senator from Massachusetts, took on the vice president of the United States, Richard Nixon, candidates became aware of the great potential of television for changing the momentum of a campaign. In general, challengers have much more to gain from debating than do incumbents. Challengers hope that the incumbent may make a

INFOTRAC

For updates and more information on debates, use the term "campaign debates" in the Subject guide.

mistake in the debate and undermine the "presidential" image. Incumbent presidents are loath to debate their challengers, because it puts their opponents on an equal footing with them.

After some negotiating about the structure and timing of debates, Vice President Al Gore and Governor George W. Bush met for three public debates before the 2000 presidential elections, and the vice presidential candidates met for one. Each of the three presidential debates featured a different format: one formal debate, one moderated discussion, and one "town meeting"–style debate. Vice President Gore was criticized for being too aggressive in one debate, and Governor Bush was criticized for either being too passive or being uninformative. The real issue was style—that is, whether a candidate could stay calm under pressure, be likable, and avoid any big mistakes. The debates were, in terms of influence on the voters, a draw.

Although debates are justified publicly as an opportunity for the voters to find out how candidates differ on the issues, what the candidates want is to capitalize on the power of television to project an image. They view the debate as a strategic opportunity to improve their own images or to point out the failures of their opponents. Candidates also know that the morning-after interpretation of the debate by the news media may play a crucial role in what the public thinks. Regardless of the risks of debating, the potential for gaining votes is so great that candidates undoubtedly will continue to seek televised debates.

The Media's Impact on the Voters

The question of how much influence the media have on voting behavior is difficult to answer. Generally, individuals watch television, read newspapers, or log on to a Web site with certain preconceived ideas about political issues and candidates. These attitudes and opinions act as a kind of perceptual screen that filters out information that makes people feel uncomfortable or that does not fit with their own ideas.

Voters watch campaign commercials and news about political campaigns with "selective attentiveness." That is, they tend to watch those commercials that support the candidates they favor and tend to pay attention to news stories about their own candidates. This selectivity also affects their perceptions of the content of the news story or commercial and whether it is remembered. Apparently, the media are most influential with those persons who have not formed an opinion about political candidates or issues. Studies have shown that the flurry of television commercials and debates immediately before election day has the most impact on those voters who are truly undecided. Few voters who have already formed their opinions change their minds under the influence of the media.

Calling Elections

In 2000, the media's worst hour came on election night. All of the networks and cable news operations vied with one another to "call" the states for one or the other of the presidential candidates. Because the media were using data from exit polls rather than actual vote counts, a number of states were "too close to call," and several were called mistakenly and later changed. Whether the rush to declare the elections over had any impact on the outcome is uncertain.

The Media and the Government

The mass media not only wield considerable power when it comes to political campaigns, but they also, in one way or another, can wield power over the affairs of government and over government officials.

The Media and the Presidency

The relationship between the media and the president is most often reciprocal: each needs the other to thrive. Because of this codependency, both the media and the president work hard to exploit the other. The media need news to report, and the president needs coverage.

In the United States, the prominence of the president is accentuated by a **White House press corps** that is assigned full-time to cover the presidency. These reporters even have a lounge in the White House where they spend their days, waiting for a story to break. Most of the time, they simply wait for the daily or twice-daily briefing by the president's **press secretary.** Because of the press corps's physical proximity to the president, the chief executive cannot even take a brief stroll around the presidential swimming pool without its becoming news. Perhaps no other democratic nation allows the press such access to its highest government official. Consequently, no other nation has its airwaves and print media so filled with absolute trivia regarding the personal lives of the chief executive and his family.

President Franklin D. Roosevelt brought new spirit to a demoralized country and led it through the Great Depression through his effective use of the media, particularly through his radio broadcasts. His radio "fireside chats" brought hope to millions. Roosevelt's speeches were masterful in their ability to forge a common emotional bond among his listeners. His decisive announcement in 1933 on the reorganization

White House Press Corps The reporters assigned full-time to cover the presidency.

Press Secretary The presidential staff member responsible for handling White House media relations and communication.

President Franklin D. Roosevelt, the first president to fully exploit the airwaves for his benefit, reported to the nation through radio "fireside chats." How did such capabilities change the nature of the presidency?

Photo Researchers

MAKING A DIFFERENCE : Be a Critical Consumer of Opinion Polls

Americans are inundated with the results of public opinion polls. The polls purport to tell us a variety of things: whether the president's popularity is up or down, whether gun control is more popular now than previously, or who is leading the pack for the next presidential nomination.

What must be kept in mind with this blizzard of information is that all poll results are not equally good or equally believable. As a critical consumer, you need to be aware of what makes one set of public opinion poll results valid and other results useless or even dangerously misleading.

SELECTION OF THE SAMPLE

Pay attention only to opinion polls that are based on scientific, or random, samples. In these so-called *probability samples,* a known probability is used to select each person interviewed. Do not give credence to the results of opinion polls that consist of shopping-mall interviews or the like. The main problem with this kind of opinion taking is that not everyone has an equal chance of being in the mall when the interview takes place. Also, it is almost certain that the people in the mall are not a reasonable cross-section of a community's entire population.

Probability samples are useful because you can calculate the range within which the results would have fallen if everybody had been interviewed. Well-designed probability samples will allow the pollster to say, for example, that he or she is 95 percent sure that 61 percent of the public, plus or minus 4 percentage points, supports national health insurance. It turns out that if you want to be twice as precise about a poll result, you need to collect a sample four times as large. This tends to make accurate polls expensive and difficult to conduct.

INTERVIEW METHOD

Pay attention as well to how people were contacted for the poll—by mail, by telephone, in person in their homes, or in some other way (such as via the Internet). Because of its lower cost, polling firms have turned more and more to telephone interviewing. This method can produce highly accurate results. Its disadvantage is that telephone interviews typically need to be short and to deal with questions that are fairly easy to answer. Interviews in person are better for getting useful information about why a particular response was given. They take much longer to complete, however. Results from mailed questionnaires should be taken with a grain of salt. Usually, only a small percentage of people send them back.

NONPOLLS

When viewers or listeners of television or radio shows are encouraged to call in their opinions to an 800 telephone number, the polling results are meaningless. Users of the Internet also have an easy way to make their views known. Only people who own computers and are interested in the topic will take the trouble to respond, however, and that group is not representative of the general public.

of the banks, for example, calmed a jittery nation and prevented the collapse of the banking industry, which was threatened by a run on banks, from which nervous depositors were withdrawing their assets. His famous Pearl Harbor speech, following the Japanese attack on the U.S. Pacific fleet on December 7, 1941 ("a day that will live in infamy"), mobilized the nation for the sacrifices and effort necessary to win World War II.

Setting the Public Agenda

According to a number of studies, the media play an important part in setting the public agenda. Evidence is strong that whatever public problems receive the most media treatment will be cited by the public in contemporary surveys as the most important problems. Although the media do not make policy decisions, they do determine to a significant extent the policy issues that need to be decided—and this is an important part of the political process. Because those who control the media are not elected representatives of the people, the agenda-setting role of the media necessarily is a controversial one. The relationship of the media to agenda setting remains complex, though, because politicians are able to manipulate media coverage to control some of its effects, as well as to exploit the media to further their agendas with the public.

KEY TERMS

consensus 119	opinion poll 120	sampling error 122
divisive opinion 120	peer group 124	sound bite 136
gender gap 127	political culture 128	spin 139
generational effect 125	political trust 129	spin doctor 139
media 126	press secretary 141	Watergate break-in 125
narrowcasting 136	public agenda 132	White House press corps 141
opinion leader 126	public opinion 119	

CHAPTER SUMMARY

❶ Public opinion is the aggregate of individual attitudes or beliefs shared by some portion of the adult population. A consensus exists when a large proportion of the public appears to express the same view on an issue. Divisive opinion exists when the public holds widely different attitudes on an issue. Sometimes a poll shows a distribution of opinion indicating that most people either have no information about an issue or are not interested enough in the issue to form a position on it.

❷ Most descriptions of public opinion are based on the results of opinion polls. The accuracy of polls depends on sampling techniques that include a representative sample of the population being polled and that ensure randomness in the selection of respondents.

❸ Problems with polls include sampling errors (which may occur when the pool of respondents is not chosen in a scientific manner), the difficulty of knowing the degree to which responses are influenced by the type and order of questions asked, the use of a yes/no format for answers to the questions, and the interviewer's techniques. Many are concerned about the use of "push polls" (in which the questions "push" the respondent toward a particular candidate). During the 1970s, telephone polling came to be widely used. Today, largely because of extensive telemarketing, people often refuse to answer calls, and nonresponse rates in telephone polling have skyrocketed.

❹ People's opinions are formed through the political socialization process. Important factors in this process are the family, educational institutions, peers and peer groups, religion, economic status, significant political events, opinion leaders, the media, demographic traits, and gender. While the family is usually seen as the most important influence in opinion formation, the media's ability to influence opinion is coming to equal that of the family.

❺ Public opinion affects the political process in many ways. The political culture provides a general environment of support for the political system, allowing the nation to weather periods of crisis. The political culture also helps Americans to evaluate their government's performance. At times, the level of trust in government has been relatively high; at other times, the level of trust has declined steeply. Similarly, Americans' confidence in government institutions varies over time, depending

on a number of circumstances. Generally, though, Americans turn to government to solve what they perceive to be the major problems facing the country. In 2003, Americans ranked terrorism and the economy as the two most significant problems facing the nation.

❻ Public opinion also plays an important role in policymaking. Politicians cannot always be guided by opinion polls, however. This is because the respondents often do not understand the costs and consequences of policy decisions or the trade-offs involved in making such decisions.

❼ The media perform a number of functions in American politics, including (a) entertainment, (b) news reporting, (c) identifying public problems, (d) socializing new generations, (e) providing a political forum, and (f) making profits. Broadcast media (television and radio) have been important means of communication since the early twentieth century. New technologies, such as cable television and the Internet, have resulted in a greater number of specialized programs.

❽ The media wield enormous political power during political campaigns and over the affairs of government and government officials by focusing attention on their actions. Today's political campaigns use political advertising and expert management of news coverage. For presidential candidates, how they appear in presidential debates is of major importance.

❾ The relationship between the media and the president is close; each has used the other—sometimes positively, sometimes negatively. The media play an important role in setting the public agenda.

SELECTED PRINT AND MEDIA RESOURCES

Suggested Readings

Abner, Herbert B. *Polling and the Public: What Every Citizen Should Know.* Washington, D.C.: CQ Press, 2001. This clearly written and often entertaining book explains what polls are, how they are conducted and interpreted, and how the wording and ordering of survey questions, as well as the interviewer's techniques, can significantly affect the respondents' answers.

Bardes, Barbara A., and Robert W. Oldendick. *Public Opinion: Measuring the American Mind*, 2d ed. Belmont, Calif.: Wadsworth Publishing Co., 2003. This examination of public opinion polling looks at the uses of public opinion data and recent technological issues in polling in addition to providing excellent coverage of public opinion on important issues over a period of decades.

Herman, Edward S., and Noam Chomsky. *Manufacturing Consent: The Political Economy of the Mass Media*. New York: Pantheon Books, 2002. In this critical look at the U.S. media, the authors contend that media ownership, advertising, official sources, and other "filters" skew the way in which the news media report the news.

Jacobsen, Clay. *Circle of Seven*. Nashville, Tenn.: Broadman & Holman, 2000. A gripping novel pitting one man, a television reporter, against a media group that manipulates opinion polls and the media to further its own ends.

NBC, Marc Robinson, Tom Brokaw, *et al. Brought to You in Living Color: Seventy-five Years of Great Moments in Television and Radio from NBC*. Somerset, N.J.: Wiley, 2002. Although this book focuses on the history of NBC, it also provides an informative history of network programming and entertainment over the past seventy-five years.

Media Resources

All the President's Men—A film, produced by Warner Brothers in 1976, starring Dustin Hoffman and Robert Redford as the two *Washington Post* reporters, Bob Woodward and Carl Bernstein, who broke the story on the Watergate scandal. The film is an excellent portrayal of the *Washington Post* newsroom and the decisions that editors make in such situations.

Disconnected: Politics, the Press, and the Public—This 2000 seminar, introduced by Peter Jennings of ABC News and moderated by Arthur Miller of Harvard Law School, examines how the media affect the national agenda and the standards of political debate. Panelists include Dan Rather of CBS News, Jeff Greenfield of CNN, Democratic Congressman Barney Frank, Republican political consultant Ed Rollins, and others.

Faith and Politics: The Christian Right—This 1995 documentary was hosted by Dan Rather and produced by CBS News. It focuses on the efforts of the Christian conservative movement to affect educational curriculums and public policy. Members of the Christian right who are interviewed include Ralph Reed and Gary Bauer. Critics of the Christian right who are interviewed include Senator Arlen Specter.

LOGGING ON

Yale University Library, one of the great research institutions, offers access to Social Science Libraries and Information Services. If you want to browse through library sources of public opinion data, this is an interesting site to visit. Go to http://www.library.yale.edu/socsci/opinion.

According to its home page, the mission of National Election Studies (NES) "is to produce high-quality data on voting, public opinion, and political participation that serves the research needs of social scientists, teachers, students, and policymakers concerned with understanding the theoretical and empirical foundations of mass politics in a democratic society." This is a good place to obtain information on public opinion. Find it at http://www.umich.edu/~nes.

The Polling Report Web site offers polls and their results organized by topic. It is up to date and easy to use. Go to http://www.pollingreport.com.

The Gallup organization's Web site offers not only polling data (although a user must pay a subscription fee to obtain access to many polling reports) but also information on how polls are constructed, conducted, and interpreted. Go to http://www.gallup.com.

Another site that features articles and polling data on public opinion is the Web site of the Zogby poll at http://www.zogby.com.

The American Review Web page critiques the media, promotes media activism, and calls for media reform. Its URL is http://www.AmericanReview.us.

To view *Slate*, an e-zine of politics and culture published by Microsoft, go to http://Slate.msn.com.

An AP–like system for college newspapers is Uwire, offered by Northwestern University and intended to provide college papers with a reliable source of infor-

mation that directly affects their readers. You can access Uwire at http://www.uwire.com.

For an Internet site that provides links to news media around the world, including alternative media, go to http://www.mediachannel.org.

USING THE INTERNET FOR POLITICAL ANALYSIS

Go to this text's Web site at http://politicalscience. wadsworth.com/schmidtbrief2004. Select "Chapter 6" in the box at the top of the window. Then, in the column on the left-hand side of the window, under "Chapter Resources," click on "Internet Exercises." The Web site will then display the following Internet

exercises that you can perform to learn more about topics covered in this chapter.

Activity 6–1: Public Opinion Research
Activity 6–2: The Gallup Poll
Activity 6–3: The Free Air Time Campaign

ONLINE STUDY GUIDE AND ADDITIONAL RESOURCES

At http://politicalscience.wadsworth.com/ schmidtbrief2004 you will find a free Study Guide to this book that includes tutorial quizzes, essay questions, practice exams, chapter outlines, learning objectives, the glossary, flashcards, crossword puzzles, and Microsoft PowerPoint presentations. Also included in the American Government Resource Center for Chapter 6:

- **InfoTrac® Reader**—Liberals and conservatives; the American left; problems with polls; political socialization; the media; media coverage of political campaigns.

- **You Are There Simulations**—Ideologies; public opinion and voting; politics and the media.

- **Participation Activities**—Discover your ideology; examine different political parties; explore your political views and political socialization; share your input with the media; write a letter to the editor.

- **MicroCase Exercises**—Ideologies; public opinion and voting; politics and the media.

- **Related Links**—Ideologies; public opinion and voting; politics and the media.

- **Video Case Studies**—History of opinion polls; problems with polls; media—the Internet revolution; media and campaigns.

- **Source Readings**—By Walt Whitman and George C. Wallace, plus selected court cases.

The site also contains the Citizen's Survival Guide, information on how to get involved in politics locally and globally, as well as regularly updated features including a Current Events Quiz, In the News, Election Links, updates on the war on terrorism, and more.

CHAPTER 7

Interest Groups and Political Parties

T HE STRUCTURE OF AMERICAN GOVERNMENT invites the participation of **interest groups** at various stages of the policymaking process. For example, after the terrorist attacks of September 11, 2001, the president's requests for antiterrorism legislation spurred fast and furious action by interest groups, which sent their **lobbyists** to persuade Congress to adopt their positions on these bills. The airlines quickly expressed their need for congressional help. They were gratified by an airline bailout bill to make up for the enormous losses they suffered as a result of the closure of U.S. airspace after the attacks and the drop in the number of passengers in the weeks that followed. After the bill passed, however, lobbyists for the many other industries that were hurt by the attacks—including car rental firms, the hotel industry, and travel and tourism companies—began asking for their own assistance packages.

Another way to attempt to influence policymaking is to become an active member of a political party and participate in the selection of political candidates, who, if elected, will hold government positions. A **political party** can be formally defined as a group of political activists who organize to win elections, operate the government, and determine public policy. This definition explains the difference between an interest group and a political party. Interest groups do not want to operate the government, and they do not put forth political candidates—even though they support candidates who will promote their interests if elected or reelected.

In this chapter, we define interest groups, describe how they try to affect the government, and summarize the legal restrictions on lobbyists. We also describe the major political parties, their history, and their organization. Finally, we explain why the two-party system has prevailed in the United States.

A Nation of Joiners

Alexis de Tocqueville observed in 1834 that "in no country of the world has the principle of association been more successfully used or applied to a greater multitude of objectives than in America."[1] The French traveler was amazed at the degree to

Interest Group An organized group of individuals sharing common objectives who actively attempt to influence policymakers.

Lobbyist An organization or individual who attempts to influence legislation and the administrative decisions of government.

Political Party A group of political activists who organize to win elections, operate the government, and determine public policy.

which Americans formed groups to solve civic problems, establish social relationships, and speak for their economic or political interests. Perhaps James Madison, when he wrote *Federalist Paper* No. 10 (see Appendix C), had already judged the character of his country's citizens similarly. He supported the creation of a large republic with many states to encourage the formation of many interests. The multitude of interests, in Madison's view, would work to discourage the formation of an oppressive majority interest.

Many Interest Groups

Surely, neither Madison nor de Tocqueville foresaw the formation of more than a hundred thousand associations in the United States. Poll data show that more than two-thirds of all Americans belong to at least one group or association. While the majority of these affiliations could not be classified as "interest groups" in the political sense, Americans do understand the principles of working in groups.

Today, interest groups range from the elementary school parent-teacher association and the local "Stop the Sewer Plant Association" to the statewide association of insurance agents. They include small groups such as local environmental organizations and national groups such as the Boy Scouts of America, the American Civil Liberties Union, the National Education Association, and the American League of Lobbyists.

Interest Groups: Elitist or Pluralist?

The elite theory of politics presumes that most Americans are uninterested in politics and are willing to let a small, elite group of citizens make decisions for them. Pluralist theory, in contrast, views politics as a struggle among various interest groups to gain benefits for their members. The pluralist approach views compromise among various competing interests as the essence of political decision making. Which of these theories best describes interest groups in American politics? To be sure, most interest groups have a middle-class or upper-class bias. Members of interest groups can afford to pay the membership fees, are generally fairly well educated, and normally participate in the political process to a greater extent than the "average" American. On the whole, however, the importance of interest groups tends to favor the pluralist theory of American politics.

Types of Interest Groups

Thousands of groups exist to influence government. Among the major types of interest groups are those that represent the main sectors of the economy. In recent years, a number of "public-interest" organizations have been formed to represent the needs of the general citizenry, including some "single-issue" groups. The interests of foreign governments and foreign businesses are also represented in the American political arena.

Economic Interest Groups

More interest groups are formed to represent economic interests than any other set of interests. The variety of economic interest groups mirrors the complexity of the American economy. The major sectors that seek influence in Washington, D.C.,

INFOTRAC

To find out more about these groups, use the term "pressure groups" in the Subject guide.

include business, agriculture, labor unions and their members, government workers, and professionals.

Business Interest Groups.

Thousands of business groups and trade associations work to influence government policies that affect their respective industries. "Umbrella groups" represent certain types of businesses or companies that deal in a particular type of product. The U.S. Chamber of Commerce, for example, is an umbrella group that represents businesses, and the National Association of Manufacturers is an umbrella group that represents only manufacturing concerns.

Some business groups are decidedly more powerful than others. The U.S. Chamber of Commerce, which has more than 200,000 member companies, can bring constituent influence to bear on every member of Congress. The National Association of Manufacturers has a staff of more than sixty people in Washington, D.C., and can mobilize dozens of well-educated, articulate lobbyists to work the corridors of Congress on issues of concern to its members. The pharmaceutical lobby, which represents many of the major drug manufacturers, is one of the most powerful interest groups in Washington because of its financial resources. This lobby has over six hundred registered lobbyists and spent close to $200 million in the 1999–2000 presidential election cycle for lobbying and campaign expenditures.

Agricultural Interest Groups.

American farmers and their employees represent less than 2 percent of the U.S. population. In spite of this, farmers' influence on legislation beneficial to their interests has been enormous. Farmers have succeeded in their aims because they have very strong interest groups. They are geographically dispersed and therefore have many representatives and senators to speak for them.

The American Farm Bureau Federation, established in 1919, has several million members (many of whom are not actually farmers) and is usually seen as conservative. It was instrumental in getting government guarantees of "fair" prices during the Great Depression in the 1930s.[2] Another important agricultural interest organization is the National Farmers' Union (NFU), which is considered more liberal.

As proof of how powerful the agricultural lobby still is in the United States, in May 2002 President George W. Bush signed the Farm Security and Rural Investment Act, which authorized the largest agricultural subsidy in U.S. history.

Labor Interest Groups.

Interest groups representing the **labor movement** date back to at least 1886, when the American Federation of Labor (AFL) was formed. In 1955, the AFL joined forces with the Congress of Industrial Organizations (CIO). Today, the combined AFL–CIO is a large union with a membership exceeding 13 million workers and an active political arm called the Committee on Political Education. In a sense, the AFL–CIO is a union of unions.

The role of unions in American society has weakened in recent years, as witnessed by a decline in union membership. In the age of automation and with the rise of the **service sector,** blue-collar workers in basic industries (autos, steel, and the like) represent a smaller and smaller percentage of the total working population. Because of this decline in the industrial sector of the economy, national unions are looking to nontraditional areas for their membership, including migrant farm workers, service workers, and, most recently, public employees—such as police officers, firefighting

Labor Movement
Generally, the economic and political expression of working-class interests; politically, the organization of working-class interests.

Service Sector The sector of the economy that provides services—such as health care, banking, and education—in contrast to the sector that produces goods.

personnel, and teachers, including college professors. Indeed, public-sector unions are the fastest-growing labor organizations.

Public Employee Unions.   The degree of unionization in the private sector has declined since 1965, but this has been partially offset by growth in the unionization of public employees. With a total membership of more than 7.1 million, public-sector unions are likely to continue expanding.

Both the American Federation of State, County, and Municipal Employees and the American Federation of Teachers are members of the AFL–CIO's Public Employee Department. Over the years, public employee unions have become quite militant and are often involved in strikes. Most of these strikes are illegal, because almost no public employees have the right to strike.

A powerful interest group lobbying on behalf of public employees is the National Education Association (NEA), a nationwide organization of about 2.5 million teachers and others connected with education. Many NEA locals function as labor unions. The NEA lobbies intensively for increased public funding of education.

Interest Groups of Professionals.   Numerous professional organizations exist, including the American Bar Association, the Association of General Contractors of America, the Institute of Electrical and Electronic Engineers, and others. Some professional groups, such as lawyers and doctors, are more influential than others because of their social status. Lawyers have a unique advantage—a large number of members of Congress share their profession. In terms of money spent on lobbying, however, one professional organization stands head and shoulders above the rest—the American Medical Association (AMA). Founded in 1847, it is now affiliated with more than 2,000 local and state medical societies and has a total membership of 300,000.

Environmental Groups

Environmental interest groups are not new. The National Audubon Society was founded in 1905 to protect the snowy egret from the commercial demand for hat decorations. The patron of the Sierra Club, John Muir, worked for the creation of national parks more than a century ago. But the blossoming of national environmental groups with mass memberships did not occur until the 1970s. Since the first Earth Day, organized in 1972, many interest groups have sprung up to protect the environment in general or unique ecological niches. The groups range from the National Wildlife Federation, with a membership of more than 4.5 million and an emphasis on education, to the more elite Environmental Defense Fund, with a membership of 300,000 and a focus on influencing federal policy. Other groups include the Nature Conservancy, which uses members' contributions to buy up threatened natural areas and either give them to state or local governments or manage them itself, and the more radical Greenpeace Society and Earth First.

Public Interest The best interests of the overall community; the national good, rather than narrow interests.

Public-Interest Groups

Public interest is a difficult term to define because, as we noted earlier, there are many publics in our nation of 295 million. It is almost impossible for one particular public policy to benefit everybody, which makes it practically impossible to define the public interest. Nonetheless, over the past few decades, a variety of lobbying organizations have been formed "in the public interest."

Nader Organizations.   The best-known and perhaps the most effective public-interest groups are those organized under the leadership of consumer activist Ralph Nader. Nader's rise to the top began after the publication, in 1965, of his book *Unsafe at Any Speed*, a lambasting critique of the purported attempt by General Motors (GM) to keep from the public detrimental information about its rear-engine Corvair. Partly as a result of Nader's book, Congress began to consider testimony in favor of an auto-mobile safety bill. GM made a clumsy attempt to discredit Nader's background. Nader sued, the media exploited the story, and when GM settled out of court for $425,000, Nader became the recognized champion of consumer interests. Since then, Nader has turned over much of his income to the more than sixty public-interest groups that he has formed or sponsored. In 2000, Nader ran for president on the ticket of the Green Party.

Other Public-Interest Groups.   One of the largest public-interest groups is Common Cause, founded in 1968. Its goal is to reorder national priorities toward "the public" and to make governmental institutions more respon-sive to the needs of the public. Other public-interest groups include the League of Women Voters, founded in 1920. Although nonpartisan, it has lobbied for the Equal Rights Amendment and for government reform. The Consumer Federation of America is an alliance of about two hundred local and national organizations interested in consumer protection. The American Civil Liberties Union dates back to World War I (1914–1918), when, under a dif-ferent name, it defended draft resisters. It gen-erally enters into legal disputes related to Bill of Rights issues.

Other Interest Groups

Single-interest groups, being narrowly focused, may be able to call more attention to their causes because they have simple and straightfor-ward goals and because their members tend to care intensely about the issues. Thus, such groups can easily motivate their members to contact legislators or to organize demonstra-tions in support of their policy goals.

A number of interest groups focus on just one issue. The abortion debate has created var-ious groups opposed to abortion (such as the

AP Photo/Paul Sakuma

Sierra Club president Adam Werbach holds a press conference in San Francisco, April 25, 1998, to announce that the Sierra Club will not call for major curbs on immigration. Why might an environmental organization take a position on immigration?

Right to Life organization) and groups in favor of abortion rights (such as NARAL Pro-Choice America). Other single-issue groups are the National Rifle Association, the Right to Work Committee (an antiunion group), and the American Israel Public Affairs Committee (a pro-Israel group).

Still other groups represent Americans who share a common characteristic, such as age or ethnicity. Such interest groups lobby for legislation that may benefit their members in terms of rights or just represent a viewpoint.

The AARP (formerly the American Association of Retired Persons) is one of the most powerful interest groups in Washington, D.C., and, according to some, the strongest lobbying group in the United States. It is certainly the nation's largest interest group, with a membership of over 35 million. The AARP has accomplished much for its members over the years. It played a significant role in the creation of Medicare and Medicaid, as well as in obtaining cost-of-living increases in Social Security payments. Recently, the AARP has been actively lobbying Congress to rein in the escalating costs of prescription drugs and to add prescription drug coverage to Medicare.

Foreign Governments

Homegrown interests are not the only players in the game. Washington, D.C., is also the center for lobbying by foreign governments as well as private foreign interests. The governments of the largest U.S. trading partners, such as Japan, South Korea, Canada, and the European Union (EU) countries, maintain substantial research and lobbying staffs. Even smaller nations, such as those in the Caribbean, engage lobbyists when vital legislation affecting their trade interests is considered. Frequently, these foreign interests hire former representatives or former senators to promote their positions on Capitol Hill.

Interest Group Strategies

Interest groups employ a wide range of techniques and strategies to promote their policy goals. The key to success for interest groups is access to government officials. To gain such access, interest groups and their representatives try to cultivate long-term relationships with legislators and government officials. The best of these relationships are based on mutual respect and cooperation. The interest group provides the official with excellent sources of information and assistance, and the official in turn gives the group opportunities to express its views.

The techniques used by interest groups can be divided into direct and indirect techniques. With **direct techniques,** the interest group and its lobbyists approach the officials personally to press their case. With **indirect techniques,** in contrast, the interest group uses the general public or individual constituents to influence the government on behalf of the interest group.

Direct Techniques

Lobbying, publicizing ratings of legislative behavior, and providing campaign assistance are three of the direct techniques used by interest groups.

Direct Technique
An interest group activity that involves interaction with government officials to further the group's goals.

Indirect Technique
A strategy employed by interest groups that uses third parties to influence government officials.

Lobbying Techniques. As might be guessed, the term *lobbying* comes from the activities of private citizens regularly congregating in the lobbies of legislative chambers before a session to petition legislators. In the latter part of the 1800s, railroad and industrial groups openly bribed state legislators to pass legislation beneficial to their interests, giving lobbying a well-deserved bad name. Most lobbyists today are professionals. They are either consultants to a company or interest group or members of one of the Washington, D.C., law firms that specialize in providing such services.

Lobbyists engage in an array of activities to influence legislation and government policy. These include the following:

1. Engaging in private meetings with public officials, including the president's advisers, to make known the interests of the lobbyists' clients. Although acting on behalf of their clients, often lobbyists furnish needed information to senators and representatives (and government agency appointees) that these officials could not easily obtain on their own. It is to the lobbyist's advantage to provide accurate information so that policymakers will rely on this source in the future.

2. Testifying before congressional committees for or against proposed legislation.

3. Testifying before executive rulemaking agencies—such as the Federal Trade Commission or the Consumer Product Safety Commission—for or against proposed rules.

4. Assisting legislators or bureaucrats in drafting legislation or prospective regulations. Often, lobbyists furnish advice on the specific details of legislation.

5. Inviting legislators to social occasions, such as cocktail parties, boating expeditions, and other events, including conferences at exotic locations. Most lobbyists believe that meeting legislators in a relaxed social setting is effective.

6. Providing political information to legislators and other government officials. Often, the lobbyists have better information than the party leadership about how other legislators are going to vote. In this case, the political information they furnish may be a key to legislative success.

7. Supplying nominations for federal appointments to the executive branch.

The Ratings Game. Many interest groups attempt to influence the overall behavior of legislators through their rating systems. Each year, the interest group selects legislation that it believes is most important to the organization's goals and then monitors how legislators vote on it. Each legislator is given a score based on the percentage of times that he or she voted in favor of the group's position. The usual scheme ranges from 0 to 100 percent. In the ratings scheme of the liberal Americans for Democratic Action, for example, a rating of 100 means that a member of Congress voted with the group on every issue and is, therefore, very liberal. Ratings are a shorthand way of describing members' voting records for interested citizens. They can also be used to embarrass members. For example, an environmental group identifies the twelve representatives who the group believes have the worst voting records on environmental issues and labels them "the Dirty Dozen."

Campaign Assistance. Interest groups have additional strategies to use in their attempts to influence government policies. Groups recognize that the greatest concern of legislators is to be reelected, so they focus on the legislators' campaign needs. Associations with large memberships, such as labor unions, are able to provide workers for political campaigns, including precinct workers to get out the vote, volunteers to put up posters and pass out literature, and people to staff telephone banks for campaign headquarters.

In many states where certain interest groups have large memberships, candidates vie for the groups' endorsements in the campaign. Gaining those endorsements may be automatic, or it may require that the candidates participate in debates or interviews with the interest groups. Endorsements are important because an interest group usually publicizes its choices in its membership publication and because the candidate can use the endorsement in her or his campaign literature. Traditionally, labor unions have endorsed Democratic Party candidates. Republican candidates, however, often try to persuade union locals at least to refrain from any endorsement. Making no endorsement can then be perceived as disapproval of the Democratic Party candidate.

Indirect Techniques

Interest groups can also try to influence government policy by working through others, who may be constituents or the general public. Indirect techniques mask the interest group's own activities and make the effort appear to be spontaneous. Furthermore, legislators and government officials are often more impressed by contacts from constituents than from an interest group's lobbyist.

Generating Public Pressure. In some instances, interest groups try to produce a "ground swell" of public pressure to influence the government. Such efforts may include advertisements in national magazines and newspapers, mass mailings, television publicity, and demonstrations. The Internet and satellite links make communication efforts even more effective. Interest groups may commission polls to find out what the public's sentiments are and then publicize the results. The intent of this activity is to convince policymakers that public opinion overwhelmingly supports the group's position.

Using Constituents as Lobbyists. Interest groups also use constituents to lobby for the group's goals. In the "shotgun" approach, the interest group tries to mobilize large numbers of constituents to write, phone, or send e-mails to their legislators or the president. Often, the group provides postcards or form letters for constituents to fill out and mail. These efforts are effective on Capitol Hill only when there is a very large number of responses, however, because legislators know that the voters did not initiate the communications on their own.

A more powerful variation of this technique uses only important constituents. With this approach, known as the "rifle" technique or the "Utah plant manager theory," the interest group might, for example, ask the manager of a local plant in Utah to contact the senator from Utah.[3] Because the constituent is seen as being responsible for many jobs or other resources, the legislator is more likely to listen carefully to the constituent's concerns about legislation than to a paid lobbyist.

Interest Groups and Campaign Money

In the last two decades, interest groups and individual companies have found new, very direct ways to contact elected officials through campaign donations. Elected officials, in turn, have become dependent on these donations to run increasingly expensive campaigns. Interest groups and corporations funnel money to political candidates through several devices: **political action committees (PACs), soft money** contributions, and **issue advocacy advertising.** These devices developed as a means of circumventing the campaign-financing reforms of the early 1970s, which limited contributions by individuals and unions to set amounts.

PACs and Political Campaigns.

The 1974 and 1976 amendments to the Federal Election Campaign Act of 1971 allow corporations, labor unions, and other interest groups to set up PACs to raise money for candidates. For a federal PAC to be legitimate, the money must be raised from at least fifty volunteer donors and must be given to at least five candidates in the federal election. PACs can contribute up to $5,000 to each candidate in each election. Each corporation or each union is limited to one PAC. As you might imagine, corporate PACs obtain funds from executives and managers in their firms, and unions obtain PAC funds from their members.

The number of PACs has grown significantly since 1977, as has the amount they spend on elections. There were about 1,000 PACs in 1976; today, there are more than 4,500. Total spending by PACs grew from $19 million in 1973 to almost $900 million in 1999–2000. About 32 percent of all campaign money spent by House candidates in 2000 came from PACs.[4]

Campaign-financing regulations clearly limit the amount that a PAC can give to any one candidate, but there is no limit on the amount that a PAC can spend on issue advocacy, either on behalf of a candidate or party or in opposition to one.

Soft Money.

In the 1999–2000 election cycle, corporations, unions, and interest groups spent more than $493 million on political campaigns for federal offices through soft money, a practice that was outlawed by the campaign-financing reform legislation of 2002. Soft money contributions have included all contributions to campaign funds that are unregulated by federal or state law. In general, such contributions were made to national party committees for certain "party-building" purposes, including voter-registration drives, the national convention, and general overhead. Soft money contributions are permitted at the state level in thirty states but are prohibited in the rest.[5]

Issue Advocacy Advertising.

Corporations and interest groups also use television, radio, the Internet, and billboards to advertise their positions on issues and to persuade the public to share their views. What is new in the last ten years is the proliferation of issue advocacy ads during political campaigns. These ads call attention to the positions or voting patterns of a candidate but do not tell the voter to "vote for" or "vote against" that person. Thus, the advertising is protected as "free speech" under the First Amendment rather than regulated as campaign advertising. The 2002 campaign-financing reform law includes a provision that prohibits issue advocacy groups from airing commercials supporting or opposing candidates

Political Action Committee (PAC) A committee set up by and representing a corporation, labor union, or special interest group. PACs raise and give campaign donations.

Soft Money Campaign contributions unregulated by federal or state law, usually given to parties and party committees to help fund general party activities.

Issue Advocacy Advertising Advertising paid for by interest groups that supports or opposes a candidate or a candidate's position on an issue without mentioning voting or elections.

INFOTRAC

For updates and more information on PACs, use the term "political action committees" in the Subject guide.

sixty days before the general election and thirty days before a primary election, however.

Regulating Lobbyists

INFOTRAC

For updates and more information on lobbying, use the term "lobbying" in the Subject guide.

Congress made its first attempt to control lobbyists and lobbying activities through Title III of the Legislative Reorganization Act of 1946, otherwise known as the Federal Regulation of Lobbying Act. The act actually provided for public disclosure more than for regulation. It required lobbyists to register and to report on their activities. Because of various shortcomings, including how *lobbyist* was defined, the act had little effect.

The reform-minded Congress of 1995–1996 overhauled the lobbying legislation, fundamentally changing the ground rules for those who seek to influence the federal government. Lobbying legislation passed in 1995 included the following provisions:

1. A lobbyist is defined as anyone who spends at least 20 percent of his or her time lobbying members of Congress, their staffs, or executive-branch officials.

2. Lobbyists must register with the clerk of the House and the secretary of the Senate within forty-five days of being hired or of making their first contact. The registra-

"A <u>very</u> special interest to see you, Senator."

tion requirement applies to organizations that spend more than $20,000 in one year or to individuals who are paid more than $5,000 annually for lobbying work.

3. Semiannual reports must disclose the general nature of the lobbying effort, specific issues and bill numbers, the estimated cost of the campaign, and a list of the branches of government contacted. The names of the individuals contacted need not be reported.

4. Representatives of U.S.–owned subsidiaries of foreign-owned firms and lawyers who represent foreign entities also are required to register.

5. The requirements exempt "grassroots" lobbying efforts and those of tax-exempt organizations, such as religious groups.

As they debated the 1995 law, both the House and the Senate adopted new rules on gifts and travel expenses: the House adopted a flat ban on gifts, and the Senate limited gifts to $50 in value and to no more than $100 in gifts from a single source in a year. There are exceptions for gifts from family members and for home-state products and souvenirs, such as T-shirts and coffee mugs. Both chambers ban all-expenses-paid trips, golf outings, and other such junkets. An exception applies for "widely attended" events, however, or if the member is a primary speaker at an event. These gift rules stopped the broad practice of taking members of Congress to lunch or dinner, but the various exemptions and exceptions have caused much controversy as the Senate and House Ethics Committees have considered individual cases.

What Is a Political Party?

Around election time, the polls and the media concentrate on the state of the political parties. Every poll asks the question, "Do you consider yourself to be a Republican, a Democrat, or an independent?" Most Americans are able to answer that question, and more than 30 percent describe themselves as **independents**—that is, they do not identify with a political party.

> **Independent** A voter or candidate who does not identify with a political party.

In the United States, being a member of a political party does not require paying dues, passing an examination, or swearing an oath of allegiance. If nothing is really required to be a member of a political party, what, then, is a political party? As mentioned earlier in this chapter, a political party is a group that seeks to win elections, operate the government, and determine public policy. Political parties are thus quite different from interest groups, which seek to influence, not run, the government.

Political parties also differ from **factions,** which are smaller groups that are trying to obtain power or benefits. Factions generally preceded the formation of political parties in American history, and the term is still used to refer to groups within parties that follow a particular leader or share a regional identification or an ideological viewpoint. For example, the Republican Party sometimes is seen as having a northeastern "moderate" faction that holds more moderate positions than the dominant conservative majority of the party. Factions are subgroups within parties that may try to capture a nomination or get a position adopted by the party. The key difference between factions and parties is that factions do not have a permanent organization, whereas political parties do.

> **Faction** A group or bloc in a legislature or political party acting in pursuit of some special interest or position.

Functions of Political Parties in the United States

Political parties in the United States engage in a wide variety of activities, many of which are discussed in the remainder of this chapter. Through these activities, parties perform a number of functions for the political system. These functions include the following:

1. *Recruiting candidates for public office.* Because it is the goal of parties to gain control of government, they must work to recruit candidates for all elective offices. Often, this means recruiting candidates to run against powerful incumbents or for unpopular jobs. Yet if parties did not search out and encourage political hopefuls, far more offices would be uncontested, and voters would have limited choices.

2. *Organizing and running elections.* Although elections are a government activity, political parties actually organize the voter-registration drives, recruit the volunteers to work at the polls, provide most of the campaign activity to stimulate interest in the election, and work to increase voter participation.

3. *Presenting alternative policies to the electorate.* In contrast to factions, which are often centered on individual politicians, parties are focused on a set of political positions. The Democrats or Republicans in Congress who vote together do so because they represent constituencies that have similar expectations and demands.

4. *Accepting responsibility for operating the government.* When a party elects the president or governor and members of the legislature, it accepts the responsibility for running the government. This includes staffing the executive branch with loyal party supporters and developing linkages among the elected officials to gain support for policies and their implementation.

5. *Acting as the organized opposition to the party in power.* The "out" party, or the one that does not control the government, is expected to articulate its own policies and oppose the winning party when appropriate. By organizing the opposition to the "in" party, the opposition party forces debate on the policy alternatives.

The major functions of American political parties are carried out by a small, relatively loose-knit nucleus of party activists. This arrangement is quite different from the more highly structured, mass-membership party organization typical of certain European working-class parties. American parties concentrate on winning elections rather than on signing up large numbers of deeply committed, dues-paying members who believe passionately in the party's program.

A Short History of Political Parties in the United States

Two-Party System A political system in which only two parties have a reasonable chance of winning.

The United States has a **two-party system,** and that system has been around since about 1800. The function and character of the political parties, as well as the emergence of the two-party system itself, have much to do with the unique historical forces operating from this country's beginning as an independent nation. Indeed, James Madison linked the emergence of political parties to the form of government created by our Constitution.

Generally, we can divide the evolution of our nation's political parties into seven periods:

1. The creation of parties, from 1789 to 1816.

2. The era of one-party rule, or personal politics, from 1816 to 1828.

3. The period from Andrew Jackson's presidency to just before the Civil War, from 1828 to 1860.

4. The Civil War and post–Civil War period, from 1860 to 1896.

5. The Republican ascendancy and the progressive period, from 1896 to 1932.

6. The New Deal period, from 1932 to 1968.

7. The modern period, from 1968 to the present.

The Formative Years: Federalists and Anti-Federalists

The first partisan political division in the United States occurred before the adoption of the Constitution. The Federalists pushed for adoption of the Constitution, whereas the Anti-Federalists were against ratification.

In September 1796, George Washington, who had served as president for almost two full terms, decided not to run again. In his farewell address, he made a somber assessment of the nation's future. Washington felt that the country might be destroyed by the "baneful effects of the spirit of party." Nevertheless, in the years after the ratification of the Constitution, Americans came to realize that something more permanent than a faction would be necessary to identify candidates for office and represent political differences among the people. The result was two political parties.

One party was the Federalists, which included John Adams, the second president (1797–1801). The Federalists represented commercial interests such as merchants and large planters. They supported a strong national government.

Thomas Jefferson led the other party, which came to be called the Republicans. (These Republicans should not be confused with the later Republican Party of Abraham Lincoln. To avoid confusion, some scholars refer to Jefferson's party as the Democratic-Republicans, but this name was never used during the time that the party existed.) Jefferson's Republicans represented artisans and farmers. They strongly supported states' rights. In 1800, when Jefferson defeated Adams in the presidential contest, one of the world's first peaceful transfers of power from one party to another was achieved.

Thomas Jefferson, founder of the first Republican Party. His election to the presidency in 1800 was one of the world's first transfers of power through a free election.

Library of Congress

The Era of Good Feelings

From 1800 to 1820, a majority of U.S. voters regularly elected Republicans to the presidency and to Congress. By 1816, the Federalist Party had virtually collapsed, and two-party competition did not really exist. Although during elections the Republicans opposed the Federalists' call for a stronger, more active central government, they undertook such active government policies as acquiring the Louisiana Territory and Florida and establishing a national bank. Because there was no real political opposition to the Republicans and thus little political debate, the administration of James Monroe (1817–1825) came to be known as the **era of good feelings.**

National Two-Party Rule: Democrats and Whigs

Organized two-party politics returned in 1824. With the election of John Quincy Adams as president, the Republican Party split in two. The followers of Adams called themselves National Republicans. The followers of Andrew Jackson, who defeated Adams in 1828, formed the **Democratic Party.** Later, the National Republicans took the name **Whig Party,** which had been a traditional name for British liberals. The Whigs stood for federal spending on "internal improvements," such as roads, and tended toward moralism in politics. The Democrats opposed both policies. The Democrats, who were the stronger of the two parties, favored personal liberty and opportunity for the "common man." It was implicitly understood that the "common man" was a white man.

The Civil War Crisis

In the 1850s, hostility between the North and South over the issue of slavery divided both parties. The Whigs were the first to split in two. The Whigs had been the party of an active federal government, but southerners had come to believe that "a government strong enough to build roads is a government strong enough to free your slaves." The southern Whigs therefore ceased to exist as an organized party. The northern Whigs united with antislavery Democrats and members of the radical antislavery Free Soil Party to form the modern **Republican Party.**

The Post–Civil War Period

After the Civil War, the Democratic Party was able to heal its divisions. Southern resentment of the Republicans' role in defeating the South and fears that the federal government would intervene on behalf of African Americans ensured that the Democrats would dominate the white South for the next century. Northern Democrats feared a strong government for other reasons. The Republicans thought that the government should promote business and economic growth, but many Republicans also wanted to use the power of government to impose evangelical Protestant moral values on society. Democrats opposed what they saw as culturally coercive measures. Many Republicans wanted to limit or even prohibit the sale of alcohol. They favored the establishment of public schools—with a Protestant curriculum. As a result, Catholics were strongly Democratic. In this period, the parties were very evenly matched in strength.

Era of Good Feelings The years from 1817 to 1825, when James Monroe was president and there was, in effect, no political opposition.

Democratic Party One of the two major American political parties evolving out of the Republican Party of Thomas Jefferson.

Whig Party A major party in the United States during the first half of the nineteenth century, formally established in 1836. The Whig Party was anti-Jackson and represented a variety of regional interests.

Republican Party One of the two major American political parties. It emerged in the 1850s as an antislavery party and consisted of former northern Whigs and antislavery Democrats.

INFOTRAC

To find out more about President Jackson, use the term "Andrew Jackson" in the Subject guide.

In the 1890s, however, the Republicans gained a decisive edge. In that decade, the populist movement emerged in the West and South to champion the interests of small farmers, who were often greatly in debt. Populists supported inflation, or the devaluation of the currency, which benefited debtors by reducing the value of outstanding debts. In 1896, when William Jennings Bryan became the Democratic candidate for president, the Democrats embraced populism. As it turned out, the few western farmers who were drawn to the Democrats by this step were greatly outnumbered by urban working-class voters who believed that inflation would reduce the value of their paychecks and who therefore became Republicans. From 1896 until

Andrew Jackson earned the name "Old Hickory" for exploits during the War of 1812. In 1828, Jackson was elected president as the candidate of the new Democratic Party.

Corbis/Bettmann

1932, the Republicans were able successfully to present themselves as the party that knew how to manage the economy.

The Progressive Interlude

In the early 1900s, a spirit of political reform arose in both major parties. Called progressivism, this spirit was compounded of a fear of the growing power of great corporations and a belief that honest, impartial government could effectively regulate the economy. In 1912, the Republican Party temporarily split as former Republican president Theodore Roosevelt campaigned for the presidency on a third-party Progressive ticket. The Republican split permitted the election of Woodrow Wilson, the Democratic candidate, along with a Democratic Congress.

Like Roosevelt, Wilson considered himself a progressive, although he and Roosevelt did not agree on how progressivism ought to be implemented. Wilson's progressivism marked the beginning of a radical change in Democratic policies. Dating back to its very foundation, the Democratic Party had been the party of limited government. Under Wilson, the Democrats became for the first time at least as receptive as the Republicans to government action in the economy.

The New Deal Era

The Republican ascendancy resumed after Wilson left office. It ended with the election of 1932, in the depths of the Great Depression. Republican Herbert Hoover was president when the depression began in 1929. While Hoover took some measures to fight the depression, they fell far short of what the public demanded. Significantly, Hoover opposed federal relief for the unemployed and the destitute. In 1932, Democrat Franklin D. Roosevelt was elected president by overwhelming margins.

The Great Depression shattered the working-class belief in Republican economic competence. Under Roosevelt, the Democrats began to make major interventions in the economy to combat the depression and to relieve the suffering of the unemployed. Roosevelt's New Deal relief programs were open to all citizens, both black and white. As a result, African Americans began to support the Democratic Party in large numbers—a development that would have stunned any American politician of the 1800s.

Roosevelt's political coalition was broad enough to establish the Democrats as the new majority party, in place of the Republicans. In the 1950s, Republican Dwight D. Eisenhower, the leading U.S. general during World War II, won two terms as president. Otherwise, with minor interruptions, the Democratic ascendancy lasted until 1968.

An Era of Divided Government

INFOTRAC

To find out more, use the term "divided government" in Keywords.

The New Deal coalition managed the unlikely feat of including both African Americans and whites who were hostile to African American advancement. This balancing act came to an end in the 1960s, a decade that was marked by the civil rights movement, by several years of "race riots" in major cities, and by the increasingly heated movement against the Vietnam War. For many economically liberal, socially conservative voters, especially in the South, social issues had become more important than economic ones, and these voters left the Democrats.

The result, since 1968, has been a nation almost evenly divided in politics. In presidential elections, the Republicans have had more success than the Democrats. Until recently, Congress remained Democratic, but official party labels can be misleading. Some of the Democrats were southern conservatives who normally voted with the Republicans on issues. As these conservative Democrats retired, they were largely replaced by Republicans.

The election of George H. W. Bush in 1988 may have signaled the beginning of a true era of **divided government.** Republican Bush won the presidency, but his Republican Party lost seats in the House and Senate. In 1992, Democrat Bill Clinton won the presidency, but his party lost congressional seats, presaging the Democrats' debacle in 1994 when the Republicans took control of both the House and the Senate. After the 2000 elections, divided government took on a new meaning. Although Republican George W. Bush won the presidency, Congress became almost evenly divided, with the Republicans holding a slim majority in the House and the Democrats holding an even narrower majority in the Senate. The Republicans succeeded in 2002 in holding on to the House and in regaining control of the Senate, but their majorities remained slim. The future impact of the events of 9/11 on party preferences is difficult to gauge—see this chapter's *America's Security* feature.

Party Organization

Each of the American political parties is often seen as having a pyramid-shaped organization, with the national chairperson and committee at the top and the local precinct chairperson on the bottom. This structure, however, does not accurately reflect the relative power of the individual parts of the **party organization.** If it did, the national

Divided Government
A situation in which one major political party controls the presidency and the other controls the chambers of Congress, or in which one party controls a state governorship and the other controls the state legislature.

Party Organization
The formal structure and leadership of a political party, including election committees; local, state, and national executives; and paid professional staff.

AMERICA'S SECURITY

Party Politics in the Aftermath of 9/11

times of crisis, voters tend to emphasize security—a concern that gives incumbents an advantage. This means that as long as Americans view security as America's most important problem, the Republican Party will hold the advantage.

WHAT HAPPENED TO THE LOYAL OPPOSITION?

Given the advantage that national security concerns gave the Republican Party, the Democrats had to ask the question: What could they oppose and still remain a loyal opposition? For some time, whenever a Democrat criticized the way the Bush administration was running the war on terrorism, Republicans and even some of the media quickly lambasted that critic. The problem for the Democrats was to come up with alternative proposals for making America safe from terrorists.

The Democrats clearly faced a dilemma. They wanted to please antiwar liberals. At the same time, they did not want to alienate moderate voters.

The political reality today is that partisanship has no place in a discussion of America's security, at least for most voters. This has made it difficult for Democrats to raise any complaints about the war on terrorism, including the war against Iraq.

FOR CRITICAL ANALYSIS

If the Democratic Party can never appear to be "weak" on America's security, does this mean that President Bush has absolute power in running the war on terrorism? What forces might stop his administration from expanding the war on terrorism too far?

U ntil 9/11, the Republican Party did not speak with a single voice. Some Republicans wanted President George W. Bush to focus on social issues. Others wanted him to focus on economic issues, such as tax cuts.

THE REPUBLICANS FIND THEIR VOICE

In the months immediately after 9/11, concerns over America's security took center stage. During

---

chairperson of the Democratic Party or the Republican Party, along with the national committee, could simply dictate how the organization was to be run, just as if it were ExxonMobil Corporation or Ford Motor Company. In reality, the political parties have a confederal structure, in which each unit has significant autonomy and is only loosely linked to the other units.

The National Party Organization

Each party has a national organization, the most clearly institutional part of which is the **national convention,** held every four years. The convention is used to nominate

National Convention
The meeting held every four years by each major party to select presidential and vice presidential candidates, to write a platform, to choose a national committee, and to conduct party business.

Party Platform A document drawn up at each national convention, outlining the policies, positions, and principles of the party.

the presidential and vice presidential candidates. In addition, the **party platform** is developed at the national convention. The platform sets forth the party's position on the issues and makes promises to be carried out if the party wins the presidency.

After the convention, the platform frequently is neglected or ignored by party candidates who disagree with it. Because candidates are trying to win votes from a wide spectrum of voters, it is counterproductive to emphasize the fairly narrow and sometimes controversial goals set forth in the platform. The work of Gerald M. Pomper has shown, however, that once elected, the parties do try to carry out platform promises and that roughly three-fourths of the promises eventually become law.[6] Of course, some general goals, such as economic prosperity, are included in the platforms of both parties.

Convention Delegates.   The party convention provides the most striking illustration of the difference between the ordinary members of a party, or party identifiers, and party activists. As a series of studies by the *New York Times* shows, delegates to the national party conventions are quite different from ordinary party identifiers. Delegates to the Democratic National Convention are far more liberal than ordinary Democratic voters. Likewise, delegates to the Republican National Convention are far more conservative than ordinary Republicans. Why does this happen? In part, it is because a person, to become a delegate, must gather votes in a primary election from party members who care enough to vote in a primary or be appointed by party leaders. Also, the primaries generally pit presidential candidates against each other on intraparty issues. Competition within each party tends to pull candidates away from the center, and delegates even more so. Often, the most important activity for the convention is making peace among the delegates who support different candidates and helping them accept a party platform that will appeal to the general electorate.

National Committee A standing committee of a national political party established to direct and coordinate party activities between national party conventions.

The National Committee.   At the national convention, each of the parties formally chooses a national standing committee, elected by the individual state parties. This **national committee** directs and coordinates party activities during the following four years. One of the jobs of the national committee is to ratify the presidential nominee's choice of a national chairperson, who in principle acts as the spokesperson for the party. (If the nominee loses, however, the chairperson is often changed.) The major responsibility of the chairperson is to manage the national election campaign. The national chairperson does such jobs as establish a national party headquarters, raise campaign funds and distribute them to state parties and to candidates, and appear in the media as a party spokesperson. The national chairperson, along with the national committee, attempts to maintain some sort of liaison among the different levels of the party organization. The fact is that the real strength and power of a national party are at the state level.

State Central Committee The principal organized structure of each political party within each state. This committee is responsible for carrying out policy decisions of the party's state convention.

The State Party Organization

Because every state party is unique, it is impossible to describe what an "average" state political party is like. Nonetheless, state parties have several organizational features in common. Each state party has a chairperson, a committee, and a number of local organizations. In theory, the role of the **state central committee**—the principal organized structure of each political party within each state—is similar in the various states. The committee has responsibility for carrying out the policy decisions of the party's state convention. The committee also has control over the use of party campaign funds during political campaigns. Usually, the state central committee has little, if any, influence on party candidates once they are elected.

State parties are also important in national politics because of the **unit rule,** which awards a state's electoral votes in presidential elections as an indivisible bloc (except in Maine and Nebraska). Presidential candidates concentrate their efforts in states in which voter preferences seem to be evenly divided or in which large numbers of electoral votes are at stake.

Unit Rule Rule by which all of a state's electoral votes are cast for the presidential candidate receiving a plurality of the popular vote in that state.

Local Party Machinery: The Grassroots

The lowest layer of party machinery is the local organization, supported by district leaders, precinct or ward captains, and party workers. In the 1800s, the institution of **patronage**—rewarding the party faithful with government jobs or contracts—held the local organization together. For immigrants and the poor, the political machine often furnished important services and protections.

Patronage Rewarding faithful party workers and followers with government employment and contracts.

The last big-city local political machine to exercise substantial power was run by Chicago's Mayor Richard J. Daley, who was also an important figure in national Democratic politics. The current mayor of Chicago, Richard M. Daley, son of the former mayor, does not have the kind of machine that his father had. City machines are now dead, mostly because their function of providing social services (and reaping the reward of votes) has been taken over by state and national agencies.

Local political organizations still provide the foot soldiers of politics—individuals who pass out literature and get out the vote on election day, which can be crucial in local elections. In many regions, local Democratic and Republican organizations still exercise some patronage, such as awarding courthouse jobs, contracts for street repair, and other lucrative construction contracts. The constitutionality of awarding—or not awarding—contracts on the basis of political affiliation has been subject to challenge, however. The Supreme Court has ruled that failing to hire or firing individuals because of their political affiliation is an infringement of the employees' First Amendment rights to free expression.[7] Local party organizations are also the most important vehicles for recruiting young adults into political work, because political involvement at the local level offers activists many opportunities to gain experience.

The Party in Government

After the election is over and the winners are announced, the focus of party activity shifts from getting out the vote to organizing and controlling the government. Party membership plays an important role in the day-to-day operations of Congress, with partisanship determining everything from office space to committee assignments and power on Capitol Hill. For the president, the political party furnishes the pool of qualified applicants for political appointments to run the government. (Although it is uncommon to do so, presidents can and occasionally do appoint executive personnel, such as cabinet members, from the opposition party.) Judicial appointments also offer a great opportunity to the winning party. For the most part, presidents are likely to appoint federal judges from their own party.

Drawing by Steiner © 1994 The New Yorker Magazine, Inc.

"The euonymus likes partial shade and does equally well under Republican and Democratic Administrations."

All of these party appointments suggest that the winning political party, whether at the national, state, or local level, has a great deal of control in the American system. Because of the checks and balances and the relative lack of cohesion in American parties, however, such control is an illusion. For some time, many Americans have seemed to prefer a "divided government," with the executive and legislative branches controlled by different parties. The trend toward **ticket splitting**— splitting votes between the president and members of Congress—has increased sharply since 1952. This practice may indicate a lack of trust in government or the relative weakness of party identification among many voters.

Ticket Splitting
Voting for candidates of two or more parties for different offices.

Why Has the Two-Party System Endured?

There are several reasons why two major parties have dominated the political landscape in the United States for almost two centuries. These reasons have to do with (1) the historical foundations of the system, (2) political socialization and practical considerations, (3) the winner-take-all electoral system, and (4) state and federal laws favoring the two-party system.

The Historical Foundations of the Two-Party System

As we have seen, during much of American history there has been one preeminent issue or dispute that divided the nation politically. In the beginning, Americans were at odds over ratifying the Constitution. After the Constitution went into effect, the power of the federal government became the major national issue. Thereafter, the dispute over slavery divided the nation by section, North versus South. At times—for example, in the North after the Civil War—cultural differences have been important, with advocates of government-sponsored morality pitted against advocates of personal liberty.

During much of the 1900s, economic differences were preeminent. In the New Deal period, the Democrats became known as the party of the working class, while the Republicans became known as the party of the middle and upper classes and commercial interests.

When politics is based on an argument between two opposing points of view, advocates of each viewpoint can mobilize most effectively by forming a single, unified party. Also, when a two-party system has been in existence for almost two centuries, it becomes hard even to imagine an alternative.

Political Socialization and Practical Considerations

Given that the majority of Americans identify with one of the two major political parties, it is not surprising that most children learn at a fairly young age to think of themselves as either Democrats or Republicans. This generates a built-in mechanism to perpetuate a two-party system. Also, many politically oriented people who aspire to work for social change consider that the only realistic way to capture political power in this country is to be either a Republican or a Democrat.

The Winner-Take-All Electoral System

At virtually every level of government in the United States, the outcome of elections is based on the **plurality,** winner-take-all principle. In a plurality system, the winner is the person who obtains the most votes, even if that person does not receive a majority (over 50 percent) of the votes. Whoever gets the most votes gets everything. Most legislators in the United States are elected from single-member districts in which only one person represents the constituency, and the candidate who finishes second in such an election receives nothing for the effort.

Electoral College Voting.   The winner-take-all system also operates in the **electoral college.** In virtually all of the states, the electors are pledged to presidential candidates chosen by their respective national party conventions. During the popular vote in November, in each of the fifty states and in the District of Columbia, the voters choose one slate of electors from those on the state ballot. If a slate of electors wins a plurality in a state, then usually *all* of the electors so chosen cast their ballots for the presidential and vice presidential candidates of the

Plurality A number of votes cast for a candidate that is greater than the number of votes for any other candidate but not necessarily a majority.

Electoral College A group of persons, called electors, who are selected by the voters in each state. This group officially elects the president and the vice president of the United States.

winning party. This means that if a particular candidate's slate of electors receives a plurality of, say, 40 percent of the votes in a state, that candidate will receive all of the state's electoral votes. Minor parties have a difficult time competing under such a system. Because voters know that minor parties cannot succeed, they often will not vote for minor-party candidates, even though the candidates are ideologically in tune with them.

Popular Election of the Governors and the President.   In most of Europe, the chief executive (usually called the prime minister) is elected by the legislature, or parliament. If the parliament contains three or more parties, as is usually the case, two or more of the parties can join together in a coalition to choose the prime minister and the other leaders of the government. In the United States, however, the people directly elect the president and the governors of all fifty states. There is no opportunity for two or more parties to negotiate a coalition. Here, too, the winner-take-all principle discriminates powerfully against any third party.

Proportional Representation.   Many other nations use a system of proportional representation with multimember districts. If, during the national election, party X obtains 12 percent of the vote, party Y gets 43 percent of the vote, and party Z gets the remaining 45 percent of the vote, then party X gets 12 percent of the seats in the legislature, party Y gets 43 percent of the seats, and party Z gets 45 percent of the seats. Because even a minor party may still obtain at least a few seats in the legislature, the smaller parties have a greater incentive to organize under such electoral systems than they do in the United States.

State and Federal Laws Favoring the Two Parties

Many state and federal election laws offer a clear advantage to the two major parties. In some states, the established major parties need to gather fewer signatures to place their candidates on the ballot than minor parties or independent candidates do. The criterion for determining how many signatures will be required is often based on the total party vote in the last general election, thus penalizing a new political party that did not compete in that election.

At the national level, minor parties face different obstacles. All of the rules and procedures of both houses of Congress divide committee seats, staff members, and other privileges on the basis of party membership. A legislator who is elected on a minor-party ticket, such as the Liberal Party of New York, must choose to be counted with one of the major parties to get a committee assignment. The Federal Election Commission (FEC) rules for campaign financing also place restrictions on minor-party candidates. Such candidates are not eligible for federal matching funds in either the primary or the general election. In the 1980 election, John Anderson, running for president as an independent, sued the FEC for campaign funds. The commission finally agreed to repay part of his campaign costs after the election in proportion to the votes he received. It is much less helpful, of course, to receive funds when the campaign is over than it is to receive funds while the campaign is still under way.

The Role of Minor Parties

For the reasons just discussed, minor parties have a difficult, if not impossible, time competing within the American two-party political system. Nonetheless, minor parties have played an important role in our political life. Frequently, dissatisfied groups have split from major parties and formed so-called **third parties,**[8] which have acted as barometers of changes in the political mood. Such barometric indicators have forced the major parties to recognize new issues or trends in the thinking of Americans. Political scientists also believe that third parties have acted as a safety valve for dissident political groups, perhaps preventing major confrontations and political unrest.

Third Party A political party other than the two major political parties (Republican and Democratic).

Current Minor Parties

Most minor parties that have endured have had a strong ideological foundation that is typically at odds with the majority mindset. Ideology has at least two functions. First, the members of the minor party regard themselves as outsiders and look to one another for support; ideology provides tremendous psychological cohesiveness. Second, because the rewards of ideological commitment are partly psychological, these minor parties do not think in terms of immediate electoral success. A poor showing at the polls therefore does not dissuade either the leadership or the grass-roots participants from continuing their quest for change in American society.

Jill Stein, the Green Party candidate for governor of Massachusetts, meets supporters outside a debate between gubernatorial candidates in 2002. Stein was not allowed to participate in the debate with the Democratic and Republican candidates. What criteria should be used to determine whether third-party candidates can participate in debates?

AP Photo/Steven Senne

Some of the notable current third parties include the Libertarian Party, the Green Party, and the Reform Party.

The Libertarian Party supports a *laissez-faire* capitalist economic program, combined with a hands-off policy on regulating matters of moral conduct. The Reform Party, founded by H. Ross Perot in 1996, seeks to reform the political process and reduce the size of government. The Green Party began as a grassroots environmentalist organization with affiliated political parties across North America and Western Europe. It was established in the United States as a national party in 1996 and nominated Ralph Nader to run for president in 2000.

Splinter Parties

Splinter Party A new party formed by a dissident faction within a major political party.

The most successful minor parties have been those that split from major parties. Perhaps the most famous **splinter party** was the "Bull Moose" Progressive Party, which split from the Republican Party in 1912. Theodore Roosevelt formed the Progressive Party, leaving the regular Republicans to support William Howard Taft. Although the party was not successful in winning the election for Roosevelt, it did succeed in splitting the Republican vote so that Democrat Woodrow Wilson won.

Another important splinter party was the American Independent Party, which supported former Democrat George Wallace in 1968. The strategy employed by Wallace was to attempt to deny Republican Richard Nixon or Democrat Hubert Humphrey the necessary majority in the electoral college. The American Independent Party emphasized mostly racial issues and, to a lesser extent, foreign policy. Wallace received 9.9 million popular votes and forty-six electoral votes.

The Impact of Minor Parties

Minor parties clearly have had an impact on American politics. What is more difficult to ascertain is how great that impact has been. Simply showing that third-party issues were taken over some years later by a major party does not prove that the third party instigated the major party's change.

INFOTRAC

To find out more on this topic, use the term "Green Party United States" in the Subject guide.

Minor parties can, however, have a serious impact on the outcomes of an election. In the 2000 presidential elections, the Green Party gathered 3 percent of the vote for its nominee, Ralph Nader, taking some votes away from Democrat Al Gore. Given the closeness of the vote in several crucial states, including Florida, the Green Party may have affected the outcome. In contrast, the Reform Party, which had won 8 percent of the vote in 1996, had little impact in 2000 because its nominee, Pat Buchanan, was too conservative for most of the party's members.

The Uncertain Future of Party Identification

Party Identification Linking oneself to a particular political party.

Polls that track **party identification** show increasing numbers of voters who identify themselves as independents. This trend extends back as far as the middle of the 1900s.

MAKING A DIFFERENCE: The Gun Control Issue

Is the easy availability of handguns a major cause of crime? Do people have a right to possess firearms to defend home and hearth? These questions are part of a long-term and heated battle between organized pro-firearm and antifirearm camps. The fight is fueled by the one million gun incidents occurring in the United States each year—murders, suicides, assaults, accidents, and robberies in which guns are involved.

ISSUES IN THE DEBATE

Issues in the debate include child-safety features on guns and the regulation of gun dealers who sell firearms at gun shows. Proponents of gun control seek safety locks and more restrictions on gun purchases—if not to ban them entirely. Proponents of firearms claim that firearms are a constitutional right and meet a vital defense need for individuals. They contend that the problem lies not in the sale and ownership of weapons but in their use by criminals.

The National Coalition to Ban Handguns favors a total ban, taking the position that handguns "serve no valid purpose, except to kill people." Such a ban is opposed by the National Rifle Association of America (NRA). The NRA, founded in 1871, is currently one of the most powerful single-issue groups in the United States. The NRA believes that gun laws will not reduce the number of crimes. It is illogical to assume, according to the NRA, that persons who refuse to obey laws prohibiting rape, murder, and other crimes will obey a gun law.

GUNS AND YOUNGER AMERICANS

Many proponents of gun control insist that controlling the purchase of weapons would reduce the availability of guns to children. In response, some states have passed laws that hold adults liable for not locking away their firearms. In addition, a number of cities have sued gun manufacturers for not controlling the flow of their products to dealers who sell guns to criminals and gang members.

FOR MORE INFORMATION

To find out more about the NRA's position, contact that organization at the following address:

> The National Rifle Association
> 11250 Waples Mill Rd.
> Fairfax, VA 22030
> 703-267-1000
> **http://www.nra.org**

To learn about the positions of gun-control advocates, contact:

> The Coalition to Stop Gun Violence
> 1023 15th St. N.W., Suite 600
> Washington, DC 20036
> 202-408-0061
> **http://www.gunfree.org**

> Brady Center to Prevent Gun Violence
> 1225 Eye St. N.W., Suite 1100
> Washington, DC 20005
> 202-289-7319
> **http://www.handguncontrol.org**

INFOTRAC
To find out more, use the term "party identification" in Keywords.

Not only have ties to the two major parties weakened in the last half century, but voters are also less willing to vote a straight ticket—that is, to vote for all the candidates of one party. In the early 1900s, straight-ticket voting was virtually universal. By midcentury, the percentage of voters who engaged in ticket splitting was 12 percent. In recent presidential elections, between 20 and 40 percent of the voters engaged in split-ticket voting. This trend, along with the increase in the number of voters who call themselves independents, suggests that parties have lost much of their hold on the loyalty of the voters.

KEY TERMS

Democratic Party **160**

direct technique **152**

divided government **162**

electoral college **167**

era of good feelings **160**

faction **157**

independent **157**

indirect technique **152**

interest group **147**

issue advocacy advertising **155**

labor movement **149**

lobbyist **147**

national committee **164**

national convention **163**

party identification **170**

party organization **162**

party platform **164**

patronage **165**

plurality **167**

political action committee (PAC) **155**

political party **147**

public interest **150**

Republican Party **160**

service sector **149**

soft money **155**

splinter party **170**

state central committee **164**

third party **169**

ticket splitting **166**

two-party system **158**

unit rule **165**

Whig Party **160**

CHAPTER SUMMARY

1 An interest group is an organization whose members share common objectives and who actively attempt to influence government policy. Interest groups proliferate in the United States because they can influence government at many points in the political structure. A political party, in contrast, is a group of political activists who organize to win elections, operate the government, and determine public policy.

2 Major types of interest groups include business, agricultural, labor, public employee, professional, and environmental groups. Other important groups

may be considered public-interest groups. In addition, special interest groups and foreign governments lobby the government.

3 Interest groups use direct and indirect techniques to influence government. Direct techniques include lobbying, publicizing ratings of legislative behavior, and providing campaign assistance. Indirect techniques include attempting to rally public sentiment and using constituents to lobby for the group's interest. Interest groups also provide financial contributions. The contributions are often made through political action committees, or PACs. Other methods of contributing include soft money, which goes directly to the parties for "party-building" purposes, and issue advocacy advertising, which is not coordinated with candidate campaigns.

4 The 1946 Legislative Reorganization Act was the first attempt to control lobbyists and their activities through registration requirements. In 1995, Congress approved new legislation requiring anyone who spends 20 percent of his or her time influencing legislation to register. Also, any organization spending $20,000 or more and any individual who is paid more than $5,000 annually for his or her work must register. Grassroots lobbying and the lobbying efforts of tax-exempt organizations are exempt from the new rules.

5 Political parties perform a number of functions for the political system. These functions include recruiting candidates for public office, organizing and running elections, presenting alternative policies to the voters, assuming responsibility for operating the government, and acting as the opposition to the party in power.

6 The evolution of our nation's political parties can be divided into seven periods: (a) the creation and formation of political parties from 1789 to 1816; (b) the era of one-party rule, or personal politics, from 1816 to 1828; (c) the period from Andrew Jackson's presidency to the Civil War, from 1828 to 1860; (d) the Civil War and post–Civil War period, from 1860 to 1896; (e) the Republican ascendency and progressive period, from 1896 to 1932; (f) the New Deal period, from 1932 to 1968; and (g) the modern period, from 1968 to the present.

7 In theory, each of the political parties has a pyramid-shaped organization with a hierarchical command structure. In reality, each level of the party—local, state, and national—has considerable autonomy. The national party organization is responsible for holding the national convention in presidential election years, writing the party platform, choosing the national committee, and conducting party business.

8 Two major parties have dominated the political landscape in the United States for almost two centuries. The reasons for this include (a) the historical foundations of the system, (b) political socialization and practical considerations, (c) the winner-take-all electoral system, and (d) state and federal laws favoring the two-party system. Minor parties have emerged from time to time, often as dissatisfied splinter groups from within major parties, and have acted as barometers of changes in political moods. Minor parties have sometimes had a serious impact on the outcomes of elections.

9 From the 1940s to the present, independent voters have formed an increasing proportion of the electorate, with a consequent decline in strongly Democratic or strongly Republican voters.

SELECTED PRINT AND MEDIA RESOURCES

Suggested Readings

Black, Earl, and Merle Black. *The Rise of Southern Republicans.* Cambridge, Mass.: Harvard University Press, 2002. This book analyzes the shift in politics in the southern states over the last four decades.

Goldstein, Kenneth M. *Interest Groups, Lobbying, and Participation in America.* New York: Cambridge University Press, 2003. What kind of people join interest groups, and how do such people seek to influ-ence legislation? The author looks for answers using survey data and interviews with activists.

Green, John C., and Paul S. Hernson, eds. *Responsible Partisanship: The Evolution of American Political Parties since 1950.* Lawrence: University Press of Kansas, 2003. This collection of scholarly essays explores the roles and functions of political parties.

Hernson, Paul S., Ronald G. Shaiko, and Clyde Wilcox, eds. *The Interest Group Connection: Electioneering,*

Lobbying, and Policymaking, 2d ed. New York: Chatham House, 2003. This book offers a collection of scholarly essays on the influence of interest groups on policymaking.

Judis, John B., and Ruy Teixeira. *The Emerging Democratic Majority.* New York: Scribner, 2002. The authors make the controversial argument that the Democrats will again become the largest party because they appeal to ethnic groups and professions that make up a growing share of the population.

Nader, Ralph. *Crashing the Party: How to Tell the Truth and Still Run for President.* New York: St. Martin's Press, 2002. This is Nader's own entertaining and detailed account of his run for the presidency as a Green in 2000.

Media Resources

Bowling for Columbine—Michael Moore's documentary won an Academy Award in 2003. Moore seeks to understand why the United States leads the industrialized world in firearms deaths. While the film is hilarious, it takes a strong position in favor of gun control and is critical of the National Rifle Association.

Norma Rae—A 1979 Hollywood movie about an attempt by a northern union organizer to unionize workers in the southern textile industry; stars Sally Field, who won an Academy Award for her performance.

Organizing America: The History of Trade Unions—A 1994 documentary that incorporates interviews, personal accounts, and archival footage to tell the story of the American labor movement. The film is a Cambridge Educational Production.

A Third Choice—A 1996 film that examines America's experience with third parties and independent candidates throughout the nation's political history.

LOGGING ON

Almost every interest group or association has its own Web site. To find one, use your favorite search engine (Google, AltaVista, or another search engine) and search for the association by name. For a sense of the breadth of the kinds of interest groups that have Web sites, take a look at one or two of those listed here.

Those interested in the gun control issue may want to visit the National Rifle Association's site at http://www.nra.org.

You can learn more about the labor movement by visiting the AFL-CIO's site at http://www.aflcio.org.

The AARP (formerly the American Association of Retired Persons) has a site at http://www.aarp.org.

The political parties all have Web sites. The Democratic Party is online at http://www.democrats.org.

The Republican National Committee is at http://www.rnc.org.

The Libertarian Party has a Web site at http://www.lp.org.

The Green Party of the United States can be found at http://www.gp.org.

Politics1.com offers extensive information on U.S. political parties, including the major parties and fifty minor parties. Go to http://www.politics1.com/parties.htm.

The Pew Research Center for the People and the Press offers survey data online on how the parties fared during the most recent elections, voter typology, and numerous other issues. To access this site, go to http://people-press.org.

USING THE INTERNET FOR POLITICAL ANALYSIS

Go to this text's Web site at **http://politicalscience. wadsworth.com/schmidtbrief2004**. Select "Chapter 7" in the box at the top of the window. Then, in the column on the left-hand side of the window, under "Chapter Resources," click on "Internet Exercises." The Web site will then display the following Internet exercises that you can perform to learn more about topics covered in this chapter.

Activity 7–1: **Common Cause**
Activity 7–2: **Special Interest Groups and Rating Systems**
Activity 7–3: **The Republicans and the Democrats**

ONLINE STUDY GUIDE AND ADDITIONAL RESOURCES

At **http://politicalscience.wadsworth.com/ schmidtbrief2004** you will find a free Study Guide to this book that includes tutorial quizzes, essay questions, practice exams, chapter outlines, learning objectives, the glossary, flashcards, crossword puzzles, and Microsoft PowerPoint presentations. Also included in the American Government Resource Center for Chapter 7:

- **InfoTrac® Reader**—The influence of interest groups; lobbying techniques; Democrats and Republicans— what's the difference; party history.

- **Simulations**—Interest groups; political parties.

- **Participation Activities**—Find an interest group that supports a cause of importance to you; find an interest group whose goals you oppose; explore political parties; volunteer for a political party.

- **MicroCase Exercises**—Interest groups; political parties.

- **Related Links**—Interest groups; political parties.

- **Video Case Studies**—The gun lobby; interest group strategies; parties—the formative years; parties—the Republicans.

- **Source Readings**—By James H. Hammond, Abraham Lincoln, and Newt Gingrich, plus selected statutes.

The site also contains the Citizen's Survival Guide, information on how to get involved in politics locally and globally, as well as regularly updated features including a Current Events Quiz, In the News, Election Links, updates on the war on terrorism, and more.

CHAPTER 8

Campaigns, Elections, and Voting Behavior

POLITICAL CAMPAIGNS ARE AT THE HEART of a democratic political system. When voters go to the polls and choose among candidates, they are exercising the fundamental right to choose the leadership of the nation and, thus, to direct national policy. The same process is repeated at every level of government in the United States: on election day, voters choose members of the town council, the county prosecuting attorney, state legislators, governors, and members of Congress, depending on the year in the political cycle. In each of these venues, candidates depend on their campaigns to sway the voters and win the election. In this chapter we discuss political campaigns, the mechanics of voting, who is most likely to vote, and some of the factors that govern decision making by voters.

The People Who Run for Office

For democracy to work, there must be candidates for office; and for voters to have a choice, there must be competing candidates. The presidential campaign provides the most colorful and exciting look at these candidates and how they prepare to compete for office. The men and women who wanted to be candidates in the 2004 presidential campaign faced a long and obstacle-filled path. First, they needed to raise enough money to tour the nation, particularly the states with early **presidential primaries,** to see if they had enough local supporters. They needed funds to create an organization, devise a plan to win primary votes, and win the party's nomination at the national convention. Finally, they needed funds to finance a successful campaign for president. Always, at every turn, there was the question of whether they would have enough funds to wage a campaign.

Presidential Primary
A statewide primary election of delegates to a political party's national convention, held to determine the party's presidential nominee.

Who Is Eligible?

There are few constitutional restrictions on who can become a candidate in the United States. As detailed in the Constitution, the formal requirements for national office are as follows:

1. *President.* Must be a natural born citizen, have attained the age of thirty-five years, and be a resident of the country for fourteen years by the time of inauguration.

2. *Vice president.* Must be a natural-born citizen, have attained the age of thirty-five years, and not be a resident of the same state as the candidate for president.[1]

3. *Senator.* Must be a citizen for at least nine years, have attained the age of thirty by the time of taking office, and be a resident of the state from which elected.

4. *Representative.* Must be a citizen for at least seven years, have attained the age of twenty-five by the time of taking office, and be a resident of the state from which elected.

The qualifications for state legislators are set by the state constitutions and likewise include age, place of residence, and citizenship. (Usually, the requirements for the upper chamber of a legislature are somewhat higher than those for the lower chamber.) The legal qualifications for running for governor or other state office are similar.

Who Runs?

In spite of these minimal legal qualifications for office at both the national and state levels, a quick look at the slate of candidates in any election—or at the current members of the U.S. House of Representatives—will reveal that not all segments of the population take advantage of these opportunities. Holders of political office in the United States are overwhelmingly white and male. Until the twentieth century, presidential candidates were always of northern European origin and Protestant heritage.[2] Laws that effectively denied voting rights made it impossible to elect African American public officials in many areas in which African Americans constituted a significant portion of the population. As a result of the passage of major civil rights

Former President Bill Clinton campaigns for Florida Democratic gubernatorial candidate Bill McBride, left, during a rally at Miami-Dade Community College in Florida, Nov. 12, 2002. How much effect do you think such rallies actually have on the voters?

AP Photo/Alan Díaz

One of the many "firsts" of the 2000 elections was the campaign of a former first lady for national office. Hillary Rodham Clinton succeeded in winning one of New York's seats in the U.S. Senate. Why might New York be willing to elect candidates who lack long-standing ties to the state?

AP Photo/Kathy Willens

legislation in the last several decades, however, the number of African American public officials has increased throughout the United States.

Until recently, women generally were considered to be appropriate candidates only for lower-level offices, such as state legislator or school board member. The last ten years have seen a tremendous increase in the number of women who run for office, not only at the state level but for the U.S. Congress as well. In 2002, for example, 135 women ran for Congress, and 62 were elected. Whereas African Americans were formerly restricted from running for office by both law and custom, women were not recruited because they had not worked their way up through the party organization or because they were thought to have no chance of winning. Today, a majority of Americans say they would vote for a qualified woman or for an African American for president of the United States.

Professional Status

Candidates are likely to be professionals, particularly lawyers. Political campaigning and officeholding are simply easier for some occupational groups than for others, and political involvement can make a valuable contribution to certain careers. Lawyers, for example, have more flexible schedules than do many other professionals, can take time off for campaigning, and can leave their jobs to hold public office full-time. Furthermore, holding political office is good publicity for their professional practice, and they usually have partners or associates to keep the firm going while they are in office. Perhaps most important, many jobs that lawyers aspire to—federal or state judgeships, state attorney offices, or work in a federal agency—can be attained by political appointment. Such appointments most often go to loyal partisans who have served their party by running for and holding office. Personal ambitions, then, are well served for certain groups by participation in the political arena, whereas it could be a sacrifice for others whose careers demand full-time attention for many years.

The Modern Campaign Machine

American political campaigns are extravagant, year-long events that produce campaign buttons and posters for collectors, hours of film and sound for the media, and, eventually, winning candidates who become the public officials of the nation. Campaigns are also enormously expensive; the total expenditures for 2002 were estimated to be several billion dollars for all congressional and local races in that year. Political campaigns exhaust candidates, their staff members, and the journalists covering the campaign—to say nothing of the public's patience.

The Changing Campaign

Campaigns seem to be getting longer and more excessive each year. The goal of the frantic activity is the same for all campaigns—to convince voters to choose a candidate or a slate of candidates for office. Part of the reason for the increased intensity

INFOTRAC

For updates on the 2004 elections, use the term "elections" in the Subject guide, and then go to the subdivision "2004."

These campaign workers have volunteered their time to support Congresswoman Loretta Sanchez, a Democrat from California who was reelected to her fourth term in 2002. Political parties and candidates at all levels would have a difficult time conducting their campaigns without such volunteers. Volunteering for a campaign is one way to participate actively in the political process.

John Nourok/PhotoEdit

of campaigns in the last decade is that they are no longer centered on the party but are centered on the candidate. The candidate-centered campaign emerged in response to several developments: changes in the electoral system, the increased importance of television in campaigns, technological innovations such as computers, and the increased cost of campaigning.

To run a successful and persuasive campaign, the candidate's organization must be able to raise funds for the effort, get coverage from the media, produce and pay for political commercials and advertising, schedule the candidate's time effectively, convey the candidate's position on the issues to the voters, conduct research on the opposing candidate, and get the voters to go to the polls. When party identification was stronger among voters and before the advent of television campaigning, a strong party organization at the local, state, or national level could furnish most of the services and expertise that the candidate needed. Political parties provided the funds for campaigning until the 1970s. Parties used their precinct organizations to distribute literature, register voters, and get out the vote on election day. Less effort was spent on advertising each candidate's positions and character, because the party label communicated that information to many voters.

One of the reasons that campaigns no longer depend on parties is that fewer people identify with them, as is evident from the increased number of political independents. In 1952, about one-fifth of adults identified themselves as independents, whereas in 2004, about one-third identified themselves as independents.

The Professional Campaign

Whether the candidate is running for the state legislature, for the governor's office, for the U.S. Congress, or for the presidency, every campaign has some fundamental tasks to accomplish. Today, most of these tasks are put into the hands of paid professionals rather than volunteers or amateur politicians.

Political Consultant
A paid professional hired to devise a campaign strategy and manage a campaign.

The most sought-after and possibly the most criticized campaign expert is the **political consultant,** who, for a large fee, devises a campaign strategy, thinks up a campaign theme, oversees the advertising, and possibly chooses the campaign colors and candidate's official portrait. The paid consultant monitors the campaign's progress, plans all media appearances, and coaches the candidate for debates. The consultants and the firms they represent are not politically neutral; most will work only for candidates from one party.

The Strategy of Winning

The goal of every political campaign is the same: to win the election. There are no rewards for a candidate who comes in second; the winner takes all. The campaign organization must plan a strategy that maximizes the candidate's chances of winning. Candidates seek to capture all the votes of their party's supporters, to convince a majority of the independent voters to vote for them, and to gain a few votes from supporters of the other party. To accomplish these goals, candidates must consider their visibility, their message, and their campaign strategy.

Candidate Visibility and Appeal

One of the most important concerns is how well known the candidate is. If she or he is a highly visible incumbent, there may be little need for campaigning except to remind the voters of the officeholder's good deeds. If, however, the candidate is an unknown challenger or a largely unfamiliar character attacking a well-known public figure, the campaign must devise a strategy to get the candidate before the public.

For an independent candidate or a candidate representing a minor party, the problem of name recognition is serious. Such candidates must present an overwhelming case for the voter to reject the major-party candidate. Both the Democratic and the Republican candidates use the strategic ploy of labeling third-party candidates as "not serious" and therefore not worth the voter's time.

The Use of Opinion Polls

One of the major sources of information for both the media and the candidates is opinion polls. Poll taking is widespread during the primaries. Presidential hopefuls have private polls taken to make sure that there is at least some chance they could be nominated and, if nominated, elected. During the presidential campaign itself, polling is even more frequent. Polls are taken not only by the regular pollsters—Roper, Harris, Gallup, and others—but also privately by each candidate's campaign organization. These private polls are for the exclusive and secret use of the candidate and his or her campaign organization. As the election approaches, many candidates use **tracking polls,** which are polls taken almost every day, to find out how well they are competing for votes. Tracking polls enable consultants to fine-tune the advertising and the candidate's speeches in the last days of the campaign.

Tracking Poll A poll taken for the candidate on a nearly daily basis as election day approaches.

Focus Groups

Another tactic is to use a **focus group** to gain insights into public perceptions of the candidate. Professional consultants organize a discussion of the candidate or of certain political issues among ten to fifteen ordinary citizens. The citizens are selected from certain target groups in the population—for example, blue-collar men, senior citizens, or young voters. The group discusses personality traits of the candidate, political advertising, and other candidate-related issues. The conversation is videotaped (and often observed from behind a mirrored wall). Focus groups are expected to reveal more emotional responses to candidates or the deeper anxieties of voters—feelings that consultants believe often are not tapped by more impersonal telephone surveys. The campaign then can shape its messages to respond to these feelings and perceptions.

Focus Group A small group of individuals who are led in discussion by a professional consultant to gather opinions on and responses to candidates and issues.

Financing the Campaign

In a book published in 1932 entitled *Money in Elections,* Louise Overacker had the following to say about campaign financing:

> The financing of elections in a democracy is a problem which is arousing increasing concern. Many are beginning to wonder if present-day methods of raising and spending

campaign funds do not clog the wheels of our elaborately constructed mechanism of popular control, and if democracies do not inevitably become [governments ruled by small groups].[3]

Although writing more than seventy years ago, Overacker touched on a sensitive issue in American political campaigns—the connection between money and elections. It is estimated that over $3 billion was spent at all levels of campaigning in the 1999–2000 presidential election cycle. At the federal level alone, a total of more than $500 million is estimated to have been spent in races for the House of Representatives, $300 million in senatorial races, and $800 million in the presidential campaign. The 2004 campaigns will certainly have cost even more when the bills are totaled. Except for the presidential campaigns, all of this money has to be provided by the candidates and their families, borrowed, or raised by contributions from individuals or political action committees. For the presidential campaigns, some of the money comes from the federal government.

Regulating Campaign Financing

The way in which campaigns are financed has changed dramatically in the last two and a half decades. Today, candidates and political parties must operate within the constraints imposed by complicated laws regulating campaign financing.

A variety of federal **corrupt practices acts** have been designed to regulate campaign financing. The first, passed in 1925, limited primary and general election expenses for congressional candidates. In addition, it required disclosure of election expenses and, in principle, put controls on contributions by corporations. There were many loopholes in the restrictions, and the acts proved to be ineffective.

The **Hatch Act** (Political Activities Act) of 1939 is best known for restricting the political activities of civil servants. The act also, however, made it unlawful for a political group to spend more than $3 million in any campaign and limited individual contributions to a political group to $5,000. Of course, such restrictions were easily circumvented by creating additional political groups.

In the 1970s, Congress passed additional legislation to reshape the nature of campaign financing. In 1971, it passed the Federal Election Campaign Act to reform the process. Then in 1974, in the wake of the Watergate scandal, Congress enacted further reforms.

Corrupt Practices Acts A series of acts passed by Congress in an attempt to limit and regulate the size and sources of contributions and expenditures in political campaigns.

Hatch Act An act passed in 1939 that restricted the political activities of government employees. It also attempted to limit campaign contributions and spending.

The Federal Election Campaign Act

The Federal Election Campaign Act (FECA) of 1971, which became effective in 1972, essentially replaced all past laws. The act placed no limit on overall spending but restricted the amount that could be spent on mass media advertising, including television. It limited the amount that candidates and their families could contribute to their own campaigns and required disclosure of all contributions and expenditures over $100. In principle, the FECA limited the role of labor unions and corporations in political campaigns. It also provided for a voluntary $1 check-off on federal income tax returns for general campaign funds to be used by major-party presidential candidates.

Further Reforms in 1974. For many, the 1971 act did not go far enough. Amendments to the FECA passed in 1974 did the following:

1. *Created the Federal Election Commission.* This commission consists of six nonpartisan administrators whose duties are to enforce compliance with the requirements of the act.

2. *Provided public financing for presidential primaries and general elections.* Any candidate running for president who is able to obtain sufficient contributions in at least twenty states can obtain a subsidy from the U.S. Treasury to help pay for primary campaigns. For example, each major party was given $15 million for its national convention in 2000. The major-party candidates have federal support for almost all of their expenses, provided they are willing to accept campaign-spending limits.

3. *Limited presidential campaign spending.* Any candidate accepting federal support has to agree to limit campaign expenditures to the amount prescribed by federal law.

4. *Limited contributions.* Under the 1974 amendments, citizens could contribute up to $1,000 to each candidate in each federal election or primary; the total limit on all contributions from an individual to all candidates was $25,000 per year. Groups could contribute up to a maximum of $5,000 to a candidate in any election. (As you will read shortly, some of these limits were changed by the 2002 campaign-reform legislation.)

5. *Required disclosure.* Each candidate must file periodic reports with the Federal Election Commission, listing who contributed, how much was spent, and for what the money was spent.

The 1976 Amendments. Further amendments to the FECA in 1976 allowed corporations, labor unions, and special interest groups to set up political action committees (PACs) to raise money for candidates. Each corporation or union is limited to one PAC.

Buckley v. Valeo. The 1971 act had limited the amount that each individual could spend on his or her own behalf. The Supreme Court declared the provision unconstitutional in 1976, in *Buckley v. Valeo*,[4] stating that it was unconstitutional to restrict in any way the amount congressional candidates or their immediate families could spend on their own behalf: "The candidate, no less than any other person, has a First Amendment right to engage in the discussion of public issues and vigorously and tirelessly to advocate his own election."

Campaign Financing beyond the Limits

Within a few years after the establishment of the tight limits on contributions, new ways to finance campaigns were developed that skirted the reforms and made it possible for huge sums of money to be raised, especially by the major political parties.

Contributions to Political Parties. Candidates, PACs, and political parties found ways to generate *soft money*—that is, campaign contributions to political parties that escaped the limits of federal election law. Although the FECA limited

contributions that would be spent on elections, there were no limits on contributions to political parties for activities such as voter education and voter-registration drives. This loophole enabled the parties to raise millions of dollars from corporations and individuals. It was not unusual for some corporations to give more than a million dollars to the Democratic National Committee or to the Republican Party.[5] As shown in Table 8–1, nearly twice as much soft money was raised in the 1999–2000 presidential election cycle as in the previous (1995–1996) presidential election cycle. The parties spent this money for their conventions, for registering voters, and for advertising to promote the general party position. The parties also sent a great deal of the money to state and local party organizations, which used it to support their own tickets.

Independent Expenditures. Business corporations, labor unions, and other interest groups discovered that it was legal to make **independent expenditures** in an election campaign so long as the expenditures were not coordinated with those of the candidate or political party. Hundreds of unique committees and organizations blossomed to take advantage of this campaign tactic. Although a 1990 United States Supreme Court decision, *Austin v. Michigan State Chamber of Commerce*,[6] upheld the right of the states and the federal government to limit independent, direct corporate expenditures (such as for advertisements) on behalf of *candidates*, the decision did not stop business and other types of groups from making independent expenditures on *issues*.

Independent Expenditures

Nonregulated contributions from PACs, organizations, and individuals. The funds may be spent on advertising or other campaign activities so long as those expenditures are not coordinated with those of a candidate.

TABLE 8–1	Soft Money Raised by Political Parties, 1994 to 2002				
	1993–1994	1995–1996	1997–1998	1999–2000	2001–2002
Democratic Party	$ 45.6 million	$122.3 million	$ 92.8 million	$243.0 million	$199.6 million
Republican Party	59.5 million	141.2 million	131.6 million	244.4 million	221.7 million
Total	105.1 million	263.5 million	224.4 million	487.4 million	421.3 million

SOURCES: *Congressional Quarterly Weekly Report,* September 6, 1997, p. 2065; and authors' update.

Although promoting issue positions is very close to promoting candidates who support those positions, the courts repeatedly have held, in accordance with the *Buckley v. Valeo* decision mentioned earlier, that interest groups have a First Amendment right to advocate their positions.

The Supreme Court clarified, in a 1996 decision,[7] that political parties may also make independent expenditures on behalf of candidates—as long as the parties do so *independently* of the candidates. In other words, the parties must not coordinate such expenditures with the candidates' campaigns or let the candidates know the specifics of how party funds are being spent.

Bundling.   Yet another way to maximize contributions to a candidate or a party is through the practice of **bundling.** Bundling entails collecting the maximum individual contribution—$1,000 until 2002, when it was raised to $2,000—from a number of individuals in the same firm or family and then sending the quite large check to the candidate of choice. While this practice is in complete compliance with the law, it makes the candidate or party more aware of the source of the funding.

Bundling The practice of adding together maximum individual campaign contributions to increase their impact on the candidate.

The effect of all of these strategies was to increase greatly the amount of money spent for campaigns and party activities. Critics of the system continued to wonder whether the voice of the individual voter or the small contributor was being drowned in the flood of big contributions. Although Congress considered reform measures every year, none was approved until 2002.

The Bipartisan Campaign Reform Act of 2002

Campaign reform had been in the air for so long that it was almost anticlimactic when President George W. Bush signed the Bipartisan Campaign Reform Act on March 27, 2002.

Key Elements of the New Law.   The 2002 law bans the large, unlimited contributions to national political parties that are known as soft money. It places curbs on, but does not entirely eliminate, the use of campaign ads by outside special interest groups advocating the election or defeat of specific candidates. Such ads are allowed up to sixty days before a general election and up to thirty days before a primary election.

In 1974, contributions by individuals to federal candidates were limited to $1,000 per individual. The 2002 act increased this limit to $2,000. In addition, the maximum amount that an individual can give to all federal candidates was raised from $25,000 per year to $95,000 over a two-year election cycle.

INFOTRAC

For updates and more information on this topic, use the term "campaign funds" in the Subject guide.

INFOTRAC

For updates and more information, use the term "campaign finance reform" in the Subject guide.

The act did not ban soft money contributions to state and local parties. These parties can accept such contributions as long as they are limited to $10,000 per year per individual.

Consequences of the 2002 Act.   One of the consequences of the 2002 act was a set of constitutional challenges by groups negatively affected. In December 2003, however, the Supreme Court upheld almost all of the clauses of the 2002 act.

The regulation prohibiting the national parties from raising unregulated "soft dollars" may have some unintended consequences. The strength of the Democratic and Republican parties has rested in part on their ability to raise large sums of money. Without large amounts of soft money, the two major parties will no longer have the power they previously had to finance get-out-the-vote drives and phone banks. This task will fall to the state parties or non-party organizations, which may not do such a good job.

Perhaps another unintended consequence of the campaign-financing reform bill will be that it benefits incumbents. According to many political scientists, the biggest immediate beneficiary will be President George W. Bush. Bush will be able to maintain a large campaign fund while his Democratic opponent will have to spend considerable time and resources trying to match it. Why? The reason is that the Democratic Party will not have large amounts of soft money to support the Democratic presidential hopeful. Therefore, the Democratic nominee will have to seek more hard money—a difficult task because the Republicans have a larger hard money donor base than the Democrats do.

Running for President: The Longest Campaign

The American presidential election is the culmination of two different campaigns linked by the parties' national conventions. The presidential primary campaign lasts from January until June of the election year, and the final presidential campaign heats up around Labor Day.

Primary elections were first mandated in 1903 in Wisconsin. The purpose of the primary was to open the nomination process to ordinary party members and to weaken the influence of party bosses in the nomination process. Until 1968, however, there were fewer than twenty primary elections for the presidency. They were often **"beauty contests"** in which candidates for the nomination competed for popular votes but the results had little or no impact on the selection of delegates to the national convention. National conventions were meetings of the party elite—legislators, mayors, county chairpersons, and loyal party workers—who were mostly appointed to their delegations. National conventions saw numerous trades and bargains among competing candidates, and the leaders of large blocs of delegate votes could direct their delegates to support a favorite candidate.

"Beauty Contest" A presidential primary in which contending candidates compete for popular votes but the results do not control the selection of delegates to the national convention.

Reforming the Primaries

In recent decades, the character of the primary process and the make-up of the national convention have changed dramatically. The mass public, rather than party elites, now generally controls the nomination process. After the disruptive riots outside the doors of the 1968 Democratic convention in Chicago, many party leaders pushed for serious reforms of the convention process. They saw the general dissatisfaction with the convention, and the riots in particular, as caused by the inability of the average party member to influence the nomination system.

The Democratic National Committee appointed a special commission to study the problems of the primary system. Referred to as the McGovern-Fraser Commission, the group over the next several years formulated new rules for delegate selection that had to be followed by state Democratic Parties.

The reforms instituted by the Democratic Party, which were imitated in most states by the Republicans, revolutionized the nomination process for the presidency. The most important changes require that most convention delegates not be nominated by the elites in either party; they must be elected by the voters in primary elections, in **caucuses** held by local parties, or at state conventions. Delegates are mostly pledged to a particular candidate, although the pledge is not always formally binding at the convention. The delegation from each state must also include a proportion of women, younger party members, and representatives of the minority groups within the party. At first, virtually no special privileges were given to elected party officials, such as senators and governors. In 1984, however, many of these officials returned to the Democratic convention as **superdelegates.**

Caucus A closed meeting of party leaders to select party candidates or to decide on policy; also, a meeting of party members designed to select candidates and propose policies.

Superdelegate A party leader or elected official who is given the right to vote at the party's national convention. Superdelegates are not elected at the state level.

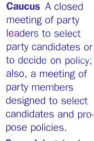

Demonstrations outside the 1968 Democratic convention in Chicago were shown on national TV. Dissatisfaction with the convention influenced the party to reform its delegate selection rules.

Paul Conklin/PhotoEdit

Types of Primaries

Primary elections differ from state to state. Among the most common types are those discussed here.

Closed Primary.   In a *closed primary*, only avowed or declared members of a party can vote in that party's primary. In other words, voters must declare their party affiliation, either when they register to vote or at the primary election. A closed-primary system tries to make sure that registered voters cannot cross over into the other party's primary in order to nominate the weakest candidate of the opposing party or to affect the ideological direction of that party.

Open Primary.   An *open primary* is a primary in which voters can vote in either party primary without disclosing their party affiliation. Basically, the voter makes the choice in the privacy of the voting booth. The voter must, however, choose one party's list from which to select candidates. Open primaries place no restrictions on independent voters.

Blanket Primary.   A *blanket primary* is one in which the voter may vote for candidates of more than one party. Alaska, Louisiana, and Washington have blanket primaries. Blanket-primary campaigns may be much more costly because each candidate for every office is trying to influence all the voters, not just those in his or her party.

   In 2000, the United States Supreme Court issued a decision that will alter significantly the use of the blanket primary. The case arose when political parties in California challenged the constitutionality of the blanket primary in that state. The parties contended that the blanket primary violated their First Amendment right of association. Because the nominees represent the party, they argued, party members—not the general electorate—should have the right to choose the party's nominee. The Supreme Court ruled in favor of the parties, holding that the blanket primary violated parties' First Amendment associational rights.[8] The Court's ruling called into question the constitutional validity of blanket primaries in other states as well.

Front-Loading the Primaries

As soon as politicians and potential presidential candidates realized that winning as many primary elections as possible guaranteed them the party's nomination for president, their tactics changed dramatically. For example, candidates running in the 2000 primaries concentrated on building organizations in states that held early, important primary elections. Candidates realized that winning early primaries, such as the New Hampshire election in February, or finishing first in the Iowa caucuses meant that the media instantly would label the winner as the **front-runner,** thus increasing the candidate's media exposure and escalating the pace of contributions to his or her campaign fund.

Front-Runner The presidential candidate who appears to be ahead at a given time in the primary season.

   The states and state political parties began to see that early primaries had a much greater effect on the outcome of the presidential election and, accordingly, began to hold their primaries earlier in the season to secure that advantage. While New Hampshire held on to its claim to hold the first primary, other states moved theirs to the next week. A group of southern states decided to hold their primaries on the same date, known as **Super Tuesday,** in the hope of nominating a moderate southerner at the Democratic convention. When California, which had held the last primary (in June), moved its primary to March, the primary season was curtailed drastically. Due to this process of **front-loading** the primaries, in 2000 the presidential nominating process was over in March, with both George W. Bush and Al Gore having enough convention delegate votes to win their nominations. This meant that the campaign was essentially without news until the conventions in August, a gap that did not appeal to the politicians or the media.

On to the National Convention

Presidential candidates have been nominated by the convention method in every election since 1832. The delegates are sent from each state and are apportioned on the basis of state representation. Extra delegates are allowed to attend from states that had voting majorities for the party in the preceding elections. Parties also accept delegates from the District of Columbia, the territories, and certain overseas groups.

Seating the Delegates.   At the convention, each political party uses a **credentials committee** to determine which delegates may participate. Controversy may arise when rival groups claim to be the official party organization for a county, district, or state. The Mississippi Democratic Party split along racial lines in 1964 at the height of the civil rights movement in the Deep South. Separate all-white and mixed white and African American sets of delegates were selected, and both factions showed up at the national convention. After much debate on party rules, the committee decided to seat the pro–civil rights delegates and exclude those who represented the traditional "white" party.

Convention Activities.   The typical convention lasts only a few days. Because delegates generally arrive at the convention committed to presidential candidates, no convention since 1952 has required more than one ballot to choose a nominee. Since 1972, candidates have usually come into the convention with enough committed delegates to win.

   In 2000, the outcome of the two conventions was so predictable that the national networks televised the convention proceedings for no more than two hours each evening. The convention planners concentrated on showing off the most important speeches during that prime-time period. Gavel-to-gavel coverage was available at several Internet sites, however.

The Electoral College

Many voters who vote for the president and vice president think that they are voting directly for a candidate. In actuality, they are voting for **electors** who will cast their ballots in the electoral college. Article II, Section 1, of the Constitution outlines in detail the number and choice of electors for president and vice president. The framers of the Constitution wanted to avoid the selection of president and vice

Super Tuesday A date on which a large number of presidential primaries are held, including those of many southern states.

Front-Loading The practice of moving presidential primary elections to the early part of the campaign, to maximize the impact of the primaries on the nomination.

Credentials Committee A committee used by political parties at their national conventions to determine which delegates may participate.

Elector A member of the electoral college, which selects the president and vice president.

FIGURE 8–1   State Electoral Votes in 2004

The map of the United States shown here is distorted to show the relative weight of the states in terms of electoral votes in 2004, following the changes required by the 2000 census. A candidate must win 270 electoral votes to be elected president.

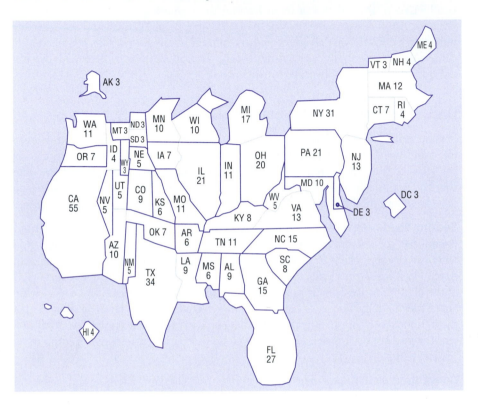

president by the excitable masses. Rather, they wished the choice to be made by a few supposedly dispassionate, reasonable men (but not women).

The Choice of Electors

Each state's electors are selected during each presidential election year. The selection is governed by state laws. After the national party convention, the electors are pledged to the candidates chosen. The total number of electors today is 538, equal to 100 senators, 435 members of the House, plus 3 electors for the District of Columbia (subsequent to the Twenty-third Amendment, ratified in 1961). Each state's number of electors equals that state's number of senators (two) plus its number of representatives. The graphic in Figure 8–1 shows how the electoral votes are apportioned by state.

The Electors' Commitment

When a plurality of voters in a state chooses a slate of electors, those electors are pledged to cast their ballots for the presidential and vice presidential candidates of their party.[9] The Constitution does not, however, *require* the electors to cast their ballots for the candidates of their party.

The ballots are counted and certified before a joint session of Congress early in January. The candidates who receive a majority of the electoral votes (270) are certified as president-elect and vice president-elect. According to the Constitution, if no candidate receives a majority of the electoral votes, the election of the president is decided in the House from among the candidates with the three highest numbers of votes, with each state having one vote (decided by a plurality of each state delegation). The selection of the vice president is determined by the Senate in a choice between the two candidates with the most votes, each senator having one vote. Congress was required to choose the president and vice president in 1801 (Thomas Jefferson and Aaron Burr), and the House chose the president in 1825 (John Quincy Adams).

It is possible for a candidate to become president without obtaining a majority of the popular vote. There have been many minority presidents in our history, including Abraham Lincoln, Woodrow Wilson, Harry Truman, John F. Kennedy, Richard Nixon (in 1968), and Bill Clinton. Such an event becomes more likely when there are major third-party candidates.

Perhaps more distressing is the possibility of a candidate's being elected when an opposing candidate receives a plurality of the popular vote. This has occurred on four occasions—in the elections of John Quincy Adams in 1824, Rutherford B. Hayes in 1876, Benjamin Harrison in 1888, and George W. Bush in 2000, all of whom won elections in which an opponent received a plurality of the popular vote.

Criticisms of the Electoral College

Besides the possibility of a candidate's becoming president even though an opponent obtains more popular votes, there are other complaints about the electoral college. The idea of the Constitution's framers was to have electors use their own discretion to decide who would make the best president. But electors no longer perform the selecting function envisioned by the founders, because they are committed to the candidate who has a plurality of popular votes in their state in the general election.[10]

It can also be argued that there is something of a bias toward states with smaller populations, because including Senate seats in the electoral vote total partly offsets the edge of the more populous states in the House. Wyoming (with two senators and one representative) gets an electoral vote for roughly each 164,594 people (based on the 2000 census), for example, whereas Iowa gets one vote for each 418,046 people, and California has a vote for every 615,848 inhabitants. Note that many of the smallest states have Republican majorities.

Many proposals for reform of the electoral college system have been advanced, particularly after the turmoil resulting from the 2000 elections. The most obvious is

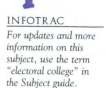

INFOTRAC

For updates and more information on this subject, use the term "electoral college" in the Subject guide.

to get rid of it completely and have a direct election, by the people, of the president and vice president. Because abolishing the electoral college would require a constitutional amendment, however, the chances of electing the president by a direct vote are remote.

The major parties are not in favor of eliminating the electoral college, fearing that it would give minor parties a more influential role. Also, less populous states are not in favor of direct election of the president because they believe they would be overwhelmed by the large-state vote.

How Are Elections Conducted?

Australian Ballot A secret ballot prepared by the government.

The United States uses the **Australian ballot**—a secret ballot that is prepared, distributed, and counted by government officials at public expense. Since 1888, all states have used the Australian ballot. Before that, many states used the alternatives of oral voting and differently colored ballots prepared by the parties. Obviously, knowing which way a person was voting made it easy to apply pressure on the person to change his or her vote, and vote buying was common.

Office-Block and Party-Column Ballots

Office-Block, or Massachusetts, Ballot A form of general election ballot in which candidates for elective office are grouped together under the title of each office.

Party-Column, or Indiana, Ballot A form of general election ballot in which all of a party's candidates for elective office are arranged in one column under the party's labels and symbols.

Coattail Effect The influence of a popular candidate on the electoral success of other candidates on the same party ticket.

Two types of Australian ballots are used in the United States in general elections. The first, called an **office-block ballot,** or sometimes a **Massachusetts ballot,** groups all the candidates for each elective office under the title of each office. Parties dislike the office-block ballot because it places more emphasis on the office than on the party; it discourages straight-ticket voting and encourages split-ticket voting.

A **party-column ballot** is a form of general election ballot in which all of a party's candidates are arranged in one column under the party's labels and symbols. It is also called the **Indiana ballot.** In some states, it allows voters to vote for all of a party's candidates for local, state, and national offices by simply marking a single "X" or by pulling a single lever. Most states use this type of ballot. As it encourages straight-ticket voting, the two major parties favor this form. When a party has an exceptionally strong presidential or gubernatorial candidate to head the ticket, the use of the party-column ballot increases the **coattail effect.**

Voting by Mail

Although voting by mail has been accepted for absentee ballots for many decades (for example, for those who are doing business away from home or for members of the armed forces), only recently have several states offered mail ballots to all of their voters. The rationale for using the mail ballot is to make voting easier and more accessible to the voters. In the 2000 presidential elections, in which Oregon voters were allowed to mail in their ballots, voter participation was over 80 percent. Although voters in a number of states now have the option of voting by mail, Oregon is the only state to have completely abandoned precinct polling places.

Norman Ornstein, an early critic of mail-in voting, has suggested that mail balloting subverts the whole election process. In part, this is because the voter casts her or his ballot at any time, perhaps before any debates or other dialogues are held between candidates. Thus, the voter may be casting an uninformed ballot.[11] Others have argued that mail-in voting deprives voters of the secrecy guaranteed by polling-place voting, provides more opportunities for fraud, and represents the abandonment of an important civic rite of going to the polls on election day. Still others, however, see the mail ballot as the best way to increase voter participation at a time when many are too busy to vote or have little interest in the process.

Vote Fraud

Vote fraud is something regularly suspected but seldom proved. Voting in the 1800s, when secret ballots were rare and people had a cavalier attitude toward the open buying of votes, was probably much more conducive to fraud than modern elections are. An investigation by Larry J. Sabato and Glenn R. Simpson, however, has revealed that the potential for vote fraud is high in many states, particularly through the use of phony voter registrations and absentee ballots.[12]

In California, for example, it is very difficult to remove a name from the polling list even if the person has not cast a ballot in the last two years. Thus, many persons are still on the rolls even though they no longer live in California. Enterprising political activists could use these names for absentee ballots. Other states have registration laws that are meant to encourage easy registration and voting. Such laws can be taken advantage of by those who seek to vote more than once.

The registration files of absentee ballots are verified at a counting facility in Fort Lauderdale, Florida, after the 2000 presidential election. Florida's election procedures came under scrutiny after the 2000 election. Is it possible to eliminate fraud entirely from the election process?

AP Photo/Wilfredo Lee

Voting in National, State, and Local Elections

In 2000, there were 200 million eligible voters. Of that number, 101 million, or 50.7 percent of eligible voters, actually went to the polls. When only half of the eligible voters participate in elections, it means, among other things, that the winner of a close presidential election may be voted in by only about one-fourth of the voting-age population (see Table 8–2).

Figure 8–2 shows **voter turnout** for presidential and congressional elections from 1900 to 2002. The last "good" year of turnout for the presidential elections was 1960, when almost 65 percent of the eligible voters actually voted. Each of the peaks in the figure represents voter turnout in a presidential election. Thus, we can also see that turnout for congressional elections is greatly influenced by whether there is a presidential election in the same year.

Voter Turnout The percentage of citizens taking part in the election process; the number of eligible voters that actually "turn out" on election day to cast their ballots.

TABLE 8–2 | Elected by a Majority?

Most presidents have won a majority of the votes cast in the election. We generally judge the extent of their victory by whether they have won more than 51 percent of the votes. Some presidential elections have been proclaimed landslides, meaning that the candidates won by an extraordinary majority of votes cast. As indicated below, however, no modern president has been elected by more than 38 percent of the total voting-age electorate.

YEAR—WINNER (PARTY)	PERCENTAGE OF TOTAL POPULAR VOTE	PERCENTAGE OF VOTING-AGE POPULATION
1932—Roosevelt (D)	57.4	30.1
1936—Roosevelt (D)	60.8	34.6
1940—Roosevelt (D)	54.7	32.2
1944—Roosevelt (D)	53.4	29.9
1948—Truman (D)	49.6	25.3
1952—Eisenhower (R)	55.1	34.0
1956—Eisenhower (R)	57.4	34.1
1960—Kennedy (D)	49.7	31.2
1964—Johnson (D)	61.1	37.8
1968—Nixon (R)	43.4	26.4
1972—Nixon (R)	60.7	33.5
1976—Carter (D)	50.1	26.8
1980—Reagan (R)	50.7	26.7
1984—Reagan (R)	58.8	31.2
1988—Bush (R)	53.4	26.8
1992—Clinton (D)	43.3	23.1
1996—Clinton (D)	49.2	23.2
2000—Bush (R)	47.8	24.9

SOURCES: *Congressional Quarterly Weekly Report*, January 31, 1989, p. 137; *The New York Times*, November 5, 1992; *The New York Times*, November 7, 1996; and *The New York Times*, November 12, 2000.

FIGURE 8–2 **Voter Turnout for Presidential and Congressional Elections, 1900 to Present**

The peaks represent turnout in presidential election years; the troughs represent turnout in off-presidential-election years.

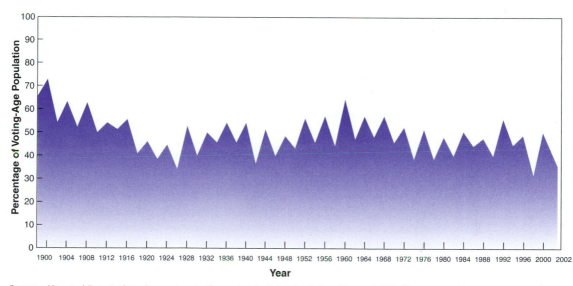

SOURCES: Historical Data Archive, Inter-university Consortium for Political and Social Research: U.S. Department of Commerce, *Statistical Abstract of the United States: 1980*, 101st ed. (Washington, D.C.: U.S. Government Printing Office, 1980), p. 515; William H. Flanigan and Nancy H. Zingale, *Political Behavior of the American Electorate*, 5th ed. (Boston: Allyn and Bacon, 1983), p. 20; *Congressional Quarterly*, various issues; and authors' updates.

The same is true at the state level. When there is a race for governor, more voters participate both in the general election for governor and in the election for state representatives. Voter participation rates in gubernatorial elections are also greater in presidential election years. The average turnout in state elections is about 14 percentage points higher when a presidential election is held.

Now consider local elections. In races for mayor, city council, county auditor, and the like, it is fairly common for only 25 percent or less of the electorate to vote. Is something amiss here? It would seem that people should be more likely to vote in elections that directly affect them. At the local level, each person's vote counts more (because there are fewer voters). Furthermore, the issues—crime control, school bonds, sewer bonds, and so on—touch the immediate interests of the voters. The facts, however, do not fit the theory. Potential voters are most interested in national elections, when a presidential choice is involved.

INFOTRAC

For more information on voting, use the term "voting" in the Subject guide.

The Effect of Low Voter Turnout

There are two schools of thought concerning low voter turnout. Some view the decline in voter participation since 1960 as a threat to our representative democratic government. Fewer and fewer individuals are deciding who wields political power in our society. Also, low voter participation presumably signals apathy about our political system in general. When only a handful of people take the time to learn about the issues, it will be easier, say the alarmists, for an authoritarian figure to take over our government.

Others are less concerned about low voter participation. They believe that a decline in voter participation simply indicates more satisfaction with the status quo. Also, they believe that representative democracy is a reality even if a very small percentage of eligible voters vote. If everyone who does not vote believes that the outcome of the election will accord with his or her own desires, then representative democracy is working.

Factors Influencing Who Votes

A clear association exists between voter participation and the following characteristics: age, educational attainment, minority status, income level, and the existence of two-party competition.

1. *Age.* Age is a strong factor in determining voter turnout on election day. The reported turnout increases with older age groups. Greater participation with age is very likely due to the fact that older voters are more settled in their lives, are already registered, and have had more time to experience voting as an expected activity.

2. *Educational attainment.* Education also influences voter turnout. In general, the more education you have, the more likely you are to vote. In the 2000 election, reported turnout was over 30 percentage points higher for those who had some college education than it was for people who had never been to high school.

3. *Minority status.* Race and ethnicity are important, too, in determining the level of voter turnout. Non-Hispanic whites in 2000 voted at a 60.4 percent rate, whereas the non-Hispanic African American turnout rate was 54.1 percent. For Hispanics, the turnout rate was 27.5 percent.

4. *Income level.* Wealthier people tend to be overrepresented among voters who turn out on election day. In 2000, turnout varied from 28.2 percent for those with annual family incomes under $5,000 to about 71.5 percent for people with annual family incomes of $75,000 or more.

5. *Two-party competition.* Another factor in voter turnout is the extent to which elections are competitive within a state. More competitive states generally have higher turnout rates, and turnout increases considerably in states where there is a highly competitive race in a particular year.

These statistics reinforce one another. White voters are likely to be wealthier than African American voters, who are also less likely to have obtained a college education.

Legal Restrictions on Voting

Legal restrictions on voter registration have existed since the founding of the nation. Most groups in the United States have been concerned with the suffrage issue at one time or another.

Historical Restrictions

In colonial times, only white males who owned property with a certain minimum value were eligible to vote, leaving a greater number of Americans ineligible than eligible to take part in the democratic process.

Property Requirements.   Many government functions concern property rights and the distribution of income and wealth, and some of the founders of our nation felt it was appropriate that only people who had an interest in property should vote on these issues. The logic behind the restriction of voting rights to property owners was questioned seriously by Thomas Paine in his pamphlet *Common Sense:*

> Here is a man who today owns a jackass, and the jackass is worth $60. Today the man is a voter and goes to the polls and deposits his vote. Tomorrow the jackass dies. The next day the man comes to vote without his jackass and cannot vote at all. Now tell me, which was the voter, the man or the jackass?[13]

The writers of the Constitution allowed the states to decide who should vote. Thus, women were allowed to vote in Wyoming in 1870 but not in the entire nation until the Nineteenth Amendment was ratified in 1920. By about 1850, most white adult males in virtually all the states could vote without any property qualification.

Further Extensions of the Franchise.   Extension of the franchise to black males occurred with the passage of the Fifteenth Amendment in 1870. This enfranchisement was short lived, however, as the "redemption" of the South by white racists had rolled back these gains by the end of the century. Not until the 1960s were African Americans, both male and female, able to participate in the electoral process in all states. Women received full national voting rights with the Nineteenth Amendment in 1920. The most recent extension of the franchise occurred when the voting age was reduced to eighteen by the Twenty-sixth Amendment in 1971.

Current Eligibility and Registration Requirements

Voting generally requires **registration,** and to register, a person must satisfy the following voter qualifications, or legal requirements: (1) citizenship, (2) age (eighteen or older), and (3) residency—the duration varies widely from state to state and with types of elections. Since 1972, states cannot impose residency requirements of more than thirty days. In addition, most states disqualify people who are mentally incompetent, prison inmates, convicted felons, or election-law violators.

Registration The entry of a person's name onto the list of eligible voters.

Each state has different qualifications for voting and registration. In 1993, Congress passed the "motor voter" bill, which requires that states provide voter-registration materials when people receive or renew driver's licenses, that all states allow voters to register by mail, and that voter-registration forms be made available at a wider variety of public places and agencies. In general, a person must register well in advance of an election, although voters in Idaho, Maine, Minnesota, Oregon, Wisconsin, and Wyoming are allowed to register up to, and on, election day. North Dakota has no voter registration.

Some argue that registration requirements are responsible for much of the non-participation in our political process. Certainly, since their introduction in the late

1800s, registration laws have had the effect of reducing the voting participation of African Americans and immigrants. There also is a partisan dimension to the debate over registration and nonvoting. Republicans generally fear that an expanded electorate would help to elect more Democrats.

How Do Voters Decide?

Political scientists and survey researchers have collected much information about voting behavior. This information sheds some light on which people vote and why people decide to vote for particular candidates. We have already discussed factors influencing voter turnout. Generally, the factors that influence voting decisions can be divided into two groups: (1) socioeconomic and demographic factors and (2) psychological factors.

Socioeconomic Status The value assigned to a person due to occupation or income. An upper-class person, for example, has high socioeconomic status.

Socioeconomic and Demographic Factors

As shown in Table 8–3, a number of socioeconomic and demographic factors appear to influence voting behavior, including (1) education, (2) income and **socioeconomic status,** (3) religion, (4) race, (5) gender, and (6) geographic region. These influences all reflect the voter's personal background and place in society. Some factors have to do with the family into which a person is born: race and (for most people) religion.

Voter registration is an important part of our political process. These workers are helping a citizen register to vote in the next election. The requirements for voter registration vary across states. Do you believe that current registration requirements are too strict, or about right?

Bob Dammrich/Stock Boston

TABLE 8–3	Votes by Groups in Presidential Elections since 1988 (in Percentages)								
	1988		1992			1996		2000	
	DUKAKIS (DEM.)	BUSH (REP.)	CLINTON (DEM.)	BUSH (REP.)	PEROT (REF.)	CLINTON (DEM.)	DOLE (REP.)	GORE (DEM.)	BUSH (REP.)
Total vote	45	53	43	38	19	49	41	48	48
Sex									
Men	41	57	41	38	21	43	44	42	53
Women	49	50	46	37	17	54	38	54	43
Race									
White	40	59	39	41	20	43	46	42	54
Black	86	12	82	11	7	84	12	90	8
Hispanic	69	30	62	25	14	72	21	67	31
Educational Attainment									
Not a high school graduate	56	43	55	28	17	59	28	59	39
High school graduate	49	50	43	36	20	51	35	48	49
College graduate	37	62	40	41	19	44	46	45	51
Postgraduate education	48	50	49	36	15	52	40	52	44
Religion									
White Protestant	33	66	33	46	21	36	53	34	63
Catholic	47	52	44	36	20	53	37	49	47
Jewish	64	35	78	12	10	78	16	79	19
White Fundamentalist	18	81	23	61	15	na	na	na	na
Union Status									
Union household	57	42	55	24	21	59	30	59	37
Family Income									
Under $15,000	62	37	59	23	18	59	28	57	37
$15,000–29,000	50	49	45	35	20	53	36	54	41
$30,000–49,000	44	56	41	38	21	48	40	49	48
Over $50,000	42	56	40	42	18	44	48	45	52
Size of Place									
Population over 500,000	62	37	58	28	13	68	25	71	26
Population 50,000 to 500,000	52	47	50	33	16	50	39	57	40
Population 10,000 to 50,000	38	61	39	42	20	48	41	38	59
Rural	44	55	39	40	20	44	46	37	59

SOURCES: *The New York Times*; Voter News Service.

Others may be the result of choices made throughout an individual's life: place of residence, educational achievement, and profession. It is also clear that many of these factors are related. People who have more education are likely to have higher incomes and to hold professional jobs. Similarly, children born into wealthier families are far more likely to complete college than children from poorer families.

Education. In the past, having a college education tended to be associated with voting for Republicans. In recent years, however, this correlation has become weaker. In particular, individuals with a postgraduate education—more than a bachelor's degree—have become increasingly Democratic. Many of these people are professionals. Also, a higher percentage of voters with only a high school education voted Republican in 2000, compared with the pattern in previous elections, in which that group of voters tended to favor Democrats. Voters with only a grade school education have voted Democratic in nearly every election.

Income and Socioeconomic Status. Traditionally, the higher a person's income, the more likely the person will be to vote Republican. Manual laborers, factory workers, and especially union members are more likely to vote Democratic. If socioeconomic status is measured by profession, then, traditionally, those of higher socioeconomic status—professionals and businesspersons, as well as white-collar workers—have tended to vote Republican. But there are no hard and fast rules. Indeed, recent research indicates that a realignment is occurring among those of higher socioeconomic status: professionals now tend to vote Democratic, while small-business owners, managers, and corporate executives tend to vote Republican.[14]

Religion. In the United States, Protestants have traditionally been more likely to vote Republican, and Catholics and Jews have been more likely to vote Democratic. Like the other patterns discussed, however, this one is somewhat fluid. Particularly notable is the degree to which religious practices, particularly church attendance, rather than denomination correlate with voting behavior. Recent studies suggest that voters who are more devout, regardless of their church affiliation, are voting Republican, while voters who are less devout are more often Democrats.

In 2000, for example, devout Protestants who regularly attend church gave 84 percent of their votes to Bush, compared with 55 percent of those who attend church less often. Among Catholics, there was a similar pattern: a majority of Catholics who attend church regularly voted Republican, while a majority of Catholics who are not regular churchgoers voted for Al Gore.[15] There are two exceptions to this trend: African Americans of all religions and Jews are strongly supportive of Democrats.

Race. African Americans voted principally for Republicans until Democrat Franklin Roosevelt's New Deal in the 1930s. Since then, they have largely identified with the Democratic Party. Indeed, Democratic presidential candidates have received, on average, more than 80 percent of the African American vote since 1956.

Gender. Until relatively recently, there seemed to be no fixed pattern of voter preference by gender in presidential elections. In recent years, however, it is clear that women have been shifting their preferences to Democratic candidates. A number of explanations for this trend have been offered, including the increase in the number of working women, feminism, and women's concerns over abortion rights and other social issues.

In their study of why women are politically moving to the left, Lena Edlund and Rohini Pande of Columbia University found that the major factor has been the disparate economic impact on men and women of not being married. In the last three decades, men and women have tended to marry later in life or to stay single even after having children. The divorce rate has also risen dramatically. Edlund and Pande argue that this decline in marriage has tended to make men richer and women poorer. Consequently, support for Democrats is high among single women, particularly single mothers.[16]

Geographic Region.   The former Solid (Democratic) South has crumbled in national elections. Only 43 percent of the votes from the southern states went to Democrat Al Gore in 2000, while 55 percent went to Republican George W. Bush. Democrats still draw much of their strength from large northern and eastern cities. Rural areas tend to be Republican (and conservative).

Psychological Factors

In addition to socioeconomic and demographic explanations for the way people vote, at least three important psychological factors play a role in voter decision making. These factors, which are rooted in attitudes and beliefs held by voters, are (1) party identification, (2) perception of the candidates, and (3) issue preferences.

Party Identification.   With the possible exception of race, party identification has been the most important determinant of voting behavior in national elections. Party affiliation is influenced by family and peer groups, by age, by the media, and by psychological attachment. In the middle to late 1960s, party identification began to weaken. Whereas independent voters were a little more than 20 percent of the eligible electorate during the 1950s, they constituted over 30 percent of all voters by

A number of factors determine how voters make decisions at the polling place. Aside from the many demographic influences that come into play, there are also psychological factors that help shape the way voters make decisions when they enter the voting booth.

MAKING A DIFFERENCE: Registering and Voting

In nearly every state, before you are allowed to cast a vote in an election, you must first register. Registration laws vary considerably from state to state.

RESIDENCY AND AGE REQUIREMENTS

What do you have to do to register and cast a vote? In general, you must be a citizen of the United States, at least eighteen years old on or before election day, and a resident of the state in which you intend to register. Most states require that you meet minimum-residency requirements. The minimum-residency requirement is very short in some states, such as one day in Alabama and ten days in New Hampshire and Wisconsin. No state requires more than thirty days. Twenty states do not have any minimum-residency requirement at all.

TIME LIMITS

Nearly every state also specifies a closing date by which you must be registered before an election. You may not be able to vote if you register too close to the day of the election. The closing date for registration varies from election day itself (Maine, Minnesota, Oregon, and Wisconsin) to thirty days before the election (Arizona). In North Dakota, no registration is necessary.

In most states, your registration can be revoked if you do not vote within a certain number of years. This process of automatically "purging" the voter-registration lists of nonactive voters varies in frequency from every two years to every ten years. Ten states do not require this purging.

AN EXAMPLE

Let us look at voter registration in Iowa as an example. Iowa voters normally register through the local county auditor or when they obtain a driver's license (under the "motor voter" law of 1993). A voter who moves to a new address within the state must change registration by contacting the auditor. Postcard registrations must be postmarked or delivered to the county auditor no later than the twenty-fifth day before an election. Postcard registration forms in Iowa are available at many public buildings, at the county auditors' offices, or from campus groups.

For more information on voting registration, contact your county or state officials, party headquarters, labor union, or local chapter of the League of Women Voters. The Web site for the League of Women Voters is **http://www.lwv.org**.

the mid-1990s. Independent voting seems to be more common among new young voters. Thus, we can still say that for established voters party identification is an important determinant in voter choice.

Perception of the Candidates.   The image of the candidate also seems to be important in a voter's choice for president. To some extent, voter attitudes toward candidates are based on emotions (such as trust) rather than on any judgment about experience or policy. In 2000, voters seemed to be attracted to candidates who appeared to have high integrity and honesty.

Issue Preferences. Issues make a difference in presidential and congressional elections. Although personality or image factors may be very persuasive, most voters have some notion of how the candidates differ on basic issues or at least know which candidates want a change in the direction of government policy.

Historically, economic issues have had the strongest influence on voters' choices. When the economy is doing well, it is very difficult for a challenger, particularly at the presidential level, to defeat the incumbent. In contrast, inflation, unemployment, or high interest rates are likely to work to the disadvantage of the incumbent. Some studies indicate that people vote on the basis of their personal economic well-being, whereas other studies seem to show that people vote on the basis of the nation's overall economic health.

KEY TERMS

Australian ballot **192**

"beauty contest" **186**

bundling **185**

caucus **187**

coattail effect **192**

corrupt practices acts **182**

credentials committee **189**

elector **189**

focus group **181**

front-loading **189**

front-runner **188**

Hatch Act **182**

independent expenditures **184**

office-block, or Massachusetts, ballot **192**

party-column, or Indiana, ballot **192**

political consultant **180**

presidential primary **176**

registration **197**

socioeconomic status **198**

superdelegate **187**

Super Tuesday **189**

tracking poll **181**

voter turnout **194**

CHAPTER SUMMARY

1 The legal qualifications for holding political office are minimal, but office holders still are predominantly white and male and are likely to be from the professional class.

2 American political campaigns are lengthy and extremely expensive. In the last decade, they have become more candidate centered rather than party centered. Candidates have begun to rely on paid consultants to wage a campaign. The crucial task of consultants is image building. The campaign organization devises a strategy to maximize the chances of winning. Candidates use public opinion polls and focus groups to gauge their popularity.

3 The amount of money spent in financing campaigns is steadily increasing. Corrupt practices acts have been passed to regulate campaign finance. The Federal Election Campaign Act of 1971 and its amendments in 1974 and 1976 limited spending and contributions. The acts allowed political action committees (PACs) to raise money for candidates. New techniques, including "soft money" contributions to the parties, independent expenditures, and bundling, were subsequently developed. The Bipartisan Campaign Reform Act of 2002 banned soft money contributions to the national parties, limited advertising by interest groups, and increased the limits on individual contributions.

❹ After the Democratic convention of 1968, the McGovern-Fraser Commission formulated new rules for primaries, which were adopted by all Democrats and by Republicans in many states. These reforms opened up the nomination process for the presidency to all voters.

❺ A presidential primary is a statewide election to help a political party determine its presidential nominee at the national convention. Some states use the caucus method of choosing convention delegates. The primary campaign recently has been shortened to the first few months of the election year.

❻ The voter technically does not vote directly for president but chooses between slates of presidential electors. The slate that wins the most popular votes throughout the state gets to cast all the electoral votes for the state. The candidate receiving a majority (270) of the electoral votes wins. Both the mechanics and the politics of the electoral college have been sharply criticized.

❼ The United States uses the Australian ballot, a secret ballot that is prepared, distributed, and counted by government officials. The office-block ballot groups candidates according to office. The party-column ballot groups candidates according to their party labels and symbols.

❽ Voter participation in the United States is low, especially when presidential candidates are not on the ballot. There is an association between voting and a person's age, education, minority status, and income level.

❾ In colonial times, only white males with a certain minimum amount of property were eligible to vote. Currently, to be eligible to vote, a person must satisfy registration, citizenship, and specified age and residency requirements. Each state has different qualifications.

❿ Socioeconomic or demographic factors that influence voting decisions include (a) education, (b) income and socioeconomic status, (c) religion, (d) race, (e) gender, and (f) geographic region. Psychological factors that influence voting decisions include (a) party identification, (b) perception of candidates, and (c) issue preferences.

SELECTED PRINT AND MEDIA RESOURCES

Suggested Readings

Abramson, Paul R., *et al. Change and Continuity in the 2000 and 2002 Elections.* Washington, D.C.: CQ Press, 2003. The authors offer a thorough and comparative analysis of two recent election cycles.

Faucheux, Ronald A. *Running for Office: The Strategies, Techniques, and Messages Modern Political Candidates Need to Win Elections.* New York: M. Evans & Co., 2002. A variety of guides on how to run a campaign are available. Typically, these guides are oriented toward first-time candidates for state or local office. Faucheaux's well-regarded manual is among the most recent.

Sabato, Larry J., ed. *Overtime! The Election 2000 Thriller.* Reading, Mass.: Addison Wesley Longman, 2001. The political and legal drama that unfolded after the 2000 elections.

Media Resources

The Candidate—A 1972 film, starring Robert Redford, that satirizes the decisions a candidate for the U.S. Senate must make. A political classic.

If You Can't Say Anything Nice—Negative campaigning seems to have become the norm in recent years. This 1999 program looks at the resulting decline in popularity of politics among the electorate and suggests approaches to restoring faith in the process.

Money Talks: The Influence of Money on American Politics—Bill Moyers reports on the influence of money on our political system. Produced in 1994.

Primary Colors—A 1998 film starring John Travolta as a southern governor who is plagued by a sex scandal during his run for the presidency.

LOGGING ON

For detailed information about current campaign-financing laws and for the latest filings of finance reports, see the site maintained by the Federal Election Commission at http://www.fec.gov.

To find excellent reports on where campaign money comes from and how it is spent, view the site maintained by the Center for Responsive Politics at http://www.opensecrets.org.

You can learn about the impact of different voting systems on election strategies and outcomes at the Center for Voting and Democracy, which maintains the following Web site: http://www.fairvote.org.

Another excellent site for investigating voting records and campaign-financing information is that of Project Vote Smart. Go to http://www.vote-smart.org.

USING THE INTERNET FOR POLITICAL ANALYSIS

Go to this text's Web site at http://politicalscience.wadsworth.com/schmidtbrief2004. Select "Chapter 8" in the box at the top of the window. Then, in the column on the left-hand side of the window, under "Chapter Resources," click on "Internet Exercises." The Web site will then display the following Internet exercises that you can perform to learn more about topics covered in this chapter.

Activity 8–1: **Voting by Mail**

Activity 8–2: **Proportional Representation**

Activity 8–3: **Campaign Contributions**

ONLINE STUDY GUIDE AND ADDITIONAL RESOURCES

At http://politicalscience.wadsworth.com/schmidtbrief2004 you will find a free Study Guide to this book that includes tutorial quizzes, essay questions, practice exams, chapter outlines, learning objectives, the glossary, flashcards, crossword puzzles, and Microsoft PowerPoint presentations. Also included in the American Government Resource Center for Chapter 8:

- **InfoTrac® Reader**—Bush vs. Gore, 2000; campaign-finance reform.

- **You Are There Simulations**—Campaign and elections; public opinion and voting.

- **Participation Activities**—Investigate what you would have to do to get on the ballot for either city council or the county board of supervisors; support a candidate running for office; research low voter turnout in the United States.

- **MicroCase Exercises**—Campaigns and elections; public opinion and voting.

- **Related Links**—Campaign and elections; public opinion and voting.

- **Video Case Studies**—Modern campaigns; running for president.

- **Source Readings**—The Federal Election Campaign Act of 1972 and 1974; *Bush v. Gore* (2000).

The site also contains the Citizen's Survival Guide, information on how to get involved in politics locally and globally, as well as regularly updated features, including a Current Events Quiz, In the News, Election Links, updates on the war on terrorism, and more.

CHAPTER 9

The Congress

MOST AMERICANS SPEND LITTLE TIME thinking about the Congress of the United States, and when they do, their opinions are frequently unflattering. For many years, the public's approval rating of Congress as a whole was about 30 percent. During the late 1990s and early 2000s, Congress's approval ratings climbed to between 40 percent and 50 percent in most polls, however, and they have continued to be relatively high. Yet the majority of voters express even higher approval ratings (in the range of 60 percent to 70 percent) for the members of Congress from their districts. This is one of the paradoxes of the relationship between the people and Congress. Members of the public hold the institution in relatively low regard compared to the satisfaction they express with their individual representatives.

> **Constituent** One of the people represented by a legislator or other elected or appointed official.

Part of the explanation for these seemingly contradictory appraisals is that members of Congress spend considerable time and effort serving their **constituents.** If the federal bureaucracy makes a mistake, the senator's or representative's office tries to resolve the issue. What most Americans see of Congress, therefore, is the work of their own representatives in their home states. Yet Congress was created to work not just for local constituents but also for the nation as a whole. Understanding the nature of the institution and the process of lawmaking is an important part of understanding how the policies that shape our lives are made.

In this chapter, we describe the functions of Congress, including constituent service, representation, lawmaking, and oversight of the government. We review how the members of Congress are elected and how Congress organizes itself when it meets. We also examine how bills pass through the legislative process.

Why Was Congress Created?

The founders of the American republic believed that the bulk of the power that would be exercised by a national government should be in the hands of the legislature. The leading role envisioned for Congress in the new government is apparent from its primacy in the Constitution. Article I deals with the structure, the powers, and the operation of Congress, beginning in Section 1 with an application of the basic principle of separation of powers: "All legislative Powers herein granted shall be vested in a Congress of the United States, which shall consist of a Senate and House of Representatives." These legislative powers are spelled out in detail in Article I and elsewhere.

The **bicameralism** of Congress—its division into two legislative houses—was in part the result of the Connecticut Compromise, which tried to balance the large-state population advantage, reflected in the House, and the small-state demand for equality in policymaking, which was satisfied in the Senate. Beyond that, the two chambers of Congress also reflected the social class biases of the founders. They wished to balance the interests and the numerical superiority of the common citizens with the property interests of the less numerous landowners, bankers, and merchants. They achieved this goal by providing in Sections 2 and 3 of Article I that members of the House of Representatives should be elected directly by "the People," whereas members of the Senate were to be chosen by the elected representatives sitting in state legislatures, who were more likely to be members of the elite. (The latter provision was changed in 1913 by the passage of the Seventeenth Amendment, which provides that senators also are to be elected directly by the people.)

The logic of separate constituencies and separate interests underlying the bicameral Congress was reinforced by differences in length of tenure. Members of the House are required to face the electorate every two years, whereas senators can serve for a much more secure term of six years—even longer than the four-year term provided for the president. Furthermore, the senators' terms are staggered so that only one-third of the senators face the electorate every two years, along with all of the House members.

Bicameralism The division of a legislature into two separate assemblies.

The Powers of Congress

The Constitution is both highly specific and extremely vague about the powers that Congress may exercise. The first seventeen clauses of Article I, Section 8, specify most of the **enumerated powers** of Congress—that is, powers expressly given to that body.

Enumerated Power A power specifically granted to the national government by the Constitution.

Enumerated Powers

The enumerated, or expressed, powers of Congress include the right to impose taxes and import tariffs; borrow money; regulate interstate commerce and international trade; establish procedures for naturalizing citizens; make laws regulating bankruptcies; coin (and print) money and regulate its value; establish standards of weights and measures; punish counterfeiters; establish post offices and postal routes; regulate copyrights and patents; establish the federal court system; punish pirates and others committing illegal acts on the high seas; declare war; raise and regulate an army and a navy; call up and regulate the state militias to enforce laws, to suppress insurrections, and to repel invasions; and govern the District of Columbia.

Representative William Jefferson, a Democrat from Louisiana, shakes hands with a constituent during a visit to his home district. Jefferson represents the Second District in Louisiana, which includes most of the city of New Orleans. After a tough fight to win his seat in 1990, Jefferson has been reelected with ease.

Philip Gould/Corbis

The most important of the domestic powers of Congress, listed in Article I, Section 8, are the rights to collect taxes, to spend, and to regulate commerce, whereas the most important foreign policy power is the power to declare war. Other sections of the Constitution give Congress a wide range of further powers. Generally, Congress is also able to establish rules for its own members, to regulate the electoral college, and to override a presidential veto. Congress may also regulate the extent of the Supreme Court's authority to review cases decided by the lower courts, regulate relations between states, and propose amendments to the Constitution.

Some functions are restricted to only one chamber. Under Article II, Section 2, the Senate must advise on, and consent to, the ratification of treaties and must accept or reject presidential nominations of ambassadors, Supreme Court justices, and "all other Officers of the United States." But the Senate may delegate to the president, the courts, or department heads the power to make lesser appointments.

The amendments to the Constitution provide for other congressional powers. Congress must certify the election of a president and a vice president or itself choose these officers if no candidate has a majority of the electoral vote (Twelfth Amendment). It may levy an income tax (Sixteenth Amendment) and determine who will be acting president in case of the death or incapacity of the president or vice president (Twentieth Amendment, Sections 3 and 4, and Twenty-fifth Amendment, Sections 2, 3, and 4). In addition, Congress explicitly is given the power to enforce, by appropriate legislation, the provisions of several other amendments.

The Necessary and Proper Clause

Beyond these numerous specific powers, Congress enjoys the right under Article I, Section 8 (the "elastic," or "necessary and proper," clause), "[t]o make all Laws which shall be necessary and proper for carrying into Execution the foregoing

Powers [of Article I], and all other Powers vested by this Constitution in the Government of the United States, or in any Department or Officer thereof." This vague statement of congressional responsibilities provided, over time, the basis for a greatly expanded national government. It also constituted, at least in theory, a check on the expansion of presidential powers.

The Functions of Congress

The Constitution provides the foundation for congressional powers. Yet a complete understanding of the role that Congress plays requires a broader study of the functions that the national legislature performs in the American political system.

Congress, as an institution of government, is expected by its members, by the public, and by other centers of political power to perform a number of functions. Our perceptions of how good a job Congress is doing overall are tied closely to evaluations of whether and how it fulfills certain specific tasks. These tasks include lawmaking, service to constituents, representation, oversight, public education, and conflict resolution.

The Lawmaking Function

The principal and most obvious function of any legislature is **lawmaking.** Congress is the highest elected body in the country charged with making binding rules for all Americans. Lawmaking requires decisions about the size of the federal budget, about health-care reform and gun control, and about the long-term prospects for war or peace. This does not mean, however, that Congress initiates most of the ideas for legislation that it eventually considers. Most of the bills that Congress acts on originate in the executive branch, and many other bills are traceable to interest groups and political party organizations. Through the processes of compromise and **logrolling** (offering to support a fellow member's bill in exchange for that member's promise to support your bill in the future), as well as debate and discussion, backers of legislation attempt to fashion a winning majority coalition.

Lawmaking The process of establishing the legal rules that govern society.

Logrolling An arrangement in which two or more members of Congress agree in advance to support each other's bills.

Service to Constituents

Individual members of Congress are expected by their constituents to act as brokers between private citizens and the imposing, often faceless federal government. This function of providing service to constituents usually takes the form of **casework.** The legislator and her or his staff spend a considerable portion of their time in casework activity, such as tracking down a missing Social Security check, explaining the meaning of particular bills to people who may be affected by them, promoting a local business interest, or interceding with a regulatory agency on behalf of constituents who disagree with proposed agency regulations.

Legislators and many analysts of congressional behavior regard this **ombudsperson** role as an activity that strongly benefits the members of Congress. A government characterized by a large, confusing bureaucracy and complex public programs offers innumerable opportunities for legislators to come to the assistance of (usually) grateful

Casework Personal work for constituents by members of Congress.

Ombudsperson A person who hears and investigates complaints by private individuals against public officials or agencies.

constituents. Morris P. Fiorina once suggested, somewhat mischievously, that senators and representatives prefer to maintain bureaucratic confusion in order to maximize their opportunities for performing good deeds on behalf of their constituents:

> Some poor, aggrieved constituent becomes enmeshed in the tentacles of an evil bureaucracy and calls upon Congressman St. George to do battle with the dragon. . . . In dealing with the bureaucracy, the congressman is not merely one vote of 435. Rather, he is a nonpartisan power, someone whose phone call snaps an office to attention. He is not kept on hold. The constituent who receives aid believes that his congressman and his congressman alone got results.[1]

The Representation Function

Representation The function of members of Congress as elected officials representing the views of their constituents.

If constituency service carries with it nothing but benefits for most members of Congress, the function of **representation** is less certain and even carries with it some danger that the legislator will lose his or her bid for reelection. Generally, representation means that the many competing interests in society should be represented in Congress. It follows that Congress should be a body acting slowly and deliberately and that its foremost concern should be to maintain a carefully crafted balance of power among competing interests.

How is representation to be achieved? There are basically two points of view on this issue.

Trustee In regard to a legislator, one who acts according to her or his conscience and the broad interests of the entire society.

The Trustee View of Representation.
The first approach to the question of how representation should be achieved is that legislators should act as **trustees** of the broad interests of the entire society and that they should vote against the narrow interests of their constituents as their conscience and their perception of national needs dictate. For example, a number of Republican legislators supported strong laws regulating the tobacco industry in spite of the views of some of their constituents.

Instructed Delegate A legislator who is an agent of the voters who elected him or her and who votes according to the views of constituents regardless of personal beliefs.

The Instructed-Delegate View of Representation.
Directly opposed to the trustee view of representation is the notion that the members of Congress should behave as **instructed delegates;** that is, they should mirror the views of the majority of the constituents who elected them to power in the first place. On the surface, this approach is plausible and rewarding. For it to work, however, we must assume that constituents actually have well-formed views on the issues that are decided in Congress and, further, that they have clear-cut preferences about these issues. Neither condition is likely to be satisfied very often. Most people generally have well-articulated views on only a few major issues.

Oversight The process by which Congress follows up on laws it has enacted to ensure that they are being enforced and administered in the way Congress intended.

Generally, most legislators hold neither a pure trustee view nor a pure instructed-delegate view. Typically, they combine both perspectives in a pragmatic mix.

The Oversight Function

Oversight of the bureaucracy is essential if the decisions made by Congress are to have any force. **Oversight** is the process by which Congress follows up on the laws it has enacted to ensure that they are being enforced and administered in the way

Congress intended. This is done by holding committee hearings and investigations, changing the size of an agency's budget, and cross-examining high-level presidential nominees to head major agencies.

Senators and representatives increasingly see their oversight function as a critically important part of their legislative activities. In part, oversight is related to the concept of constituency service, particularly when Congress investigates alleged arbitrariness or wrongdoing by bureaucratic agencies.

The Public-Education Function

Educating the public is a function that is performed whenever Congress holds public hearings, exercises oversight over the bureaucracy, or engages in committee and floor debate on such major issues and topics as political assassinations, aging, illegal drugs, and the concerns of small businesses. In so doing, Congress presents a range of viewpoints on pressing national questions. Congress also decides what issues will come up for discussion and decision; this **agenda setting** is a major facet of its public-education function.

Agenda Setting
Determining which public-policy questions will be debated or considered.

The Conflict-Resolution Function

Congress is commonly seen as an institution for resolving conflicts within American society. Organized interest groups and representatives of different racial, religious, economic, and ideological interests look on Congress as an access point for airing their grievances and seeking help. This puts Congress in the position of trying to resolve the differences among competing points of view by passing laws to accommodate as many interested parties as possible. To the extent that Congress meets pluralist expectations in accommodating competing interests, it tends to build support for the entire political process.

House-Senate Differences

Congress is composed of two markedly different—but co-equal—chambers. Although the Senate and the House of Representatives exist within the same legislative institution, each has developed certain features that clearly distinguish one from the other.

Size and Rules

The central difference between the House and the Senate is simply that the House is much larger than the Senate. The House has 435 representatives, plus delegates from the District of Columbia, Puerto Rico, Guam, American Samoa, and the Virgin Islands, compared with just 100 senators. This size difference means that a greater number of formal rules are needed to govern activity in the House, whereas correspondingly looser procedures can be followed in the less crowded Senate. This difference is most obvious in the rules governing debate on the floors of the two chambers.

Rules Committee A standing committee of the House of Representatives that provides special rules under which specific bills can be debated, amended, and considered by the House.

INFOTRAC

To find out more about filibusters, use the term "filibuster" in Keywords.

The Senate normally permits extended debate on all issues that arise before it. In contrast, the House operates with an elaborate system in which its **Rules Committee** normally proposes time limitations on debate for any bill and a majority of the entire body accepts or modifies those suggested time limits. As a consequence of its stricter time limits on debate, the House, despite its greater size, often is able to act on legislation more quickly than the Senate.

Debate and Filibustering

The Senate tradition of *filibustering*, or employing unlimited debate as a blocking tactic, dates back to 1790. In that year, a proposal to move the U.S. capital from New York to Philadelphia was stalled by such time-wasting tactics. This unlimited-debate tradition is not absolute, however. Under Senate Rule 22, debate may be ended by invoking *cloture*, which shuts off discussion on a bill. Rule 22 states that debate may be closed off on a bill if sixteen senators sign a petition requesting it and if three-fifths of the entire membership vote for cloture. After cloture is invoked, each senator may speak on a bill for a maximum of one hour before a vote is taken. In 1979, the Senate refined Rule 22 to ensure that a final vote must take place within one hundred hours of debate after cloture has been imposed.

Prestige

As a consequence of the greater size of the House, representatives generally cannot achieve as much individual recognition and public prestige as can members of the Senate. Senators are better able to gain media exposure and to establish careers as spokespersons for large national constituencies.

Congresspersons and the Citizenry: A Comparison

Members of the U.S. Senate and the U.S. House of Representatives are not typical American citizens. Members of Congress are older than most Americans, partly because of constitutional age requirements and partly because a good deal of political experience normally is an advantage in running for national office. Members of Congress are also disproportionately white, male, and trained in high-status occupations. Lawyers are by far the largest occupational group among congresspersons, although the proportion of lawyers in the House is lower now than it was in the past. Compared with the average American citizen, members of Congress are well paid. In 2003, annual congressional salaries were $154,700. Increasingly, members of Congress are also much wealthier than the average citizen. Whereas fewer than 1 percent of Americans have assets exceeding $1 million, about one-third of the members of Congress are millionaires. Table 9–1 summarizes selected characteristics of the members of Congress.

TABLE 9–1	Characteristics of the 108th Congress, 2003–2005		
CHARACTERISTIC	U.S. POPULATION (2000)*	HOUSE	SENATE
Age (median)	35.3	54.0	59.5
Percentage minority	24.9	15.4	3
Religion			
Percentage church members	61.0	98.4	99
Percentage Roman Catholic	39.0	28.5	24
Percentage Protestant	56.0	56.6	53
Percentage Jewish	4.0	6.0	11
Percentage female	50.9	14.3	14
Percentage with college degrees	25.1	92.0	97
Occupation			
Percentage with law degrees	2.8	41.0	59
Percentage blue-collar workers	20.1	1.4	0
Family income			
Percentage of families earning over $50,000 annually	22.0	100.0	100
Personal wealth			
Percentage of population with assets over $1 million[†]	0.7	16.0	33

*Estimates based on 2000 census.
[†]107th Congress.

Congressional Elections

The process of electing members of Congress is decentralized. Congressional elections are operated by the individual state governments, which must conform to the rules established by the U.S. Constitution and by national statutes. The Constitution states that representatives are to be elected every second year by popular ballot and the number of seats awarded to each state is to be determined by the results of the decennial census. Each state has at least one representative, with most congressional districts having about half a million residents. Senators are elected by popular vote (since the passage of the Seventeenth Amendment) every six years; approximately one-third of the seats are chosen every two years. Each state has two senators. Under Article I, Section 4, of the Constitution, state legislatures are given control over "[t]he Times, Places and Manner of holding Elections for Senators and Representatives"; however, "the Congress may at any time by Law make or alter such Regulations."

Candidates for Congressional Elections

Candidates for congressional seats may be self-selected, or they may be recruited by the local party leadership. Candidates may resemble the voters of the district in ethnicity or religion, but they are also likely to be very successful individuals who have been active in politics before.

INFOTRAC

For updates and more information on congressional elections, use the term "United States Congress" in the Subject guide, and then go to the subdivision "elections."

Congressional Campaigns and Elections. Congressional campaigns have changed considerably in the past two decades. Like all other campaigns, they are much more expensive, with the average cost of a winning Senate campaign now $5 million and a winning House campaign averaging more than $770,000. Campaign funds include direct contributions by individuals, contributions by political action committees (PACs), and "soft money" funneled through state party committees. All of these contributions are regulated by laws, including the Federal Election Campaign Act of 1971, as amended, and most recently the Bipartisan Campaign Reform Act of 2002. Once in office, legislators spend some time almost every day raising funds for their next campaign.

Direct Primary An intraparty election in which the voters select the candidates who will run on a party's ticket in the subsequent general election.

Most candidates for Congress must win the nomination through a **direct primary,** in which **party identifiers** vote for the candidate who will be on the party ticket in the general election. To win the primary, candidates may take more liberal or more conservative positions to get the votes of party identifiers. In the general election, they may moderate their views to attract the votes of independents and voters from the other party.

Party Identifier A person who identifies with a political party.

Presidential Effects. Congressional candidates are always hopeful that a strong presidential candidate on the ticket will have "coattails" that will sweep in senators and representatives of the same party. In fact, coattail effects have been quite limited, and in the last two presidential elections, have not materialized at all. Members of Congress who are from contested districts or who are in their first term are more likely to experience the effect of midterm elections, which are held in the even-numbered years in between presidential contests. In these years, voter turnout falls sharply, and the party controlling the White House normally loses seats in Congress. Table 9–2 shows the pattern for midterm elections since 1942.

TABLE 9–2	Midterm Gains and Losses by the Party of the President, 1942 to 2002

Seats gained or lost by the party of the president in the House of Representatives

1942	−45 (D.)
1946	−55 (D.)
1950	−29 (D.)
1954	−18 (R.)
1958	−47 (R.)
1962	−4 (D.)
1966	−47 (D.)
1970	−12 (R.)
1974	−48 (R.)
1978	−15 (D.)
1982	−26 (R.)
1986	−5 (R.)
1990	−8 (R.)
1994	−52 (D.)
1998	+5 (D.)
2002	+5 (R.)

The Power of Incumbency

The power of incumbency in the outcome of congressional elections cannot be overemphasized. Table 9–3 shows that the overwhelming majority of representatives and a smaller proportion of senators who decide to run for reelection are successful. A number of scholars contend that the pursuit of reelection is the strongest motivation behind the activities of members of Congress. The reelection goal is pursued in several ways. Incumbents can use the mass media, make personal appearances with constituents, and send newsletters—all to produce a favorable image and to make the incumbent's name a household word. Members of Congress generally try to present themselves as informed, experienced, and responsive to people's needs. Legislators also can point to things that they have done to benefit their constituents—by fulfilling

TABLE 9–3	The Power of Incumbency												
	PRESIDENTIAL-YEAR ELECTIONS						MIDTERM ELECTIONS						
	1980	1984	1988	1992	1996	2000	1978	1982	1986	1990	1994	1998	2002
House													
Number of incumbent candidates	398	411	409	368	384	403	382	393	394	406	387	402	393
Reelected	361	392	402	325	361	394	358	354	385	390	349	395	383
Percentage of total	90.7	95.4	98.3	88.3	94.0	97.8	93.7	90.1	97.7	96.0	90.2	98.3	97.5
Defeated	37	19	7	43	23	9	24	39	9	16	38	7	10
In primary	6	3	1	19	2	3	5	10	3	1	4	1	3
In general election	31	16	6	24	21	6	19	29	6	15	34	6	7
Senate													
Number of incumbent candidates	29	29	27	28	21	29	25	30	28	32	26	29	28
Reelected	16	26	23	23	19	23	15	28	21	31	24	26	24
Percentage of total	55.2	89.6	85.2	82.1	90.5	79.3	60.0	93.3	75.0	96.9	92.3	89.7	85.7
Defeated	13	3	4	5	2	6	10	2	7	1	2	3	4
In primary	4	0	0	1	1	0	3	0	0	0	0	0	1
In general election	9	3	4	4	1	6	7	2	7	1	2	3	3

SOURCES: Norman Ornstein, Thomas E. Mann, and Michael J. Malbin, *Vital Statistics on Congress, 2001–2002* (Washington, D.C.: The AEI Press, 2002); and authors' update.

the congressional casework function or bringing money for mass transit to the district, for example. Finally, incumbents can demonstrate the positions that they have taken on key issues by referring to their voting records in Congress.

Congress after the 2002 Elections

The Republican wins in the House and Senate in 2002 left the Democrats scrambling to find issues and leaders that would galvanize voters over the next two years. Many Democrats came away from the 2002 elections believing that voters saw them as lacking vision and leadership. The Republicans emerged from the elections the stronger and more focused party, benefiting from the leadership shown by President Bush in the war on terrorism. The Republican majority in Congress is slim, however. The Republicans now have a twenty-two-seat majority in the House and only a two-seat majority in the Senate. These slight leads may force the Senate Republicans to work in a bipartisan fashion on some issues.

Congressional Reapportionment

By far the most complicated aspects of the mechanics of congressional elections are the issues of **reapportionment** (the allocation of seats in the House to each state after each census) and **redistricting** (the redrawing of the boundaries of the districts

Reapportionment The allocation of seats in the House of Representatives to each state after each census.

Redistricting The redrawing of the boundaries of the congressional districts within each state.

Justiciable Question
A question that may be raised and reviewed in court.

INFOTRAC

For more information on reapportionment, use the term "United States Congress" in the Subject guide, and then go to the subdivision "election districts."

Gerrymandering The drawing of legislative district boundary lines for the purpose of obtaining partisan or factional advantage.

within each state). In a landmark six-to-two vote in 1962, the Supreme Court made reapportionment a **justiciable** (that is, a reviewable) **question** in the Tennessee case of *Baker v. Carr*[2] by invoking the Fourteenth Amendment principle that no state can deny to any person "the equal protection of the laws." Therefore, a state legislature must be apportioned so that all districts are equal in population. This "one person, one vote" principle was applied to congressional districts in the 1964 case of *Wesberry v. Sanders*,[3] based on Article I, Section 2, of the Constitution, which requires that congresspersons be chosen "by the People of the several States."

Severe malapportionment of congressional districts before *Wesberry* resulted in some districts containing two or three times the populations of other districts in the same state, thereby diluting the effect of a vote cast in the more populous districts. This system generally benefited the conservative populations of rural areas and small towns and harmed the interests of the more heavily populated and liberal urban areas.

Gerrymandering

Although the general issue of reapportionment has been dealt with fairly successfully by the one person, one vote principle, the **gerrymandering** issue has not yet been resolved. This term refers to the legislative boundary-drawing tactics that were used under Elbridge Gerry, the governor of Massachusetts, in the 1812 elections (see Figure 9–1). A district is said to have been gerrymandered when its shape is altered substantially by the dominant party in a state legislature to maximize its electoral strength at the expense of the minority party.

In 1986, the Supreme Court heard a case that challenged gerrymandered congressional districts in Indiana. The Court ruled for the first time that redistricting for the political benefit of one group could be challenged on constitutional grounds. In this specific case, *Davis v. Bandemer*,[4] however, the Court did not agree that the districts were drawn unfairly, because it could not be proved that a group of voters would consistently be deprived of influence at the polls as a result of the new districts.

In the meantime, political gerrymandering continues. Redistricting decisions are often made by a small group of political leaders within a state legislature. Typically, their goal is to shape voting districts in such a way as to maximize their party's chances of winning state legislative seats as well as seats in Congress. One of the techniques they use is called "packing and cracking." With the use of powerful computers and software, they pack voters supporting the opposing party into as few districts as possible or crack the opposing party's supporters into different districts.

Clearly, partisan redistricting aids incumbents. Perhaps, though, there is an alternative, a possibility that we examine in this chapter's *At Issue* feature on page 219.

"Minority-Majority" Districts

Under the mandate of the Voting Rights Act of 1965, the Justice Department issued directives to states after the 1990 census instructing them to create congressional districts that would maximize the voting power of minority groups—that

FIGURE 9–1 The Original Gerrymander

The practice of "gerrymandering"—the excessive manipulation of the shape of a legislative district to benefit a certain incumbent or party—is probably as old as the republic, but the name originated in 1812. In that year, the Massachusetts legislature carved out of Essex County a district that historian John Fiske said had a "dragonlike contour." When the painter Gilbert Stuart saw the misshapen district, he penciled in a head, wings, and claws and exclaimed, "That will do for a salamander!" Editor Benjamin Russell replied, "Better say a Gerrymander" (after Elbridge Gerry, then governor of Massachusetts).

SOURCE: *Congressional Quarterly's Guide to Congress,* 3d ed. (Washington, D.C.: Congressional Quarterly Press, 1982), p. 695.

is, create districts in which minority voters were the majority. The result was a number of creatively drawn congressional districts—see, for example, Illinois's Fourth Congressional District in Figure 9–2 on the following page.

Many of these "minority-majority" districts were challenged in court by citizens who claimed that to create districts based on race or ethnicity alone violates the equal protection clause of the Constitution. In 2001, the Supreme Court reviewed a case involving North Carolina's Twelfth District. The district was 165 miles long, following Interstate 85 for the most part. According to a local joke, the district was so narrow that a car traveling down the interstate highway with both doors open would kill most of the voters in the district. In 1996, the Supreme Court had held that the district was unconstitutional because race had been the dominant factor in drawing the district's boundaries. Shortly thereafter, the boundaries were redrawn, but the district was again challenged as a racial gerrymander. A federal district court agreed and invalidated the new boundaries as unconstitutional. In 2001, however, the Supreme Court held that there was insufficient evidence for the lower court's

FIGURE 9–2 The Fourth Congressional District of Illinois

This district, which is mostly within Chicago's city limits, was drawn to connect two Hispanic neighborhoods separated by an African American majority district.

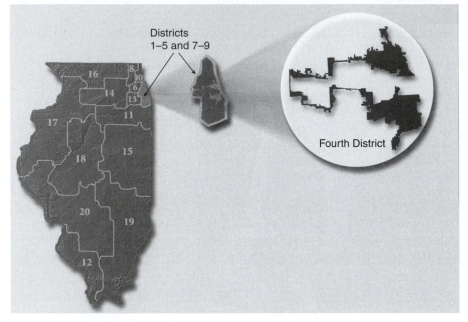

SOURCE: *The New York Times,* July 15, 2001, p. 16.

conclusion that race had been the dominant factor when the boundaries were redrawn.[5]

Staff and Privileges

Members of Congress enjoy a number of benefits. Among these benefits are permanent professional staffs and special privileges and immunities.

Permanent Professional Staffs

More than 30,000 people are employed in the Capitol Hill bureaucracy. About half of them are personal and committee staff members. The personal staff includes office clerks and secretaries; professionals who deal with media relations, draft legislation, and satisfy constituency requests for service; and staffers who maintain local offices in the member's home district or state.

The average Senate office on Capitol Hill employs about thirty staff members, and twice that number work on the personal staffs of senators from the most populous states. House office staffs typically are about half as large as those of the Senate. The number of staff members has increased dramatically since 1960.

AT ISSUE: Should Nonpartisan Boards Take Charge of Redistricting?

As you have already learned, incumbents are routinely reelected to office. One of the reasons this is so is the partisan nature of the redistricting process each decade. Those in Congress enlist the help of party leaders in their states, who redistrict in such a way as to make congressional members' seats safe for reelection if they choose to run.

REDISTRICTING SHOULD NO LONGER BE PARTISAN

It used to be that on election day, Americans chose their representatives. Today, however, the opposite seems to be occurring—the representatives are choosing the voters through the political redistricting process. As mentioned, this gives incumbents an advantage.

Some have suggested that to ensure neutrality in redistricting, nonpartisan state commissions should be established to make redistricting decisions. Iowa and Arizona already use nonpartisan boards to redistrict. Canada and Britain use this process, too, with great success. The boundaries are universally respected, and the legislative seats are more competitive.

"IF IT AIN'T BROKE, DON'T FIX IT"

Others contend that there is no truly neutral way to engage in this complicated activity every ten years. Indeed, when the Supreme Court looked at this issue in 1993 in *Shaw v. Reno,*[*] it found nothing wrong with traditional redistricting criteria or methods; that is, the Supreme Court accepted the current process as constitutional even though it often results in protecting the seats of incumbent legislators and improving their political advantages.

One of the reasons the American democratic system has remained so stable is that we respect political tradition. The so-called faults of partisan redistricting have been part of that system for over two hundred years. Why should we change it if the end result has been a strong republic?

FOR CRITICAL ANALYSIS

If you were on a nonpartisan redistricting commission, how might you go about redrawing congressional district boundaries after each census?

[*]509 U.S. 630 (1993).

Privileges and Immunities under the Law

Members of Congress also benefit from a number of special constitutional protections. Under Article I, Section 6, of the Constitution, for example, "for any Speech or Debate in either House, they shall not be questioned in any other Place." The "speech or debate" clause means that a member may make any allegations or other statements he or she wishes in connection with official duties and normally not be sued for libel or slander or otherwise be subject to legal action.

The Committee Structure

Most of the actual work of legislating is performed by the committees and subcommittees within Congress. Thousands of bills are introduced in every session of Congress, and no single member can possibly be adequately informed on all the

Discharge Petition A procedure by which a bill in the House of Representatives may be forced (discharged) out of a committee that has refused to report it for consideration by the House.

Standing Committee A permanent committee in the House or Senate that considers bills within a certain subject area.

issues that arise. The committee system is a way to provide for specialization, or a division of the legislative labor. Members of a committee can concentrate on just one area or topic—such as taxation or energy—and develop sufficient expertise to draft appropriate legislation when needed. The flow of legislation through both the House and the Senate is determined largely by the speed with which the members of these committees act on bills and resolutions.

The Power of Committees

Sometimes called "little legislatures," committees usually have the final say on pieces of legislation.[6] Committee actions may be overturned on the floor by the House or Senate, but this rarely happens. Legislators normally defer to the expertise of the chairperson and other members of the committee who speak on the floor in defense of a committee decision. Chairpersons of committees exercise control over the scheduling of hearings and formal action on a bill. They also decide which subcommittee will act on legislation falling within their committee's jurisdiction.

Committees only very rarely are deprived of control over a bill—although this kind of action is provided for in the rules of each chamber. In the House, if a bill has been considered by a standing committee for thirty days, the signatures of a majority (218) of the House membership on a **discharge petition** can pry a bill out of an uncooperative committee's hands. From 1909 to 2003, however, although over nine hundred such petitions were initiated, only slightly more than two dozen resulted in successful discharge efforts. Of those, twenty resulted in bills that passed the House.[7]

Senate Democratic leader Tom Daschle lashes out at President George W. Bush for having failed "miserably" at diplomacy prior to launching the military attack on Iraq in March 2003. Daschle was one of the few Democrats to speak out so forcibly against the president's actions. How much influence should the Senate have on the president's conduct of foreign policy?

Types of Congressional Committees

Over the past two centuries, Congress has created several different types of committees, each of which serves particular needs of the institution.

Standing Committees.   By far the most important committees in Congress are the **standing committees**—permanent bodies that are established by the rules of each chamber of Congress and that continue from session to session. A list of the standing committees of the 108th Congress is presented in Table 9–4 on page 222. In addition, most of the standing committees have created subcommittees to carry out their work. In the 108th Congress, there were 68 subcommittees in the Senate and 88 in the

House.[8] Each standing committee is given a specific area of legislative policy jurisdiction, and almost all legislative measures are considered by the appropriate standing committees.

Because of the importance of their work and the traditional influence of their members in Congress, certain committees are considered to be more prestigious than others. Seats on standing committees that handle spending issues are especially sought after because members can use these positions to benefit their constituents. Committees that control spending include the Appropriations Committee in either chamber and the Ways and Means Committee in the House. Members also normally seek seats on committees that handle matters of special interest to their constituents. A member of the House from an agricultural district, for example, will have an interest in joining the House Agriculture Committee.

Select Committees. In principle, a **select committee** is created for a limited period of time and for a specific legislative purpose. For example, a select committee may be formed to investigate a public problem, such as child nutrition or aging. In practice, a select committee, such as the Select Committee on Intelligence in each chamber, may continue indefinitely. Select committees rarely create original legislation.

Select Committee A temporary legislative committee established for a limited time period and for a special purpose.

Joint Committees. A **joint committee** is formed by the concurrent action of both chambers of Congress and consists of members from each chamber. Joint committees, which may be permanent or temporary, have dealt with the economy, taxation, and the Library of Congress.

Joint Committee A legislative committee composed of members from both chambers of Congress.

Conference Committees. Special types of joint committees—**conference committees**—are formed for the purpose of achieving agreement between the House and the Senate on the exact wording of legislative acts when the two chambers pass legislative proposals in different forms. No bill can be sent to the White House to be signed into law unless it first passes both chambers in identical form. Sometimes called the "third house" of Congress, conference committees are in a position to make significant alterations in legislation and frequently become the focal point of policy debates.

Conference Committee A special joint committee appointed to reconcile differences when bills pass the two chambers of Congress in different forms.

The House Rules Committee. Because of its special "gatekeeping" power over the terms on which legislation will reach the floor of the House of Representatives, the House Rules Committee holds a uniquely powerful position. A special committee rule sets the time limit on debate and determines whether and how a bill may be amended. This practice dates back to 1883. The Rules Committee has the unusual power to meet while the House is in session, to have its resolutions considered immediately on the floor, and to initiate legislation on its own.

The Selection of Committee Members

In both chambers, members are appointed to standing committees by the Steering Committee of their party. The majority-party member with the longest term of continuous service on a standing committee is given preference when the committee selects its chairperson. This is not a law but an informal, traditional process, and it

Seniority System A custom followed in both chambers of Congress specifying that the member with the longest term of continuous service will be given preference when a committee chairperson (or holders of other significant posts) is selected.

Safe Seat A district that returns a legislator with 55 percent of the vote or more.

applies to other significant posts in Congress as well. The **seniority system,** although it deliberately treats members unequally, provides a predictable means of assigning positions of power within Congress.

The general pattern until the 1970s was that members of the House or Senate who represented **safe seats** would be reelected continually and eventually would accumulate enough years of continuous committee service to enable them to become the chairpersons of their committees. In the 1970s, a number of reforms in the chairperson selection process somewhat modified the seniority system. The reforms introduced the use of a secret ballot in electing House committee chairpersons and allowed for the possibility of choosing a chairperson on a basis other than seniority. The Democrats immediately replaced three senior chairpersons who were out of step with the rest of their party. In 1995, under Speaker Newt Gingrich, the Republicans chose relatively junior House members as chairpersons of several key committees, thus ensuring conservative control of the committees. The Republicans also passed a rule limiting the term of a chairperson to six years.

The Formal Leadership

The limited amount of centralized power that exists in Congress is exercised through party-based mechanisms. Congress is organized by party. When the Democratic Party, for example, wins a majority of seats in either the House or the Senate,

TABLE 9–4	Standing Committees of the 108th Congress, 2003–2005
HOUSE COMMITTEES	SENATE COMMITTEES
Agriculture	Agriculture, Nutrition, and Forestry
Appropriations	Appropriations
Armed Services	Armed Services
Budget	Banking, Housing, and Urban Affairs
Education and the Workforce	Budget
Energy and Commerce	Commerce, Science, and Transportation
Financial Services	Energy and Natural Resources
Government Reform	Environment and Public Works
House Administration	Finance
International Relations	Foreign Relations
Judiciary	Governmental Affairs
Resources	Health, Education, Labor, and Pensions
Rules	Judiciary
Science	Rules and Administration
Small Business	Small Business and Entrepreneurship
Standards of Official Conduct	Veterans Affairs
Transportation and Infrastructure	
Veterans Affairs	
Ways and Means	

Democrats control the official positions of power in that chamber, and every important committee has a Democratic chairperson and a majority of Democratic members. The same process holds when Republicans are in the majority.

We consider the formal leadership positions in the House and Senate separately, but you will note some broad similarities in the way leaders are selected and in the ways they exercise power in the two chambers.

Leadership in the House

The House leadership is made up of the Speaker, the majority and minority leaders, and the party whips.

The Speaker.   The foremost power holder in the House of Representatives is the **Speaker of the House.** The Speaker's position is technically a nonpartisan one, but in fact, for the better part of two centuries, the Speaker has been the official leader of the majority party in the House. When a new Congress convenes in January of odd-numbered years, each party nominates a candidate for Speaker. All Democratic members of the House vote for their party's nominee, and all Republicans support their candidate. The vote to organize the House is the one vote in which representatives must vote with their party. In a sense, this vote defines a member's partisan status.

The influence of modern-day Speakers is based primarily on their personal prestige, persuasive ability, and knowledge of the legislative process—plus the acquiescence or

Speaker of the House The presiding officer in the House of Representatives. The Speaker is always a member of the majority party and is the most powerful and influential member of the House.

Dennis Hastert, a Republican member of Congress from Illinois, became Speaker of the House in 1999 during the contentious impeachment action against President Bill Clinton.

AP Photo/Ron Edmonds

active support of other representatives. The major formal powers of the Speaker include the following:

INFOTRAC

For updates and more information, use the term "United States Congress House" in the Subject Guide, and then go to "Speaker."

1. Presiding over meetings of the House.

2. Appointing members of joint committees and conference committees.

3. Scheduling legislation for floor action.

4. Deciding points of order and interpreting the rules with the advice of the House parliamentarian.

5. Referring bills and resolutions to the appropriate standing committees of the House.

A Speaker may take part in floor debate and vote, as can any other member of Congress, but recent Speakers usually have voted only to break a tie.

Majority Leader of the House The party leader elected by the majority party in the House.

The Majority Leader.   The **majority leader of the House** is elected by a caucus of the majority party to foster cohesion among party members and to act as a spokesperson for the party. The majority leader influences the scheduling of debate and acts as the chief supporter of the Speaker. The majority leader cooperates with the Speaker and other party leaders, both inside and outside Congress, to formulate the party's legislative program and to guide it through the legislative process in the House. The parties often recruit future Speakers from those who hold that position.

Minority Leader of the House The party leader elected by the minority party in the House.

The Minority Leader.   The **minority leader of the House** is the candidate nominated for Speaker by a caucus of the minority party. Like the majority leader, the leader of the minority party has as her or his primary responsibility the maintaining of cohesion within the party's ranks. The minority leader also speaks on behalf of the president if the minority party controls the White House. In relations with the majority party, the minority leader consults with both the Speaker and the majority leader on recognizing members who wish to speak on the floor, on House rules and procedures, and on the scheduling of legislation. Minority leaders have no actual power in these areas, however.

Whip A member of Congress who aids the majority or minority leader of the House or the Senate.

Whips.   The leadership of each party includes assistants to the majority and minority leaders, who are known as **whips.** The whips are members of Congress who assist the party leaders by passing information down from the leadership to party members and by ensuring that members show up for floor debate and cast their votes on important issues. Whips conduct polls among party members about the members' views on legislation, inform the leaders about whose vote is doubtful and whose is certain, and may exert pressure on members to support the leaders' positions.

Leadership in the Senate

The Senate is less than one-fourth the size of the House. This fact alone probably explains why a formal, complex, and centralized leadership structure is less necessary in the Senate than it is in the House.

The two highest-ranking formal leadership positions in the Senate are essentially ceremonial in nature. Under the Constitution, the vice president of the United

AP Photo/Mark Humphrey; AP Photo/Susan Walsh

Senator William Frist (R., Tenn.), left, was elected unanimously as Senate majority leader on December 23, 2002. Trent Lott (R., Miss.), the former Senate majority leader, had stepped down from the post due to the furor touched off by his racist-sounding remarks during a 100th-birthday tribute to Senator Strom Thurmond (R., S.C.). Nancy Pelosi (D., Calif.), right, is the first woman to hold a leadership position in Congress. She was elected to the post of House minority whip in 2001 and House minority leader in 2002.

States is the president (that is, the presiding officer) of the Senate and may vote to break a tie. The vice president, however, is only rarely present for a meeting of the Senate. The Senate elects instead a **president pro tempore** ("pro tem") to preside over the Senate in the vice president's absence. Ordinarily, the president pro tem is the member of the majority party with the longest continuous term of service in the Senate. The president pro tem is mostly a ceremonial position. Junior senators take turns actually presiding over the sessions of the Senate.

The real leadership power in the Senate rests in the hands of the **Senate majority leader,** the **Senate minority leader,** and their respective whips. The Senate majority and minority leaders have the right to be recognized first in debate on the floor and generally exercise the same powers available to the House majority and minority leaders. They control the scheduling of debate on the floor in conjunction with the majority party's Policy Committee, influence the allocation of committee assignments for new members or for senators attempting to transfer to a new committee, influence the selection of other party officials, and participate in selecting members of conference committees. The leaders are expected to mobilize support for partisan legislative initiatives or for the proposals of a president who belongs to their party. The leaders act as liaisons with the White House when the president is of their party, try to obtain the

President Pro Tempore The temporary presiding officer of the Senate in the absence of the vice president.

Senate Majority Leader The chief spokesperson of the majority party in the Senate, who directs the legislative program and party strategy.

Senate Minority Leader The party officer in the Senate who commands the minority party's legislative program and strategy.

cooperation of committee chairpersons, and seek to facilitate the smooth functioning of the Senate through the senators' unanimous consent. Floor leaders are elected by their respective party caucuses.

Senate party whips, like their House counterparts, maintain communication within the party on platform positions and try to ensure that party colleagues are present for floor debate and important votes. The Senate whip system is far less elaborate than its counterpart in the House, simply because there are fewer members to track.

How a Bill Becomes Law

Each year, Congress and the president propose and approve many laws. Some are budget and appropriation laws that require extensive bargaining but must be passed for the government to continue to function. Other laws are relatively free of controversy and are passed with little dissension. Still other proposed legislation is extremely controversial and reaches to the roots of differences between Democrats and Republicans and between the executive and legislative branches. (In times of crisis, Congress may act quickly to pass legislation that later may not seem so necessary to many groups in the public. See, for example, the discussion of the controversial airline bailout bill in this chapter's *America's Security* feature on page 228.)

As detailed in Figure 9–3, each law begins as a bill, which must be introduced in either the House or the Senate. Often, similar bills are introduced in both chambers. A "money bill," however, must start in the House. In each chamber, the bill follows similar steps. It is referred to a committee and its subcommittees for study, discussion, hearings, and rewriting ("markup"). When the bill is reported out to the full chamber, it must be scheduled for debate (by the Rules Committee in the House and by the leadership in the Senate). After the bill has been passed in each chamber, if it contains different provisions, a conference committee is formed to write a compromise bill, which must be approved by both chambers before it is sent to the president to sign or veto.

How Much Will the Government Spend?

The Constitution is extremely clear about where the power of the purse lies in the national government: all taxing or spending bills must originate in the House of Representatives. Today, much of the business of Congress is concerned with approving government expenditures through the budget process and with raising the revenues to pay for government programs.

Executive Budget
The budget prepared and submitted by the president to Congress.

From 1922, when Congress required the president to prepare and present to the legislature an **executive budget,** until 1974, the congressional budget process was so disjointed that it was difficult to visualize the total picture of government finances. The president presented the executive budget to Congress in January. It was broken down into thirteen or more appropriations bills. Some time later, after all of the bills were debated, amended, and passed, it was more or less possible to estimate total government spending for the next year.

FIGURE 9–3 How a Bill Becomes Law

This illustration shows the most typical way in which proposed legislation is enacted into law. Most legislation begins as similar bills introduced into each chamber of Congress. The process is illustrated here with two hypothetical bills, House bill No. 100 (HR 100) and Senate bill No. 200 (S 200). The path of HR 100 is shown on the left, and that of S 200, on the right.

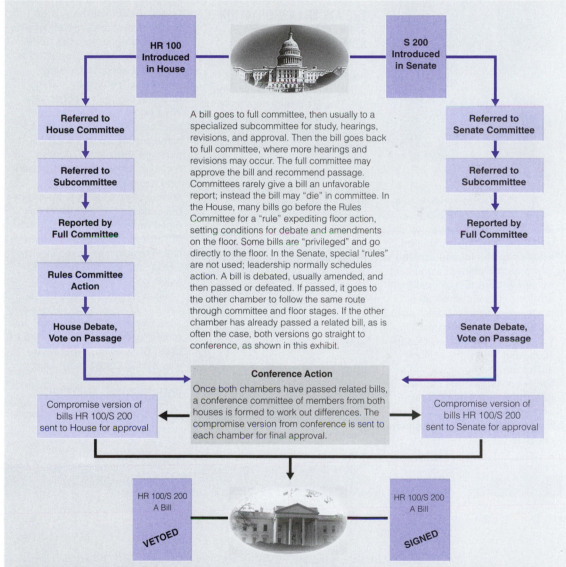

HR 100 Introduced in House

S 200 Introduced in Senate

Referred to House Committee

Referred to Subcommittee

Reported by Full Committee

Rules Committee Action

House Debate, Vote on Passage

Referred to Senate Committee

Referred to Subcommittee

Reported by Full Committee

Senate Debate, Vote on Passage

A bill goes to full committee, then usually to a specialized subcommittee for study, hearings, revisions, and approval. Then the bill goes back to full committee, where more hearings and revisions may occur. The full committee may approve the bill and recommend passage. Committees rarely give a bill an unfavorable report; instead the bill may "die" in committee. In the House, many bills go before the Rules Committee for a "rule" expediting floor action, setting conditions for debate and amendments on the floor. Some bills are "privileged" and go directly to the floor. In the Senate, special "rules" are not used; leadership normally schedules action. A bill is debated, usually amended, and then passed or defeated. If passed, it goes to the other chamber to follow the same route through committee and floor stages. If the other chamber has already passed a related bill, as is often the case, both versions go straight to conference, as shown in this exhibit.

Conference Action

Once both chambers have passed related bills, a conference committee of members from both houses is formed to work out differences. The compromise version from conference is sent to each chamber for final approval.

Compromise version of bills HR 100/S 200 sent to House for approval

Compromise version of bills HR 100/S 200 sent to Senate for approval

HR 100/S 200 A Bill

VETOED

HR 100/S 200 A Bill

SIGNED

A compromise bill approved by both houses is sent to the president, who can sign it into law or veto it and return it to Congress. Congress may override a veto by a two-thirds majority vote in both houses; the bill then becomes law without the president s signature.

AMERICA'S SECURITY

Was the Airline Bailout Necessary?

After the terrorist acts in September 2001, American airline companies were severely weakened. In addition to the losses due to the four crashed planes, significant revenues were lost immediately after the attacks when all airports were closed. Some, such as Reagan National Airport in Washington, D.C., were closed for weeks. Then the airlines suffered their worst decline in travel bookings ever, caused in part by new security fears and in part by concerns about real and imagined hassles during check-in.

THE AIR TRANSPORTATION SAFETY AND SYSTEM STABILIZATION ACT

Two weeks after 9/11, Congress passed the Air Transportation Safety and System Stabilization Act. This act provided up to $5 billion in payments to the airlines for losses resulting from airport shutdowns, as well as federal loans of up to $10 billion. It also provided for expanded federally guaranteed aviation insurance, limiting air carriers' liability for losses to no more than $100 million for claims arising because of an act of terrorism.

The justification given for these new subsidies was that the airlines play a crucial role in the nation's economy. The airlines, already in trouble before 9/11, saw their losses multiply two- and threefold to literally billions of dollars in 2002.

WHO SHOULD PAY THE CONSEQUENCES?

Not everyone agreed that the nation's security required a federal bailout of the airline industry.

Critics argued that the airlines themselves were partly responsible for the disasters because, in their efforts to cut costs, they failed to implement adequate security measures. The airlines should therefore pay the consequences. What would the consequences have been? Without the bailout, some airlines would have gone bankrupt. The assets of these bankrupt airlines would have been sold to stronger airlines. The demise of some airlines would not have caused the collapse of the American airline industry. Rather, the strongest and best-managed airlines would have taken over the weaker and less well managed airlines.

As it turned out, despite the bailout, by early 2003 some airlines had entered bankruptcy, and others faced grave financial problems. Once again, the industry was asking Congress for help.

FOR CRITICAL ANALYSIS

To what extent should an industry be expected to pay for catastrophic disasters of any nature?

Frustrated by the president's ability to impound funds and dissatisfied with the entire budget process, Congress passed the Budget and Impoundment Control Act of 1974 to regain some control over the nation's spending. The act required the president to spend the funds that Congress had appropriated, ending the president's ability to kill programs by withholding funds. The other major accomplishment of the act was to force Congress to examine total national taxing and spending at least twice in each budget cycle.

The budget cycle of the federal government is described in the following subsections. (See Figure 9–4 for a graphic illustration of the budget cycle.)

Preparing the Budget

The federal government operates on a **fiscal year (FY)** cycle. The fiscal year runs from October through September, so that fiscal 2005, or FY05, runs from October 1, 2004, through September 30, 2005. Eighteen months before a fiscal year starts, the executive branch begins preparing the budget. The Office of Management and Budget (OMB) receives advice from the Council of Economic Advisers (CEA) and the Treasury Department. The OMB outlines the budget and then sends it to the various departments and agencies. Bargaining follows, in which—to use only two of many examples—the Department of Health and Human Services argues for fewer welfare spending cuts and the armed forces argue for more defense spending.

Even though the OMB has only six hundred employees, it is one of the most powerful agencies in Washington. It assembles the budget documents and monitors federal agencies throughout each year. Every year, it begins the budget process with a **spring review,** in which it requires all of the agencies to review their programs, activities, and goals. At the beginning of each summer, the OMB sends out a letter instructing agencies to submit their requests for funding for the next fiscal year. By the end of the summer, each agency must submit a formal request to the OMB.

In actuality, the "budget season" begins with the **fall review.** At this time, the OMB looks at budget requests and, in almost all cases, routinely cuts them back. Although the OMB works within guidelines established by the president, specific decisions often are left to the OMB director and the director's associates. By the beginning of November, the director's review begins. The director meets with cabinet secretaries and budget officers. Time becomes crucial. The budget must be completed by January so that it can be included in the *Economic Report of the President.*

Fiscal Year (FY) A twelve-month period used for accounting purposes. The fiscal year does not coincide with the calendar year.

Spring Review A process in which the Office of Management and Budget (OMB) requires federal agencies to review their programs and submit requests for funding for the next fiscal year.

Fall Review A process in which the OMB, after receiving federal agency requests for funding for the next fiscal year, reviews the requests, makes changes, and submits its recommendations to the president.

FIGURE 9–4 The Budget Cycle

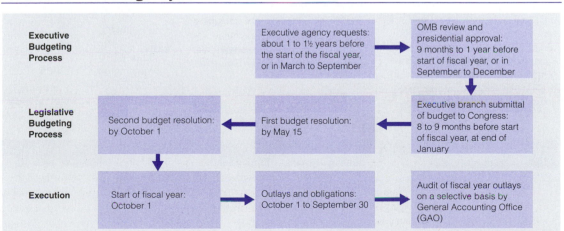

MAKING A DIFFERENCE: Learn about Your Representatives

To cast an informed vote, you need to know how your congressional representatives stand on the issues and, if they are incumbents, how they have voted on bills that are important to you.

CONTACT YOUR REPRESENTATIVES

You can start by going to the Web sites of the U.S. House of Representatives (at **http://www.house.gov**) and the U.S. Senate (at **http://www.senate.gov**). From these Web sites, you can search for your representative by state or zip code, send an e-mail to your representative directly from a form on the Web site, or link to your representative's own Web site.

Although you can communicate easily with your representatives by e-mail, using e-mail has drawbacks. Representatives and senators are now receiving large volumes of e-mail, and they rarely read it themselves. They have staff members who read and respond to e-mail, instead. Many interest groups argue that U.S.

mail, or even express mail or a phone call, is more likely to capture the attention of the representative than e-mail. You can contact your representatives directly at the Capitol using one of the following addresses or phone numbers:

United States House of Representatives
Washington, DC 20515
202-224-3121

United States Senate
Washington, DC 20510
202-224-3121

TRACK VOTING RECORDS AND PERFORMANCE EVALUATIONS

Interest groups also track the voting records of members of Congress and rate the members on the issues. Project Vote Smart tracks the performance of over 13,000 political leaders, including their campaign finances, issue positions, and voting records. You can contact Project Vote Smart at:

Project Vote Smart
One Common Ground
Philipsburg, MT 59858
Voter Hotline toll free
1-888-VOTE-SMART
(1-888-868-3762)
http://www.vote-smart.org

You can also scroll down the site map at this Web site and click on "Ratings." When that page opens, you can learn how various interest groups rate members of Congress on key issues, such as abortion and civil rights.

Finally, if you want to know how your representatives funded their campaigns, contact the Center for Responsive Politics (CRP), a research group that tracks money in politics and campaign fundraising. You can contact the CRP at:

The Center for Responsive Politics
1101 14th St. N.W., Suite 1030
Washington, DC 20005
202-857-0044
http://www.opensecrets.org

Congress Faces the Budget

In January, nine months before the fiscal year starts, the president takes the OMB's proposed budget, approves it, and submits it to Congress. Then the congressional budgeting process takes over. The budgeting process involves two steps. First, Congress must authorize funds to be spent. The **authorization** is a formal declaration by the appropriate congressional committee that a certain amount of funding may be available to an agency. Congressional committees and subcommittees look at the proposals from the executive branch and the Congressional Budget Office (CBO) in making the decision to authorize funds. After the funds are authorized, they must be appropriated by Congress. The appropriations committees of both the House and the Senate forward spending bills to their respective bodies. The **appropriation** of funds occurs when the final bill is passed.

Authorization A formal declaration by a legislative committee that a certain amount of funding may be available to an agency.

Appropriation The passage, by Congress, of a spending bill specifying the amount of authorized funds that actually will be allocated for an agency's use.

Budget Resolutions

The first budget resolution by Congress is supposed to be passed in May. It sets overall revenue goals and spending targets. During the summer, bargaining among all the concerned parties takes place. Spending and tax laws that are drawn up during this period are supposed to be guided by the May congressional budget resolution.

By September, Congress is supposed to pass its second budget resolution, one that will set "binding" limits on taxes and spending for the fiscal year beginning October 1. Bills passed before that date that do not fit within the limits of the budget resolution are supposed to be changed.

In actuality, between 1978 and 1996, Congress did not pass a complete budget by October 1. In other words, generally, Congress does not follow its own rules. Budget resolutions are passed late, and when they are passed, they are not treated as binding. In each fiscal year that starts without a budget, every agency operates on the basis of a **continuing resolution,** which enables the agencies to keep on doing whatever they were doing the previous year with the same amount of funding. Even continuing resolutions have not always been passed on time.

Continuing Resolution A temporary funding law that Congress passes when an appropriations bill has not been decided by the beginning of the new fiscal year on October 1.

KEY TERMS

agenda setting **211**

appropriation **231**

authorization **231**

bicameralism **207**

casework **209**

conference committee **221**

constituent **206**

continuing resolution **231**

direct primary **214**

discharge petition **220**

enumerated power **207**

executive budget **226**

fall review **229**

fiscal year (FY) **229**

gerrymandering **216**

instructed delegate **210**

joint committee **221**

justiciable question **216**

lawmaking **209**

logrolling **209**

majority leader of the House **224**

minority leader of the House **224**

ombudsperson **209**

oversight **210**

party identifier **214**

CHAPTER SUMMARY

1 The authors of the Constitution believed that the bulk of national power should be in the legislature. The Constitution states that Congress will consist of two chambers. A result of the Connecticut Compromise, this bicameral structure established a balanced legislature, with the membership in the House of Representatives based on population and the membership in the Senate based on the equality of states.

2 The first seventeen clauses of Article I, Section 8, of the Constitution specify most of the enumerated, or expressed, powers of Congress, including the right to impose taxes, to borrow money, to regulate commerce, and to declare war. Besides its enumerated powers, Congress enjoys the right to "make all Laws which shall be necessary and proper for carrying into Execution the foregoing Powers, and all other Powers vested by this Constitution in the Government of the United States, or in any Department or Officer thereof." This is called the elastic, or necessary and proper, clause.

3 The functions of Congress include (a) lawmaking, (b) service to constituents, (c) representation, (d) oversight, (e) public education, and (f) conflict resolution.

4 There are 435 members in the House of Representatives and 100 members in the Senate. Owing to its larger size, the House has a greater number of formal rules. The Senate tradition of unlimited debate dates back to 1790 and has been used over the years to frustrate the passage of bills. Under Senate Rule 22, cloture can be used to shut off debate on a bill.

5 Members of Congress are not typical American citizens. They are older and wealthier than most Americans, disproportionately white and male, and more likely to be trained in professional occupations.

6 Congressional elections are operated by the individual state governments, which must abide by rules established by the Constitution and national statutes. Most candidates for Congress must win nomination through a direct primary. The overwhelming majority of incumbent representatives and a smaller proportion of senators who run for reelection are successful. The most complicated aspect of the mechanics of congressional elections is reapportionment—the allocation of legislative seats to constituencies. The Supreme Court's "one person, one vote" rule has been applied to equalize the populations of congressional and state legislative districts.

7 Most of the actual work of legislating is performed by committees and subcommittees within Congress. Legislation introduced into the House or Senate is assigned to the appropriate standing committees for review. Select committees are created for a limited time for a specific purpose. Joint committees are formed by the concurrent action of both chambers and consist of members from each chamber. Conference committees are special joint committees set up to achieve agreement between the House and the Senate on the exact wording of legislative acts passed by both chambers in different forms. The seniority rule, which is usually followed, specifies that the longest-serving member of the majority party will be the chairperson of a committee.

8 The foremost power holder in the House of Representatives is the Speaker of the House. Other leaders are the House majority leader, the House minority leader, and the majority and minority whips. Formally, the vice president is the presiding officer of the Senate, with the most senior member of the majority party serving as the president pro tempore to preside when the vice president is absent. Actual leadership in the Senate rests with the majority leader, the minority leader, and their whips.

9 A bill becomes law by progressing through both chambers of Congress and their appropriate standing and joint committees to the president.

10 The budget process for a fiscal year begins with the preparation of an executive budget by the president. This is reviewed by the Office of Management and Budget and then sent to Congress, which is supposed to pass a final budget by the end of September. Since 1978, Congress has generally not followed its own time rules.

SELECTED PRINT AND MEDIA RESOURCES

Suggested Readings

Barone, Michael, and Grant Ujifusa. *The Almanac of American Politics, 2004*. Washington, D.C.: National Journal, 2003. This book, which is published biannually, is a comprehensive summary of current political information on each member of Congress, his or her state or congressional district, recent congressional election results, key votes, ratings by various organizations, sources of campaign contributions, and records of campaign expenditures.

Davidson, Roger H., and Walter J. Oleszek. *Congress and Its Members*, 8th ed. Washington, D.C.: CQ Press, 2002. This updated classic looks carefully at the "two Congresses," the one in Washington and the role played by congresspersons at home.

Just, Ward S. *The Congressman Who Loved Flaubert*. New York: Carrol and Graf Publishers, 1990. This fictional account of a career politician was first published in 1973 and is still a favorite with students of political science. Ward Just is renowned for his political fiction and particularly for his examination of character and motivation.

Rosenthal, Cindy Simon, ed. *Women Transforming Congress (Congressional Studies Series, Vol. 4)*. Norman: University of Oklahoma Press, 2003. This collection of essays written by women in the political arena focuses on how the political activities of women have transformed the predominantly male institution of Congress.

Silverberg, David. *Congress for Dummies*. Hoboken, N.J.: For Dummies, 2002. This introduction to how Congress works has forewords by Speaker of the House Dennis Hastert and Senate Minority Leader Tom Daschle. Silverberg is the editor of *The Hill*, a weekly that covers Congress. He has covered Congress as a reporter for over twenty years.

Media Resources

The Congress—In one of his earlier efforts (1988), filmmaker Ken Burns profiles the history of the Congress. Narration is by David McCullough, and those interviewed include David Broker, Alistair Cooke, and Cokie Roberts. PBS Home Video rereleased this film on DVD in 2003.

Congress: A Day in the Life of a Representative—From political meetings to social functions to campaigning, this 1995 program examines what politicians really do. Featured representatives are Tim Roemer (D. Indiana) and Sue Myrick (R. North Carolina).

Mr. Smith Goes to Washington—A 1939 film in which Jimmy Stewart plays the naïve congressman who is quickly educated in Washington. A true American political classic.

The Seduction of Joe Tynan—A 1979 film in which Alan Alda plays a young senator who must face serious decisions about his political role and his private life.

LOGGING ON

To find out about the schedule of activities in Congress, use the following Web sites:
http://www.senate.gov
http://www.house.gov

The Congressional Budget Office is online at http://www.cbo.gov.

The URL for the Government Printing Office is http://www.access.gpo.gov.

For the real inside facts on what is going on in Washington, D.C., you can look at the following resources.

RollCall, the newspaper of the Capitol: http://www.rollcall.com.

Congressional Quarterly, a publication that reports on Congress: http://www.cq.com.

The Hill, which investigates various activities of Congress: http://www.hillnews.com.

USING THE INTERNET FOR POLITICAL ANALYSIS

Go to this text's Web site at http://politicalscience. wadsworth.com/schmidtbrief2004. Select "Chapter 9" in the box at the top of the window. Then, in the column on the left-hand side of the window, under "Chapter Resources," click on "Internet Exercises." The Web site will then display the following exercises

that you can perform to learn more about topics covered in this chapter.

Activity 9–1: Reading *Roll Call*
Activity 9–2: The Thomas Web Site
Activity 9–2: The *Congressional Quarterly*

ONLINE STUDY GUIDE AND ADDITIONAL RESOURCES

At http://politicalscience.wadsworth.com/ schmidtbrief2004 you will find a free Study Guide to this book that includes tutorial quizzes, essay questions, practice exams, chapter outlines, learning objectives, the glossary, flashcards, crossword puzzles, and Microsoft PowerPoint presentations. Also included in the American Government Resource Center for Chapter 9:

- **InfoTrac® Reader**—Shaping congressional districts; the power of Congress.
- **You Are There Simulations**—Congress.
- **Participation Activities**—You can lobby Congress; explore the issue of term limits.

- **MicroCase Exercise**—Congress.
- **Related Links**—Congress.
- **Video Case Study**—Congressional election costs.
- **Source Readings**—By James Madison, plus a selected court case.

The site also contains the Citizen's Survival Guide, information on how to get involved in politics locally and globally, as well as regularly updated features including a Current Events Quiz, In the News, Election Links, updates on the war on terrorism, and more.

CHAPTER 10

The Presidency

THE WRITERS OF THE CONSTITUTION created the presidency of the United States without any models on which to draw. Nowhere else in the world was there a democratically selected chief executive. What the founders did not want was a king. In fact, given their previous experience with royal governors in the colonies, many of the delegates to the Constitutional Convention wanted to create a very weak executive who could not veto legislation. Other delegates, especially those who had witnessed the need for a strong leader in the Revolutionary Army, believed a strong executive to be necessary for the republic. The delegates, after much debate, created a chief executive who had enough powers granted in the Constitution to balance those of Congress.[1] In this chapter, after looking at who can become president and at the process involved, we examine closely the nature and extent of the constitutional powers held by the president.

Who Can Become President?

The requirements for becoming president, as outlined in Article II, Section 1, of the Constitution, are not overwhelmingly stringent:

> No person except a natural born Citizen, or a Citizen of the United States, at the time of the Adoption of this Constitution, shall be eligible to the Office of President; neither shall any Person be eligible to that Office who shall not have attained to the Age of thirty-five Years, and been fourteen Years a Resident within the United States.

The "natural born citizen" rule has prevented a number of popular figures from contemplating a run at the presidency, including California governor Arnold Schwarzenegger (born in Austria), Michigan governor Jennifer Granholm (born in Canada), and former secretaries of state Henry Kissinger and Madeleine Albright. Kissinger was born in Germany and Albright was born in Czechoslovakia (in what is now the Czech Republic). An interesting question is whether a "natural born citizen" must be born in the United States and its territories. What about a child born to a U.S. citizen or to a couple who are U.S. citizens visiting or living abroad?

The Supreme Court has never dealt with this question, which was debated when Michigan governor George Romney, born in Chihuahua, Mexico, to American parents, made a serious bid for the Republican presidential nomination in the 1960s.[2]

Although the Constitution states that the minimum-age requirement for the presidency is thirty-five years, most presidents have been much older than that when they assumed office. John F. Kennedy, at the age of forty-three, was the youngest elected president, and the oldest was Ronald Reagan, at age sixty-nine. The average age at inauguration has been fifty-four. There has clearly been a demographic bias in the selection of presidents. All have been male, white, and from the Protestant tradition, except for John F. Kennedy, a Roman Catholic.

The Process of Becoming President

Twelfth Amendment
An amendment to the Constitution, adopted in 1804, that specifies the separate election of the president and vice president by the electoral college.

Major and minor political parties nominate candidates for president and vice president at national conventions every four years. As we have seen, the nation's voters do not elect a president and vice president directly but rather cast ballots for presidential electors, who then vote for president and vice president in the electoral college.

Because the election is governed by a majority in the electoral college, it is conceivable that someone could be elected to the office of the presidency without having a plurality of the popular vote cast. Indeed, in four cases, candidates won elections even though their major opponents received more popular votes. One of those cases occurred in 2000, when George W. Bush won the electoral college vote and became president even though his opponent, Al Gore, won the popular vote. In elections when more than two candidates were running for office, many presidential candidates have won with less than 50 percent of the total popular votes cast for all candidates—including Abraham Lincoln, Woodrow Wilson, Harry Truman, John F. Kennedy, Richard Nixon, and, in 1992, Bill Clinton.

On occasion, the electoral college has failed to give any candidate a majority. At this point, the election is thrown into the House of Representatives. The president is then chosen from among the three candidates having the most electoral college votes. Only two times in our past has the House had to decide on a president. Thomas Jefferson and Aaron Burr tied in the electoral college in 1800. This happened because the Constitution had not been explicit in indicating which of the two electoral votes was for president and which was for vice president. In 1804, the **Twelfth Amendment** clarified the matter by requiring that the president and vice president be chosen separately. In 1824, the House again had to make a choice, this time among William H. Crawford, Andrew Jackson, and John Quincy Adams. It chose Adams, even though Jackson had more electoral and popular votes.

From left to right, the first cabinet—Henry Knox, Thomas Jefferson, Edmund Randolph, Alexander Hamilton—and the first president, George Washington.

The Many Roles of the President

The Constitution speaks briefly about the duties and obligations of the president. Based on this brief list of powers and on the precedents of history, the presidency has grown into a very complicated job that requires balancing at least five constitutional roles. These are (1) chief of state, (2) chief executive, (3) commander in chief of the armed forces, (4) chief diplomat, and (5) chief legislator of the United States. Here we examine each of these significant presidential functions, or roles. It is worth noting that one person plays all these roles simultaneously and that the needs of these roles may at times come into conflict.

Chief of State

Every nation has at least one person who is the ceremonial head of state. In most democratic governments, the role of **chief of state** is given to someone other than the chief executive, who is the head of the executive branch of government. In Britain, for example, the chief of state is the queen. In much of Europe, the prime minister is the chief executive, and the chief of state is the president. But in the United States, the president is both chief executive and chief of state.

According to William Howard Taft, as chief of state the president symbolizes the "dignity and majesty" of the American people. In this role, the president engages in a number of activities that are largely symbolic or ceremonial, such as decorating war heroes, throwing out the first ball to open the baseball season, and dedicating parks and post offices.

Some students of the American political system believe that having the president serve as both the chief executive and the chief of state drastically limits the time available to do "real" work. Not all presidents have agreed with this conclusion, however—particularly those presidents who have skillfully blended these two roles with their role as politician. Being chief of state gives the president tremendous public exposure, which can be an important asset in a campaign for reelection. When that exposure is positive, it helps the president deal with Congress over proposed legislation and increases the chances of being reelected—or getting the candidates of the president's party elected.

Chief of State The role of the president as ceremonial head of the government.

Chief Executive

According to the Constitution, "The executive Power shall be vested in a President of the United States of America. . . . [H]e may require the Opinion, in writing, of the principal Officer in each of the executive Departments, upon any Subject relating to the Duties of their respective Offices . . . and he shall nominate, and by and with the Advice and Consent of the Senate, shall appoint . . . Officers of the United States. . . . [H]e shall take Care that the Laws be faithfully executed."

As **chief executive,** the president is constitutionally bound to enforce the acts of Congress, the judgments of federal courts, and treaties signed by the United States. The duty to "faithfully execute" the laws has been a source of constitutional power for presidents. To assist in the various tasks of the chief executive, the president has

Chief Executive The role of the president as head of the executive branch of the government.

President George W. Bush is shown here working in the Oval Office. This oval-shaped office in the White House is often used to represent the power of the presidency and of the United States.

AP Photo/Doug Mills

Civil Service A collective term for the body of employees working for the government.

Appointment Power The authority vested in the president to fill a government office or position.

Reprieve A formal postponement of the execution of a sentence imposed by a court of law.

Pardon A release from the punishment for or legal consequences of a crime.

a federal bureaucracy, which currently consists of over 2.7 million federal civilian employees.

The Powers of Appointment and Removal.   You might think that the president, as head of the largest bureaucracy in the United States, wields enormous power. The president, however, only nominally runs the executive bureaucracy. Most government positions are filled by **civil service** employees, who generally gain government employment through a merit system rather than presidential appointment. Therefore, even though the president has important **appointment power,** it is limited to cabinet and subcabinet jobs, federal judgeships, agency heads, and about two thousand lesser jobs. This means that most of the 2.7 million federal employees owe no political allegiance to the president. They are more likely to owe loyalty to congressional committees or to interest groups representing the sector of the society that they serve.

The president's power to remove from office those officials who are not doing a good job or who do not agree with the president is not explicitly granted by the Constitution and has been limited. In 1926, however, a Supreme Court decision prevented Congress from interfering with the president's ability to fire those executive-branch officials whom the president had appointed with Senate approval.[3]

Harry Truman spoke candidly of the difficulties a president faces in trying to control the executive bureaucracy. On leaving office, he referred to the problems that Dwight Eisenhower, as a former general of the army, was going to have: "He'll sit here and he'll say do this! do that! and nothing will happen. Poor Ike—it won't be a bit like the Army. He'll find it very frustrating."[4]

The Power to Grant Reprieves and Pardons.   Section 2 of Article II of the Constitution gives the president the power to grant **reprieves** and **pardons** for offenses against the United States except in cases of impeachment. All pardons are administered by the Office of the Pardon Attorney in the Department of Justice. In principle, a pardon is granted to remedy a mistake made in a conviction.

The Supreme Court upheld the president's power to grant reprieves and pardons in a 1925 case concerning a pardon granted by the president to an individual convicted of contempt of court. The judiciary had contended that only judges had the authority to convict individuals for contempt of court when court orders were violated and that the courts should be free from interference by the executive branch. The Supreme Court simply stated that the president could grant reprieves or pardons for all offenses "either before trial, during trial, or after trial, by individuals, or by classes, conditionally or absolutely, and this without modification or regulation by Congress."[5]

In a controversial decision, President Gerald Ford pardoned former president Richard Nixon for his role in the Watergate affair before any charges were brought in court. Just before George W. Bush's inauguration in 2001, President Bill Clinton announced pardons for more than one hundred persons. Some of these pardons were controversial.

INFOTRAC
To find out more about pardons, use the term "Clinton pardons" in Keywords.

Commander in Chief

The president, according to the Constitution, "shall be Commander in Chief of the Army and Navy of the United States, and of the Militia of the several States, when called into the actual Service of the United States." In other words, the armed forces are under civilian, rather than military, control.

Commander in Chief
The role of the president as supreme commander of the military forces of the United States.

Wartime Powers. Certainly, those who wrote the Constitution had George Washington in mind when they made the president the **commander in chief.** Although we no longer expect our president to lead the troops into battle, presidents as commanders in chief have wielded dramatic power. Harry Truman made the awesome decision to drop atomic bombs on Hiroshima and Nagasaki in 1945 to force Japan to surrender and thus bring to an end World War II. Lyndon Johnson ordered bombing missions against North Vietnam in the 1960s, and he personally selected some of the targets. Richard Nixon decided to invade Cambodia in 1970. George H. W. Bush sent troops to Panama in 1989 and to the Middle East in 1990. Bill

After September 11, 2001, President George W. Bush met frequently with his key military advisers, National Security Adviser Condoleezza Rice, left, and Defense Secretary Donald Rumsfeld, right. President Bush's role as commander in chief was even more pronounced during the wars in Afghanistan (2001) and Iraq (2003).

AP Photo/Doug Mills

Clinton sent troops to Haiti in 1994 and to Bosnia in 1995 and sent American planes to bomb Serbia in 1999. Most recently, George W. Bush invaded Iraq in 2003.

The president is the ultimate decision maker in military matters. Everywhere the president goes, so too goes the "football"—a briefcase filled with all the codes necessary to order a nuclear attack. Only the president has the power to order the use of nuclear force.

As commander in chief, the president has probably exercised more authority than in any other role. Constitutionally, Congress has the sole power to declare war, but the president can send the armed forces into a country in situations that are certainly the equivalent of war. Harry Truman dispatched troops to Korea in 1950. Kennedy, Johnson, and Nixon waged an undeclared war in Southeast Asia, where more than 58,000 Americans were killed and 300,000 were wounded. In neither of these situations had Congress declared war. (For a further discussion of the president's role in wartime, see this chapter's *America's Security* feature.)

The War Powers Resolution.   In an attempt to gain more control over such military activities, in 1973 Congress passed the **War Powers Resolution**—over President Nixon's veto—requiring that the president consult with Congress when sending American forces into action. Once they are sent, the president must report to Congress within forty-eight hours. Unless Congress approves the use of troops within sixty days or extends the sixty-day time limit, the forces must be withdrawn.

In spite of the War Powers Resolution, the powers of the president as commander in chief are more extensive today than they were in the past. These powers are linked closely to the president's powers as chief diplomat, or chief crafter of foreign policy.

Chief Diplomat

The Constitution gives the president the power to recognize foreign governments, to make treaties with the **advice and consent** of the Senate, and to make special agreements with other heads of state that do not require congressional approval. In addition, the president nominates ambassadors. As **chief diplomat,** the president dominates American foreign policy, a role that has been supported many times by the Supreme Court.

Diplomatic Recognition.   An important power of the president as chief diplomat is that of **diplomatic recognition,** or the power to recognize—or refuse to recognize— foreign governments. In the role of ceremonial head of state, the president has always received foreign diplomats. In modern times, the simple act of receiving a foreign diplomat has been equivalent to accrediting the diplomat and officially recognizing his or her government. Such recognition of the legitimacy of another country's government is a prerequisite to diplomatic relations or negotiations between that country and the United States.

Deciding when to recognize a foreign power is not always simple. The United States, for example, did not recognize the Soviet Union until 1933—sixteen years after the Russian Revolution of 1917. In December 1978, long after the Communist victory in China in 1949, Jimmy Carter finally granted official recognition to the People's Republic of China.

INFOTRAC

For more information on this topic, use the term "War Powers Resolution of 1973" in the Subject guide.

War Powers Resolution A law passed in 1973 spelling out the conditions under which the president can commit troops without congressional approval.

Advice and Consent Terms in the Constitution describing the U.S. Senate's power to review and approve treaties and presidential appointments.

Chief Diplomat The role of the president in recognizing foreign governments, making treaties, and making executive agreements.

Diplomatic Recognition The formal acknowledgment of a foreign government as legitimate.

AMERICA'S SECURITY

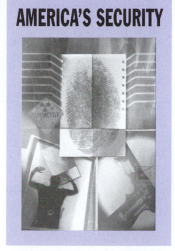

The President's Role in Wartime

Americans look to their government, especially their president, to exercise leadership during times of crisis. Like previous presidents who were in office during wartime, President George W. Bush reacted vigorously to a crisis—the terrorist attacks of 9/11. Among the first steps Bush took was to go to war with the Taliban government of Afghanistan, which was complicit in the 9/11 attacks.

THE ROAD TO IRAQ

During 2002 and early 2003, President Bush contended that Iraq posed a major threat to our national security because of its attempts to produce nuclear and chemical weapons that could be used to attack U.S. citizens at home and abroad. The administration spent months trying to convince the United Nations to share the U.S. view. In October 2002, the United Nations Security Council passed a resolution supporting the use of force against Iraq if that country refused to cooperate with inspectors searching for evidence of weapons of mass destruction. In 2003, when the Security Council opposed the Bush administration's request for authorization of war against Iraq, the United States went to war based on the 2002 resolution. The United States invaded Iraq in March 2003, supported by some thirty other nations.

Some argue that Bush's wartime powers rival those of President Franklin Roosevelt during World War II. As Tim Lynch, director of the Project on Criminal Justice at the Cato Institute, noted, "the power President Bush is wielding today is truly breathtaking."

WAR AND PRESIDENTIAL POPULARITY

Historically, presidents' approval ratings have soared when the United States has entered wars. The use of American forces initially spurs a "rally 'round the flag" reaction.

President Bush saw his ratings skyrocket immediately after 9/11. They reached an unprecedented 90 percent during the successful war against the Taliban in Afghanistan. Bush's ratings started to slip to the 70 percent range by the spring of 2002, however, and by early 2003 they had dipped to 58 percent. When the war against Iraq was launched, the president's ratings climbed again—to over 70 percent. Since then, they have fallen once more.

FOR CRITICAL ANALYSIS

Never before has a U.S. commander in chief permitted military action against another nation for the sole purpose of changing its political regime. What might be some of the unintended consequences of Bush's doctrine of "preemptive war"—or war to prevent future threats to our national security?

Proposal and Ratification of Treaties.   The president has the sole power to negotiate treaties with other nations. These treaties must be presented to the Senate, where they may be modified and must be approved by a two-thirds vote. After ratification, the president can approve the senatorial version of the treaty. Approval poses a problem when the Senate has tacked on substantive amendments or reservations to a treaty, particularly when such changes may require reopening negotiations with the other signatory governments. Sometimes a president may decide to withdraw a treaty if the senatorial changes are too extensive—as Woodrow Wilson did

In the roles of chief of state and chief diplomat, the U.S. president frequently visits or receives foreign diplomats and heads of state. Here, President George W. Bush talks with Egyptian President Hosni Mubarak at Camp David, Maryland, in 2002. How much effect do the president's personal relationships with foreign leaders have on U.S. policy objectives?

AP Photo/Kenneth Lambert

with the Versailles Treaty in 1919. Wilson believed that the senatorial reservations would weaken the treaty so much that it would be ineffective. His refusal to accept the senatorial version of the treaty led to the eventual refusal of the United States to join the League of Nations.

Before September 11, 2001, President George W. Bush indicated his intention to steer the United States in a unilateral direction on foreign policy, citing the priority of domestic concerns over the need for international cooperation. He rejected the Kyoto Agreement on global warming and proposed ending the 1972 Anti-Ballistic Missile (ABM) Treaty. After the terrorist attacks of 9/11, however, President Bush sought cooperation from U.S. allies in the war on terrorism. His attempts to gain international support for a war against Iraq to overthrow that country's government were not as successful as he had hoped.

Executive Agreements.

Executive Agreement An international agreement made by the president, without senatorial ratification, with the head of a foreign state.

Presidential power in foreign affairs is enhanced greatly by the use of **executive agreements** made between the president and other heads of state. Such agreements do not require Senate approval, although the House and Senate may refuse to appropriate the funds necessary to implement them. Whereas treaties are binding on all succeeding administrations, executive agreements require each new president's consent to remain in effect.

Among the advantages of executive agreements are speed and secrecy. The former is essential during a crisis; the latter is important when the administration fears that open senatorial debate may be detrimental to the best interests of the United States or to the interests of the president.[6] There have been far more executive agreements (about 9,000) than treaties (about 1,300). Many executive agreements contain secret provisions calling for American military assistance or other support.

Chief Legislator

Constitutionally, presidents must recommend to Congress legislation that they judge necessary and expedient. Not all presidents have wielded their powers as **chief legislator** in the same manner. Some presidents have been almost completely unsuccessful in getting their legislative programs implemented by Congress. Presidents Franklin Roosevelt and Lyndon Johnson, however, saw much of their proposed legislation put into effect.

In modern times, the president has played a dominant role in creating the congressional agenda. In the president's annual **State of the Union message,** which is required by the Constitution (Article II, Section 3) and is usually given in late January shortly after Congress reconvenes, the president as chief legislator presents a program. The message gives a broad, comprehensive view of what the president wishes the legislature to accomplish during its session. It is as much a message to the American people and to the world as it is to Congress. Its impact on public opinion can determine the way in which Congress responds to the president's agenda.

Chief Legislator The role of the president in influencing the making of laws.

State of the Union Message An annual message to Congress in which the president proposes a legislative program.

Getting Legislation Passed.

The president can propose legislation. Congress, however, is not required to pass—or even introduce—any of the administration's bills. How, then, does the president get those proposals made into law? One way is by exercising the power of persuasion. The president writes to, telephones, and meets with various congressional leaders; makes public announcements to influence public opinion; and, as head of the party, exercises legislative leadership through the congresspersons of that party.

A president whose party holds a majority in both chambers of Congress may have an easier time getting legislation passed than does a president who faces a hostile Congress. But one of the ways in which a president who faces a hostile Congress still can wield power is through the ability to veto legislation.

Saying No to Legislation.

The president has the power to say no to legislation through use of the veto, by which the White House returns a bill unsigned to Congress with a **veto message** attached.[7] Because the Constitution requires that every bill passed by the House and the Senate be sent to the president before it becomes law, the president must act on each bill.

Veto Message The president's formal explanation of a veto when legislation is returned to Congress.

1. If the bill is signed, it becomes law.
2. If the bill is not sent back to Congress after ten congressional working days, it becomes law without the president's signature.
3. The president can reject the bill and send it back to Congress with a veto message setting forth objections. Congress then can change the bill, hoping to secure presidential approval and repass it. Or Congress can simply reject the president's objections by overriding the veto with a two-thirds roll-call vote of the members present in each house.

Each year the president presents the State of the Union message, which is required by Article II, Section 3, of the Constitution and is usually given in late January. Attendees include all members of Congress and usually also include the justices of the U.S. Supreme Court and the heads of most of the executive departments.

AP Photo/Doug Mills

4. If the president refuses to sign the bill and Congress adjourns within ten working days after the bill has been submitted to the president, the bill is killed for that session of Congress. This is called a **pocket veto.** If Congress wishes the bill to be reconsidered, the bill must be reintroduced during the following session.

Presidents employed the veto power infrequently until after the Civil War, but it has been used with increasing vigor since then.

The Line-Item Veto.   Ronald Reagan lobbied strenuously for Congress to give another tool to the president—the **line-item veto,** which would allow the president to veto *specific* spending provisions of legislation that was passed by Congress. Reagan saw the line-item veto as the only way that he could control overall congressional spending. In 1996, Congress passed the Line Item Veto Act, which provided for the line-item veto. President Clinton used this new power on several occasions, but the act was challenged in court. In 1998, by a six-to-three vote, the United States Supreme Court overturned the act. The Court stated that "there is no provision in the Constitution that authorizes the president to enact, to amend or to repeal statutes."[8]

Congress's Power to Override Presidential Vetoes.   A veto is a clear-cut indication of the president's dissatisfaction with congressional legislation. Congress, however, can override a presidential veto, although it rarely exercises this power. Consider that two-thirds of the members of each chamber who are present must vote to override the president's veto in a roll-call vote. This means that if only one-third plus one of the members voting in one of the chambers of Congress do not agree to override the veto, the veto holds. In all of American history, only about 7 percent of vetoes have been overridden.

Pocket Veto A special veto exercised by the chief executive after a legislative body has adjourned. Bills not signed by the chief executive die after a specified period of time.

Line-Item Veto A veto of individual lines or items within a piece of legislation rather than of the entire bill.

Other Presidential Powers

The powers of the president just discussed are called **constitutional powers,** because their basis lies in the Constitution. In addition, Congress has established by law, or statute, numerous other presidential powers—such as the ability to declare national emergencies. These are called **statutory powers.** Both constitutional and statutory powers have been labeled the **expressed powers** of the president, because they are expressly written into the Constitution or into law.

Presidents also have what have come to be known as **inherent powers.** These depend on the loosely worded statements in the Constitution that "the executive Power shall be vested in a President" and that the president should "take Care that the Laws be faithfully executed." The most common example of inherent powers are those emergency powers invoked by the president during wartime. Franklin Roosevelt, for example, used his inherent powers to move the Japanese and Japanese Americans living in the United States into internment camps for the duration of World War II.

The President as Party Chief and Superpolitician

Presidents are by no means above political partisanship, and one of their many roles is that of chief of party. Although the Constitution says nothing about the function of the president within a political party (the mere concept of political parties was abhorrent to most of the authors of the Constitution), today presidents are the actual leaders of their parties.

The President as Chief of Party

As party leader, the president chooses the national committee chairperson and can try to discipline party members who fail to support presidential policies. One way of exerting political power within the party is through **patronage**—appointing individuals to government or public jobs. This power was more extensive in the past, before the establishment of the civil service in 1883, but the president still retains important patronage power. As we noted earlier, the president can appoint several thousand individuals to jobs in the cabinet, the White House, and the federal regulatory agencies.

Perhaps the most important partisan role that the president played in the late 1990s and early 2000s was that of fund-raiser. The president is able to raise large amounts of money for the party through appearances at dinners, speaking engagements, and other social occasions. President Clinton may have raised more than half a billion dollars for the Democratic Party during his two terms. President Bush is on course to be even more successful than Clinton.

Presidents have a number of other ways of exerting influence as party chief. The president may make it known that a particular congressperson's choice for federal judge will not be appointed unless that member of Congress is more supportive of the president's legislative program. The president may agree to campaign for a particular program or for

Constitutional Power A power vested in the president by Article II of the Constitution.

Statutory Power A power created for the president through laws enacted by Congress.

Expressed Power A power of the president that is expressly written into the Constitution or into statutory law.

Inherent Power A power of the president derived from the statements in the Constitution that "the executive Power shall be vested in a President" and that the president should "take Care that the Laws be faithfully executed"; defined through practice rather than through law.

Patronage The practice of rewarding faithful party workers and followers with government employment and contracts.

"I don't think you can distance yourself from the White House on this one. After all, you <u>are</u> the President."

a particular candidate. Presidents also reward loyal members of Congress by supporting funding for local projects, tax breaks for regional industries, and other forms of "pork."

Constituencies and Public Approval

All politicians worry about their constituencies, and presidents are no exception. Presidents are also concerned with public approval ratings.

Presidential Constituencies.   Presidents have many constituencies. In principle, they are beholden to the entire electorate—the public of the United States—even those who did not vote. They are certainly beholden to their party, because its members helped to put them in office. The president's constituencies also include members of the opposing party whose cooperation the president needs. Finally, the president has to take into consideration a constituency that has come to be called the **Washington community.** This community consists of individuals who—whether in or out of political office—are intimately familiar with the workings of government, thrive on gossip, and measure on a daily basis the political power of the president.

Washington Community
Individuals regularly involved with politics in Washington, D.C.

Public Approval.   All of these constituencies are impressed by presidents who maintain a high level of public approval, partly because this is very difficult to accomplish. Presidential popularity, as measured by national polls, gives the president an extra political resource to use in persuading legislators or bureaucrats to pass legislation.

President George W. Bush received an unprecedented approval rating of 90 percent after the September 11, 2001, terrorist attacks. Before the attacks, Bush's approval ratings had hovered between 50 and 60 percent. This rally of public support behind the president allowed Bush to achieve legislative successes, such as an antiterrorism act in late 2001 and an education reform act in 2002. By early 2003, Bush's approval ratings had fallen back to the 50 to 60 percent range. Bush's approval ratings soared again during the war in Iraq, but by the end of 2003 they had returned to the 50 percent range.

"Going Public."   Since the early 1900s, presidents have spoken more to the public and less to Congress. In the 1800s, only 7 percent of presidential speeches were addressed to the public; since 1900, 50 percent have been addressed to the public.

One scholar, Samuel Kernell, has proposed that the style of presidential leadership has changed since World War II, owing partly to the influence of television, with a resulting change in the balance of national politics.[9] Presidents frequently go

INFOTRAC

For updates on public approval, use the term "Bush approval" in Keywords.

over the heads of Congress and the political elites, taking their cases directly to the people. This strategy, which Kernell dubbed "going public," gives the president additional power through the ability to persuade and manipulate public opinion. By identifying their own positions so clearly, presidents make compromises with Congress much more difficult and weaken the legislators' positions. Given the increasing importance of the media as the major source of political information for citizens and elites, presidents will continue to use public opinion as part of their arsenal of weapons to gain support from Congress and to achieve their policy goals.

Special Uses of Presidential Power

Presidents have at their disposal a variety of special powers and privileges not available in the other branches of the U.S. government. These include (1) emergency powers, (2) executive orders, and (3) executive privilege.

Emergency Powers

If you were to read the Constitution, you would find no mention of the additional powers that the executive office may exercise during national emergencies. Indeed, the Supreme Court has indicated that an "emergency does not create power."[10] But it is clear that presidents have used their inherent powers during times of emergency, particularly in the realm of foreign affairs. The **emergency powers** of the president were first enunciated in the Supreme Court's decision in *United States v. Curtiss-Wright Export Corp.*[11] In that case, President Franklin Roosevelt, without authorization by Congress, ordered an embargo on the shipment of weapons to two warring South American countries. The Court recognized that the president may exercise inherent powers in foreign affairs and that the national government has primacy in foreign affairs.

Emergency Power
An inherent power exercised by the president during a period of national crisis.

Examples of emergency powers are abundant, coinciding with crises in domestic and foreign affairs. Abraham Lincoln's suspension of civil liberties at the beginning of the Civil War (1861–1865), his calling of the state militias into national service, and his subsequent governance of conquered areas and even of areas of northern states were justified by claims that such actions were essential to preserve the Union. Franklin Roosevelt declared an "unlimited national emergency" following the fall of France in World War II (1939–1945) and mobilized the federal budget and the economy for war.

President Harry Truman authorized the federal seizure of steel plants and their operation by the national government in 1952 during the Korean War. Truman claimed that he was using his inherent emergency power as chief executive and commander in chief to safeguard the nation's security, as an ongoing steel mill strike threatened the supply of weapons to the armed forces. The Supreme Court did not agree, holding that the president had no authority under the Constitution to seize private property or to legislate such action.[12] According to legal scholars, this was the first time a limit was placed on the exercise of the president's emergency powers.

Executive Orders

Executive Order A rule or regulation issued by the president that has the effect of law.

Congress allows the president (as well as administrative agencies) to issue **executive orders** that have the force of law. These executive orders can do the following: (1) enforce legislative statutes, (2) enforce the Constitution or treaties with foreign nations, and (3) establish or modify rules and practices of executive administrative agencies.

An executive order, then, represents the president's legislative power. The only apparent requirement is that under the Administrative Procedure Act of 1946, all executive orders must be published in the *Federal Register,* a daily publication of the U.S. government. Executive orders have been used to establish procedures for appointing noncareer administrators, to implement national affirmative action regulations, to restructure the White House bureaucracy, to ration consumer goods and to administer wage and price controls under emergency conditions, to classify government information as secret, to regulate the export of restricted items, and to establish military tribunals for suspected terrorists.

Federal Register A publication of the U.S. government that prints executive orders, rules, and regulations.

Executive Privilege

Executive Privilege The right of executive officials to withhold information from or to refuse to appear before a legislative committee.

Another inherent executive power that has been claimed by presidents concerns the ability of the president and the president's executive officials to withhold information from or to refuse to appear before Congress or the courts. This is called **executive privilege,** and it relies on the constitutional separation of powers for its basis.

Presidents have frequently invoked executive privilege to avoid having to disclose information to Congress on actions of the executive branch. For example, President George W. Bush claimed executive privilege to keep the head of the newly established Office of Homeland Security, Tom Ridge, from testifying before Congress. The Bush administration also resisted attempts by the congressional General Accounting Office to obtain information about meetings and documents related to Vice President Dick Cheney's actions as chair of the administration's energy policy task force. Bush, like presidents before him, claimed that a certain degree of secrecy is essential to national security. Critics of executive privilege believe that it can be used to shield from public scrutiny actions of the executive branch that should be open to Congress and to the American public.

Limiting Executive Privilege. Limits to executive privilege went untested until the Watergate affair in the early 1970s. Five men had broken into the headquarters of the Democratic National Committee and were caught searching for documents that would damage the candidacy of the Democratic nominee, George McGovern. Later investigation showed that the break-in was planned by members of Richard Nixon's campaign committee and that Nixon and his closest advisers had devised a strategy for impeding the investigation of the crime. After it became known that all of the conversations held in the Oval Office had been tape-recorded on a secret system, Nixon was ordered to turn over the tapes to the special prosecutor.

Nixon refused to do so, claiming executive privilege. He argued that "no president could function if the private papers of his office, prepared by his personal staff, were open to public scrutiny." In 1974, in one of the Supreme Court's most famous cases, *United States v. Nixon,*[13] the justices unanimously ruled that Nixon had to hand over

INFOTRAC

For more information on this subject, use the term "executive privilege" in the Subject guide.

the tapes. The Court held that executive privilege could not be used to prevent evidence from being heard in criminal proceedings.

Clinton's Attempted Use of Executive Privilege.   The claim of executive privilege was also raised by the Clinton administration as a defense against the aggressive investigation of Clinton's relationship with Monica Lewinsky by Independent Counsel Kenneth Starr. The federal judge overseeing the case denied the claims of privilege, however, and the decision was upheld on appeal.

Abuses of Executive Power and Impeachment

Presidents normally leave office either because their first term has expired and they have not sought (or won) reelection or because, having served two full terms, they are not allowed to be elected for a third term (owing to the Twenty-second Amendment, passed in 1951). Eight presidents have died in office. But there is still another way for a president to leave office—by **impeachment** and conviction. Articles I and II of the Constitution authorize the House and Senate to remove the president, the vice president, or other civil officers of the United States for committing "Treason, Bribery, or other high Crimes and Misdemeanors." According to the Constitution, the impeachment process begins in the House, which impeaches (accuses) the federal officer involved. If the House votes to impeach the officer, it draws up articles of impeachment and submits them to the Senate, which conducts the actual trial.

> **Impeachment** An action by the House of Representatives to accuse the president, vice president, or other civil officers of the United States of committing "Treason, Bribery, or other high Crimes and Misdemeanors."

In the history of the United States, no president has ever actually been impeached and also convicted—and thus removed from office—by means of this process. President Andrew Johnson (1865–1869), who succeeded to the office after the assassination of Abraham Lincoln, was impeached by the House but acquitted by the Senate. More than a century later, the House Judiciary Committee approved articles of impeachment against President Richard Nixon for his involvement in the cover-up of the Watergate break-in of 1972. Informed by members of his own party that he had no hope of surviving the trial in the Senate, Nixon resigned on August 9, 1974, before the full House voted on the articles. Nixon is the only president to resign from the office.

The second president to be impeached by the House but not convicted by the Senate was President Bill Clinton. In September 1998, Independent Counsel Kenneth Starr sent to Congress the findings of his investigation of the president on the charges of perjury and obstruction of justice. The House approved two charges against Clinton: lying to the grand jury about his affair with Monica Lewinsky and obstruction of justice. The articles of impeachment were then sent to the Senate, which acquitted Clinton.

INFOTRAC
To find out more about impeachment, use the term "Clinton impeachment" in Keywords.

The Executive Organization

Gone are the days when presidents answered their own mail, as George Washington did. It was not until 1857 that Congress authorized a private secretary for the president, to be paid by the federal government. Woodrow Wilson typed most of his correspondence, even though he did have several secretaries. At the beginning of Franklin Roosevelt's long tenure in the White House, the entire staff consisted of thirty-seven employees. With the New Deal and World War II, however, the presidential staff became a sizable organization.

The Cabinet

Cabinet An advisory group selected by the president to aid in making decisions. The cabinet includes the heads of fifteen executive departments and others named by the president.

Although the Constitution does not include the word *cabinet,* it does state that the president "may require the Opinion, in writing, of the principal Officer in each of the executive Departments." Since the time of George Washington, there has been an advisory group, or **cabinet,** to which the president turns for counsel.

Members of the Cabinet.　Originally, the cabinet consisted of only four officials—the secretaries of state, treasury, and war and the attorney general. Today, the cabinet numbers fourteen department secretaries and the attorney general. The cabinet may include others as well. The president at his or her discretion can, for example, ascribe cabinet rank to the vice president, the head of the Office of Management and Budget, the national security adviser, the ambassador to the United Nations, or others.

Kitchen Cabinet The informal advisers to the president.

Often, a president will use a **kitchen cabinet** to replace the formal cabinet as a major source of advice. The term *kitchen cabinet* originated during the presidency of Andrew Jackson, who relied on the counsel of close friends who often met with him in the kitchen of the White House. A kitchen cabinet is a very informal group of advisers; usually, they are friends with whom the president worked before being elected.

Presidential Use of Cabinets.　Because neither the Constitution nor statutory law requires the president to consult with the cabinet, its use is purely discretionary. Some presidents have relied on the counsel of their cabinets more than others. Dwight Eisenhower frequently turned to his cabinet for advice on a wide range of governmental policies—perhaps because he was used to the team approach to solving problems from his experience in the U.S. Army. More often, presidents have solicited the opinions of their cabinets and then did what they wanted to do anyway. Lincoln supposedly said—after a cabinet meeting in which a vote was seven nays against his one aye—"Seven nays and one aye, the ayes have it." In general, few presidents have relied heavily on the advice of their cabinet members.

It is not surprising that presidents tend not to rely on their cabinet members' advice. Often, the departmental heads are more responsive to the wishes of their own staffs or to their own political ambitions than they are to the president. They may be more concerned with obtaining resources for their departments than with achieving the goals of the president. So there is often a strong conflict of interest between presidents and their cabinet members.

The Executive Office of the President

Executive Office of the President (EOP) An organization established by President Franklin D. Roosevelt to assist the president in carrying out major duties.

When President Franklin Roosevelt appointed a special committee on administrative management, he knew that the committee would conclude that the president needed help. Indeed, the committee proposed a major reorganization of the executive branch. Congress did not approve the entire reorganization, but it did create the **Executive Office of the President (EOP)** to provide staff assistance for the chief executive and to help coordinate the executive bureaucracy. Since that time, a number of agencies have been created within the EOP to supply the president with advice and staff help. These agencies include the following:

- White House Office.
- White House Military Office.
- Office of the Vice President.
- Council of Economic Advisors.
- Council on Environmental Quality.
- National Security Council.
- Office of Management and Budget.
- Office of National AIDS Policy.
- Office of National Drug Control Policy.
- Office of Science and Technology Policy.
- Office of the United States Trade Representative.
- President's Critical Infrastructure Protection Board.
- President's Foreign Intelligence Advisory Board.

Several of the offices within the EOP are especially important, including the White House Office, the Office of Management and Budget, and the National Security Council.

The White House Office.

The **White House Office** includes most of the key personal and political advisers to the president. Among the jobs held by these aides are those of legal counsel to the president, secretary, press secretary, and appointments secretary. Often, the individuals who hold these positions are recruited from the president's campaign staff. Their duties—mainly protecting the president's political interests—are similar to campaign functions. In all recent administrations, one member of the White House Office has been named **chief of staff.** This person, who is responsible for coordinating the office, is also one of the president's chief advisers.

The president may establish special advisory units within the White House to address topics the president finds especially important. Such units include the long-established Domestic Policy Council and the National Economic Council. Under George W. Bush, these units also include the Office of Faith-Based and Community Initiatives and the USA Freedom Corps. The White House Office also includes the staff members who support the first lady.

In addition to civilian advisers, the president is supported by a large number of military personnel, who are organized under the White House Military Office. These members of the military provide communications, transportation, medical care, and food services to the president and the White House staff.

Employees of the White House Office have been both envied and criticized. The White House Office, according to most former staffers, grants its employees access and power. They are able to use the resources of the White House to contact virtually anyone in the world by telephone, cable, fax, or electronic mail as well as to use the influence of the White House to persuade legislators and citizens. Because of this

White House Office The personal office of the president, which tends to presidential political needs and manages the media.

Chief of Staff The person who is named to direct the White House Office and advise the president.

influence, staffers are often criticized for overstepping the bounds of the office. It is the appointments secretary who is able to grant or deny senators, representatives, and cabinet secretaries access to the president. It is the press secretary who grants to the press and television journalists access to any information about the president.

The Office of Management and Budget.   The **Office of Management and Budget (OMB)** was originally the Bureau of the Budget, which was created in 1921 within the Department of the Treasury. Recognizing the importance of this agency, Franklin Roosevelt moved it into the White House Office in 1939. Richard Nixon reorganized the Bureau of the Budget in 1970 and changed its name to reflect its new managerial function. It is headed by a director, who must make up the annual federal budget that the president presents to Congress each January for approval. In principle, the director of the OMB has broad fiscal powers in planning and estimating various parts of the federal budget, because all agencies must submit their proposed budget to the OMB for approval. In reality, it is not so clear that the OMB truly can affect the greater scope of the federal budget. The OMB may be more important as a clearinghouse for legislative proposals initiated in the executive agencies.

The National Security Council.   The **National Security Council (NSC)** is a link between the president's key foreign and military advisers and the president. Its members consist of the president, the vice president, and the secretaries of state and defense, plus other informal members. Included in the NSC is the president's special assistant for national security affairs. In 2001, Condoleezza Rice became the first woman to serve as the president's national security adviser.

Office of Management and Budget (OMB) A division of the Executive Office of the President. The OMB assists the president in preparing the annual budget, clearing and coordinating departmental agency budgets, and supervising the administration of the budget.

National Security Council (NSC) An agency in the Executive Office of the President that advises the president on national security.

The Vice Presidency

The Constitution does not give much power to the vice president. The only formal duty is to preside over the Senate—which is rarely necessary. This obligation is fulfilled when the Senate organizes and adopts its rules and when the vice president is needed to decide a tie vote. In all other cases, the president pro tem manages parliamentary procedures in the Senate. The vice president is expected to participate only informally in senatorial deliberations, if at all.

The Vice President's Job

Vice presidents have traditionally been chosen by presidential nominees to balance the ticket to attract groups of voters or appease party factions. If a presidential nominee is from the North, it is not a bad idea to have a vice presidential nominee who is from the South. If the presidential nominee is from a rural state, perhaps someone with an urban background would be most suitable as a running mate. Presidential nominees who are strongly conservative or strongly liberal would do well to have vice presidential nominees who are more in the middle of the political road.

In recent presidential elections, vice presidents have been selected for other reasons. Bill Clinton picked Al Gore to be his running mate in 1992 even though both were southern and moderates. The ticket appealed to southerners and moderates, both of whom were crucial to the election. In 2000, both vice presidential selections

Vice President Dick Cheney assembled a task force in 2001 to advise the president on his energy policy. The task force recommended the disbursement of millions of federal dollars to energy companies. The General Accounting Office, the investigative arm of Congress, sued Cheney for release of documents prepared for the task force. Cheney claimed that release of the information would affect the president's ability to get candid opinions from people outside government.

were intended to shore up the respective presidential candidates' perceived weaknesses. Republican George W. Bush, who was subject to criticism for his lack of government experience and his "lightweight" personality, chose Dick Cheney, a former member of Congress who had also served as secretary of defense. Democrat Al Gore chose Senator Joe Lieberman of Connecticut, whose reputation for moral integrity (as an Orthodox Jew) could help counteract the effects of Bill Clinton's sex scandals.

The job of vice president is not extremely demanding, even when the president gives some specific task to the vice president. Typically, vice presidents spend their time supporting the president's activities. Of course, the vice presidency takes on more significance if the president becomes disabled or dies in office—and the vice president becomes president.

Presidential Succession

Eight vice presidents have become president because of the death of the president. John Tyler, the first to do so, took over William Henry Harrison's position after only one month. No one knew whether Tyler should simply be a caretaker until a new president could be elected three and a half years later or whether he actually should be president. Tyler assumed that he was supposed to be the chief executive, and he acted as such—although he was commonly referred to as "His Accidency." Since then, vice presidents taking over the position of the presidency because of the incumbent's death have assumed the presidential powers.

But what should a vice president do if a president becomes incapable of carrying out necessary duties while in office? When James Garfield was shot in 1881, he stayed alive for two and a half months. What was Vice President Chester Arthur's role?

This question was not addressed in the original Constitution. Article II, Section 1, says only that "[i]n Case of the Removal of the President from Office, or of his Death, Resignation, or Inability to discharge the Powers and Duties of the said Office, the same shall devolve on [the same powers shall be exercised by] the Vice President." There have been many instances of presidential disability. When Dwight Eisenhower became ill a second time in 1958, he entered into a pact with Richard Nixon that provided that the vice president could determine whether the president was incapable of carrying out his duties if the president could not communicate. John Kennedy and Lyndon Johnson entered into similar agreements with their vice presidents. Finally, in 1967, the **Twenty-fifth Amendment** was passed, establishing procedures in case of presidential incapacity.

Twenty-fifth Amendment A 1967 amendment to the Constitution that establishes procedures for filling presidential and vice presidential vacancies and makes provisions for presidential disability.

The Twenty-Fifth Amendment

According to the Twenty-fifth Amendment, when a president believes that he or she is incapable of performing the duties of his office, the president must inform Congress in writing. Then the vice president serves as acting president until the president can resume normal duties. When the president is unable to communicate, a majority of the cabinet, including the vice president, can declare that fact to Congress. Then the vice president serves as acting president until the president resumes normal duties. If a dispute arises over the return of the president's ability, a two-thirds vote of Congress is required to decide whether the vice president shall remain acting president or whether the president shall resume normal duties.

TABLE 10–1	Line of Succession to the Presidency of the United States

1. Vice president
2. Speaker of the House of Representatives
3. Senate president *pro tempore*
4. Secretary of state
5. Secretary of the treasury
6. Secretary of defense
7. Attorney general (heads Justice Department)
8. Secretary of the interior
9. Secretary of agriculture
10. Secretary of commerce
11. Secretary of labor
12. Secretary of health and human services
13. Secretary of housing and urban development
14. Secretary of transportation
15. Secretary of energy
16. Secretary of education
17. Secretary of veterans affairs
18. Secretary of homeland security

When the Vice Presidency Becomes Vacant

The Twenty-fifth Amendment also addresses the issue of how the president should fill a vacant vice presidency. Section 2 of the amendment simply states, "Whenever there is a vacancy in the office of the Vice President, the President shall nominate a Vice President who shall take office upon confirmation by a majority vote of both Houses of Congress."

The question of who shall be president if both the president and vice president die is answered by the Succession Act of 1947. If the president and vice president die, resign, or are disabled, the Speaker of the House will become president, after resigning from Congress. Next in line is the president pro tem of the Senate, followed by the cabinet officers in the order of the creation of their departments (see Table 10–1).

MAKING A DIFFERENCE: Communicating with the White House

Writing to the president of the United States has long been a way for citizens to express their political opinions. The most traditional form of communication is, of course, by letter. Letters to the president should be addressed to:

**The President
of the United States**
The White House
1600 Pennsylvania Avenue N.W.
Washington, DC 20500

Letters may be sent to the first lady at the same address. Will you get an answer? Almost certainly. The White House mail room is staffed by volunteers and paid employees who sort the mail for the president and tally the public's concerns. You may receive a standard response to your comments or a more personal, detailed response.

TELEPHONE THE WHITE HOUSE

You can also call the White House on the telephone and leave a mes-sage for the president or first lady. To call the switchboard, call 202-456-1414, a number publicized by former Secretary of State James Baker when he told the Israelis through the media, "When you're serious about peace, call us at . . . ." The switchboard received more than eight thousand calls in the next twenty-four hours.

The White House also has a round-the-clock comment line, which you can reach at 202-456-1111. When you call that number, an operator will take down your comments and forward them to the president's office.

USE THE INTERNET

The home page for the White House is

www.whitehouse.gov

It is designed to be entertaining and to convey information about the president. You can also send your comments and ideas to the White House using e-mail. Send comments to the president at

President@whitehouse.gov

Address e-mail to the first lady at

First.Lady@whitehouse.gov

In 2003, the White House deployed a new and somewhat complicated system for sending messages to President Bush. It involves navigating successive Web pages and filling out a form. You must choose one of a limited number of topics selected by the White House. Once the message is sent, the writer must wait for an automated e-mail response that asks for a confirmation.

KEY TERMS

advice and consent 240

appointment power 238

cabinet 250

chief diplomat 240

chief executive 237

chief legislator 243

chief of staff 251

chief of state 237

civil service 238

commander in chief 239

constitutional power 245

diplomatic recognition 240

emergency power 247

executive agreement 242

Executive Office of the
   President (EOP) 250

executive order 248

executive privilege 248

expressed power 245

Federal Register 248

impeachment 249

inherent power 245

kitchen cabinet 250

line-item veto 244

National Security Council
   (NSC) 252

Office of Management and
   Budget (OMB) 252

pardon 238

patronage 245

pocket veto 244

reprieve 238

State of the Union
   message 243

statutory power 245

Twelfth Amendment 236

Twenty-fifth Amendment 254

veto message 243

War Powers Resolution 240

Washington community 246

White House Office 251

CHAPTER SUMMARY

1 The office of the presidency in the United States, combining as it does the functions of chief of state and chief executive, was, when created, unique. The framers of the Constitution were divided over whether the president should be a weak or a strong executive.

2 The requirements for the office of the presidency are outlined in Article II, Section 1, of the Constitution. The president's roles include both formal and informal duties. The roles of the president include chief of state, chief executive, commander in chief, chief diplomat, chief legislator, and party chief.

3 As chief of state, the president is ceremonial head of the government. As chief executive, the president is bound to enforce the acts of Congress, the judgments of the federal courts, and treaties. The chief executive has the power of appointment and the power to grant reprieves and pardons.

4 As commander in chief, the president is the ultimate decision maker in military matters. As chief diplomat, the president recognizes foreign governments, negotiates treaties, signs agreements, and nominates and receives ambassadors. The role of chief legislator includes recommending legislation to Congress, lobbying for the legislation, approving laws, and exercising the veto power.

5 In addition to constitutional powers, the president has statutory powers written into law by Congress and inherent powers. Presidents are also leaders of their political parties. Presidents use their power to persuade and their access to the media to fulfill this function.

6 Presidents have a variety of special powers not available to other branches of the government. These include emergency powers and the power to issue executive orders and invoke executive privilege.

7 Abuses of executive power are dealt with by Articles I and II of the Constitution, which authorize the House and Senate to impeach and remove the president, vice president, or other officers of the federal government for committing "Treason, Bribery, or other high Crimes and Misdemeanors."

8 The president receives assistance from the cabinet and from the Executive Office of the President (including the White House Office).

9 The vice president is the constitutional officer assigned to preside over the Senate and to assume the presidency in case of the death, resignation, removal, or disability of the president. The Twenty-fifth Amendment, passed in 1967, established procedures to be followed in case of presidential incapacity and when filling a vacant vice presidency.

SELECTED PRINT AND MEDIA RESOURCES

Suggested Readings

Clinton, Hillary. *Living History*. New York: Simon & Schuster, 2003. The former first lady and current senator from New York provides her own explanation of the events of her husband's presidency.

Frum, David. *The Right Man: The Surprise Presidency of George Bush*. New York: Random House, 2003. The author, who was a speechwriter for George W. Bush during his first year as president, provides an inside look at this period of the Bush presidency.

Greenfield, Meg. *Washington*. New York: Public Affairs, 2001. The author, a long-time *Washington Post* reporter, takes a candid look at Washington, D.C., politics and political players.

Greenstein, Fred I. *The Presidential Difference: Leadership Style from Roosevelt to Clinton*. Old Tappan, N.J.: Free Press, 2000. In this book, an eminent presidential scholar examines and discusses the leadership styles of eleven chief executives. Greenstein assesses each president in several categories, including organization, skill, vision, and emotional intelligence.

Woodward, Bob. *Bush at War*. New York: Simon & Schuster, 2002. Noted investigative journalist Woodward takes a close look at presidential decision making in the months following the terrorist attacks of September 11, 2001. His account of the Bush White House and his analysis of President Bush's leadership style are especially notable.

Media Resources

CNN—Election 2000—A politically balanced look at the extraordinarily close presidential election of 2000, which pitted Republican George W. Bush against Democrat Al Gore. The race was eventually settled by the United States Supreme Court. CNN's Bill Hemmer narrates this 2001 production.

LBJ: A Biography—An acclaimed biography of Lyndon Johnson that covers his rise to power, his presidency, and the events of the Vietnam War, which ended his presidency; produced in 1991 as part of PBS's *The American Experience* series.

Nixon—An excellent 1995 film exposing the events of Richard Nixon's troubled presidency. Anthony Hopkins plays the embattled but brilliant chief executive.

Sunrise at Campobello—An excellent portrait of one of the greatest presidents, Franklin Delano Roosevelt; produced in 1960 and starring Ralph Bellamy.

LOGGING ON

This site offers extensive information on the White House and the presidency: http://www.whitehouse.gov.

Inaugural addresses of American presidents from George Washington to George W. Bush can be found at http://www.bartleby.com/124.

You can find an excellent collection of data and maps describing all U.S. presidential elections at Dave Leip's Atlas of U.S. Presidential Elections. Go to http://uselectionatlas.org.

USING THE INTERNET FOR POLITICAL ANALYSIS

Go to this text's Web site at **http://politicalscience. wadsworth.com/schmidtbrief2004**. Select "Chapter 10" in the box at the top of the window. Then, in the column on the left-hand side of the window, under "Chapter Resources," click on "Internet Exercises." The Web site will then display the following Internet

exercises that you can perform to learn more about topics covered in this chapter.

Activity 10–1: Managing the News
Activity 10–2: The National Security Council
Activity 10–3: The Office of the Vice President

ONLINE STUDY GUIDE AND ADDITIONAL RESOURCES

At **http://politicalscience.wadsworth.com/ schmidtbrief2004** you will find a free Study Guide to this book that includes tutorial quizzes, essay questions, practice exams, chapter outlines, learning objectives, the glossary, flashcards, crossword puzzles, and Microsoft PowerPoint presentations. Also included in the American Government Resource Center for Chapter 10:

- **InfoTrac® Reader**—Evaluating Bill Clinton and George W. Bush; does President Bush exercise too much power?
- **You Are There Simulation**—The presidency.
- **Participation Activities**—Contact the president about a policy change; find a newsgroup discussion about the president.

- **MicroCase Exercise**—The presidency.
- **Related Links**—The presidency.
- **Video Case Study**—The presidency—Clinton style; Nixon and Ford style.
- **Source Readings**—By Alexander Hamilton and Louis Fisher, plus selected court cases and proceedings.

The site also contains the Citizen's Survival Guide, information on how to get involved in politics locally and globally, as well as regularly updated features including a Current Events Quiz, In the News, Election Links, updates on the war on terrorism, and more.

CHAPTER 11

The Bureaucracy

FACELESS BUREAUCRATS—THIS IMAGE provokes a negative reaction from many, if not most, Americans. Polls consistently report that the majority of Americans support "less government." The same polls, however, report that the majority of Americans support almost every specific program that the government undertakes. The conflict between the desire for small government and the benefits that only a large government can provide has been a constant feature of American politics. For example, the goal of preserving endangered species has widespread support. At the same time, many people believe that restrictions imposed under the Endangered Species Act violate the rights of landowners. Helping the elderly pay their medical bills is a popular objective, but hardly anyone enjoys paying the Medicare tax that supports this effort.

In this chapter, we describe the size, organization, and staffing of the federal bureaucracy. We review modern attempts at bureaucratic reform and the process by which Congress exerts ultimate control over the bureaucracy. We also discuss the bureaucracy's role in making rules and setting policy.

The Nature of Bureaucracy

Every modern president, at one time or another, has proclaimed that his administration was going to "fix government." All modern presidents also have put forth plans to end government waste and inefficiency (see Table 11–1 on page 260). Their success has been, in a word, underwhelming. Presidents have been generally powerless to affect significantly the structure and operation of the federal bureaucracy.

A **bureaucracy** is the name given to a large organization that is structured hierarchically to carry out specific functions. Generally, most bureaucracies are characterized by an organization chart. The units of the organization are divided according to the specialization and expertise of the employees.

Bureaucracy A large organization that is structured hierarchically to carry out specific functions.

259

TABLE 11–1	**Selected Presidential Plans to End Government Inefficiency**
PRESIDENT	NAME OF PLAN
Lyndon Johnson (1963–1969)	Programming, Planning, and Budgeting Systems
Richard Nixon (1969–1974)	Management by Objectives
Jimmy Carter (1977–1981)	Zero-Based Budgeting
Ronald Reagan (1981–1989)	President's Private Sector Survey on Cost Control (the Grace Commission)
George H. W. Bush (1989–1993)	Right-Sizing Government
Bill Clinton (1993–2001)	Reinventing Government
George W. Bush (2001–)	Performance-Based Budgeting

Public and Private Bureaucracies

We should not think of bureaucracy as unique to government. Any large corporation or university can be considered a bureaucratic organization. The fact is that the handling of complex problems requires a division of labor. Individuals must concentrate their skills on specific, well-defined aspects of a problem and depend on others to solve the rest of it.

Public or government bureaucracies differ from private organizations in some important ways, however. A private corporation, such as Microsoft, has a single set of leaders, its board of directors. Public bureaucracies, in contrast, do not have a single set of leaders. Although the president is the chief administrator of the federal system, all bureaucratic agencies are subject to Congress for their funding, staffing, and, indeed, their continued existence. Furthermore, public bureaucracies supposedly serve the citizen rather than the stockholder.

One other important difference between private corporations and government bureaucracies is that government bureaucracies are not organized to make a profit. Rather, they are supposed to perform their functions as efficiently as possible to conserve the taxpayers' dollars. Perhaps it is this ideal that makes citizens hostile toward government bureaucracy when they experience inefficiency and red tape.

Models of Bureaucracy

Several theories have been offered to help us better understand the ways in which bureaucracies function. Each of these theories focuses on specific features of bureaucracies.

Weberian Model.   The classic model, or **Weberian model,** of the modern bureaucracy was proposed by the German sociologist Max Weber.[1] He argued that the increasingly complex nature of modern life, coupled with the steadily growing demands placed on governments by their citizens, made the formation of bureaucracies inevitable. According to Weber, most bureaucracies—whether in the public or private sector—are hierarchically organized and governed by formal procedures. The power in a bureaucracy flows from the top downward. Decision-making processes in bureaucracies are shaped by detailed technical rules that promote similar decisions in

INFOTRAC

For more information about this topic, use the term "public administration" in the Subject guide.

Weberian Model A model of bureaucracy developed by sociologist Max Weber, who viewed bureaucracies as rational, hierarchical organizations in which decisions are based on logical reasoning.

similar situations. Bureaucrats are specialists who attempt to resolve problems through logical reasoning and data analysis instead of "gut feelings" and guesswork. Individual advancement in bureaucracies is supposed to be based on merit rather than political connections. Indeed, the modern bureaucracy, according to Weber, should be an apolitical organization.

Acquisitive Model.

Other theorists do not view bureaucracies in terms as benign as Weber's. Some believe that bureaucracies are acquisitive in nature. Proponents of the **acquisitive model** argue that top level bureaucrats will always try to expand, or at least to avoid any reductions in, the size of their budgets. Although government bureaucracies are not-for-profit enterprises, bureaucrats want to maximize the size of their budgets and staff, because these things are the most visible trappings of power in the public sector. These efforts are also prompted by the desire of bureaucrats to "sell" their products—national defense, public housing, agricultural subsidies, and so on—to both Congress and the public.

Monopolistic Model.

Because government bureaucracies seldom have competitors, some theorists have suggested that these bureaucratic organizations may be explained best by a **monopolistic model.** The analysis is similar to that used by economists to examine the behavior of monopolistic firms. Monopolistic bureaucracies—like monopolistic firms—essentially have no competitors and act accordingly. Because monopolistic bureaucracies usually are not penalized for chronic inefficiency, they have little reason to adopt cost-saving measures or to make more productive use of their resources. Some economists have argued that such problems can be cured only by privatizing certain bureaucratic functions.

Acquisitive Model A model of bureaucracy that views top level bureaucrats as seeking to expand the size of their budgets and staff to gain greater power.

Monopolistic Model A model of bureaucracy that compares bureaucracies to monopolistic business firms. Lack of competition in either case leads to inefficient and costly operations.

The Department of Agriculture inspects meat-packing facilities throughout the United States, certifying the quality and condition of the meat to be sold. Why might the packing industry welcome federal grading of beef?

David Frazier/PhotoResearchers

The Size of the Bureaucracy

In 1789, the new government's bureaucracy was minuscule. There were three departments—State (with nine employees), War (with two employees), and Treasury (with thirty-nine employees)—and the Office of the Attorney General (which later became the Department of Justice). The bureaucracy was still small in 1798. At that time, the secretary of state had seven clerks and spent a total of $500 (about $6,200 in 2004 dollars) on stationery and printing. In that same year, the Appropriations Act allocated $1.4 million to the War Department (or $17.3 million in 2004 dollars).[2]

Times have changed. Excluding the military, the federal bureaucracy includes approximately 2.7 million government employees. That number has remained relatively stable for the last several decades. It is somewhat deceiving, however, because many other individuals work directly or indirectly for the federal government as subcontractors or consultants and in other capacities. In fact, according to some studies, the federal work force vastly exceeds the number of official federal workers.[3]

Cabinet Department
One of the fifteen departments of the executive branch.

Line Organization In the federal government, an administrative unit that is directly accountable to the president.

The figures for federal government employment are only part of the story. Figure 11–1 shows the growth in government employment at the federal, state, and local levels. Since 1970, this growth has been mainly at the state and local levels. (The current financial crisis of the states shows up as a drop in the number of local employees in 2002.) If all government employees are counted, more than 15 percent of all civilian employment is accounted for by government.

The costs of the bureaucracy are commensurately high. The share of the gross national product accounted for by all government spending was only 8.5 percent in 1929. Today, it is about 30 percent.

FIGURE 11–1 Government Employment at the Federal, State, and Local Levels

There are more local government employees than federal and state employees combined.

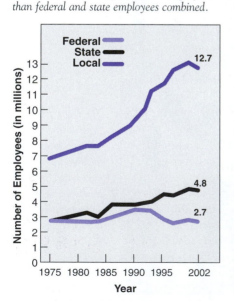

The Organization of the Federal Bureaucracy

Within the federal bureaucracy are a number of different types of government agencies and organizations. Figure 11–2 outlines the several bureaucracies within the executive branch, as well as the separate organizations that provide services to Congress, to the courts, and directly to the president. The executive branch, which employs most of the government's staff, has four major types of structures. They are (1) cabinet departments, (2) independent executive agencies, (3) independent regulatory agencies, and (4) government corporations. Each has a distinctive relationship to the president, and some have unusual internal structures, overall goals, and grants of power.

Cabinet Departments

The fifteen **cabinet departments** are the major service organizations of the federal government. They can also be described in management terms as **line organizations.** This means that

FIGURE 11–2 Organization Chart of the Federal Government

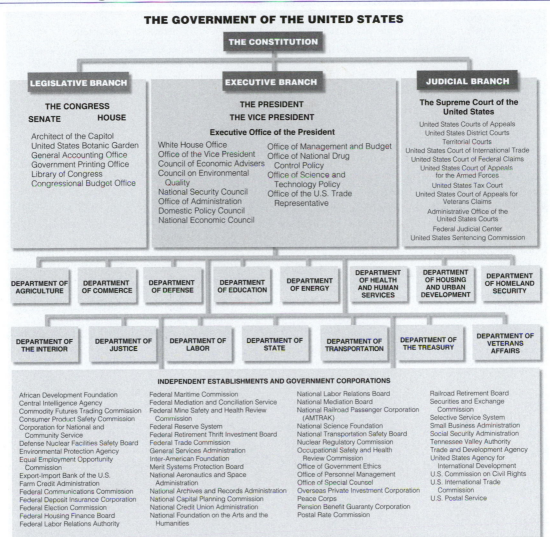

THE GOVERNMENT OF THE UNITED STATES

THE CONSTITUTION

LEGISLATIVE BRANCH

THE CONGRESS

SENATE   HOUSE

Architect of the Capitol
United States Botanic Garden
General Accounting Office
Government Printing Office
Library of Congress
Congressional Budget Office

EXECUTIVE BRANCH

THE PRESIDENT
THE VICE PRESIDENT
Executive Office of the President

White House Office
Office of the Vice President
Council of Economic Advisers
Council on Environmental
  Quality
National Security Council
Office of Administration
Domestic Policy Council
National Economic Council

Office of Management and Budget
Office of National Drug
  Control Policy
Office of Science and
  Technology Policy
Office of the U.S. Trade
  Representative

JUDICIAL BRANCH

**The Supreme Court of the
United States**

United States Courts of Appeals
United States District Courts
Territorial Courts
United States Court of International Trade
United States Court of Federal Claims
United States Court of Appeals
  for the Armed Forces
United States Tax Court
United States Court of Appeals for
  Veterans Claims
Administrative Office of the
  United States Courts
Federal Judicial Center
United States Sentencing Commission

DEPARTMENT OF AGRICULTURE | **DEPARTMENT OF COMMERCE** | **DEPARTMENT OF DEFENSE** | **DEPARTMENT OF EDUCATION** | **DEPARTMENT OF ENERGY** | **DEPARTMENT OF HEALTH AND HUMAN SERVICES** | **DEPARTMENT OF HOUSING AND URBAN DEVELOPMENT** | **DEPARTMENT OF HOMELAND SECURITY**

DEPARTMENT OF THE INTERIOR | **DEPARTMENT OF JUSTICE** | **DEPARTMENT OF LABOR** | **DEPARTMENT OF STATE** | **DEPARTMENT OF TRANSPORTATION** | **DEPARTMENT OF THE TREASURY** | **DEPARTMENT OF VETERANS AFFAIRS**

INDEPENDENT ESTABLISHMENTS AND GOVERNMENT CORPORATIONS

African Development Foundation
Central Intelligence Agency
Commodity Futures Trading Commission
Consumer Product Safety Commission
Corporation for National and
  Community Service
Defense Nuclear Facilities Safety Board
Environmental Protection Agency
Equal Employment Opportunity
  Commission
Export-Import Bank of the U.S.
Farm Credit Administration
Federal Communications Commission
Federal Deposit Insurance Corporation
Federal Election Commission
Federal Housing Finance Board
Federal Labor Relations Authority

Federal Maritime Commission
Federal Mediation and Conciliation Service
Federal Mine Safety and Health Review
  Commission
Federal Reserve System
Federal Retirement Thrift Investment Board
Federal Trade Commission
General Services Administration
Inter-American Foundation
Merit Systems Protection Board
National Aeronautics and Space
  Administration
National Archives and Records Administration
National Capital Planning Commission
National Credit Union Administration
National Foundation on the Arts and the
  Humanities

National Labor Relations Board
National Mediation Board
National Railroad Passenger Corporation
  (AMTRAK)
National Science Foundation
National Transportation Safety Board
Nuclear Regulatory Commission
Occupational Safety and Health
  Review Commission
Office of Government Ethics
Office of Personnel Management
Office of Special Counsel
Overseas Private Investment Corporation
Peace Corps
Pension Benefit Guaranty Corporation
Postal Rate Commission

Railroad Retirement Board
Securities and Exchange
  Commission
Selective Service System
Small Business Administration
Social Security Administration
Tennessee Valley Authority
Trade and Development Agency
United States Agency for
  International Development
U.S. Commission on Civil Rights
U.S. International Trade
  Commission
U.S. Postal Service

SOURCE: *United States Government Manual, 2003–2004* (Washington, D.C.: U.S. Government Printing Office, 2003).

they are directly accountable to the president and are responsible for performing government functions, such as printing money and training troops. These departments were created by Congress when the need for each department arose. The first department to be created was State, and the most recent one was Homeland Security, established in 2002. A president might ask that a new department be created or an old one abolished, but the president has no power to do so without legislative approval from Congress.

TABLE 11–2	Executive Departments	
DEPARTMENT AND YEAR ESTABLISHED	PRINCIPAL FUNCTIONS	SELECTED SUBAGENCIES
State (1789) (31,916 employees)	Negotiates treaties; develops foreign policy; protects citizens abroad.	Passport Agency; Bureau of Diplomatic Security; Foreign Service; Bureau of Human Rights and Humanitarian Affairs; Bureau of Consular Affairs.
Treasury (1789) (131,872 employees)	Pays all federal bills; borrows money; collects federal taxes; mints coins and prints paper currency; supervises national banks.	Internal Revenue Service; U.S. Mint.
Interior (1849) (71,005 employees)	Supervises federally owned lands and parks; supervises Native American affairs.	U.S. Fish and Wildlife Service; National Park Service; Bureau of Indian Affairs; Bureau of Land Management.
Justice (1870)* (101,392 employees)	Furnishes legal advice to the president; enforces federal criminal laws; supervises the federal prisons.	Federal Bureau of Investigation; Drug Enforcement Administration; Bureau of Prisons.
Agriculture (1889) (98,879 employees)	Provides assistance to farmers and ranchers; conducts agricultural research; works to protect forests.	Soil Conservation Service; Agricultural Research Service; Food Safety and Inspection Service; Federal Crop Insurance Corporation.
Commerce (1913)† (37,087 employees)	Grants patents and trademarks; conducts a national census; monitors the weather; protects the interests of businesses.	Bureau of the Census; Bureau of Economic Analysis; Patent and Trademark Office; National Oceanic and Atmospheric Administration.
Labor (1913) (16,144 employees)	Administers federal labor laws; promotes the interests of workers.	Occupational Safety and Health Administration; Bureau of Labor Statistics; Employment Standards Administration; Employment and Training Administration.
Defense (1947)‡ (684,446 employees)	Manages the armed forces (army, navy, air force, and marines); operates military bases; is responsible for civil defense.	National Security Agency; Joint Chiefs of Staff; Departments of the Air Force, Navy, Army; Defense Advanced Research Projects Agency; Defense Intelligence Agency; the service academies.

*Formed from the Office of the Attorney General (created in 1789).
†Formed from the Department of Commerce and Labor (created in 1903).
‡Formed from the Department of War (created in 1789) and the Department of Navy (created in 1798).

Each department is headed by a secretary (except for the Justice Department, which is headed by the attorney general). Each also has several levels of undersecretaries, assistant secretaries, and so on.

Presidents theoretically have considerable control over the cabinet departments, because presidents are able to appoint or fire all of the top officials. Even cabinet departments do not always respond to the president's wishes, though. One reason that presidents are frequently unhappy with their departments is that the entire bureaucratic structure below the top political levels is staffed by permanent employees, many of whom are committed to established programs or procedures and who resist change. As we can see from Table 11–2, each cabinet department employs thousands of individuals, only a handful of whom are under the control of the president. The table also describes some of the functions of each of the departments.

TABLE 11–2	Executive Departments—Continued	
DEPARTMENT AND YEAR ESTABLISHED	PRINCIPAL FUNCTIONS	SELECTED SUBAGENCIES
Housing and Urban Development (1965) (10,643 employees)	Deals with the nation's housing needs; develops and rehabilitates urban communities; overseas resale of mortgages.	Government National Mortgage Association; Office of Community Planning and Development; Office of Fair Housing and Equal Opportunity.
Transportation (1967) (58,819 employees)	Finances improvements in mass transit; develops and administers programs for highways, railroads, and aviation.	Federal Aviation Administration; Federal Highway Administration; National Highway Traffic Safety Administration; Federal Transit Administration.
Energy (1977) (15,789 employees)	Promotes the conservation of energy and resources; analyzes energy data; conducts research and development.	Federal Energy Regulatory Commission; National Nuclear Security Administration.
Health and Human Services (1979)[§] (67,091 employees)	Promotes public health; enforces pure food and drug laws; conducts and sponsors health-related research.	Food and Drug Administration; Public Health Service; Centers for Disease Control; National Institutes of Health; Centers for Medicare and Medicaid Services.
Education (1979)[§] (4,592 employees)	Coordinates federal programs and policies for education; administers aid to education; promotes educational research.	Office of Special Education and Rehabilitation Service; Office of Elementary and Secondary Education; Office of Postsecondary Education; Office of Federal Student Aid.
Veterans Affairs (1988) (225,159 employees)	Promotes the welfare of veterans of the U.S. armed forces.	Veterans Health Administration; Veterans Benefits Administration; National Cemetery Systems.
Homeland Security (2002) (151,813 employees)	Attempts to prevent terrorist attacks within the United States, control America's borders, and minimize the damage from natural disasters.	U.S. Customs Service; U.S. Coast Guard; Secret Service; Federal Emergency Management Agency; Bureau of Citizenship and Immigration Services.

[§]Formed from the Department of Health, Education, and Welfare (created in 1953).
Employment figures as of March 2003.

Independent Executive Agencies

Independent executive agencies are bureaucratic organizations that are not located within a department but report directly to the president, who appoints their chief officials. When a new federal agency is created—the Environmental Protection Agency, for example—Congress decides where it will be located in the bureaucracy. In recent decades, presidents often have asked that a new organization be kept separate or independent rather than added to an existing department, particularly if a department may in fact be hostile to the agency's creation.

Independent Regulatory Agencies

The **independent regulatory agencies** are typically responsible for a specific type of public policy. Their function is to make and implement rules and regulations in a particular sphere of action to protect the public interest.

Independent Executive Agency A federal agency that is not part of a cabinet department but reports directly to the president.

Independent Regulatory Agency An agency outside the major executive departments charged with making and implementing rules and regulations.

In practice, the regulatory agencies are administered independently of all three branches of government. They were set up because Congress felt it was unable to handle the complexities and technicalities required to carry out specific laws in the public interest. The regulatory commissions in fact combine some functions of all three branches of government—executive, legislative, and judicial. They are legislative in that they make rules that have the force of law. They are executive in that they provide for the enforcement of those rules. They are judicial in that they decide disputes involving the rules they have made.

Members of regulatory agency boards or commissions are appointed by the president with the consent of the Senate, although they do not report to the president. By law, the members of regulatory agencies cannot all be from the same political party. Presidents can influence regulatory agency behavior by appointing people of their own parties or people who share their political views when vacancies occur, in particular when the chair is vacant. Members may be removed by the president only for causes specified in the law creating the agency.

Agency Capture.   Over the last several decades, some observers have concluded that these agencies, although nominally independent, may in fact not always be so. They contend that many independent regulatory agencies have been **captured** by the very industries and firms that they were supposed to regulate. The results have been less competition rather than more competition, higher prices rather than lower prices, and less choice rather than more choice for consumers.

Deregulation and Reregulation.   During the presidency of Ronald Reagan (1981–1989), some significant deregulation (the removal of regulatory restraints—the opposite of regulation) occurred, much of which had started under President Jimmy Carter (1977–1981). For example, President Carter appointed a chairperson of the Civil Aeronautics Board (CAB) who gradually eliminated regulation of airline fares and routes. Then, under Reagan, the CAB was eliminated on January 1, 1985.

During the first Bush administration (1989–1993), calls for reregulation of many businesses increased. Indeed, during that administration, the Americans with Disabilities Act of 1990, the Civil Rights Act of 1991, and the Clean Air Act Amendments of 1991, all of which increased or changed the regulation of many businesses, were passed. Additionally, the Cable Reregulation Act of 1992 was passed.

Under President Bill Clinton (1993–2001), the Interstate Commerce Commission was eliminated, and the banking and telecommunications industries, along with many other sectors of the economy, were deregulated. At the same time, there was extensive regulation to protect the environment.

Government Corporations

Another form of bureaucratic organization in the United States is the **government corporation.** Although the concept is borrowed from the world of business, distinct differences exist between public and private corporations.

A private corporation has shareholders (stockholders) who elect a board of directors, who in turn choose the corporate officers, such as president and vice president. When a private corporation makes a profit, it must pay taxes (unless it avoids them

Capture The act by which an industry being regulated by a government agency gains direct or indirect control over agency personnel and decision makers.

INFOTRAC

For more information about deregulation, use the term "deregulation" in the Subject guide.

Government Corporation An agency of government that administers a quasi-business enterprise.

through various legal loopholes). It either distributes part or all of the after-tax profits to shareholders as dividends or plows the profits back into the corporation to make new investments.

A government corporation has a board of directors and managers, but it does not have any stockholders. We cannot buy shares of stock in a government corporation. If the government corporation makes a profit, it does not distribute the profit as dividends. Also, if it makes a profit, it does not have to pay taxes; the profits remain in the corporation.

Staffing the Bureaucracy

There are two categories of bureaucrats: political appointees and civil servants. As noted earlier, the president is able to make political appointments to most of the top jobs in the federal bureaucracy. The president also can appoint ambassadors to foreign posts. The rest of the individuals who work for the national government belong to the civil service and obtain their jobs through a much more formal process.

Political Appointees

When making political appointments, the president and the president's advisers solicit suggestions from politicians, businesspersons, and other prominent individuals. Appointments to these positions offer the president a way to pay off outstanding political debts. But the president must also take into consideration such things as the candidate's work experience, intelligence, political affiliations, and personal characteristics. Presidents have differed in the importance they attach to appointing women and minorities to top bureaucratic positions. Presidents often use ambassadorships, however, to reward individuals for their campaign contributions.

The Aristocracy of the Federal Government.   Political appointees are in some sense the aristocracy of the federal government. But their powers, although appearing formidable on paper, are often exaggerated. Like the president, a political appointee will occupy her or his position for a comparatively brief time. Political appointees often leave office before the president's term actually ends. In fact, the average term of service for political appointees is less than two years. As a result, most appointees have little background for their positions and may be mere figureheads. Often, they only respond to the paperwork that flows up from below. Additionally, the professional civil servants who make up the permanent civil service may not feel compelled to carry out their current boss's directives quickly, because they know that he or she will not be around for very long.

The Difficulty in Firing Civil Servants.   This inertia is compounded by the fact that it is extremely difficult to discharge civil servants. In recent years, fewer than one-tenth of 1 percent of federal employees have been fired for incompetence. Because discharged employees may appeal their dismissals, many months or even years may pass before the issue is resolved conclusively. This occupational rigidity helps to ensure that most political appointees, no matter how competent or driven, will not be able to exert much meaningful influence over their subordinates, let alone implement dramatic changes in the bureaucracy itself.

History of the Federal Civil Service

When the federal government was formed in 1789, it had no career public servants but rather consisted of amateurs who were almost all Federalists. When Thomas Jefferson took over as president, few in his party were holding federal administrative jobs, so he fired more than one hundred officials and replaced them with his own supporters. For the next twenty-five years, a growing body of federal administrators gained experience and expertise, becoming in the process professional public servants. These administrators stayed in office regardless of who was elected president. The bureaucracy had become a self-maintaining, long-term element within government.

To the Victor Belong the Spoils.   When Andrew Jackson took over the White House in 1828, he could not believe how many appointed officials (appointed before he became president, that is) were overtly hostile toward him and his Democratic Party. As the bureaucracy was reluctant to carry out his programs, Jackson did the obvious: he fired federal officials—more than had all his predecessors combined. The **spoils system**—an application of the principle that to the victor belong the spoils— became the standard method of filling federal positions. Whenever a new president was elected from a party different from the party of the previous president, there would be an almost complete turnover in the staffing of the federal government.

Spoils System The awarding of government jobs to political supporters and friends.

The Civil Service Reform Act of 1883.   Jackson's spoils system survived for a number of years, but it became increasingly corrupt. Also, as the size of the bureaucracy increased by 300 percent between 1851 and 1881, the cry for civil service reform became louder. Reformers began to look to the example of several European countries, which had established a professional civil service that operated under a **merit system** in which job appointments were based on competitive examinations.

In 1883, the **Pendleton Act**—or **Civil Service Reform Act**—was passed, placing the first limits on the spoils system. The act established the principle of employment on the basis of open, competitive examinations and created the **Civil Service Commission** to administer the personnel service. Only 10 percent of federal employees were initially covered by the merit system. Later laws, amendments, and executive orders, however, increased the coverage to more than 90 percent of federal employees. The effects of these reforms were felt at all levels of government.

The Supreme Court strengthened the civil service system in *Elrod v. Burns*[4] in 1976 and *Branti v. Finkel*[5] in 1980. In those two cases, the Court used the First Amendment to forbid government officials from discharging or threatening to discharge public employees solely for not being supporters of the political party in power unless party affiliation is an appropriate requirement for the position. Additional enhancements to the civil service system were added in *Rutan v. Republican Party of Illinois*[6] in 1990. The Court's ruling effectively prevented the use of partisan political considerations as the basis for hiring, promoting, or transferring most public employees. An exception was permitted, however, for senior policymaking positions, which usually go to officials who will support the programs of the elected leaders.

Merit System The selection, retention, and promotion of government employees on the basis of competitive examinations.

Pendleton Act (Civil Service Reform Act) An act that established the principle of employment on the basis of merit and created the Civil Service Commission to administer the personnel service.

Civil Service Commission The initial central personnel agency of the national government; created in 1883.

The Civil Service Reform Act of 1978. In 1978, the Civil Service Reform Act abolished the Civil Service Commission and created two new federal agencies to perform its duties. To administer the civil service laws, rules, and regulations, the act created the Office of Personnel Management (OPM). The OPM is empowered to recruit, interview, and test potential government workers and determine who should be hired. The OPM makes recommendations to the individual agencies as to which persons meet the standards (typically, the top three applicants for a position), and the agencies then decide whom to hire. To oversee promotions, employees' rights, and other employment matters, the act created the Merit Systems Protection Board (MSPB). The MSPB evaluates charges of wrongdoing, hears employee appeals from agency decisions, and can order corrective action against agencies and employees.

Federal Employees and Political Campaigns. In 1933, when President Franklin Roosevelt set up his New Deal, a virtual army of civil servants was hired to staff the many new agencies that were created. Because the individuals who worked in these agencies owed their jobs to the Democratic Party, it seemed natural for them to campaign for Democratic candidates. The Democrats controlling Congress in the mid-1930s did not object. But in 1938, a coalition of conservative Democrats and Republicans took control of Congress and forced through the Hatch Act—or Political Activities Act—of 1939. The act prohibited federal employees from actively participating in the political management of campaigns. It also forbade the use of federal authority to influence nominations and elections and outlawed the use of bureaucratic rank to pressure federal employees to make political contributions.

The Hatch Act created a controversy that lasted for decades. Many contended that the act deprived federal employees of their First Amendment freedoms of speech and association. In 1972, a federal district court declared the act unconstitutional. The United States Supreme Court, however, reaffirmed the challenged portion of the act in 1973, stating that the government's interest in preserving a nonpartisan civil service was so great that the prohibitions should remain.[7] Twenty years later, Congress addressed the criticisms of the Hatch Act by passing the Federal Employees Political Activities Act of 1993. This act, which amended the Hatch Act, lessened the harshness of the 1939 act in several ways. Among other things, the 1993 act allowed federal employees to run for office in nonpartisan elections, participate in voter-registration drives, make campaign contributions to political organizations, and campaign for candidates in partisan elections.

Modern Attempts at Bureaucratic Reform

As long as the federal bureaucracy exists, there will be attempts to make it more open, efficient, and responsive to the needs of U.S. citizens. The most important actual and proposed reforms in the last several decades include sunshine and sunset laws, privatization, and more protection for so-called whistleblowers.

Sunshine Laws

In 1976, Congress enacted the **Government in the Sunshine Act.** It required for the
first time that all multiheaded federal agencies—agencies headed by a committee
instead of an individual—hold their meetings regularly in public session. The bill
defined *meeting* as almost any gathering, formal or informal, of agency members,
including a conference telephone call. The only exceptions to this rule of openness
are discussions of matters such as court proceedings or personnel problems, and these
exceptions are specifically listed in the bill. Sunshine laws now exist at all levels of
government.

Sunset Laws

Potentially, the size and scope of the federal bureaucracy can be controlled through
sunset legislation, which places government programs on a definite schedule for
congressional consideration. Unless Congress specifically reauthorizes a particular
federally operated program at the end of a designated period, it would be terminated
automatically; that is, its sun would set.

The idea of sunset legislation was initially suggested by Franklin Roosevelt when
he created the plethora of New Deal agencies. His assistant, William O. Douglas,
recommended that each agency's charter should include a provision allowing for its
termination in ten years. Only an act of Congress could revitalize it. The proposal
was never adopted. It was not until 1976 that a state legislature—Colorado's—
adopted sunset legislation for state regulatory commissions, giving them a life of six
years before their suns set. Today, most states have some type of sunset law.

"*Who do I see to get big government off my back?*"

Privatization

Another approach to bureaucratic reform is **privatization,** which occurs when government services are replaced by services from the private sector. For example, the government might contract with private firms to operate prisons. Supporters of privatization argue that some services could be provided more efficiently by the private sector. Another scheme is to furnish vouchers to "clients" in lieu of services. For example, instead of supplying housing, the government could offer vouchers that recipients could use to "pay" for housing in privately owned buildings.

The privatization, or contracting out, strategy has been most successful on the local level. Municipalities, for example, can form contracts with private companies for such things as trash collection. This approach is not a cure-all, however, as there are many functions, particularly on the national level, that cannot be contracted out in any meaningful way. For example, the federal government could not contract out most of the Defense Department's functions to private firms.

Incentives for Efficiency and Productivity

An increasing number of state governments are beginning to experiment with a variety of schemes to run their operations more efficiently and capably. They focus on maximizing the efficiency and productivity of government workers by providing incentives for improved performance.[8] For example, many governors, mayors, and city administrators are considering ways in which government can be made more entrepreneurial. Some of the most promising measures have included such tactics as permitting agencies that do not spend their entire budgets to keep some of the difference and rewarding employees with performance-based bonuses.

At the federal level, the Government Performance and Results Act of 1997 was designed to improve efficiency in the federal work force. The act required that all government agencies (except the Central Intelligence Agency) describe their new goals and establish methods for determining whether those goals are met. Goals may be broadly crafted (for example, reducing the time it takes to test a new drug before allowing it to be marketed) or narrowly crafted (for example, reducing the number of times a telephone rings before it is answered).

The "performance-based budgeting" implemented by President George W. Bush takes this results-oriented approach a step further. Performance-based budgeting links agency funding to actual agency performance. Agencies are given specific performance criteria to meet, and the Office of Management and Budget rates each agency to determine how well it has performed. The amount of funds that each agency will receive in the next annual budget is determined by the extent to which it has met the performance criteria.

Helping Out the Whistleblowers

The term **whistleblower** as applied to the federal bureaucracy has a special meaning: it is someone who blows the whistle on a gross governmental inefficiency or illegal action. Whistleblowers may be clerical workers, managers, or even specialists, such

Privatization The replacement of government services with services provided by private firms.

INFOTRAC
For more information about privatization, use the term "privatization" in the Subject guide.

Whistleblower Someone who brings to public attention gross governmental inefficiency or an illegal action.

as scientists. The 1978 Civil Service Reform Act prohibits reprisals against whistle-blowers by their superiors, and it set up the Merit Systems Protection Board as part of this protection. Many federal agencies also have toll-free hot lines that employees can use anonymously to report bureaucratic waste and inappropriate behavior. About 35 percent of all calls result in agency action or follow-up.

Further protection for whistleblowers was provided in 1989, when Congress passed the Whistle-Blower Protection Act. That act established an independent agency, the Office of Special Counsel (OSC), to investigate complaints brought by government employees who have been demoted, fired, or otherwise sanctioned for reporting government fraud or waste. There is little evidence, though, that potential whistleblowers truly have received more protection as a result of these endeavors. More than 40 percent of the employees who turned to the OSC for assistance in a recent three-year period stated that they were no longer employees of the government agencies on which they blew the whistle.

Some state and federal laws encourage employees to blow the whistle on their employers' wrongful actions by providing monetary incentives to the whistleblowers. At the federal level, for example, the False Claims Act of 1986 allows a whistle-blower who has disclosed information about a fraud perpetrated against the U.S. government to receive a monetary award. If the government chooses to prosecute the case, the whistleblower receives between 15 and 25 percent of the proceeds. If the government declines to intervene, the whistleblower can bring suit on behalf of the government and will receive between 25 and 30 percent of the proceeds.

INFOTRAC

For more information about this topic, use the term "whistleblowing" in the Subject guide.

Bureaucrats as Politicians and Policymakers

Enabling Legislation
A statute enacted by Congress that authorizes the creation of an administrative agency and specifies the name, purpose, composition, functions, and powers of the agency being created.

Because Congress is unable to oversee the day-to-day administration of its programs, it must delegate certain powers to administrative agencies. Congress delegates the power to implement legislation to agencies through what is called **enabling legislation.** For example, the Federal Trade Commission was created by the Federal Trade Commission Act of 1914, the Equal Employment Opportunity Commission was created by the Civil Rights Act of 1964, and the Occupational Safety and Health Administration was created by the Occupational Safety and Health Act of 1970. The enabling legislation generally specifies the name, purpose, composition, functions, and powers of the agency.

In theory, the agencies should put into effect laws passed by Congress. Laws are often drafted in such vague and general terms, however, that they provide little guidance to agency administrators as to how the laws should be implemented. This means that the agencies themselves must decide how best to carry out the wishes of Congress.

The discretion given to administrative agencies is not accidental. Congress has long realized that it lacks the technical expertise and the resources to monitor the implementation of its laws. Hence, the administrative agency is created to fill the gaps. This gap-filling role requires the agency to formulate administrative rules (regulations) to put flesh on the bones of the law. But it also forces the agency itself to become an unelected policymaker.

The Rulemaking Environment

Rulemaking does not occur in a vacuum. Suppose that Congress passes a new air-pollution law. The Environmental Protection Agency (EPA) might decide to implement the new law through a technical regulation on factory emissions. This proposed regulation would be published in the *Federal Register,* a daily government publication, so that interested parties would have an opportunity to comment on it. Individuals and companies that opposed parts or all of the rule might then try to convince the EPA to revise or redraft the regulation. Some parties might try to persuade the agency to withdraw the proposed regulation altogether. In any event, the EPA would consider these comments in drafting the final version of the regulation following the expiration of the comment period.

Once the final regulation has been published in the *Federal Register,* there is a sixty-day waiting period before the rule can be enforced. During that period, businesses, individuals, and state and local governments can ask Congress to overturn the regulation. After that sixty-day period has lapsed, the regulation can still be challenged in court by a party having a direct interest in the rule, such as a company that expects to incur significant costs in complying with it. The company could argue that the rule misinterprets the applicable law or goes beyond the agency's statutory purview. An allegation by the company that the EPA made a mistake in judgment probably would not be enough to convince the court to throw out the rule. The company instead would have to demonstrate that the rule itself was "arbitrary and capricious." To meet this standard, the company would have to show that the rule reflected a serious flaw in the EPA's judgment—such as a steadfast refusal by the agency to consider reasonable alternatives to its rule.

How agencies implement, administer, and enforce certain legislation has resulted in controversy. For example, decisions made by agencies charged with implementing and administering the Endangered Species Act have led to protests from farmers, ranchers, and others. For a recent controversy over this act's implementation, see this chapter's *At Issue* feature on the following page.

INFOTRAC

For more information about the EPA, use the term "Environmental Protection Agency" in Keywords.

Negotiated Rulemaking

Since the end of World War II (1939–1945), companies, environmentalists, and other special interest groups have challenged government regulations in court. In the 1980s, however, the sheer wastefulness of attempting to regulate through litigation became more and more apparent. Today, a growing number of federal agencies encourage businesses and public-interest groups to become directly involved in the drafting of regulations. Agencies hope that such participation may help to prevent later courtroom battles over the meaning, applicability, and legal effect of the regulations.

Congress formally approved such a process, which is called *negotiated rulemaking,* in the Negotiated Rulemaking Act of 1990. The act authorizes agencies to allow those who will be affected by a new rule to participate in the rule-drafting process. If an agency chooses to engage in negotiated rulemaking, it must publish in the *Federal Register* the subject and scope of the rule to be developed, the parties that will be affected significantly by the rule, and other information. Representatives of the

AT ISSUE: Does the Endangered Species Act Cause More Harm Than It Prevents?

Congress passed the Endangered Species Act (ESA) almost three decades ago. Both Republicans and Democrats supported the legislation. The ESA's goal was straightforward: to protect species that are on the brink of extinction.

SAVING SPECIES IS ALWAYS WORTH THE COST

Proponents of the ESA argue that we should do everything possible to maintain existing fish, wildlife, and flora, in part because we may discover additional uses for them in years to come. Maintaining diversity in species may allow us to develop lifesaving cures in the future, for example. Although some humans may suffer harm—for example, loss of jobs—because of certain environmental regulations, that is the price we have to pay to guarantee biodiversity. We have to protect endangered species so that our children, our grandchildren, and generations to come will be able to enjoy the same diversity of animal, insect, and plant life that we now enjoy.

COSTS MUST BE TAKEN INTO ACCOUNT

While few people argue against the goals of the ESA, some are unhappy with its implementation. These critics believe that its costs are greater than its benefits. As one example, they cite a National Academy of Sciences (NAS) investigation of the gov-ernment's decision to cut off the flow of irrigation water from Klamath Lake in Oregon in the summer of 2001. That action, which affected irrigation water for more than one thousand farms in southern Oregon and northern California, was undertaken to save endangered suckerfish and local salmon. It was believed that the lake's water level was so low that further use of the lake water for irrigation would harm these fish. The results of this decision were devastating for many farmers. The NAS report claimed that the government had not based its decision on scientific investigation. According to the report, the low water level never really threatened the suckerfish, and it may actually have helped the salmon population.

Critics of the ESA argue that all actions have costs and that those costs must be examined. If one hundred thousand people must lose their jobs to save an insect, plant, or animal, perhaps there should be a nationwide policy debate before such action is undertaken.

FOR CRITICAL ANALYSIS

Is it possible to calculate the benefits of saving species? If not, then how can we compare the benefits of saving species with the costs? How should we decide when, where, and how to save species?

affected groups and other interested parties then may apply to be members of the negotiating committee. The agency is represented on the committee, but a neutral third party (not the agency) presides over the proceedings. Once the committee members have reached agreement on the terms of the proposed rule, notice of the proposed rule is published in the *Federal Register*, followed by a period for comments by any person or organization interested in the proposed rule. Negotiated rulemaking often is conducted under the condition that the participants promise not to challenge in court the outcome of any agreement to which they were a party.

Bureaucrats Are Policymakers

Theories of public administration once assumed that bureaucrats do not make policy decisions but only implement the laws and policies promulgated by the president and legislative bodies. Many people continue to make this assumption. A more realistic view, which is now held by most bureaucrats and elected officials, is that the agencies and departments of government play important roles in policymaking. As we have seen, many government rules, regulations, and programs are in fact initiated by the bureaucracy, based on its expertise and scientific studies. How a law passed by Congress eventually is translated into concrete action—from the forms to be filled out to decisions about who gets the benefits—usually is determined within each agency or department. Even the evaluation of whether a policy has achieved its purpose usually is based on studies that are commissioned and interpreted by the agency administering the program.

The bureaucracy's policymaking role often has been depicted by what traditionally has been called the "iron triangle." Recently, the concept of an "issue network" has been viewed as a more accurate description of the policymaking process.

Iron Triangles.   In the past, scholars often described the bureaucracy's role in the policymaking process by using the concept of an **iron triangle**—a three-way alliance among legislators in Congress, bureaucrats, and interest groups. Consider as an example the development of agricultural policy. Congress, as one component of the triangle, includes two major committees concerned with agricultural policy: the House Committee on Agriculture and the Senate Committee on Agriculture, Nutrition, and Forestry. The Department of Agriculture, the second component of the triangle, has almost 100,000 employees, plus thousands of contractors and consultants. Agricultural interest groups, the third component of the iron triangle in agricultural policymaking, include many large and powerful associations, such as the American Farm Bureau Federation, the National Cattleman's Association, and the Corn Growers Association. These three components of the iron triangle work together, formally or informally, to create policy.

For example, the various agricultural interest groups lobby Congress to develop policies that benefit their groups' interests. Members of Congress cannot afford to ignore the wishes of interest groups because those groups are potential sources of voter support and campaign contributions. The legislators in Congress also work closely with the Department of Agriculture, which, in implementing a policy, can develop rules that benefit—or are not adverse to—certain industries or groups. The Department of Agriculture, in turn, supports policies that enhance the department's budget and powers. In this way, according to theory, agricultural policy is created that benefits all three components of the iron triangle. In 2002, the result was the Farm Security and Rural Investment Act, the largest agricultural subsidy act in U.S. history.

Issue Networks.   To be sure, the preceding discussion presents a much simplified picture of how the iron triangle works. With the growth in the complexity of government, policymaking also has become more complex. The bureaucracy is larger, Congress has more committees and subcommittees, and interest groups are more powerful than ever. Although iron triangles still exist, often they are inadequate as

Iron Triangle The three-way alliance among legislators, bureaucrats, and interest groups to make or preserve policies that benefit their respective interests.

descriptions of how policy is actually made. Frequently, different interest groups concerned about a certain area of policy have conflicting demands, which makes agency decision making difficult. Additionally, divided government in recent years has meant that departments are pressured by the president to take one approach and by Congress to take another.

Many scholars now use the term *issue network* to describe the policymaking process. An **issue network** is a group of individuals or organizations that support a particular policy position on the environment, taxation, consumer safety, or some other issue. Typically, an issue network includes legislators and/or their staff members, interest groups, bureaucrats, scholars and other experts, and representatives from the media. Members of a particular issue network work together to influence the president, members of Congress, administrative agencies, and the courts to affect public policy on a specific issue. Each policy issue may involve conflicting positions taken by two or more issue networks.

Issue Network A group of individuals or organizations— which may consist of legislators and legislative staff members, interest group leaders, bureaucrats, the media, scholars, and other experts— that supports a particular policy position on a given issue.

Congressional Control of the Bureaucracy

Many political pundits doubt whether Congress can meaningfully control the federal bureaucracy. These commentators forget that Congress specifies in an agency's "enabling legislation" the powers of the agency and the parameters within which it can operate. Additionally, Congress has the power of the purse and could, theoretically, refuse to authorize or appropriate funds for a particular agency. Whether Congress would actually take such a drastic measure would depend on the circumstances. It is clear, however, that Congress does have the legal authority to decide whether to fund or not to fund administrative agencies. Congress also can exercise oversight over agencies through investigations and hearings.

Congressional committees conduct investigations and hold hearings to oversee an agency's actions, reviewing them to ensure compliance with congressional intentions. The agency's officers and employees can be ordered to testify before a committee about the details of an action. Through these oversight activities, especially in the qustions and comments of members of the House or Senate during the hearings, Congress indicates its positions on specific programs and issues.

Congress can ask the General Accounting Office (GAO) to investigate particular agency actions as well. The Congressional Budget Office (CBO) also conducts oversight studies. The results of a GAO or CBO study may encourage Congress to hold further hearings or make changes in the law. Even if a law is not changed explicitly by Congress, however, the views expressed in any investigations and hearings are taken seriously by agency officials, who often act on those views.

In 1996, Congress passed the Congressional Review Act. The act created special procedures that can be used to express congressional disapproval of particular agency actions. These procedures have rarely been used, however. Since the act's passage, the executive branch has issued over 15,000 regulations. Yet only eight resolutions of disapproval have been introduced, and none of these was passed by either chamber.

MAKING A DIFFERENCE: What the Government Knows about You

The federal government collects billions of pieces of information on tens of millions of Americans each year. These data are stored in files and sometimes are exchanged among agencies. You are probably the subject of several federal records (for example, in the Social Security Administration; the Internal Revenue Service; and, if you are a male, the Selective Service).

THE FOIA

The 1966 Freedom of Information Act (FOIA) requires that the federal government release, at your request, any identifiable information it has about you or about any other subject. Ten categories of material are exempted, however (classified material, confidential material on trade secrets, internal personnel rules, personal medical files, and the like). To request material, write directly to the Freedom of Information Act officer

at the agency in question (say, the Department of Education). You must have a relatively specific idea about the document or information you want to obtain.

THE PRIVACY ACT

A second law, the Privacy Act of 1974, gives you access specifically to information the government may have collected about you. This law allows you to review records on file with federal agencies and to check those records for possible inaccuracies. Cases exist in which the records of two people with similar names have become confused. In some cases, innocent persons have had the criminal records of other persons erroneously inserted into their files.

If you want to look at any records or find out if an agency has a record on you, write to the agency head or Privacy Act officer, and address your letter to the specific agency. State that "under the

provisions of the Privacy Act of 1974, 5 U.S.C. 522a, I hereby request a copy of (or access to) _____." Then describe the record that you wish to investigate.

CONTACT THE ACLU

The American Civil Liberties Union (ACLU) has published a manual, called *Your Right to Government Information,* that guides you through the steps of obtaining information from the federal government. You can order it online at the following Web site:

http://www.aclu.org

In the search box at the bottom of the page, enter "Marwick" (the name of the author). Alternatively, you can order the manual from the ACLU at the following address:

ACLU Publications
P.O. Box 4713
Trenton, NJ 08650-4713
1-800-775-ACLU

KEY TERMS

acquisitive model **261**

bureaucracy **259**

cabinet department **262**

capture **266**

Civil Service Commission **268**

enabling legislation **272**

government corporation **266**

Government in the
    Sunshine Act **270**

independent executive
    agency **265**

independent regulatory
    agency **265**

iron triangle **275**

issue network **276**

line organization **262**

merit system **268**

monopolistic model **261**

Pendleton Act (Civil Service
    Reform Act) **268**

privatization **271**

spoils system **268**

sunset legislation **270**

Weberian model **260**

whistleblower **271**

CHAPTER SUMMARY

① Bureaucracies are hierarchical organizations characterized by division of labor and extensive procedural rules. Bureaucracy is the primary form of organization of most major corporations and universities as well as governments.

② Several theories have been offered to explain bureaucracies. The Weberian model posits that bureaucracies are rational, hierarchical organizations in which decisions are based on logical reasoning. The acquisitive model views top level bureaucrats as pressing for ever-larger budgets and staff to augment their own sense of power and security. The monopolistic model focuses on the environment in which most government bureaucracies operate, stating that bureaucracies are inefficient and excessively costly to operate because they have no competitors.

③ Since the founding of the United States, the federal bureaucracy has grown from 50 to about 2.7 million employees (excluding the military). Federal, state, and local employees together make up over 15 percent of the nation's civilian labor force. The federal bureaucracy consists of fifteen cabinet departments, as well as a large number of independent executive agencies, independent regulatory agencies, and government corporations. These entities enjoy varying degrees of autonomy, visibility, and political support.

④ A federal bureaucracy of career civil servants was formed during Thomas Jefferson's presidency. Andrew Jackson implemented a spoils system through which he appointed his own political supporters. A civil service based on professionalism and merit was the goal of the Civil Service Reform Act of 1883. Concerns that the civil service be freed from the pressures of politics prompted the passage of the Hatch Act in 1939. Significant changes in the administration of the civil service were made by the Civil Service Reform Act of 1978.

⑤ There have been many attempts to make the federal bureaucracy more open, efficient, and responsive to the needs of U.S. citizens. The most important reforms have included sunshine and sunset laws, privatization, strategies to provide incentives for increased productivity and efficiency, and protection for whistleblowers.

⑥ Congress delegates much of its authority to federal agencies when it creates new laws. The bureaucrats who run these agencies may become important policymakers, because Congress has neither the time nor the technical expertise to oversee the administration of its laws. In the agency rulemaking process, a proposed regulation is published. A comment period follows, during which interested parties may offer suggestions for changes. Because companies and other organizations have challenged many regulations in court, federal agencies now are authorized to allow parties that will be affected by new regulations to participate in the rule-drafting process.

7 Congress exerts ultimate control over all federal agencies, because it controls the federal government's purse strings. It also establishes the general guidelines by which regulatory agencies must abide. The appropriations process may also provide a way to send messages of approval or disapproval to particular agencies, as do congressional hearings and investigations of agency actions.

SELECTED PRINT AND MEDIA RESOURCES

Suggested Readings

Gronlund, Ake, ed. *Electronic Government: Design, Applications, and Management.* Hershey, Pa.: Idea Group Publishing, 2002. This collection of essays focuses on how electronic government might improve government services as well as increase citizen participation in democratic processes.

Heller, Joseph. *Catch 22.* New York: Simon & Schuster, 1961. Joseph Heller's classic novel is often considered an antiwar or antimilitary novel, but its satirical humor is also directed at the culture, corruption, and contradictions of bureaucratic institutions generally.

Hilts, Philip J. *Protecting America's Health: The FDA, Business, and One Hundred Years of Regulation.* New York: Knopf, 2003. This history of the Food and Drug Administration (FDA) explains the origin and nature of the drug-approval process and the importance of clinical trials. The book provides a thorough examination of an important regulatory agency. Hilts is sympathetic to the FDA and relatively critical of the pharmaceutical industry.

Light, Paul C. *Government's Greatest Achievements: From Civil Rights to Homeland Security.* Washington, D.C.: The Brookings Institution, 2002. The author stresses that for all of the criticisms made about the bureaucracy, the government does work—as witnessed by its many achievements over the past half-century.

Wilson, James Q. *Bureaucracy: What Government Agencies Do and Why They Do It.* New York: Basic Books, 2000. Wilson provides a thorough description of the federal bureaucracy, with examples. He argues that bureaucracy behaves in consistent—and therefore predictable—ways and that institutional culture is a major determinant of an agency's behavior.

Media Resources

The Bureaucracy of Government: John Lukacs—A 1988 Bill Moyers special. Historian John Lukacs discusses the common political lament over the giant but invisible mechanism called bureaucracy.

The Missiles of October—A movie retelling the events of October 1962, when the Kennedy administration decided to blockade Cuba to force the Soviet Union to remove its missiles from Cuba. The 1974 film, starring William Devane and Martin Sheen, gives an excellent inside view of policymaking involving the State Department, the Defense Department, and the president.

Yes, Minister—A new member of the British cabinet bumps up against the machinations of a top civil servant in a comedy of manners. This popular 1980 BBC comedy is now available on DVD.

LOGGING ON

Numerous links to federal agencies and information on the federal government can be found at the U.S. government's official Web site. Go to **http://www.firstgov.gov**.

The Federal Web Locator is an excellent site to access if you want to find information on the bureaucracy. Its URL is **http://www.infoctr.edu/fwl**.

You may want to examine two publications available from the federal government to learn more about the federal bureaucracy. The first is the *Federal Register*, which is the official publication for executive-branch documents. You can find it at: **http://www.gpoaccess.gov/fr/browse.html**.

The second is the *United States Government Manual*, which describes the origins, purposes, and administrators of every federal department and agency. It is available at: **http://www.gpoaccess.gov/gmanual/browse.html**.

"The Plum Book," which lists the bureaucratic positions that can be filled by presidential appointment, is online at **http://www.gpoaccess.gov/plumbook/index.html**.

To find telephone numbers for government agencies and personnel, you can go to **http://www.firstgov.gov/Agencies.shtml**.

USING THE INTERNET FOR POLITICAL ANALYSIS

Go to this text's Web site at **http://politicalscience.wadsworth.com/schmidtbrief2004**. Select "Chapter 11" in the box at the top of the window. Then, in the column on the left-hand side of the window, under "Chapter Resources," click on "Internet Exercises." The Web site will then display the following Internet exercises that you can perform to learn more about topics covered in this chapter.

Activity 11–1: The FirstGov Web Site
Activity 11–2: The U.S. Department of Agriculture
Activity 11–3: The National Labor Relations Board

ONLINE STUDY GUIDE AND ADDITIONAL RESOURCES

At **http://politicalscience.wadsworth.com/schmidtbrief2004** you will find a free Study Guide to this book that includes tutorial quizzes, essay questions, practice exams, chapter outlines, learning objectives, the glossary, flashcards, crossword puzzles, and Microsoft PowerPoint presentations. Also included in the American Government Resource Center for Chapter 11:

- **InfoTrac® Reader**—Homeland security; privatization.
- **You Are There Simulations**—The Department of Agriculture; the Cabinet.
- **Participation Activities**—Take a closer look at a specific bureaucratic agency; find a newsgroup discussion about a bureaucratic issue that interests you.

- **MicroCase Exercise**—Bureaucracy.
- **Related Links**—Bureaucracy.
- **Video Case Study**—Bureaucratic rulemaking.
- **Source Readings**—Selected statutes.

The site also contains the Citizen's Survival Guide, information on how to get involved in politics locally and globally, as well as regularly updated features including a Current Events Quiz, In the News, Election Links, updates on the war on terrorism, and more.

CHAPTER 12

The Judiciary

T HE JUSTICES OF THE SUPREME COURT are not elected but rather are appointed by the president and confirmed by the Senate. The same is true for all other federal court judges. This fact does not mean that the federal judiciary is apolitical, however. Indeed, our courts play a larger role in making public policy than courts in any other country in the world today.

As Alexis de Tocqueville, a nineteenth-century French commentator on American society, noted, "scarcely any political question arises in the United States that is not resolved, sooner or later, into a judicial question."[1] Our judiciary forms part of our political process. The instant that judges interpret the law, they become actors in the political arena—policymakers working within a political institution. The most important political force within our judiciary is the United States Supreme Court.

How do courts make policy? Why do the federal courts play such an important role in American government? The answers to these questions lie, in part, in our colonial heritage. Most of American law is based on the English system, particularly the English common law tradition. In that tradition, the decisions made by judges constitute an important source of law.

We open this chapter with a look at this tradition and at the various sources of American law. We then examine the federal court system—its organization, how its judges are selected, how these judges affect policy, and how they are restrained by our system of checks and balances.

The Common Law Tradition

In 1066, the Normans conquered England, and William the Conqueror and his successors began the process of unifying the country under their rule. One of the ways they did this was to establish the king's courts. Before the conquest, disputes had been settled according to local custom. The king's courts sought to establish a common or uniform set of rules for the whole country. As the number of courts and cases increased, portions of the most important decisions of each year were gathered together and recorded in *Year Books*. Judges settling disputes similar to ones that had been decided before used the *Year Books* as the basis for their decisions. If a case was unique, judges had to create new laws, but they based their decisions on the general principles suggested by earlier cases. The body of judge-made law that developed under this system is still used today and is known as the **common law.**

The practice of deciding new cases with reference to former decisions—that is, according to **precedent**—became a cornerstone of the English and American judicial systems and is embodied in the doctrine of ***stare decisis*** (pronounced *ster*-ay dih-*si*-ses), a Latin phrase that means "to stand on decided cases." The doctrine of *stare decisis* obligates judges to follow the precedents set previously by their own courts or by higher courts that have authority over them.

For example, a lower state court in California would be obligated to follow a precedent set by the California Supreme Court. That lower court, however, would not be obligated to follow a precedent set by the supreme court of another state, because each state court system is independent. Of course, when the United States Supreme Court decides an issue, all of the nation's other courts are obligated to abide by the Court's decision—because the Supreme Court is the highest court in the land.

The doctrine of *stare decisis* provides a basis for judicial decision making in all countries that have common law systems. Today, the United States, Britain, and several dozen other countries have common law systems. Generally, those countries that were once colonies of Great Britain, including countries such as Australia, Canada, India, and New Zealand, have retained their English common law heritage.

Common Law Judge-made law that originated in England from decisions shaped according to prevailing custom. Decisions were applied to similar situations and gradually became common to the nation.

Precedent A court rule bearing on subsequent legal decisions in similar cases. Judges rely on precedents in deciding cases.

Stare Decisis To stand on decided cases; the judicial policy of following precedents established by past decisions.

Sources of American Law

The body of American law includes the federal and state constitutions, statutes passed by legislative bodies, administrative law, and case law—the legal principles expressed in court decisions.

Constitutions

The constitutions of the federal government and the states set forth the general organization, powers, and limits of government. The U.S. Constitution is the supreme law of the land. A law in violation of the Constitution, no matter what its source, may be declared unconstitutional and thereafter cannot be enforced. Similarly, the state constitutions are supreme within their respective borders (unless they conflict with the U.S. Constitution or federal laws and treaties made in accordance with it). The Constitution thus defines the political playing field on which state and federal powers are reconciled.

Statutes and Administrative Regulations

Although the English common law provides the basis for both our civil and criminal legal systems, statutes (laws enacted by legislatures) increasingly have become important in defining the rights and obligations of individuals. Federal statutes may relate to any subject that is a concern of the federal government and may cover areas ranging from hazardous waste to federal taxation. State statutes include criminal codes, commercial laws, and laws covering a variety of other matters. Cities, counties, and other local political bodies also pass statutes, which are called ordinances. These ordinances may deal with such issues as zoning proposals and public safety. Rules and regulations issued by administrative agencies are another source of law. Today, much of the work of the courts consists of interpreting these laws and regulations and applying them to circumstances in cases before the courts.

Case Law

Because we have a common law tradition, in which the doctrine of *stare decisis* plays an important role, the decisions rendered by the courts also form an important body of law, collectively referred to as **case law.** Case law includes judicial interpretations of common law principles and doctrines as well as interpretations of the types of law just mentioned—constitutional provisions, statutes, and administrative agency regulations. It is up to the courts, and particularly the Supreme Court, to decide what a constitutional provision or a statutory phrase means. In doing so, the courts, in effect, establish law. (We will discuss this policymaking function of the courts in more detail later in the chapter.)

Case Law Judicial interpretations of common law principles and doctrines, as well as interpretations of constitutional law, statutory law, and administrative law.

The Federal Court System

The United States has a dual court system. There are state courts and federal courts. Each of the fifty states, as well as the District of Columbia, has its own independent system of courts. Here we focus on the federal courts. (For a discussion of additional federal courts, see this chapter's *America's Security* feature on the next page.)

Jurisdiction The authority of a court to decide certain cases.

Basic Judicial Requirements

The federal court system derives its power from Article III, Section 1, of the U.S. Constitution. That section limits the **jurisdiction** (the authority to hear and decide cases) of the federal courts to cases that involve either a federal question or diversity of citizenship. A **federal question** arises when a case is based, at least in part, on the U.S. Constitution, a treaty, or a federal law. A person who claims that her or his rights under the Constitution, such as the right to free speech, have been violated could bring a case in a federal court. **Diversity of citizenship** exists when the parties to a lawsuit are from different states or (more rarely) when the suit involves a U.S. citizen and a government or citizen of a foreign country. The amount in controversy must be at least $75,000 before a federal court can take jurisdiction in a diversity case, however.

Federal Question A question that pertains to the U.S. Constitution, acts of Congress, or treaties. A federal question provides a basis for federal jurisdiction.

Diversity of Citizenship The condition that exists when the parties to a lawsuit are citizens of different states or citizens of a U.S. state and citizens or a government of a foreign country. Diversity of citizenship provides a basis for federal jurisdiction.

Types of Federal Courts

As you can see in Figure 12–1 on page 285, the federal court system is basically a three-tiered model consisting of (1) U.S. district courts and various specialized courts

AMERICA'S SECURITY

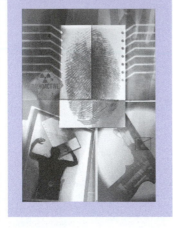

Does National Security Require Secret Courts?

Since the terrorist attacks on September 11, 2001, many Americans are rethinking their safety and what they need to do to protect it. The federal government, however, has been concerned with protecting the nation against terrorism for some time. Among other things, the government's efforts to curb terrorism have involved the establishment of "secret courts."

THE FISA COURT

The federal government created the first secret court in 1978. In that year, Congress passed the Foreign Intelligence Surveillance Act (FISA), which established a court to hear requests for warrants for the surveillance of suspected spies. Officials can request warrants without having to reveal to the suspect or to the public the information used to justify the warrant. The FISA court has approved almost all of the thousands of requests for warrants that officials have submitted. There is no public access to the court's proceedings or records.

In the aftermath of the terrorist attacks on September 11, 2001, the Bush administration expanded the powers of the FISA court. Previously, the FISA allowed secret domestic surveillance only if "the purpose" was foreign intelligence. Recent amendments to the FISA changed this wording to "a significant purpose"—meaning that warrants may now be requested to obtain evidence that can be used in criminal trials. Additionally, the court has the authority to approve physical as well as electronic searches, which means that officials may search a suspect's property without obtaining a warrant in open court and without notifying the subject.

ALIEN "REMOVAL COURTS"

The FISA court is not the only court in which suspects' rights have been reduced. In response to the Oklahoma City bombing in 1995, Congress passed the Anti-Terrorism and Effective Death Penalty Act of 1996. The act included a provision creating an alien "removal court" to hear evidence against suspected "alien terrorists." The judges rule on whether there is probable cause for deportation. If so, a public deportation proceeding is held in a U.S. district court. The prosecution does not need to follow procedures that normally apply in criminal cases. In addition, the defendant cannot see the evidence that the prosecution used to secure the hearing.

FOR CRITICAL ANALYSIS

Do you think that exceptions should be made to constitutional rights if it means greater national security?

Trial Court The court in which most cases begin.

General Jurisdiction Exists when a court's authority to hear cases is not significantly restricted.

of limited jurisdiction (not all of the latter are shown in the figure), (2) intermediate U.S. courts of appeals, and (3) the United States Supreme Court.

U.S. District Courts.   The U.S. district courts are trial courts. **Trial courts** are what their name implies—courts in which trials are held and testimony is taken. The U.S. district courts are courts of **general jurisdiction,** meaning that they can hear cases involving a broad array of issues. Federal cases involving most matters typically are heard in district courts. (The other courts on the lower tier of the model shown

FIGURE 12–1 The Federal Court System

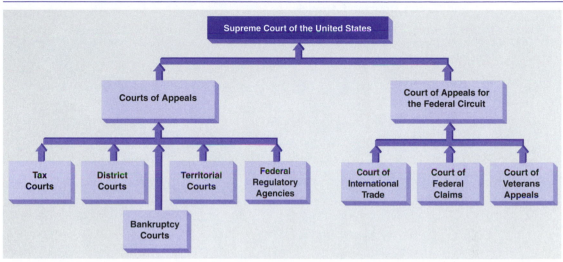

in Figure 12–1 are courts of **limited jurisdiction,** meaning that they can try cases involving only certain types of claims, such as tax claims or bankruptcy petitions.)

There is at least one federal district court in every state. The number of judicial districts can vary over time, owing to population changes and corresponding case loads. Currently, there are ninety-four federal judicial districts. A party who is dissatisfied with the decision of a district court can appeal the case to the appropriate U.S. court of appeals, or federal **appellate court.** Figure 12–2 on page 286 shows the jurisdictional boundaries of the district courts (which are state boundaries, unless otherwise indicated by dotted lines within a state) and of the U.S. courts of appeals.

U.S. Courts of Appeals.

There are thirteen U.S. courts of appeals—also referred to as U.S. circuit courts of appeals. Twelve of these courts, including the U.S. Court of Appeals for the District of Columbia, hear appeals from the federal district courts located within their respective judicial circuits (geographic areas over which they exercise jurisdiction). The Court of Appeals for the Thirteenth Circuit, called the Federal Circuit, has national appellate jurisdiction over certain types of cases, such as cases involving patent law and those in which the U.S. government is a defendant.

Note that when an appellate court reviews a case decided in a district court, the appellate court does not conduct another trial. Rather, a panel of three or more judges reviews the record of the case on appeal, which includes a transcript of the trial proceedings, and determines whether the trial court committed an error. Usually, appellate courts do not look at questions of *fact* (such as whether a party did, in fact, commit a certain action, such as burning a flag) but at questions of *law* (such as whether the act of flag-burning is a form of speech protected by the First Amendment to the Constitution). An appellate court will challenge a trial court's finding of fact only when the finding is clearly contrary to the evidence presented at trial or when there is no evidence to support the finding.

Limited Jurisdiction Exists when a court's authority to hear cases is restricted to certain types of claims, such as tax claims or bankruptcy petitions.

Appellate Court A court having jurisdiction to review cases and issues that were originally tried in lower courts.

FIGURE 12–2 Geographic Boundaries of Federal District Courts and Circuit Courts of Appeals

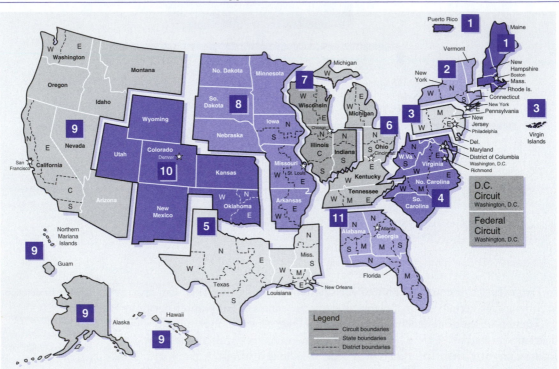

SOURCE: Administrative Office of the United States Courts.

A party can petition the United States Supreme Court to review an appellate court's decision. The likelihood that the Supreme Court will grant the petition is slim, however, because the Court reviews only a very few of the cases decided by the appellate courts. This means that decisions made by appellate judges usually are final.

The United States Supreme Court. The highest level of the three-tiered model of the federal court system is the United States Supreme Court. Although the Supreme Court can exercise original jurisdiction (that is, act as a trial court) in certain cases, such as those affecting foreign diplomats and those in which a state is a party, most of its work is as an appellate court. The Court hears appeals not only from the federal appellate courts but also from the highest state courts. Note, though, that the United States Supreme Court can review a state supreme court decision only if a federal question is involved. Because of its importance in the federal court system, we will look more closely at the Supreme Court in the next section.

Parties to Lawsuits

In most lawsuits, the parties are the plaintiff (the person or organization that initiates the lawsuit) and the defendant (the person or organization against whom the lawsuit is brought). There may be several plaintiffs and defendants in a single lawsuit. In the last several decades, many lawsuits have been brought by interest groups. Interest groups play an important role in our judicial system, because they **litigate**— bring to trial—or assist in litigating most cases of racial or gender-based discrimination, virtually all civil liberties cases, and more than one-third of the cases involving business matters. Interest groups also file **amicus curiae** (pronounced ah-*mee*-kous *kur*-ee-eye) **briefs,** or "friend of the court" briefs, in more than 50 percent of these kinds of cases.

Sometimes, interest groups or other plaintiffs will bring a **class-action suit,** in which whatever the court decides will affect all members of a class similarly situated (such as users of a particular product manufactured by the defendant in the lawsuit). The strategy of class-action lawsuits was pioneered by such groups as the National Association for the Advancement of Colored People (NAACP), the Legal Defense Fund, and the Sierra Club, whose members believed that the courts would offer a more sympathetic forum for their views than would Congress.

Procedural Rules

Both the federal and the state courts have established procedural rules that shape the litigation process. These rules are designed to protect the rights and interests of the parties, to ensure that the litigation proceeds in a fair and orderly manner, and to identify the issues that must be decided by the court—thus saving court time and costs. Court decisions may also apply to trial procedures. For example, the Supreme Court has held that the parties' attorneys cannot discriminate against prospective jurors on the basis of race or gender. Some lower courts have also held that people cannot be excluded from juries because of their sexual orientation or religion.

The parties must comply with procedural rules and with any orders given by the judge during the course of the litigation. When a party does not follow a court's order, the court can cite him or her for contempt. A party who commits *civil* contempt (failing to comply with a court's order for the benefit of another party to the proceeding) can be taken into custody, fined, or both, until the party complies with the court's order. A party who commits *criminal* contempt (obstructing the administration of justice or bringing the court into disrepect) also can be taken into custody and fined but cannot avoid punishment by complying with a previous order.

The Supreme Court at Work

The Supreme Court, by law, begins its regular annual term on the first Monday in October and usually adjourns in late June or early July of the next year. Special sessions may be held after the regular term is over, but only a few cases are decided in this way. More commonly, cases are carried over until the next regular session.

Of the total number of cases that are decided each year, those reviewed by the Supreme Court represent less than one-half of 1 percent. Included in these, however, are decisions that profoundly affect our lives. In recent years, the United States Supreme Court has decided issues involving capital punishment, affirmative action programs, religious freedom, assisted suicide, abortion, busing, term limits for congresspersons,

Litigate To engage in a legal proceeding or seek relief in a court of law; to carry on a lawsuit.

Amicus Curiae Brief A brief (a document containing a legal argument supporting a desired outcome in a particular case) filed by a third party, or *amicus curiae* (Latin for "friend of the court"), who is not directly involved in the litigation.

Class-Action Suit A lawsuit filed by an individual seeking damages for "all persons similarly situated."

"Do you ever have one of those days when everything seems un-Constitutional?"

sexual harassment, pornography, states' rights, limits on federal jurisdiction, and many other matters with significant consequences for the nation. Because the Supreme Court exercises a great deal of discretion over the types of cases it hears, it can influence the nation's policies by issuing decisions in some types of cases and refusing to hear appeals in others, thereby allowing lower court decisions to stand.

Which Cases Reach the Supreme Court?

Many people are surprised to learn that in a typical case, there is no absolute right of appeal to the United States Supreme Court. The Court's appellate jurisdiction is almost entirely discretionary—the Court can choose which cases it will decide. The justices never explain their reasons for hearing certain cases and not others, so it is difficult to predict which case or type of case the Court might select.

Factors That Bear on the Decision.   Factors that bear on the decision include whether a legal question has been decided differently by various lower courts and needs resolution by the highest court, whether a lower court's decision conflicts with an existing Supreme Court ruling, and whether the issue could have significance beyond the parties to the dispute. Another factor is whether the solicitor general is pressuring the Court to take a case. The solicitor general, a high-ranking presidential appointee within the Justice Department, represents the national government before the Supreme Court and promotes presidential policies in the federal courts.

INFOTRAC

For more information about the Supreme Court, use the term "United States Supreme Court" in the Subject guide.

He or she decides what cases the government should ask the Supreme Court to review and what position the government should take in cases before the Court.

Granting Petitions for Review.   If the Court decides to grant a petition for review, it will issue a **writ of *certiorari*** (pronounced sur-shee-uh-*rah*-ree). The writ orders a lower court to send the Supreme Court a record of the case for review. More than 90 percent of the petitions for review are denied. A denial is not a decision on the merits of a case, nor does it indicate agreement with the lower court's opinion. (The judgment of the lower court remains in force, however.) Therefore, denial of the writ has no value as a precedent. The Court will not issue a writ unless at least four of the nine justices approve of it. This is called the **rule of four.**[2]

Deciding Cases

Once the Supreme Cour grants *certiorari* in a particular case, the justices do extensive research on the legal issues and facts involved in the case. (Of course, some preliminary research was necessary before deciding to grant the petition for review.) Each justice is entitled to four law clerks, who undertake much of the research and preliminary drafting necessary for the justice to form an opinion.[3]

The Court normally does not hear any evidence, as is true with all appeals courts. The Court's consideration of a case is based on the abstracts, the record, and the briefs. The attorneys are permitted to present **oral arguments.** All statements and the justices' questions are tape-recorded during these sessions. Unlike the practice in most courts, lawyers addressing the Supreme Court can be (and often are) questioned by the justices at any time during oral argument.

The justices meet to discuss and vote on cases in conferences held throughout the term. In these conferences, in addition to deciding cases currently before the Court, the justices decide which new petitions for *certiorari* to grant. These conferences take place in the oak-paneled chamber and are strictly private—no stenographers, tape recorders, or video cameras are allowed.

Decisions and Opinions

When the Court has reached a decision, its opinion is written. The **opinion** contains the Court's ruling on the issue or issues presented, the reasons for its decision, the rules of law that apply, and other information. In many cases, the decision of the lower court is **affirmed,** resulting in the enforcement of that court's judgment or decree. If the Supreme Court feels that a reversible error was committed during the trial or that the jury was instructed improperly, however, the decision will be **reversed.** Sometimes the case will be **remanded** (sent back to the court that originally heard the case) for a new trial or other proceeding. For example, a lower court might have held that a party was not entitled to bring a lawsuit under a particular law. If the Supreme Court holds to the contrary, it will remand (send back) the case to the trial court with instructions that the trial go forward.

The Court's written opinion sometimes is unsigned; this is called an opinion *per curiam* ("by the court"). Typically, the Court's opinion is signed by all the justices who agree with it. When in the majority, the chief justice assigns the opinion and

Writ of *Certiorari* An order issued by a higher court to a lower court to send up the record of a case for review.

Rule of Four A United States Supreme Court procedure by which four justices must vote to grant a petition for review for the case to come before the full Court.

Oral Arguments The verbal arguments presented in person by attorneys to an appellate court.

Opinion The statement by a judge or a court of the decision reached in a case. The opinion sets forth the applicable law and details the reasoning on which the ruling was based.

Affirm To declare that a court ruling is valid and must stand.

Reverse To annul or make void a court ruling on account of some error or irregularity.

Remand To send a case back to the court that originally heard it.

often writes it personally. When the chief justice is in the minority, the senior justice on the majority side decides who writes the opinion.

When all justices unanimously agree on an opinion, the opinion is written for the entire Court (all the justices) and can be deemed a **unanimous opinion.** When there is not a unanimous opinion, a **majority opinion** is written, outlining the views of the majority of the justices involved in the case. Often, one or more justices who feel strongly about making or emphasizing a particular point that is not made or emphasized in the unanimous or majority written opinion will write a **concurring opinion.** That means the justice writing the concurring opinion agrees (concurs) with the conclusion given in the majority written opinion, but for different reasons. Finally, in other than unanimous opinions, one or more dissenting opinions are usually written by those justices who do not agree with the majority. The **dissenting opinion** is important because it often forms the basis of the arguments used years later if the Court reverses the previous decision and establishes a new precedent.

Shortly after the opinion is written, the Supreme Court announces its decision from the bench. At that time, the opinion is made available to the public at the office of the clerk of the Court. The clerk also releases the opinion for online publication. Ultimately, the opinion is published in the *United States Reports*, which is the official printed record of the Court's decisions.

The Selection of Federal Judges

All federal judges are appointed. The Constitution, in Article II, Section 2, states that the president appoints the justices of the Supreme Court with the advice and consent of the Senate. Congress has provided the same procedure for staffing other federal courts. This means that the Senate and the president jointly decide who shall fill every vacant judicial position, no matter what the level.

There are over 850 federal judgeships in the United States. Once appointed to such a judgeship, a person holds that job for life. Judges serve until they resign, retire voluntarily, or die. Federal judges who engage in blatantly illegal conduct may be removed through impeachment, although such action is rare.

Judicial Appointments

Judicial candidates for federal judgeships are suggested to the president by the Department of Justice, senators, other judges, the candidates themselves, and lawyers' associations and other interest groups. In selecting a candidate to nominate for a judgeship, the president considers not only the person's competence but also other factors, including the person's political philosophy (as will be discussed shortly), ethnicity, and gender.

The nomination process—no matter how the nominees are obtained—always works the same way. The president makes the actual nomination, transmitting the name to the Senate. The Senate then either confirms or rejects the nomination. To reach a conclusion, the Senate Judiciary Committee (operating through subcommittees) invites testimony, both written and oral, at its various hearings. A practice used in the Senate, called **senatorial courtesy,** is a constraint on the president's freedom

---

Unanimous Opinion A court opinion or determination on which all judges agree.

Majority Opinion A court opinion reflecting the views of the majority of the judges.

Concurring Opinion A separate opinion prepared by a judge who supports the decision of the majority of the court but who wants to make a particular point.

Dissenting Opinion A separate opinion in which a judge dissents from (disagrees with) the conclusion reached by the majority on the court.

Senatorial Courtesy In federal district court judgeship nominations, a tradition allowing a senator of the president's political party to veto a judicial appointment in his or her state.

to appoint federal district judges. Senatorial courtesy allows a senator of the president's political party to veto a judicial appointment in her or his state.

Federal District Court Judgeship Nominations.
Although the president nominates federal judges, the nomination of federal district court judges typically originates with a senator or senators of the president's party from the state in which there is a vacancy. If the nominee is deemed unqualified, as a matter of political courtesy the president will discuss with the senator or senators who originated the nomination whether the nomination should be withdrawn. Also, when a nomination is unacceptable politically to the president, the president will consult with the appropriate senator or senators, indicate that the nomination is unacceptable, and work with the senator or senators to seek an alternative candidate.

Federal Courts of Appeals Appointments.
There are many fewer federal courts of appeals appointments than federal district court appointments, but they are more important. This is because federal appellate judges handle more important matters, at least from the point of view of the president, and therefore presidents take a keener interest in the nomination process for such judgeships. Also, the U.S. courts of appeals have become "steppingstones" to the Supreme Court. Typically, the president culls the Circuit Judge Nominating Commission's list of nominees for potential candidates. The president may also use this list to oppose senators' recommendations that may be unacceptable politically to the president.

"Before we begin today, may I say that both my client and I were astonished that Your Honor was not nominated for the Supreme Court?"

TABLE 12–1	Background of Supreme Court Justices to 2004
	NUMBER OF JUSTICES (108 = TOTAL)
Occupational Position before Appointment	
Private legal practice	25
State judgeship	21
Federal judgeship	28
U.S. attorney general	7
Deputy or assistant U.S. attorney general	2
U.S. solicitor general	2
U.S. senator	6
U.S. representative	2
State governor	3
Federal executive post	9
Other	3
Religious Background	
Protestant	83
Roman Catholic	11
Jewish	6
Unitarian	7
No religious affiliation	1
Age on Appointment	
Under 40	5
41–50	31
51–60	58
61–70	14
Political Party Affiliation	
Federalist (to 1835)	13
Jeffersonian Republican (to 1828)	7
Whig (to 1861)	1
Democrat	44
Republican	42
Independent	1
Educational Background	
College graduate	92
Not a college graduate	16
Gender	
Male	106
Female	2
Race	
White	106
African American	2

SOURCES: Congressional Quarterly, *Congressional Quarterly's Guide to the U.S. Supreme Court* (Washington, D.C.: Congressional Quarterly Press, 1996); and authors' update.

Supreme Court Appointments.   As we have described, the president nominates Supreme Court justices.[4] As you can see in Table 12–1, which summarizes the background of all Supreme Court justices to 2004, the most common occupational background of the justices at the time of their appointment has been private legal practice or state or federal judgeship.

Partisanship and Judicial Appointments

Ideology plays an important role in the president's choices for judicial appointments. In most cases, the president appoints judges or justices who belong to the president's political party. Presidents see their federal judiciary appointments as the one sure way to institutionalize their political views long after they have left office. By 1993, for example, Presidents Ronald Reagan and George H. W. Bush together had appointed nearly three-quarters of all federal court judges. This preponderance of Republican-appointed federal judges strengthened the legal moorings of the conservative social agenda on a variety of issues, ranging from abortion to civil rights. Nevertheless, President Bill Clinton had the opportunity to appoint about two hundred federal judges, thereby shifting the ideological make-up of the federal judiciary.

By the time you read this book, one or more of the Supreme Court justices may have retired. Should this happen, President George W. Bush will be in a position to exercise considerable influence over the future ideological make-up of the Supreme Court. As many presidents have learned, however, there is no guarantee that once a justice is appointed to the bench, that justice's decisions will please the president.

The Senate's Role

Ideology also plays a large role in the Senate's confirmation hearings, and presidential nominees to the Supreme Court have not always been confirmed. In fact, almost 20 percent of presidential nominations to the Supreme Court have been either rejected or not acted on by the Senate. There have been many acrimonious battles over Supreme Court appointments when the Senate and the president have not seen eye to eye about political matters. From 1968 through 1987, four presidential nominees to the highest court were rejected. One of the most controversial Supreme Court nominations was that of Clarence Thomas, who underwent an extremely volatile confirmation hearing in 1991, replete with charges of sexual harassment against him. He was ultimately confirmed by the Senate, however.

President Bill Clinton had little trouble gaining approval for both of his nominees to the Supreme Court: Ruth Bader Ginsburg and Stephen Breyer. Clinton found it more difficult, however, to secure Senate approval for his judicial nominations to the lower courts. In fact, during the late 1990s and early 2000s the duel between the Senate and the president aroused considerable concern about the consequences of the increasingly partisan and ideological tension over federal judicial appointments. As a result of Senate delays in confirming nominations, the number of judicial vacancies mounted, as did the backlog of cases pending in the federal courts.

INFOTRAC

For updates and more information on this subject, use the term "Senate Committee on the Judiciary" in the Subject guide.

Policymaking and the Courts

The partisan battles over judicial appointments reflect an important reality in today's American government: the importance of the judiciary in national politics. Because appointments to the federal benches are for life, the ideology of judicial appointees can affect national policy for years to come. Although the primary function of judges in our system of government is to interpret and apply the laws, inevitably judges make policy when carrying out this task. One of the major policymaking tools of the federal courts is their power of judicial review.

Judicial Review

The power of the courts to determine whether a law or action by the other branches of government is constitutional is known as the power of *judicial review*. This power enables the judicial branch to act as a check on the other two branches of government, in line with the checks and balances system established by the U.S. Constitution.

The power of judicial review is not mentioned in the Constitution, however. Rather, it was established by the United States Supreme Court's decision in *Marbury v. Madison*.[5] In that case, in which the Court declared that a law passed by Congress violated the Constitution, the Court claimed such a power for the judiciary:

> It is emphatically the province and duty of the Judicial Department to say what the law is. Those who apply the rule to a particular case, must of necessity expound and interpret that rule. If two laws conflict with each other, the courts must decide on the operation of each.

If a federal court declares that a federal or state law or policy is unconstitutional, the court's decision affects the application of the law or policy only within that court's jurisdiction. For this reason, the higher the level of the court, the greater the impact of the decision on society. Because of the Supreme Court's national jurisdiction, its decisions have the greatest impact. For example, when the Supreme Court held that an Arkansas state constitutional amendment limiting the terms of congresspersons was unconstitutional, laws establishing term limits in twenty-three other states also were invalidated.[6]

Judicial Activism and Judicial Restraint

Judicial scholars like to characterize different judges and justices as being either "activist" or "restraintist." The doctrine of **judicial activism** rests on the conviction that the federal judiciary should take an active role by using its powers to check the activities of Congress, state legislatures, and administrative agencies when those government bodies exceed their authority. One of the Supreme Court's most activist eras was the period from 1953 to 1969, when the Court was headed by Chief Justice Earl Warren. The Warren Court propelled the civil rights movement forward by holding, among other things, that laws permitting racial segregation violated the equal protection clause.

In contrast, the doctrine of **judicial restraint** rests on the assumption that the courts should defer to the decisions made by the legislative and executive branches, because members of Congress and the president are elected by the people whereas members of the federal judiciary are not. Because administrative agency personnel normally have more expertise than the courts do in the areas regulated by the agencies, the courts likewise should defer to agency rules and decisions. In other words, under the doctrine of judicial restraint, the courts should not thwart the implementation of legislative acts and agency rules unless they are clearly unconstitutional.

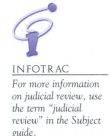
INFOTRAC
For more information on judicial review, use the term "judicial review" in the Subject guide.

Judicial Activism A doctrine holding that the Supreme Court should take an active role by using its powers to check the activities of governmental bodies when those bodies exceed their authority.

Judicial Restraint A doctrine holding that the Supreme Court should defer to the decisions made by the elected representatives of the people in the legislative and executive branches.

Judicial activism sometimes is linked with liberalism, and judicial restraint with conservatism. In fact, though, a conservative judge can be activist, just as a liberal judge can be restraintist. In the 1950s and 1960s, the Supreme Court was activist and liberal. Some observers believe that the Rehnquist Court, with its conservative majority, has become increasingly activist since the 1990s. Some go even further and claim that the federal courts, including the Supreme Court, wield too much power in our democracy.

Ideology and the Rehnquist Court

William H. Rehnquist became the sixteenth chief justice of the Supreme Court in 1986, after fifteen years as an associate justice. He was known as a strong anchor of the Court's conservative wing. With Rehnquist's appointment as chief justice, it seemed to observers that the Court necessarily would become more conservative.

INFOTRAC

For more information on the chief justice, use the term "William Rehnquist" in the Subject guide.

This, in fact, has happened. The Court began to take a rightward shift shortly after Rehnquist became chief justice, and the Court's rightward movement continued as other conservative appointments to the bench were made during the Reagan and George H. W. Bush administrations. Today, three of the justices (William Rehnquist, Antonin Scalia, and Clarence Thomas) are notably conservative in their views. Four of the justices (John Paul Stevens, David Souter, Ruth Bader Ginsburg, and Stephen Breyer) hold liberal-to-moderate views. The middle of the Court is now occupied by two moderate-to-conservative justices, Sandra Day O'Connor and Anthony Kennedy. O'Connor and Kennedy usually provide the "swing votes" on the Court in controversial cases. The ideological alignments on the Court vary, however, depending on the issues involved in particular cases.

Certainly, today's Supreme Court has moved far from the liberal positions taken by the Court under Earl Warren (1953–1969) and under Warren Burger (1969–1986). Since the mid-1990s, the Court has issued a large number of conservative rulings.

Federalism.   Several of these rulings reflect a conservative approach to constitutional law that emphasizes states' rights. For example, in 1995 the Court curbed—for the first time in sixty years—the national government's constitutional power under the commerce clause to regulate intrastate activities. The Court held that a federal law regulating the possession of guns in school zones had nothing to do with interstate commerce and therefore Congress had overreached its powers by attempting to regulate this activity.[7] In 2000, the Court held that Congress had overreached its authority under the commerce clause when it included a federal remedy for gender-motivated violence, such as rape or stalking, in the federal Violence against Women Act of 1994. The Court concluded that the effect of such violence on interstate commerce was not sufficient to justify national regulation of noneconomic, violent criminal conduct.[8] The Court has also bolstered states' rights in its decisions holding that states have sovereign immunity, under the Eleventh Amendment, from lawsuits brought by state employees under federal laws prohibiting certain types of discrimination. Some observers fear that the Court's recent decisions on states' rights are threatening the federal structure of the nation.[9]

The Rehnquist Court

LIBERAL/MODERATE

John Paul Stevens   David Souter   Ruth Bader Ginsburg   Stephen Breyer

SWING VOTES   CONSERVATIVE

Sandra Day O'Connor   Anthony Kennedy   William Rehnquist   Antonin Scalia   Clarence Thomas

In view of the Court's support for states' rights, many scholars were surprised when the Court involved itself in the dispute over the manual recounting of the Florida votes after the 2000 elections. Nonetheless, in a historic decision, the Court reversed the Florida Supreme Court's order to manually recount the votes in selected Florida counties—a decision that effectively handed the presidency to George W. Bush.[10]

Civil Rights.   In civil rights cases, the Rehnquist Court's generally conservative ("strict") interpretation of the Constitution has had mixed results. In one decision, the Court refused to extend the constitutional right to privacy to include the right of terminally ill persons to end their lives through physician-assisted suicide. Therefore, a state law banning this practice did not violate the Constitution.[11] (Essentially, the Court left it up to the states to decide whether to ban—or to permit—assisted suicide; to date, only one state, Oregon, has passed a law permitting the practice.) In another decision, the Court held that a federal statute expanding religious liberties was an unconstitutional attempt by Congress to rewrite the Constitution.[12]

A series of cases decided by the Court in 2003 had a major impact on civil rights issues. In two cases involving the University of Michigan, the Court held that limited affirmative action plans in pursuit of diversity were constitutional.[13] In a Texas case, the Court ruled that laws against homosexual conduct violate the due process clause of the Fourteenth Amendment.[14]

What Checks Our Courts?

Our judicial system is probably the most independent in the world. But the courts do not have absolute independence, for they are part of the political process. Political checks limit the extent to which courts can exercise judicial review and engage in an activist policy. These checks are exercised by the executive branch, the legislature, the public, and, finally, the judiciary itself.

Executive Checks

President Andrew Jackson was once supposed to have said, after Chief Justice John Marshall made an unpopular decision, "John Marshall has made his decision; now let him enforce it."[15] This purported remark goes to the heart of **judicial implementation**—the enforcement of judicial decisions in such a way that those decisions are translated into policy. The Supreme Court simply does not have any enforcement powers, and whether a decision will be implemented depends on the cooperation of the other two branches of government. Rarely, though, will a president refuse to enforce a Supreme Court decision, as President Jackson did. More commonly, presidents exercise influence over the judiciary by appointing new judges and justices as federal judicial seats become vacant.

Judicial Implementation The way in which court decisions are translated into action.

AP Photo/Steve Helber

In December 2000, with the outcome of the presidential election still in doubt, the United States Supreme Court agreed to hear an appeal from George W. Bush to stop the manual recount of ballots in Florida. Many people considered the Court's involvement in the disputed election unwarranted.

Executives at the state level also may refuse to implement court decisions with which they disagree. A notable example of such a refusal occurred in Arkansas after the Supreme Court ordered schools to desegregate "with all deliberate speed" in 1955.[16] Arkansas governor Orval Faubus refused to cooperate with the decision and used the state's National Guard to block the integration of Central High School in Little Rock. Ultimately, President Dwight Eisenhower had to federalize the Arkansas National Guard and send federal troops to Little Rock to quell the violence that had erupted.

Legislative Checks

Courts may make rulings, but often the legislatures at local, state, and federal levels are required to appropriate funds to carry out the courts' rulings. A court, for example, may decide that prison conditions must be improved, but it is up to the legislature to authorize the funds necessary to carry out the ruling. When such funds are not appropriated, the court that made the ruling, in effect, has been checked.

Courts' rulings can be overturned by constitutional amendments at both the federal and state levels. Many of the amendments to the U.S. Constitution (such as the Fourteenth, Fifteenth, and Twenty-sixth Amendments) check the state courts' ability to allow discrimination, for example. Proposed constitutional amendments that were created in an effort to reverse courts' decisions on school prayer and abortion have failed.

Finally, Congress or a state legislature can rewrite (amend) old laws or enact new ones to overturn a court's rulings if the legislature concludes that the court is interpreting laws or legislative intentions erroneously. For example, Congress passed the Civil Rights Act of 1991 in part to overturn a series of conservative rulings in employment discrimination cases.

In 1993, Congress enacted the Religious Freedom Restoration Act (RFRA), which broadened religious liberties, after Congress concluded that a 1990 Supreme Court ruling restricted religious freedom to an unacceptable extent.[17] On signing the RFRA, President Clinton stated that the elected government's view of religious liberty was "far more consistent with the intent of the founders than [was] the Supreme Court." The Supreme Court responded in kind. In 1997, it invalidated the RFRA, declaring that the act represented an unconstitutional attempt by Congress to add new rights to the Constitution.[18] The Court proclaimed horror at the prospect that "[s]hifting legislative majorities could change the Constitution."

Public Opinion

Public opinion plays a significant role in shaping government policy, and certainly the judiciary is not excepted from this rule. For one thing, persons affected by a Supreme Court decision that is noticeably at odds with their views may simply ignore it. Officially sponsored prayers were banned in public schools in 1962, yet it was widely known that the ban was (and still is) ignored in many southern districts. What can the courts do in this situation? Unless someone complains about the prayers and initiates a lawsuit, the courts can do nothing.

The public also can pressure state and local government officials to refuse to enforce a certain decision. As already mentioned, judicial implementation requires the cooperation of government officials at all levels, and public opinion in various regions of the country will influence whether or not such cooperation is forthcoming.

Additionally, the courts themselves necessarily are influenced by public opinion to some extent. After all, judges are not "islands" in our society; their attitudes are influenced by social trends, just as the attitudes and beliefs of all persons are. Courts generally tend to avoid issuing decisions that they know will be noticeably at odds with public opinion. In part, this is because the judiciary, as a branch of the government, prefers to avoid creating divisiveness among the public. Also, a court—particularly the Supreme Court—may lose stature if it decides a case in a way that markedly diverges from public opinion. For example, in 2002 the Supreme Court ruled that the execution of mentally retarded criminals violates the Eighth Amendment's ban on cruel and unusual punishment. In its ruling, the Court indicated that standards of what constitutes cruel and unusual punishment are determined by public opinion and that there is "powerful evidence that today our society views mentally retarded offenders as categorically less culpable than the average criminal."[19]

Judicial Traditions and Doctrines

Supreme Court justices (and other federal judges) typically exercise self-restraint in fashioning their decisions. In part, this restraint stems from their knowledge that the other two branches of government and the public can exercise checks on the judiciary, as previously discussed. To a large extent, however, this restraint is mandated by various judicially established traditions and doctrines. For example, in exercising its discretion to hear appeals, the Supreme Court will not hear a meritless appeal just so it can rule on the issue. Also, when reviewing a case, the Supreme Court typically narrows its focus to just one issue or one aspect of an issue involved in the case. The Court rarely makes broad, sweeping decisions on issues. Furthermore, the doctrine of *stare decisis* acts as a restraint because it obligates the courts, including the Supreme Court, to follow established precedents when deciding cases. Only rarely will courts overrule a precedent.

Other judicial doctrines and practices also act as restraints. For example, the courts will hear only what are called justiciable disputes—disputes that arise out of actual cases. In other words, a court will not hear a case that involves a merely hypothetical issue. Additionally, if a political question is involved, the Supreme Court often will exercise judicial restraint and refuse to rule on the matter. A **political question** is one that the Supreme Court declares should be decided by the elected branches of government—the executive branch, the legislative branch, or those two branches acting together. For example, the Supreme Court has refused to rule on the controversy regarding the rights of gay men and lesbians in the military, preferring instead to defer to the executive branch's decisions on the matter. Generally, fewer questions are deemed political questions by the Supreme Court today than in the past.

Political Question An issue that a court believes should be decided by the executive or legislative branch.

Higher courts can reverse the decisions of lower courts. Lower courts can act as a check on higher courts, too. Lower courts can ignore—and have ignored—Supreme

MAKING A DIFFERENCE: Changing the Legal System

The U.S. legal system may seem too complex to be influenced by one individual, but its power nonetheless depends on the support of individuals. The public has many ways of resisting, modifying, or overturning statutes and rulings of the courts.

AN EXAMPLE—MOTHERS AGAINST DRUNK DRIVING

One example of the kind of pressure that can be exerted on the legal system began with a tragedy. In 1980, thirteen-year-old Cari Lightner was hit from behind and killed by a drunk driver while she was walking in a bicycle lane. The driver was a forty-seven-year-old man with two prior drunk-driving convictions. He was at that time out on bail after a third arrest. Cari's mother, Candy, quit her job as a real estate agent to form

Mothers Against Drunk Driving (MADD) and launched a campaign to stiffen penalties for drunk-driving convictions.

The organization now has three million members and supporters. Outraged by the thousands of lives lost every year because of drunk driving, the group seeks stiff penalties against drunk drivers. MADD, by becoming involved, has gotten results. Owing to its efforts and the efforts of other citizen-activist groups, many states have responded with stiffer penalties and deterrents. If you feel strongly about this issue and want to get involved, contact:

MADD
P.O. Box 541688
Dallas, TX 75354-1688
1-800-GET-MADD
http://www.madd.org

INFORMATION ABOUT THE SUPREME COURT

If you want information about the Supreme Court, contact the following by telephone or letter:

Clerk of the Court
The Supreme Court of the
   United States
1 First St. N.E.
Washington, DC 20543
202-479-3000

You can access online information about the Supreme Court at the following site:

http://www.oyez.org/oyez/
frontpage

Court decisions. Usually, this is done indirectly. A lower court might conclude, for example, that the precedent set by the Supreme Court does not apply to the exact circumstances in the case before the court; or the lower court may decide that the Supreme Court's decision was ambiguous with respect to the issue before the lower court. The fact that the Supreme Court rarely makes broad and clear-cut statements on any issue makes it easier for the lower courts to interpret the Court's decisions in different ways.

KEY TERMS

affirm **289**

amicus curiae brief **287**

appellate court **285**

case law **283**

class-action suit **287**

common law **282**

concurring opinion **290**

dissenting opinion **290**

diversity of citizenship **283**

federal question **283**

general jurisdiction **284**

judicial activism **294**

judicial implementation **297**

judicial restraint **294**

jurisdiction **283**

limited jurisdiction **285**

litigate **287**

majority opinion **290**

opinion **289**

oral arguments **289**

political question **299**

precedent **282**

remand **289**

reverse **289**

rule of four **289**

senatorial courtesy **290**

stare decisis **282**

trial court **284**

unanimous opinion **290**

writ of *certiorari* **289**

CHAPTER SUMMARY

1 American law is rooted in the common law tradition, which is part of our heritage from England. The common law doctrine of *stare decisis* (which means "to stand on decided cases") obligates judges to follow precedents established previously by their own courts or by higher courts that have authority over them. Precedents established by the United States Supreme Court, the highest court in the land, are binding on all lower courts. Fundamental sources of American law include the U.S. Constitution and state constitutions, statutes enacted by legislative bodies, regulations issued by administrative agencies, and case law.

2 Article III, Section 1, of the U.S. Constitution limits the jurisdiction of the federal courts to cases involving (a) a federal question—which is a question based, at least in part, on the U.S. Constitution, a treaty, or a federal law; or (b) diversity of citizenship—which arises when the parties to a lawsuit are from different states or when the lawsuit involves a foreign citizen or government. The federal court system is a three-tiered model consisting of (a) U.S. district (trial) courts and various lower courts of limited jurisdiction; (b) U.S. courts of appeals; and (c) the

United States Supreme Court. Cases may be appealed from the district courts to the appellate courts. In most cases, the decisions of the federal appellate courts are final because the Supreme Court hears relatively few cases.

3 The Supreme Court's decision to review a case is influenced by many factors, including the significance of the issues involved and whether the solicitor general is pressing the Court to take the case. After a case is accepted, the justices undertake research (with the help of their law clerks) on the issues involved in the case, hear oral arguments from the parties, meet in conference to discuss and vote on the issue, and announce the opinion, which is then released for publication.

4 Federal judges are nominated by the president and confirmed by the Senate. Once appointed, they hold office for life, barring gross misconduct. The nomination and confirmation process, particularly for Supreme Court justices, is often extremely politicized. Democrats and Republicans alike realize that justices may occupy seats on the Court for decades and naturally want to have persons appointed who share their basic views. Nearly 20 percent of all Supreme Court appointments have been either rejected or not acted on by the Senate.

5 In interpreting and applying the law, judges inevitably become policymakers. The most important policymaking tool of the federal courts is the power of judicial review. This power was not mentioned specifically in the Constitution, but John Marshall claimed the power for the Court in his 1803 decision in *Marbury v. Madison*.

6 Judges who take an active role in checking the activities of the other branches of government sometimes are characterized as "activist" judges,

and judges who defer to the other branches' decisions sometimes are regarded as "restraintist" judges. The Warren Court of the 1950s and 1960s was activist in a liberal direction, whereas today's Rehnquist Court seems to be increasingly activist in a conservative direction. Several politicians and scholars argue that judicial activism has gotten out of hand.

7 Checks on the powers of the federal courts include executive checks, legislative checks, public opinion, and judicial traditions and doctrines.

SELECTED PRINT AND MEDIA RESOURCES

Suggested Readings

Finkelman, Paul, and Melvin I. Urofsky. *Landmark Decisions of the United States Supreme Court.* Washington, D.C.: CQ Press, 2002. The authors look at numerous Supreme Court decisions in U.S. history and analyze their impact on American society.

Murphy, Bruce Allen. *Wild Bill: The Legend and Life of William O. Douglas.* New York: Random House, 2003. As a member of the Supreme Court from 1939 to 1975, William O. Douglas played a leading role in championing individual liberties. Murphy's biography provides much detail not only on the Court but also on American politics in general. (Murphy also reveals that the private Douglas was much less admirable than the public figure.)

Noonan, John T., Jr. *Narrowing the Nation's Power: The Supreme Court Sides with the States.* Berkeley: University of California Press, 2002. The author, a judge on the Court of Appeals for the Ninth Circuit (appointed by Ronald Reagan), takes issue with the Supreme Court's conservative states' rights agenda. He believes that the Court's entry into "uncharted territory" is threatening our democracy.

O'Connor, Sandra Day. *The Majesty of the Law: Reflections of a Supreme Court Justice.* New York: Random House, 2003. As the Supreme Court's most prominent swing vote, Justice O'Connor may be the most powerful member of that body. O'Connor gives a basic introduction to the Court, reflects on past dis-

crimination against women in the law, tells amusing stories about fellow justices, and calls for improving the treatment of jury members.

Media Resources

Amistad—A 1997 movie, starring Anthony Hopkins, about a slave ship mutiny in 1839. Much of the story revolves around the prosecution, ending at the Supreme Court, of the slave who led the revolt.

Court TV—This TV channel covers high-profile trials, including those of O. J. Simpson, the Unabomber, British nanny Louise Woodward, and Timothy McVeigh. (You can learn how to access Court TV from your area at its Web site—see the *Logging On* section for its URL.)

Gideon's Trumpet—A 1980 film, starring Henry Fonda as the small-time criminal James Earl Gideon, which makes clear the path that a case takes to the Supreme Court and the importance of cases decided there.

Justice Sandra Day O'Connor—In a 1994 program, Bill Moyers conducts Justice O'Connor's first television interview. Topics include women's rights, O'Connor's role as the Supreme Court's first woman justice, and her difficulties breaking into the male-dominated legal profession. O'Connor defends her positions on affirmative action and abortion.

Marbury v. Madison—A 1987 video on the famous 1803 case that established the principle of judicial review.

LOGGING ON

The home page of the federal courts is a good starting point for learning about the federal court system in general. At this site, you can even follow the "path" of a case as it moves through the federal court system. Go to **http://www.uscourts.gov**.

To access the Supreme Court's official Web site, on which Supreme Court decisions are made available within hours of their release, go to **http://supremecourtus.gov**.

Several Web sites offer searchable databases of Supreme Court decisions. You can access Supreme Court cases since 1970 at FindLaw's site: **http://www.findlaw.com**.

The following Web site also offers an easily searchable index to Supreme Court opinions, including some important historic decisions: **http://supct.law.cornell.edu/supct**.

You can find information on the justices of the Supreme Court, as well as their decisions, at **http://www.oyez.org/oyez/frontpage**.

Court TV's Web site offers information ranging from its program schedule and how you can find Court TV in your area to famous cases and the wills of celebrities. For each case included on the site, you can read a complete history as well as selected documents filed with the court and court transcripts. You can access this site at **http://www.courttv.com**.

USING THE INTERNET FOR POLITICAL ANALYSIS

Go to this text's Web site at **http://politicalscience.wadsworth.com/schmidtbrief2004**. Select "Chapter 12" in the box at the top of the window. Then, in the column on the left-hand side of the window, under "Chapter Resources," click on "Internet Exercises." The Web site will then display the following Internet exercises that you can perform to learn more about topics covered in this chapter.

Activity 12–1: The FindLaw Web Site
Activity 12–2: The United States Federal Courts
Activity 12–3: The United States Supreme Court

ONLINE STUDY GUIDE AND ADDITIONAL RESOURCES

At **http://politicalscience.wadsworth.com/schmidtbrief2004** you will find a free Study Guide to this book that includes tutorial quizzes, essay questions, practice exams, chapter outlines, learning objectives, the glossary, flashcards, crossword puzzles, and Microsoft PowerPoint presentations. Also included in the American Government Resource Center for Chapter 12:

- **InfoTrac® Reader**—The Supreme Court and constitutional protections; politics and the federal courts.
- **You Are There Simulations**—Court cases; the Supreme Court.
- **Participation Activities**—Learn about HALT; find a newsgroup discussion about a judiciary topic that interests you.

- **MicroCase Exercise**—The judiciary.
- **Related Links**—The judiciary.
- **Video Case Study**—Judge selection; legislative checks.
- **Source Readings**—By Alexander Hamilton and John Marshall, plus a selected statute.

The site also contains the Citizen's Survival Guide, information on how to get involved in politics locally and globally, as well as regularly updated features including a Current Events Quiz, In the News, Election Links, updates on the war on terrorism, and more.

CHAPTER 13

Domestic and Economic Policy

TYPICALLY, WHENEVER A POLICY DECISION is made, some groups will be better off and some groups will be hurt. All policymaking generally involves such a dilemma.

Part of the public-policy debate in our nation involves domestic problems. **Domestic policy** can be defined as all of the laws, government planning, and government actions that affect each individual's daily life in the United States. Consequently, the span of such policies is enormous. Domestic policies range from relatively simple issues, such as what the speed limit should be on interstate highways, to more complex ones, such as how best to protect our environment. Many of our domestic policies are formulated and implemented by the federal government, but a number of others are the result of the combined efforts of federal, state, and local governments.

In this chapter, we look at domestic policy issues involving airline safety, poverty and welfare, crime, and the environment. We also examine national economic policies undertaken solely by the federal government. Before we start our analysis, though, we must look at how public policies are made.

Domestic Policy
Public plans or courses of action that concern internal issues of national importance, such as poverty, crime, and the environment.

The Policymaking Process

How does any issue get resolved? First, of course, the issue has to be identified as a problem. Often, policymakers simply have to open their local newspapers—or letters from their constituents—to discover that a problem is brewing. On rare occasions, a crisis, such as that brought about by the terrorist attacks of September 11, 2001, creates the need to formulate policy. Like most Americans, however, policymakers receive much of their information from the national media. Finally, various lobbying groups provide information to members of Congress.

A challenging issue after 9/11 was how to increase the safety of airline travel. In response to concerns over this issue, Congress passed the Aviation Security Act, which was signed by President George W. Bush in November 2001. This legislation provides a good example of the steps involved in the policymaking process.

No matter how simple or how complex the problem, those who make policy follow a number of steps. We can divide the process of policymaking into at least five steps: agenda building, policy formulation, policy adoption, policy implementation, and policy evaluation.

Agenda Building

First of all, the issue must get on the agenda. In other words, Congress must become aware that an issue requires congressional action. Agenda building may occur as the result of a crisis, technological change, or mass media campaigns, as well as through the efforts of strong political personalities and effective lobbying groups.

The crisis of 9/11 put the issue of aviation security on the agenda immediately after the attacks. A number of groups pressured Congress to take prompt action, which Congress did by enacting the Aviation Transportation Act (more commonly known as the Aviation Security Act) of 2001.

Policy Formulation

During the next step in the policymaking process, various policy proposals are discussed among government officials and the public. Such discussions may take place in the printed media, on television, and in the halls of Congress. Congress holds hearings, the president voices the administration's views, and the topic may even become a campaign issue.

When developing the Aviation Security Act, members of Congress worked closely with representatives from a number of groups and trade associations, including representatives from the airline industry, pilots' associations, private security contractors, manufacturers of airport screening equipment, employees' unions, immigrant groups, and many others. Not surprisingly, the debates focused on the question of whether airport security should become the responsibility of the federal government.

Generally, the Senate thought that the federal government should assume this responsibility and that all airport screening personnel should become federal employees. Some groups objected to this idea on ideological grounds. They believed that the federal government should not take over a function that can be performed by private businesses, which is how airport security had been handled in the past. Many members of the House of Representatives urged that airport security be left in the hands of private contractors but subject to federal supervision and requirements.

Policy Adoption

The third step in the policymaking process involves choosing a specific strategy from among the proposals that have been discussed. The bill that finally passed the House and Senate was a compromise: airport security was federalized, but not necessarily permanently. For three years, all airport screening was to be under the supervision of the government. Screening personnel would have to be U.S. citizens and become federal employees. During this three-year period, five airports of differing sizes would be allowed to test various screening procedures in pilot programs. At the end of the period, airports could opt out of the federal worker program and use private security contractors—but under federal supervision.

House Republicans who had objected to the federalization of airport security were satisfied with the compromise and also with the final bill's inclusion of additional provisions proposed by the House. These provisions included steps that would increase security for caterers, checked baggage, and runways and other areas.

Policy Implementation

The fourth step in the policymaking process involves the implementation of the policy alternative chosen by Congress. Government action must be implemented by bureaucrats, the courts, police, and individual citizens. Implementation of the Aviation Security Act began immediately. Airport screening workers who wanted to retain their jobs were required to apply to the federal government for employment. Full implementation of the act, of course, would take time. For example, the requirement that new equipment to detect explosives be installed in airports would take months or even years to put in place.

Policy Evaluation

After a policy has been implemented, it is evaluated. Groups inside and outside the government conduct studies to determine what actually happens after a policy has been implemented for a given period of time. Based on this feedback and the perceived success or failure of the policy, a new round of policymaking initiatives will be undertaken to improve on the effort. How effective the Aviation Security Act will be in providing greater aviation security remains to be seen. Within a few more years, though, Congress will have received significant feedback on the results of the act's implementation.

Poverty and Welfare

Throughout the world, poverty has historically been accepted as inevitable. The United States and other industrialized nations, however, have sustained enough economic growth in the past several hundred years to eliminate mass poverty. In fact, considering the wealth and high standard of living in the United States, the persistence of poverty here appears bizarre and anomalous. How can there still be so much poverty in a nation of so much abundance? And what can be done about it?

Income Transfer A transfer of income from some individuals in the economy to other individuals. This is generally done by way of the government.

A traditional solution has been **income transfers.** These are methods of transferring income from relatively well-to-do to relatively poor groups in society, and as a nation, we have been using such methods for a long time. Before we examine these efforts, let us look at the concept of poverty in more detail and at the characteristics of the poor.

The Low-Income Population

We can see in Figure 13–1 that the number of people classified as poor fell steadily from 1961 to 1968—that is, during the presidencies of John Kennedy and Lyndon Johnson. The number remained level until the recession of 1981–1982, under

FIGURE 13–1   The Official Number of Poor in the United States

The number of individuals classified as poor fell steadily from 1961 through 1968. It then increased during the 1981–1982 recession. After 1994, the number fell steadily until 2000, when it started to rise again.

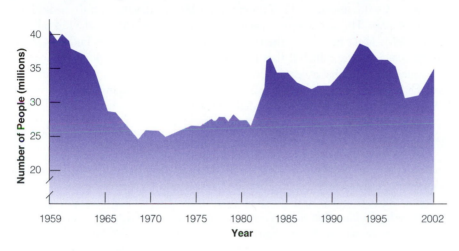

Ronald Reagan, when it increased substantially. The number fell during the "Internet boom" of 1994–2000, but then it started to rise again.

The threshold income level that is used to determine who falls into the poverty category was originally based on the cost of a nutritionally adequate food plan designed by the U.S. Department of Agriculture in 1963. The threshold was determined by multiplying the food-plan cost times three, on the assumption that food expenses constitute approximately one-third of a poor family's expenditures. Until 1969, annual revisions of the threshold level were based only on price changes in food. After 1969, the adjustments were made on the basis of changes in the consumer price index (CPI). The CPI is based on the average prices of a specified set of goods and services bought by wage earners in urban areas.

The low-income poverty threshold thus represents the income needed to maintain a specified standard of living as of 1963, with the purchasing-power value increased year by year to reflect the general increase in prices. For 2003, for example, the official poverty level for a family of four was about $18,300.

The official poverty level is based on pretax income, including cash but not in-kind subsidies—food stamps, housing vouchers, and the like. If we correct poverty levels for such benefits, the percentage of the population that is below the poverty line drops dramatically.

The Antipoverty Budget

It is not always easy to determine how much the government spends to combat poverty. In part, this is because it is not always easy to decide whether a particular program is an antipoverty program. Are grants to foster parents an antipoverty measure? What about job-training programs? Are college scholarships for low-income students an

In-Kind Subsidy A good or service—such as food stamps, housing, or medical care—provided by the government to low-income groups.

INFOTRAC
For updates and more information on welfare reform, use the term "welfare reform" in the Subject guide.

antipoverty measure? President George W. Bush's federal budget for 2004 allocated $14.5 billion for such scholarships.

Bush's 2004 budget allocated about $375 billion, or about one-sixth of all federal expenditures, to federal programs that support persons of limited income (scholarships included).[1] Of this amount, $177 billion was for Medicaid, which funds medical services to the poor. The states were expected to contribute an additional $134 billion to Medicaid. Medical care is by far the largest portion of the antipoverty budget. One reason medical spending is high is that there is a widespread belief that everyone should receive medical care that at least approximates the care received by an average person. No such belief supports spending for other purposes, such as shelter or transportation. Elderly people receive 70 percent of Medicaid spending.

Basic Welfare

Temporary Assistance to Needy Families (TANF) A state-administered program in which grants from the national government are used to provide welfare benefits. The TANF program replaced the Aid to Families with Dependent Children (AFDC) program.

The program that most people think of when they hear the word *welfare* is called **Temporary Assistance to Needy Families (TANF).** With the passage in 1996 of the Personal Responsibility and Work Opportunity Reconciliation Act, popularly known as the Welfare Reform Act, the government created TANF to replace an earlier program known as Aid to Families with Dependent Children (AFDC). The AFDC program provided "cash support for low-income families with dependent children who have been deprived of parental support due to death, disability, continued absence of a parent, or unemployment."

Under the TANF program, the U.S. government turned over to the states, in the form of block grants, funds targeted for welfare assistance. The states, not the national government, now bear the burden of any increased welfare spending. For example, if a state wishes to increase the amount of TANF payments over what the national government supports, the state has to pay the additional costs.

One of the aims of the Welfare Reform Act was to reduce welfare spending. To do this, the act made two significant changes in the basic welfare program. One change was to limit most welfare recipients to only two years of assistance at a time. The second change was to impose a lifetime limit on welfare assistance of five years. The Welfare Reform Act has largely met its objectives. During the first five years after the act was passed, the number of families receiving welfare payments was cut in half. The 2004 federal budget allocated $19 billion to the TANF block grants.

Other Forms of Government Assistance

Supplemental Security Income (SSI) A federal program established to provide assistance to elderly persons and persons with disabilities.

The **Supplemental Security Income (SSI)** program was established in 1974 to provide a nationwide minimum income for elderly persons and persons with disabilities who do not qualify for Social Security benefits. The 2004 budget allocated $37 billion to this program.

Food Stamps Coupons issued by the federal government to low-income individuals to be used for the purchase of food.

The government also issues **food stamps,** coupons that can be used to purchase food. Food stamps are available to low-income individuals and families. Recipients must prove that they qualify by showing that they have a low income (or no income at all). Food stamps go to a much larger group of people than TANF payments. President Bush's 2004 budget allocated $26 billion to the food stamp program. The

Less than one hundred yards from the White House, a homeless man sleeps, with his head on a cart containing all of his possessions. What do you think are the most likely causes of this man's condition? What policy recommendations follow from these causes?

Jeff Lawrence/Stock Boston

food stamp program has become a major part of the welfare system in the United States, although it was started in 1964 mainly to benefit farmers by distributing surplus food through retail channels.

The **earned-income tax credit (EITC) program** was created in 1975 to help low-income workers by giving back part or all of their Social Security taxes. Currently, more than 20 percent of all taxpayers claim an EITC, and an estimated $34 billion a year is rebated to taxpayers through the program.

Homelessness—Still a Problem

The plight of the homeless remains a problem. Indeed, some observers argue that the Welfare Reform Act of 1996 has increased the number of homeless persons. There are no hard statistics on the homeless, but estimates of the number of people without a home on any given night in the United States range from a low of 230,000 to as many as 750,000 people.

It is difficult to estimate how many people are homeless because the number depends on how the homeless are defined. There are *street people*—those who sleep in bus stations, parks, and other areas. Many of these people are youthful runaways. There are the so-called *sheltered homeless*—those who sleep in government-supported or privately funded shelters. Many of these individuals used to live with their families or friends. While street people are almost always single, the sheltered homeless

Earned-Income Tax Credit (EITC) Program A government program that helps low-income workers by giving back part or all of their Social Security taxes.

INFOTRAC

For more information on the homeless, use the term "homelessness" in the Subject guide.

include many families with children. Homeless families are the fastest-growing subgroup of the homeless population.

The homeless problem pits liberals against conservatives. Conservatives argue that there are not really that many homeless people and that most of them are alcoholics, drug users, or the mentally ill. Conservatives contend that these individuals should be dealt with by either the mental-health system or the criminal justice system. In contrast, many liberals argue that homelessness is caused by a reduction in welfare benefits and by excessively priced housing. They want more shelters to be built for the homeless.

Some cities have "criminalized" homelessness. Many municipalities have outlawed sleeping on park benches and sidewalks, as well as panhandling and leaving personal property on public property. In some cities, police sweeps remove the homeless, who then become part of the criminal justice system.

Crime in the Twenty-first Century

Although crime rates have fallen, on average, in the last several years, virtually all polls taken in the United States in the last decade show that crime is one of the major concerns of the public. A related issue that has been on the domestic policy agenda for decades is controlling the use and sale of illegal drugs—activities that are often associated with crimes of violence. More recently, finding ways to deal with terrorism has become a priority for the nation's policymakers.

Crime in American History

In every period in the history of this nation, people have voiced their apprehension about crime. Some criminologists argue that crime was probably as frequent around the time of the American Revolution as it is currently. During the Civil War, mob violence and riots erupted in several cities. After the Civil War, people in San Francisco were told that "no decent man is in safety to walk the streets after dark; while at all hours, both night and day, his property is jeopardized by incendiarism [arson] and burglary."[2] From 1860 to 1890, the crime rate rose twice as fast as the population.[3] Only during the three-decade period from the mid-1930s to the early 1960s did the United States experience, for the first time in its history, stable or slightly declining overall crime rates.

What most Americans are worried about is violent crime. From the mid-1980s to 1994, its rate rose relentlessly. The murder rate per 100,000 people in 1964 was 4.9, whereas in 1994 it was estimated at 9.3, an increase of almost 100 percent. Since 1995, however, violent crime rates have declined. Some argue that the cause of this decline is the booming economy the United States has generally enjoyed since about 1993. Others claim that the $3 billion of additional funds the federal government has spent to curb crime in the last few years has led to less crime. Still others argue that an increase in the number of persons who are jailed or imprisoned is responsible for the reduction in crime. Some have even argued that legalized abortion has reduced the population that is likely to commit crimes.

Ayman Gheith, right, and Omar Choudhary, left, were among three men detained by police in Florida on September 13, 2002. A woman reported to police that she had overheard them making terrorist threats while dining at a restaurant. The men were later cleared of any wrongdoing. The incident led Muslim Americans to claim that they were victims of racial profiling.

AP Photo/J. Pat Carter

Federal Drug Policy

Illegal drugs are a major cause of crime in America. A rising percentage of arrests are for illegal drug use or drug trafficking. The violence that often accompanies the illegal drug trade occurs for several reasons. One is that drug dealers engage in "turf wars" over the territories in which drugs can be sold. Another is that when drug deals go bad, drug dealers cannot turn to the legal system for help, so they turn to violence.

The war on drugs and the increased spending on drug interdiction over the years have had virtually no effect on overall illegal drug consumption in the United States. Indeed, mandatory sentences, which have been imposed by the federal government since the late 1980s for all federal offenses, including the sale or possession of illegal drugs, lead to a further problem—overcrowded prisons. Furthermore, almost half of the 1.5 million people arrested each year in the United States on drug charges are arrested on marijuana charges—and of these, almost 90 percent are charged with possession only.

While the federal government has done little to modify its drug policy, state and local governments have been experimenting with new approaches to the problem. Many states now have special "drug courts" for those arrested for illegal drug use. In these courts, offenders typically are "sentenced" to a rehabilitation program. (For a further discussion of this topic, see this chapter's *At Issue* feature on the next page.)

AT ISSUE: The Debate over Marijuana

In the last decade, eight states—Alaska, Arizona, California, Colorado, Maine, Nevada, Oregon, and Washington—and Washington, D.C., have adopted laws legalizing marijuana, or cannabis, for medical use. Typically, laws legalizing marijuana use for medical reasons allow physicians to prescribe marijuana only for patients who are suffering from a terminal illness, such as cancer or AIDS.

The adoption of "medical marijuana" laws has triggered further debate over whether marijuana should be legalized for certain purposes. Because federal drug policy prohibits the use of marijuana for any purpose, the debate is whether drug policy should be dictated by the federal government or left to the states.

NATIONAL DRUG POLICY PREVAILS

State laws legalizing marijuana for medical purposes directly conflict with the federal Controlled Substances Act of 1970. This act defines marijuana as a substance subject to federal control, and those who possess marijuana are subject to federal criminal penalties. The Constitution states, in the supremacy clause, that the Constitution and federal laws and treaties are the supreme law of the land. Thus, if a state law conflicts with a federal law, the federal law takes priority. This means that state laws authorizing the use of marijuana for medical purposes, when challenged, may be invalidated by the courts. In one case involving an Oakland, California, cooperative that distributed cannabis to those who wanted it for medical purposes, the United States Supreme Court held that the federal law prevailed.*

*United States v. Oakland Cannabis Buyers' Cooperative, 532 U.S. 483 (2001).

(In December 2003, however, a federal appeals court ruled that the federal government may have no authority when medical marijuana is not sold or transported across state lines. This case will likely go to the Supreme Court.)

Many Americans believe that drug policy should be left in the hands of the federal government. They argue that if each state could create its own laws on drugs, citizens would not have uniform protection against the problems stemming from drug use and abuse. After all, the use and sale of illegal drugs are nationwide problems.

LET THE STATES DECIDE

Proponents of medical marijuana argue that the federal government should respect the wishes of the majority of the voters in the states that have legalized marijuana use for medical purposes. If this means revising federal drug policy, then that should be done. They also point out that several other nations, including England and Canada, have legalized medical marijuana. Why shouldn't the United States do so as well?

Some supporters of medical marijuana go even further and contend that the mere possession of small amounts of marijuana for any purpose should be decriminalized. These advocates contend that marijuana is more like alcohol than like heroin or cocaine and therefore it should not be treated like heroin or cocaine by the law.

FOR CRITICAL ANALYSIS

If an initiative to legalize the use of marijuana for medical purposes were placed on your state's ballot, how would you vote? Why?

Confronting Terrorism

Of all of the different types of crimes, terrorism can be the most devastating. The victims of terrorist attacks can number in the hundreds—or even in the thousands, as was the case when hijacked airplanes crashed into the Pentagon and the World Trade Center on September 11, 2001. Additionally, locating the perpetrators is often extremely difficult. In a suicide bombing, the perpetrators have themselves been killed, so the search is not for the perpetrators but for others who might have conspired with them in planning the attack.

Terrorism is certainly not a new phenomenon in the world, but it is a relatively new occurrence on U.S. soil. And certainly, the 9/11 attacks made many Americans aware for the first time of the hatred of America harbored by some foreigners—in this case, a network of religious fundamentalists in foreign countries.

Environmental Policy

The government has been responding to pollution problems since before the American Revolution, when the Massachusetts Bay Colony issued regulations to try to stop the pollution of Boston Harbor. In the 1800s, states passed laws controlling water pollution after scientists and medical researchers convinced most policymakers that dumping sewage into drinking and bathing water caused disease. Table 13–1 on the following page describes the major environmental legislation in the United States.

SALVAGE FREEDOM NOT TIMBER

Kicking Sa....am's

MORE TREES LESS BUSH

AP Photo/Don Ryan, File

Protesters in Central Point, Oregon, held signs during a visit to the area by President George W. Bush in 2002. Environmentalists vowed to fight Bush's proposal to increase logging in national forests.

The National Environmental Policy Act

The year 1969 marked the start of the most concerted national government involvement in solving pollution problems. In that year, the conflict between oil-exploration interests and environmental interests literally erupted when an oil well six miles off the coast of Santa Barbara, California, exploded, releasing 235,000 gallons of crude oil. The result was an oil slick, covering an area of eight hundred square miles, that washed up on the city's beaches and killed plant life, birds, and fish. Congress soon passed the National Environmental Policy Act of 1969. This landmark legislation established, among other things, the Council on Environmental Quality. It also mandated that an **environmental impact statement (EIS)** be prepared for all major federal actions that could significantly affect the quality of the environment. The act gave citizens and public-interest groups concerned with the environment a weapon against the unnecessary and inappropriate use of natural resources by the government.

Environmental Impact Statement (EIS) A report that must show the costs and benefits of major federal actions that could significantly affect the quality of the environment.

Curbing Air Pollution

After years of lobbying by environmentalists and counterlobbying by industry, the Clean Air Act of 1990 was passed. This act required automobile manufacturers to cut new automobiles' exhaust emissions of nitrogen oxide by 60 percent and emissions of other pollutants by 35 percent. By 1998, all new automobiles had to meet this standard. Regulations that went into effect beginning with 2004 model cars call for

TABLE 13–1	Major Federal Environmental Legislation

1899 Refuse Act. Made it unlawful to dump refuse into navigable waters without a permit. A 1966 court decision made all industrial wastes subject to this act.

1948 Federal Water Pollution Control Act. Set standards for the treatment of municipal water waste before discharge. Revisions to this act were passed in 1965 and 1967.

1955 Air Pollution Control Act. Authorized federal research programs for air-pollution control.

1963 Clean Air Act. Assisted local and state governments in establishing control programs and coordinating research.

1965 Clean Air Act Amendments. Authorized the establishment of federal standards for automobile exhaust emissions, beginning with 1968 models.

1965 Solid Waste Disposal Act. Provided assistance to local and state governments for control programs and authorized research in this area.

1965 Water Quality Act. Authorized the setting of standards for discharges into waters.

1967 Air Quality Act. Established air-quality regions and acceptable regional pollution levels. Required local and state governments to implement approved control programs or be subject to federal controls.

1969 National Environmental Policy Act. Established the Council on Environmental Quality (CEQ) for the purpose of coordinating all federal pollution-control programs. Authorized the establishment of the Environmental Protection Agency (EPA) to implement CEQ policies on a case-by-case basis.

1970 Clean Air Act Amendments. Authorized the EPA to set national air-pollution standards and restricted the discharge of six major pollutants into the lower atmosphere. Automobile manufacturers were required to reduce nitrogen oxide, hydrocarbon, and carbon monoxide emissions by 90 percent (in addition to the 1965 requirements) during the 1970s.

1972 Clean Water Act (Federal Water Pollution Control Act Amendments). Set national water-quality goal of restoring polluted waters to swimmable, fishable waters by 1983.

1972 Federal Environmental Pesticide Control Act. Required that all pesticides used in interstate commerce be approved and certified as effective for their stated purpose. Required certification that they were harmless to humans, animal life, animal feed, and crops.

1974 Clean Water Act. Originally called the Safe Drinking Water Act, this law set (for the first time) federal standards for water suppliers serving more than twenty-five people, having more than fifteen service connections, or operating more than sixty days a year.

1976 Resource Conservation and Recovery Act. Encouraged the conservation and recovery of resources. Put hazardous waste under government control. Prohibited the opening of new dumping sites. Required that all existing open dumps be closed or upgraded to sanitary landfills by 1983. Set standards for providing technical, financial, and marketing assistance to encourage solid waste management.

1977 Clean Air Act Amendments. Postponed the deadline for automobile emission requirements.

1980 Comprehensive Environmental Response, Compensation, and Liability Act. Established a "Superfund" to clean up toxic waste dumps.

1990 Clean Air Act Amendments. Provided for precise formulas for new gasoline to be burned in the smoggiest cities, further reduction in carbon monoxide and other exhaust emissions in certain areas that still had dangerous ozone levels in the year 2003, and a cap on total emissions of sulfur dioxide from electricity plants. Placed new restrictions on toxic pollutants.

1990 Oil Pollution Act. Established liability for the clean-up of navigable waters after oil-spill disasters.

1996 Food Quality and Protection Act. Amended the Federal Food, Drug, and Cosmetic Act of 1938 to regulate the use of pesticides in the cultivation and marketing of food products.

1999 Chemical Safety Information, Site Security, and Fuels Regulatory Relief Act. Established new provisions to regulate risk management plans at certain chemical and fuel facilities to reduce the risk of chemical explosions and to lessen the vulnerability of these facilities to criminal and terrorist activities.

INFOTRAC

For more information on air pollution, use the term "air pollution" in the Subject guide.

cutting nitrogen oxide tailpipe emissions by nearly 10 percent by 2007. For the first time, sport utility vehicles and light trucks will be required to meet the same emission standards as automobiles.

Stationary sources of air pollution were also made subject to more regulation under the 1990 act. The act required 110 of the oldest coal-burning power plants in the United States to cut their emissions 40 percent by 2001. Controls were placed on other factories and businesses in an attempt to reduce ground-level ozone pollution in ninety-six cities to healthful levels by 2005 (except in Los Angeles, which has until 2010 to meet the standards). The act also required that the production of chlorofluorocarbons (CFCs) be stopped completely by the year 2002. CFCs are thought to deplete the ozone layer in the upper atmosphere and increase the levels of harmful radiation reaching the earth's surface. CFCs were used in air-conditioning and other refrigeration units.

In 1997, in light of evidence that very small particles (2.5 microns, or millionths of a meter) of soot might be dangerous to our health, the Environmental Protection Agency (EPA) issued new particulate standards for motor vehicle exhaust systems and other sources of pollution. The EPA also established a more rigorous standard for ground-level ozone, which is formed when sunlight combines with pollutants from cars and other sources. Ozone is a major component of smog.

The Politics of Economic Decision Making

Nowhere are the principles of public policymaking more obvious than in the economic decisions made by the federal government. The president and Congress (and, to a growing extent, the judiciary) are faced constantly with questions concerning economic policy. Three economic policy areas of particular concern are taxes, Social Security, and monetary policy.

Each policy action that affects one of these three areas carries with it costs and benefits, known as **policy trade-offs.** The costs are typically borne by one group and the benefits enjoyed by another group.

Policy Trade-Offs The cost to the nation of undertaking any one policy in terms of all of the other policies that could have been undertaken.

The Politics of Taxes and Subsidies

Taxes are voted on by members of Congress. Members of Congress also vote on *subsidies*, which are a type of negative taxes that benefit certain businesses and individuals. The Internal Revenue Code encompasses thousands of pages, thousands of sections, and thousands of subsections—our tax system is not very simple.

Tax Rates.   Individuals and businesses pay taxes based on tax rates. Not all of your income is taxed at the same rate. The first few dollars you make are not taxed at all. The highest rate is imposed on the "last" dollar you make. This highest rate is the *marginal* tax rate. Table 13–2 on the following page shows the 2003 marginal tax rates for individuals and married couples. The higher the tax rate—the action on the part of the government—the greater the public's reaction to that tax rate. If the highest tax rate you pay on the income you make is 15 percent, then any method you can use to reduce your taxable income by one dollar saves you fifteen cents in tax liabilities that you owe the federal government. Individuals paying a 15 percent rate have a relatively small incentive to avoid paying taxes, but consider individuals who were faced with a tax rate of 94 percent in the 1940s. They had a tremendous incentive to find legal ways to reduce their taxable incomes. For every dollar of income that was somehow deemed nontaxable, these taxpayers would reduce tax liabilities by ninety-four cents.

TABLE 13–2	Marginal Tax Rates for Single Persons and Married Couples (2003)		
SINGLE PERSONS		MARRIED COUPLES	
MARGINAL TAX BRACKET	MARGINAL TAX RATE	MARGINAL TAX BRACKET	MARGINAL TAX RATE
$ 0–$ 7,000	10%	$ 0–$ 14,000	10%
$ 7,000–$ 28,400	15%	$ 14,000–$ 56,800	15%
$ 28,400–$ 68,800	25%	$ 56,800–$114,650	25%
$ 68,800–$143,500	28%	$114,650–$174,700	28%
$143,500–$311,950	33%	$174,700–$311,950	33%
$311,950 and above	35%	$311,950 and above	35%

Loopholes and Lowered Taxes.   Individuals and corporations facing high tax rates will adjust their earning and spending behavior to reduce their taxes. They will also make concerted attempts to get Congress to add **loopholes** to the tax law that allow them to reduce their taxable incomes. When the Internal Revenue Code imposed very high tax rates on high incomes, it also provided for more loopholes than it does today. For example, special provisions enabled investors in oil and gas wells to reduce their taxable incomes.

Loophole A legal method by which individuals and businesses are allowed to reduce the tax liabilities owed to the government.

In 2001, President George W. Bush fulfilled a campaign pledge by persuading Congress to enact new legislation lowering tax rates. In 2003, rates were lowered again, retroactive to January 2003. Table 13–2 gives the resulting rates. As a result of other changes contained in the new tax laws, the U.S. tax code became even more complicated than it was before.

The Social Security Problem

Closely related to the question of taxes in the United States is the viability of the Social Security system. Social Security taxes came into existence when the Federal Insurance Contribution Act (FICA) was passed in 1935. Social Security was established as a means of guaranteeing a minimum level of pension benefits to all persons. Today, many people regard Social Security as a kind of "social compact"—a national promise to successive generations that they will receive support in their old age.

As of 2003, a 6.2 percent rate is imposed on each employee's wages up to a maximum of $87,000 to pay for Social Security. Employers must pay in ("contribute") an equal percentage. In addition, a combined employer/employee 2.9 percent tax rate is assessed for Medicare on all wage income, with no upper limit. Medicare is a federal program, begun in 1965, that pays hospital and physicians' bills for persons over the age of sixty-five.

Social Security Is Not a Pension Fund.   One of the problems with the Social Security system is that people who pay into Social Security think that they are actually paying into a fund, perhaps with their name on it. This is what you do when you pay into a private pension plan. It is not the case, however, with the federal Social Security system. That system is basically a pay-as-you-go transfer system in which those who are working are paying benefits to those who are retired.

Currently, the number of people who are working relative to the number of people who are retiring is declining. Therefore, those who continue to work will have to pay more in Social Security taxes to fund the benefits of those who retire. In 2025, when the retirement of the Baby Boomer generation is complete, benefits are projected to cost almost 25 percent of taxable payroll income in the economy, compared with the current rate of 16 percent. In today's dollars, that amounts to more than a trillion dollars of additional taxes annually.

Workers per Retiree.   One way to think about the future bill that today's college students (and their successors) could face in the absence of fundamental changes in Social Security is to consider the number of workers available to support each retiree. As you can see in Figure 13–2 on the following page, roughly three workers now provide for each retiree's Social Security, *plus* his or her Medicare benefits. Unless the current system is changed, by 2030 only two workers will be available to pay the Social Security and Medicare benefits due each recipient.

The growing number of people claiming the Social Security retirement benefit may pose less of a problem than the ballooning cost of Medicare. In the first place, an older population will require greater expenditures on medical care. In addition, however, medical expenditures *per person* are also going up rapidly. Given the continuing advances in medical science, Americans may logically wish to devote an ever-greater share of the national income to medical care. This choice puts serious

FIGURE 13–2 Workers per Retiree

The average number of workers per Social Security retiree has declined dramatically since the program's inception.

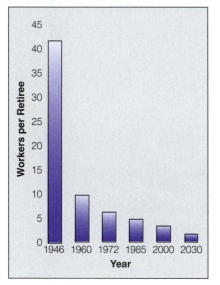

SOURCES: Social Security Administration and authors' estimates.

INFOTRAC

For more information on Social Security, use the term "Social Security reform" in the Subject guide.

pressure on federal and state budgets, however, because a large part of the nation's medical bill is funded by the government.

What Will It Take to Salvage Social Security?

The facts just discussed illustrate why efforts to reform Social Security and Medicare have begun to dominate the nation's public agenda. What remains to be seen is how the government ultimately will resolve the problem. What, if anything, might be done?

Raise Taxes. One option is to raise the Social Security payroll tax rate. A 2.2 percentage point hike in the payroll tax rate, to an overall rate of 17.5 percent, would yield an $80 billion annual increase in contributions. Such a tax increase would keep current taxes above current benefits until 2020, after which the system would again technically be in "deficit." Another option is to eliminate the current cap on the level of wages to which the payroll tax is applied; this measure would also generate about $80 billion per year in additional tax revenues. Nevertheless, even a combined policy of eliminating the wage cap and implementing a 2.2 percentage point tax increase would not keep tax collections above benefit payments over the long run.

Other Options. Proposals are also on the table to increase the age of full benefit eligibility, perhaps to as high as seventy. In addition, many experts believe that increases in immigration offer the best hope of dealing with the tax burdens and work force shrinkage of the future. Unless Congress changes the existing immigration system to permit the admission of a much larger number of working-age immigrants with useful skills, however, immigration is unlikely to relieve much of the pressure building due to our aging population.

Privatizing Social Security. Still another proposal calls for partially privatizing the Social Security system in the hope of increasing the rate of return on individuals' retirement contributions. Privatization would allow workers to invest a specified portion of their Social Security payroll taxes in the stock market. Although such a solution would have been unthinkable in past decades, today there is some support for the idea. Indeed, President George W. Bush's proposal that Social Security be partially privatized in this way has drawn significant support.

A number of groups oppose the concept of partial privatization, however. These groups fear that the diversion of Social Security funds into individual stock portfolios could jeopardize the welfare of future retirees, who would be at the mercy of the volatile stock market. Opponents of partial privatization also worry that such a change could be a first step down the slippery slope toward full privatization—and the end of government-guaranteed retirement income.

The Politics of Fiscal and Monetary Policy

Changes in the tax code sometimes form part of an overall fiscal policy change. **Fiscal policy** is defined as the use of changes in government expenditures and taxes to alter national economic variables, such as the rate of inflation, the rate of unemployment, the level of interest rates, and the rate of economic growth. The federal government also controls **monetary policy,** defined as the use of changes in the amount of money in circulation to affect interest rates, credit markets, the rate of inflation, and employment. Fiscal policy is the domain of Congress and the president. Monetary policy, as we shall see, is not under the control of Congress and the president, because the monetary authority in the United States—the Federal Reserve System, or the Fed—is an independent agency not directly controlled by either Congress or the president.

Fiscal Policy: Theory and Reality.

The theory behind fiscal policy is relatively straightforward: When the economy is going into a recession (and, as a result, unemployment is rising), the federal government should stimulate economic activity by increasing government expenditures, decreasing taxes, or both. When the economy is becoming overheated, with rapid increases in employment and rising prices (a condition of inflation), fiscal policy should become contractionary. That is, government expenditures should be reduced and taxes increased. This view of fiscal policy was first implemented in the 1960s. It was an outgrowth of the economic theories of the English economist John Maynard Keynes (pronounced *kaynz*), first published during the Great Depression of the 1930s.

Keynes believed that the forces of supply and demand operated too slowly in a serious recession and that government should step in to stimulate the economy. According to **Keynesian economics,** for example, the Great Depression resulted from a serious imbalance in the economy. The public was saving more than usual, and businesses were investing less than usual. At the beginning of the depression, the government should have filled the gap that was created when businesses began limiting their investments. The government could have done so by increasing government spending or cutting taxes. A practical problem is that changes in taxes and spending take time to work their way through Congress—there can be lengthy time lags.

Monetary Policy: Politics and Reality.

The theory behind monetary policy, like that behind fiscal policy, is relatively straightforward. In periods of recession and high unemployment, we should stimulate the economy by expanding the rate of growth of the money supply. (The money supply is defined loosely as checking account balances and currency.) An easy-money policy is supposed to lower interest rates and induce consumers to spend more and producers to invest more. With rising inflation, we should do the reverse: reduce the rate of growth of the amount of money in circulation. Interest rates should rise, choking off some consumer spending and some business investment. This is called a tight money policy. But the world is never so simple as the theory we use to explain it. If the nation experiences stagflation—rising inflation *and* rising unemployment, as we experienced in the 1970s—then neither an easy nor a tight money policy will provide an immediate solution.

Fiscal Policy The use of changes in government spending or taxation to alter national economic variables, such as the rate of unemployment.

Monetary Policy The use of changes in the amount of money in circulation to alter credit markets, employment, and the rate of inflation.

Keynesian Economics An economic theory associated with the use of fiscal policy to alter national economic variables—for example, increased government spending during times of economic downturns.

AP Photo/Ron Edmonds

Alan Greenspan, the chairman of the Federal Reserve. The Federal Reserve is responsible for our nation's monetary policy. Greenspan is often called to testify before various congressional committees. He frequently finds himself in the "hot seat" when the economy enters a recession.

Federal Open Market Committee (FOMC) The most important body within the Federal Reserve System. The FOMC decides how monetary policy should be carried out.

U.S. Treasury Bond Debt issued by the federal government.

Public Debt, or National Debt The total amount of debt carried by the federal government.

The Monetary Authority—The Federal Reserve System. Congress established our modern central bank, the Federal Reserve System, in 1913. It is managed by a board of governors consisting of seven members, including the very powerful chairperson. All of the governors, including the chairperson, are nominated by the president and approved by the Senate. Their appointments are for fourteen years.

Through the Federal Reserve System, called the Fed, and its **Federal Open Market Committee (FOMC),** decisions about monetary policy are made eight times a year. The Board of Governors of the Federal Reserve System is independent. The president can attempt to convince the board, and Congress can threaten to merge the Fed with the Treasury, but as long as the Fed retains its independence, its chairperson and governors can do what they please. Hence, any talk about "the president's monetary policy" or "Congress's monetary policy" is inaccurate. To be sure, the Fed has, on occasion, yielded to presidential pressure, and for a while the Fed's chairperson felt constrained to follow a congressional resolution requiring him to report monetary targets over each six-month period. But now, more than ever before, the Fed remains one of the truly independent sources of economic power in the government.

Monetary Policy and Lags. Monetary policy does not suffer from the lengthy time lags that affect fiscal policy, because the Fed can, within a very short period, put its policy into effect. Nonetheless, researchers have estimated that it takes almost fourteen months for a change in monetary policy to become effective, measured from the time the economy either slows down or speeds up too much to the time the economy feels the policy change. This means that by the time monetary policy goes into effect, a different policy might be appropriate.

Budget Deficits and the Public Debt

From 1960 until the late 1990s, the federal government ran a deficit—spent more than it received—in every year except two. Every time a budget deficit occurred, the federal government issued debt instruments in the form of **U.S. Treasury bonds.** The sale of these bonds to corporations, private individuals, pension plans, foreign governments, foreign businesses, and foreign individuals added to the **public debt,** or **national debt,** defined as the total amount owed by the federal government. Thus, if the public debt is, say, $4 trillion this year and the federal budget deficit is $150 billion during the year, then at the end of the year the public debt will be $4.15 trillion. Table 13–3 shows what has happened to the net public debt over time.

It would seem that the nation has been increasingly mortgaging its future. But this table does not take into account two important variables: inflation and increases in population. A better way to examine the relative importance of the public debt is to compare it with total national output. We do this in Figure 13–3. There you see that, as a percentage of total national output, the public debt reached its peak during World War II and fell steadily thereafter until the mid-1970s. Since then, except for a slight reduction in 1990, it rose until 1995, when it again started to fall, only to start rising again in 2002.

The New Reality of Federal Government Deficits

The economy had already gone into the beginnings of a recession in 2001 when terrorists attacked the Pentagon and the World Trade Center towers. The blow to the nation's economy helped keep it in a recession for many months to follow. Thus, federal government revenues from taxes did not rise as planned. At the same time, federal government expenditures increased rather dramatically because of the new war on terrorism. For example, Congress immediately passed an emergency $40 billion funding bill for the war on terrorism and has increased spending for defense and homeland security in subsequent budgets.

Occasionally, Congress and the president used the war on terrorism as an excuse to fund all sorts of additional programs in the name of "security." One of those was a farm bill that

TABLE 13–3	Net Public Debt of the Federal Government
YEAR	TOTAL (BILLIONS OF CURRENT DOLLARS)
1940	$ 42.7
1945	235.2
1950	219.0
1960	237.2
1970	284.9
1980	709.3
1990	2,410.1
1992	2,998.6
1993	3,247.5
1994	3,432.1
1995	3,603.4
1996	3,747.1
1997	3,900.0
1998	3,870.0
1999	3,632.9
2000	3,448.6
2001	3,200.3
2002	3,528.7
2003	3,878.4
2004	4,254.5*
*Estimate.	

SOURCE: U.S. Office of Management and Budget.

FIGURE 13–3 Net Public Debt as a Percentage of National Output

The public debt as a percentage of national output reached its peak during World War II and then dropped consistently until about 1975. It then grew steadily until the mid-1990s, when it again started to fall, only to start rising again in 2002.

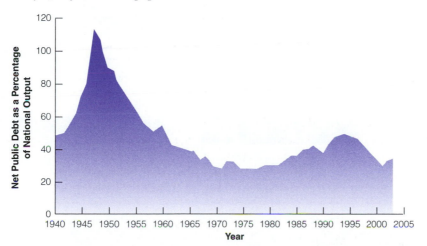

INFOTRAC

For more information on the Federal Reserve, use the term "Alan Greenspan" in the Subject guide.

MAKING A DIFFERENCE: Learning about Social Security

The growing number of elderly people and increases in the cost of medical care will force changes in the Social Security and Medicare programs in years to come. The nature of these changes is still an open question. Should Social Security and Medicare be changed as little as possible, to keep the system at least close to what currently exists? Or should we make more radical changes, such as replacing the existing programs with a system of private pensions? You can develop your own opinions by learning more about the Social Security issue.

ADVOCATES OF PRIVATIZATION

There are a variety of proposals for privatizing Social Security. Some call for a complete replacement of the existing system. Others call for combining a market-based plan with parts of the existing program. In general, advocates of privatization believe that the government should not be in the business of providing pensions and that pensions and health insurance are best left to the private sector. The

following organizations advocate privatization:

National Center for Policy
Analysis
12655 N. Central Expy.,
Suite 720
Dallas, TX 75243–1739
972-386-6272
http://www.ncpa.org
http://www.
mysocialsecurity.org

Institute for Policy Innovation
250 S. Stemmons Freeway,
Suite 215
Lewisville, TX 75067
972-874-5139
http://www.ipi.org

The Cato Institute
1000 Massachusetts
Avenue N.W.
Washington, DC 20001-5403
202-842-0200
http://www.cato.org
http://socialsecurity.org

OPPONENTS OF PRIVATIZATION

A variety of organizations oppose privatization in the belief that it will lead to reduced benefits for some

or all older people. Opponents of privatization believe that privatization plans are motivated more by ideology than by practical considerations. Organizations opposing privatization include:

AARP
601 E. Street N.W.
Washington, DC 20049
800-424-3410
http://www.aarp.org/
socialsecurity

National Committee to Preserve
Social Security and Medicare
10 G Street N.E., Suite 600
Washington, DC 20002
202-216-0420
http://www.ncpssm.org

The Social Security Network
c/o The Century Foundation
41 East 70th St.
New York, NY 10021
212-452-7743
http://www.socsec.org

even supporters of President Bush labeled "a blow to rationality in government spending." The farm bill added $73.5 billion over ten years to the $98.5 billion previously legislated to maintain current government agricultural subsidy programs.

We can expect to see federal government deficits, and therefore increases in the net public debt, for some years to come. Certainly, the war against Iraq will be costly and contribute to a larger budget deficit.

The Problem of "Crowding Out"

The prospect of an increasing public debt is worrisome to many economists. As we have seen, a large public debt is made up of a series of annual federal government budget deficits. Each time the federal government runs a deficit, we know that it must go into the financial marketplace to borrow the money. This process, in which the U.S. Treasury sells U.S. Treasury bonds, is called **public debt financing.** Public debt financing can "crowd out" private borrowing. Consider that to borrow, say, $100 billion, the federal government must bid for loanable funds in the marketplace, just as any business does. It bids for those loanable funds by offering to pay higher interest rates. Consequently, interest rates are increased when the federal government runs large deficits and borrows money to cover them. Higher interest rates can stifle or slow business investment, which reduces the rate of economic growth. This assumes, of course, that the Fed is not simultaneously increasing the money supply to hold down interest rates.

INFOTRAC
For updates and more information on public debts, use the term "public debts" in the Subject guide.

Public Debt Financing
The government's spending more than it receives in taxes and paying for the difference by issuing U.S. Treasury bonds, thereby adding to the public debt.

KEY TERMS

domestic policy **304**

earned-income tax credit (EITC) program **309**

environmental impact statement (EIS) **313**

Federal Open Market Committee (FOMC) **320**

fiscal policy **319**

food stamps **308**

income transfer **306**

in-kind subsidy **307**

Keynesian economics **319**

loophole **316**

monetary policy **319**

national debt **320**

policy trade-offs **315**

public debt **320**

public debt financing **323**

Supplemental Security Income (SSI) **308**

Temporary Assistance to Needy Families (TANF) **308**

U.S. Treasury bond **320**

CHAPTER SUMMARY

1 Domestic policy consists of all of the laws, government planning, and government actions that affect the daily lives of American citizens. Policies are created in response to public problems or public demand for government action. Major policy problems discussed in this chapter include aviation security, poverty and welfare, crime, the environment, and Social Security.

2 The policymaking process is initiated when policymakers become aware—through the media or from their constituents—of a problem that needs to be addressed by the legislature and the president. The process of policymaking includes five steps: agenda building, policy formulation, policy adoption, policy implementation, and policy evaluation. All policy actions necessarily result in both costs and benefits for society.

3 In spite of the wealth of the United States, a significant number of Americans live in poverty or are homeless. The low-income poverty threshold represents the income needed to maintain a specified standard of living as of 1963, with the purchasing-power value increased year by year based on the general increase in prices. The official poverty level is based on pretax income, including cash, and does not take into consideration in-kind subsidies (food stamps, housing vouchers, and so on).

4 The 1996 Welfare Reform Act transferred more control over welfare programs to the states, limited the number of years people can receive welfare assistance, and imposed work requirements on welfare recipients. The reform act succeeded in reducing the number of welfare recipients in the United States by at least 50 percent.

5 There is widespread concern in this country about violent crime. The overall rate of violent crime has been declining since 1995, however. Crimes associated with illegal drug sales and use have also challenged policymakers. A controversial issue today is whether federal drug policy should take priority over state laws that legalize the use of marijuana for certain medical purposes. A pressing issue facing Americans and their government today, of course, is terrorism—one of the most devastating forms of crime.

6 Pollution problems continue to plague the United States and the world. Since the nineteenth century, a number of significant federal acts have been passed in an attempt to curb the pollution of our environment. The National Environmental Policy Act of 1969 established the Council on Environmental Quality. That act also mandated that environmental impact statements be prepared for all legislation or major federal actions that might significantly affect the quality of the environment. The Clean Air Act amendments of 1990 constituted one significant government attempt at cleaning up our environment.

7 As a general rule, individuals and corporations that pay taxes at the highest rates will try to pressure Congress to create tax loopholes. (Loopholes allow high-income earners to reduce their taxable incomes.)

8 Closely related to the question of taxes is the viability of the Social Security system. As the number of people who are retired increases relative to the number of people who are working, those who work will have to pay more Social Security taxes to pay for the benefits of those who retire. Proposed solutions to the Social Security problem include raising taxes, reducing benefits payouts, reforming immigration policies, and partially privatizing the Social Security system in the hope of obtaining higher rates of return on contributions.

9 Fiscal policy is the use of changes in government expenditures and taxes to alter national economic variables, such as the rate of inflation or unemployment. Monetary policy is the use of changes in the amount of money in circulation to affect interest rates, credit markets, the rate of inflation, and employment. Fiscal policy usually means increasing government spending during recessionary periods and increasing taxes during inflationary boom periods. A problem with both fiscal policy and monetary policy is the lag between the time a problem occurs in the economy and the time when policy changes are actually felt in the economy.

10 Whenever the federal government spends more than it receives, it runs a deficit. The deficit is met by U.S. Treasury borrowing. This adds to the public debt of the federal government. Those who oppose deficit spending argue that one effect of the federal deficit is the crowding out of private investment. Although the federal budget deficit had virtually disappeared by 1998, by 2002 it was clear that Americans would once again see budget deficits, and thus increases in the net public debt, for years to come.

SELECTED PRINT AND MEDIA RESOURCES

Suggested Readings

Friedman, Milton, and Walter Heller. *Monetary versus Fiscal Policy*. New York: Norton, 1969. This is a classic presentation of the pros and cons of monetary and fiscal policy given by a noninterventionist (Friedman) and an advocate of federal government intervention in the economy (Heller).

Lomborg, Bjorn. *The Skeptical Environmentalist: Measuring the Real State of the World*. New York: Cambridge University Press, 2001. Lomborg's work is one of the most controversial books published on any topic in recent years. Lomborg argues that the condition of the environment is currently getting better, not worse, and that much environmental alarm is not based on facts.

Miller, Roger LeRoy, *et al. The Economics of Public Issues*, 14th ed. Reading, Mass.: Addison-Wesley, 2003. Chapters 4, 8, 11, 13, 19, 20, 22, 24, and 27 are especially useful. The authors use short essays of three to seven pages to explain the purely economic aspects of numerous social problems, including health care, the environment, and poverty.

President's Council of Economic Advisers. *Economic Report of the President*. Washington, D.C.: U.S. Government Printing Office, published annually. This volume contains a wealth of details concerning current monetary and fiscal policy and what is happening to the economy.

Rosenbaum, Walter A. *Environmental Politics and Policy*, 5th ed. Washington, D.C.: CQ Press, 2002. The author examines U.S. environmental policy since 1970, including issues such as nuclear waste, air and water pollution, the battle for public lands, and global environmentalism.

Media Resources

The Age of Terror: A Survey of Modern Terrorism—A four-part series, released in 2002, that contains unprecedented interviews with bombers, gunmen, hijackers, and kidnappers. The interviews are combined with photos from police and news archives. The four tapes are *In the Name of Liberation*, *In the Name of Revolution*, *In the Name of God*, and *In the Name of the State*.

Alan Greenspan—This rather laudatory biography of the chairman of the Federal Reserve was released in 1999. Using Greenspan, the film looks at factors that influence the world and national economies.

A Day's Work, A Day's Pay—This 2002 documentary by Jonathan Skurnik and Kathy Leichter follows three welfare recipients in New York City from 1997 to 2000. When forced to work at city jobs for well below the prevailing wage and not allowed to go to school, the three fight for programs that will help them get better jobs.

Drugs and Punishment: Are America's Drug Policies Fair?—In this 1996 BBC production, British journalist Charles Wheeler examines America's drug use and the hail of new drug laws instituted under the Reagan administration. Former drug czar William Bennett defends the government's position.

Traffic—A 2001 film, starring Michael Douglas and Benicio Del Toro, that offers compelling insights into the consequences of failed drug policies. (*Authors' note:* This film contains material of a violent and sexual nature that may be offensive.)

LOGGING ON

For current statistics on poverty in the United States, go to http://www.census.gov/hhes/www/poverty.html.

The National Governors Association offers information on the current status of welfare reform and other topics at http://www.nga.org.

The Federal Bureau of Investigation offers information about crime rates at its Web site: http://www.fbi.gov/ucr/ucr.htm.

You can also find statistics and other information on crime in the United States at the Web site of the Bureau of Justice Statistics. Go to http://www.ojp.usdoj.gov/bjs.

To find more information on poverty in the United States and the latest research on this topic, go to the site of the Institute for Research on Poverty at http://www.ssc.wisc.edu/irp.

You can keep up with actions taken by the Federal Reserve by checking the home page of the Federal Reserve Bank of San Francisco at http://www.frbsf.org.

For further information on Social Security, access the Social Security Administration's home page at http://www.ssa.gov.

For information on the 2004 budget of the U.S. government, go to http://www.whitehouse.gov/omb/budget/fy2004.

USING THE INTERNET FOR POLITICAL ANALYSIS

Go to this text's Web site at http://politicalscience.wadsworth.com/schmidtbrief2004. Select "Chapter 13" in the box at the top of the window. Then, in the column on the left-hand side of the window, under "Chapter Resources," click on "Internet Exercises." The Web site will then display the following Internet exercises that you can perform to learn more about topics covered in this chapter.

Activity 13–1: Medicaid and the Uninsured
Activity 13–2: Simulating the National Budget
Activity 13–3: The Federal Reserve System

ONLINE STUDY GUIDE AND ADDITIONAL RESOURCES

At http://politicalscience.wadsworth.com/schmidtbrief2004 you will find a free Study Guide to this book that includes tutorial quizzes, essay questions, practice exams, chapter outlines, learning objectives, the glossary, flashcards, crossword puzzles, and Microsoft PowerPoint presentations. Also included in the American Government Resource Center for Chapter 13:

- **InfoTrac® Reader**—The future of Social Security; tax policy; George W. Bush and the environment.

- **You Are There Simulations**—The Controlled Substances Act; the death penalty; economic policy.

- **Participation Activities**—Research a current social-policy issue; learn about one environmentalist group and one property rights/pro–free enterprise group; research the president's proposed budget; find a news-

group discussion about an economic policy issue that interests you.

- **MicroCase Exercises**—Social policy; economic policy.

- **Related Links**—Social policy; economic policy.

- **Video Case Study**—Environmental policy.

- **Source Readings**—By John Dewey and presidents Bill Clinton, Dwight Eisenhower, and Ronald Reagan, plus selected court cases and statutes.

The site also contains the Citizen's Survival Guide, information on how to get involved in politics locally and globally, as well as regularly updated features including a Current Events Quiz, In the News, Election Links, updates on the war on terrorism, and more.

CHAPTER 14

Foreign Policy

O N SEPTEMBER 11, 2001, AMERICANS were forced to change their view of national security and of our relations with the rest of the world—literally overnight. No longer could citizens of the United States believe that national security issues involved only threats overseas or that the American homeland could not be attacked. No longer could Americans believe that regional conflicts in other parts of the world had no direct impact on the United States.

Within a few days, it became known that the attacks on the World Trade Center and on the Pentagon had been planned and carried out by a terrorist network named al Qaeda that was funded and directed by the radical Islamic leader Osama bin Laden. The network was closely linked to the Taliban government of Afghanistan, which had ruled that nation since 1996.

Americans were shocked by the complexity and the success of the attacks. They wondered how our airport security systems could have failed so drastically. How could the Pentagon, the heart of the nation's defense, have been successfully attacked? Shouldn't our intelligence community have known about and defended against this network? And, finally, how could our foreign policy have been so blind to the anger voiced by Islamic groups throughout the world?

In this chapter, we examine the tools of foreign policy and national security policy in light of the many challenges facing the United States today. One of the major challenges for U.S. foreign policymakers is how best to respond to the threat of terrorism. We also review the history of American foreign policy.

INFOTRAC
To learn more about Osama bin Laden, use the term "Osama bin Laden" in the Subject guide.

Facing the World: Foreign and Defense Policy

The United States is only one nation in a world with almost two hundred independent countries, many located in regions where armed conflict is ongoing. What tools does our nation have to deal with the many challenges to its peace and

Foreign Policy A nation's external goals and the techniques and strategies used to achieve them.

Diplomacy The process by which states carry on political relations with each other; settling conflicts among nations by peaceful means.

Economic Aid Assistance to other nations in the form of grants, loans, or credits to buy the assisting nation's products.

Technical Assistance The practice of sending experts in such areas as agriculture, engineering, or business to aid other nations.

Foreign Policy Process The steps by which foreign policy goals are decided and acted on.

National Security Policy Policy that is concerned with the safety and defense of the nation.

Defense Policy A subset of national security policy—policies having to do with the U.S. armed forces.

prosperity? One tool is **foreign policy.** By this term, we mean both the goals the government wants to achieve in the world and the techniques and strategies to achieve them. For example, if one national goal is to achieve stability in the Middle East and to encourage the formation of pro-American governments there, U.S. foreign policy in that area may be carried out through **diplomacy, economic aid, technical assistance,** or military intervention. Sometimes foreign policies are restricted to statements of goals or ideas, such as helping to end world poverty, whereas at other times foreign policies are comprehensive efforts to achieve particular objectives, such as changing the regime in Iraq.

As you will read later in this chapter, in the United States, the **foreign policy process** usually originates with the president and those agencies that provide advice on foreign policy matters. Foreign policy formulation often is affected by congressional action and national public debate.

National Security Policy

As one aspect of overall foreign policy, **national security policy** is designed primarily to protect the independence and the political integrity of the United States. It concerns itself with the defense of the United States against actual or potential (real or imagined) enemies, domestic or foreign.

U.S. national security policy is based on determinations made by the Department of Defense, the Department of State, and a number of other federal agencies, including the National Security Council (NSC). The NSC acts as an advisory body to the president, but it has increasingly become a rival to the State Department in influencing the foreign policy process.

Defense policy is a subset of national security policy. Generally, defense policy refers to the set of policies that direct the scale and size of the U.S. armed forces. Defense policies are proposed by the leaders of the nation's military forces and the secretary of defense and are greatly influenced by congressional decision makers.

Diplomacy

Diplomacy is another aspect of foreign policy. Diplomacy includes all of a nation's external relationships, from routine diplomatic communications to summit meetings among heads of state. More specifically, diplomacy refers to the settling of disputes and conflicts among nations by peaceful methods. Diplomacy is the set of negotiating techniques by which a nation attempts to carry out its foreign policy.

Diplomacy may or may not be successful, depending on the willingness of the parties to negotiate. For example, in 1993, after years of refusing to negotiate or even recognize each other's legitimacy, Israel and representatives of the Palestine Liberation Organization (the PLO) reached an agreement under which Israel returned control of Jericho and part of the West Bank to the Palestinians. As of 2004, however, relations between Israel and the Palestinians continued to erupt in conflict, and the United States, together with the leaders of the European Union, continued to use diplomatic tools to try to get the parties to resume peace negotiations.

Morality versus Reality in Foreign Policy

From the earliest years of the republic, Americans have believed that their nation had a special destiny. The American experiment in democratic government and capitalism, it was thought, would provide the best possible life for men and women and be a model for other nations. As the United States assumed greater status as a power in world politics, Americans came to believe that the nation's actions on the world stage should be guided by American political and moral principles.

INFOTRAC

For more information on the NSC, use the term "United States National Security Council" in the Subject guide.

Moral Idealism

This view of America's mission has led to the adoption of many foreign policy initiatives that are rooted in **moral idealism.** This philosophy sees the world as fundamentally benign and assumes that most nations can be persuaded to take moral considerations into account when setting their policies. In this perspective, nations should come together and agree to keep the peace, as President Woodrow Wilson (1913–1921) proposed for the League of Nations. Many of the foreign policy initiatives taken by the United States have been based on this idealistic view of the world. The Peace Corps, which was created by President John Kennedy in 1961, is one example of an effort to spread American goodwill and technology that has achieved some of its goals.

Moral Idealism A philosophy that sees all nations as willing to cooperate and agree on moral standards for conduct.

Political Realism A philosophy that sees each nation as acting principally in its own interest.

Political Realism

In opposition to the moral perspective is **political realism.** Realists see the world as a dangerous place in which each nation strives for its own survival and interests regardless of moral considerations. The United States must also base its foreign policy decisions on cold calculations without regard for morality. Realists believe that the United States must be prepared militarily to defend itself, because all other nations are, by definition, out to improve their own situations. The practice of political realism in foreign policy allows the United States to sell weapons to military

Raquib Jamal is a business volunteer in Ghana helping farmers develop and run tourism businesses. Her work is an example of the moral idealism that is an important component of American foreign policy.

Peace Corps photo

dictators who will support its policies, to support American business around the globe, and to repel terrorism through the use of force.

American Foreign Policy—A Mixture of Both

It is important to note that the United States never has been guided by only one of these principles. Instead, both moral idealism and political realism affect foreign policymaking. President George W. Bush drew on the tradition of morality in foreign policy when he declared that the al Qaeda network of Osama bin Laden was "evil" and that fighting terrorism was fighting evil. To actually wage war on the Taliban in Afghanistan, however, U.S. forces needed the right to use the airspace of India and Pakistan, neighbors of Afghanistan. The United States had previously criticized both of these South Asian nations because they had developed and tested nuclear weapons. To work with India and Pakistan, the United States switched to a realist policy, promising aid and support to both regimes in return for their assistance in the war on terrorism.

The second Gulf War, in 2003, also revealed a mixture of idealism and realism. While the primary motive for invading Iraq was realistic (in the interests of U.S. security), another goal of the war reflected idealism (the liberation of the Iraqi people from an oppressive regime).

Challenges in World Politics

The foreign policy of the United States, whether moralist, realist, or both, must be formulated to deal with world conditions. Early in its history, the United States was a weak, new nation facing older nations well equipped for world domination. In the twenty-first century, the United States faces different challenges. Now it must devise foreign and defense policies that will enhance its security in a world in which it is the global superpower and has no equal.

The Emergence of Terrorism

Dissident groups, rebels, and other revolutionaries have long engaged in terrorism to gain attention and to force their enemies to the bargaining table. Over the last two decades, however, terrorism has increasingly threatened world peace and the lives of ordinary citizens.

Terrorism and Regional Strife.   Terrorism can be a weapon of choice in regional or domestic strife. The conflict in the Middle East between Israel and the Arab states is an example. Until recently, the conflict had been lessened by a series of painfully negotiated agreements between Israel and some of the Arab states. Those opposed to the peace process, however, have continued to disrupt the negotiations through assassinations, mass murders, and bomb blasts in the streets of major cities within Israel.

Terrorist Attacks against Foreign Civilians.   In other cases, terrorist acts are planned against civilians of foreign nations traveling abroad to make an interna-

Terrorist bombings have become increasingly destructive in recent decades. In the Palestinian-Israeli conflict, Palestinian suicide bombers target crowded public places, such as bus stops, as depicted in the photo on the right. Above, Palestinians carry sacks of food through the remains of a market in Bethlehem, destroyed after a stand-off between Israeli troops and Palestinians in the fall of 2002.

tional statement and to frighten the citizens of a faraway land. One of the most striking of these attacks was that launched by Palestinian terrorists against Israeli athletes at the Munich Olympics in 1972, during which eleven athletes were killed. Other attacks have included ship and airplane hijackings, as well as bombings of government facilities abroad, such as embassies or military bases. For example, in 1998, terrorist bombings of two American embassies in Africa killed 257 people, including 12 Americans, and injured over 5,500 others.

September 11. In 2001, terrorism came home to the United States in ways that few Americans could have imagined. In a well-coordinated attack, nineteen terrorists hijacked four airplanes and crashed three of them into buildings—two into the World Trade Center towers in New York City and one into the Pentagon in Washington, D.C. The fourth airplane crashed in a field in Pennsylvania after the passengers fought the hijackers. Why did the al Qaeda network plan and launch attacks on the United States? Apparently, the leaders of the network, including Osama bin Laden, were angered by the presence of U.S. troops on the soil of Saudi Arabia, which they regard as sacred. They also saw the United States as the primary defender of Israel against the Palestinians. The attacks were intended to frighten and demoralize the American people, thus convincing their leaders to withdraw American troops from the Middle East.

The War on Terrorism

After 9/11, President George W. Bush immediately implemented stronger security measures to protect homeland security and U.S. facilities and personnel abroad. The president sought and received congressional support for heightened airport security,

INFOTRAC

For updates and more information on terrorism, use the term "terrorism" in the Subject guide.

A satellite image of lower Manhattan shows the devastation after the collapse of the World Trade Center towers on September 11, 2001. Terrorists crashed two commercial airplanes into the twin towers. Three thousand people were killed in the terrorist attacks at the World Trade Center and the Pentagon.

Department of Defense photo

new laws allowing greater domestic surveillance of potential terrorists, and new funding for the military.

Military Responses.   The first military effort was directed against al Qaeda camps in Afghanistan and the Taliban regime, which had ruled that country since 1996. In late 2001, after building a coalition of international allies and anti-Taliban rebels within Afghanistan, the United States defeated the Taliban and supported the creation of an interim government that did not support terrorism.

During 2002 and early 2003, the U.S. government focused its attention on the threat posed by Saddam Hussein's government in Iraq. As you will read later in this chapter, after the first Gulf War, in 1991, Hussein was subject to various United

Nations (UN) resolutions. These resolutions included mandates that Iraq allow UN weapons inspectors to search for and oversee the elimination of weapons of mass destruction and related research facilities. Iraq's failure to comply with the UN requirements led to a stand-off that lasted for over a decade.

Having tried and failed to convince the UN Security Council that the UN should take action to enforce its resolutions, President Bush decided to take unilateral action against Iraq. In March 2003, supported by a coalition of thirty-five other nations, including Great Britain, the United States invaded Iraq. Within three weeks, Hussein's government had toppled. An irregular resistance to the coalition forces followed, however. In December 2003, Hussein was finally located and arrested. The difficult task facing the victors continues to be establishing a new governing regime. (For a further discussion of the decision to act without UN approval, see this chapter's *At Issue* feature on the following page.)

A New Kind of War.   In September 2002, President Bush enunciated what has since become known as the "Bush doctrine":

> We will . . . [defend] the United States, the American people, and our interests at home and abroad by identifying and destroying the threat before it reaches our borders. While the United States will constantly strive to enlist the support of the international community, we will not hesitate to act alone, if necessary to exercise our right of self-defense by acting preemptively against such terrorists, to prevent them from doing harm against our people and our country.[1]

The concept of "preemptive war" as a defense strategy is a new element in U.S. foreign policy. The concept is based on the assumption that in the war on terrorism, self-defense must be *anticipatory*. As President Bush stated on March 17, 2003, just before launching the invasion of Iraq, "Responding to such enemies only after they have struck first is not self-defense, it is suicide."

The Bush doctrine has not been without its critics. Some point out that preemptive wars against other nations have traditionally been waged by dictators and rogue states—not democratic nations. By employing such tactics, the United States would seem to be contradicting its basic values. Others claim that launching preemptive wars will make it difficult for the United States to further world peace in the future. By endorsing such a policy itself, the United States could hardly argue against the decisions of other nations to do likewise when they feel potentially threatened.

Nuclear Proliferation

In 1945, the United States was the only nation to possess nuclear weapons. Several nations quickly joined the "nuclear club," however, including the Soviet Union in 1949, Great Britain in 1952, France in 1960, and China in 1964. India and Pakistan detonated nuclear devices within a few weeks of each other in 1998. Many other nations are suspected of possessing nuclear weapons or the capability to produce them in a short time.

More than 32,000 nuclear warheads are known to be in stock worldwide, although the exact number is uncertain because some countries do not reveal the extent of their

INFOTRAC

For up-to-date coverage of developments in Iraq, use the term "Iraq War" in the Subject guide.

AT ISSUE: Should the United States Abandon the UN and Go It Alone?

On September 12, 2002, in a speech to the United Nations (UN) General Assembly, President George W. Bush asked that the UN take action against Iraq. The UN Security Council first approved the United States's call for weapons inspections and then, in February 2003, backed away from supporting any use of force against Iraq.

The UN's refusal to take action convinced the Bush administration that the United States would have to act alone to overthrow the government in Baghdad. The UN's inaction also raised an important question: Should the United States abandon attempts to work with the UN in the future and "go it alone" in the world arena?

THE UNITED STATES SHOULD ACT ALONE

Many believe that the United States should go its own way in the world and not rely on the UN. After all, time and again the UN has proved itself to be incapable of undertaking decisive action to maintain international peace and security. For one thing, the organization lacks sufficient funding. For another, member nations, including the United States, often put their own national interests above those of the international community.

Finally, the UN is structurally flawed in that all nations (except for the five permanent members of the Security Council) have equal powers, regardless of size, financial contribution, or political system. How can the UN possibly reach a consensus on a policy decision when member nations, such as the United States and North Korea, hold widely diverse views on human rights, democracy, and nuclear proliferation? Why should America, as the world's only superpower, put its foreign policy under an institution that functions so imperfectly?

THE UNITED STATES CANNOT AFFORD TO ACT ALONE

Other groups argue that although the UN may not be perfect, it is nonetheless essential that the United States support its activities and refrain from acting unilaterally. The UN is one of a number of multilateral organizations that were designed after World War II (1939–1945) to prevent the world from again plunging into war. For the most part, these organizations have served us well. Just because a majority of the members of the UN Security Council do not agree with the government of the United States is no reason to abandon a half-century of efforts toward an organization that unites all nations.

Additionally, many Americans believe that we will be far less secure if we continue to act alone. Refusing to cooperate with the UN may have a profound effect on the willingness of other countries to cooperate with the United States on important matters. Drug trafficking, global warming, and terrorism are just three examples of problems that require as much international cooperation as possible. Surrendering some American freedom of action is more than worth the gains from acting jointly with other nations through the UN.

FOR CRITICAL ANALYSIS

Do you believe that the United States should act unilaterally in the war on terrorism, or should we do everything we can to work with the UN? Which approach would better further U.S. interests in the long run?

Cold War The ideological, political, and economic impasse that existed between the United States and the Soviet Union following World War II.

nuclear stockpiles. Although the United States and Russia have dismantled some of their nuclear weapons systems since the end of the **Cold War** and the dissolution of the Soviet Union in 1991 (discussed later in this chapter), both still retain sizable nuclear arsenals. Even more troublesome is *nuclear proliferation*—the development of nuclear weapons by additional nations. We discuss the threat that terrorists might obtain nuclear weapons in this chapter's *America's Security* feature on page 336.

The New Power: China

Since Richard Nixon's visit to China in 1972, American policy has been to gradually engage the Chinese in diplomatic and economic relationships in the hope of turning the nation in a more pro-Western direction. In 1989, however, when Chinese students engaged in extraordinary demonstrations against the government, the Chinese government crushed the demonstrations, killing a number of students and protesters and imprisoning others. The result was a distinct chill in Chinese-American relations.

Chinese-American Trade Ties.
After initially criticizing the administration of George H. W. Bush (1989–1993) for not being hard enough on China, President Bill Clinton came around to a policy of diplomatic outreach to the Chinese. An important reason for this change was the large and growing trade ties between the two countries. China was granted **most-favored-nation status** for tariffs and trade policy on a year-to-year basis. (To prevent confusion, in 1998 the status was renamed *normal trade relations* status, or NTR.) In 2000, over objections from organized labor and human rights groups, Congress approved a permanent grant of NTR status to China.

In 2001, Congress endorsed China's application to join the World Trade Organization (WTO), which effectively guaranteed China's admission to that body. For a country that is officially communist, China already permits a striking degree of free enterprise, and the rules China must follow as a WTO member will further increase the role of the private sector in China's economy.

Chinese-American Tensions.
China has one of the fastest-growing economies in the world. Given China's large population, projections suggest that the gross domestic product of China may match or exceed that of the United States during the coming century. This prospect has led to alarm in some quarters. Some U.S. observers and officials have argued that China is destined to become a great rival—or even an enemy—of the United States. Tensions have been increased by allegations that China or ethnic Chinese from Southeast Asia have made illegal campaign contributions in the United States.

In 1999, Wen Ho Lee, a Taiwanese-American nuclear scientist, was accused of spying for China and placed in solitary confinement for nine months. Asian American leaders contended that the Lee case was being used to stir up racial hostility toward Asian Americans. In 2000, a court found that while Lee had violated certain security guidelines, he was innocent of espionage. The judge apologized to Lee for the way in which the government had mishandled the case. Tensions between the Chinese and U.S. governments were also enhanced in 2001 by a dispute that followed a collision between a U.S. spy plane and a Chinese fighter jet. Still, after the September 11 attacks, China offered its full support to the United States in the war on terrorism and, for the first time ever, supplied intelligence to the United States about terrorist activities. The Chinese, however, did not support the American military action to overthrow Saddam Hussein.

Most-Favored-Nation Status A status granted by an international treaty by which each member nation must treat other members at least as well as it treats the country that receives its most favorable treatment.

Regional Conflicts

The United States played a role—sometimes alone, sometimes with other powers—in many regional conflicts during the 1990s and early 2000s.

AMERICA'S SECURITY

Nuclear Proliferation and Terrorists

I n the 1980s and 1990s, the United States and the Soviet Union negotiated several treaties aimed at reducing the threat that their nuclear arsenals pose to the world. In addition, the United States has attempted to influence late arrivals to the "nuclear club" through a combination of rewards and punishments. In some cases, the United States has promised aid to a nation to gain cooperation. In other cases, such as those of India and Pakistan, it has imposed economic sanctions as a punishment for carrying out nuclear tests.

THE NUCLEAR TEST BAN TREATY

In 1999, President Clinton presented the Comprehensive Nuclear Test Ban Treaty to the Senate for ratification. The treaty, formed in 1996, prohibits all nuclear test explosions worldwide and provides for the establishment of a global network of monitoring stations. Ninety-three nations have ratified the treaty. Among those that have not are China, Israel, India, and Pakistan. In a defeat for the Clinton administration, the U.S. Senate rejected the treaty in 1999.

Has the defeat of the treaty increased the nuclear threat? It is possible that pressure from nations that had ratified the treaty would be instrumental in imposing greater security measures on existing weapons materials and technology, thus helping to keep them out of the hands of terrorists. The United States may have lost moral authority to lobby other nations to improve their security measures when it failed to ratify the test ban treaty.

TERRORISTS COULD OBTAIN NUCLEAR WEAPONS

Among the nations suspected of having nuclear weapons programs are Algeria, Iran, Libya, North Korea, and Syria. All of these nations have been described by the United States as "states of concern," "terrorist regimes," or "rogue states." The fear exists that one of these nations could supply nuclear materials to terrorists. Also, since the dissolution of the Soviet Union in 1991, the security of its nuclear arsenal has declined. There have been reported thefts of nuclear material from the former Soviet Union in the past decade.*

With nuclear weapons, materials, and technology available worldwide, it is conceivable that terrorists could develop a nuclear device and use it in a terrorist act.

FOR CRITICAL ANALYSIS

Other than the use of military force, what methods could the United States or other countries use to prevent the spread of nuclear technology to terrorists?

*Rensselaer Lee, *Smuggling Armageddon: The Nuclear Black Market in the Former Soviet Union and Europe* (New York: St. Martin's Press, 2000).

The Middle East.   As a long-time supporter of Israel, the United States has undertaken to persuade the Israelis to negotiate with the Palestinians who live in the territories occupied by the state of Israel. The conflict, which began in 1948, has been extremely hard to resolve. The internationally recognized solution is for Israel to yield the West Bank and the Gaza Strip to the Palestinians in return for effective security commitments and abandonment by the Palestinians of any right of return to Israel proper. Unfortunately, the Palestinians have been unwilling to stop terrorist attacks on Israel, and Israel has been unwilling to dismantle its settlements in the occupied territories. Further, the two parties have been unable to come to an agreement on how much of the West Bank should go to the Palestinians and on what compensation (if any) the Palestinians should receive for abandoning all claims to settlement in Israel proper.

In December 1988, the United States began talking directly to the Palestine Liberation Organization (PLO), and in 1991, under great pressure from the United States, the Israelis opened talks with representatives of the Palestinians and other Arab states. In 1993, the Israeli-Palestinian peace talks reached a breakthrough, with both parties agreeing to set up Palestinian self-government in the West Bank and the Gaza Strip. The historic agreement, signed in Cairo on May 4, 1994, put in place a process by which the Palestinians would assume self-rule in the Gaza Strip and in the town of Jericho. In the months that followed, Israeli troops withdrew from much of the occupied territory, Palestinians assumed police duties, and many Palestinian prisoners were freed by the Israelis.

Although negotiations between the Israelis and the Palestinians resulted in more agreements in Oslo, Norway, in 2000, the agreements were rejected by Palestinian radicals, who began a campaign of suicide bombings in Israeli cities. In 2002, the Israeli government responded by moving tanks and troops into Palestinian towns to kill or capture the terrorists. The crisis seemed to doom all further peace agreements. How the U.S.–led invasion of Iraq and the toppling of Saddam Hussein's regime in 2003 will affect Arab-Israeli relations in the future remains to be seen.

The Persian Gulf—The First Gulf War.   On August 2, 1990, the Persian Gulf became the setting for a major challenge to the international system set up after World War II (1939–1945). President Saddam Hussein of Iraq sent troops into the neighboring oil sheikdom of Kuwait, occupying that country. This was the most clear-cut case of aggression against an independent nation in half a century. At the formal request of the king of Saudi Arabia, American troops were dispatched to set up a defensive line at the Kuwaiti border. After the United Nations (UN) approved a resolution authorizing the use of force if Saddam Hussein did not respond to sanctions, the U.S. Congress reluctantly also approved such an authorization. On January 17, 1991, two days after a deadline for President Hussein to withdraw, U.S.–led coalition forces launched a massive air attack on Iraq. After several weeks, the ground offensive began. Iraqi troops retreated from Kuwait a few days later, and the first Gulf War ended, although many Americans criticized President George H. W. Bush for not sending troops to Baghdad and deposing Saddam Hussein.

As part of the cease-fire that ended the Gulf War, Iraq agreed to abide by all UN resolutions and to allow UN weapons inspectors to oversee the destruction of its medium-range missiles and all chemical- and nuclear-weapons research facilities. Economic sanctions would continue to be imposed on Iraq until the weapons inspectors finished their jobs. In 1999, however, Iraq placed such obstacles in the path of the UN inspectors that they withdrew from the country.

As part of the war on terrorism, the United States destroyed the Taliban regime in Afghanistan that allowed terrorists to train in that country. Here, an F-18 Hornet is launched from the aircraft carrier USS Carl Vinson. A fleet of aircraft carrier battle groups allows the U.S. military to launch bombing raids anywhere in the world.

Department of Defense photo by Petty Officer First Class Greg Messier, U.S. Navy

The Persian Gulf—The Second Gulf War.   After the terrorist attacks on the United States on September 11, 2001, President George W. Bush called Iraq and Saddam Hussein part of an "axis of evil" that threatened world peace. In 2002 and early 2003, Bush called for a "regime change" in Iraq and began assembling an international coalition that might support further military action in Iraq.

As already discussed, Bush was unable to convince the UN Security Council that military force was necessary in Iraq, so the United States took the initiative. In March 2003, U.S. and British forces invaded Iraq and within a month had ended Hussein's decades-old dictatorship. The coalition forces then turned to the task of assisting Iraq in recovering from the war and establishing a new government.

Bosnia.   After the end of the Cold War, Eastern Europe, a region that had been extremely stable while under Soviet domination, suddenly became an unknown quantity in U.S. policy. In Yugoslavia, a federation of six republics, the new leader— Slobodan Milosevic—attempted to replace communism with Serbian nationalism as the motivating ideology of government. As a result, four Yugoslav republics with non-Serb majorities seceded from the union in 1992. Two of these new nations— Croatia and Bosnia—contained sizable Serb-populated districts. Using the Yugoslav armed forces and, later, local Serb militias, the Serbs attempted to regain control of the Serb districts, plus additional territory. In Bosnia, the result was a four-year civil war among Serb, Croatian, and Bosnian Muslim forces.

As the front stabilized, the various parties engaged in "ethnic cleansing," or driving members of the opposing ethnic groups from their homes. Atrocities, including the murder of civilians and officially sponsored rapes, were common. Serb forces were responsible for the greater share of these, though Croatian forces also behaved badly.

In July 1995, the Muslim-inhabited, UN–sponsored "safe area" of Srebrenica was overrun by Bosnian Serbs, who killed virtually the entire male population of the zone. This was the worst war crime committed in Europe since the end of World War II.

The fall of Srebrenica spurred the Western powers toward greater efforts to end the war. In August 1995, the army of Croatia, covertly equipped by Western interests, regained full control of that country's territory and began a sweep through Serb-controlled Bosnia. Together with a Western bombing campaign, this forced the Bosnian Serbs to accept a cease-fire. Under the North Atlantic Treaty Organization (NATO), forces from the United States and European nations maintained the resulting peace and oversaw the reconstruction of Bosnia.

Kosovo. In 1998, a second major crisis broke out in former Yugoslavia. For some years, the Albanian majority in the Serb province of Kosovo had agitated for independence from what remained of Yugoslavia. In 1998, Yugoslav forces responded to the agitation by attempting to drive the entire Albanian population out of the province. Through NATO, the United States mounted a bombing campaign in 1999 that forced Yugoslav forces to leave Kosovo. NATO and Russian forces then occupied the province.

Southern Africa. During the mid-1990s and early 2000s, Africa experienced great strides toward freedom but also suffered from civil wars and other disasters. In South Africa, the first all-race elections, held in 1994, were seen as a positive and inspiring development throughout most of the world. Nelson Mandela was elected the first president under the new constitution. South Africans of all races seemed ready to support the new regime. Economic sanctions imposed by the United States and other countries had helped lead to this result.

A negative development was the spread of the disease AIDS (acquired immune deficiency syndrome). This disease infects one-fourth of the populations of Botswana and Zimbabwe and is endemic in most other nations in the southernmost part of the continent. Millions of adults are dying from AIDS, leaving orphaned children. The epidemic is taking a huge economic toll on the affected countries because of the cost of caring for patients and the loss of skilled workers. The disease may be the greatest single threat to world stability emanating from Africa. The Bush administration has announced a special aid package directed at this problem.

African Civil Wars. The year 1994 brought disaster to the African nation of Rwanda. Following the accidental death of that country's president, members of the Hutu tribe launched a campaign of genocide against the Tutsi tribe. More than half a million people were killed in a matter of weeks, with many bodies dumped in the rivers. The United Nations called for troops to assist in relief efforts but to no avail. The genocide campaign came to an abrupt end as a Tutsi guerrilla force, sponsored by neighboring Uganda, overthrew the Rwandan government. A large number of Hutus then fled from Rwanda. The United States played almost no part in this crisis until small military and civilian contingents were sent to assist the Hutu refugees.

Africa has been home to a number of what have been called "failed states"—that is, countries in which the central government has collapsed, resulting in long-running civil wars. Somalia, Sierra Leone, and Liberia are examples. In Sierra Leone, a decade of civil war came to an end in 2002 with the introduction of British peace-keeping forces. In 2003, a long-running civil war in Liberia resulted in international calls for American intervention. (Liberia was founded in the 1800s by African Americans who had returned to the continent.) By late 2003, however, the Liberian situation had stabilized without the need for U.S. peacekeeping forces.

In Angola, wars dating back as far as 1961 came to an end in 2002 with the death of rebel leader Jonas Savimbi, who had received U.S. support for several years in the 1970s. In 1996, civil war broke out in Zaire (now named Congo-Kinshasa). Rebels were aided by Rwandan and Ugandan forces, while Angolan and Zimbabwean forces entered the country to support the government. The civil war officially came to an end in 2002, and a coalition government was established in 2003. Several million deaths, primarily due to disease and malnutrition, were attributed to the war.

Who Makes Foreign Policy?

Is foreign policy made by the president, Congress, or by both acting jointly? There is no easy answer to this question, because, as constitutional authority Edwin S. Corwin once observed, the U.S. Constitution created an "invitation to struggle" between the president and Congress for control over the foreign policy process.

In October 2002, President George W. Bush signed a joint resolution from Congress authorizing the use of military force against Iraq to dismantle all of Iraq's weapons of mass destruction.

AP Photo/Ron Edmonds

Powers of the President

Article II, Section 2, of the Constitution designates the president as "Commander in Chief of the Army and Navy of the United States" and gives the president the power to make treaties, provided that two-thirds of the senators present concur. In addition to this formal treaty-making power, the president can make use of executive agreements. Since World War II, executive agreements have accounted for almost 95 percent of the understandings reached between the United States and other nations. An additional power conferred on the president in Article II, Section 2, is the right to appoint ambassadors, other public ministers, and consuls. In Section 3 of that article, the president is given the power to recognize foreign governments through receiving their ambassadors.

Other broad sources of presidential power in the U.S. foreign policy process are tradition, precedent, and the president's personality. The president can employ a host of informal techniques that give the White House overwhelming superiority within the government in foreign policy leadership.

First, the president has access to information. More information is available to the president from the Central Intelligence Agency, the State Department, and the Defense Department than to any other governmental official. This information carries with it the ability to make quick decisions—and that ability is used often. Second, the president is a legislative leader who can influence the amount of funds that are allocated for different programs. Third, the president can influence public opinion. President Theodore Roosevelt once made the following statement:

> People used to say to me that I was an astonishingly good politician and divined what the people are going to think. . . . I did not "divine" how the people were going to think; I simply made up my mind what they ought to think and then did my best to get them to think it.[2]

Presidents are without equal in influencing public opinion, partly because of their ability to command the media. Depending on their skill in appealing to patriotic sentiment (and sometimes fear), they can make people think that their course in foreign affairs is right and necessary.

Finally, the president can commit the nation morally to a course of action in foreign affairs. Because the president is the head of state and the leader of one of the most powerful nations on earth, once the president has made a commitment for the United States, it is difficult for Congress or anyone else to back down from that commitment.

Other Sources of Foreign Policymaking

There are at least four foreign policymaking sources within the executive branch, in addition to the president. These are (1) the Department of State, (2) the National Security Council, (3) the intelligence community, and (4) the Department of Defense.

The Department of State.   In principle, the State Department is the executive agency that has primary authority over foreign affairs. It supervises U.S. relations with the nearly two hundred independent nations around the world and with the

United Nations and other multinational groups, such as the Organization of American States. It staffs embassies and consulates throughout the world. It has about 32,000 employees. This number may sound impressive, but it is small compared with, say, the 67,000 employees of the Department of Health and Human Services. Also, the State Department had a total annual budget of only $10.2 billion in fiscal year 2004, one of the smallest budgets of the cabinet departments.

Newly elected presidents usually tell the American public that the new secretary of state is the nation's chief foreign policy adviser. Nonetheless, the State Department's preeminence in foreign policy has declined dramatically since World War II. The State Department's image is often poor—some see it as a slow, plodding, bureaucratic maze of inefficient, indecisive individuals.

Negative Constituents
Citizens who openly oppose government policies.

It is not surprising that the State Department has been overshadowed in foreign policy. It has no natural domestic constituency as does, for example, the Department of Defense, which can call on defense contractors for support. Instead, the State Department has what might be called **negative constituents**—U.S. citizens who openly oppose American foreign policy. One of the State Department's major functions, administering foreign aid, often elicits criticisms. There is a widespread belief that the United States spends much more on foreign aid than it actually does. In 2004, President Bush's budget request allocated $12.4 billion to foreign economic aid, or about fifty-five cents for every one hundred dollars of federal spending.

The National Security Council.

The job of the National Security Council (NSC), created by the National Security Act of 1947, is to advise the president on the integration of "domestic, foreign, and military policies relating to the national security." Its larger purpose is to provide policy continuity from one administration to the next. As it has turned out, the NSC—consisting of the president, the vice president, the secretaries of state and defense, the director of emergency planning, and often the chairperson of the joint chiefs of staff and the director of the CIA—is used in just about any way the president wants to use it.

The role of national security adviser to the president seems to adjust to fit the player. Some advisers have come into conflict with heads of the State Department. Henry Kissinger, Nixon's flamboyant and aggressive national security adviser, rapidly gained ascendancy over William Rogers, the secretary of state, in foreign policy. Although there were rumors of divisions over policy within George W. Bush's national security team, Secretary of State Colin Powell, National Security Adviser Condoleezza Rice, and Secretary of Defense Donald Rumsfeld all became important players and spokespersons for the administration.

The Intelligence Community.

Intelligence Community The government agencies that gather information about the capabilities and intentions of foreign governments or that engage in covert actions.

No discussion of foreign policy would be complete without some mention of the **intelligence community.** This consists of the forty or more government agencies or bureaus that are involved in intelligence activities, informational and otherwise. The CIA, created as part of the National Security Act of 1947, is a key official member of the intelligence community.

Intelligence activities consist mostly of overt information gathering, but covert actions also are undertaken. Covert actions, as the name implies, are done secretly, and rarely does the American public find out about them. In the late 1940s and early 1950s, the CIA covertly subsidized anti-Communist labor unions in Western Europe.

The CIA covertly aided in the overthrow of the Mossadegh regime in Iran, which allowed the restoration of the shah in 1953.

During the mid-1970s, the "dark side" of the CIA was at least partly uncovered when the Senate undertook an investigation of its activities. One of the major findings of the Senate Select Committee on Intelligence was that the CIA had routinely spied on American citizens domestically—supposedly, a strictly prohibited activity. Consequently, the CIA came under the scrutiny of oversight committees within Congress, which restricted the scope of its activity. By 1980, however, the CIA had regained much of its lost power to engage in covert activities.

By 2001, the agency had come under fire for a number of intelligence lapses, including the failure to detect the nuclear arsenals of Pakistan and India and the failure to have advance knowledge about the terrorist attack on the United States on September 11. With the rise of terrorism, the intelligence agencies have received more funding and enhanced surveillance powers, but these moves have also aroused fear that the agencies are being given too much authority to spy on citizens and legal residents of the United States.

INFOTRAC

For updates and more information on the CIA, use the term "Central Intelligence Agency" in the Subject guide.

The Department of Defense.   The Department of Defense (DOD) was created in 1947 to bring all of the various activities of the American military establishment under the jurisdiction of a single department headed by a civilian secretary of defense. At the same time, the joint chiefs of staff, consisting of the commanders of the various military branches and a chairperson, was created to formulate a unified military strategy.

Although the Department of Defense is larger than any other federal department, it declined in size after the fall of the Soviet Union in 1991. In the subsequent ten years, the total number of civilian employees was reduced by about 400,000, to about 670,000. Military personnel were also reduced in number. The defense budget has remained relatively flat in recent years, but with the advent of the war on terrorism and the use of military forces in Afghanistan and Iraq, funding is being increased again.

Congress Balances the Presidency

A new interest in the balance of power between Congress and the president on foreign policy questions developed during the Vietnam War (1964–1975). Sensitive to public frustration over the long and costly war and angry at Richard Nixon for some of his other actions as president, Congress attempted to establish limits on the power of the president in setting foreign and defense policy. In 1973, Congress passed the War Powers Resolution over President Nixon's veto. The act limited the president's use of troops in military action without congressional approval. Most presidents, however, have not interpreted the "consultation" provisions of the act as meaning that Congress should be consulted before military action is taken. Instead, Presidents Ford, Carter, Reagan, Bush, and Clinton ordered troop movements and then informed congressional leaders. Critics note that it is quite possible for a president to commit troops to a situation from which the nation could not withdraw without incurring heavy losses, whether or not Congress is consulted.

At times, Congress can take the initiative in foreign policy. In 1986, Congress initiated and passed a bill instituting economic sanctions against South Africa to pressure that nation into ending its policy of racial segregation (apartheid). President Ronald Reagan vetoed the bill, but the veto was overridden by large majorities in both the House and the Senate.

Domestic Sources of Foreign Policy

The president's power to make foreign policy may also be limited by the public. Although the sense of patriotism among Americans tends to throw public opinion behind the president, some segments of the population are more likely to debate the issues and create publicity through the media. Elites in American business, education, communications, labor, and religion try to influence presidential decision making through several strategies. The segment of the population called the **attentive public,** which probably constitutes 10 to 20 percent of all citizens, is more interested in foreign affairs than most Americans. These Americans are also likely to transmit their opinions to the less interested members of the public through conversation and local leadership.

Attentive Public That portion of the general public that pays attention to policy issues.

The **military-industrial complex,** the mutually beneficial relationship between the armed forces and defense contractors, can also exert influence on foreign policy. President Eisenhower, in his last official speech, on January 17, 1961, warned that "we must guard against the acquisition of unwarranted influence" by the military-industrial complex in the creation of foreign policy.

Military-Industrial Complex The mutually beneficial relationship between the armed forces and defense contractors.

The Pentagon has supported a large sector of our economy through defense contracts. Perhaps the Pentagon's strongest allies have been members of Congress whose districts or states benefit from the economic power of military bases or contracts. After the Cold War ended in the late 1980s, the defense industry looked abroad for new customers. Sales of some military equipment to China raised serious issues for the Clinton administration. The war on terrorism provoked a new debate about what types of weaponry would be needed to safeguard the nation in the future. When President George W. Bush proposed legislation in 2002 to increase the Defense Department's budget substantially, weapons manufacturers looked forward to increased sales and profits.

INFOTRAC

For more information on the military-industrial complex, use the term "military-industrial complex" in the Subject guide.

The Major Foreign Policy Themes

Although some observers suggest that U.S. foreign policy is inconsistent and changes with the current occupant of the White House, the long view of American diplomatic ventures reveals some major themes underlying foreign policy. In the early years of the nation, presidents and the people generally agreed that the United States should avoid foreign entanglements and concentrate instead on its own development. From the beginning of the twentieth century until today, however, a major theme has been increasing global involvement. The theme of the post–World War II years was the containment of communism. The major theme for the twenty-first century has not yet emerged. Some have suggested, however, that the theme may well be the containment of terrorism.

The Formative Years: Avoiding Entanglements

During the formative years of the United States, the new nation was operating under the Articles of Confederation. The national government had no right to levy or collect taxes, no control over commerce, no right to make commercial treaties, and no power to raise an army (the Revolutionary army was disbanded in 1783). The government's lack of international power was made clear when Barbary pirates seized American hostages in the Mediterranean. The United States was unable to rescue the hostages and ignominiously had to purchase them in a treaty with Morocco.

The founders of this nation had a basic mistrust of European governments. George Washington said it was the U.S. policy "to steer clear of permanent alliances," and Thomas Jefferson echoed this sentiment when he said America wanted peace with all nations but "entangling alliances with none." This was also a logical position at a time when the United States was so weak militarily that it could not influence European development directly. Moreover, being protected by oceans that took weeks to traverse certainly allowed the nation to avoid entangling alliances. During the 1700s and 1800s, the United States generally stayed out of European conflicts and politics.

The Monroe Doctrine.   President James Monroe, in his message to Congress on December 2, 1823, stated that this country would not accept foreign intervention in the Western Hemisphere. In return, the United States would not meddle in European affairs. The **Monroe Doctrine** was the underpinning of the U.S. **isolationist foreign policy** toward Europe, which continued throughout the 1800s.

In this hemisphere, however, the United States pursued an actively expansionist policy. The nation purchased Louisiana in 1803, annexed Texas in 1845, gained substantial territory from Mexico in 1848, purchased Alaska in 1867, and annexed Hawaii in 1898.

The Spanish-American War and World War I.   The end of the isolationist policy started with the Spanish-American War in 1898. Winning the war gave the United States possession of Guam, Puerto Rico, and the Philippines (which gained independence in 1946). On the heels of that war came World War I (1914–1918). The United States declared war on Germany on April 6, 1917, because that country refused to give up its campaign of sinking all ships headed for Britain, including passenger ships. (Large passenger ships of that time commonly held over a thousand people, so the sinking of such a ship was a disaster comparable to the attack on the World Trade Center.) In the 1920s, the United States went "back to normalcy," as President Warren G. Harding urged it to do. U.S. military forces were largely disbanded, defense spending dropped to about 1 percent of total annual national income, and the nation returned to a period of isolationism.

The Era of Internationalism

Isolationism was permanently shattered by the bombing of the U.S. naval base at Pearl Harbor, Hawaii, on December 7, 1941. The surprise attack by the Japanese

Monroe Doctrine A policy statement by President James Monroe in 1823: (1) European nations should not establish new colonies in the Western Hemisphere, (2) European nations should not intervene in the affairs of independent nations of the Western Hemisphere, and (3) the United States would not interfere in the affairs of European nations.

Isolationist Foreign Policy A nation's policy of abstaining from an active role in international affairs or alliances.

A lone U.S. soldier walks in a trench in France during World War I. Under President Woodrow Wilson, the United States entered the war on April 6, 1917. More than eight million soldiers and an even larger number of civilians died before the war ended on Armistice Day, November 11, 1918.

National Archives photo

INFOTRAC

For more information on the Cold War, use the term "Cold War" in the Subject guide.

Soviet Bloc The Eastern European countries that installed Communist regimes after World War II.

Iron Curtain The term used to describe the division of Europe between the Soviet Union and the West; popularized by Winston Churchill.

caused the deaths of 2,403 American servicemen and the wounding of 1,143 others. Eighteen warships were sunk or seriously damaged, and 188 planes were destroyed at the airfields. President Franklin Roosevelt asked Congress to declare war on Japan immediately, and the United States entered World War II.

The United States was the only major participating country to emerge from World War II with its economy intact, and even strengthened. The Soviet Union, Japan, Italy, France, Germany, Britain, and a number of minor participants in the war were all economically devastated. The United States was also the only country to have control over operational nuclear weapons. President Harry Truman had personally made the decision to use two atomic bombs, on August 6 and August 9, 1945, to end the war with Japan. (Historians still argue over the necessity of this action, which ultimately killed more than 100,000 Japanese civilians and left an equal number permanently injured.) The United States truly had become the world's superpower.

The Cold War.   The United States had become an uncomfortable ally of the Soviet Union after Adolf Hitler's invasion of Soviet territory. Soon after World War II ended, relations between the Soviet Union and the West deteriorated. The Soviet Union wanted a weakened Germany, and to achieve this, it insisted that the country be divided in two, with East Germany becoming a buffer against the West. Little by little, the Soviet Union helped to install Communist governments in Eastern European countries, which began to be referred to collectively as the **Soviet bloc.** In response, the United States encouraged the rearming of Western Europe. The Cold War had begun.[3]

In Fulton, Missouri, on March 5, 1946, Winston Churchill, in a striking metaphor, declared that from the Baltic to the Adriatic Sea "an iron curtain has descended across the [European] continent." The term **iron curtain** became even more appropriate when Soviet-dominated East Germany built a wall separating East Berlin from West Berlin in August 1961.

CORBIS/Bettmann

British Prime Minister Winston Churchill, U.S. President Franklin Roosevelt, and Soviet leader Joseph Stalin met at Yalta from February 4 to 11, 1945, to resolve their differences over the shape that the international community would take after World War II.

Containment Policy. In 1947, a remarkable article was published in *Foreign Affairs*. The article was signed by "X." The actual author was George F. Kennan, chief of the policy-planning staff for the State Department. The doctrine of **containment** set forth in the article became—according to many—the Bible of Western foreign policy. "X" argued that whenever and wherever the Soviet Union could successfully challenge the West, it would do so. He recommended that our policy toward the Soviet Union be "firm and vigilant containment of Russian expansive tendencies."[4]

The containment theory was expressed clearly in the **Truman Doctrine,** which was enunciated by President Harry Truman in his historic address to Congress on March 12, 1947. In that address, he announced that the United States must help countries in which a Communist takeover seemed likely. Later that year, he backed the Marshall Plan, an economic assistance plan for Europe that was intended to prevent the expansion of Communist influence there. By 1950, the United States had entered into a military alliance with the European nations called the North Atlantic Treaty Organization, or NATO. The combined military power of the United States and the European nations worked to contain Soviet influence to Eastern Europe and to maintain a credible threat to any Soviet military attack on Western Europe.

Containment A U.S. diplomatic policy adopted by the Truman administration to contain Communist power within its existing boundaries.

Truman Doctrine The policy adopted by President Harry Truman in 1947 to halt Communist expansion in southeastern Europe.

INFOTRAC

For more information on George F. Kennan, use the term "George Kennan" in the Subject guide.

Superpower Relations

During the Cold War, there was never any direct military confrontation between the United States and the Soviet Union. Rather, confrontations among "client" nations were used to carry out the policies of the superpowers. Only on occasion did the United States directly enter a conflict in a significant way. Two such occasions were in Korea and Vietnam.

After the end of World War II, northern Korea was occupied by the Soviet Union, and southern Korea was occupied by the United States. The result was two rival Korean governments. In 1950, North Korea invaded South Korea. The United States entered the war, which prevented an almost certain South Korean defeat. When U.S. forces were on the brink of conquering North Korea, however, China joined the war on the side of the north, resulting in a stalemate. An armistice signed in 1953 led to the two Koreas that exist today. U.S. forces have remained in South Korea ever since.

The Vietnam War (1964–1975) also involved the United States in a civil war between a Communist North and pro-Western South. U.S. military support of the South Vietnamese government escalated under Presidents Kennedy and Johnson. American forces in Vietnam at the height of the U.S. involvement totaled more than 500,000 troops. A peace agreement in 1973 allowed U.S. troops to leave the country, and in 1975 North Vietnam easily occupied Saigon and unified the nation. The debate over U.S. involvement in Vietnam became extremely heated and, as mentioned previously, spurred congressional efforts to limit the ability of the president to commit forces to armed combat.

The Cuban Missile Crisis. Perhaps the closest the two superpowers ever came to a nuclear confrontation was the Cuban missile crisis in 1962. The Soviets placed missiles in Cuba, ninety miles off the U.S. coast, in response to Cuban fears of an American invasion and to try to balance an American nuclear advantage. President Kennedy and his advisers rejected the option of armed intervention, setting up a naval blockade around the island instead. When Soviet vessels appeared near Cuban waters, the tension reached its height. After intense negotiations between Washington and Moscow, the Soviet ships turned around on October 25, and on October 28 the Soviet Union announced the withdrawal of its missile operations from Cuba. In exchange, the United States agreed not to invade Cuba and to remove some of its own missiles that were located near the Soviet border in Turkey.

A Period of Détente. The French word **détente** means a relaxation of tensions. By the end of the 1960s, it was clear that some efforts had to be made to reduce the threat of nuclear war between the United States and the Soviet Union. Each nation had acquired the military capacity to destroy the other with nuclear weapons.

As the result of lengthy negotiations, the United States and the Soviet Union signed the **Strategic Arms Limitation Treaty (SALT I)** in May 1972. That treaty "permanently" limited the development and deployment of antiballistic missiles (ABMs), and it limited the number of offensive missiles each country could deploy.

The policy of détente was not limited to the U.S. relationship with the Soviet Union. President Nixon visited the People's Republic of China in 1972 and set the stage for the formal diplomatic recognition of that country, which occurred during the Carter administration (1977–1981).

Détente A French word meaning a relaxation of tensions. The term characterizes U.S.–Soviet policy as it developed under President Richard Nixon.

Strategic Arms Limitation Treaty (SALT I) A treaty between the United States and the Soviet Union to stabilize the nuclear arms competition between the two countries.

President Bush met with Russian President Vladimir Putin on November 13, 2001, to discuss, among other things, reducing nuclear weapons stockpiles in the two countries. Why might such reductions have become easier after the collapse of the Soviet Union?

AP Photo/Ron Edmonds

The Reagan-Bush Years. President Ronald Reagan took a hard line against the Soviet Union during his first term, proposing the strategic defense initiative (SDI), or "Star Wars," in 1983. SDI was designed to serve as a space-based defense against enemy missiles. In November 1985, however, President Reagan and Mikhail Gorbachev, the Soviet leader, began to work on an arms reduction agreement. In 1987, the negotiations resulted in the Intermediate-Range Nuclear Force (INF) Treaty, which required the superpowers to dismantle a total of four thousand intermediate-range missiles within the first three years of the agreement.

The Dissolution of the Soviet Union. The end of the Cold War and the dissolution of the Soviet Union by 1991 brought sweeping changes in world politics and challenged U.S. foreign policy in ways that were unimaginable only a few years before. In August 1991, a military coup to overthrow Gorbachev and reverse his political changes was thwarted. Boris Yeltsin declared Russia an independent state, and the remaining former Soviet republics soon followed suit.

American strategists worried as much about who now controlled the Soviet nuclear arsenal as about completing arms treaty negotiations. In 1992, the United States signed the Strategic Arms Reduction Treaty (START) with four former Soviet republics—Russia, Ukraine, Belarus, and Kazakhstan—to reduce the number of long-range nuclear weapons.

President George W. Bush changed directions in 2001, announcing that the United States was withdrawing from the 1972 ABM treaty. Six months later, however, Bush and Russian President Vladimir Putin signed an agreement greatly reducing the number of nuclear weapons on each side over the next few years. As the United States launched its war on terrorism, Putin stood by Bush's side as an ally. Nonetheless, Russia objected to the use of military forces in Iraq in early 2003, believing that a war against Iraq was unjustified.

MAKING A DIFFERENCE : Working for Human Rights

In many countries throughout the world, human rights are not protected. In some nations, people are imprisoned, tortured, or killed because they oppose the regime. In other nations, ethnic or racial groups are oppressed by the majority population. In nations such as Somalia, where civil war caused starvation among millions of people, international efforts to send food relief to refugee camps were hampered by the fighting among rival factions.

JOINING AN ORGANIZATION

What can you do to work for the improvement of human rights in other nations? One way is to join an organization that attempts to keep watch over human rights violations. (Two such organizations are listed at the end of this feature.) By publicizing human rights violations, such organizations try to pressure nations into changing their tactics. Sometimes, these organizations are able to apply

enough pressure and cause enough embarrassment that victims may be freed from prison or allowed to emigrate.

KEEPING INFORMED

Another way to work for human rights is to keep informed about the state of affairs in other nations and to write personally to governments that violate human rights or to their embassies, asking them to cease these violations. Again, the organizations listed at the end of the feature have publications to keep you aware of developments in other nations.

If you want to receive general information about the position of the United States on human rights violations, you can contact the State Department:

> U.S. Department of State
> Bureau of Democracy,
>   Human Rights, and Labor
> 2201 C St. N.W.

Washington, DC 20520
202-647-4000
http://www.state.gov/g/drl/hr

You can also contact the United Nations:

United Nations
777 United Nations Plaza
New York, NY 10017
212-963-1234
http://www.un.org

The following organizations are well known for their watchdog efforts in countries that violate human rights for political reasons:

Amnesty International U.S.A.
322 Eighth Ave., Fl. 10
New York, NY 10001
212-807-8400
http://www.amnestyusa.org

American Friends Service
   Committee
1501 Cherry St.
Philadelphia, PA 19102
215-241-7000
http://www.afsc.org

KEY TERMS

attentive public **344**

Cold War **334**

containment **347**

defense policy **328**

détente **348**

diplomacy **328**

economic aid **328**

foreign policy **328**

foreign policy process **328**

CHAPTER SUMMARY

1 Foreign policy includes national goals and the techniques used to achieve them. National security policy, which is one aspect of foreign policy, is designed to protect the independence and the political and economic integrity of the United States. Diplomacy involves the nation's external relationships and is an attempt to resolve conflict without resort to arms. U.S. foreign policy is sometimes based on moral idealism and sometimes based on political realism.

2 Terrorism has become a major challenge facing the United States and other nations. The United States waged war on terrorism after the September 11 attacks. U.S. armed forces occupied Afghanistan in 2001 as part of the military response to terrorism and occupied Iraq in 2003.

3 Nuclear proliferation continues to be an issue due to the breakup of the Soviet Union and the loss of control over its nuclear arsenal, along with the continued efforts of other nations to gain nuclear warheads. The number of warheads is known to be more than 32,000.

4 Ethnic tensions and political instability in many regions of the world provide challenges to the United States. Negotiations have brought agreement in South Africa, but civil wars have torn apart Rwanda, Yugoslavia, and other countries. The Middle East continues to be a hotbed of conflict despite efforts to continue the peace process. In 1991 and again in 2003, the United States sent combat troops to Iraq. The second Gulf War, in 2003, succeeded in toppling the decades-long dictatorship in Iraq.

5 The formal power of the president to make foreign policy derives from the U.S. Constitution, which designates the president as commander in chief of the army and navy. Presidents have interpreted this authority broadly. They also have the power to make treaties and executive agreements. In principle, the State Department is the executive agency with primary authority over foreign affairs. The National Security Council also plays a major role. The intelligence community consists of government agencies engaged in activities varying from information gathering to covert actions. In response to presidential actions in the Vietnam War, Congress attempted to establish some limits on the power of the president to intervene abroad by passing the War Powers Resolution in 1973.

6 Three major themes have guided U.S. foreign policy. In the early years of the nation, isolationism was the primary focus. With the start of the twentieth century, this view gave way to global involvement. From the end of World War II through the 1980s, the major goal was to contain communism and the influence of the Soviet Union.

7 During the 1700s and 1800s, the United States had little international power and generally stayed out of European conflicts and politics. The 1800s have been called the period of isolationism. The Monroe Doctrine of 1823 stated that the United States would not accept foreign intervention in the Western Hemisphere and would not meddle in European affairs. The United States pursued an actively expansionist policy in the Americas and the Pacific area, however.

8 The end of the policy of isolationism toward Europe started with the Spanish-American War of 1898. U.S. involvement in European politics became more extensive when the United States entered World War I on April 6, 1917. World War II marked a lasting change in American foreign policy. The United States was the only major country to emerge from the war with its economy intact and the only country with operating nuclear weapons.

9 Soon after the close of World War II, the uncomfortable alliance between the United States and the Soviet Union ended, and the Cold War began. A policy of containment, which assumed an expansionist Soviet Union, was enunciated in the Truman Doctrine. Following the frustrations of the Vietnam War and the apparent arms equality of the United States and the Soviet Union, the United States adopted a policy of détente. Although President Reagan took a tough stance toward the Soviet Union during his first term, his second term saw serious negotiations toward arms reduction, culminating in the signing of the Intermediate-Range Nuclear Force Treaty in 1987. After the fall of the Soviet Union, Russia emerged as a less threatening state and signed the Strategic Arms Reduction Treaty with the United States in 1992. The United States and Russia have agreed on some issues in recent years, such as the fight against terrorism, but have disagreed on other matters, such as the war against Iraq in 2003.

SELECTED PRINT AND MEDIA RESOURCES

Suggested Readings

Hoge, James F., Jr., and Gideon Rose. *How Did This Happen? Terrorism and the New War.* New York: Public Affairs, 2001. Compiled after the September 11 attacks, this book of essays discusses the causes of terrorism and the foreign policy and defense initiatives that must be taken to confront it.

Lewis, Bernard. *What Went Wrong? Western Impact and Middle Eastern Response.* Oxford: Oxford University Press, 2002. Lewis, an outstanding scholar of the Middle East, provides a brief history of how the West and the Middle East have taken different paths in the last few centuries and how those choices bring them into conflict.

Nye, Joseph S., Jr. *The Paradox of American Power: Why the World's Only Superpower Can't Go It Alone.* New York: Oxford University Press, 2002. Former assistant secretary of defense and now dean of Harvard's Kennedy School of Government, Joseph Nye stresses the importance of U.S. cooperation with the international community and indicates why the United States cannot "go it alone" in today's world arena.

Rashid, Ahmed. *Taliban: Militant Islam, Oil, and Fundamentalism in Central Asia.* New Haven, Conn.: Yale University Press, 2001. Written by a reporter who spent twenty-one years in Afghanistan, this book examines the causes of Islamic radicalism and of the anger against the United States expressed by the Taliban when that government was in power.

Media Resources

The Aftermath: A Visit to Postwar Iraq—A 2003 program that features interviews with Iraqi clerics, businessmen, scholars, and street protestors, and also with U.S. soldiers and their commanders.

Black Hawk Down—This 2002 film recounts the events in Mogadishu, Somalia, in October 1993, during which two U.S. Black Hawk helicopters were shot down. The film, which is based on reporter Mark Bowden's best-selling book by the same name, contains graphic scenes of terrifying urban warfare.

The Fall of Milosevic—A highly acclaimed 2003 documentary by Norma Percy and Brian Lapping. This film covers the final years of the crisis in former Yugoslavia, including the war in Kosovo and the fall of Slobodan Milosevic, Serb nationalist leader and alleged war criminal. Except for Milosevic himself, almost all top Serb and Albanian leaders are interviewed, as are President Bill Clinton and British Prime Minister Tony Blair.

The 50 Years War—Israel and the Arabs—A two-volume PBS Home Video released in 2000. More balanced than some accounts, this film includes interviews with many leaders involved in the struggle, including:

from Israel, Yitzhak Rabin, Shimon Peres, Benjamin Netanyahu, and Ariel Sharon; from the Arab world, Egypt's Anwar al-Sadat, Jordan's King Hussein, and Yasir Arafat; and from the United States, presidents Jimmy Carter, George H. W. Bush, and Bill Clinton.

Osama bin Laden: In the Name of Allah—A 2001 biography of the leader responsible for the terrorist attacks of September 11, 2001.

LOGGING ON

Our government and the governments of other nations maintain hundreds of Web sites on foreign and defense policy. If you are interested in information about visas, passports, and individual countries, you can access the site maintained by the Department of State at http://www.state.gov.

For information about human rights, national security, and other issues from a European point of view, check the Web site maintained by the Swiss government, the International Relations and Security Network, at http://www.fsk.ethz.ch.

The Brookings Institution, a Washington, D.C., think tank, provides access to its research reports at the following Web site: http://www.brook.edu.

The Global Affairs Agenda, an interest group that promotes a progressive or liberal foreign policy, provides information about many topics at http://www.foreignpolicy-infocus.org.

For information about the intelligence community and about foreign countries, go to the Web site of the Central Intelligence Agency at http://www.cia.gov.

Freedom House, an organization that promotes its vision of democracy around the world, rates all nations on their democratic practices at http://www.freedomhouse.org.

USING THE INTERNET FOR POLITICAL ANALYSIS

Go to this text's Web site at http://politicalscience.wadsworth.com/schmidtbrief2004. Select "Chapter 14" in the box at the top of the window. Then, in the column on the left-hand side of the window, under "Chapter Resources," click on "Internet Exercises." The Web site will then display the following Internet exercises that you can perform to learn more about topics covered in this chapter.

Activity 14–1: **Land Mines**
Activity 14–2: **The United Nations**
Activity 14–2: **The World Trade Organization**

ONLINE STUDY GUIDE AND ADDITIONAL RESOURCES

At http://politicalscience.wadsworth.com/schmidtbrief2004 you will find a free Study Guide to this book and a wealth of other material. For Chapter 14, you will also find in the American Government Resource Center:

- **InfoTrac® Reader**—International relations; September 11 and American foreign policy.

- **You Are There Simulation**—Foreign policy.

- **Participation Activities**—Visit several Web sites of interest groups that focus on foreign policy issues that

concern you; research a specific foreign policy issue currently discussed in Congress.

- **MicroCase Exercise**—Foreign policy.

- **Related Links**—Foreign policy.

- **Source Readings**—By presidents George Washington and Lyndon Johnson, plus the *Tonkin Gulf Resolution*.

Notes

Chapter 1
The Foundations of American Government

1. James Madison, in Alexander Hamilton, James Madison, and John Jay, *The Federalist Papers*, No. 10. See Appendix C, page 382.

2. Alexander Hamilton, "Speech on the Constitutional Convention on a Plan of Government," in *Selected Writings and Speeches of Alexander Hamilton*, ed. Morton J. Frisch (Washington, D.C.: American Enterprise Institute, 1985), p. 108.

3. Michael Parenti, *Democracy for the Few*, 7th ed. (New York: St. Martin's Press, 1995).

4. *Roe v. Wade*, 410 U.S. 113 (1973).

5. *Lawrence v. Texas*, 123 S.Ct. 2472 (2003).

6. Richard J. Ellis, "Rival Visions of Equality in American Political Culture," *Review of Politics*, Vol. 54 (Spring 1992), p. 254.

Chapter 2
Forging a New Government: The Constitution

1. John Camp, *Out of the Wilderness: The Emergence of an American Identity in Colonial New England* (Middleton, Conn.: Wesleyan University Press, 1990).

2. See Morison's "The Mayflower Compact" in Daniel J. Boorstin, ed., *An American Primer* (Chicago: University of Chicago Press, 1966), p. 18.

3. *The Political Writings of Thomas Paine*, Vol. 1 (Boston: J. P. Mendum Investigator Office, 1870), p. 46.

4. Not all scholars believe that Jefferson was truly influenced by Locke. For example, Jay Fliegelman states that "Jefferson's fascination with Homer, Ossian, Patrick Henry, and the violin is of greater significance than his indebtedness to Locke." Jay Fliegelman, *Declaring Independence: Jefferson, Natural Language, and the Culture of Performance* (Stanford, Calif.: Stanford University Press, 1993).

5. The State House was later named Independence Hall. This was the same room in which the Declaration of Independence had been signed eleven years earlier.

6. There is some irony here. At the Constitutional Convention, those opposed to a strong central government pushed for a federal system because such a system would allow the states to retain some of their sovereign rights (see Chapter 3). The label *Anti-Federalists* thus contradicted their essential views.

7. Some scholars believe that *The Federalist Papers* played only a minor role in securing ratification of the Constitution. Even if this is true, they still have lasting value as an authoritative explanation of the Constitution.

8. Of particular interest is the view of the Anti-Federalist position contained in Herbert J. Storing, *What the Anti-Federalists Were For* (Chicago: University of Chicago Press, 1981). Storing also edited seven volumes of the Anti-Federalist writings, *The Complete Anti-Federalist* (Chicago: University of Chicago Press, 1981). See also Josephine F. Pacheco, *Antifederalism: The Legacy of George Mason* (Fairfax, Va.: George Mason University Press, 1992).

9. 5 U.S. 137 (1803). See Chapter 12 for a further discussion of the *Marbury v. Madison* case.

10. *Brown v. Board of Education of Topeka*, 347 U.S. 483 (1954).

Chapter 3
Federalism

1. Recent legislation has altered somewhat the unitary character of the French political system. In Britain, the unitary nature of the government has been modified by the creation of the Scottish Parliament.

2. *New State Ice Co. v. Liebmann*, 285 U.S. 262 (1932).

3. Text of the address by the president to the National Conference of State Legislatures, Atlanta, Georgia (Washington, D.C.: The White House, Office of the Press Secretary, July 30, 1981), as quoted in Edward Millican, *One United People: The Federalist Papers and the National Idea* (Lexington, Ky.: The University Press of Kentucky, 1990).

4. 4 Wheaton 316 (1819).

5. An excellent example of this is President Dwight Eisenhower's disciplining of Arkansas governor Orval Faubus in 1957 by federalizing the National Guard to enforce the court-ordered desegregation of Little Rock High School.

6. 4 Wheaton 316 (1819).

7. 9 Wheaton 1 (1824).

8. The future of the national government's powerful role was cemented with the passage of the Sixteenth Amendment (ratified in 1913), which authorized the federal income tax.

9. *Hammer v. Dagenhart*, 247 U.S. 251 (1918). This decision was overruled in *United States v. Darby*, 312 U.S. 100 (1940).

10. 514 U.S. 549 (1995).

11. 529 U.S. 598 (2000).

12. 527 U.S. 706 (1999).

13. 528 U.S. 62 (2000).

14. 123 S.Ct. 1972 (2003).

15. 521 U.S. 898 (1997).

Chapter 4
Civil Liberties

1. 7 Peters 243 (1833).

2. 268 U.S. 652 (1925).

3. *Everson v. Board of Education*, 330 U.S. 1 (1947).

4. 403 U.S. 602 (1971).

5. 473 U.S. 402 (1985).

6. 521 U.S. 203 (1997).

7. 370 U.S. 421 (1962).

8. 472 U.S. 38 (1985).

9. 505 U.S. 577 (1992).

10. *Doe v. Santa Fe Independent School District*, 168 F.3d 806 (5th Cir. 1999).

11. *Santa Fe Independent School District v. Doe*, 530 U.S. 290 (2000).

12. 393 U.S. 97 (1968).

13. 482 U.S. 578 (1987).

14. *Freiler v. Tangipahoa Parish Board of Education*, 201 F.3d 602 (5th Cir. 2000).

15. 515 U.S. 819 (1995).

16. 494 U.S. 872 (1990).

17. 521 U.S. 507 (1997).

18. 403 U.S. 713 (1971).

19. *Aguilar v. Avis Rent A Car System*, 21 Cal.4th 121 (1999).

20. 393 U.S. 503 (1969).

21. 488 U.S. 884 (1989).

22. *United States v. Eichman*, 496 U.S. 310 (1990).

23. *Virginia v. Black*, 123 S.Ct. 1536 (2003).

24. *Virginia State Board of Pharmacy v. Virginia Citizens Consumer Council, Inc.*, 425 U.S. 748 (1976).

25. 119 Cal.Rptr.2d 296 (2002).

26. *Schenck v. United States*, 249 U.S. 47 (1919).

27. 268 U.S. 652 (1925).

28. 395 U.S. 444 (1969).

29. 378 U.S. 184 (1964).

30. 413 U.S. 5 (1973).

31. 495 U.S. 103 (1990).

32. *Doe v. University of Michigan*, 721 F.Supp. 852 (1989).

33. Shannon P. Duffy, "Right to a 'Redneck' T-Shirt," *The National Law Journal*, October 14, 2002, p. A4.

34. 376 U.S. 254 (1964).

35. 427 U.S. 539 (1976).

36. 443 U.S. 368 (1979).

37. *Smith v. Collin*, 439 U.S. 916 (1978).

38. 381 U.S. 479 (1965).

39. 410 U.S. 113 (1973). Jane Roe was not the real name of the woman in this case. It is a common legal pseudonym used to protect a person's privacy.

40. 492 U.S. 490 (1989).

41. 505 U.S. 833 (1992).

42. *Schenck v. ProChoice Network*, 519 U.S. 357 (1997).

43. *Stenberg v. Carhart*, 530 U.S. 914 (2000).

44. *In re Quinlan*, 70 N.J. 10 (1976).

45. 521 U.S. 702 (1997).

46. 372 U.S. 335 (1963).

47. 316 U.S. 455 (1942).

48. 384 U.S. 436 (1966).

49. *Dickerson v. United States*, 530 U.S. 428 (2000).

50. *Arizona v. Fulminante*, 499 U.S. 279 (1991).

51. *Davis v. United States*, 512 U.S. 452 (1994).

52. 367 U.S. 643 (1961).

53. *Nix v. Williams*, 467 U.S. 431 (1984).

54. *Massachusetts v. Sheppard*, 468 U.S. 981 (1984).

Chapter 5
Civil Rights

1. 19 Howard 393 (1857).

2. 109 U.S. 3 (1883).

3. *Plessy v. Ferguson*, 163 U.S. 537 (1896).

4. 321 U.S. 649 (1944).

5. 347 U.S. 483 (1954).

6. 349 U.S. 294 (1955).

7. *Belk v. Charlotte-Mecklenburg Board of Education*, 269 F.3d 305 (4th Cir. 2001).

8. *Dothard v. Rawlinson*, 433 U.S. 321 (1977).

9. *Arizona v. Norris*, 463 U.S. 1073 (1983).

10. *United States v. Virginia*, 518 U.S. 515 (1996).

11. 438 U.S. 265 (1978).

12. 515 U.S. 200 (1995).

13. 84 F.3d 720 (5th Cir. 1996).

14. *Gratz v. Bollinger*, 123 S.Ct. 2411 (2003).

15. *Grutter v. Bollinger*, 123 S.Ct. 2325 (2003).

16. 414 U.S. 563 (1974).

17. *O'Connor v. Consolidated Coil Caterers Corp.*, 517 U.S. 308 (1996).

18. 527 U.S. 471 (1999).

19. *Toyota Manufacturing, Kentucky, Inc. v. Williams*, 534 U.S. 184 (2002).

20. *Boy Scouts of America v. Dale*, 530 U.S. 640 (2000).

21. 478 U.S. 186 (1986).

22. *Lawrence v. Texas*, 123 S.Ct. 2472 (2003).

23. California, Connecticut, Hawaii, Maryland, Massachusetts, Minnesota, Nevada, New Hampshire, New Jersey, Rhode Island, Vermont, and Wisconsin. Maine also had a law protecting gay and lesbian rights until February 1998, when the law was repealed in a referendum.

24. 517 U.S. 620 (1996).

Chapter 6
Public Opinion, Political Socialization, and the Media

1. See the discussion of the media's influence on politics in Richard Davis and Diana Owens, *New Media and American Politics* (New York: Oxford University Press, 1998).

2. Barbara A. Bardes and Robert W. Oldendick, *Public Opinion: Measuring the American Mind*, 2d ed. (Belmont, Calif.: Wadsworth Publishing Co., 2003), p. 73.

3. *The Press and Foreign Policy* (Princeton, N.J.: Princeton University Press, 1963), p. 81.

4. See Doris A. Graber, *Mass Media and American Politics*, 6th ed. (Chicago: University of Chicago Press, 2001).

5. From a letter to W. T. Barry, August 4, 1822. See Philip R. Fendall ed., *Letters and Other Writings of James Madison Published by Order of Congress* (Philadelphia: Lippincott, 1865), Vol. III, p. 276.

6. As quoted in Kathleen Hall Jamieson, *Packaging the Presidency: A History and Criticism of Presidential Campaign Advertising*, 3d ed. (New York: Oxford

University Press, 1996), p. 200.

7. Doris Graber, *Mass Media and American Politics*, 5th ed. (Washington, D.C.: Congressional Quarterly Press, 1997), p. 59.

Chapter 7
Interest Groups and Political Parties

1. Alexis de Tocqueville, *Democracy in America*, Vol. 1, edited by Phillips Bradley (New York: Knopf, 1980), p. 191.

2. The Agricultural Adjustment Act of 1933 (declared unconstitutional) was replaced by the 1937 Agricultural Adjustment Act and later changed and amended several times.

3. Kay Lehman Schlozman and John T. Tierney, *Organized Interests and American Democracy* (New York: Harper & Row, 1986), p. 293.

4. Federal Election Commission, 2003.

5. Charles S. Mack, *Business, Politics, and the Practice of Government Relations* (Westport, Conn.: Quorum Books, 1997), p. 226.

6. Gerald M. Pomper and Susan S. Lederman, *Elections in America: Control and Influence in Democratic Politics*, 2d ed. (New York: Longman, 1980).

7. *Rutan v. Republican Party of Illinois*, 497 U.S. 62 (1990).

8. The term *third party* is erroneous, because sometimes there have been third, fourth, fifth, and even sixth parties, and so on. Because it has endured, however, we will use the term here.

Chapter 8
Campaigns, Elections, and Voting Behavior

1. Technically, a presidential and vice presidential candidate can be from the same state, but if they are, one of the two must forfeit the electoral votes of their home state.

2. A number of early presidents were Unitarian. The Unitarian Church is not Protestant, but it is historically rooted in the Protestant tradition.

3. Louise Overacker, *Money in Elections* (New York: Macmillan, 1932), p. vii.

4. 424 U.S. 1 (1976).

5. Paul Allen Beck, *Party Politics in America*, 8th ed. (New York: Longman Publishers, 1997), pp. 293–294.

6. 494 U.S. 652 (1990).

7. *Colorado Republican Federal Campaign Committee v. Federal Election Commission*, 518 U.S. 604 (1996).

8. *California Democratic Party v. Jones*, 530 U.S. 567 (2000).

9. In Maine and Nebraska, electoral votes are based on congressional districts. Each district chooses one elector. The remaining two electors are chosen statewide.

10. Note, however, that there have been revolts by so-called faithless electors in 1796, 1820, 1948, 1956, 1960, 1968, 1972, 1976, 1988, and 2000.

11. Norman Ornstein, "Vote-by-Mail: Is It Good for Democracy?" *Campaigns and Elections*, May 1996, p. 47.

12. Larry J. Sabato and Glenn R. Simpson, *Dirty Little Secrets: The Persistence of Corruption in American Politics* (New York: Random House, 1996).

13. Thomas Paine, *Common Sense* (London: H. D. Symonds, 1792), p. 28.

14. Thomas B. Edsall, "Voters Thinking Less with Their Wallets," *International Herald Tribune*, March 27, 2001, p. 3.

15. Ronald Brownstein, "Attendance, Not Affiliation, Key to Religious Voters," *The Los Angeles Times*, July 16, 2001, p. A10.

16. Lena Edlund and Rohini Pande, "Why Have Women Become Left-Wing? The Political Gender Gap and the Decline in Marriage," *The Quarterly Journal of Economics*, Vol. 117, Issue 3 (August 2002), p. 917.

Chapter 9
The Congress

1. Morris P. Fiorina, *Congress: Keystone of the Washington Establishment*, 2d ed. (New Haven, Conn.: Yale University Press, 1989), pp. 44, 47.

2. 369 U.S. 186 (1962). The term *justiciable* is pronounced juhs-*tish*-a-buhl.

3. 376 U.S. 1 (1964).

4. 478 U.S. 109 (1986).

5. *Easley v. Cromartie*, 532 U.S. 234 (2001).

6. The term *little legislatures* is from Woodrow Wilson, *Congressional Government* (New York: Meridian Books, 1956 [first published in 1885]).

7. Congressional Quarterly, Inc., *Guide to Congress*, 5th ed. (Washington, D.C.: CQ Press, 2000); and authors' update.

8. *Congressional Directory* (Washington, D.C.: U.S. Government Printing Office, various editions).

Chapter 10
The Presidency

1. Forrest McDonald, *The American Presidency: An Intellectual History* (Lawrence: University Press of Kansas, 1994), p. 179.

2. George Romney was governor of Michigan from 1963 to 1969. Romney was not nominated, and the issue remains unresolved.

3. *Meyers v. United States*, 272 U.S. 52 (1926).

4. Quoted in Richard E. Neustadt, *Presidential Power: The Politics of Leadership* (New York: Wiley, 1960), p. 9. Truman may not have considered the amount of politics involved in decision making in the upper reaches of the army.

5. *Ex parte Grossman*, 267 U.S. 87 (1925).

6. The Case Act of 1972 requires that an executive agreement be transmitted to Congress within sixty days after the agreement takes effect. Secret agreements are transmitted to the foreign relations committees as classified information.

7. *Veto* in Latin means "I forbid."

8. *Clinton v. City of New York*, 524 U.S. 417 (1998).

9. Samuel Kernell, *Going Public: New Strategies of Presidential Leadership*, 3d ed. (Washington, D.C.: Congressional Quarterly Press, 1997).

10. *Home Building and Loan Association v. Blaisdell*, 290 U.S. 398 (1934).

11. 299 U.S. 304 (1936).

12. *Youngstown Sheet and Tube Co. v. Sawyer*, 343 U.S. 579 (1952).

13. 318 U.S. 683 (1974).

Chapter 11
The Bureaucracy

1. Max Weber, *Theory of Social and Economic Organization*, ed. Talcott Parsons (1947; repr., Glencoe, Ill.: Free Press, 1997).

2. Leonard D. White, *The Federalists: A Study in Administrative History, 1789–1801* (New York: Free Press, 1948).

3. See, for example, Paul C. Light, *The True Size of Government* (Washington, D.C.: Brookings Institution Press, 1999).

4. 427 U.S. 347 (1976).

5. 445 U.S. 507 (1980).

6. 497 U.S. 62 (1990).

7. *United States Civil Service Commission v. National Association of Letter Carriers*, 413 U.S. 548 (1973).

8. See, for example, David Osborne and Ted Gaebler, *Reinventing Government: How the Entrepreneurial Spirit Is Transforming the Public Sector* (Reading, Mass.: Addison-Wesley, 1992); and David Osborne and Peter Plastrik, *Banishing Bureaucracy: The Five Strategies for Reinventing Government* (Reading, Mass.: Addison-Wesley, 1997).

Chapter 12
The Judiciary

1. Alexis de Tocqueville, *Democracy in America* (1835 and 1840; repr., New York: Harper & Row, 1966), p. 248.

2. The "rule of four" is modified when seven or fewer justices participate, which occurs from time to time. When that happens, as few as three justices can grant *certiorari*.

3. For a former Supreme Court law clerk's account of the role these clerks play in the high court's decision-making process, see Edward Lazarus, *Closed Chambers: The First Eyewitness Account of the Epic Struggles inside the Supreme Court* (New York: Times Books, 1998).

4. For a discussion of the factors that may come into play during the process of nominating Supreme Court justices, see David A. Yalof, *Pursuit of Justices: Presidential Politics and the Selection of Supreme Court Nominees* (Chicago: University of Chicago Press, 1999).

5. 5 U.S. 137 (1803).

6. *U.S. Term Limits v. Thornton*, 514 U.S. 779 (1995).

7. *United States v. Lopez*, 514 U.S. 549 (1995).

8. *United States v. Morrison*, 529 U.S. 598 (2000).

9. See, for example, John T. Noonan, Jr., *Narrowing the Nation's Power: The Supreme Court Sides with the States* (Berkeley: University of California Press, 2002); and Simon Lazarus, "The Most Dangerous Branch," *The Atlantic Monthly*, June 2002.

10. *Bush v. Gore*, 531 U.S. 98 (2000).

11. *Washington v. Glucksberg*, 521 U.S. 702 (1997).

12. *City of Boerne v. Flores*, 521 U.S. 507 (1997).

13. *Gratz v. Bollinger*, 123 S.Ct. 2411 (2003); and *Grutter v. Bollinger*, 123 S.Ct. 2325 (2003).

14. *Lawrence v. Texas*, 123 S.Ct. 2472 (2003).

15. The decision referred to was *Cherokee Nation v. Georgia*, 30 U.S. 1 (1831).

16. *Brown v. Board of Education*, 349 U.S. 294 (1955)—the second *Brown* decision.

17. *Employment Division, Department of Human Resources of Oregon v. Smith*, 494 U.S. 872 (1990).

18. *City of Boerne v. Flores*, 521 U.S. 507 (1997).

19. *Atkins v. Virginia*, 536 U.S. 304 (2002).

Chapter 13
Domestic and Economic Policy

1. This sum does not include the Earned Income Tax Credit, which is not part of the federal budget.

2. President's Commission on Law Enforcement and Administration of Justice, *Challenge of Crime in a Free Society* (Washington, D.C.: Government Printing Office, 1967), p. 19.

3. Richard Shenkman, *Legends, Lies and Cherished Myths of American History* (New York: HarperCollins, 1988), p. 158.

Chapter 14
Foreign Policy

1. George W. Bush, September 17, 2002. The full text of the document from which this statement is taken can be accessed at **http://www.whitehouse.gov/nsc/nssall.html**. Other speeches and press releases made by President Bush prior to the attack on Iraq are available online at **http://www.whitehouse.gov/response/index.html**.

2. Sidney Warren, *The President as World Leader* (New York: McGraw-Hill, 1964), p. 23.

3. See John Lewis Gaddis, *The United Nations and the Origins of the Cold War* (New York: Columbia University Press, 1972).

4. X, "The Sources of Soviet Conduct," *Foreign Affairs*, July 1947, p. 575.

The Declaration of Independence

In Congress, July 4, 1776

A Declaration by the Representatives of the United States of America, in General Congress assembled. When in the Course of human Events, it becomes necessary for one People to dissolve the Political Bands which have connected them with another, and to assume among the Powers of the Earth, the separate and equal Station to which the Laws of Nature and of Nature's God entitle them, a decent Respect to the Opinions of Mankind requires that they should declare the causes which impel them to the Separation.

We hold these Truths to be self-evident, that all Men are created equal, that they are endowed by their Creator with certain unalienable Rights, that among these are Life, Liberty, and the Pursuit of Happiness—That to secure these Rights, Governments are instituted among Men, deriving their just Powers from the Consent of the Governed, that whenever any Form of Government becomes destructive of these Ends, it is the Right of the People to alter or to abolish it, and to institute new Government, laying its Foundation on such Principles, and organizing its Powers in such Forms, as to them shall seem most likely to effect their Safety and Happiness. Prudence, indeed, will dictate that Governments long established should not be changed for light and transient Causes; and accordingly all Experience hath shewn, that Mankind are more disposed to suffer, while Evils are sufferable, than to right themselves by abolishing the Forms to which they are accustomed. But when a long Train of Abuses and Usurpations, pursuing invariably the same Object, evinces a Design to reduce them under absolute Despotism, it is their Right, it is their Duty, to throw off such Government, and to provide new Guards for their future Security. Such has been the patient Sufferance of these Colonies; and such is now the Necessity which constrains them to alter their former Systems of Government. The History of the present King of Great-Britain is a History of repeated Injuries and Usurpations, all having in direct Object the Establishment of an absolute Tyranny over these States. To prove this, let Facts be submitted to a candid World.

He has refused his Assent to Laws, the most wholesome and necessary for the public Good.

He has forbidden his Governors to pass Laws of immediate and pressing Importance, unless suspended in their Operation till his Assent should be obtained; and when so suspended, he has utterly neglected to attend to them.

He has refused to pass other Laws for the Accommodation of large Districts of People, unless those People would relinquish the Right of Representation in the Legislature, a Right inestimable to them, and formidable to Tyrants only.

He has called together Legislative Bodies at Places unusual, uncomfortable, and distant from the Depository of their Public Records, for the sole Purpose of fatiguing them into Compliance with his Measures.

He has dissolved Representative Houses repeatedly, for opposing with manly Firmness his Invasions on the Rights of the People.

He has refused for a long Time, after such Dissolutions, to cause others to be elected; whereby the Legislative Powers, incapable of Annihilation, have returned to the People at large for their exercise; the State remaining in the mean time exposed to all the Dangers of Invasion from without, and Convulsions within.

He has endeavoured to prevent the Population of these States; for that Purpose obstructing the Laws for Naturalization of Foreigners; refusing to pass others to encourage their Migrations hither, and raising the Conditions of new Appropriations of Lands.

He has obstructed the Administration of Justice, by refusing his Assent to Laws for establishing Judiciary Powers.

He has made Judges dependent on his Will alone, for the Tenure of their offices, and the Amount and payment of their Salaries.

He has erected a Multitude of new Offices, and sent hither Swarms of Officers to harrass our People, and eat out their Substance.

He has kept among us, in Times of Peace, Standing Armies, without the consent of our Legislatures.

He has affected to render the Military independent of, and superior to the Civil Power.

He has combined with others to subject us to a Jurisdiction foreign to our Constitution, and unacknowledged by our Laws; giving his Assent to their Acts of pretended Legislation:

For quartering large Bodies of Armed Troops among us:

For protecting them, by a mock Trial, from Punishment for any Murders which they should commit on the Inhabitants of these States:

For cutting off our Trade with all Parts of the World:

For imposing Taxes on us without our Consent:

For depriving us, in many cases, of the Benefits of Trial by Jury:

For transporting us beyond Seas to be tried for pretended Offences:

For abolishing the free System of English Laws in a neighbouring Province, establishing therein an arbitrary Government, and enlarging its Boundaries, so as to render it at once an Example and fit Instrument for introducing the same absolute Rule into these Colonies:

For taking away our Charters, abolishing our most valuable Laws, and altering fundamentally the Forms of our Governments:

For suspending our own Legislatures, and declaring themselves invested with Power to legislate for us in all Cases whatsoever.

He has abdicated Government here, by declaring us out of his Protection and waging War against us.

He has plundered our Seas, ravaged our Coasts, burnt our towns, and destroyed the Lives of our People.

He is, at this Time, transporting large Armies of foreign Mercenaries to compleat the works of Death, Desolation, and Tyranny, already begun with circumstances of Cruelty and Perfidy, scarcely paralleled in the most barbarous Ages, and totally unworthy the Head of a civilized Nation.

He has constrained our fellow Citizens taken Captive on the high Seas to bear Arms against their Country, to become the Executioners of their Friends and Brethren, or to fall themselves by their Hands.

He has excited domestic Insurrections amongst us, and has endeavoured to bring on the Inhabitants of our Frontiers, the merciless Indian Savages, whose known Rule of Warfare, is an undistinguished Destruction, of all Ages, Sexes and Conditions.

In every state of these Oppressions we have Petitioned for Redress in the most humble Terms: Our repeated Petitions have been answered only by repeated Injury. A Prince, whose Character is thus marked by every act which may define a Tyrant, is unfit to be the Ruler of a free People.

Nor have we been wanting in Attentions to our British Brethren. We have warned them from Time to Time of Attempts by their Legislature to extend an unwarrantable Jurisdiction over us. We have reminded them of the Circumstances of our Emigration and Settlement here. We have appealed to their native Justice and Magnanimity, and we have conjured them by the Ties of our common Kindred to disavow these Usurpations, which, would inevitably interrupt our Connections and Correspondence. They too have been deaf to the Voice of Justice and of Consanguinity. We must, therefore, acquiesce in the Necessity, which denounces our Separation, and hold them, as we hold the rest of Mankind, Enemies in War, in Peace, Friends.

We, therefore, the Representatives of the UNITED STATES OF AMERICA, in General Congress Assembled, appealing to the Supreme Judge of the World for the Rectitude of our Intentions, do, in the Name, and by the Authority of the good People of these Colonies, solemnly Publish and Declare, That these United Colonies are, and of Right ought to be, Free and Independent States; that they are absolved from all Allegiance to the British Crown, and that all political Connection between them and the State of Great-Britain, is and ought to be totally dissolved; and that as Free and Independent States, they have full Power to levy War, conclude Peace, contract Alliances, establish Commerce, and to do all other Acts and Things which Independent States may of right do. And for the support of this declaration, with a firm Reliance on the Protection of divine Providence, we mutually pledge to each other our lives, our Fortunes, and our sacred Honor.

The Constitution of the United States of America*

The Preamble

We the People of the United States, in Order to form a more perfect Union, establish Justice, insure domestic Tranquility, provide for the common defence, promote the general Welfare, and secure the Blessings of Liberty to ourselves and our Posterity, do ordain and establish this Constitution for the United States of America.

The Preamble declares that "We the People" are the authority for the Constitution (unlike the Articles of Confederation, which derived their authority from the states). The Preamble also sets out the purposes of the Constitution.

Article I. (Legislative Branch)

The first part of the Constitution, Article 1, deals with the organization and powers of the lawmaking branch of the national government, the Congress.

Section 1. Legislative Powers

All legislative Powers herein granted shall be vested in a Congress of the United States, which shall consist of a Senate and House of Representatives.

Section 2. House of Representatives

Clause 1: Composition and Election of Members. The House of Representatives shall be composed of Members

chosen every second Year by the People of the several States, and the Electors in each State shall have the Qualifications requisite for Electors of the most numerous Branch of the State Legislature.

Each state has the power to decide who may vote for members of Congress. Within each state, those who may vote for state legislators may also vote for members of the House of Representatives (and, under the Seventeenth Amendment, for U.S. senators). When the Constitution was written, nearly all states limited voting rights to white male property owners or taxpayers at least twenty-one years old. Subsequent amendments granted voting power to African American men, all women, and eighteen-year-olds.

Clause 2: Qualifications. No Person shall be a Representative who shall not have attained to the Age of twenty five Years, and been seven Years a Citizen of the United States, and who shall not, when elected, be an Inhabitant of that State in which he shall be chosen.

Each member of the House must (1) be at least twenty-five years old, (2) have been a U.S. citizen for at least seven years, and (3) be a resident of the state in which she or he is elected.

Clause 3: Apportionment of Representatives and Direct Taxes. Representatives [and direct Taxes][1] shall be apportioned among the several States which may be included within this Union, according to their respective Numbers [which shall be determined by adding to the

---

*The spelling, capitalization, and punctuation of the original have been retained here. Brackets indicate passages that have been altered by amendments to the Constitution. We have added article titles (in parentheses), section titles, and clause designatories. We have inserted annotations in italics.

[1] Modified by the Sixteenth Amendment.

whole Number of free Persons, including those bound to Service for a Term of Years, and excluding Indians not taxed, three fifths of all other Persons].[2] The actual Enumeration shall be made within three Years after the first Meeting of the Congress of the United States, and within every subsequent Term of ten Years, in such Manner as they shall by Law direct. The Number of Representatives shall not exceed one for every thirty Thousand, but each State shall have at Least one Representative; and until such enumeration shall be made, the State of New Hampshire shall be entitled to chuse three, Massachusetts eight, Rhode Island and Providence Plantations one, Connecticut five, New York six, New Jersey four, Pennsylvania eight, Delaware one, Maryland six, Virginia ten, North Carolina five, South Carolina five, and Georgia three.

A state's representation in the House is based on the size of its population. Population is counted in each decade's census, after which Congress reapportions House seats. Since early in the twentieth century, the number of seats has been limited to 435.

Clause 4: Vacancies. When vacancies happen in the Representation from any State, the Executive Authority thereof shall issue Writs of Election to fill such Vacancies.

The "Executive Authority" is the state's governor. When a vacancy occurs in the House, the governor calls a special election to fill it.

Clause 5: Officers and Impeachment. The House of Representatives shall chuse their Speaker and other Officers; and shall have the sole Power of Impeachment.

The power to impeach is the power to accuse. In this case, it is the power to accuse members of the executive or judicial branch of wrongdoing or abuse of power. Once a bill of impeachment is issued, the Senate holds the trial.

Section 3. The Senate

Clause 1: Term and Number of Members. The Senate of the United States shall be composed of two Senators from each State [chosen by the Legislature thereof],[3] for six Years; and each Senator shall have one Vote.

Every state has two senators, each of whom serves for six years and has one vote in the upper chamber. Since the

Seventeenth Amendment in 1913, all senators are elected directly by voters of the state during the regular election.

Clause 2: Classification of Senators. Immediately after they shall be assembled in Consequence of the first Election, they shall be divided as equally as may be into three Classes. The Seats of the Senators of the first Class shall be vacated at the Expiration of the second Year, of the second Class at the Expiration of the fourth Year, and of the third Class at the Expiration of the sixth Year, so that one third may be chosen every second Year; [and if Vacancies happen by Resignation, or otherwise, during the Recess of the Legislature of any State, the Executive thereof may make temporary Appointments until the next Meeting of the Legislature, which shall then fill such Vacancies].[4]

One-third of the Senate's seats are open to election every two years (in contrast, all members of the House are elected simultaneously).

Clause 3: Qualifications. No Person shall be a Senator who shall not have attained to the Age of thirty Years, and been nine Years a Citizen of the United States, and who shall not, when elected, be an Inhabitant of that State for which he shall be chosen.

Every senator must be at least thirty years old, a citizen of the United States for a minimum of nine years, and a resident of the state in which he or she is elected.

Clause 4: The Role of the Vice President. The Vice President of the United States shall be President of the Senate, but shall have no Vote, unless they be equally divided.

The vice president presides over meetings of the Senate but cannot vote unless there is a tie. The Constitution gives no other official duties to the vice president.

Clause 5: Other Officers. The Senate shall chuse their other Officers, and also a President pro tempore, in the Absence of the Vice President, or when he shall exercise the Office of President of the United States.

The Senate votes for one of its members to preside when the vice president is absent. This person is usually called the pres-

---

[2] Modified by the Fourteenth Amendment.

[3] Repealed by the Seventeenth Amendment.

[4] Modified by the Seventeenth Amendment.

ident pro tempore because of the temporary situation of the position.

Clause 6: Impeachment Trials. The Senate shall have the sole Power to try all Impeachments. When sitting for that Purpose, they shall be on Oath or Affirmation. When the President of the United States is tried, the Chief Justice shall preside: And no Person shall be convicted without the Concurrence of two thirds of the Members present.

The Senate conducts trials of officials that the House impeaches. The Senate sits as a jury, with the vice president presiding if the president is not on trial.

Clause 7: Penalties for Conviction. Judgment in Cases of Impeachment shall not extend further than to removal from Office, and disqualification to hold and enjoy any Office of honor, Trust, or Profit under the United States: but the Party convicted shall nevertheless be liable and subject to Indictment, Trial, Judgment, and Punishment, according to Law.

On conviction of impeachment charges, the Senate can only force an official to leave office and prevent him or her from holding another office in the federal government. The individual, however, can still be tried in a regular court.

Section 4. Congressional Elections: Times, Manner, and Places

Clause 1: Elections. The Times, Places and Manner of holding Elections for Senators and Representatives, shall be prescribed in each State by the Legislature thereof; but the Congress may at any time by Law make or alter such Regulations, except as to the Places of chusing Senators.

Congress set the Tuesday after the first Monday in November in even-numbered years as the date for congressional elections. In states with more than one seat in the House, Congress requires that representatives be elected from districts within each state. Under the Seventeenth Amendment, senators are elected at the same places as other officials.

Clause 2: Sessions of Congress. [The Congress shall assemble at least once in every Year, and such Meeting shall be on the first Monday in December, unless they shall by Law appoint a different Day.][5]

_____
[5] Changed by the Twentieth Amendment.

Congress has to meet every year at least once. The regular session now begins at noon on January 3 of each year, subsequent to the Twentieth Amendment, unless Congress passes a law to fix a different date. Congress stays in session until its members vote to adjourn. Additionally, the president may call a special session.

Section 5. Powers and Duties of the Houses

Clause 1: Admitting Members and Quorum. Each House shall be the Judge of the Elections, Returns, and Qualifications of its own Members, and a Majority of each shall constitute a Quorum to do Business; but a smaller Number may adjourn from day to day, and may be authorized to compel the Attendance of absent Members, in such Manner, and under such Penalties as each House may provide.

Each chamber may exclude or refuse to seat a member-elect.
The quorum rule requires that 218 members of the House and 51 members of the Senate be present in order to conduct business. This rule is normally not enforced in the handling of routine matters.

Clause 2: Rules and Discipline of Members. Each House may determine the Rules of its Proceedings, punish its Members for disorderly Behaviour, and, with the Concurrence of two thirds, expel a Member.

The House and the Senate may adopt their own rules to guide their proceedings. Each may also discipline its members for conduct that is deemed unacceptable. No member may be expelled without a two-thirds majority vote in favor of expulsion.

Clause 3: Keeping a Record. Each House shall keep a Journal of its Proceedings, and from time to time publish the same, excepting such Parts as may in their Judgment require Secrecy; and the Yeas and Nays of the Members of either House on any question shall, at the Desire of one fifth of those Present, be entered on the Journal.

The journals of the two houses are published at the end of each session of Congress.

Clause 4: Adjournment. Neither House, during the Session of Congress, shall, without the Consent of the other, adjourn for more than three days, nor to any other Place than that in which the two Houses shall be sitting.

Congress has the power to determine when and where to meet, provided, however, that both houses meet in the same city. *Neither chamber may recess for more than three days without the consent of the other.*

Section 6. Rights of Members
Clause 1: Compensation and Privileges. The Senators and Representatives shall receive a Compensation for their services, to be ascertained by Law, and paid out of the Treasury of the United States. They shall in all Cases, except Treason, Felony and Breach of the Peace, be privileged from Arrest during their Attendance at the Session of their respective Houses, and in going to and returning from the same; and for any Speech or Debate in either House, they shall not be questioned in any other Place.

Congressional salaries are to be paid by the U.S. Treasury rather than by the members' respective states. The original salaries were $6 per day; in 1857 they were $3,000 per year. Both representatives and senators were paid $154,700 in 2003.

Treason is defined in Article III, Section 3. A felony is any serious crime. A breach of the peace is any indictable offense less than treason or a felony. Members cannot be arrested for things they say during speeches and debates in Congress. This immunity applies to the Capitol Building itself and not to their private lives.

Clause 2: Restrictions. No Senator or Representative shall, during the Time for which he was elected, be appointed to any civil Office under the Authority of the United States, which shall have been created, or the Emoluments whereof shall have been encreased during such time; and no Person holding any Office under the United States, shall be a Member of either House during his Continuance in Office.

During the term for which a member was elected, he or she cannot concurrently accept another federal government position.

Section 7. Legislative Powers:
Bills and Resolutions
Clause 1: Revenue Bills. All Bills for raising Revenue shall originate in the House of Representatives; but the Senate may propose or concur with Amendments as on other Bills.

All tax and appropriation bills for raising money have to originate in the House of Representatives. The Senate, though, often amends such bills and may even substitute an entirely different bill.

Clause 2: The Presidential Veto. Every Bill which shall have passed the House of Representatives and the Senate, shall, before it becomes a Law, be presented to the President of the United States; If he approve he shall sign it, but if not he shall return it, with his Objections to the House in which it shall have originated, who shall enter the Objections at large on their Journal, and proceed to reconsider it. If after such Reconsideration two thirds of that House shall agree to pass the Bill, it shall be sent together with the Objections, to the other House, by which it shall likewise be reconsidered, and if approved by two thirds of that House, it shall become a Law. But in all such Cases the Votes of both Houses shall be determined by Yeas and Nays, and the Names of the Persons voting for and against the Bill shall be entered on the Journal of each House respectively. If any Bill shall not be returned by the President within ten Days (Sundays excepted) after it shall have been presented to him, the Same shall be a Law, in like Manner as if he had signed it, unless the Congress by their Adjournment prevent its Return in which Case it shall not be a Law.

When Congress sends the president a bill, he or she can sign it (in which case it becomes law) or send it back to the house in which it originated. If it is sent back, a two-thirds majority of each house must pass it again for it to become law. If the president neither signs it nor sends it back within ten days, it becomes law anyway, unless Congress adjourns in the meantime.

Clause 3: Actions on Other Matters. Every Order, Resolution, or Vote to which the Concurrence of the Senate and House of Representatives may be necessary (except on a question of Adjournment) shall be presented to the President of the United States; and before the Same shall take Effect, shall be approved by him, or being disapproved by him, shall be repassed by two thirds of the Senate and House of Representatives, according to the Rules and Limitations prescribed in the Case of a Bill.

The president must either sign or veto everything that Congress passes, except votes to adjourn and resolutions not having the force of law.

Section 8. The Powers of Congress
Clause 1: Taxing. The Congress shall have Power To lay and collect Taxes, Duties, Imposts and Excises, to pay the Debts and provide for the common Defence and general Welfare of the United States; but all Duties, Imposts and Excises shall be uniform throughout the United States;

Duties are taxes on imports and exports. Impost is a generic term for tax. Excises are taxes on the manufacture, sale, or use of goods.

Clause 2: Borrowing. To borrow Money on the credit of the United States;

Congress has the power to borrow money, which is normally carried out through the sale of U.S. treasury bonds on which interest is paid. Note that the Constitution places no limit on the amount of government borrowing.

Clause 3: Regulation of Commerce. To regulate Commerce with foreign Nations, and among the several States, and with the Indian Tribes;

This is the commerce clause, which gives to the Congress the power to regulate interstate and foreign trade. Much of the activity of Congress is based on this clause.

Clause 4: Naturalization and Bankruptcy. To establish a uniform Rule of Naturalization, and uniform Laws on the subject of Bankruptcies throughout the United States;

Only Congress may determine how aliens can become citizens of the United States. Congress may make laws with respect to bankruptcy.

Clause 5: Money and Standards. To coin Money, regulate the Value thereof, and of foreign Coin, and fix the Standard of Weights and Measures;

Congress mints coins and prints and circulates paper money. Congress can establish uniform measures of time, distance, weight, and so on. In 1838, Congress adopted the English system of weights and measurements as our national standard.

Clause 6: Punishing Counterfeiters. To provide for the Punishment of counterfeiting the Securities and current Coin of the United States;

Congress has the power to punish those who copy American money and pass it off as real. Currently, the fine is up to $5,000 and/or imprisonment for up to fifteen years.

Clause 7: Roads and Post Offices. To establish Post Offices and post Roads;

Post roads include all routes over which mail is carried—highways, railways, waterways, and airways.

Clause 8: Patents and Copyrights. To promote the Progress of Science and useful Arts, by securing for limited Times to Authors and Inventors the exclusive Right to their respective Writings and Discoveries;

Authors' and composers' works are protected by copyrights established by copyright law, which currently is the Copyright Act of 1976, as amended. Copyrights are valid for the life of the author or composer plus seventy years. Inventors' works are protected by patents, which vary in length of protection from fourteen to twenty years. A patent gives a person the exclusive right to control the manufacture or sale of her or his invention.

Clause 9: Lower Courts. To constitute Tribunals inferior to the supreme Court;

Congress has the authority to set up all federal courts, except the Supreme Court, and to decide what cases those courts will hear.

Clause 10: Punishment for Piracy. To define and punish Piracies and Felonies committed on the high Seas, and Offences against the Law of Nations;

Congress has the authority to prohibit the commission of certain acts outside U.S. territory and to punish certain violations of international law.

Clause 11: Declaration of War. To declare War, grant Letters of Marque and Reprisal, and make Rules concerning Captures on Land and Water;

Only Congress can declare war, although the president, as commander in chief, can make war without Congress's formal declaration. Letters of marque and reprisal authorized private parties to capture and destroy enemy ships in wartime. Since the middle of the nineteenth century, international law has prohibited letters of marque and reprisal, and the United States has honored the ban.

Clause 12: The Army. To raise and support Armies, but no Appropriation of Money to that Use shall be for a longer Term than two Years;

Congress has the power to create an army; the money used to pay for it must be appropriated for no more than two-year intervals. This latter restriction gives ultimate control of the army to civilians.

Clause 13: Creation of a Navy. To provide and maintain a Navy;

This clause allows for the maintenance of a navy. In 1947, Congress created the U.S. Air Force.

Clause 14: Regulation of the Armed Forces. To make Rules for the Government and Regulation of the land and naval Forces;

Congress sets the rules for the military mainly by way of the Uniform Code of Military Justice, which was enacted in 1950 by Congress.

Clause 15: The Militia. To provide for calling forth the Militia to execute the Laws of the Union, suppress Insurrections and repel Invasions;

The militia is known today as the National Guard. Both Congress and the president have the authority to call the National Guard into federal service.

Clause 16: How the Militia Is Organized. To provide for organizing, arming, and disciplining the Militia, and for governing such Part of them as may be employed in the Service of the United States, reserving to the States respectively, the Appointment of the Officers, and the Authority of training the Militia according to the discipline prescribed by Congress;

This clause gives Congress the power to "federalize" state militia (National Guard). When called into such service, the National Guard is subject to the same rules that Congress has set forth for the regular armed services.

Clause 17: Creation of the District of Columbia. To exercise exclusive Legislation in all Cases whatsoever, over such District (not exceeding ten Miles square) as may, by Cession of particular States, and the Acceptance of Congress, become the Seat of the Government of the United States, and to exercise like Authority over all Places purchased by the Consent of the Legislature of the State in which the Same shall be, for the Erection of Forts, Magazines, Arsenals, dock-Yards, and other needful Buildings;—And

Congress established the District of Columbia as the national capital in 1791. Virginia and Maryland had granted land for the District, but Virginia's grant was returned because it was believed it would not be needed. Today, the District covers sixty-nine square miles.

Clause 18: The Elastic Clause. To make all Laws which shall be necessary and proper for carrying into Execution the foregoing Powers, and all other Powers vested by this Constitution in the Government of the United States, or in any Department or Officer thereof.

This clause—the necessary and proper clause, or the elastic clause—grants no specific powers, and thus it can be stretched to fit different circumstances. It has allowed Congress to adapt the government to changing needs and times.

Section 9. The Powers Denied to Congress

Clause 1: Question of Slavery. The Migration or Importation of such Persons as any of the States now existing shall think proper to admit, shall not be prohibited by the Congress prior to the Year one thousand eight hundred and eight, but a Tax or duty may be imposed on such Importation, not exceeding ten dollars for each Person.

"Persons" referred to slaves. Congress outlawed the slave trade in 1808.

Clause 2: Habeas Corpus. The privilege of the Writ of Habeas Corpus shall not be suspended, unless when in Cases of Rebellion or Invasion the public Safety may require it.

A writ of habeas corpus is a court order directing a sheriff or other public officer who is detaining another person to "produce the body" of the detainee so the court can assess the legality of the detention.

Clause 3: Special Bills. No Bill of Attainder or ex post facto Law shall be passed.

A bill of attainder is a law that inflicts punishment without a trial. An ex post facto law is a law that inflicts punishment for an act that was not illegal when it was committed.

Clause 4: Direct Taxes. [No Capitation, or other direct, Tax shall be laid, unless in Proportion to the Census or Enumeration herein before directed to be taken.][6]

A capitation is a tax on a person. A direct tax is a tax paid directly to the government, such as a property tax. This clause

---

[6] Modified by the Sixteenth Amendment.

was intended to prevent Congress from levying a tax on slaves per person and thereby taxing slavery out of existence.

Clause 5: Export Taxes. No Tax or Duty shall be laid on Articles exported from any State.

Congress may not tax any goods sold from one state to another or from one state to a foreign country. (Congress does have the power to tax goods that are bought from other countries, however.)

Clause 6: Interstate Commerce. No Preference shall be given by any Regulation of Commerce or Revenue to the Ports of one State over those of another: nor shall Vessels bound to, or from, one State, be obliged to enter, clear, or pay Duties in another.

Congress may not treat different ports within the United States differently in terms of taxing and commerce powers. Congress may not tax goods sent from one state to another. Finally, Congress may not give one state's port a legal advantage over the ports of another state.

Clause 7: Treasury Withdrawals. No Money shall be drawn from the Treasury, but in Consequence of Appropriations made by Law; and a regular Statement and Account of the Receipts and Expenditures of all public Money shall be published from time to time.

Federal funds can be spent only as Congress authorizes. This is a significant check on the president's power.

Clause 8: Titles of Nobility. No Title of Nobility shall be granted by the United States: And no Person holding any Office of Profit or Trust under them, shall, without the Consent of the Congress, accept of any present, Emolument, Office, or Title, of any kind whatever, from any King, Prince, or foreign State.

No person in the United States may hold a title of nobility, such as duke or duchess. This clause also discourages bribery of American officials by foreign governments.

Section 10. Those Powers Denied to the States

Clause 1: Treaties and Coinage. No State shall enter into any Treaty, Alliance, or Confederation; grant Letters of Marque and Reprisal; coin Money; emit Bills of Credit; make any Thing but gold and silver Coin a Tender in Payment of Debts; pass any Bill of Attainder, ex post facto Law, or Law impairing the Obligation of Contracts, or grant any Title of Nobility.

Prohibiting state laws "impairing the Obligation of Contracts" was intended to protect creditors. (Shays' Rebellion—an attempt to prevent courts from giving effect to creditors' legal actions against debtors—occurred only one year before the Constitution was written.)

Clause 2: Duties and Imposts. No State shall, without the Consent of the Congress, lay any Imposts or Duties on Imports or Exports, except what may be absolutely necessary for executing its inspection Laws; and the net Produce of all Duties and Imposts, laid by any State on Imports or Exports, shall be for the Use of the Treasury of the United States; and all such Laws shall be subject to the Revision and Controul of the Congress.

Only Congress can tax imports. Further, the states cannot tax exports.

Clause 3: War. No State shall, without the Consent of Congress, lay any Duty of Tonnage, keep Troops, or Ships of War in time of Peace, enter into any Agreement or Compact with another State, or with a foreign Power or engage in War, unless actually invaded, or in such imminent Danger as will not admit of delay.

A duty of tonnage is a tax on ships according to their cargo capacity. No states may effectively tax ships according to their cargo unless Congress agrees. Additionally, this clause forbids any state to keep troops or warships during peacetime or to make a compact with another state or foreign nation unless Congress so agrees. A state can, in contrast, maintain a militia, but its use has to be limited to disorders that occur within the state—unless, of course, the militia is called into federal service.

Article II. (Executive Branch)

Section 1. The Nature and Scope of Presidential Power

Clause 1: Four-Year Term. The executive Power shall be vested in a President of the United States of America. He shall hold his Office during the Term of four Years, and, together with the Vice President, chosen for the same Term, be elected, as follows.

The president has the power to carry out laws made by Congress, called the executive power. He or she serves in office for a four-year term after election. The Twenty-second Amendment limits the number of times a person may be elected president.

Clause 2: *Choosing Electors from Each State.*   Each State shall appoint, in such Manner as the Legislature thereof may direct, a Number of Electors, equal to the whole Number of Senators and Representatives to which the State may be entitled in the Congress; but no Senator or Representative, or Person holding an Office of Trust or Profit under the United States, shall be appointed an Elector.

The "Electors" are more commonly known as the "electoral college." The president is elected by electors—that is, representatives chosen by the people—rather than by the people directly.

Clause 3: *The Former System of Elections.*   [The Electors shall meet in their respective States, and vote by Ballot for two Persons, of whom one at least shall not be an Inhabitant of the same State with themselves. And they shall make a List of all the Persons voted for, and of the Number of Votes for each; which List they shall sign and certify, and transmit sealed to the Seat of the Government of the United States, directed to the President of the Senate. The President of the Senate shall, in the Presence of the Senate and House of Representatives, open all the Certificates, and the Votes shall then be counted. The Person having the greatest Number of Votes shall be the President, if such Number be a Majority of the whole Number of Electors appointed; and if there be more than one who have such Majority, and have an equal Number of Votes, then the House of Representatives shall immediately chuse by Ballot one of them for President; and if no Person have a Majority, then from the five highest on the List the said House shall in like Manner chuse the President. But in chusing the President, the Votes shall be taken by States, the Representation from each State having one Vote; A quorum for this Purpose shall consist of a Member or Members from two thirds of the States, and a Majority of all the States shall be necessary to a Choice. In every Case, after the Choice of the President, the Person having the greater Number of Votes of the Electors shall be the Vice President. But if there should

remain two or more who have equal Votes, the Senate shall chuse from them by Ballot the Vice President.][7]

The original method of selecting the president and vice president was replaced by the Twelfth Amendment. Apparently, the framers did not anticipate the rise of political parties and the development of primaries and conventions.

Clause 4: *The Time of Elections.*   The Congress may determine the Time of chusing the Electors, and the Day on which they shall give their Votes; which Day shall be the same throughout the United States.

Congress set the Tuesday after the first Monday in November every fourth year as the date for choosing electors. The electors cast their votes on the Monday after the second Wednesday in December of that year.

Clause 5: *Qualifications for President.*   No person except a natural born Citizen, or a Citizen of the United States, at the time of the Adoption of this Constitution, shall be eligible to the Office of President; neither shall any Person be eligible to that Office who shall not have attained to the Age of thirty five Years, and been fourteen Years a Resident within the United States.

The president must be a natural-born citizen, be at least thirty-five years of age when taking office, and have been a resident within the United States for at least fourteen years.

Clause 6: *Succession of the Vice President.*   [In Case of the Removal of the President from Office, or of his Death, Resignation or Inability to discharge the Powers and Duties of the said Office, the same shall devolve on the Vice President, and the Congress may by Law provide for the Case of Removal, Death, Resignation or Inability, both of the President and Vice President, declaring what Officer shall then act as President, and such Officer shall act accordingly, until the Disability be removed, or a President shall be elected.][8]

This former section provided for the method by which the vice president was to succeed to the presidency, but its wording is ambiguous. It was replaced by the Twenty-fifth Amendment.

---

[7] Changed by the Twelfth Amendment.

[8] Modified by the Twenty-fifth Amendment.

Clause 7: The President's Salary. The President shall, at stated Times, receive for his Services, a Compensation, which shall neither be encreased nor diminished during the Period for which he shall have been elected, and he shall not receive within that Period any other Emolument from the United States, or any of them.

The president maintains the same salary during each four-year term. Moreover, she or he may not receive additional cash payments from the government. Originally set at $25,000 per year, the salary is currently $400,000 a year plus a $50,000 nontaxable expense account.

Clause 8: The Oath of Office. Before he enter on the Execution of his Office, he shall take the following Oath or Affirmation: "I do solemnly swear (or affirm) that I will faithfully execute the Office of President of the United States, and will to the best of my Ability, preserve, protect and defend the Constitution of the United States."

The president is "sworn in" prior to beginning the duties of the office. Currently, the taking of the oath of office occurs on January 20, following the November election. The ceremony is called the inauguration. The oath of office is administered by the chief justice of the United States Supreme Court.

Section 2. Powers of the President

Clause 1: Commander in Chief. The President shall be Commander in Chief of the Army and Navy of the United States, and of the Militia of the several States, when called into the actual Service of the United States; he may require the Opinion, in writing, of the principal Officer in each of the executive Departments, upon any Subject relating to the Duties of their respective Offices, and he shall have Power to grant Reprieves and Pardons for Offences against the United States, except in Cases of Impeachment.

The armed forces are placed under civilian control because the president is a civilian but still commander in chief of the military. The president may ask for the help of the head of each of the executive departments (thereby creating the cabinet). The cabinet members are chosen by the president with the consent of the Senate, but they can be removed without Senate approval.

The president's clemency powers extend only to federal cases. In those cases, he or she may grant a full or conditional pardon or reduce a prison term or fine.

Clause 2: Treaties and Appointment. He shall have Power, by and with the Advice and Consent of the Senate, to make Treaties, provided two thirds of the Senators present concur; and he shall nominate, and by and with the Advice and Consent of the Senate, shall appoint Ambassadors, other public Ministers and Consuls, Judges of the supreme Court, and all other Officers of the United States, whose Appointments are not herein otherwise provided for, and which shall be established by Law; but the Congress may by Law vest the Appointment of such inferior Officers, as they think proper, in the President alone, in the Courts of Law, or in the Heads of Departments.

Many of the major powers of the president are identified in this clause, including the power to make treaties with foreign governments (with the approval of the Senate by a two-thirds vote) and the power to appoint ambassadors, Supreme Court justices, and other government officials. Most such appointments require Senate approval.

Clause 3: Vacancies. The President shall have Power to fill up all Vacancies that may happen during the Recess of the Senate, by granting Commissions which shall expire at the end of their next Session.

The president has the power to appoint temporary officials to fill vacant federal offices without Senate approval if Congress is not in session. Such appointments expire automatically at the end of Congress's next term.

Section 3. Duties of the President

He shall from time to time give to the Congress Information of the State of the Union, and recommend to their Consideration such Measures as he shall judge necessary and expedient; he may, on extraordinary Occasions, convene both Houses, or either of them, and in Case of Disagreement between them, with Respect to the Time of Adjournment, he may adjourn them to such Time as he shall think proper; he shall receive Ambassadors and other public Ministers; he shall take Care that the Laws be faithfully executed, and shall Commission all the Officers of the United States.

Annually, the president reports on the state of the union to Congress, recommends legislative measures, and proposes a federal budget. The State of the Union speech is a statement not only to Congress but also to the American people. After it is given, the president proposes a federal budget and presents an economic report. At any time, the president may send special messages to Congress while it is in session. The president has the power to call special sessions, to adjourn Congress when its two houses do not agree on when to adjourn, to receive diplomatic representatives of other governments, and to ensure the proper execution of all federal laws. The president further has the ability to empower federal officers to hold their positions and to perform their duties.

Section 4. Impeachment
The President, Vice President and all civil Officers of the United States, shall be removed from Office on Impeachment for, and Conviction of, Treason, Bribery, or other high Crimes and Misdemeanors.

Treason denotes giving aid to the nation's enemies. The definition of high crimes and misdemeanors is usually given as serious abuses of political power. In either case, the president or vice president may be accused by the House (called an impeachment) and then removed from office if convicted by the Senate. (Note that impeachment does not mean removal but rather refers to an accusation of treason or high crimes and misdemeanors.)

Article III. (Judicial Branch)

Section 1. Judicial Powers, Courts, and Judges
The judicial Power of the United States, shall be vested in one supreme Court, and in such inferior Courts as the Congress may from time to time ordain and establish. The Judges, both of the supreme and inferior Courts, shall hold their Offices during good Behaviour, and shall, at stated Times, receive for their Services a Compensation, which shall not be diminished during their Continuance in Office.

The Supreme Court is vested with judicial power, as are the lower federal courts that Congress creates. Federal judges serve in their offices for life unless they are impeached and convicted by Congress. The payment of federal judges may not be reduced during their time in office.

Section 2. Jurisdiction
Clause 1: Cases under Federal Jurisdiction. The judicial Power shall extend to all Cases, in Law and Equity, arising under this Constitution, the Laws of the United States, and Treaties made, or which shall be made, under their Authority;—to all Cases affecting Ambassadors, other public Ministers and Consuls;—to all Cases of admiralty and maritime Jurisdiction;—to Controversies to which the United States shall be a Party;—to

Controversies between two or more States; [—between a State and Citizens of another State;—][9] between Citizens of different States;—between Citizens of the same State claiming Lands under Grants of different States, [and between a State, or the Citizens thereof, and foreign States, Citizens or Subjects.][10]

The federal courts take on cases that concern the meaning of the U.S. Constitution, all federal laws, and treaties. They also can take on cases involving citizens of different states and citizens of foreign nations.

Clause 2: Cases for the Supreme Court. In all Cases affecting Ambassadors, other public Ministers and Consuls, and those in which a State shall be a Party, the supreme Court shall have original Jurisdiction. In all the other Cases before mentioned, the supreme Court shall have appellate Jurisdiction, both as to Law and Fact, with such Exceptions, and under such Regulations as the Congress shall make.

In a limited number of situations, the Supreme Court acts as a trial court and has original jurisdiction. These cases involve a representative from another country or involve a state. In all other situations, the cases must first be tried in the lower courts and then can be appealed to the Supreme Court. Congress may, however, make exceptions. Today the Supreme Court acts as a trial court of first instance on rare occasions.

Clause 3: The Conduct of Trials. The Trial of all Crimes, except in Cases of Impeachment, shall be by Jury; and such Trial shall be held in the State where the said Crimes shall have been committed; but when not committed within any State, the Trial shall be at such Place or Places as the Congress may by Law have directed.

Any person accused of a federal crime is granted the right to a trial by jury in a federal court in that state in which the crime was committed. Trials of impeachment are an exception.

Section 3. Treason
Clause 1: The Definition of Treason. Treason against the United States, shall consist only in levying War against them, or, in adhering to their Enemies, giving them Aid and Comfort. No Person shall be convicted of Treason unless on the Testimony of two Witnesses to the same overt Act, or on Confession in open Court.

---

[9] Modified by the Eleventh Amendment.
[10] Modified by the Eleventh Amendment.

Treason is the making of war against the United States or giving aid to its enemies.

Clause 2: Punishment. The Congress shall have Power to declare the Punishment of Treason, but no Attainder of Treason shall work Corruption of Blood, or Forfeiture except during the Life of the Person attainted.

Congress has provided that the punishment for treason ranges from a minimum of five years in prison and/or a $10,000 fine to a maximum of death. "No Attainder of Treason shall work Corruption of Blood" prohibits punishment of the traitor's heirs.

Article IV.
(Relations among the States)

Section 1. Full Faith and Credit
Full Faith and Credit shall be given in each State to the public Acts, Records, and judicial Proceedings of every other State. And the Congress may by general Laws prescribe the Manner in which such Acts, Records and Proceedings shall be proved, and the Effect thereof.

All states are required to respect one another's laws, records, and lawful decisions. There are exceptions, however. A state does not have to enforce another state's criminal code. Nor does it have to recognize another state's grant of a divorce if the person obtaining the divorce did not establish legal residence in the state in which it was given.

Section 2. Treatment of Citizens
Clause 1: Privileges and Immunities. The Citizens of each State shall be entitled to all Privileges and Immunities of Citizens in the several States.

A citizen of a state has the same rights and privileges as the citizens of another state in which he or she happens to be.

Clause 2: Extradition. A Person charged in any State with Treason, Felony, or other Crime, who shall flee from Justice, and be found in another State, shall on Demand of the executive Authority of the State from which he fled, be delivered up, to be removed to the State having Jurisdiction of the Crime.

Any person accused of a crime who flees to another state must be returned to the state in which the crime occurred.

Clause 3: Fugitive Slaves. [No Person held to Service or Labour in one State, under the Laws thereof, escaping into another, shall, in Consequence of any Law or Regulation therein, be discharged from such Service or Labour, but shall be delivered up on Claim of the Party to whom such Service or Labour may be due.][11]

This clause was struck down by the Thirteenth Amendment, which abolished slavery in 1865.

Section 3. Admission of States
Clause 1: The Process. New States may be admitted by the Congress into this Union; but no new State shall be formed or erected within the Jurisdiction of any other State; nor any State be formed by the Junction of two or more States, or Parts of States, without the Consent of the Legislatures of the States concerned as well as of the Congress.

Only Congress has the power to admit new states to the union. No state may be created by taking territory from an existing state unless the state's legislature so consents.

Clause 2: Public Land. The Congress shall have Power to dispose of and make all needful Rules and Regulations respecting the Territory or other Property belonging to the United States; and nothing in this Constitution shall be so construed as to Prejudice any Claims of the United States, or of any particular State.

The federal government has the exclusive right to administer federal government public lands.

Section 4. Republican Form of Government
The United States shall guarantee to every State in this Union a Republican Form of Government, and shall protect each of them against Invasion; and on Application of the Legislature, or of the Executive (when the Legislature cannot be convened) against domestic Violence.

Each state is promised a republican form of government; that is, one in which the people elect their representatives. The federal government is bound to protect states against any attack by foreigners or during times of trouble within a state.

Article V. (Methods of Amendment)

The Congress, whenever two thirds of both Houses shall deem it necessary, shall propose Amendments to this

---

[11] Repealed by the Thirteenth Amendment.

Constitution, or on the Application of the Legislatures of two thirds of the several States, shall call a Convention for proposing Amendments, which, in either Case, shall be valid to all Intents and Purposes, as Part of this Constitution, when ratified by the Legislatures of three fourths of the several States, or by Conventions in three fourths thereof, as the one or the other Mode of Ratification may be proposed by the Congress; Provided that no Amendment which may be made prior to the Year One thousand eight hundred and eight shall in any Manner affect the first and fourth Clauses in the Ninth Section of the First Article; and that no State, without its Consent, shall be deprived of its equal Suffrage in the Senate.

Amendments may be proposed in either of two ways: a two-thirds vote of each chamber (Congress) or at the request of two-thirds of the states. Ratification of amendments may be carried out in two ways: by the legislatures of three-fourths of the states or by the voters in three-fourths of the states. No state may be denied equal representation in the Senate.

Article VI. (National Supremacy)

Clause 1: Existing Obligations. All Debts contracted and Engagements entered into, before the Adoption of this Constitution shall be as valid against the United States under this Constitution, as under the Confederation.

During the Revolutionary War and the years of the Confederation, Congress borrowed large sums. This clause pledged that the new federal government would assume those financial obligations.

Clause 2: Supreme Law of the Land. This Constitution, and the Laws of the United States which shall be made in Pursuance thereof; and all Treaties made, or which shall be made, under the Authority of the United States, shall be the supreme Law of the Land; and the Judges in every State shall be bound thereby, any Thing in the Constitution or Laws of any State to the Contrary notwithstanding.

This is typically called the supremacy clause; it declares that federal law takes precedence over all forms of state law. No government at the local or state level may make or enforce any law that conflicts with any provision of the Constitution, acts of Congress, treaties, or other rules and regulations issued by the president and his or her subordinates in the executive branch of the federal government.

Clause 3: Oath of Office. The Senators and Representatives before mentioned, and the Members of the several State Legislatures, and all executive and judicial Officers, both of the United States and of the several States, shall be bound by Oath or Affirmation, to support this Constitution; but no religious Test shall ever be required as a Qualification to any Office or public Trust under the United States.

Every federal and state official must take an oath of office promising to support the U.S. Constitution. Religion may not be used as a qualification to serve in any federal office.

Article VII. (Ratification)

The Ratification of the Conventions of nine States shall be sufficient for the Establishment of this Constitution between the States so ratifying the Same.

Nine states were required to ratify the Constitution. Delaware was the first and New Hampshire the ninth.

Done in Convention by the Unanimous Consent of the States present the Seventeenth Day of September in the Year of our Lord one thousand seven hundred and Eighty seven and of the Independence of the United States of America the Twelfth. In witness whereof we have hereunto subscribed our Names, Articles in addition to, and amendment of the Constitution of the United States of America, proposed by Congress and ratified by the Legislatures of the several states, pursuant to the Fifth Article of the original Constitution.

Go. WASHINGTON
Presid't. and deputy from Virginia

Attest

WILLIAM JACKSON
Secretary

DELAWARE
Geo. Read
Gunning Bedford jun
John Dickinson
Richard Bassett
Jaco. Broom

MASSACHUSETTS
Nathaniel Gorham
Rufus King

CONNECTICUT
Wm. Saml. Johnson
Roger Sherman

NEW YORK
Alexander Hamilton

NEW JERSEY
Wh. Livingston
David Brearley
Wm. Paterson
Jona. Dayton

PENNSYLVANIA
B. Franklin
Thomas Mifflin
Robt. Morris
Geo. Clymer
Thos. FitzSimons
Jared Ingersoll
James Wilson
Gouv. Morris

NEW HAMPSHIRE
John Langdon
Nicholas Gilman

MARYLAND
James McHenry
Dan of St. Thos. Jenifer
Danl. Carroll

VIRGINIA
John Blair
James Madison Jr.

NORTH CAROLINA
Wm. Blount
Richd. Dobbs Spaight
Hu. Willaimson

SOUTH CAROLINA
J. Rutledge
Charles Cotesworth
    Pinckney
Charles Pinckney
Pierce Butler

GEORGIA
William Few
Abr. Baldwin

Amendments to the Constitution of the United States

(The Bill of Rights[12])

Amendment I.
(Religion, Speech, Assembly, and Petition)

Congress shall make no law respecting an establishment of religion, or prohibiting the free exercise thereof; or abridging the freedom of speech, or of the press; or the right of the people peaceably to assemble, and to petition the Government for a redress of grievances.

Congress may not create an official church or enact laws limiting the freedom of religion, speech, the press, assembly, and petition. These guarantees, like the others in the Bill of Rights (the first ten amendments), are not absolute—each may be exercised only with regard to the rights of other persons.

Amendment II.
(Militia and the Right to Bear Arms)

A well regulated Militia, being necessary to the security of a free State, the right of the people to keep and bear Arms, shall not be infringed.

To protect itself, each state has the right to maintain a volunteer armed force. States and the federal government regulate the possession and use of firearms by individuals.

Amendment III.
The Quartering of Soldiers

No Soldier shall, in time of peace be quartered in any house, without the consent of the Owner, nor in time of war, but in a manner to be prescribed by law.

Before the Revolutionary War, it had been common British practice to quarter soldiers in colonists' homes. Military troops do not have the power to take over private houses during peacetime.

Amendment IV.
(Searches and Seizures)

The right of the people to be secure in their persons, houses, papers, and effects, against unreasonable searches and seizures, shall not be violated, and no Warrants shall issue, but upon probable cause, supported by Oath or affirmation, and particularly describing the place to be searched, and the persons or things to be seized.

Here the word warrant *means "justification" and refers to a document issued by a magistrate or judge indicating the name, address, and possible offense committed. Anyone asking for the warrant, such as a police officer, must be able to convince the magistrate or judge that an offense probably has been committed.*

Amendment V.
(Grand Juries, Self-Incrimination, Double Jeopardy, Due Process, and Eminent Domain)

No person shall be held to answer for a capital, or otherwise infamous crime, unless on a presentment or indictment of a Grand Jury, except in cases arising in the land or naval forces, or in the Militia, when in actual service in time of War or public danger; nor shall any person be subject for the same offence to be twice put in jeopardy of life or limb; nor shall be compelled in any criminal case to be a witness against himself, nor be deprived of life, liberty, or property, without due process of law; nor shall private property be taken for public use, without just compensation.

There are two types of juries. A grand jury considers physical evidence and the testimony of witnesses and decides whether there is sufficient reason to bring a case to trial. A petit jury hears the case at trial and decides it. "For the same offence to be twice put in jeopardy of life or limb" means to be tried twice for the same crime. A person may not be tried for the same crime twice or forced to give evidence against herself or himself. No person's right to life, liberty, or property may

---

[12] On September 25, 1789, Congress transmitted to the state legislatures twelve proposed amendments, two of which, having to do with congressional representation and congressional pay, were not adopted. The remaining ten amendments became the Bill of Rights. In 1992, the amendment concerning congressional pay was adopted as the Twenty-seventh Amendment.

be taken away except by lawful means, called the due process of law. *Private property taken for use in public purposes must be paid for by the government.*

Amendment VI.
(Criminal Court Procedures)

In all criminal prosecutions, the accused shall enjoy the right to a speedy and public trial, by an impartial jury of the State and district wherein the crime shall have been committed, which district shall have been previously ascertained by law, and to be informed of the nature and cause of the accusation; to be confronted with the witnesses against him; to have compulsory process for obtaining witnesses in his favor, and to have the Assistance of Counsel for his defence.

Any person accused of a crime has the right to a fair and public trial by a jury in the state in which the crime took place. The charges against that person must be so indicated. Any accused person has the right to a lawyer to defend him or her and to question those who testify against him or her, as well as the right to call people to speak in his or her favor at trial.

Amendment VII.
(Trial by Jury in Civil Cases)

In Suits at common law, where the value in controversy shall exceed twenty dollars, the right of trial by jury shall be preserved, and no fact tried by jury, shall be otherwise re-examined in any Court of the United States, than according to the rules of the common law.

A jury trial may be requested by either party in a dispute in any case involving more than $20. If both parties agree to a trial by a judge without a jury, the right to a jury trial may be put aside.

Amendment VIII.
(Bail, Cruel and Unusual Punishment)

Excessive bail shall not be required, nor excessive fines imposed, nor cruel and unusual punishments inflicted.

Bail is that amount of money that a person accused of a crime may be required to deposit with the court as a guarantee that she or he will appear in court when requested. The amount of bail required or the fine imposed as punishment for a crime

must be reasonable compared with the seriousness of the crime involved. Any punishment judged to be too harsh or too severe for a crime shall be prohibited.

Amendment IX.
(The Rights Retained by the People)

The enumeration in the Constitution, of certain rights, shall not be construed to deny or disparage others retained by the people.

Many civil rights that are not explicitly enumerated in the Constitution are still held by the people.

Amendment X.
(Reserved Powers of the States)

The powers not delegated to the United States by the Constitution, nor prohibited by it to the States, are reserved to the States respectively, or to the people.

Those powers not delegated by the Constitution to the federal government or expressly denied to the states belong to the states and to the people. This amendment in essence allows the states to pass laws under their "police powers."

Amendment XI
(Ratified on February 7, 1795—
Suits against States)

The Judicial power of the United States shall not be construed to extend to any suit in law or equity, commenced or prosecuted against one of the United States by Citizens of another State, or by Citizens or Subjects of any Foreign State.

This amendment has been interpreted to mean that a state cannot be sued in federal court by one of its own citizens, by a citizen of another state, or by a foreign country.

Amendment XII
(Ratified on June 15, 1804—
Election of the President)

The Electors shall meet in their respective states, and vote by ballot for President and Vice-President, one of whom, at least, shall not be an inhabitant of the same State with themselves; they shall name in their ballots the person voted for as President, and in distinct ballots the person voted for as Vice-President, and they shall make distinct lists of all persons voted for as President, and of all persons voted for as Vice-President, and of the number of votes for each, which lists they shall sign and certify, and transmit sealed to the seat of the government of the United States, directed to the President of the Senate;—The President of the Senate shall, in the presence of the Senate and House of Representatives, open all the certificates and the votes shall then be counted;—The person having the greatest number of votes for President, shall be the President, if such number be a majority of the whole number of Electors appointed; and if no person have such majority, then from the persons having the highest numbers not exceeding three on the list of those voted for as President, the House of Representatives shall choose immediately, by ballot, the President. But in choosing the President, the votes shall be taken by States, the representation from each State having one vote; a quorum for this purpose shall consist of a member or members from two-thirds of the States, and a majority of all States shall be necessary to a choice. [And if the House of Representatives shall not choose a President whenever the right of choice shall devolve upon them, before the fourth day of March next following, then the Vice-President shall act as President, as in the case of the death or other constitutional disability of the President.][13]—The person having the greatest number of votes as Vice-President, shall be the Vice-President, if such number be a majority of the whole number of Electors appointed, and if no person have a majority, then from the two highest numbers on the list, the Senate shall choose the Vice-President; a quorum for the purpose shall consist of two-thirds of the whole number of Senators, and a majority of the whole number shall be necessary to a choice. But no person constitutionally ineligible to the office of President shall be eligible to that of Vice-President of the United States.

The original procedure set out for the election of president and vice president in Article II, Section 1, resulted in a tie in 1800 between Thomas Jefferson and Aaron Burr. It was not until the next year that the House of Representatives chose Jefferson to be president. This amendment changed the procedure by providing for separate ballots for president and vice president.

Amendment XIII
(Ratified on December 6, 1865— Prohibition of Slavery)

Section 1.

Neither slavery nor involuntary servitude, except as a punishment for crime whereof the party shall have been duly convicted, shall exist within the United States, or any place subject to their jurisdiction.

Some slaves had been freed during the Civil War. This amendment freed the others and abolished slavery.

Section 2.

Congress shall have power to enforce this article by appropriate legislation.

Amendment XIV
(Ratified on July 9, 1868— Citizenship, Due Process, and Equal Protection of the Laws)

Section 1.

All persons born or naturalized in the United States, and subject to the jurisdiction thereof, are citizens of the United States and of the State wherein they reside. No State shall make or enforce any law which shall abridge the privileges or immunities of citizens of the United States; nor shall any State deprive any person of life, liberty, or property, without due process of law; nor deny to any person within its jurisdiction the equal protection of the laws.

Under this provision, states cannot make or enforce laws that take away rights given to all citizens by the federal government. States cannot act unfairly or arbitrarily toward, or discriminate against, any person.

Section 2.

Representatives shall be apportioned among the several States according to their respective numbers, counting the whole number of persons in each State, excluding Indians not taxed. But when the right to vote at any election for the choice of electors for President and Vice President of the United States, Representatives in Congress, the Executive and Judicial officers of a State, or the members of the Legislature thereof, is denied to any of the male inhabitants of such State, being [twenty-one][14] years of age, and

---

[13] Changed by the Twentieth Amendment.

[14] Changed by the Twenty-sixth Amendment.

citizens of the United States, or in any way abridged, except for participation in rebellion, or other crime, the basis of representation therein shall be reduced in the proportion which the number of such male citizens shall bear to the whole number of male citizens twenty-one years of age in such State.

Section 3.

No person shall be a Senator or Representative in Congress, or elector of President and Vice President, or hold any office, civil or military, under the United States, or under any State, who having previously taken an oath, as a member of Congress, or as an officer of the United States, or as a member of any State legislature, or as an executive or judicial officer of any State, to support the Constitution of the United States, shall have engaged in insurrection or rebellion against the same, or given aid or comfort to the enemies thereof. But Congress may by a vote of two-thirds of each House, remove such disability.

This provision forbade former state or federal government officials who had acted in support of the Confederacy during the Civil War to hold office again. It limited the president's power to pardon those persons. Congress removed this "disability" in 1898.

Section 4.

The validity of the public debt of the United States, authorized by law, including debts incurred for payment of pensions and bounties for services in suppressing insurrection or rebellion, shall not be questioned. But neither the United States nor any State shall assume or pay any debt or obligation incurred in aid of insurrection or rebellion against the United States, or any claim for the loss or emancipation of any slave, but all such debts, obligations and claims shall be held illegal and void.

Section 5.

The Congress shall have power to enforce, by appropriate legislation, the provisions of this article.

Amendment XV
(Ratified on February 3, 1870—
The Right to Vote)

Section 1.

The right of citizens of the United States to vote shall not be denied or abridged by the United States or by any State on account of race, color, or previous condition of servitude.

No citizen can be refused the right to vote simply because of race or color or because that person was once a slave.

Section 2.

The Congress shall have power to enforce this article by appropriate legislation.

Amendment XVI
(Ratified on February 3, 1913—
Income Taxes)

The Congress shall have power to lay and collect taxes on incomes, from whatever source derived, without apportionment among the several States, and without regard to any census or enumeration.

This amendment allows Congress to tax income without sharing the revenue so obtained with the states according to their population.

Amendment XVII
(Ratified on April 8, 1913—
The Popular Election of Senators)

Section 1.

The Senate of the United States shall be composed of two Senators from each State, elected by the people thereof, for six years; and each Senator shall have one vote. The electors in each State shall have the qualifications requisite for electors of the most numerous branch of the State legislatures.

Section 2.

When vacancies happen in the representation of any State in the Senate, the executive authority of such State shall issue writs of election to fill such vacancies: *Provided,* That the legislature of any State may empower the executive thereof to make temporary appointments until the people fill the vacancies by election as the legislature may direct.

Section 3.

This amendment shall not be so construed as to affect the election or term of any Senator chosen before it becomes valid as part of the Constitution.

This amendment modified portions of Article I, Section 3, that related to election of senators. Senators are now elected by the voters in each state directly. When a vacancy occurs, either the state may fill the vacancy by a special election, or the governor of the state involved may appoint someone to fill the seat until the next election.

Amendment XVIII
(Ratified on January 16, 1919—
Prohibition)

Section 1.

After one year from the ratification of this article the manufacture, sale, or transportation of intoxicating liquors within, the importation thereof into, or the exportation thereof from the United States and all territory subject to the jurisdiction thereof for beverage purposes is hereby prohibited.

Section 2.

The Congress and the several States shall have concurrent power to enforce this article by appropriate legislation.

Section 3.

This article shall be inoperative unless it shall have been ratified as an amendment to the Constitution by the legislatures of the several States, as provided in the Constitution, within seven years from the date of the submission hereof to the States by the Congress.[15]

This amendment made it illegal to manufacture, sell, and transport alcoholic beverages in the United States. It was repealed by the Twenty-first Amendment.

Amendment XIX
(Ratified on August 18, 1920—
Women's Right to Vote)

Section 1.

The right of citizens of the United States to vote shall not be denied or abridged by the United States or by any State on account of sex.

Section 2.

Congress shall have power to enforce this article by appropriate legislation.

Women were given the right to vote by this amendment, and Congress was given the power to enforce this right.

---

[15] The Eighteenth Amendment was repealed by the Twenty-first Amendment.

Amendment XX
(Ratified on January 23, 1933—
The Lame Duck Amendment)

Section 1.

The terms of the President and Vice President shall end at noon on the 20th day of January, and the terms of Senators and Representatives at noon on the 3d day of January, of the years in which such terms would have ended if this article had not been ratified; and the terms of their successors shall then begin.

This amendment modified Article I, Section 4, Clause 2, and other provisions relating to the president in the Twelfth Amendment. The taking of the oath of office was moved from March 4 to January 20.

Section 2.

The Congress shall assemble at least once in every year, and such meeting shall begin at noon on the 3d day of January, unless they shall by law appoint a different day.

Congress changed the beginning of its term to January 3. The reason the Twentieth Amendment is called the Lame Duck Amendment is because it shortens the time between when a member of Congress is defeated for reelection and when he or she leaves office.

Section 3.

If, at the time fixed for the beginning of the term of the President, the President elect shall have died, the Vice President elect shall become President. If a President shall not have been chosen before the time fixed for the beginning of his term, or if the President elect shall have failed to qualify, then the Vice President elect shall act as President until a President shall have qualified; and the Congress may by law provide for the case wherein neither a President elect nor a Vice President elect shall have qualified, declaring who shall then act as President, or the manner in which one who is to act shall be selected, and such person shall act accordingly until a President or Vice President shall have qualified.

This part of the amendment deals with problem areas left ambiguous by Article II and the Twelfth Amendment. If the president dies before January 20 or fails to qualify for office, the presidency is to be filled in the order given in this section.

Section 4.

The Congress may by law provide for the case of the death of any of the persons from whom the House of Representatives may choose a President whenever the rights of choice shall have devolved upon them, and for the case of the death of any of the persons from whom the Senate may choose a Vice President whenever the right of choice shall have devolved upon them.

Congress has never created legislation subsequent to this section.

Section 5.

Sections 1 and 2 shall take effect on the 15th day of October following the ratification of this article.

Section 6.

This article shall be inoperative unless it shall have been ratified as an amendment to the Constitution by the legislatures of three-fourths of the several States within seven years from the date of its submission.

Amendment XXI
(Ratified on December 5, 1933—
The Repeal of Prohibition)

Section 1.

The eighteenth article of amendment to the Constitution of the United States is hereby repealed.

Section 2.

The transportation or importation into any State, Territory, or possession of the United States for delivery or use therein of intoxicating liquors, in violation of the laws thereof, is hereby prohibited.

Section 3.

This article shall be inoperative unless it shall have been ratified as an amendment to the Constitution by conventions in the several States, as provided in the Constitution, within seven years from the date of the submission hereof to the States by the Congress.

The amendment repealed the Eighteenth Amendment but did not make alcoholic beverages legal everywhere. Rather, they remained illegal in any state that so designated them. Many such "dry" states existed for a number of years after 1933. Today, there are still "dry" counties within the United States, in which the sale of alcoholic beverages is illegal.

Amendment XXII
(Ratified on February 27, 1951—
Limitation of Presidential Terms)

Section 1.

No person shall be elected to the office of the President more than twice, and no person who has held the office of President, or acted as President, for more than two years of a term to which some other person was elected President shall be elected to the office of President more than once. But this Article shall not apply to any person holding the office of President when this Article was proposed by the Congress, and shall not prevent any person who may be holding the office of President, or acting as President, during the term within which this Article becomes operative from holding the office of President or acting as President during the remainder of such term.

Section 2.

This article shall be inoperative unless it shall have been ratified as an amendment to the Constitution by the legislatures of three-fourths of the several States within seven years from the date of its submission to the States by the Congress.

No president may serve more than two elected terms. If, however, a president has succeeded to the office after the halfway point of a term in which another president was originally elected, then that president may serve for more than eight years, but not to exceed ten years.

Amendment XXIII
(Ratified on March 29, 1961—
Presidential Electors for
the District of Columbia)

Section 1.

The District constituting the seat of Government of the United States shall appoint in such manner as the Congress may direct:

A number of electors of President and Vice President equal to the whole number of Senators and Representatives in Congress to which the District would be entitled if it were a State, but in no event more than the least populous State; they shall be in addition to those appointed by the States, but they shall be considered, for the purposes of the election of President and Vice President, to be electors appointed by a State; and they shall meet in the District and perform such duties as provided by the twelfth article of amendment.

Section 2.

The Congress shall have power to enforce this article by appropriate legislation.

Citizens living in the District of Columbia have the right to vote in elections for president and vice president. The District of Columbia has three presidential electors, whereas before this amendment it had none.

Amendment XXIV
(Ratified on January 23, 1964—
The Anti–Poll Tax Amendment)

Section 1.

The right of citizens of the United States to vote in any primary or other election for President or Vice President, for electors for President or Vice President, or for Senator or Representative in Congress, shall not be denied or abridged by the United States, or any State by reason of failure to pay any poll tax or other tax.

Section 2.

The Congress shall have power to enforce this article by appropriate legislation.

No government shall require a person to pay a poll tax in order to vote in any federal election.

Amendment XXV
(Ratified on February 10, 1967—
Presidential Disability and Vice
Presidential Vacancies)

Section 1.

In case of the removal of the President from office or of his death or resignation, the Vice President shall become President.

Whenever a president dies or resigns from office, the vice president becomes president.

Section 2.

Whenever there is a vacancy in the office of the Vice President, the President shall nominate a Vice President who shall take office upon confirmation by a majority vote of both Houses of Congress.

Whenever the office of the vice presidency becomes vacant, the president may appoint someone to fill this office, provided Congress consents.

Section 3.

Whenever the President transmits to the President pro tempore of the Senate and the Speaker of the House of Representatives his written declaration that he is unable to discharge the powers and duties of his office, and until he transmits to them a written declaration to the contrary, such powers and duties shall be discharged by the Vice President as Acting President.

Whenever the president believes she or he is unable to carry out the duties of the office, she or he shall so indicate to Congress in writing. The vice president then acts as president until the president declares that she or he is again able to properly carry out the duties of the office.

Section 4.

Whenever the Vice President and a majority of either the principal officers of the executive departments or of such other body as Congress may by law provide, transmit to the President pro tempore of the Senate and the Speaker of the House of Representatives their written declaration that the President is unable to discharge the powers and duties of his office, the Vice President shall immediately assume the powers and duties of the office as Acting President.

Thereafter, when the President transmits to the President pro tempore of the Senate and the Speaker of the House of Representatives his written declaration that no inability exists, he shall resume the powers and duties of his office unless the Vice President and a majority of either the principal officers of the executive department or of such other body as Congress may by law provide, transmit within four days to the President pro tempore of the Senate and the Speaker of the House of Representatives their written declaration that the President is unable to discharge the powers and duties of his office. Thereupon Congress shall decide the issue, assembling within forty-eight hours for that purpose if not in session. If the Congress, within twenty-one days after receipt of the latter written declaration, or, if Congress is not in session, within twenty-one days after Congress is required to assemble, determines by two-thirds vote of both Houses that the President is unable to discharge the powers and duties of his office, the Vice President shall continue to discharge the same as Acting President; otherwise, the President shall resume the powers and duties of his office.

Whenever the vice president and a majority of the members of the cabinet believe that the president cannot carry out his or her duties, they shall so indicate in writing to Congress. The vice president shall then act as president. When the president believes that she or he is able to carry out her or his duties again, she or he shall so indicate to the Congress. If, though, the vice president and a majority of the cabinet do not agree, Congress must decide by a two-thirds vote within three weeks who shall act as president.

Amendment XXVI (Ratified on July 1, 1971— The Eighteen-Year-Old Vote)

Section 1.
The right of citizens of the United States, who are eighteen years of age or older, to vote shall not be denied or abridged by the United States or by any State on account of age.

No one over eighteen years of age can be denied the right to vote in federal or state elections by virtue of age.

Section 2.
The Congress shall have power to enforce this article by appropriate legislation.

Amendment XXVII (Ratified on May 7, 1992— Congressional Pay)

No law varying the compensation for the services of the Senators and Representatives shall take effect, until an election of representatives shall have intervened.

This amendment allows the voters to have some control over increases in salaries for congressional members. Originally submitted to the states for ratification in 1789, it was not ratified until 203 years later, in 1992.

APPENDIX C

Federalist Papers No. 10 and No. 51

In 1787, after the newly drafted U.S. Constitution was submitted to the thirteen states for ratification, a major political debate ensued between the Federalists (who favored ratification) and the Anti-Federalists (who opposed ratification). Anti-Federalists in New York were particularly critical of the Constitution, and in response to their objections, Federalists Alexander Hamilton, James Madison, and John Jay wrote a series of eighty-five essays in defense of the Constitution. The essays were published in New York newspapers and reprinted in other newspapers throughout the country.

For students of American government, the essays, collectively known as The Federalist Papers, are particularly important because they provide a glimpse of the founders' political philosophy and intentions in designing the Constitution—and, consequently, in shaping the American philosophy of government.

We have included in this appendix two of these essays: Federalist Papers No. 10 and No. 51. Both essays have been annotated by the authors to indicate their importance in American political thought and to clarify the meaning of particular passages.

Federalist Paper No. 10

Federalist Paper No. 10, penned by James Madison, has often been singled out as a key document in American political thought. In this essay, Madison attacks the Anti-Federalists' fear that a republican form of government will inevitably give rise to "factions"—small political parties or groups united by a common interest—that will control the government. Factions will be harmful to the country because they will implement policies beneficial to their own interests but adverse to other people's rights and to the public good. In this essay, Madison attempts to lay to rest this fear by explaining how, in a large republic such as the United States, there will be so many different factions, held together by regional or local interests, that no single one of them will dominate national politics.

Madison opens his essay with a paragraph discussing how important it is to devise a plan of government that can control the "instability, injustice, and confusion" brought about by factions.

Among the numerous advantages promised by a well-constructed Union, none deserves to be more accurately developed than its tendency to break and control the violence of faction. The friend of popular governments never finds himself so much alarmed for their character and fate as when he contemplates their propensity to this dangerous vice. He will not fail, therefore, to set a due value on any plan which, without violating the principles to which he is attached, provides a proper cure for it. The instability, injustice, and confusion introduced into the public councils have, in truth, been the mortal diseases under which popular governments have everywhere perished, as they continue to be the favorite and fruitful topics from which the adversaries to liberty derive their most specious declamations. The valuable improvements made by the American constitutions on the popular models, both ancient and modern, cannot certainly be too much admired; but it would be an unwarrantable partiality to contend that they have as effectually obviated the danger on this side, as was wished and expected. Complaints are everywhere heard from our most considerate and virtuous citizens, equally the friends of public and private faith and of public and personal liberty, that our governments are too unstable, that the public good is disregarded in the conflicts of rival parties, and that measures are too often decided, not according to the rules of justice and the rights of the minor party, but by the superior force of an interested and overbearing majority. However anxiously we may wish that these complaints had no foundation, the evidence of known facts will not permit us to deny that they are in some degree true. It will be found, indeed, on a candid review of our situation, that some of the distresses under which we labor have been erroneously charged on the operation of our governments; but it will be found, at the same time, that other causes will not alone account for many of our heaviest misfortunes; and, particularly, for that prevailing and increasing distrust of public engagements and alarm for private rights which are echoed from one end of the continent to the other. These must be chiefly, if not wholly, effects of the unsteadiness and injustice with which a factious spirit has tainted our public administration.

Madison now defines what he means by the term faction.

By a faction I understand a number of citizens, whether amounting to a majority or minority of the whole, who are united and actuated by some common impulse of passion, or of interest, adverse to the rights of other citizens, or the permanent and aggregate interests of the community.

Madison next contends that there are two methods by which the "mischiefs of faction" can be cured: by removing the causes of faction or by controlling their effects. In the following paragraphs, Madison explains how liberty itself nourishes factions. Therefore, to abolish factions would involve abolishing liberty—a cure "worse than the disease."

There are two methods of curing the mischiefs of faction: the one, by removing its causes; the other, by controlling its effects.

There are again two methods of removing the causes of faction: the one, by destroying the liberty which is essential to its existence; the other, by giving to every citizen the same opinions, the same passions, and the same interests.

It could never be more truly said than of the first remedy that it was worse than the disease. Liberty is to fac-

tion what air is to fire, an aliment without which it instantly expires. But it could not be a less folly to abolish liberty, which is essential to political life, because it nourishes faction than it would be to wish the annihilation of air, which is essential to animal life, because it imparts to fire its destructive agency.

The second expedient is as impracticable as the first would be unwise. As long as the reason of man continues fallible, and he is at liberty to exercise it, different opinions will be formed. As long as the connection subsists between his reason and his self-love, his opinions and his passions will have a reciprocal influence on each other; and the former will be objects to which the latter will attach themselves. The diversity in the faculties of men, from which the rights of property originate, is not less an insuperable obstacle to a uniformity of interests. The protection of these faculties is the first object of government. From the protection of different and unequal faculties of acquiring property, the possession of different degrees and kinds of property immediately results; and from the influence of these on the sentiments and views of the respective proprietors ensues a division of the society into different interests and parties.

The latent causes of faction are thus sown in the nature of man; and we see them everywhere brought into different degrees of activity, according to the different circumstances of civil society. A zeal for different opinions concerning religion, concerning government, and many other points, as well of speculation as of practice; an attachment to different leaders ambitiously contending for pre-eminence and power; or to persons of other descriptions whose fortunes have been interesting to the human passions, have, in turn, divided mankind into parties, inflamed them with mutual animosity, and rendered them much more disposed to vex and oppress each other than to co-operate for their common good. So strong is this propensity of mankind to fall into mutual animosities that where no substantial occasion presents itself the most frivolous and fanciful distinctions have been sufficient to kindle their unfriendly passions and excite their most violent conflicts. But the most common and durable source of factions has been the various and unequal distribution of property. Those who hold and those who are without property have ever formed distinct interests in society. Those who are creditors, and those who are debtors, fall under a like discrimination. A landed interest, a manufacturing interest, a mercantile interest, a moneyed interest, with many lesser interests, grow up of necessity in civilized nations, and divide them into different classes, actuated by different sentiments and views. The regulation of these various and interfering interests forms the principal task of modern legislation and involves the spirit of party and faction in the necessary and ordinary operations of government.

No man is allowed to be a judge in his own cause, because his interest would certainly bias his judgment, and, not improbably, corrupt his integrity. With equal, nay with greater reason, a body of men are unfit to be both judges and parties at the same time; yet what are many of the most important acts of legislation but so many judicial determinations, not indeed concerning the rights of single persons, but concerning the rights of large bodies of citizens? And what are the different classes of legislators but advocates and parties to the causes which they determine? Is a law proposed concerning private debts? It is a question to which the creditors are parties on one side and the debtors on the other. Justice ought to hold the balance between them. Yet the parties are, and must be, themselves the judges; and the most numerous party, or in other words, the most powerful faction must be expected to prevail. Shall domestic manufacturers be encouraged, and in what degree, by restrictions on foreign manufacturers? [These] are questions which would be differently decided by the landed and the manufacturing classes, and probably by neither with a sole regard to justice and the public good. The apportionment of taxes on the various descriptions of property is an act which seems to require the most exact impartiality; yet there is, perhaps, no legislative act in which greater opportunity and temptation are given to a predominant party to trample on the rules of justice. Every shilling with which they overburden the inferior number is a shilling saved to their own pockets.

It is in vain to say that enlightened statesmen will be able to adjust these clashing interests and render them all subservient to the public good. Enlightened statesmen will not always be at the helm. Nor, in many cases, can such an adjustment be made at all without taking into view indirect and remote considerations, which will rarely prevail over the immediate interest which one party may find in disregarding the rights of another or the good of the whole.

The inference to which we are brought is that the *causes* of faction cannot be removed and that relief is only to be sought in the means of controlling its *effects*.

Having concluded that "the causes of faction cannot be removed," Madison now looks in some detail at the other method by which factions can be cured—by controlling their *effects. This is the heart of his essay. He begins by positing a significant question: How can you have self-government without risking the possibility that a ruling faction, particularly a majority faction, might tyrannize over the rights of others?*

If a faction consists of less than a majority, relief is supplied by the republican principle, which enables the majority to defeat its sinister views by regular vote. It may clog the administration, it may convulse the society; but it will be unable to execute and mask its violence under the forms of the Constitution. When a majority is included in a faction, the form of popular government, on the other hand, enables it to sacrifice to its ruling passion or interest both the public good and the rights of other citizens. To secure the public good and private rights against the danger of such a faction, and at the same time to preserve the spirit and the form of popular government, is then the great object to which our inquiries are directed. Let me add that it is the great desideratum by which alone this form of government can be rescued from the opprobrium under which it has so long labored and be recommended to the esteem and adoption of mankind.

Madison now sets forth the idea that one way to control the effects of factions is to ensure that the majority are rendered incapable of acting in concert in order to "carry into effect schemes of oppression." He goes on to state that in a democracy, in which all citizens participate personally in government decision making, there is no way to prevent the majority from communicating with each other and, as a result, acting in concert.

By what means is this object attainable? Evidently by one of two only. Either the existence of the same passion or interest in a majority at the same time must be prevented, or the majority, having such coexistent passion or interest, must be rendered, by their number and local situation, unable to concert and carry into effect schemes of oppression. If the impulse and the opportunity be suffered to coincide, we well know that neither moral nor religious motives can be relied on as an adequate control. They are not found to be such on the injustice and violence of individuals, and lose their efficacy in proportion to the number combined together, that is, in proportion as their efficacy becomes needful.

From this view of the subject it may be concluded that a pure democracy, by which I mean a society consisting of a small number of citizens, who assemble and administer the government in person, can admit of no cure for the mischiefs of faction. A common passion or interest will, in almost every case, be felt by a majority of the whole; a communication and concert results from the form of government itself; and there is nothing to check the inducements to sacrifice the weaker party or an obnoxious individual. Hence it is that such democracies have ever been spectacles of turbulence and contention; have ever been found incompatible with personal security or the rights of property; and have in general been as short in their lives as they have been violent in their deaths. Theoretic politicians, who have patronized this species of government, have erroneously supposed that by reducing mankind to a perfect equality in their political rights, they would at the same time be perfectly equalized and assimilated in their possessions, their opinions, and their passions.

Madison now moves on to discuss the benefits of a republic with respect to controlling the effects of factions. He begins by defining a republic and then pointing out the "two great points of difference" between a republic and a democracy: a republic is governed by a small body of elected representatives, not by the people directly; and a republic can extend over a much larger territory and embrace more citizens than a democracy can.

A republic, by which I mean a government in which the scheme of representation takes place, opens a different prospect and promises the cure for which we are seeking. Let us examine the points in which it varies from pure democracy, and we shall comprehend both the nature of the cure and the efficacy which it must derive from the Union.

The two great points of difference between a democracy and a republic are: first, the delegation of the government, in the latter, to a small number of citizens elected by the rest; secondly, the greater number of citizens and greater sphere of country over which the latter may be extended.

In the following four paragraphs, Madison explains how in a republic, particularly a large republic, the delegation of authority to elected representatives will increase the likelihood that those who govern will be "fit" for their positions and that a proper balance will be achieved between local (factional) interests and national interests. Note how he stresses that the new federal Constitution, by dividing powers between state governments and the national government, provides a "happy combination in this respect."

The effect of the first difference is, on the one hand, to refine and enlarge the public views by passing them through the medium of a chosen body of citizens, whose wisdom may best discern the true interest of their country and whose patriotism and love of justice will be least likely to sacrifice it to temporary or partial considerations. Under such a regulation it may well happen that the public voice, pronounced by the representatives of the people, will be more consonant to the public good than if pronounced by the people themselves, convened for the purpose. On the other hand, the effect may be inverted. Men of factious tempers, of local prejudices, or of sinister designs, may, by intrigue, by corruption, or by other means, first obtain the suffrages, and then betray the interests of the people. The question resulting is, whether small or extensive republics are most favorable to the election of proper guardians of the public weal; and it is clearly decided in favor of the latter by two obvious considerations.

In the first place it is to be remarked that however small the republic may be the representatives must be raised to a certain number in order to guard against the cabals of a few; and that however large it may be they must be limited to a certain number in order to guard against the confusion of a multitude. Hence, the number of representatives in the two cases not being in proportion to that of the constituents, and being proportionally greatest in the small republic, it follows that if the proportion of fit characters be not less in the large than in the small republic, the former will present a greater option, and consequently a greater probability of a fit choice.

In the next place, as each representative will be chosen by a greater number of citizens in the large than in the small republic, it will be more difficult for unworthy candidates to practice with success the vicious arts by which elections are too often carried; and the suffrages of the people being more free, will be more likely to center on men who possess the most attractive merit and the most diffusive and established characters.

It must be confessed that in this, as in most other cases, there is a mean, on both sides of which inconveniencies will be found to lie. By enlarging too much the number of electors, you render the representative too little acquainted with all their local circumstances and lesser interests; as by reducing it too much, you render him unduly attached to these, and too little fit to comprehend and pursue great and national objects. The federal Constitution forms a happy combination in this respect; the great and aggregate interests being referred to the national, the local and particular to the State legislatures.

Madison now looks more closely at the other difference between a republic and a democracy—namely, that a republic can encompass a larger territory and more citizens than a democracy can. In the remaining paragraphs of his essay, Madison concludes that in a large republic, it will be difficult for factions to act in concert. Although a factious group—religious, political, economic, or otherwise—may control a local or regional government, it will have little chance of gathering a national following. This is because in a large republic, there will be numerous factions whose work will offset the work of any one particular faction ("sect"). As Madison phrases it, these numerous factions will "secure the national councils against any danger from that source."

The other point of difference is the greater number of citizens and extent of territory which may be brought within the compass of republican than of democratic government; and it is this circumstance principally which renders factious combinations less to be dreaded in the former than in the latter. The smaller the society, the fewer probably will be the distinct parties and interests composing it; the fewer the distinct parties and interests, the more frequently will a majority be found of the same party; and the smaller the number of individuals composing a majority, and the smaller the compass within which they are placed, the more easily will they concert and execute their plans of oppression. Extend the sphere and you take in a greater variety of parties and interests; you make it less probable that a majority of the whole will have a common motive to invade the rights of other citizens; or if such a common motive exists, it will be more difficult for all who feel it to discover their own strength and to act in unison with each other. Besides other impediments, it may be remarked that, where there is a consciousness of unjust or dishonorable purposes, communication is always checked by distrust in proportion to the number whose concurrence is necessary.

Hence, it clearly appears that the same advantage which a republic has over a democracy in controlling the effects of faction is enjoyed by a large over a small republic—is enjoyed by the Union over the States composing it. Does this advantage consist in the substitution of representatives whose enlightened views and virtuous sentiments render them superior to local prejudices and to schemes of injustice? It will not be denied that the representation of the Union will be most likely to possess these requisite endowments. Does it consist in the greater security afforded by a greater variety of parties, against the event of any one party being able to outnumber and oppress the rest? In an equal degree does the increased variety of parties comprised within the Union increase this security. Does it, in fine, consist in the greater obstacles opposed to the concert and accomplishment of the secret wishes of an unjust and interested majority? Here again the extent of the Union gives it the most palpable advantage.

The influence of factious leaders may kindle a flame within their particular States but will be unable to spread a general conflagration through the other States. A religious sect may degenerate into a political faction in a part of the Confederacy; but the variety of sects dispersed over the entire face of it must secure the national councils against any danger from that source. A rage for paper money, for an abolition of debts, for an equal division of property, or for any other improper or wicked project, will be less apt to pervade the whole body of the Union than a particular member of it, in the same proportion as such a malady is more likely to taint a particular county or district than an entire State.

In the extent and proper structure of the Union, therefore, we behold a republican remedy for the diseases most incident to republican government. And according to the degree of pleasure and pride we feel in being republicans ought to be our zeal in cherishing the spirit and supporting the character of federalists.

Publius
(James Madison)

Federalist Paper No. 51

Federalist Paper No. 51, also authored by James Madison, is another classic in American political theory. Although the Federalists wanted a strong national government, they had not abandoned the traditional American view, particularly notable during the revolutionary era, that those holding powerful government positions could not be trusted to put national interests and the common good above their own personal interests. In this essay, Madison explains why the separation of the national government's powers into three branches—executive, legislative, and judicial—and a federal structure of government offer the best protection against tyranny.

To what expedient, then, shall we finally resort, for maintaining in practice the necessary partition of power among the several departments as laid down in the Constitution? The only answer that can be given is that as all these exterior provisions are found to be inadequate the defect must be supplied, by so contriving the interior structure of the government as that its several constituent parts may, by their mutual relations, be the means of keeping each other in their proper places. Without presuming to undertake a full development of this important idea I will hazard a few general observations which may perhaps place it in a clearer light, and enable us to form a more correct judgment of the principles and structure of the government planned by the convention.

In the next two paragraphs, Madison stresses that for the powers of the different branches (departments) of government to be truly separated, the personnel in one branch should not be dependent on another branch for their appointment or for the "emoluments" (compensation) attached to their offices.

In order to lay a due foundation for that separate and distinct exercise of the different powers of government, which to a certain extent is admitted on all hands to be essential to the preservation of liberty, it is evident that each department should have a will of its own; and consequently should be so constituted that the members of each should have as little agency as possible in the appointment of the members of the others. Were this principle rigorously adhered to, it would require that all the appointments for the supreme executive, legislative, and judiciary magistracies should be drawn from the same fountain of authority, the people, through channels having no communication whatever with one another. Perhaps such a plan of constructing the several depart-

ments would be less difficult in practice than it may in contemplation appear. Some difficulties, however, and some additional expense would attend the execution of it. Some deviations, therefore, from the principle must be admitted. In the constitution of the judiciary department in particular, it might be inexpedient to insist rigorously on the principle: first, because peculiar qualifications being essential in the members, the primary consideration ought to be to select that mode of choice which best secures these qualifications; second, because the permanent tenure by which the appointments are held in that department must soon destroy all sense of dependence on the authority conferring them.

It is equally evident that the members of each department should be as little dependent as possible on those of the others for the emoluments annexed to their offices. Were the executive magistrate, or the judges, not independent of the legislature in this particular, their independence in every other would be merely nominal.

In the following passages, which are among the most widely quoted of Madison's writings, he explains how the separation of the powers of government into three branches helps to counter the effects of personal ambition on government. The separation of powers allows personal motives to be linked to the constitutional rights of a branch of government. In effect, rival personal interests in each branch will help to keep the powers of the three government branches separate and, in so doing, will help to guard the public interest.

But the great security against a gradual concentration of the several powers in the same department consists in giving to those who administer each department the necessary constitutional means and personal motives to resist encroachments of the others. The provision for defense must in this, as in all other cases, be made commensurate to the danger of attack. Ambition must be made to counteract ambition. The interest of the man must be connected with the constitutional rights of the place. It may be a reflection on human nature that such devices should be necessary to control the abuses of government. But what is government itself but the greatest of all reflections on human nature? If men were angels, no government would be necessary. If angels were to govern men, neither external nor internal controls on government would be necessary. In framing a government which is to be administered by men over men, the great difficulty lies in this: you must first enable the government to control the governed; and in the next place oblige it to control itself. A dependence on the people is, no doubt, the primary control on the government; but experience has taught mankind the necessity of auxiliary precautions.

This policy of supplying, by opposite and rival interests, the defect of better motives, might be traced through the whole system of human affairs, private as well as public. We see it particularly displayed in all the subordinate distributions of power, where the constant aim is to divide and arrange the several offices in such a manner as that each may be a check on the other—that the private interest of every individual may be a sentinel over the public rights. These inventions of prudence cannot be less requisite in the distribution of the supreme powers of the State.

Madison now addresses the issue of equality between the branches of government. The legislature will necessarily predominate, but if the executive is given an "absolute negative" (absolute veto power) over legislative actions, this also could lead to an abuse of power. Madison concludes that the division of the legislature into two "branches" (parts, or chambers) will act as a check on the legislature's powers.

But it is not possible to give to each department an equal power of self-defense. In republican government, the legislative authority necessarily predominates. The remedy for this inconveniency is to divide the legislature into different branches; and to render them, by different modes of election and different principles of action, as little connected with each other as the nature of their common functions and their common dependence on the society will admit. It may even be necessary to guard against dangerous encroachments by still further precautions. As the weight of the legislative authority requires that it should be thus divided, the weakness of the executive may require, on the other hand, that it should be fortified. An absolute negative on the legislature appears, at first view, to be the natural defense with which the executive magistrate should be armed. But perhaps it would be neither altogether safe nor alone sufficient. On ordinary occasions it might not be exerted with the requisite firmness, and on extraordinary occasions it might be perfidiously abused. May not this defect of an absolute negative be supplied by some qualified connection between this weaker department and the weaker branch of the stronger department, by which the latter may be led to support the constitutional rights of the former, without being too much detached from the rights of its own department?

If the principles on which these observations are founded be just, as I persuade myself they are, and they be applied as a criterion to the several State constitutions, and to the federal Constitution, it will be found that if the latter does not perfectly correspond with them, the former are infinitely less able to bear such a test.

In the remainder of the essay, Madison discusses how a federal system of government, in which powers are divided between the states and the national government, offers "double security" against tyranny.

There are, moreover, two considerations particularly applicable to the federal system of America, which place that system in a very interesting point of view.

First. In a single republic, all the power surrendered by the people is submitted to the administration of a single government; and the usurpations are guarded against by a division of the government into distinct and separate departments. In the compound republic of America, the power surrendered by the people is first divided between two distinct governments, and then the portion allotted to each subdivided among distinct and separate departments. Hence a double security arises to the rights of the people. The different governments will control each other, at the same time that each will be controlled by itself.

Second. It is of great importance in a republic not only to guard the society against the oppression of its rulers, but to guard one part of the society against the injustice of the other part. Different interests necessarily exist in different classes of citizens. If a majority be united by a common interest, the rights of the minority will be insecure. There are but two methods of providing against this evil: the one by creating a will in the community independent of the majority—that is, of the society itself; the other, by comprehending in the society so many separate descriptions of citizens as will render an unjust combination of a majority of the whole very improbable, if not impracticable. The first method prevails in all governments possessing an hereditary or self-appointed authority. This, at best, is but a precarious security; because a power independent of the society may as well espouse the unjust views of the major as the rightful interests of the minor party, and may possibly be turned against both parties. The second method will be exemplified in the federal republic of the United States. Whilst all authority in it will be derived from and dependent on the society, the society itself will be broken into so many parts, interests and classes of citizens, that the rights of individuals, or of the minority, will be in little danger from interested combinations of the majority. In a free government the security for civil rights must be the same as that for religious rights. It consists in the one case in the multiplicity of interests, and in the other in the multiplicity of sects. The degree of security in both cases will depend on the number of interests and sects; and this may be presumed to depend on the extent of country and number of people comprehended under the same government. This view of the subject must particularly recommend a proper federal system to all the sincere and considerate friends of republican government, since it shows that in exact proportion as the territory of the Union may be formed into more circumscribed Confederacies, or States, oppressive combinations of a majority will be facilitated; the best security, under the republican forms, for the rights of every class of citizen, will be diminished; and consequently the stability and independence of some member of the government, the only other security, must be proportionally increased. Justice is the end of government. It is the end of civil society. It ever has been and ever will be pursued until it be obtained, or until liberty be lost in the pursuit. In a society under the forms of which the stronger faction can readily unite and oppress the weaker, anarchy may as truly be said to reign as in a state of nature, where the weaker individual is not secured against the violence of the stronger; and as, in the latter state, even the stronger individuals are prompted, by the uncertainty of their condition, to submit to a government which may protect the weak as well as themselves; so, in the former state, will the more powerful factions or parties be gradually induced, by a like motive, to wish for a government which will protect all parties, the weaker as well as the more powerful. It can be little doubted that if the State of Rhode Island was separated from the Confederacy and left to itself, the insecurity of rights under the popular form of government within such narrow limits would be displayed by such reiterated oppressions of factious majorities that some power altogether independent of the people would soon be called for by the voice of the very factions whose misrule had proved the necessity of it. In the extended republic of the United States, and among the great variety of interests, parties, and sects which it embraces, a coalition of a majority of the whole society could seldom take place on any other principles than those of justice and the general good; whilst there being thus less danger to a minor from the will of a major party, there must be less pretext, also, to provide for the security of the former, by introducing into the government a will not dependent on the latter, or, in other words, a will independent of the society itself. It is no less certain than it is important, notwithstanding the contrary opinions which have been entertained, that the larger the society, provided it lie within a practicable sphere, the more duly capable it will be of self-government. And happily for the republican cause, the practicable sphere may be carried to a very great extent by a judicious modification and mixture of the *federal principle*.

Publius
(James Madison)

Glossary

A

Acquisitive Model   A model of bureaucracy that views top level bureaucrats as seeking constantly to expand the size of their budgets and the staffs of their departments or agencies so as to gain greater power and influence in the public sector.

Actual Malice   In libel cases, either knowledge of a deflamatory statement's falsity or a reckless disregard for the truth.

Advice and Consent   The power vested in the U.S. Senate by the Constitution (Article II, Section 2) to give its advice and consent to the president on treaties and presidential appointments.

Affirm   To declare that a court ruling is valid and must stand.

Affirmative Action   A policy in educational admissions or job hiring that gives special consideration or compensatory treatment to traditionally disadvantaged groups in an effort to overcome present effects of past discrimination.

Agenda Setting   Determining which public-policy questions will be debated or considered.

Amicus Curiae Brief   A brief (a document containing a legal argument supporting a desired outcome in a particular case) filed by a third party, or *amicus curiae* (Latin for "friend of the court"), who is not directly involved in the litigation but who has an interest in the outcome of the case.

Anti-Federalist   An individual who opposed the ratification of the new Constitution in 1787. The Anti-Federalists were opposed to a strong central government.

Appellate Court   A court having jurisdiction to review cases and issues that were originally tried in lower courts.

Appointment Power   The authority vested in the president to fill a government office or position. Positions filled by presidential appointment include those in the executive branch and the federal judiciary, commissioned officers in the armed forces, and members of the independent regulatory commissions.

Appropriation   The passage, by Congress, of a spending bill, specifying the amount of authorized funds that actually will be allocated for an agency's use.

Aristocracy   Rule by the "best"; in reality, rule by an upper class.

Attentive Public   That portion of the general public that pays attention to policy issues.

Australian Ballot   A secret ballot prepared, distributed, and tabulated by government officials at public expense. Since 1888, all states have used the Australian ballot rather than an open, public ballot.

Authoritarianism   A type of regime in which only the government itself is fully controlled by the ruler. Social and economic institutions exist that are not under the government's control. Contrast *totalitarianism*.

Authorization   A formal declaration by a legislative committee that a certain amount of funding may be available to an agency. Some authorizations terminate in a year; others are renewable automatically without further congressional action.

B

Bad-Tendency Rule   A rule stating that speech or other First Amendment freedoms may be curtailed if there is a possibility that such expression might lead to some "evil."

"Beauty Contest"   A presidential primary in which contending candidates compete for popular votes but the results have little or no impact on the selection of delegates to the national convention.

Bicameral Legislature   A legislature made up of two chambers, or parts. The U.S. Congress, composed of the House of Representatives and the Senate, is a bicameral legislature.

Bicameralism   The division of a legislature into two separate assemblies.

Block Grants   Federal programs that provide funds to state and local governments for general functional areas, such as criminal justice or mental-health programs.

Bundling   The practice of adding together maximum individual campaign contributions to increase their impact on the candidate.

Bureaucracy   A large organization that is structured hierarchically to carry out specific functions.

Busing In the context of civil rights, the transportation of public school students from areas where they live to schools in other areas to eliminate school segregation based on residential patterns.

C

Cabinet An advisory group selected by the president to aid in decision making. The cabinet includes the heads of fifteen executive departments and others named by the president. Depending on the president, the cabinet may be highly influential or relatively insignificant in its advisory role.

Cabinet Department One of the fifteen departments of the executive branch (State, Treasury, Defense, Justice, Interior, Agriculture, Commerce, Labor, Health and Human Services, Housing and Urban Development, Education, Energy, Transportation, Veterans Affairs, and Homeland Security).

Capture The act of gaining direct or indirect control over agency personnel and decision makers by the industry that is being regulated.

Case Law The rules and principles announced in court decisions. Case law includes judicial interpretations of common law principles and doctrines as well as interpretations of constitutional law, statutory law, and administrative law.

Casework Personal work for constituents by members of Congress.

Categorical Grants-in-Aid Federal grants-in-aid to states or local governments that are for very specific programs or projects.

Caucus A closed meeting of party leaders to select party candidates or to decide on policy; also, a meeting of party members designed to select candidates and propose policies.

Checks and Balances A major principle of the American government system whereby each branch of the government exercises a check on the actions of the others.

Chief Diplomat The role of the president in recognizing foreign governments, making treaties, and making executive agreements.

Chief Executive The role of the president as head of the executive branch of the government.

Chief Legislator The role of the president in influencing the making of laws.

Chief of Staff The person who is named to direct the White House Office and advise the president.

Chief of State The role of the president as ceremonial head of the government.

Civil Liberties Those personal freedoms that are protected for all individuals and that generally deal with individual freedom. Civil liberties typically involve restraining the government's actions against individuals.

Civil Rights Generally, all rights rooted in the Fourteenth Amendment's guarantee of equal protection under the law.

Civil Service A collective term for the body of employees working for the government. Generally, the term is understood to apply to all those who gain government employment through a merit system.

Civil Service Commission The initial central personnel agency of the national government; created in 1883.

Class-Action Suit A lawsuit filed by an individual seeking damages for "all persons similarly situated."

Clear and Present Danger Test The test proposed by Justice Holmes for determining when government may restrict free speech. Restrictions are permissible, he argued, only when speech presents a "clear and present danger" to the public order.

Coattail Effect The influence of a popular candidate on the electoral success of other candidates on the same party ticket. The effect is increased by the party-column ballot, which encourages straight-ticket voting.

Cold War The ideological, political, and economic impasse that existed between the United States and the Soviet Union following World War II.

Commander in Chief The role of the president as supreme commander of the military forces of the United States and of the state National Guard units when they are called into federal service.

Commerce Clause The section of the Constitution in which Congress is given the power to regulate trade among the states and with foreign countries.

Commercial Speech Advertising statements, which increasingly have been given First Amendment protection.

Common Law Judge-made law that originated in England from decisions shaped according to prevailing customs. Decisions were applied to similar situations and thus gradually became common to the nation.

Concurrent Powers Powers held jointly by the national and state governments.

Concurring Opinion A separate opinion prepared by a judge who supports the decision of the majority of the court but who wants to make or clarify a particular point or to voice disapproval of the grounds on which the decision was made.

Confederal System A system of government consisting of a league of independent states, each having essentially sovereign powers. The central government created by such a league has only limited powers over the states.

Confederation A political system in which states or regional governments retain ultimate authority except for those powers they expressly delegate to a central government. A voluntary association of independent states, in which the member states agree to limited restraints on their freedom of action.

Conference Committee A special joint committee appointed to reconcile differences when bills pass the two chambers of Congress in different forms.

Consensus General agreement among the citizenry on an issue.

Consent of the People The idea that governments and laws derive their legitimacy from the consent of the governed.

Conservatism A set of beliefs that includes a limited role for the national government in helping individuals, support for traditional values and lifestyles, and a cautious response to change.

Constituent One of the people represented by a legislator or other elected or appointed official.

Constitutional Power A power vested in the president by Article II of the Constitution.

Containment A U.S. diplomatic policy adopted by the Truman administration to "build situations of strength" around the globe to contain Communist power within its existing boundaries.

Continuing Resolution A temporary law that Congress passes when an appropriations bill has not been decided by the beginning of the new fiscal year on October 1.

Cooperative Federalism The theory that the states and the national government should cooperate in solving problems.

Corrupt Practices Acts A series of acts passed by Congress in an attempt to limit and regulate the size and sources of contributions and expenditures in political campaigns.

Credentials Committee A committee used by political parties at their national conventions to determine which delegates may participate. The committee inspects the claim of each prospective delegate to be seated as a legitimate representative of his or her state.

D

De Facto Segregation Racial segregation that occurs because of past social and economic conditions and residential patterns.

De Jure Segregation Racial segregation that occurs because of laws or administrative decisions by public agencies.

Defamation of Character Wrongfully hurting a person's good reputation. The law has imposed a general duty on all persons to refrain from making false, defamatory statements about others.

Defense Policy A subset of national security policy that generally refers to the set of policies that direct the scale and size of the U.S. armed forces.

Democracy A system of government in which ultimate political authority is vested in the people. Derived from the Greek words *demos* ("the people") and *kratos* ("authority").

Democratic Party One of the two major American political parties that evolved out of the Republican Party of Thomas Jefferson.

Détente A French word meaning a relaxation of tensions. The term characterizes U.S.–Soviet policy as it developed under President Richard Nixon and Secretary of State Henry Kissinger. Détente stressed direct cooperative dealings with Cold War rivals but avoided ideological accommodation.

Diplomacy The total process by which states carry on political relations with each other; the settling of conflicts among nations by peaceful means.

Diplomatic Recognition The formal acknowledgment of a foreign government as legitimate.

Direct Democracy A system of government in which political decisions are made by the people directly, rather than by their elected representatives; probably possible only in small political communities.

Direct Primary An intraparty election in which the voters select the candidates who will run on a party's ticket in the subsequent general election.

Direct Technique An interest group activity that involves interaction with government officials to further the group's goals.

Discharge Petition A procedure by which a bill in the House of Representatives may be forced out of a committee (discharged) that has refused to report it for consideration by the House. The discharge petition must be signed by an absolute majority (218) of representatives and is used only on rare occasions.

Dissenting Opinion A separate opinion in which a judge dissents from (disagrees with) the conclusion reached by the majority on the court and expounds his or her own views about the case.

Diversity of Citizenship A basis for federal court jurisdiction over a lawsuit that involves citizens of different states or (more rarely) citizens of a U.S. state and citizens or subjects of a foreign country. The amount in controversy must be at least $75,000 before a federal court can take jurisdiction in such cases.

Divided Government A situation in which one major political party controls the presidency and the other controls the chambers of Congress or in which one party controls a state governorship and the other controls the state legislature.

Divisive Opinion Public opinion that is polarized between two quite different positions.

Domestic Policy Public plans or courses of action that concern internal issues of national importance, such as poverty, crime, and the environment.

Dominant Culture The values, customs, language, and ideals established by the group or groups in a society that traditionally have controlled politics and government institutions in that society.

Dual Federalism A system of government in which the states and the national government each remain supreme within their own spheres. The doctrine looks on nation and state as coequal sovereign powers. It holds that acts of states within their reserved powers are legitimate limitations on the powers of the national government.

E

Earned-Income Tax Credit (EITC) Program A government program that helps low-income workers by giving back part or all of their Social Security taxes.

Economic Aid Assistance to other nations in the form of grants, loans, or credits to buy the assisting nation's products.

Elastic Clause, or Necessary and Proper Clause The clause in Article I, Section 8, that grants Congress the power to do whatever is necessary to execute its specifically delegated powers.

Elector A person on the partisan slate that is selected early in the presidential election year according to state laws and the applicable political party apparatus to cast ballots for president and vice president. The number of electors in each state is equal to that state's number of representatives in both chambers of Congress.

Electoral College A group of persons called electors selected by the voters in each state and Washington, D.C.; this group officially elects the president and vice president of the United States. The number of electors in each state is equal to the number of each state's representatives in both chambers of Congress. The Twenty-third Amendment to the Constitution permits Washington, D.C., to have as many electors as the smallest state.

Elite An upper socioeconomic class that controls political and economic affairs.

Elite Theory A perspective holding that society is ruled by a small number of people who exercise power in their self-interest.

Emergency Power An inherent power exercised by the

president during a period of national crisis, particularly in foreign affairs.

Enabling Legislation   A statute enacted by Congress that authorizes the creation of an administrative agency and specifies the name, purpose, composition, functions, and powers of the agency being created.

Enumerated Powers   Powers specifically granted to the national government by the Constitution. The first seventeen clauses of Article I, Section 8, specify most of the enumerated powers of Congress.

Environmental Impact Statement (EIS)   As a requirement mandated by the National Environmental Policy Act, a report that must show the costs and benefits of major federal actions that could significantly affect the quality of the environment.

Equality   As a political value, the idea that all people are of equal worth.

Era of Good Feelings   The years from 1817 to 1825, when James Monroe was president and there was, in effect, no political opposition.

Establishment Clause   The part of the First Amendment prohibiting the establishment of a church officially supported by the national government. It is applied to questions of state and local government aid to religious organizations and schools, questions of the legality of allowing or requiring school prayers, and questions of the teaching of evolution versus fundamentalist theories of creation.

Exclusionary Rule   A policy forbidding the admission at trial of illegally seized evidence.

Executive Agreement   An international agreement made by the president, without senatorial ratification, with the head of a foreign state.

Executive Budget   The budget prepared and submitted by the president to Congress.

Executive Office of the President (EOP)   An organization established by President Franklin D. Roosevelt by executive order under the Reorganization Act of 1939 to assist the president in carrying out major duties.

Executive Order   A rule or regulation issued by the president that has the effect of law. Executive orders can implement and give administrative effect to provisions in the Constitution, to treaties, and to statutes.

Executive Privilege   The right of executive officials to withhold information from or to refuse to appear before a legislative committee. Executive privilege is enjoyed by the president and by those executive officials accorded that right by the president.

Expressed Power   A constitutional or statutory power of the president that is expressly written into the Constitution or into statutory law.

F

Faction   A group or bloc in a legislature or political party acting in pursuit of some special interest or position.

Fall Review   The time every year when, after receiving formal federal agency requests for funding for the next fiscal year, the Office of Management and Budget reviews the requests, makes changes, and submits its recommendations to the president.

Federal Mandate   A requirement in federal legislation that forces states and municipalities to comply with certain rules.

Federal Open Market Committee (FOMC)   The most important body within the Federal Reserve System. The FOMC decides how monetary policy should be carried out by the Federal Reserve System.

Federal Question   A question that pertains to the U.S. Constitution, acts of Congress, or treaties. A federal question provides a basis for federal jurisdiction.

Federal Register   A publication of the executive branch of the U.S. government that prints executive orders, rules, and regulations.

Federal System   A system of government in which power is divided between a central government and regional, or subdivisional, governments. Each level must have some domain in which its policies are dominant and some genuine political or constitutional guarantee of its authority.

Federalist   The name given to one who was in favor of the adoption of the U.S. Constitution and the creation of a federal union with a strong central government.

Feminism   The movement that supports political, economic, and social equality for women.

Fiscal Policy   The use of changes in government spending or taxation to alter national economic variables, such as the rate of unemployment.

Fiscal Year (FY)   A twelve-month period that is used for bookkeeping, or accounting, purposes. Usually, the fiscal year does not coincide with the calendar year. For example, the federal government's fiscal year runs from October 1 through September 30.

Focus Group   A small group of individuals who are led in discussion by a professional consultant to gather opinions on and responses to candidates and issues.

Food Stamps   Coupons issued by the federal government to low-income individuals to be used for the purchase of food.

Foreign Policy   A nation's external goals and the techniques and strategies used to achieve them.

Foreign Policy Process   The steps by which external goals are decided and acted on.

Free Exercise Clause   The provision of the First Amendment guaranteeing the free exercise of religion.

Front-Loading   The practice of moving presidential primary elections to the early part of the campaign, to maximize the impact of certain states or regions on the nomination.

Front-Runner   The presidential candidate who appears to be ahead at a given time in the primary season.

G

Gag Order   An order issued by a judge restricting the publication of news about a trial in progress or a pretrial hearing in order to protect the accused's right to a fair trial.

Gender Discrimination   Any practice, policy, or procedure that denies equality of treatment to an individual or to a group because of gender.

Gender Gap   A term most often used to describe the difference between the percentage of women who vote for a particular candidate and the percentage of men who vote for the candidate. The term came into use after the 1980 presidential elections.

General Jurisdiction Exists when a court's authority to hear cases is not significantly restricted. A court of general jurisdiction normally can hear a broad range of cases.

Generational Effect A long-lasting effect of events of a particular time period on the political opinions or preferences of those who came of political age at that time.

Gerrymandering The drawing of legislative district boundary lines for the purpose of obtaining partisan or factional advantage. A district is said to be gerrymandered when its shape is manipulated by the dominant party in the state legislature to maximize electoral strength at the expense of the minority party.

Government The institution in which decisions are made that resolve conflicts or allocate benefits and privileges. It is unique because it has the ultimate authority within society.

Government Corporation An agency of government that administers a quasi-business enterprise. These corporations are used when activities are primarily commercial. They produce revenue for their continued existence, and they require greater flexibility than is permitted for departments and agencies.

Government in the Sunshine Act A law that requires all multiheaded federal agencies to conduct their business regularly in public session.

Grandfather Clause A device used by southern states to exempt whites from state taxes and literacy laws originally intended to disenfranchise African American voters. It restricted the voting franchise to those who could prove that their grandfathers had voted before 1867.

Great Compromise The compromise between the New Jersey and the Virginia plans that created one chamber of Congress based on population and one chamber representing each state equally; also called the Connecticut Compromise.

H

Hatch Act An act passed in 1939 that restricted the political activities of government employees. It also prohibited a political group from spending more than $3 million in any campaign and limited individual contributions to a committee to $5,000. The act was designed to control political influence buying.

I

Ideology A comprehensive set of beliefs about the nature of people and about the institutions and role of government.

Impeachment As authorized by Articles I and II of the Constitution, an action by the House of Representatives to accuse the president, vice president, or civil officers of the United States of committing "Treason, Bribery, or other high Crimes and Misdemeanors."

Income Transfer A transfer of income from some individuals in the economy to other individuals. This is generally done by way of the government. It is a transfer in the sense that no current services are rendered by the recipients.

Incorporation Theory The view that most of the protections of the Bill of Rights apply to state governments through the Fourteenth Amendment's due process clause.

Independent A voter or candidate who does not identify with a political party.

Independent Executive Agency A federal agency that is not part of a cabinet department but reports directly to the president.

Independent Expenditures Nonregulated contributions from PACs, ideological organizations, and individuals. The groups may spend funds on advertising or other campaign activities so long as those expenditures are not coordinated with those of a candidate.

Independent Regulatory Agency An agency outside the major executive departments charged with making and implementing rules and regulations to protect the public interest.

Indiana Ballot See *Party-Column Ballot*.

Indirect Technique A strategy employed by interest groups that uses third parties to influence government officials.

Inherent Power A power of the president derived from the loosely worded statements in the Constitution that "the executive Power shall be vested in a President" and that the president should "take Care that the Laws be faithfully executed"; defined through practice rather than through constitutional or statutory law.

Initiative A procedure by which voters can propose a law or a constitutional amendment.

In-Kind Subsidy A good or service—such as food stamps, housing, or medical care—provided by the government to low-income groups.

Institution An ongoing organization that performs certain functions for society.

Instructed Delegate A legislator who is an agent of the voters who elected him or her and who votes according to the views of constituents regardless of personal assessments.

Intelligence Community The government agencies that are involved in gathering information about the capabilities and intentions of foreign governments and that engage in covert activities to further U.S. foreign policy aims.

Interest Group An organized group of individuals sharing common objectives who actively attempt to influence policymakers.

Iron Curtain The term used to describe the division of Europe between the Soviet Union and the West; popularized by Winston Churchill in a speech portraying Europe as being divided by an iron curtain, with the nations of Eastern Europe behind the curtain and increasingly under Soviet control.

Iron Triangle The three-way alliance among legislators, bureaucrats, and interest groups to make or preserve policies that benefit their respective interests.

Isolationist Foreign Policy Abstaining from an active role in international affairs or alliances, which characterized U.S. foreign policy toward Europe during most of the 1800s.

Issue Advocacy Advertising Advertising paid for by interest groups that supports or opposes a candidate or candidate's position on an issue without mentioning voting or elections.

Issue Network A group of individuals or organizations— which may consist of legislators or legislative staff members, interest group leaders, bureaucrats, the media, scholars, and other experts—that support a particular policy position on a given issue, such as one on the environment, taxation, or consumer safety.

Item Veto   The power to veto particular sections or items of an appropriations bill while signing the remainder of the bill into law. The governors of most states have this power.

J

Joint Committee   A legislative committee composed of members from both chambers of Congress.

Judicial Activism   A doctrine holding that the Supreme Court should take an active role in using its powers to check the activities of Congress, state legislatures, and administrative agencies when those government bodies exceed their authority.

Judicial Implementation   The way in which court decisions are translated into action.

Judicial Restraint   A doctrine holding that the Supreme Court should defer to the decisions made by the elected representatives of the people in the legislative and executive branches.

Judicial Review   The power of the Supreme Court or any court to declare unconstitutional federal or state laws and other acts of government.

Jurisdiction   The authority of a court to decide certain cases. Not all courts have the authority to decide all cases. Where a case arises and what its subject matter is are two jurisdictional factors.

Justiciable Question   A question that may be raised and reviewed in court.

K

Keynesian Economics   An economic theory named after English economist John Maynard Keynes and typically associated with the use of fiscal policy to alter national economic variables—for example, increased government spending during times of economic downturns.

Kitchen Cabinet   The informal advisers to the president.

L

Labor Movement   Generally, the full range of economic and political expression of working-class interests; politically, the organization of working-class interests.

Lawmaking   The process of deciding the legal rules that govern society. Such laws may regulate minor affairs or establish broad national policies.

Legislature   A governmental body primarily responsible for the making of laws.

Libel   A written defamation of a person's character, reputation, business, or property rights. To a limited degree, the First Amendment protects the press from libel actions.

Liberalism   A set of beliefs that includes the advocacy of positive government action to improve the welfare of individuals, support for civil rights, and tolerance for political and social change.

Libertarianism   A political ideology based on skepticism or opposition toward almost all government activities.

Liberty   The greatest freedom of individuals that is consistent with the freedom of other individuals in the society.

Limited Government   A form of government based on the principle that the powers of government should be clearly limited either through a written document or through wide public understanding; characterized by institutional checks to ensure that government serves the public rather than private interests.

Limited Jurisdiction   Exists when a court's authority to hear cases is restricted to certain types of claims, such as tax claims or bankruptcy petitions.

Line Organization   With respect to the federal government, an administrative unit that is directly accountable to the president.

Line-Item Veto   The power of an executive to veto individual lines or items within a piece of legislation without vetoing the entire bill.

Literacy Test   A test administered as a precondition for voting, often used to prevent African Americans from exercising their right to vote.

Litigate   To engage in a legal proceeding or seek relief in a court of law; to carry on a lawsuit.

Lobbyist   An organization or individual that attempts to influence the passage, defeat, or contents of legislation and the administrative decisions of government.

Logrolling   An arrangement in which two or more members of Congress agree in advance to support each other's bills.

Loophole   A legal method by which individuals and businesses are allowed to reduce the tax liabilities owed to the government.

M

Madisonian Model   A structure of government proposed by James Madison in which the powers of the government are separated into three branches: executive, legislative, and judicial.

Majoritarianism   A political theory holding that in a democracy, the government ought to do what the majority of the people want.

Majority Leader of the House   A legislative position held by an important party member in the House of Representatives. The majority leader is selected by the majority party in caucus or conference to foster cohesion among party members and to act as spokesperson for the majority party in the House.

Majority Opinion   A court opinion reflecting the views of the majority of the judges.

Majority Rule   A basic principle of democracy asserting that the greatest number of citizens in any political unit should select officials and determine policies.

Mandatory Retirement   Forced retirement when a person reaches a certain age.

Massachusetts Ballot   See *Office-Block Ballot.*

Media   The channels of communication with mass audiences.

Merit System   The selection, retention, and promotion of government employees on the basis of competitive examinations.

Military-Industrial Complex The mutually beneficial relationship between the armed forces and defense contractors.

Minority Leader of the House The party leader elected by the minority party in the House.

Monetary Policy The use of changes in the amount of money in circulation to alter credit markets, employment, and the rate of inflation.

Monopolistic Model A model of bureaucracy that compares bureaucracies to monopolistic business firms. Lack of competition within a bureaucracy leads to inefficient and costly operations. Because bureaucracies are not penalized for inefficiency, there is no incentive to reduce costs or use resources more productively.

Monroe Doctrine A policy statement included in President James Monroe's 1823 annual message to Congress, which set out three principles: (1) European nations should not establish new colonies in the Western Hemisphere, (2) European nations should not intervene in the affairs of independent nations of the Western Hemisphere, and (3) the United States would not interfere in the affairs of European nations.

Moral Idealism A philosophy that sees all nations as willing to cooperate and agree on moral standards for conduct.

Most-Favored-Nation Status A status granted by an international treaty by which each member nation must treat other members at least as well as it treats the country that receives its most favorable treatment.

N

Narrowcasting Broadcasting that is targeted to one small sector of the population.

National Committee A standing committee of a national political party established to direct and coordinate party activities during the four-year period between national party conventions.

National Convention The meeting held every four years by each major party to select presidential and vice presidential candidates, to write a platform, to choose a national committee, and to conduct party business. In theory, the national convention is at the top of a hierarchy of party conventions (the local and state conventions are below it) that consider candidates and issues.

National Debt See *Public Debt.*

National Security Council (NSC) A staff agency in the Executive Office of the President established by the National Security Act of 1947. The NSC advises the president on domestic and foreign matters involving national security.

National Security Policy Foreign and domestic policy designed to protect the independence and political and economic integrity of a nation; policy that is concerned with the safety and defense of the nation.

Natural Rights Rights held to be inherent in natural law, not dependent on governments. John Locke stated that natural law, being superior to human law, specifies certain rights of "life, liberty, and property." These rights, altered to become "life, liberty, and the pursuit of happiness," are asserted in the Declaration of Independence.

Necessary and Proper Clause See *Elastic Clause.*

Negative Constituents Citizens who openly oppose government policies.

O

Office of Management and Budget (OMB) A division of the Executive Office of the President created by executive order in 1970 to replace the Bureau of the Budget. The OMB's main functions are to assist the president in preparing the annual budget, to clear and coordinate all departmental agency budgets, to help set fiscal policy, and to supervise the administration of the federal budget.

Office-Block, or Massachusetts, Ballot A form of general election ballot in which candidates for elective office are grouped together under the title of each office. It emphasizes voting for the office and the individual candidate, rather than for the party.

Oligarchy Rule by a few members of the elite.

Ombudsperson A person who hears and investigates complaints by private individuals against public officials or agencies.

Opinion The statement by a judge or a court of the decision reached in a case tried or argued before it. The opinion sets forth the law that applies to the case and details the legal reasoning on which the ruling was based.

Opinion Leader One who is able to influence the opinions of others because of position, expertise, or personality. Such leaders help to shape public opinion.

Opinion Poll A method of systematically questioning a small, selected sample of respondents who are deemed representative of the total population. Opinion polls are widely used by government, business, university scholars, political candidates, and voluntary groups to provide reasonably accurate data on public attitudes, beliefs, expectations, and behavior.

Oral Arguments The verbal arguments presented in person by attorneys to an appellate court. Each attorney presents reasons to the court why the court should rule in her or his client's favor.

Order A state of peace and security. Maintaining order by protecting members of society from violence and criminal activity is the oldest purpose of government.

Oversight The responsibility Congress has for following up on laws it has enacted to ensure that they are being enforced and administered in the way Congress intended.

P

Pardon A release from the punishment for or legal consequences of a crime; a pardon can be granted by the president before or after a conviction.

Party Identification Linking oneself to a particular political party.

Party Identifier A person who identifies with a political party.

Party Organization The formal structure and leadership of a political party, including election committees; local, state, and national executives; and paid professional staff.

Party Platform A document drawn up by the platform

committee at each national convention, outlining the policies, positions, and principles of the party; it is then submitted to the entire convention for approval.

Party-Column, or Indiana, Ballot A form of general election ballot in which candidates for elective office are arranged in columns under their respective party labels and symbols. It emphasizes voting for the party, rather than for the office or individual.

Patronage Rewarding faithful party workers and followers with government employment and contracts.

Peer Group A group consisting of members sharing common relevant social characteristics. These groups play an important part in the socialization process, helping to shape attitudes and beliefs.

Pendleton Act (Civil Service Reform Act) The law, as amended over the years, that remains the basic statute regulating federal employment personnel policies. It established the principle of employment on the basis of merit and created the Civil Service Commission to administer the personnel service.

Pluralism A theory that views politics as a conflict among interest groups. Political decision making is characterized by bargaining and compromise.

Plurality The total votes cast for a candidate who receives more votes than any other candidate but not necessarily a majority. Most national, state, and local electoral laws provide for winning elections by a plurality vote.

Pocket Veto A special veto power exercised by the chief executive after a legislative body has adjourned. Bills not signed by the chief executive die after a specified period of time. If Congress wishes to reconsider such a bill, it must be reintroduced in the following session of Congress.

Police Power The authority to legislate for the protection of the health, morals, safety, and welfare of the people. In the United States, most police power is a reserved power of the states.

Policy Trade-Offs The cost to the nation of undertaking any one policy in terms of all of the other policies that could have been undertaken. For example, an increase in the expenditures on one federal program means either a reduction in expenditures on another program or an increase in federal taxes (or the deficit).

Political Action Committee (PAC) A committee set up by and representing a corporation, labor union, or special interest group. PACs raise and give campaign donations on behalf of the organizations or groups they represent.

Political Consultant A paid professional hired to devise a campaign strategy and manage a campaign. Image building is the crucial task of the political consultant.

Political Culture The collection of beliefs and attitudes toward government and the political process held by a community or nation.

Political Party A group of political activists who organize to win elections, operate the government, and determine public policy.

Political Question An issue that a court believes should be decided by the executive or legislative branch.

Political Realism A philosophy that sees each nation acting principally in its own interest.

Political Socialization The process through which individuals learn a set of political attitudes and form opinions about social issues. The family and the educational system are two of the most important forces in the political socialization process.

Political Trust The degree to which individuals express trust in the government and political institutions, usually measured through a specific series of survey questions.

Politics The struggle or process to decide which members of society get certain benefits or privileges and which members of society are excluded from benefits or privileges; more specifically, the struggle over power or influence within organizations or informal groups that can grant benefits or privileges.

Poll Tax A special tax that must be paid as a qualification for voting. The Twenty-fourth Amendment to the Constitution outlawed the poll tax in national elections, and in 1966 the Supreme Court declared it unconstitutional in all elections.

Popular Sovereignty The concept that ultimate political authority is based on the will of the people.

Precedent A court rule bearing on subsequent legal decisions in similar cases. Judges rely on precedents in deciding cases.

President Pro Tempore The temporary presiding officer of the Senate in the absence of the vice president.

Presidential Primary A statewide primary election of delegates to a political party's national convention to help a party determine its presidential nominee. Such delegates are either pledged to a particular candidate or unpledged.

Press Secretary The individual responsible for representing the White House before the media. The press secretary writes news releases, provides background information, sets up press conferences, and generally handles communication for the White House.

Prior Restraint Restraining an action before it has actually occurred. In relation to the press, prior restraint means censorship.

Privatization The replacement of government services with services provided by private firms.

Property Anything that is or may be subject to ownership. As conceived by the political philosopher John Locke, the right to property is a natural right superior to human law (laws made by government).

Public Agenda Issues that commonly are perceived by members of the political community as meriting public attention and governmental action. The media play an important role in setting the public agenda by focusing attention on certain topics.

Public Debt, or National Debt The total amount of debt carried by the federal government.

Public Debt Financing The government's spending more than it receives in taxes and paying for the difference by issuing U.S. Treasury bonds, thereby adding to the public debt.

Public Figures Public officials, movie stars, and generally all persons who become known to the public because of their positions or activities.

Public Interest The best interests of the collective, overall community; the national good, rather than the narrow interests of a self-serving group.

Public Opinion The aggregate of individual attitudes or beliefs shared by some portion of the adult population. There is no one public opinion, because there are many different "publics."

R

Ratification Formal approval.

Reapportionment The allocation of seats in the House of Representatives to each state after each census.

Recall A procedure allowing the people to vote to dismiss an elected official from state office before his or her term has expired.

Redistricting The redrawing of the boundaries of the congressional districts within a state.

Referendum An electoral device whereby legislative or constitutional measures are referred by the legislature to the voters for approval or disapproval.

Registration The entry of a person's name onto the list of eligible voters for elections. To register, a person must meet certain legal requirements relating to age, citizenship, and residency.

Remand To send a case back to the court that originally heard it.

Representation The function of members of Congress as elected officials in representing the views of their constituents.

Representative Assembly A legislature composed of individuals who represent the population.

Representative Democracy A form of government in which representatives elected by the people make and enforce laws and policies.

Reprieve Postponement of the execution of a sentence imposed by a court of law; usually done for humanitarian reasons or to await new evidence.

Republic A form of government in which sovereignty rests with the people, who elect agents to represent them in lawmaking and other decisions.

Republican Party One of the two major American political parties, which emerged in the 1850s as an antislavery party. It consisted of former northern Whigs and antislavery Democrats.

Reverse To annul or make void a court ruling on account of some error or irregularity.

Reverse Discrimination The charge that affirmative action programs requiring preferential treatment or quotas discriminate against those who do not have minority status.

Rule of Four A United States Supreme Court procedure according to which four justices must vote to hear a case in order for the case to come before the full Court.

Rules Committee A standing committee of the House of Representatives that provides special rules under which specific bills can be debated, amended, and considered by the House.

S

Safe Seat A district that returns the legislator with 55 percent of the vote or more.

Sampling Error The difference between sample results and the true result if the entire population had been interviewed.

Select Committee A temporary legislative committee established for a limited time period and for a special purpose.

Senate Majority Leader The chief spokesperson of the majority party in the Senate, who directs the legislative program and party strategy.

Senate Minority Leader The party officer in the Senate who commands the minority party's opposition to the policies of the majority party and directs the legislative program and strategy of his or her party.

Senatorial Courtesy In federal district court judgeship nominations, a Senate tradition allowing a senator of the president's political party to veto a judicial appointment in his or her state by indicating that the appointment is personally not acceptable. At that point, the Senate may reject the nomination, or the president may withdraw consideration of the nominee.

Seniority System A custom followed in both chambers of Congress specifying that the member of the majority party with the longest term of continuous service will be given preference when a committee chairperson (or holders of other significant posts) is selected.

Separate-but-Equal Doctrine The doctrine holding that segregation in schools and public accommodations does not imply that one race is superior to another and that separate-but-equal facilities do not violate the equal protection clause.

Separation of Powers The principle of dividing governmental powers among the executive, the legislative, and the judicial branches of government.

Service Sector The sector of the economy that provides services—such as health care, banking, and education—in contrast to the sector of the economy that produces goods.

Sexual Harassment Unwanted physical or verbal conduct or abuse of a sexual nature that interferes with a recipient's job performance, creates a hostile environment, or carries with it an implicit or explicit threat of adverse employment consequences.

Slander The public uttering of a false statement that harms the good reputation of another. The statement must be made to, or within the hearing of, persons other than the defamed party.

Social Contract A voluntary agreement among individuals to secure their rights and welfare by creating a government and abiding by its rules.

Socialism A political ideology based on strong support for economic and social equality. Socialists traditionally envisioned a society in which large privately owned businesses were taken over by the government or by employee cooperatives.

Socioeconomic Status The value assigned to a person due to occupation or income. An upper-class person, for example, has high socioeconomic status.

Soft Money Campaign contributions unregulated by federal or state law, given to parties and party committees to help fund general party activities. Soft money has been used to evade contribution limits.

Sound Bite A brief, memorable comment that easily can be fit into news broadcasts.

Soviet Bloc The Eastern European countries that installed Communist regimes after World War II.

Speaker of the House The presiding officer in the House of Representatives. The Speaker is always a member of the majority party and is the most powerful and influential member of the House.

Spin An interpretation of campaign events or election results that is favorable to the candidate's campaign strategy.

Spin Doctor   A political campaign adviser who tries to convince journalists of the truth of a particular interpretation of events.

Splinter Party   A new party formed by a dissident faction within a major political party. Usually, splinter parties have emerged when a particular personality was at odds with the major party.

Spoils System   The awarding of government jobs to political supporters and friends; generally associated with President Andrew Jackson.

Spring Review   The time every year when the Office of Management and Budget requires federal agencies to review their programs, activities, and goals and submit their requests for funding for the next fiscal year.

Standing Committee   A permanent committee in the House or Senate that considers bills within a certain subject area.

Stare Decisis   To stand on decided cases; the judicial policy of following precedents established by past decisions.

State   A group of people occupying a specific area and organized under one government; may be either a nation or a subunit of a nation.

State Central Committee   The principal organized structure of each political party within each state. This committee is responsible for carrying out policy decisions of the party's state convention.

State of the Union Message   An annual message to Congress in which the president proposes a legislative program. The message is addressed not only to Congress but also to the American people and to the world. It offers the opportunity to dramatize policies and objectives and to gain public support.

Statutory Power   A power created through laws enacted by Congress.

Strategic Arms Limitation Treaty (SALT I)   A treaty between the United States and the Soviet Union to stabilize the nuclear arms competition between the two countries. SALT I talks began in 1969, and agreements were signed on May 26, 1972.

Suffrage   The right to vote; the franchise.

Sunset Legislation   A law requiring that an existing program be reviewed regularly for its effectiveness and be terminated unless specifically extended as a result of this review.

Super Tuesday   A date on which a large number of presidential primaries are held, including those of many southern states.

Superdelegate   A party leader or elected official who is given the right to vote at the party's national convention. Superdelegates are not elected at the state level.

Supplemental Security Income (SSI)   A federal program established to provide assistance to elderly persons and disabled persons.

Supremacy Clause   The constitutional provision that makes the Constitution and federal laws superior to all conflicting state and local laws.

Supremacy Doctrine   A doctrine that asserts the superiority of national law over state or regional laws. This principle is rooted in Article VI of the Constitution, which provides that the Constitution, the laws passed by the national government under its constitutional powers, and all treaties constitute the supreme law of the land.

Symbolic Speech   Nonverbal expression of beliefs, which is given substantial protection by the courts.

T

Technical Assistance   The practice of sending experts with technical skills in such areas as agriculture, engineering, or business to aid other nations.

Temporary Assistance to Needy Families (TANF)   A state-administered program in which grants from the national government are given to the states, which use the funds to provide assistance to those eligible to receive welfare benefits. The TANF program was created by the Welfare Reform Act of 1996 and replaced the former AFDC program.

Third Party   A political party other than the two major political parties (Republican and Democratic). Often, third parties are composed of dissatisfied groups that have split from the major parties. They act as indicators of political trends and as safety valves for dissident groups.

Ticket Splitting   Voting for candidates of two or more parties for different offices. For example, a voter splits her ticket if she votes for a Republican presidential candidate and for a Democratic congressional candidate.

Totalitarian Regime   A form of government that controls all aspects of the political and social life of a nation. All power resides with the government. The citizens have no power to choose the leadership or policies of the country.

Tracking Poll   A poll taken for the candidate on a nearly daily basis as election day approaches.

Trial Court   The court in which most cases begin and in which questions of fact are examined.

Truman Doctrine   The policy adopted by President Harry Truman in 1947 to halt Communist expansion in southeastern Europe.

Trustee   In regard to a legislator, one who acts according to her or his conscience and the broad interests of the entire society.

Twelfth Amendment   An amendment to the Constitution adopted in 1804 that specifies the separate election of the president and vice president by the electoral college.

Twenty-fifth Amendment   An amendment to the Constitution adopted in 1967 that establishes procedures for filling vacancies in the two top executive offices and that makes provisions for situations involving presidential disability.

Two-Party System   A political system in which only two parties have a reasonable chance of winning.

U

U.S. Treasury Bond   Evidence of debt issued by the federal government; similar to corporate bonds but issued by the U.S. Treasury.

Unanimous Opinion   A court opinion or determination on which all judges agree.

Unicameral Legislature   A legislature with only one legislative body, as compared with a bicameral (two-house) legislature, such as the U.S. Congress. Nebraska is the only state in the Union with a unicameral legislature.

Unit Rule   Rule by which all of a state's electoral votes are cast for the presidential candidate receiving a plurality of the popular vote in that state.

Unitary System   A centralized governmental system in which local or subdivisional governments exercise only those powers given to them by the central government.

Universal Suffrage   The right of all adults to vote for their representatives.

V

Veto Message   The president's formal explanation of a veto when legislation is returned to Congress.

Voter Turnout   The percentage of citizens taking part in the election process; the number of eligible voters that actually "turn out" on election day to cast their ballots.

W

War Powers Resolution   A law passed in 1973 spelling out the conditions under which the president can commit troops without congressional approval.

Washington Community   Individuals regularly involved with politics in Washington, D.C.

Watergate Break-In   The 1972 illegal entry into the Democratic National Committee offices by participants in President Richard Nixon's reelection campaign.

Weberian Model   A model of bureaucracy developed by the German sociologist Max Weber, who viewed bureaucracies as rational, hierarchical organizations in which power flows from the top downward and decisions are based on logical reasoning and data analysis.

Whig Party   A major political party in the United States during the first half of the nineteenth century, formally established in 1836. The Whig Party was dominated by anti-Jackson elements and represented a variety of regional interests. It fell apart as a national party in the early 1850s.

Whip   A member of Congress who aids the majority or minority leader of the House or the Senate.

Whistleblower   An insider who brings to public attention gross governmental inefficiency or an illegal action.

White House Office   The personal office of the president, which tends to presidential political needs and manages the media.

White House Press Corps   A group of reporters assigned full-time to cover the presidency.

White Primary   A state primary election that restricts voting to whites only; outlawed by the Supreme Court in 1944.

Writ of *Certiorari*   An order issued by a higher court to a lower court to send up the record of a case for review. It is the principal vehicle for United States Supreme Court review.

Writ of *Habeas Corpus*   *Habeas corpus* means, literally, "you have the body." A writ of *habeas corpus* is an order that requires jailers to bring a person before a court or judge and explain why the person is being held in prison.

Index

Photo Credits

Cover Image: Getty Chapter Openers: page 1 Stock Boston, Christopher Brown 19 Corbis 45 Corbis, Joseph Sohm, ChromoSohm, Inc. 69 PhotoEdit, Elana Rooraid 94 Corbis 147 AP Photo, The Capital Times, David Sandell 176 AP Photo, John Russell 206 PhotoEdit, Tom McCarthy 259 Corbis, Eye Ubiquitous 235 AP Photo, Eric Draper 304 AP Photo, Susan Walsh 327 AP Photo